LIKE OUR MOUNTAINS

MCGILL-QUEEN'S STUDIES IN ETHNIC HISTORY
SERIES ONE: DONALD HARMAN AKENSON, EDITOR

1 Irish Migrants in the Canadas
A New Approach
Bruce S. Elliott

2 Critical Years in Immigration
Canada and Australia Compared
Freda Hawkins
(Second edition, 1991)

3 Italians in Toronto
Development of a National Identity, 1875–1935
John E. Zucchi

4 Linguistics and Poetics of Latvian Folk Songs
Essays in Honour of the Sesquicentennial of the Birth of Kr. Barons
Vaira Vikis-Freibergs

5 Johan Schrøder's Travels in Canada, 1863
Orm Øverland

6 Class, Ethnicity, and Social Inequality
Christopher McAll

7 The Victorian Interpretation of Racial Conflict
The Maori, the British, and the New Zealand Wars
James Belich

8 White Canada Forever
Popular Attitudes and Public Policy toward Orientals in British Columbia
W. Peter Ward
(Second edition, 1990)

9 The People of Glengarry
Highlanders in Transition, 1745–1820
Marianne McLean

10 Vancouver's Chinatown
Racial Discourse in Canada, 1875–1980
Kay J. Anderson

11 Best Left as Indians
Native-White Relations in the Yukon Territory, 1840–1973
Ken Coates

12 Such Hardworking People
Italian Immigrants in Postwar Toronto
Franca Iacovetta

13 The Little Slaves of the Harp
Italian Child Street Musicians in Nineteenth-Century Paris, London, and New York
John E. Zucchi

14 The Light of Nature and the Law of God
Antislavery in Ontario, 1833–1877
Allen P. Stouffer

15 Drum Songs
Glimpses of Dene History
Kerry Abel

16 Louis Rosenberg
Canada's Jews
Edited by Morton Weinfeld

17 A New Lease on Life
Landlords, Tenants, and Immigrants in Ireland and Canada
Catharine Anne Wilson

18 In Search of Paradise
The Odyssey of an Italian Family
Susan Gabori

19 Ethnicity in the Mainstream
Three Studies of English Canadian Culture in Ontario
Pauline Greenhill

20 Patriots and Proletarians
The Politicization of Hungarian Immigrants in Canada, 1923–1939
Carmela Patrias

21 The Four Quarters of the Night
The Life-Journey of an Emigrant Sikh
Tara Singh Bains and Hugh Johnston

22 Cultural Power, Resistance and Pluralism
Colonial Guyana, 1838–1900
Brian L. Moore

23 Search Out the Land
The Jews and the Growth of Equality in British Colonial America, 1740–1867
Sheldon J. Godfrey and Judith C. Godfrey

24 The Development of Elites in
Acadian New Brunswick,
1861–1881
Sheila M. Andrew

25 Journey to Vaja
Reconstructing the World of
a Hungarian-Jewish Family
Elaine Kalman Naves

MCGILL-QUEEN'S STUDIES IN ETHNIC HISTORY
SERIES TWO: JOHN ZUCCHI, EDITOR

1 Inside Ethnic Families
Three Generations of Portuguese-Canadians
Edite Noivo

2 A House of Words
Jewish Writing, Identity, and Memory
Norman Ravvin

3 Oatmeal and the Catechism
Scottish Gaelic Settlers in Quebec
Margaret Bennett

4 With Scarcely a Ripple
Anglo-Canadian Migration into the
United States and Western Canada,
1880–1920
Randy William Widdis

5 Creating Societies
Immigrant Lives in Canada
Dirk Hoerder

6 Social Discredit
Anti-Semitism, Social Credit,
and the Jewish Response
Janine Stingel

7 Coalescence of Styles
The Ethnic Heritage of St John
River Valley Regional Furniture,
1763–1851
Jane L. Cook

8 Brigh an Orain / A Story in Every Song
The Songs and Tales of
Lauchie MacLellan
Translated and edited by John Shaw

9 Demography, State and Society
Irish Migration to Britain,
1921–1971
Enda Delaney

10 The West Indians of Costa Rica
Race, Class, and the Integration of
an Ethnic Minority
Ronald N. Harpelle

11 Canada and the Ukrainian Question, 1939–1945
Bohdan S. Kordan

12 Tortillas and Tomatoes
Transmigrant Mexican Harvesters
in Canada
Tanya Basok

13 Old and New World Highland Bagpiping
John G. Gibson

14 Nationalism from the Margins
The Negotiation of Nationalism
and Ethnic Identities among Italian
Immigrants in Alberta and British
Columbia
Patricia Wood

15 Colonization and Community
The Vancouver Island Coalfield
and the Making of the British
Columbia Working Class
John Douglas Belshaw

16 Enemy Aliens, Prisoners of War
Internment in Canada during the
Great War
Bohdan S. Kordan

17 Like Our Mountains
A History of Armenians in Canada
Isabel Kaprielian-Churchill

Like Our Mountains

A History of Armenians in Canada

ISABEL KAPRIELIAN-CHURCHILL

McGill-Queen's University Press
Montreal & Kingston • London • Ithaca

© Isabel Kaprielian-Churchill 2005
ISBN 0-7735-2663-3

Legal deposit second quarter 2005
Bibliothèque nationale du Québec

Printed in Canada on acid-free paper.

This book has been published with the help of grants from the Department of Canadian Heritage / Patrimoine Canada, Government of Canada.

McGill-Queen's University Press acknowledges the support of the Canada Council for the Arts for our publishing program. We also acknowledge the financial support of the Government of Canada through the Book Publishing Industry Development Program (BPIDP) for our publishing activities.

National Library of Canada Cataloguing in Publication

Kaprielian-Churchill, Isabel, 1935–
    Like our mountains : a history of Armenians in Canada / Isabel Kaprielian-Churchill.

(McGill-Queen's studies in ethnic history, ISSN 0846-8869 ; 17)
Includes bibliographical references and index.
ISBN 0-7735-2663-3

    1. Armenians – Canada – History. 2. Armenian Canadians – History. 3. Armenian Canadians – Social conditions. I. Title. II. Series.

FC106.A7K36 2004   971.004'991992   C2004-904450-8

Typeset in 10/12 Sabon by True to Type

THIS BOOK IS DEDICATED TO

Aristakes and Marta Kaprielian
Tateos and Azniv Zakarian
Kapriel and Loussaper Kaprielian
Norman Sarkis Kaprielian
Paul Vardkes and Eleanor Kaprielian
John Zaven Kaprielian
Albert and Anoush Kaprielian
Aris Kurken Kaprielian
Laurence Gabriel Kaprielian
Haig and Marina Seferian
Matthew Gabriel Seferian
Zoie Lucine Seferian
and to my husband, Stacy Churchill

Mount Ararat

We were peaceful like our mountains,
You invaded us like ferocious winds.
We confronted you like our mountains,
You growled fiercely like ferocious winds.
But we are eternal like our mountains,
You will perish like ferocious winds.
                              Hovannes Shiraz

Contents

Illustrations and Maps xiii

Acknowledgments xvii

Introduction xxiii

Note on Transliteration xlv

Acronyms xlvii

PART ONE   THE OLD WORLD   1

1 Keghi: Land of Mountains   3
2 Changing Horizons   23

PART TWO   ARMENIAN PIONEERS IN CANADA   45

3 The First Wave: To World War I   47
4 Family and Work   65
5 Community Development: The Formative Years   80

PART THREE   GENOCIDE, SURVIVAL, AND THE RESPONSE OF CANADIANS   111

6 Genocide and Survival   113
7 The Impact of Genocide   137

PART FOUR REFUGEE ENTRY INTO CANADA,
REHABILITATION, AND REPARATIONS 153

8 "A Drop in the Bucket": Armenian Refugees and Their Entry into Canada 155

9 Refugee Resettlement in Canada: The Early Years 179

10 The Quest for Reparations 205

PART FIVE RECONSTRUCTING NEW WORLDS 235

11 Foundations of Material Life: St Catharines 237

12 The Church and Politics: Background, 1914–1930 269

13 The Church and Politics: Crisis in St Catharines, 1930–1933 283

14 Aftermath of the Church Crisis: 1933–1950 300

15 Family and Community in Hamilton: From Being Armenian to Being Armenian-Canadian 322

PART SIX OLD FOUNDATIONS, NEW COMMUNITIES 349

16 Old Foundations: Montreal and Toronto to 1950 351

17 New Communities: The Third Wave, 1950–1988 373

18 Settlement of the Third Wave: 1950–1988 401

19 Institutional and Organizational Life 416

20 Armenian Integration, Maintenance, and Societal Recognition 453

Conclusion and Epilogue 478

Notes 487

Bibliography 567

Index 615

Illustrations

Mount Ararat   viii

Main centres of Armenian settlement in Canada   xxi

Map of the Old World   xxii

Catholicos Vazken I of Echmiadzin and Catholicos Karekin II of Cilicia   xliv

A list of pre-1914 Armenian and part-Armenian villages in Keghi   facing page 44

Portrait of mother and son, Van, pre-1914   facing page 45

Paul Courian, Toronto, ca 1900   facing page 45

Following page 152

The killing fields of Keghi

Attestation paper of Samuel Harry Chickegian (Chichakian)

Discharge paper of Hagop (Jack) Kaprielian

Excerpt frm an article about the Armenian Relief Society

Young Armenian survivors in an orphanage in Aleppo, early 1920s

Courtship photograph of Kapriel Kaprielian sent to a bride-to-be in Syria, ca 1920s

Passport issued by French authorities in Syria for a refugee girl

Young picture brides with their first-born children, Hamilton, ca 1926

The Georgetown Boys thank Canada

Questionnaire submitted in pursuit of reparations

Following page 234

Postcard of the Armenian General Benevolent Union, ca 1920

Crocheted and needleworked handkerchiefs

Book cover of revolutionary and patriotic songs

Group photo of a picnic in Hamilton, ca 1936–37

Tombstone, Brantford

Statement of goals expressed by Armenian community leaders

Two boys, 1931

Following page 348

Pasdermajian brothers standing in front of Yervant's Oriental Rugs

Interior of a rug store in Toronto, ca 1980s

Marriage ceremony, Toronto

Celebrating Easter by cracking traditional coloured eggs

Growing up Armenian Canadian – the fourth generation

Hnchak poster of Armenian heroes with Mother Armenia

Modern statue of Mother Armenia, Republic of Armenia

Holy Trinity Armenian Apostolic Church

St Mary's Armenian Apostolic Church

St Gregory the Illuminator Armenian Catholic Church

Armenian Evangelical Church

Cover of *Sovetakan Hayasta*n (Soviet Armenia), Yerevan, 1987

Poster of David of Sasun marking the erathquake in Armenia in 1988   oo

Following page 452

Abaka, an Armenian-, English-, and French-language weekly

Horizon, an Armenian-, English-, and French-language weekly

Annual demonstration protesting Turkey's unwillingness to recognize the Genocide

Armenian schoolchildren in concert, Toronto, 1990s

Armenian sculpture of the Virgin and Child

Sculpture of stone cross and eagle remembering 1915

Statue erected by Armenians in Montreal to commemorate the Genocide

Canadian stamp commemorating Armenia's conversion to Christianity

Armenians thank Canada, 21 April 2004

Acknowledgments

This book has taken me on an adventurous and unforgettable journey into the homes, institutions, and organizations of Armenians in Canada. It has allowed me to probe the minds and hearts of Armenian Canadians, and it is to them that I owe my greatest debt of gratitude. After so many years, I can at last express my deep appreciation to them and hope that my writing conveys their passion, complexity, and indomitable spirit.

A book of this type depends on many people and to them all I wish to express my profound gratitude. Although space does not allow me to mention everyone's name, I wish to thank some who were exceptionally helpful. Intellectually, I owe much to the late Professor Robert F. Harney, who was my thesis supervisor and guided my earlier thought and work. He taught me that immigration and ethnic history and the history of Armenians in Canada were valid academic pursuits and that they had meaning, relevance, and importance. Dr Robert Mirak and Professor Raymond Breton gave invaluable guidance as members of my thesis committee. They have continued to counsel me and have remained sources of knowledge, inspiration, and friendship throughout the preparation of this book. I would also like to thank Professor Richard Hovannisian, who not only read and commented on parts of this book but who has provided a model of scholarship and an unerring reference point about the old country.

The Armenian Apostolic Church in Canada, both the Diocese and the Prelacy gave me permission to access church documents, as did the Anglican and United Churches. Armenian organizations, especially the

Armenian Revolutionary Federation, opened their archives, which proved to be a crucial source for the early period.

I was fortunate to have archivists and librarians working closely with me and I wish to thank them all, but in particular I must mention Myron Momryk of the National Archives of Canada and John Burtniak, Special Collections, Brock University, St Catharines. Their knowledge of the sources at their disposal opened many new channels for me. The Archives of Ontario assisted me in a number of ways, especially with the use of their photography collection. I am also pleased to express my appreciation to Alice Samuelian Aslanian and Armen Samuelian of the Librairie Orientale in Paris, who always managed to find exactly the book I needed. In this regard, I owe a note of thanks to Isabelle Gibb, interlibrary loan librarian at OISE, who located books in far-off corners of the world.

In the early phase of my studies I worked as a researcher with the Multicultural History Society of Ontario, where I deposited much of the material that I had gathered, some of which remained with the Society and some of which was transferred to the Archives of Ontario. These documents and photographs are open to the public, and it is my hope that scholars will use them, as I have done in the preparation of this book.

With affection and respect I acknowledge my debt to two friends and advisors, the late Reverend Sempad Der Meksian and Archbishop Khajag Hagopian, the prelate of the Armenian Prelacy of Canada. Three people never failed to respond to my many requests for information, photographs, or documents: Dikranouhi Artinian, Aris Babikian, and Eugenie Shehirian. I would also like to thank those who read and commented on parts of the manuscript, suggested pertinent readings, found useful material in local institutions, assisted me with almost illegible hand-written documents, transcribed taped interviews, or helped me in other ways: Lily Adourian, Berj Aloian, Aram Arkun, John Avedisian, Margaret Campbell, MP, Garo Chichekian, Angel Dardarian, Salpi Der Ghazarian, Professor Donna Gabaccia, Nora Halagian Langton, Charles Houghton, John Hovsepian, Hasmig Injejikian, Kohar Kasparian, Professor Raymond Kévorkian, Reverend Krikor Maksoudian, Dr Dickran Malatjalian, Professor Armen Manougian, Giro Manoyan, Alma Margossian, Dr Edward Melkonian, Serpouhie Messerlian, Gary Muir, Dr Dennis Papazian, Gerald Ottenbreit Jr, Boghos Seferian, Haig Seferian, Senator Raymond Setlakwé, Paul Solomonian, and Perouz and Antranig Yoldjian.

Oral sources form one of the most critical components of this book. I am grateful to everyone who shared their painful, but also happy memories with me. In this respect, let me mention the principals, teachers, and students of the Armenian schools in Toronto for carrying out oral history projects. The students interviewed older members of the community, thus broadening the scope of our knowledge of what I describe in this book as the third wave. I am also indebted to respondents who loaned me photographs, documents, and books, in particular those who opened their extensive personal collections to me, including Harold Bedoukian and Janice (Summers) Bedoukian, Markar Begian, Alexander B. Davies (Mooradian collection), Eleanor Koldofsky (Babayan collection), Robert Melkonian, Yervant Pasdermajian, and Nevart Sarkissian.

I am pleased to pay special thanks to Hygus Torosian and Alice Torosian, dear friends with whom I had many stimulating debates about the St Catharines community. They gave me a wealth of material and, like so many others, opened their home to me. It is with sadness that I mention Hygus's death at the age of ninety, before the publication of the book he so wanted to see. Indeed, my greatest regret is that this book took far too long to be published, for many who were looking forward to its publication are now gone.

The Ontario Institute for Studies in Education of the University of Toronto generously assisted this endeavour through grants and release time for research and writing. I completed a major part of the manuscript while at the University of Toronto as a graduate student, postdoctoral fellow, research associate, and lecturer, before taking up a post at California State University, Fresno. The Department of History at Fresno welcomed me and has remained a steady source of encouragement. It gave me the opportunity to develop and teach two new history courses: Armenians in North America and the Armenian Genocide in Comparative Context. The genocide course gave me the chance to move beyond the political perspective of the Genocide to examine an aspect of the catastrophe that has not been emphasized – the survival, especially of women and children.

I would like to thank the staff at McGill-Queen's University Press for their cooperation and thoughtfulness, especially Professor John Zucchi, general editor of McGill-Queen's Studies in Ethnic History; Joan McGilvray, coordinating editor; and Ron Curtis, who meticulously copyedited the manuscript and prepared the index. It has also been a pleasure to work with Jane Davie (Geography Department of the University of Toronto), who prepared the maps. The insightful and constructive suggestions made by the anonymous reviewers of earlier drafts of the manuscript are also greatly appreciated.

I wish to thank the Social Sciences and Humanities Research Council of Canada for doctoral and postdoctoral fellowships and the federal Department of the Secretary of State, the Government of Ontario, and the Multicultural History Society of Ontario for steady and unfailing research assistance. The Bertha and John Garabedian Charitable Foundation (Fresno) lightened my teaching load during crucial stages of this book. I am especially grateful to the Department of Canadian Heritage for providing the funds to publish this book. Originally the history of Armenians in Canada was to be part of the Generations Series; when that series ended, the commitment to publish this study was kept, thanks to the interest of the Honourable Sheila Copps, Minister of Canadian Heritage at the time.

Finally, I would like to pay tribute to my family. My brothers, Norman and Paul, were immeasurably helpful in my research. Beyond their contributions to this book, I would like to thank them for instilling in me a love of history. Norman has always been fascinated with American and Armenian history and Paul with British history and Canadian military history. Together with my father, a spellbinding storyteller who regaled us with riveting tales of life in Keghi, they created a world where stories were a focus of family dynamics. My maternal grandmother combined her faith with her musical talent as soloist in the Cathedral in Erzerum and my mother passed on her legacy. She filled our home with the enchantment of poetry and music and taught me to sing folk melodies, chant prayers and hymns, and belt out patriotic and revolutionary songs, and she bequeathed to me an abiding love of music and of the "sunbaked taste of Armenian words" (from Yeghishé Charents.)

My dear children, Albert, Lance, and Marina, grew up with this book, first, when it was part of my doctoral thesis, and later, when I broadened the scope, in my commitment to my Canadian and Armenian heritages. They listened with great curiosity as I recounted my day's adventures, my impressions, and the new information I had gathered. My husband, Stacy Churchill, has been at my side all along the way. He has given me intellectual and moral support, enthusiastically discussed my observations, ideas, and analyses with me, and lightened the work with his wit and humour. To everyone, thank you.

Parts of this book have appeared in the following journals: *Ararat Quarterly*; *The Armenian Review*; *Canadian Historical Review*; *Canadian Woman Studies*; *International Migration Review*; *Journal of American Ethnic History*; *Journal of Armenian Studies*, various issues of *Polyphony: Bulletin of the Multicultural History Society of Ontario*, and *Resources for Feminist Research*. Parts have also appeared in the following books: *Anatomy of Genocide: State-Sponsored Mass-Killings in the Twentieth Century*; *Armenian Karin/Erzerum*; *Armenian Women in a Changing World*; *Dictionary of Canadian Biography*; *Encyclopedia of Canada's Peoples*; *Voices of Armenian Women*; *Pulse of the World: Refugees in our Schools*; *Looking into my Sister's Eyes: An Exploration in Women's History*; and *Sisters or Strangers? Immigrant, Ethnic, and Racialized Women in Canadian History*.

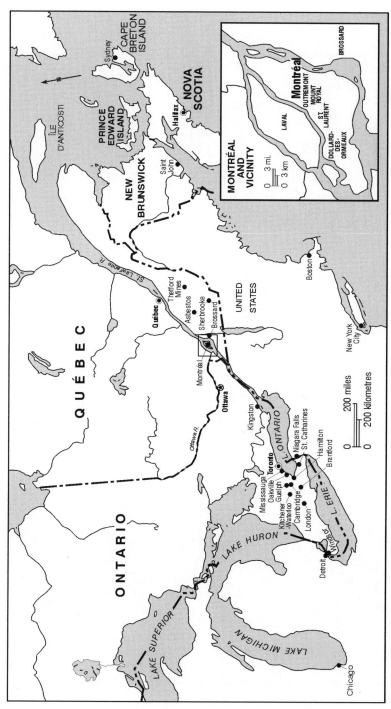

Main centres of Armenian settlement in Canada. Courtesy Department of Geography, University of Toronto. Cartographer, Jane Davie.

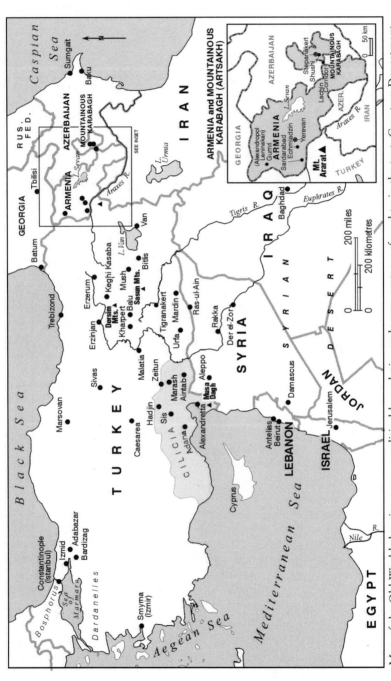

Map of the Old World showing current political boundaries and some centres referred to in the text. Courtesy Department of Geography, University of Toronto. Cartographer, Jane Davie.

Introduction

> Memory is the key to resurrection.
> Northrop Frye

My objective in writing this book was to examine how Armenians came and settled in Canada, what type of world they refashioned in the new country, how they integrated into Canadian society, and to what extent they retained their ethnocultural identity and a measure of continuity for a period of one hundred years. The result is a story of balance – balance between the old and new worlds, balance between attachment to Armenia and Armenian culture, traditions, and values and attachment to Canada and Canadian culture, traditions, and values.

When Armenians came to Canada, they carried with them centuries of experience of being a minority and well-honed traditions and techniques of ethnonational survival. For them, to safeguard their national symbols and to function as a viable minority in North America while contributing to the host society seemed neither incongruous nor contradictory. With their expertise in retaining their language and religion while speaking other languages in business and living in a pluralist society, Armenians knew they could reconcile the diversities inherent in a complex new society like Canada.[1]

The transatlantic crossing brought Armenians from a Moslem country to a Christian land where they endeavoured to balance their Armenian heritage with their Canadian identity. Gradually, with increasing self-confidence, they created not only an Armenian diaspora but a vibrant ethnic community that contributed to Canadian society through participation in Canada's industrial and business development, in Canada's war effort, in Canada's professional life, and in Canada's artistic blossoming.

Such a balance was possible partly because of historic traditions entrenched in the British North America Act, which created the Dominion of Canada in 1867 (now referred to as the Constitution Act, 1867). By its terms, the concept of a monolithic nation-state on the European model was rejected in favour of a state that recognized more than one ethnocultural component. The concept of minority rights – albeit rights for "official" minorities – was established in the nineteenth century, and although minority rights have had a turbulent history in Canada, they would lead to the development of bilingualism and multiculturalism in the Canadian polity by the end of the twentieth century.[2]

The evolution towards multiculturalism as an official Canadian policy (1970) and the recognition and legitimization of diverse groups received setbacks during the twentieth century, particularly during the 1920s, when immigration was curtailed and for some, like Armenians, Jews, Africans, and Asians, almost totally prohibited. Restrictive immigration policies reinforced a society of inequality dominated by established British and French Canadian élites. Still, the transformation of Canadian society during the twentieth century is reflected in substantial changes affecting individuals and ethnic groups. In 1940 people with Armenian names were refused work in the offices of iron factories where Armenian men had toiled for decades. But in 2003, film director Atom Egoyan stood at the forefront of Canadian cinema; his film ARARAT won five Genie Awards, including Arsinée Khanjian's honours for actress in a leading role. In music, Peter Oundjian was the newly appointed conductor of the Toronto Symphony Orchestra, and Nurhan Arman was conductor of the New Brunswick Symphony Orchestra and musical director of the Toronto Sinfonia Chamber Orchestra, while Raffi Armenian, former conductor of the Kitchener-Waterloo Symphony Orchestra, and Gerard Kantarjian continued to play a major role in classical music in Canada. Brilliant young artists, soprano Isabel Bayrakdarian, composer and jazz guitarist Levon Ishkhanian, pianist Serouj Kradjian, and violinist Catherine Manoukian illuminated the musical scene, reaping awards and winning international acclaim. Theatre director and playwright Hrant Alianak and Richard Ouzounian, drama critic for the *Toronto Star*, were noted in Canadian theatre. And two brothers, Yousuf Karsh and Malak, who passed away in 2002 and 2001, bequeathed a magnificent legacy of photography. In the political arena, Sarkis Assadourian, federal member of Parliament, and Senator Raymond Setlakwé strived to have the Armenian Genocide recognized by the Parliament of Canada. These are but examples of a symbolic shift with ramifications in all aspects of Canadian life; they resonate with societal changes, along with a continued, vigorous ethnocultural presence.

The story of the Armenian ethnic group during the twentieth century reveals that the total surrender of an ethnocultural heritage, either by an individual or a group, is neither inevitable nor necessary. Diversity can be reconciled with integration in Canadian society. Competing claims and tensions among different heritages can be resolved, for in its evolution, Canada has developed the flexibility and the breadth to incorporate diversity within the overarching unity of Canadian values of democracy, tolerance, liberalism, human rights, and the rule of law, which are now entrenched in the Canadian Charter of Rights and Freedoms. Recognition of and respect for individuals and groups are inalienable and nonnegotiable, and since they apply to everyone – though perhaps not always equally – they are fundamental unifying forces in Canadian society.[3]

Like accounts of other ethnic groups in Canada, this study is written within the framework of developments in Canada and is, therefore, part of Canadian history.[4] But the history of Armenians in Canada cannot be divorced from events in the Armenian homeland and in other parts of the diaspora. To make the Armenian experience in Canada more comprehensible, therefore, I have adopted a broader scope in this study, so that while Armenians came to Canada and created their own new world with its own dynamism and history, their story also forms part of the history of the far-flung Armenian diaspora, a diaspora that has sometimes claimed more Armenians than the homeland itself.[5]

The examination of the Armenian diaspora in North America is still in its infancy. Perhaps the trauma of genocide induced Armenian immigrants to focus first on reestablishing themselves in a new world and then on setting down for posterity the history of the beloved homeland, lost to them forever. The accounts of Armenian life in old country cities and villages – a prominent genre of post-Genocide writing – have received recent impetus with Richard Hovannisian's UCLA conferences on ancient Armenian cities. His publication of conference papers has justifiably generated growing interest in the lost world of our ancestors. Hovannisian is currently dealing with the Armenian diaspora with two conferences on the Armenians of Persia/Iran, commemorating their deportations from Armenia, especially Julfa, to Persia, notably to New Julfa (near Isfahan) four hundred years ago.

Armenian diasporan studies seemed to be moving forward twenty years ago when Robert Mirak established the parameters of the history of Armenians in the United States with his outstanding pioneering work *Torn between Two Lands: Armenians in America, 1890 to World War I*. But few have followed in his footsteps, since scholars in different disciplines have concentrated on the Genocide, partly in response to the Turkish government's denials, lobbies, and academic inducements. Armenian communities in various North American cities have received some attention, for example in Arpena Mesrobian's *Like One Family: The Armenians of Syracuse, the History of Armenians in America* and Richard T. LaPiere's doctoral dissertation, "The Armenian Colony in Fresno County, California: A Study in Social Psychology." Anny Bakalian's *Armenian-Americans: From Being to Feeling Armenian* and George Kooshian's recent doctoral dissertation "The Armenian Immigrant Community of California, 1880–1935," are excellent regional studies. Unfortunately the study of the involvement of Armenians in the rug trade, the jewellery industry, and the sciences, arts, and philanthropy in North America has not been seriously undertaken. Nor has the study of Armenian participation in the labour movement in the United States, either as factory workers or as union activists. Aside from Father Oshagan Minassian's dissertation, "A History of the Armenian Holy Apostolic Orthodox Church in the United States (1888–1944)," no in-depth examinations of the church crises of 1933 and 1956 have appeared, despite the release of formerly inaccessible documents.

Going beyond the United States, I have yet to unearth an account of Armenians in Mexico or in Cuba, even though active Armenian settlements thrived in these countries following the Genocide. In Canada, the history of Armenians of different cohorts, in different cities, or in different lines of work has been pitifully sparse; Armenian institutional and organizational history has been equally neglected. Kévork Baghdjian's *La Communauté Arménienne Catholique de Montréal* and his *Les Arméniens au Québec: Aperçu historique*, as well as Garo Chichekian's demographic studies of Armenians in Quebec, notably *The Armenian Community of Quebec* contribute to our understanding of the Quebec community, and Jack Apramian's *Georgetown Boys* is an invaluable description of the Armenian orphan refugee children who were brought to Canada after the Genocide.

Increasing numbers of Armenians are tracing their family histories – histories truncated by the Genocide. One important quantitative source is the ship passenger list. Mark B. Arslan, for example, in researching his family's history, has made his findings of Keghi immigrants who landed at Ellis Island available on the web. Such sources, added to traditional historical documentation such as census data and coupled with city and regional accounts, are necessary early building blocks of Armenian diasporan history in North America. It is to be hoped that in the near future – before records disappear and participants vanish from the historical field – we will see a synthesis of these various studies for a broader perspective of the Armenian diasporan experience.[6]

My history of Armenians in Canada is intended to provide a piece of the great puzzle of the Armenian dispersion and diaspora. It covers approximately one hundred years of Armenian settlement in Canada, from 1887, when the first Armenian is known to have come to this country, to 1988, when Soviet Armenia was shattered by one traumatic event after another: the massacre of Armenians in Sumgait and Baku by Azerbaijanis and the flight of Armenian refugees to Armenia and other parts of the Soviet Union, a devastating earthquake, a crippling blockade imposed by Azerbaijan and Turkey on Armenia and on the Republic of Mountainous Karabagh (Artsakh), and a war between Karabagh and Armenia, on one side, and Azerbaijan on the other.

The declaration of independence on 9 September 1991 by the Republic of Mountainous Karabagh and on 21 September by the Republic of Armenia transformed the diaspora and changed its priorities. The focus of attention has shifted once more to Armenia and Artsakh, because their very existence is at stake. In the press and at meetings – wherever people come together – the same issues are debated, as individuals and groups weigh the needs of Armenia and the responsibilities of the diaspora. Because of these great changes and their impact on the diaspora, it seemed appropriate to end this study before they began and to leave the period after 1988 for others to examine, even though I frequently refer to developments after this date.

In defining the terms of reference for this study, several pressing questions arose. Was it to be about the same people over time, for example, an examination of a family over a period of a hundred years? Or was it to be about a particular group in a particular place, for example, a history of Armenians in Toronto in the twentieth century? Neither option seemed appropriate, because different cohorts of Armenians had settled in different parts of Canada at different times. Armenians in St Catharines, Ontario, in 1925 were not the same as Armenians in Montreal, Quebec, in 1985. Yet both groups identified themselves as Armenian, both were part of the broader Armenian community in Canada, and, most significantly, both could claim a certain amalgamation and continuity.

To deal with these issues, I have structured the book, first, on the basis of the three major waves of immigration: pre–World War I, post–World War I, and post–World War II, drawing out the specificities of each immigrant cohort. Within each section, I have endeavoured to integrate various aspects of community life: immigration, settlement, work, organizations and institutions, and family and community.

Typically, the story begins in a mountainous and remote part of the Ottoman Empire, the home of the earliest Canadian pioneers. Part 1 sketches Armenian life in the district of Keghi within the context of emigration and serves as a case study of Armenian exodus from the historic Armenian provinces in the Ottoman Empire: Erzerum (Karin),

Van, Bitlis, Tigranakert (Diarbakir), Mamuret ul-Aziz (Kharput, Kharpert), and Sivas (Sebastia). Whether the early settlers left as permanent emigrants or as sojourners, their homeland and their identity formed a powerful component of their world.[7]

In spite of stringent immigration regulations obstructing the entry of Armenians, who were classified as Asians, about two thousand entered Canada from the late 1880s to the outbreak of World War I. As shown in part 2, they settled and worked primarily in the growing industrial towns of southern Ontario – Brantford, St Catharines, Hamilton, and Galt – where they established the foundations of community life, even though many intended to return home. But the Genocide changed the course of their lives and transformed forever the nature, composition, and size of these fledgling settlements, as discussed in part 3. Historian Aristakes of Lastivert describes the destruction of Ani, the glorious city of 1001 churches: "Men were slaughtered in the streets, women carried away, infants crushed on the pavements; the comely faces of the young were disfigured, virgins were violated in public, young boys murdered before the eyes of the aged, whose venerable white hairs became bloody and whose corpses rolled on the earth."[8]

This eleventh-century account of the Turkish invasion of the land of Armenia might well have been written about the twentieth century. In 1915 the Ottoman Turks embarked on a well-planned and systematic scheme to annihilate the Armenian people, just as their Turkish ancestors, emerging from the distant reaches of Asia, had wiped out many other peoples living in Anatolia. One and a half million Armenians were lost and the remnant were driven from their homeland and scattered in the Caucasus, the Mediterranean, and Middle Eastern countries. The Genocide is a watershed in the life of the Armenian people, and neither the homeland nor the diaspora can be understood outside the context of events between 1915 and 1923.

After World War I, the mostly male settlers in Canada set about to reconstitute family life. They tried to locate surviving family members and to find suitable wives in orphanages and refugee camps. If Canadian immigration authorities had obstructed entry before 1914, they virtually barricaded the gates after the war, as shown in part 4. In a frenzy of racism, government bureaucrats clamped down to prohibit the entry of Asians, and in a drive to keep out potential "public charges," they banned the admission of refugees. As a result of restrictions, scarcely thirteen hundred Armenians managed to enter Canada from 1915 to 1945. The majority were women and children, reflecting the survival ratios; most were linked to the pre-1914 settlers either as kith or kin.

Part 5 shows that the location of settlement expanded to Guelph,

Preston, Windsor, Toronto, and Montreal. As nuclear family structures replaced the predominantly male society of the pre-1914 period, boardinghouses gave way to single-family homes. From the 1920s to the 1940s, factory labour remained the principal, though not the only, source of family income. Armenian involvement in the factory brought men in touch with the union movement; and Armenians in St Catharines, Brantford, and present-day Cambridge played a leading role in union formation. For many the factory was a bridge to little businesses. Entrepreneurial activity was particularly popular in Toronto, which emerged as the centre of the carpet industry, with a variety of spin-offs. Meanwhile, the younger generation educated in Canada began moving into the professions and the arts, notably medicine, teaching, and music.

Political and religious conflicts were triggered by events largely outside the Armenian Canadian scene. The fall of the independent Armenian republic in 1920, the sovietization of Armenia, the involvement of Russian communism in Armenian affairs, and the murder of an archbishop in New York City in 1933 all had a profound impact on the national consciousness of diasporan Armenians. Like a tidal wave, hostility between the different ideological groups overwhelmed every Armenian settlement in North America and engulfed every aspect of immigrant life.

The Second World War brought a temporary respite, but the Cold War and the split on political grounds in the Armenian Church in 1956 between Echmiadzin, situated in Soviet Armenia, and Cilicia, located in Lebanon, further distanced the warring factions. Gradually, two different communities emerged, with Armenians living in the same neighbourhood, working in the same factories, and attending the same Canadian schools, but each with its own political and religious agendas, community structures, and activities. Each group undertook to perpetuate the Armenian heritage by supporting theatrical and choral groups and supplementary schools, by building churches and community centres, and by establishing political, regional, cultural, sports, youth, and benevolent organizations. The intensity of their commitment is evident: from 1930 to 1960, through great sacrifice and expense, they built or acquired at least six community centres and three churches – a rather impressive feat for an ethnic group numbering fewer than ten thousand people and spread out over Southern Ontario and Quebec.

Like the first two cohorts of Armenian immigration to Canada, the third movement, covered in part 6, was precipitated by upheaval, this time in the Middle Eastern countries where Armenians had found hospitality after the Genocide. Destabilization in the Middle East coincided with the gradual relaxation of Canadian immigration regulations during the 1960s and 1970s. Unlike previous immigration, the flow of Armenians to Canada in the post–World War II period occurred initially through the auspices of an immigration aid organization, the Canadian Armenian Congress, led by Yervant Pasdermajian. The newcomers migrated from big cities like Cairo, Alexandria, Istanbul, Beirut, Athens, and Aleppo and settled mainly in the large urban centres of Montreal and Toronto. Statistics based on the 1981 census reveal that 19.7 percent of the respondents who gave Armenian as their ethnic origin were born in Canada, leaving a full 80 percent as foreign-born. Thus by the 1980s immigrants dominated Armenian community life in Canada, even though Armenians had settled in Canada for almost a hundred years. In spite of the multifarious and multifaceted character of the Armenian diaspora, a strong sense of Armenianness permeated the community, but it was inevitably defined by different groups in different terms.

Although interest in and concern for Armenians overseas continued, the principal focus of the third wave, until 1988 at least, was the North American diaspora. Indeed, Armenians have clearly demonstrated this fact in the last forty years by building community centres and churches of various denominations, launching new diasporan organizations, and establishing full-day Armenian schools.

Within the framework of the three immigration flows, I have examined Armenians in different cities at different times, moving from place to place, analyzing the group in a particular city, at a given time. Three principal factors dictated my choices: the dominance of a city at a specific time, the extent to which developments characterized Armenian community life, and, finally, the availability of sources. For the pioneering period, I concentrate on Brantford, the largest Armenian settlement in Canada before World War I. For the years between World War I and World War II, St Catharines became the principal centre of activity, and during the 1940s and 1950s Hamilton emerged as an important settlement. For the latter part of the twentieth century, I focus on Montreal and Toronto, the main targets of recent Armenian immigration. While each of these five cities has had a specific history, with different outlooks and different priorities, together they represent the experience and the evolution of the Armenian community in Canada and its interaction with Canadian society and life.

Moving more deeply into the structure of the book, I have delineated four major themes that seemed to me to represent the Armenian experience in Canada and demonstrate the transformation from a mentality of exile to a mentality of belonging and from a psychology of homelessness to a psychology of rootedness: 1 attachment to the homeland

and the impact of its loss and revival, 2 determination to retain Armenian ethnic identity in the diaspora, 3 the Genocide and its enduring impact, and 4 loyalty to Canada, the land of refuge.

Armenians show an attachment to their homeland, whether it lies in Turkey, Russia, the Soviet Union, the first independent republic (1918–20), or the current republic (founded in 1991). This affiliation drives internal community dynamics, sometimes in a divisive way, as in the church conflict covered in chapters 12 to 14. More often, the homeland has mobilized different factions to stand united, whether in the educational associations in the pre–World War I period, the fundraising for Genocide survivors, the protests and demonstrations at various levels of government in Canada, the striking mobilization of the community for 1988 earthquake victims, or the current All-Armenia Fund which raises money for schools, hospitals, and highways in the republics of Armenia and mountainous Karabagh. The relationship between homeland and diaspora highlights the interplay between international and local, a dimension that has distinguished the Armenian community since the pioneer period of settlement. Unfortunately our language to describe or define diaspora/homeland consciousness, whether created by voluntary exodus or forced expulsion, is underdeveloped, if not nonexistent. While it is difficult to label the nature and range of diaspora nationalisms/transnationalisms and to pinpoint diaspora nationalisms within different contexts such as religion or politics, I use the term ethnopatriotism as an all-encompassing general word to refer to the sentiments and loyalties of the diaspora toward the homeland.

While Armenians show a strong bond with their homeland and with the concept of a free and independent nation-state, they have responded to their twentieth-century history of genocide and dispersal by embracing the idea of a global nation, a nation that supercedes political boundaries. This diasporan mentality, this ethnoversion, reflects on the next major theme: the desire to retain an Armenian ethnic identity within the larger Canadian society. The ability to remain Armenian, to cling to religion, culture, and history, and, at the same time, to live and participate successfully in a larger non-Armenian society "adds up," says Christopher Walker, "to a national characteristic, if such a thing exists."[9]

Third, I endeavour to portray the lasting legacy of the Genocide. Every Armenian was traumatized by the events from 1915 to 1923. During the atrocities, properties and buildings were destroyed, a culture was decimated, and a nation was reduced to skeletal proportions. The Genocide is a living nightmare that continues to trouble the victims and their descendents. The tragic events have united the various generations, immigration cohorts, and political and religious factions at the same time that the Turkish government's denial that a genocide was perpetrated has, perforce, politicized the Genocide.

During the twentieth century, Armenians were a people on the move. They were forced out of their ancestral homeland, found sanctuary in various Middle Eastern, Mediterranean, and Caucasian countries, then moved again when turmoil and upheaval put life at risk once more. In Canada immigrants encountered a civilized and peaceful world; they found safety and security and lived and worked in a society that accepted them. Armenians – from the earliest settlers fleeing persecution, to refugees seeking sanctuary, to more recent immigrants searching for peace – are deeply grateful to call Canada home. This strong commitment to Canada, in turn, raises the issue of multiple loyalties and civic and private identities, a topic that I refer to in the conclusion and epilogue.

In addition to these four major themes, I have also dealt with a number of subthemes that channel the discourse throughout the narrative: the importance of the factory and the rug industry to economic stability and community development; the role played by the rank and file in establishing and maintaining community development, especially in the early years; the role of women and children in creating and sustaining community life; the backdrop of Canadian institutions, such as the Anglican Church, as vital mechanisms for adjustment to Canada; neighbourhoods as a means of retaining community cohesion and their replacement by large compounds that encompass church, community centre, school, and gym; the various networks that bound Armenians in Canada to each other and to Armenians in other parts of the world; and the melding of people from different diasporas, bringing with them different languages, different forms of the Armenian language, different traditions, and different histories and finding their common denominator in both their ancient Armenian and newly created Canadian identities.

SOURCES

I have tried to link the present to the past in order to understand current developments within the Armenian Canadian community by using a variety of secondary and primary sources: government and non-government archives in Canada, France, Switzerland, the United Kingdom, Armenia, and the United States; Armenian and non-Armenian church records; autobiographies, biographies, memoirs, letters, diaries, and memorabilia; newspapers in Armenian, English, and French; census data; and factory, school, organizational, and cemetery records.

In addition to written sources – both published and unpublished – this book allows the actors to speak for themselves. From the late

1970s to 2002, I interviewed many Armenians in different cities. I have used excerpts from these oral interviews throughout the text. The work of other interviewers is duly acknowledged in the notes. For most of the interviewees I have used pseudonyms to protect their privacy, but I give the actual names, places, and dates of interviews in the bibliography.

When I started researching Armenians in Canada, very little had been published about this group. Not only were secondary sources scarce, but no Armenian archive, library, or collection of primary material could be easily tapped. Aside from documents in the National Archives of Canada and some in the Archives of Ontario, I found – initially at least – that my principal sources were Armenian Canadians themselves. Not only did they disclose factual information about the Old World, their immigration to Canada, and their settlement in this country, but they also gave me access to their personal memorabilia, including memoirs, letters, and photographs. I deposited these "subjective documents" belonging to individuals and Armenian organizations and institutions in the Archives of Ontario and in the Multicultural History Society of Ontario. These resources provide a basis from which future research can now move on a sound footing.

The oral interviews opened up new avenues of research. Reparations, which are covered in chapter 10, provide a case in point. Informants' references led me to search for archival documents to substantiate their accounts about their long and tortuous efforts to receive reparations. Oral sources also enabled me to see patterns of mobility, of work, and of political and religious affiliation. Interviewees shed light on the frequency of sojourning, the places of sojourn, and the length of sojourning by men from the region of Keghi. Similarly, individual life histories of people who were strangers to each other confirmed past events. In recounting their genocide experiences, for example, several informants described the Kurdish and Turkish attacks on unarmed civilians – men, women, and children – near the village of Koulakan in Keghi. Such testimony is all the more precious because these informants personally witnessed and experienced the deportations, refugeeism, and rehabilitation; because they were the last generation from the home soil; and because the destruction of Armenian libraries, archives, manuscripts, and records during and after the Genocide has been exceedingly thorough.

My role as interviewer and investigator was one of involvement. I used a series of interview schedules ranging from the premigration period, the Genocide, survival experiences, and resettlement in Canada. But I did not rigidly follow my questionnaires, preferring to allow the informants to narrate their own story. I tried to distance myself, to be objective, and to avoid leading questions, but in the final analysis, I, as historian, guided the interview by my questions and by restraining the informant from digressing too far afield. At times – depending on the informant and on the topic – the interview moved beyond uncovering facts and evolved into a discussion/debate between the informant and the historian. Thus, the interview itself became a historical text – a vivid reflection and manifestation of the informant's and the investigator's historical experience and vision. The dynamics of the interview could be an object of analysis: a woman who refused to allow her father to discuss his leftist political ideology revealed as much about her relationship with her father as about her own values and outlook.[10]

Oral interviews remain controversial historical sources. Certainly, one must be constantly on the alert for mythologizing, self-aggrandizement, personal prejudices, and outright fabrications. It is as obligatory to corroborate information from the spoken word as it is to verify information from the written one. What emerged from my encounters, aside from factual material, were people's own emotions, their impressions, perspectives, attitudes, and values. These aspects of reality – including the fabrications and the prejudices – are as historically revealing as are census data, government archives, and organizational records.

Oral sources have been criticized because they rely on memory, and memory is fragile, ephemeral. But memory can also be powerful and enduring. I recall a colleague some years ago questioning me on the authenticity of oral sources, considering that I was interviewing people about events – the Genocide, notably – that had taken place decades before. He brushed aside the soundness of memory, particularly of elderly people. But he remained silent when I repeated what an interviewee had told me after I remarked on her ability to remember the most minute detail of her experience. "I never forgot. I think of those events every day of my life." Who can forget seeing a young friend buried up to his neck, then a grown man, swinging by on horseback and decapitating him? How can a child forget seeing his mother stabbed to death? How can a mother forget the rape of her daughter, the murder of her children? Individuals do not forget tragedies and triumphs; neither do groups. Nor should they. It is their defiance against their adversaries and the key to their resurrection.

This book is far from a complete history, however. An analysis, for instance, of Armenian Canadian artistic achievement might examine Old and New World influences on creativity; the Armenian boys at the Georgetown farm/home/school merit a separate history; and an examination of the relationship between the Canadian diaspora and the newly created Armenian republic still demands attention.

AUDIENCE

My approach in presenting multiple voices based on hundreds of original sources, in analyzing gender roles and relationships within families and communities, and in viewing community organizations and institutions as points of rivalry between discourses about national symbols is intended for the general reader interested in the diverse population of Canada. Fortunately, in the last few decades the social history of ethnic groups has advanced as a legitimate field of academic research and writing. The academic reader will easily recognize perspectives and techniques that reflect recent developments in social-history methodology, some of which I have tried to incorporate in a seamless and subtle manner.

I have also written this book for those of Armenian descent who are trying to understand part of their heritage. This book is for the young woman who recreated her identity as an adult, learning to speak and read Armenian on her own, since her parents had rejected their Armenian identity in an attempt to be Canadian. It is for the young woman whose father was dissowned by his parents for marrying a non-Armenian. It is for the young man who is ashamed of his background because his grandmother, overwhelmed by her terrible experiences during the Genocide, was eventually driven to a mental institution. This work is for all those who grew up in an atmosphere of woe and lamentation and who too seldom rejoiced in the victory and successes of their people.

Finally, I should comment about my own role in this study. It has been both difficult and rewarding. To examine the Armenian experience in Canada, I have relied heavily on my own memory of that experience. Luckily, I was blessed with a family who had a sense of history. We discussed and analyzed all local events, marriages and funerals, visitors to the city, feuds, gossip, attitudes, and ideas. World events were also topics of family conversation, but always within the context of the impact on Armenia and Armenians. In a way, then, this history has been an attempt to cull the depths of my own memory, like looking into a huge mass of ice, where I tried to see deep into the centre of the block.

But looking at myself and my world was not my only role, since I was and continue to be a participant in and observer of Armenian community life. I am still touched by the melancholy eyes and quivering lips of the all too few survivors as they describe their terror during the Genocide. I am still moved by the forlorn mountain music. I still laugh at the lusty humour, partake of the feasts, join in the animated dancing, and weep at the tragedy of a people. To be a participant and an observer and to write about it gave me a new perspective on events, people, and developments, and it required self-restraint, for I had to set aside my personal feelings and prejudices in order to try to present as balanced and as accurate an account as I could, based on the information I had gathered. The experience was like looking at myself in a pool of water, where the water was not always still. Sometimes it became turbulent and I was obliged to wait until the waters had calmed down.

And this brings me to the role of historian: studying and analyzing the world of an intriguing group of people, reading the documents, examining the photos, interviewing the participants. It was like looking through a glass window at a distant, complex, and multilayered cityscape to probe the streets and alleyways, the houses and temples, the offices and concert halls, the shops and schools and to try to understand the people who made the city alive and robust. In a way, this story is from the inside out, for I have tried to grasp the heartbeat, the mentality, and the very soul of the community by blending memory, compassion, and distance. I hope I have done justice to the men, women, and children who made it all happen.

PRELUDE

Although we are small and very limited in numbers, not a powerful people, and many times have been subjugated by foreign kingdoms, yet too, many deeds of bravery have been performed in our land which are worthy of record, but which no one has troubled to write down.
Movses Khorenatsi, *History of the Armenians*

Since ancient times, faith and geography have personified the Armenian spirit. Even before Armenia adopted Christianity as a state religion in 301, religion and rock formed part of the people's folklore and psyche. Legend has it that there was once a *vishap* (dragon) that attacked flocks of sheep and their shepherds. One of the shepherds beseeched the intervention of the god Peer and vowed that if the sheep was spared, he would sacrifice twelve sheep to the god. The shepherd's request was granted and the dragon was petrified into a gigantic mountain called Ahjdahai Mountain. The shepherd's reluctance to fulfill his end of the bargain, however, infuriated the god, who then turned sheep and shepherds into rock.

Since the time Christianity was brought to Armenians, religion and rock have continued to mesh, but now in the form of stone churches, stone sculptures, and stone crosses. *Khachkars* (literally, cross stones) were used as tombstones and thus symbolize death, but they also symbolize the rock land of Armenia, the rock land of eternity. The magnificent designs – both geometric and floral – entwine the cross, each line cut with such precision that "the stark white of the surface is a brilliant foil to the shadowy grooves." These elegant designs reflect the tension of the cross itself, symbol both of creativity and suffering, the symbol of "a culture crossed and double-crossed because of her Christianity and her idealistic expectations of other Christian powers." [11] The stone cross epitomizes a land crisscrossed by the cultures of East and West, North and South, and by warring armies stamping across the land of Armenia, the land of rock. Typically, the cross stone has accompanied another cross – the cross sword, the symbol of temporal, worldly, and secular power. The cross and the sword have intersected just as religion and politics have intercrossed in the long and remarkable history of these mountain people and their great empires, mighty armies, magnificent cities, radiant churches, beautiful literature, and exquisite art and architecture.

It is characteristic of Armenians, then, that in 2001 they celebrated two very important church and state events: the seventeen hundredth anniversary of the adoption of Christianity as the state religion of Armenia and the tenth anniversary of the independence of the Republic of Armenia and the Republic of Mountainous Karabagh. Festivities, pilgrimages, concerts, colloquia, and special divine services were held in every country where an Armenian community existed. But the principal events took place in the Republic of Armenia, where religion and politics have been the nucleus and the underpinnings of relations with the widely dispersed Armenian diaspora.

On 20 September 2001, His Holiness Karekin II, Catholicos of the Mother See at Echmiadzin, led a pilgrimage of distinguished leaders of Christian churches to the Monastery of Khor Virap. The entourage included His Holiness Aram I, Catholicos of the Great House of Cilicia, and the Armenian Patriarchs of Jerusalem and Constantinople (Istanbul); heads of the Oriental Orthodox churches and the Russian Orthodox Church; delegations from the Greek, Romanian, and Georgian Orthodox Churches; and the Archbishop of the Anglican Church. Khor Virap is the dungeon where St Gregory the Illuminator, founder of the Armenian Church, was interred for thirteen years in the third century, before converting King Tiridates III and ushering in state Christianity in Armenia in 301.

After prayers at Khor Virap, the pilgrimage travelled to Tsitsernakaberd, the memorial monument dedicated to the martyrs of the Armenian Genocide (1915-23). "These two visits have great significance for us," remarked Archbishop Hovnan Derderian, Primate of the Armenian Diocese in Canada and Executive Secretary of the Seventeen Hundredth Anniversary Celebrations Ecclesiastical Committee. "If the

Monastery of Khor Virap symbolizes the Christian 'birth' of the Armenians, then Tsitsernakaberd symbolizes our resurrection." On Saturday, 22 September, the Ceremony of the Blessing of the Holy Chrism (Muron), the holy oil, took place on the newly built altar of Holy Echmiadzin, and on the following day, the new cathedral in Yerevan, St Gregory the Illuminator, was consecrated.

The second phase of ceremonies took place from 25 to 27 September, when His Holiness Pope John Paul II visited Armenia, the first Roman Catholic pontiff to do so. The Holy Father celebrated Divine Liturgy in Echmiadzin and an ecumenical service in the Cathedral of St Gregory the Illuminator in Yerevan. In 2001, on the occasion of Catholicos Karekin II's visit to the Vatican, Pope John Paul II presented him with priceless relics of St Gregory "as a testimony of love and brotherhood between the two churches." For more than five hundred years these relics of the first Armenian Catholicos had lain at the Cathedral of San Gregorio Armeno in Naples. On the occasion of the Pope's visit, these relics were solemnly installed in St Gregory's Cathedral in the Armenian capital. On 27 September, the Pope and the Catholicos signed a historic joint declaration that stated, in part: "The extermination of a million and a half Armenian Christians, in what is generally referred to as the first genocide of the Twentieth Century, and the subsequent annihilation of thousands under the former totalitarian regime are tragedies that still live in the memory of the present-day generation."[12]

During September, Armenians throughout the world celebrated the tenth anniversary of the independence of Armenia and of Mountainous Karabagh. After six hundred years of conquest, the first independent republic, founded in 1918, fell to the combined invasion of Turkey and Communist Russia. What little remained of historic Armenia emerged as Soviet Armenia, which dominated the homeland scene and influenced the diaspora for seventy years, covering most of the twentieth century. With the collapse of the Soviet Union, a new republic was born in 1991, once again transforming the relations between homeland and diaspora.

BACKGROUND

Here is a people who have learned to rejoice in the genius of the soul.

Yeghishé Charents

Armenians are a Caucasian people, and they speak an Indo-European language. For three thousand years they inhabited the area around Lake Van, Lake Sevan, Mt Ararat, and the upper reaches of the

Euphrates and Tigris rivers. At the crossroads between East and West, North and South, "Armenia has been the theatre of perpetual war" (Edward Gibbon).

Armenians are indigenous to a region that straddles present-day Turkey, Iran, and parts of the Caucasus that were formerly under Russian/Soviet domination. Before 1914, between two and two and one-quarter million Armenians lived in the Ottoman empire, and about one to one and one-half million in the Caucasus region of the Russian empire. Large enclaves resided in Tiflis, Constantinople, and Cilicia, which encompassed the lands of the last Armenian kingdom (1080–1375) and is located in present-day southern Turkey. Most Armenians lived in the six Armenian provinces: Erzerum, Van, Bitlis, Tigranakert, Kharput, and Sebastia. Today the Republic of Armenia is home to about three million Armenians of a total world population of about six and one-half million.

The interrelationship between old land and new is further complicated by the fact that Armenians are also linked to a widespread diaspora, the result of oppression and deportation. In contemporary times Armenian communities in various Middle Eastern countries, including Lebanon, Syria, Egypt, and Iran, expanded and multiplied. Armenians also settled in large numbers in France, notably in and around Paris, Lyons, and Marseilles. In the United States they put down roots in New England, New York, and California well over a hundred years ago. Clearly, to understand the Armenians, it is essential to see them not only in their local environment in Canada but also in the context of the old land and the extensive diaspora.

Armenian identity cannot be separated from the Armenian Church. The Holy Armenian Apostolic Church is both national and apostolic, the result of the proselytizing work of the apostles St Thaddeus and St Bartholomew between AD 43 and AD 68. Even before AD 301 Armenians had established a number of bishoprics, most notably in the region of Erzerum. But 301 is significant because in that year, through the mission of St Gregory the Illuminator, Armenians adopted Christianity as a state religion, the first nation to do so. Conversion to Christianity ushered in a great revolution among the Armenian people, not only in the religious sphere, moving from a pantheon of gods to one God, faith in Jesus Christ, and belief in the Trinity, but also in the social and moral spheres. The treatment of women and children, for example, changed dramatically as polygamy and infanticide were denounced and practised less and less.

The spiritual head of the Armenian Church, the Catholicos, was traditionally and universally recognized at Echmiadzin, the Mother See. However, Echmiadzin was not the only Catholicosate. Because of the vagaries of Armenian history, the Holy See had to be transferred to other places after 453: to Ani in Anatolia and Sis in Cilicia (1293). Sis was the capital of the Armenian Kingdom of Cilicia, created following the flight of Armenians from Seljuk invaders in the thirteenth and fourteenth centuries. In 1441 Echmiadzin was revived and recognized as the principal Armenian See. It exercised jurisdiction over Greater Armenia, and the Catholicos carried the title Catholicos of All Armenians. The Catholicos of Cilicia carried the title of Catholicos of the Great House of Cilicia and exercised control over Cilicia and the Levant. Echmiadzin and Cilicia carefully guarded the dioceses under their respective jurisdictions. By the turn of the twentieth century, the Armenian church reflected the political vicissitudes of the nation: the spiritual head of the Armenian church, the Catholicos, resided in the Mother See of Echmiadzin, near Yerevan, in the Russian Empire. The Cilician See, in the Ottoman Empire, recognized the Mother See and shared the same dogma, theology, and liturgy but remained administratively separate.

During the Genocide, the Turks exiled the Catholicos of Cilicia, Sahag II, from Sis; in 1921 he and his flock found refuge in Lebanon. Eight years later, as its own operations were winding down, the Near East Relief placed under the disposition of the Holy Father the buildings of a former orphanage in Antelias, outside the city of Beirut. Through the generosity of Armenian benefactors, the church eventually purchased the property. At the same time, with the sovietization of the independent Armenian republic in the 1920s, the Mother See was stifled by the Communist regime.

During the twentieth century, both Catholicoses have exercised jurisdiction over Armenians in North America, the division having been generated by political rather than doctrinal differences. With the collapse of Communism, the Mother See breathes freely once again, after seventy years of bondage. The church's liberation has intensified efforts to bring about union of the two jurisdictions of the Holy Armenian Apostolic Church.

The two sees do not differ in dogma, doctrine, liturgy, or rites. Both view the Apostolic Church as the national church of the Armenians, whereby the church and the people, regardless of where they might be, constitute an indivisible whole. They admit as essential the dogmatic definitions of the first three church councils only and accordingly uphold the Nicene Creed. By contrast, the Roman Catholic and Orthodox Churches accept the decisions of subsequent councils. Tolerant towards other denominations, the Apostolic Church accepts all who believe in the Trinity, the Incarnation, and the Redemption of Christ as part of the Universal Church.

One of the major strengths of the Apostolic Church lies in its democratic foundation and character. Joint lay and clerical councils elect all clergy, including the Catholicos; and elected lay and ecclesiastic representatives share all church governance. Priests are ordained by bishops. The lower-order priests, or *kahanas*, are allowed to marry, but not the *vardapets* (masters of divinity), from whose ranks the church hierarchy is chosen.

The liturgy is still celebrated in classical Armenian, though the sermon and some prayers and readings may be said in the vernacular language, in English or French, depending on circumstances. Usually, the chants and hymns are from the music of Makar Yekmalian or Komitas Vardapet. To accommodate parishioners, the church has had the Bible translated into the modern vernacular, has shortened the length of the *patarag* (Mass) and reduced the number of services, and has embarked on an educational program to explain the ancient rituals and their symbolism to the faithful. Unlike other churches with seven sacraments, the Apostolic Church combines Baptism, Confirmation, and First Communion in one sacrament shortly after birth. Confession is public, with ritualized prayers, and Unction (not Extreme Unction) is administered in the visitation of the ill. Armenians celebrate five main feasts, namely, the Nativity (6 January), Easter, Transfiguration, the Assumption of Mary, and the Exaltation of the Cross. St Gregory the Illuminator, as founder of the Armenian Church, St James (Surp Hagop), and St Mesrob Mashtots are the principal saints. Flexible in doctrine and liberal in outlook, the Apostolic Church has endured for seventeen hundred years. For the last five hundred years, as is the case today, the two sees have responded to the pastoral needs of Armenians embracing different political or state allegiances.

The Catholicosates should not to be confused with the Patriarchate of Constantinople or with the Patriarchate of Jerusalem, which are administrative units. Following the conquest of Armenia by the Ottoman Turks, Armenians were designated a "millet," or religious community, under the supervision of the Armenian bishop of Constantinople, who eventually earned the title of patriarch. In doctrinal matters the patriarch looked and continues to look to Echmiadzin, but as the leader of the Apostolic millet, he represented his flock to the Turkish government and holds a measure of responsibility for Armenian churches, schools, hospitals, and social services in Turkey. Another Armenian patriarch resides in Jerusalem, with his seat at the Cathedral of St James. The Armenian church shares the premises of the Church of the Holy Sepulchre in Jerusalem and the Church of the Nativity in Bethlehem with the Roman Catholic and Greek Orthodox Churches.

Before the Genocide, about 95 percent of Armenians in both Turkey and Russia belonged to the Apostolic Church. The remainder adhered to the Catholic or Protestant faiths, also classified as millets by the Turkish government. The Catholics, led by their patriarch in Constantinople, achieved the status of millet in 1830. Their most outstanding monk was Mkhitar of Sivas (1676–1749), founder of the Mkhitarist order (1701) and the monastery on the Island of San Lazarro, off the coast of Venice, Italy, in 1715. With their emphasis on education and printing, the Mkhitarists have acted as a vital bridge between Europe and the Armenians.

Protestant missionaries, particularly from the United States, started proselytizing among Armenians in the Ottoman empire in the early nineteenth century. In 1850, they, too, were granted the status of millet by Turkish authorities. Like the Catholics, the Protestant missionaries did not succeed in making great inroads to converting the masses, but their impact on education, printing, and health services contributed immeasurably to the progress and Westernization of the Armenian people. Today, the majority of Armenians in Canada adhere to the Apostolic Church, but Catholic and Protestant Churches also have their faithful followers.

In the sphere of Armenian language and literature, the role of religious forces has been multifaceted. In AD 404–5, Mesrob Mashtots, with the support and inspiration of Catholicos Sahag, developed the Armenian alphabet, which, like the autocephalic Armenian Church itself, is unique. The formation of the alphabet – in effect, Armenianizing Christianity – ushered in, during the fifth century, the Golden Age of Armenian literature, the most outstanding achievement of which was the translation of the Bible, "the Queen of Versions."[13] The *grabar*, or classical language, was used in church services and on formal occasions, while the people spoke a vernacular form. During the Armenian Reawakening, or *Zartonk*, of the nineteenth century, the vernacular language became more commonly used in popular literature and in mass education. Many of the nineteenth-century intellectual, social, and political innovations owed much to Armenians living and studying abroad, a flourishing intelligentsia among Armenians in Russia and Turkey, the endeavours of the Armenian Catholic Mkhitarist monks in Venice and Vienna, the work and influence of American Protestant missionaries and the enormous reforms carried out by the Armenian Apostolic Church and its supporters. The vernacular itself was and continues to be rent by two major forms of the language – Eastern Armenian, spoken in Armenia and Iran, and Western Armenian, used everywhere else.

The complexities of language usage in Canada seem limitless. Aside from trying to balance Armenian, English, and French, Armenians must deal with the classical in church services and the vernacular in day-to-day life. Until the last twenty years, the most common form of the vernacular among Armenian immigrants was the Western. With the recent movement from Iran and Armenia, the Eastern form has become increasingly popular, a fact that may cause tension, especially in full-day Armenian-language schools. Some immigrants, furthermore, who identify as Armenians do not speak any form of the language, but, depending on their background, function most frequently in English, French, Arabic, or Turkish. The ramifications of language proliferation seep into the veins and arteries of the community and affect everyday life in a multitude of ways.

The twentieth century has not been kind to the Armenian people. Genocide, famine, dispersal, internecine strife, earthquake, and war pummelled this small nation. A collective burden of victimization and martyrdom, evil foreboding and cursed fate traumatized the Armenian psyche. And yet the Armenian nation survived. Like seeds cast on fertile ground, the Armenian people, at home and abroad, were reborn. The blows of destiny did not break the spirit of the Armenians. Instead, they strengthened a determination to survive and not vanish into the shadows of history. In spite of losses, or perhaps because of them, in spite of small numbers, or perhaps because of them, the will of a people, scattered though they are, has not dissolved in the face of tragedy. Only a people with such tenacity, resolve, and creativity could write these words:

> Yes, we are small
> the smallest pebble
> in a field of stones.
> But have you felt the hurtle
> of pebbles pitched
> from a mountain top?
> Small, yes,
> you have compressed us world.
> into a diamond.[14]

His Holiness Vazken I, Catholicos of all Armenians (Echmiadzin, Armenia), at left and His Holiness Karekin II of the Great House of Cilicia (Antelias, Lebanon) in brotherly harmony after mass in Armenia after the 1988 earthquake.
Following the death of Catholicos Vazken I, Catholicos Karekin II of Cilicia was elected Catholicos Karekin I of Echmiadzin in 1995. He served until his premature death in 1999.
Photographer Harry L. Koundakjian.

NOTE ON TRANSLITERATION

Generally, I have transliterated Armenian words according to the phonetic values of Eastern and Classical Armenian without diacritical marks. The principal exception is in the use of proper names. As a rule, I spell names of people and organizations according to their own usage. For example, General Andranik's name takes the Eastern form while a Canadian resident would more usually have preferred the Western form, Antranig. Similarly with Gabriel and Kapriel, Surp and Surb (Saint). This shifting between Eastern and Western forms may be confusing to the reader, but I considered it the only appropriate way to deal with language complexities. Of course in direct quotations the original spelling is preserved.

Transliteration Key

Ա	ա	a	Ծ	ծ	ds	Ձ	ձ	dj
Բ	բ	b	Կ	կ	k	Ռ	ռ	r
Գ	գ	g	Հ	հ	h	Ս	ս	s
Դ	դ	d	Ձ	ձ	dz	Վ	վ	v
Ե	ե	ye,[1] e	Ղ	ղ	gh	Տ	տ	t
Զ	զ	z	Ճ	ճ	j	Ր	ր	r
Է	է	e	Մ	մ	m	Ց	ց	ts
Ը	ը	e	Յ	յ	h,[1] y,[2]	Ւ	ւ	v
Թ	թ	t	Ն	ն	n	Փ	փ	p
Ժ	ժ	zh	Շ	շ	sh	Ք	ք	k
Ի	ի	i	Ո	ո	vo,[1] o	Օ	օ	o
Լ	լ	l	Չ	չ	ch	Ֆ	ֆ	f
Խ	խ	kh	Պ	պ	p			

Diphthongs

ու u, v[3]   եա ia, ya[4]

ոյ ui, oy,[3] o[2]   յա ya[4]

այ ai, ay[3], a[2]

---

[1] In the initial position.
[2] The letter յ is not transliterated in the final position.
[3] When followed by a vowel.
[4] When preceded by a vowel.

Acronyms

ABCFM   American Board of Commissioners for Foreign Missions
ACP   Armenian Communist Party
ACYOA   Armenian Church Youth Organization of America
ACYOC   Armenian Church Youth Organization of Canada
ADL   Armenian Democratic Liberal Organization (Ramgavar)
AFL   American Federation of Labour
AGBU   Armenian General Benevolent Union
AMAA   Armenian Missionary Association of America
ANC   Armenian National Committee
ANCC   Armenian National Committee of Canada
ANCHA   Armenian National Committee to Aid Homeless Armenians
ARAC   Armenian Relief Association of Canada
ARF   Armenian Revolutionary Federation (Dashnak)
ARS   Armenian Relief Society
AUM   Armenian Union of Montreal
AYA   Armenian Youth Association
AYF   Armenian Youth Federation
CAC   Canadian Armenian Congress
CAU   Canadian Armenian Union
CAYPA   Canadian Armenian Young Peoples' Association
CCC   Canadian Council of Churches
CCF   Co-operative Commonwealth Federation
CCL   Canadian Congress of Labour
CEF   Canadian Expeditionary Force
CCP   Canadian Communist Party

CIO	Committee for Industrial Organization, Congress of Industrial Organizations
CUP	Committee of Union and Progress
GM	General Motors
HMEM	Armenian General Sports Union
HOG	Relief Committee for Armenia
M.E.G.	Cultural Alumni of Mkhitarian, Esayan, and Getronagan Colleges
NA	National Archives of Canada
NEI	Near East Industries
NER	Near East Relief
PRO	Public Record Office
RG	Record Group
SDH	Social Democrat Hnchakian
SWOC	Steel Workers' Organizing Committee
UAA	United Armenian Association
UCA	United Church Archives
UCC	United Church of Canada
WUL	Workers' Unity League

PART ONE

The Old World

I

Keghi: Land of Mountains

The mountain of St. Light was their symbol of liberty and strength.

The nineteenth-century traveller who veered off the ancient caravan route from Trebizond to Tabriz at Erzerum to head southward towards Keghi penetrated a majestically beautiful but remote land, a region of danger and violence. With its soaring mountain peaks and sweeping gorges, Keghi rose up like an earthly paradise. Indeed, its ancient name, Khorshian, Khortsine, or Xorjean – deep sound – conjured up the mystery of wind and thunder echoing from mountain to mountain. Situated approximately seventeen hundred metres above sea level, with mountain peaks scaling more than three thousand metres, and cut by the Gayl (Wolf) River, the *kaza*, or district or township, of Keghi (Geghi, Kgi, Kigi, Kghi, Keli) lay surrounded by the Dersim, Bingol, and Sheytan mountain ranges.[1]

The settled population of Keghi, primarily small farmers, eked out an existence from the harsh land, while fending off ruthless Kurdish brigands, great semifeudal Moslem landowners and tribes, and a central administration intent on squeezing the last penny out of the peasants but unwilling or unable to protect and defend them. Young and adventurous men ventured out of the region to seek their fortunes in other places: cosmopolitan Smyrna and Constantinople, fabled Alexandria and Aleppo, industrializing centres of the Caucasus in czarist Russia, or the developing Balkan countries. These were the trailblazers who sailed across many seas and set down roots of Armenian settlement in a far-off British dominion. Some newcomers embarked on their way to Canada from intermediate countries, such as Bulgaria or the United States, while others travelled from the Ottoman empire, either after a sojourn in cities like Constantinople or directly from their home village. The people of Keghi, called Keghetsis, were joined by coreligionists from all the Armenian provinces, including Erzerum (Karin), Van, Bitlis, Diarbakir (Tigranakert), Mamuret-ul-Aziz (Kharpert, Kharput), and Sivas (Sebastia), and especially from areas in and around the towns of Mush, Balu, Kharput, Bitlis, Van, and Jabaghjur and from the great metropolis of Constantinople (Bolis, Polis). Except for the small group of Constantinople immigrants, the newcomers were largely men of the agricultural, artisan, and small entrepreneurial classes, and they shared similar social, cultural, religious, economic, and political backgrounds.

Because about 90 percent of Armenian pioneers came originally from Keghi, this part, which focuses on old-country origins, sketches Armenian life in Keghi from the late nineteenth century to 1914, roughly during the reign of Sultan Abdul Hamid II (1878–1908) and the early years of the Young Turk regime. This brief study of Keghi examines the reasons Armenians left the Ottoman empire and sheds light on the experiences, values, and priorities that shaped their lives. How, for example, does a man whose sister was abducted by Kurdish outlaws protect his daughter in Canada? How does a boy who saw Turkish gendarmes beat his father to death react to government and police in North America? How does a Christian minority that for centuries coped with persecution by Moslems deal with the openness and freedom of a Christian society? This portrayal of Keghi will represent, furthermore, a microcosm of rural life among Armenians in the interior, where approximately 80 to 85 percent of the Armenian population was engaged in agriculture.[2] Keghi was neither separate nor unique. It was part of the Armenian nation, and the fate of its people was inextricably entwined with the fate of all Armenians in the Ottoman Empire.

CONDITIONS IN KEGHI

As in other regions of Anatolia, Keghi was marked by complex racial, linguistic, and religious structures. Keghi district lay in the *sanjak*, or county, of Erzerum in the *vilayet*, or province, of Erzerum. In the early twentieth century, approximately half the population of Keghi were Armenians and the remainder Shiite Kurds; about 10 percent of the total were Sunni Turks, mostly government officials, great landowners, and soldiers. Statistics concerning the total number of inhabitants in Keghi at the turn of the century vary from forty to sixty thousand and concerning the number of Armenians from twenty to thirty-five thousand. Some of the statistical discrepancies are no doubt due to whether or not sojourners and emigrants were included in the calculations.³ Before World War 1 about 363 large and small villages, including 51 Armenian and part-Armenian villages and hamlets, dotted the countryside and fell under the governance of a *kaimakam* (an appointed ruler) operating from Keghi Kasaba, the only town in the district and the region's administrative, religious, educational, and judicial capital.⁴ The sedentary Christian Armenians, mostly yeomen and peasants, artisans, and small merchants struggled to survive and to retain a measure of their identity in the midst of their Moslem neighbours: Kurdish and Turkish "country notables," nomadic and transhumance Kurdish tribes, government officials, and subsistence farmers. Shepherds and day labourers – both Christian and Moslem – fell to the bottom of the social and economic order.

The Armenians of Keghi – hardy mountain folk – were rugged individualists, yet they nurtured a strong communal society. Aside from the family and clan, which were like a fortress itself, the most important structure of community organization was the village, typically consisting of a cluster of small mud-brick or stone buildings, with pastures and fields beyond the inhabited area. Where racial and religious diversity did not complicate or dissipate village loyalty, village inhabitants were committed to defending the village's reputation and its boundaries and to serving the village and its people. To the Armenians the village represented a unit of self-sufficiency, self-help, and self-defence. If, for instance, the village depended on irrigation, it was the collective responsibility of all households to keep the canals clean and in good repair and to regulate the water supply equitably. If the government or its agents levied a tax on the village, the obligation fell on the whole village, and the village leaders, directed by the elected *rais*, or headman, divided the load among various households according to their ability to pay. In turn, each family expected the villagers to rally to it in times of need: to build a barn, extinguish a fire, repel an attack.

The village was composed of distinct patrilineal and patrilocal *tuner* (households). In Keghi households extended vertically from the nuclear family, or *entanik*, and included father, mother, both bachelor and married sons with their families, unmarried daughters, and perhaps single or widowed elderly relatives. Under the authority of the family patriarch, all members of the household pooled their property and resources and contributed their time and talents to the welfare and well-being of the household.⁵

Each *tun* occupied a small dwelling attached to or above a stable. Household members lived in one room, in which they ate, sat, and slept, rolling out their mattresses at night around the fireplace. Some families also had a small room with a *tonir*, an inverted, brick-lined cone oven dug into the floor and used for baking bread. Usually *kertastan*, or kin, lived in a block of interconnected buildings constructed as a "labyrinthine ... warren in which people could hide themselves and their valuables" at the time of an attack.[6] In the late nineteenth century these dwellings became overcrowded. It was not unusual to find fifteen people living in a space approximately twelve feet by twenty-five feet. To deal with such overcrowding, families sometimes partitioned the land and built new dwellings, thus creating more households.

The kinship group ran through the male line from a common ancestor at least three or four generations back. Although the rights and duties of members may not have been precisely defined, the kinship ties always remained very intimate and extremely intense. A villager would generally identify himself by referring to his clan name first, then his village of origin. Frequently the kinship network broadened out beyond the village – either through out-marriage or godfathering – to create new and vital channels for economic, political, religious, and familial activities. This extension, in turn, forged new kinship ties.

Land tenure consisted of a mixture of small, privately owned, fragmented, and dispersed strips; usufructuary and emphyteutic lands in the hands of local and absentee Moslem landlords (*beys and aghas*: semi-feudal lords or tribal chieftains) who allowed the peasants to use the land and to pass on to their heirs the rights of use; and government-owned pastures and forests. In a list noting the holdings of seventeen Keghi families, the size of the farms ranges from fifteen to three hundred acres, with nine farms of more than a hundred acres. As the mountain sides afforded good pasturage, sheep and goat farming evolved as the most profitable and reliable means of livelihood in Keghi. Each spring, villagers, especially women and children, migrated up to the *oba*, the summer encampment in the mountains. While the sheep and goats were grazing, villagers collected herbs and prepared food for winter consumption. Although they planted primarily grain, their attempts to cultivate crops on a large scale were thwarted by geographic factors: little arable land, a short and dry growing season, long harsh winters, and periodic drought. Moreover, local implements – the crotched stick-plow, the long-tined wooden winnowing fork, the ox-drawn threshing sledge were as crude as the methods of farming. The laborious and unsatisfactory means of breaking up the soil impressed an observer who noted that use of the wooden plow, with eight or ten yoke of oxen was so inefficient that "the amount turned per day would not equal a few hours plowing with an up-to-date plow and a strong team of horses." Despite the primitive methods and tools, British consular representatives and American and Canadian missionaries regarded Armenians as comparatively good farmers. British vice-consul in Van, C.M. Hallward, for instance, was not surprised when a Moslem lord in Bitlis replaced the Kurds in one of his villages by Armenian farmers in order to increase production; and the Canadian missionary Rev. Dr Robert Chambers repeatedly praised Armenian skill in viticulture and silk production.[7]

While the village agricultural economy relied principally on raising sheep and goats and cultivating grain, the need for self-sufficiency and the prospect for profit combined to generate trade and commerce in the township. For the shoes, sickles, scythes, woolens, and linens that they produced, the villagers of Tarman (Darman, Temran), for example, bartered for butter, cheese, madsun (yogurt), nuts, and grains with friendly Kurdish villagers. As the main road, dangerous though it was, wound through the valley of the Gayl River (Keghi Su), enterprising villages profited from feeding and housing caravaneers and from purchasing their wares for trade. Individual craftsmen such as tinkers, stone masons, tailors, cobblers, iron mongers, carpenters, weavers, potters, dye makers, blacksmiths, and honey and candle makers contributed their talents to local endeavour and to trade with surrounding areas, including Mush, Kharput, Balu, and Erzerum.[8]

In Keghi, farmers were entrepreneurs with respect both to selling their harvest and to generating additional resources through diversification of work. Lines between agricultural activity, on the one hand, and artisanal and commercial endeavours, on the other, were often blurred in a mixed economy as farmers engaged in commerce and merchants engaged in farming. Lines between rural and urban also merged as farmers maintained regular links with different cities, but especially with the district town of Keghi Kasaba and with the more distant provincial capital of Erzerum, both of which were imbedded in an agricultural economy.

While most large villages had a cobbler, a dry goods store, and a barber/bonesetter/midwife, the main focus of merchant and artisanal activity remained Keghi Kasaba. Vera Laligian, for example, described how her father and uncle ran a dry goods and shoe shop in town, selling new shoes and repairing used ones. Gulnaz Bakaian's father operated a café, and Antranig Shamigian's great grandfather, a master craftsman, constructed such buildings as baths and flour mills.[9]

Industrious in their daily toil, attached to their homeland, and loyal both to their church and the sultan, thousands of Keghi Armenians, nevertheless, left their beloved country. The causes of this exodus were as intricate as the manifold racial, religious, social, political, and economic complexities that plagued the region. A 1911 report by the Armenian Revolutionary Federation fieldworker, Simon Vratsian, following his travels through Keghi, described the tough living conditions. Only one-tenth of Keghi benefited from the mountain springs, while nine-tenths of the *kaza* suffered from lack of water. Yet with proper irrigation and some simple agricultural improvements the region could have overcome the problems of drought and famine and easily sustained the sparse population. Rich mineral deposits in the Keghi mountains lay untouched. Private entrepreneurs eager to develop these resources were not only discouraged but often viewed with suspicion by officials who regarded such venturers as ripe for the plucking.

Roads and bridges, the report continued, were dirty, unkempt, broken-down, and hazardous. Travellers, goods, and the mail were perpetually at the mercy of bandits: "Like a slaughterhouse, blood flowed along the highways." The perils of travel and transportation exposed the peasants' vulnerability. Unable to transport their surplus produce to market, Keghi farmers found themselves time and again in desperate straits and were compelled to sell their merchandise to local buyers at rock-bottom prices. For want of a doctor, a nurse, or a dispensary, people died needlessly. Government buildings were run-down and decrepit, jails unfit for human habitation, and bureaucrats and police corrupt and inefficient.[10]

At a time when the Ottoman state was beleaguered by successive wars and rebellions, it was further weakened by financial and economic mismanagement and corruption. In 1854, during the Crimean War, the Ottoman government borrowed £3 million at 6 percent interest from European countries. By 1881 the public debt had escalated to £200 million, resulting in the creation of the Public Debt Administration and eventually the establishment of the Ottoman Bank, both of which were controlled by and responsible to foreign creditors. During the latter part of the nineteenth century, European investment in Ottoman finances and the economy expanded. Most infrastructure construction, like road, bridge, tram, railway, port, and quay construction; most gas, electrical, and water development; some of the small number of mines and factories; and, significantly, the production and export of tobacco were dominated by Europeans. Western states, furthermore, flooded the Ottoman market with cheap manufactured goods, especially textiles, with the consequent ruination of native handicraft industries, which could not compete with the inexpensive and superior European products.[11]

Ruben Khan-Azad (Nshan Karapetian), one of the young founders of the Social Democratic Hnchak political party, criticized Turkish leaders for their failure to protect local industries and agriculture: "In order to maintain their race and religion, the government used every means to resist European enlightenment and progress. Yet the same government allowed European goods to enter, almost duty free, resulting in the collapse of local industries. Since in Anatolia, Armenians controlled a good part of the crafts and trades, they sustained great losses and many small businesses sank into bankruptcy. In order to repay its loans, to modernize the army and bureaucracy, to enlarge the police force, and to fund the Sultan's extravagances, the Turkish government squeezed the unfortunate people with exorbitant taxes which it demanded in money rather than in kind." "Where," asks Khan-Azad, "were the common people to find cash for taxes in a country with limited commerce, few factories, meagre trade facilities, and no trains to transport materials?" The farmer, unable to export his surplus produce, was obliged to sell his harvest to local buyers at low prices. To make ends meet, he often sold next year's harvest even before it was sowed.[12] How appropriate, then, the complaint of a Keghetsi: "We were not living. It was not living."[13]

The ruination of the countryside and the alienation of the peasantry was symptomatic of a regime marked by misgovernment. Moslem robber barons, rapacious landlords, and ignorant and greedy civil servants made life intolerable for the Anatolian masses – both Christians and Moslems alike. An inefficient system of taxation and tax farming gave rise to unjust demands on agriculturalists, and an unequal and cruel judicial and penal structure undermined efforts at reform. Kurdish brigands, "against whom little redress is afforded by the Government," and persecution of Armenians as a Christian minority drove Keghetsis deeper into poverty and heightened their discontent.[14] Cicero's description of the looting and desecration of Sicily pales in the light of the pillaging of Anatolia and the suffering of the people.

The flagrant confiscation of peasant land erupted into a national scandal. Before the 1870s property in the interior was chiefly held "without the aid of Government certificates or title deeds, each district having its peculiar traditional customs." In an effort to restructure land tenure and tighten its hold on the provinces, the government passed regulations for the registration and certification of property. The general intention was to extend and confirm the rights of use, of possession, and of ownership. But the plan led to a dislocation of the old communal agrarian order, transformed tax-farmers into freeholders, and added "distraint and eviction to the immemorial sufferings of the peasantry."[15]

In Keghi, the *beys* (feudal or clan chiefs or war lords) offered to help the villagers carry out the complicated operations of registration. After getting possession of the villagers' papers, however, the unscrupulous lords registered the lands in their own names. By such trickery, four *beys* usurped the fields of twelve villages. In the village of Tarman, for example, Keghetsis describe how a *bey* seized two pasture lands that the villagers had bought 130 years before and prevented their flocks from grazing on them.[16] Any who dared defy the *beys* were beaten, looted, or, worse still, murdered by hired gangs of thugs. Meanwhile, appeals to civil, judicial, and military authorities whose job it was to protect the people proved futile.[17] In many cases, officials colluded with landlords at the expense of the peasants or, intimidated by the wrath of such dangerous and powerful families, refused to take action against them. British consular officials were appalled that commissioners dispatched to probe the Keghi land scandal were being entertained by the very *beys* they were sent to investigate. Extensive litigation, letters to the sultan, and representation to the British Embassy failed to help the Keghi villagers regain their lands. Instead, many villagers lost the rights to the land they cultivated, slipped into debt, were evicted, or became share-croppers and farm labourers.[18]

Although the Moslem peasant struggled alongside his Christian neighbour, he could at least bear arms to defend himself and could seek compensation for grievances in the courts. Both these avenues were virtually closed to Christians, because they were not allowed to carry arms and their testimony against a Moslem was usually inadmissible. To make matters more difficult, attempts to petition the government for assistance and consideration were met with "the condemnation of a 'people plotting revolution,'" which, wrote a British consular official, "the Armenian people in this country are far from contemplating.[19]

THE BURDENS OF TAXATION

Christian and Moslem alike suffered from the tax burden: of the taxes paid by Keghetsis in 1909, the government spent scarcely one-fifth on the region; the remainder found its way into the government treasury or private coffers. Tax inequities weighed down even more heavily on the Armenian religious minority, for although they made up approximately half of Keghi's population, they paid approximately four-fifths of the tax burden, without receiving commensurate services.[20]

The system of levying and collecting taxes provided limitless opportunities for abuse. Customarily, the government sold tithes by annual auction to the highest bidder. After paying the government its share, the tithe-farmer could pocket whatever he managed to extract from the villagers in his jurisdiction. For a whole year the tithe-farmer could "work his will with the inhabitants and their property without any interference from the [central] Government." The legal tithes stood at about 11¾ percent of the produce, but tax-farmers often extorted as much as 25 percent of the harvest. According to law, villagers were obliged to keep the harvest on the threshing floor until the tithe-farmer took his share. Often his agent arrived late in the season, after the grain had been exposed to the elements. From the unspoiled portion he took the tithe-farmer's share, as well as his own, leaving the villagers, especially in bad years, with inadequate supplies of good grain for the winter. To add to their burden, the villagers were required to provide free food and quarter for the tax collectors and their animals. Such hospitality did not deter the unwelcome guests from insisting on double payment or returning a few months later to extract more produce.[21]

In a report dated 25 January 1870, Keghi leaders deplored the scandalously high price of grain. They described the attempts of Mardiros Agha Alemian, a well-to-do Armenian landowner, to alleviate the people's anguish by buying grain and selling it to the Christian and Moslem masses at the lower price of the previous year. By contrast, the government sent out abusive tax collectors demanding new taxes: twenty-four *khurush* from every man between the ages of fifteen and sixty and twenty-four *khurush* for every pair of cattle. This unexpected and illegal tax piled burden after burden on the poor people, and their torment knew no bounds. Eight years later, in a letter to the patriarch, eighteen Keghi leaders listed their grievances. The people could tolerate no more. If crime and wrongdoing went unpunished, if the government did nothing to help the people, and if they never saw the face of peace, what was left for them to do but to follow in the footsteps of their compatriots, abandon their homes and their lands, and emigrate.[22]

Similar offenses were described by a Captain Everett in 1880, during crop failures following the Russo-Turkish war (1877–78). The unfortunate people, he wrote, are "inexorably pursued by the tax gatherers, and imprisoned by the authorities when unable to pay, and this notwithstanding that the Government owed many of these same people considerable sums of money for supplies furnished during the war." Tithes in certain villages, he reported, had been bought by a company run by members of the government in Erzerum who sold their wheat in winter at exorbitant prices.[23] In 1894, Vice-consul C.M. Hallward noted that the tithes "have increased in inverse proportion to the wealth of the peasants." He continued, quoting a Turkish official, who complained that "whereas in former times ten or fifteen horsemen could always obtain in plenty all the food they wanted for themselves and their horses in any Armenian village, nowadays one horseman can sometimes scarcely obtain barley for his horse."[24]

Usually the tithes were purchased by speculators who had no personal interest in the welfare of the peasants or of the village. Frequently tithe-farmers acted in collusion with civil, judicial, and military officials; sometimes they were the same people. Emin Pasha, a Kurd, for instance, bought the tithes of twenty-four villages for twenty-four thousand piastres, perhaps one-third of their real value. He managed to make such a good bargain because "he frightened away all competitors since he was a colonel in the Hamidiyeh regiment." In Keghi tax-farmers gradually coalesced with the *beys* and *aghas* to form a freeholding landed aristocracy known as the "country notables," or *derebeys*. Especially in isolated areas, the country notables assumed the role of local autocrats, even to the point of raising their own armies.[25]

Other taxes, such as the animal tax, provided further means for extortion. Frequently, tax collectors made no allowance for dead or stolen sheep, recorded a higher number of sheep than actually existed, and pocketed the overpayment. In one case, when villagers objected to such injustice, the official threatened to accuse them of harbouring political fugitives if they proved uncooperative. "To rob the people," observed Captain Everett in 1880, "is no crime, for every man's hand is against them. To rob the Government needs only discretion and money. So long as sufficient payment is made in the right place there is seldom any objection."[26]

In the latter part of the nineteenth century, exacting *prima noce* and collecting tribute (*hafir*) were still prevalent in the countryside and regarded by the lords as a proprietary right to be sold or bequeathed as inheritance. When a *bey* married, the villagers were expected to offer him presents, and when one of the villagers was betrothed or married, the lord expected gifts and often demanded the young bride on her wedding night (prima noce). To secure the assistance and protection of the lord against thieves and cutthroats, the villagers paid an annual tribute that typically consisted of bushels of grain, cattle, sheep, chickens, butter, tobacco, madsun (yogurt), salt, clothing, ribbons, spoons, agricultural implements, and money. They were also obliged to furnish him with their labour without wages. Although villagers fulfilled their end of the bargain, many *beys* failed to provide adequate protection and frequently used these ancient rights only as means of extortion or retribution. In the village of Oror, for instance, when a Protestant objected to Sunday labour, the *bey* had him beaten with thirty lashes and imprisoned for refusing to work for him on the Sabbath.[27]

The law further required each adult male to provide four days' free labour to the government every year for building and repairing roads and bridges. No more than one-third of the village men were to be requisitioned at a time for the road tax, or corvée, known in Turkey as the *amaliat*. In 1871 British consul Taylor described how farmers were dragged from far-off villages for forced labour on the Erzerum-Trebizond highway. The men were compelled to give the government twenty days' work without wages or without its equivalent in kind. Gratuitous labour for five years was thus exacted from the men without the guarantee of exemption from future service. Twenty-five years later Vice-consul Crow noted that sometimes half or three-quarters of the village men were called out at one time and detained for ten or fifteen days unless they paid bribes. Upon completing the work, the men were entitled to certificates, but these were often withheld and villagers were driven to work a second time. Forced from their own fields, even at harvest time, the men were made to work long hours with inadequate rations and filthy lodgings. "As the population is entirely agricultural," Vice-consul Crow concluded, "it necessarily follows that the work of a whole village is sometimes interrupted while the *amaliat* lasts and the most serious loss entailed on the population in consequence."[28]

Although a general conscription law had been passed in the 1850s, Turkish rulers were not anxious to enlist non-Moslems in the army. In order to commute military service and add to the sultan's coffers, Christians were permitted to pay a military exemption tax, or *bedel*. Before 1908 the government collected sums for men of military age, but it also collected indiscriminately for children, old men, priests, the infirm, and the absent. After widespread property damage during the 1894–97 massacres, imperial regulations called for a remission of this tax for two years. But government agents demanded from survivors the share of those who had been killed, who had disappeared, or who had emigrated – doubtless with an eye on funds sent from abroad to help Armenians rebuild their homes and businesses.[29]

Villagers also resented providing for troops and billeting them in their homes. As Keghi was strategically located near the Russian frontier between the army headquarters in Erzinjan and Erzerum and as it bordered on the impregnable Dersim Mountains, Keghi villagers were regularly called upon to supply the army. Rarely did they receive full value for the provisions procured, and the requisitioned goods ended more often in the homes of government officials than in the hands of the army. Such graft had become part of daily life, but quartering soldiers in their homes was another matter and caused immeasurable anxiety and frustration. In 1907, for example, the government sent fifteen hundred Hamidiyeh troops from the Hasanatsi Kurdish tribe into Keghi to subjugate the obdurate Dersim Kurds. For twenty days the Keghetsis fed and quartered the unruly troops and their horses. Food and bedding aside, the villagers justifiably feared for theft of their belongings and, more seriously, for violations against women and children.[30]

THE RELATIONSHIP BETWEEN THE ARMENIANS AND THE KURDS

According to British consul Taylor, most of the Kurdish clans in the province of Erzerum had been deported from Syria and Iraq following the Kurdish rebellions of the mid–nineteenth century. In order to offset Kurdish resistance to extensions of Ottoman power and to neutralize the movement for an independent Kurdistan, the Turkish government had uprooted and relocated them to Anatolia. In Keghi, these relative newcomers represented several different elements: the sedentary population, transhumance clans, nomadic tribes, robber bands, and the Hamidiyeh regiments.[31]

According to Keghi historians, the relationship between sedentary Kurdish peasants and Armenians was tolerable and usually friendly. Oral interviewees confirm that good relations existed between Armenian and Kurdish farmers, to the point that Kurdish children attended Armenian schools and, although infrequent, god-parenting and marriage took place between the two peoples. As for the transhumance Kurdish clans, particularly those inhabiting the Keghi side of the Dersim Mountains, oral sources relate that they were as friendly with their Christian neighbours as they were hostile towards Turkish religious and political authorities. They objected to Turkish efforts to convert them to the Sunni sect and opposed all attempts to subdue them and destroy their semiautonomous status. According to some Keghetsis, these clans, though classified as Moslem Kurds, were remnants of Christian Armenian renegades who had been forced to flee and convert in times past. As proof, Armenians describe the Dersim villagers' language as a mixture of Kurdish and Armenian, point to their reverence of the Christian St Sarkis, and note their custom of drawing a cross rather than a crescent on their bread.[32]

By contrast, other Kurdish tribes treated the Christian population as a patrimonial source of extortion and pillage. Ensconced in their mountain fastnesses these warlords regularly swooped down and raided defenceless villages. They behaved as if any act of violence against Armenians would be overlooked, if not indeed rewarded, by the government. Their coreligionists, the nomadic Kurdish clans, were yet another drain on the villagers' livelihood. The British traveller, H.F.B Lynch, remarked upon the "continuous throng of sheep and goats and horses and weather-worn people of either sex and every age" lumbering northward every spring in search of pasturage. "These yearly migrations of the Kurdish tribes are not conducted without great suffering on the part of the settled population; their granaries are plundered by the shepherd army, and the land which they might have cultivated is occupied by the nomads during winter as pasture for their flocks." The ancient right of quarter, or *kishlak*, was particularly abhorrent to the Keghetsis, because these tribes intruded into the privacy of their homes, sometimes for an entire winter, which in Keghi could last as long as six or seven months. "We had to feed them and their horses," recalled an interviewee. "Not only did they eat, drink, and sleep, they also stole. We were helpless. They were armed and it was against the law for us to bear arms." Complaints to government officials about the loss of privacy, maltreatment, robbery, rape, and murder at the hands of these nomads fell on deaf ears.[33] According to custom the nomads paid a tax to the local authorities for the right of *kishlak*; in return, the villagers were to receive a credit in their taxes for the food, fuel, and fodder that the Kurds had consumed. Instead, government employees lined their pockets with the *kishlak* tax and heaped financial loss and psychological torment on the villagers.

Appeals to the *beys* or government agents resulted either in the immediate arrest or punishment of the complainant or simply in inaction by the officials, leaving the accused to revenge themselves in their own way. It would be pointless, wrote Hallward, to complain to the government about Mami the Kurd, "a lawless savage," since he acts "under auspices of the Government which confers on him the title of Pasha." "During the last year ten Armenians were killed and forty wounded because they had the temerity to complain to the authorities about the oppression at the hands of the Kurds."[34]

Inevitably, the juxtaposition of Armenian and Kurd, Christian and Moslem, sedentary cultivator and nomadic herdsman, and toiler and brigand generated perpetual friction in the interior. The plight of the Armenian peasant is immortalized in Bedros Tourian's poem, "The New Dark Days":

The peasant sows but never reaps
He hungers evermore,
He eats his bread in bitterness
Lo! tears and blood together
Drop from his pallid face;
And these are our own brothers,
Of our own blood and race!
Give back our sisters' roses,
Our brothers who have died
The crosses of our churches,
Our nation's peace and pride!
O Sultan, we demand of thee

And with our hearts entreat –
Give us protection from the Koord
Or arms his arms to meet.³⁵

The attacks, exactions, and depredations by both Kurdish tribes and bandits were a source of deep-rooted discontent among the Armenians in Keghi, highlighting, as they did, the Turkish government's disinclination to establish peace and harmony.³⁶ In 1869, British consul Taylor described the deserted villages, ruined churches, and desolate fields in the province of Erzerum: "People who formerly possessed thirty or forty buffaloes besides sheep and cows, at the same time working ten ploughs, are now begging their bread; and within the last two years the Christian villages of —— have been utterly abandoned by the Armenians owing to the depredations of the [Kurds]." In many of the deserted sites, he continued, where Armenian churches had withstood the ravages of time as well as the "implacable hostility to everything Christian to destroy them," decreasing numbers of Armenians still clung with "affectionate pertinacity," to their church and their language, "dragging on an existence" under Moslem overlords who had "dispossessed the Christians of the lands and villages about." Thirty years later, Consul Crow confirmed that conditions in the interior had not improved. "Yet," he noted, "the Kurds, nomads or sedentary, owe direct obedience to a Pasha, a Bey, or an Agha, of their own denomination, and are therefore easy to control, and, if the Central Government, instead of being content to see the country rendered uninhabitable, would hold these Pashas, Beys, and Aghas responsible for the acts of their tribesmen, and send direct orders ... to stop their plundering ... the insecurity would cease instantaneously."³⁷

Kurdish-Armenian relations were never simple, for as Christopher Walker noted, "the Turkish government regularly ascribed the massacre of Armenians to the actions of wild, unsubdued Kurdish tribes, whereas in each case the 'thinning out' or straightforward extermination of Armenians was a matter of considered government policy. The 'Kurdish cover-up' is very frequently met, and only really ended when the Turkish government embarked on deporting and massacring the Kurds themselves, by which time there were, anyway, scarcely any Armenians left."³⁸

Periodically, Kurdish tribes rebelled against Turkish incursions on their status, against attempts to centralize power in Constantinople, and against the establishment of a standing army in the provinces. Eager to subdue this rebellious multitude and win its support, Sultan Abdul Hamid exploited their internecine feuds and religious differences and extended a measure of control over many Kurdish tribes, culminating in the creation of the Hamidiyeh regiments in 1891–92. By providing the Kurds with arms, uniforms, and his personal colours, Hamid legitimized one of the fiercest and most lawless elements in the Empire. In doing so, he deepened the hostility between Christian Armenian and Moslem Kurd. The Armenians in the interior, banned from bearing arms, saw the Hamidiyeh as a violent force set up to terrorize them under the pretext of a frontier corps. Indeed, Kurds enrolled wholesale in the regiments and considered themselves outside the jurisdiction of the law; they "simply laughed" at the police if they attempted to arrest them. The formation of the Hamidiyeh and the attitude of some Kurds led to an escalation of crime and brigandage in the interior, rather than peace and order. Should any attempts be made to enforce disciplined military service on the Hamidiyeh, reported Hallward, "these paper regiments would ... speedily dissolve in the air of their native mountains."[39]

FORCED CONVERSION

Sultan Abdul Hamid II carried out other practices to drive the wedge deeper between Christians and Moslems. Traditionally, the millet system had allowed the Turks to rule conquered people of diverse races, different languages, and various religions. The millet structure, based on the principle of separate and unequal, consolidated power in the hands of the Moslem Turks and, cumbersome and undemocratic though it was, maintained a measure of peace in the land. Ideally, the separation of religious groups would safeguard and protect each from the religious, linguistic, and cultural encroachments of the others, though in practice Christians were always under threat of forced conversion. Sultan Abdul Hamid II manipulated Moslem and Turkish extremism to his political ends. He managed to mediate some of the differences among various Moslem sects and nationalities to unite them against religious and ethnic minorities. By fusing faith in Islam with loyalty to the Turkish state and by embodying both in himself – the caliph and sultan – Hamid sought to isolate, divide, and repress the minorities, including Armenians, Greeks, Assyrians, and Jews, as well as Moslems of different ethnicities. And as Turkey moved toward the European concept of the nation-state during the latter part of the nineteenth century, the rallying cry for Turkification spread throughout the country. In their turn, the Christian Armenians, who were determined to maintain both their religion and language, found themselves increasingly marginalized, the target of discrimination, contempt, and oppression by Moslem officials, aristocrats, and the *ulema* (holy men).[40]

Armenians in Keghi – the vast majority – belonged to their traditional church, the Armenian Apostolic Church, and were proud that Keghi had been the site of one of the early Christian bishoprics in historic Armenia. In 1910 they supported fifty-six parishes and fifty-one churches.[41] Like their coreligionists in other areas, Keghetsis recognized that the adoption of Christianity had marked a revolutionary reshaping of the Armenian people and that their perseverence in preserving their religious culture symbolized both their identity and their destiny.

Most villages, even small ones, had their own apostolic church structure. But churches and altars, priests and parishioners were not enough to ward off forced conversions. In 1868 a group of Keghi leaders lamented the increase in the number of forced conversions in their region. In a short time, they wrote, not a single Armenian in Keghi will write an Armenian name. British consul Cumberbatch, writing to Ambassador Currie in 1895, recounted events in some outlying villages. The leading men of one of the villages were taken from the church in which they had sought refuge and given the choice of life or conversion. Thirty, among them the priest, refused and were killed at the church door. At another village, ten Protestant Armenians were murdered for refusing to convert and fifty-five men, women, and children threw themselves into the Euphrates rather than change religions. Another report described how the Armenians were suffering great anguish because their children were unbaptized, their dead were buried according to Moslem rites, the men were forcibly circumcised, and all were prohibited from communicating with an Armenian priest. It was impossible, wrote Vice-consul Crow, for Armenians "to remain Christian and live." When an Armenian converted to Islam, he lost not only his religious identity but his ethnic identity as well. All converts to Islam ceased to be Armenian. Hence the significance of conversions.[42]

The persecution of Armenian Christians was further carried out by attacks on Armenian clergy, who were particularly at risk, since they were regarded by Moslems as evil men, blasphemers deserving of insult, revulsion, and death. With impunity Moslems desecrated churches, pillaged and destroyed church property, and burned ancient and priceless manuscripts, paintings, and sculptures. In 1869 British consul Taylor recounted how Kurdish marauders "stormed and completely plundered the venerable church and convent ... of Surb Ohann, near the town of Mush" and carried off all the church plate, ornaments, and embroidered robes. He was particularly saddened by the irreparable loss of the valuable old manuscript collection. Twenty-five years later, Kurdish thieves sacked the beautiful monastery of Surb Garabed in Hakstun in Keghi and fled with the flocks belonging to the monastery. For such outrage the Armenians were awarded no redress and the robbers handed no punishment.[43]

Moslems showed no greater respect for Protestants. When Armenians converted to Protestantism, they became part of a separate millet. Under the guidance of the American Protestant missionaries, the Armenian Protestants learned their rights and how to protect them. Accordingly, Protestant villagers in Keghi refused to submit to an extended corvée. As a desperate last resort, they made representations to the British embassy. In the face of loss of revenue followed by such defiance and boldness, the *beys* swore vengeance on Protestants. To make an example, they beat up the Protestant leader of one of the villages, on the pretense that he had failed to meet the needs of the army. They deliberately billeted soldiers in a Protestant chapel and scoffed at charges that the men were defiling the chapel and depriving the people of a place of public worship. If the Protestants denounced the practice of billeting soldiers in their homes and churches, the *bey* simply "increased the number of soldiers in a family as often as complaints were repeated."[44]

Women were always under the threat of rape and abduction.[45] Villagers recount how Kurds brazenly "broke down the doors of the houses of three men who were absent and violated their wives." A thirteen-year-old Armenian girl, sent to fetch water at the village fountain was abducted by Kurds and when her father and brother chased the abductors to get her back, they were beaten up and shot. The girl was forced to adopt Islam. The religious laws of the state were such that "a girl must possess more than ordinary courage and determination to declare herself a Christian after she has been in the hands of the Musslumans [sic] even for one day." The vice-consul reporting the incident added that any Moslem could legally rob Christian children from their parents and with the aid of the authorities forcibly convert the children to Islam.[46]

Keghetsis found hope in the occasional victory. The villagers of Tarman, for example, proudly described their successful revolt against Ismail Bey who, like other *beys*, enclosed the fields. Anxious about their thirsty animals, which the *bey* had forbidden water access, the villagers marched towards the corral, beat up the *bey*'s guards, and tore apart his fences. Ismail brought a suit against the villagers but the presiding judge remonstrated with him and instructed him to "make up with your villagers."[47] Keghetsis also praised Mehmet Ali Bey, the *kaimakam* of Keghi. Rarely had they seen such a man. Mehmet governed well and justly, defended the villages from brigands, refused all bribes, made no distinction between Moslems and Christians, and worked for the benefit of the state and the tranquility of the inhabitants. Unfortunately Mehmet was removed on the grounds that he was pro-Christian.[48]

MASSACRES: 1890S

In the face of growing nationalism among Turks, the sultan's opposition to reforms, and increasing intolerance among fundamentalist Moslems, Armenians tried more fervently to retain their religious and cultural identity, to stabilize their social and economic status, and to resist misrule and injustice. During the 1890s, Armenians petitioned the government, organized demonstrations, and engaged in local armed combat against attack and theft. In punishment, particularly for the "revolt" of the Armenians of Sasun against double taxation, the army, the police, and Moslem mobs looted and destroyed property and murdered between one hundred and three hundred thousand Armenian men, women, and children throughout the empire from 1892 to 1897. In a confidential letter dated 22 February 1896, H.A. Cumberbatch, British consul in Erzerum, informed the British ambassador in Constantinople about Armenian reaction to these massacres: "From this town alone over five hundred have already left furnished with Turkish passports and as many more without. So far the exodus has been confined to the male members of town families, the women folk intending to follow later on, and the chief inducement to leave the country appears to be the fear of further massacres or arrests ... but there are also signs of the intentions of the rural population to follow the example of the townspeople ... if the Government shows unmistakable signs ... to take effective measures to protect the Christian subjects ... from future molestation ... many Armenians, who, as a rule, are attached to the soil, would gladly remain, but at present the emigration movement is gaining ground daily."[49]

Keghetsis describe their suffering and their resistance to Kurdish attacks. In the village of Khups, for example, news reached the defending villagers that, as in Sasun, regular government troops, armed with heavy artillery, had been despatched to back up the Kurds and quell the Khups "rebellion." Silently, during the night, the villagers buried some of their possessions, and carrying what they could, fled to the nearby mountain. The next day the Kurds pillaged the deserted village, carried off sheep and grain, fodder and furniture. What they did not steal, they burned. Village after village met the same fate. The entire region of Keghi lay charred and ruined.[50]

In the midst of such chaos and destruction, swarms of tax collectors descended on the villages, backed by the army, demanding with typical vigour the full tax load. In one village, the women and children were forced to stand in the burning sun without water until the money was paid.⁵¹ Having no recourse to justice and unable to cope with the Kurds and tax collectors who were backed by local government officials and the military, the Keghetsis sent a series of six telegrams to the sultan describing the cruelties and hardships to which they were subjected and beseeched His Majesty to intervene on their behalf. Unable to pay their taxes because of damage to their property and theft of their goods, Keghetsi men were tortured and imprisoned, women were raped, clergymen were mistreated, and children were beaten. In one village the tax collectors tried to extort the tax debt of absentees and indigents, and when they failed to gather all they demanded from the people, they called in the police who seized furniture and sheep belonging to other villagers. The police chief, the villagers wrote, sold them for a quarter of their true value to the local Moslems. Sultan Abdul Hamid took no action and their supplications went unheeded.⁵²

Villagers who were not evicted were driven deeper into the clutches of usurers, who charged the peasants interest rates that "took the wind out of their sails." Peasants borrowed on the security of future crops, promising repayment in kind at high interest rates. Instead of loaning money to the villagers at 8 percent according to regulations, the Agricultural Bank loaned money "to some people" who, in turn, loaned it to the villagers at 20 percent interest. The majority of the creditors were Moslems, and they were gradually becoming proprietors of land formerly in Armenian hands.⁵³ As land ownership became more centralized in the possession of a small number of Moslem beys, Armenian farmers fell deeper into poverty.

RESISTANCE AND EMIGRATION

By the latter part of the nineteenth century, exploitation, anarchy, and violence had plunged Keghi into a dark world of insecurity and backwardness. The settled population was tormented by ruthless brigands, corrupt officials, and avaricious *derebeys*. Instead of relying on the government, its administrators, judges, and police to defend them and their interests, Armenians could expect nothing more than further abuse and outrage.

The Armenians of Keghi were peaceful but not passive. They were sons of mountain and rock – dauntless, strong-willed, tenacious, and proudly independent. Their beloved mountains, some towering over nine thousand feet, were entrenched in their history, their myths and folklore, and most notably in their psyche.⁵⁴ On craggy precipices they built their monasteries to be close to God and to find sanctuary and safety during attack. Keghetsis were mountain men, shaped and toughened as much by geography as by religion and oppression. They resisted persecution, retaliated against theft and brigandage, and challenged injustice. They organized self-defence bands and took up arms to protect their families, their properties, and their honour.

Keghetsis reacted to the worsening conditions by staying and setting up more efficient measures of policing, self-defence, and mutual assistance, for they saw hope in reform, and if not in reform, in armed resistance. Others despaired about the future, faced as they were with incessant economic hardship, collusion between government and Moslem *derebeys*, heavily armed opposition, persecution of Christians, and massacres sanctioned and instigated by the government. How could they cope with a government whose troops and police were in the pay of great landowners and whose courts disdained the law and conspired against Christians? They fled their homeland forever, openly if they could afford to bribe their way out or secretly if they could find no other means of escape. Still others, perhaps less prosperous or more attached to their patrimonial lands, took up sojourning as a compromise – a means of bringing in outside capital while holding fast the bonds of family and village. In sojourning, the sons of Keghi would find respite from tyranny and a taste of liberty.

2

Changing Horizons

> As long as they [the Turks] claimed Armenia did not exist, they [the Armenians] clung all the more persistently to the fact of their existence.
>
> Paul Cambon

Although Keghi was isolated, it was not inaccessible. The region was land-locked and mountainous, but Keghetsis did not function in a closed world. Rather, there was a steady stream of internal movement in the area. Religious festivals held in monastery grounds, fairs and markets, travellers, troubadours, caravans, itinerant tradesmen, god-parenting, and out-marriage established contacts between different villages. Nor was it unusual for families to relocate from one village to another or for Keghetsis to migrate beyond the region.

They travelled far afield: they married outside the region, emigrated to urban centres to acquire an education or find a job, and journeyed to Erzerum, Aleppo, and Constantinople to import and export merchandise. Levon Musheghian, of the village of Chanakhchi, for example, describes how his people sold woven articles to the Kurds in return for sheep. In the spring they took their huge flock to graze in Mush, Khnus, and the Bingol Mountains. With the onset of fall, they drove their entire flock to Aleppo, where they exchanged the sheep for cloth. This merchandise they then sold to village shops, the shops in Keghi Kasaba, and to an uncle engaged in the textile business in Erzerum.[1]

THE TRADITION OF SOJOURNING

Some migrants quit the village forever and followed in the footsteps of their ancestors who had formed Armenian settlements in Asia as in Persia or India and in European countries such as Russia, Poland, Italy, or France. But many others worked in different places and remitted funds back home; and when they eventually returned, they introduced new ways of thinking and behaving. Pilag Evarian's grandfather, from the village of Arek, for instance, rose to the position of secretary to Hagop Pasha in Constantinople, all the while sending funds to his family in the village and establishing important links between the region and the capital. Zadur Amirghanian, who, after a ten-year sojourn, returned to Keghi as an architect, brought new building methods to the region with his churches, schools, bridges, and viaducts.[2]

Of the 180,000 Armenians in Constantinople (Bolis) before 1895, it was estimated that 80,000 were sojourners from the provinces.[3] Some, like the Mooradian family, were engaged in entrepreneurial activities: a brother in the capital city, another in the village of Arek, and two nephews in Erzerum carried on a wide-ranging importing and exporting business, especially of textiles. "Even before I was born," recalled another interviewee, "my father went to Bolis to work. He returned when I was 8 or 10 and stayed for a whole year. That's when my brother was born. My father operated an inn in Bolis with a coffee shop on the main floor. He was the manager. His cousin was his partner. Every year he would send us money. And not only money. Also trunk loads of goods, fabrics."[4] Other sojourners found menial work in Constantinople as waiters or servants, for example, or engaged in artisanal activities as cooks or tailors or took on backbreaking labour as porters, stevedores, or construction workers.

In Bolis, these men came into contact with the intellectual ferment that was making a profound impact on the Armenian middle classes. They learned to read and write, attended Bible classes, formed regional societies, listened to lectures about Armenian history and the current condition of the Armenian people, and became politically active.

Always at risk of disease, injury, and death, men nevertheless made the choice to work away from home in order to cope with poverty, overcrowding, and unemployment and to pursue the promise of opportunity. Sojourning provided funds necessary to secure the household economy, while keeping the family, especially the next generation, on home soil. Thus, temporary migration served private necessity, family stability, and national loyalty.

So entrenched was the sojourning tradition, so institutionalized among the rural population, that migrant workers, especially the longshoremen and porters in Constantinople, appear frequently in Armenian literature, usually in tragic circumstances, like the lonely, dying man in Daniel Varoujan's poem, "He is ill":

> Abandoned in the dim corner of an inn, the pitiful sojourner is sick. Bit by bit the dampness draws his body to the grave.

He has no doctor and whatever money he had saved is gone. The pain is severe. How pitiable. There is not a loving heart to pour her goodness on his thirsty lips ...
He is still in the prime of his life. A groom. Far away from Bolis [Constantinople] in Van, they need food. His bride and parents want him back. It is yet too early to die ...
He will die. He is gravely ill. In his coffin he will not have the tears of his loved ones, nor the last oath of faithfulness.

He will die. And in his native land his bride, longing for his love, will in vain wait for his return.
Poor lady of Van. Sure of hope's promises for happiness you smile at the stars, while on the firmament of life is being drawn the lightning of his death ...
For whom are you still guarding the touch of his kisses beneath your veil? Tomorrow, poor soul, a traveller will break the news: "They buried him, longing for his loved ones."[5]

The practice of sojourning in the capital, where jobs were plentiful and wages relatively good, suffered a blow in the mid-1890s when, in retaliation to Armenian demonstrations against oppression and persecution, Turkish police and angry Moslem mobs hounded Armenians and brutalized and murdered them.[6] Hundreds of Armenians took refuge on ships docked in the harbour and escaped to the Balkans or other Mediterranean countries; Ottoman authorities immediately proscribed their reentry into the empire. The government deported others back to their villages and prohibited large-scale movement of Armenian provincials to Constantinople. Those who fled the country, as well as those who were sent back to the interior, left their mark on their home environments, for they extended the chain of migration, enhanced the network of kith and kin around the globe, and exposed villagers to new ideas and a vision of different possibilities.

At the same time, the increasing flow of European manufactured goods into the Ottoman Empire and spreading industrialization in parts of the empire disrupted local industry, wrought economic havoc, and drove growing numbers of the rural/village population to seek salvation in urban centres, often in foreign cities. Small businessmen, craftsmen, and farmers were being shaken by the changing industrial and economic conditions. But brigandage, destruction, and massacre stepped up the process of out-migration among the Armenians of Anatolia. In 1910, for example, a traveller estimated that of the thirty thousand Armenians in Keghi, approximately three thousand, between the ages of twenty and forty had taken up the "sojourner's cane." Another account, giving the population of Keghi as twenty thousand Armenians calculated that over four thousand Armenians had left the district by 1913–14. The extent of Keghi emigration is confirmed by an examination of ship passenger lists. One such account has yielded the names of approximately 1,925 people from Keghi who entered the United States at Ellis Island roughly from 1900 to 1914. Almost all these immigrants indicated they were joining a relative or friend. If we assume that all 1,925 were indeed from Keghi, if we allow 25 percent for repeated names and repeat visits, and if we make a conservative assumption that 75 percent of those kith and kin already in the United States were also from Keghi, we are left with an overall estimate of just under 3,000 Keghetsis away from home from about 1900 to 1914. Actually the number of emigrants from Keghi would certainly have been greater, since these statistics do not account for Keghetsis whose Ellis Island records are not included in that list, who entered the United States at other ports, or who headed for other points of the Keghi diaspora, including Russia, the Balkans, France, Mexico, and Canada.[7]

Keghetsis first headed for Turkish and Russian centres, seeking work in factories, mines, forests, the Baku oil fields and refineries, and bridge, road, tramway, and railroad construction. As they heard about job opportunities in other countries, the peripatetic men of Keghi broadened their horizons from Trebizond, Erzerum, and the Caucasus to Egypt and the Balkans. Informants give a sense of the patterns, frequency, and extent of Keghetsi globe-trotting:

My other grandfather had lived in Bolis for thirty-five years and knew Turkish very well. He had gone there to work ... was working for a doctor. His wife had stayed behind. He would work and send money home.

My maternal grandfather had a hotel with two friends ... in Trebizond. He also cooked at the French school in Trebizond ... He learned gourmet cooking ... became a renowned chef. [He] used to come once a year to the village, stay a couple of weeks' holiday and then he'd return ... For many years he stayed there [in Trebizond] and sent his earnings home to the village ... He spent his life sojourning. When I was a little boy, he'd ... bring me European suits when I was two. I'd wear European clothes when I was little.[8]

They used to go to Russia from our area ... They would go to Alexandropol or Kars. Workers. Made a bit of gold and returned. ... Sometime in the late 1880s or early 1890s Daniel Navoian and his brother left our village of Djerman to work in Bolis. They were *hamals* [porters]. Carried goods on their backs.[9]

Hovannes Melkonian, from the village of Arek, tried his luck in Egypt. He migrated to Cairo, in the latter part of the nineteenth century, when he was in his mid-teens and was hired as a cook by the family of Nubar Pasha (1825-99), prime minister of Egypt. They sent young Hovannes to study culinary art at the Hotel Carlton, in London, and later to Paris, probably at the Ritz. In an arranged match, Hovannes married the stunningly beautiful Virginia Mooradian, who was secretly spirited out of Arek to escape the lascivious desires of the local *bey*.[10] Hovannes and Virginia, whose family ran an import-export business in Arek, Erzerum, and Constantinople (mentioned above) invited her father, mother, brother, and two sisters to join them in Egypt in 1912. Seven years earlier, a cousin, Yeghishé Mooradian, had left Erzerum and emigrated to Brantford, Ontario (1905), to join friends and relatives and shortly afterwards brought his parents and brothers to Canada as well. Thus the family had links in Arek, Erzerum, Constantinople, Cairo, and Brantford.

Other informants talked about their links with the Balkans: "My grandfather lived [in Rumania] for seven years. He was married, but he went alone." Another described how her "father went from Astghapert (Astghaberd, Astghpert) village to Bulgaria. There he got married and had three children ... He had a brother in Brantford [Ontario]."[11]

Like other migrants from Europe, Armenian men were drawn to the industries and capital in North America. Daniel Navoian, of Djerman village, recalled an interviewee, "fled to Bulgaria [from Bolis in 1896] with many other Armenians. He disappeared. His name was not heard of again in our land. He did not write. After spending years in Bulgaria, he migrated to the United States and ended up in Troy, New York."[12] Compelled thus to live and work outside the region, the sons of Keghi, already accustomed to periodic migration to closer targets, gradually expanded their frontiers across the Atlantic to the beckoning industries of North America.[13]

According to Robert Mirak, students, clergy, artisans, merchants, and professionals led the movement of Armenians to the United States in the latter half of the nineteenth century. As North America became more accessible and familiar to the peasantry, from the 1890s onward, more agriculturalists and labouring classes joined the movement. The first Keghetsis to travel to North America were probably students either sponsored by the Protestant missionaries at Euphrates College in Kharput or influenced by them.[14] Arsen Damkhajian, for instance, who later changed his name to Arsen Diran and who was the son of a Protestant preacher, was born in Keghi Kasaba. After graduating from Euphrates College, Arsen, just twenty-one, migrated to Boston around 1892. With a speaking knowledge of English, he started working at

Semajian's Photo Studio in that city and after six months of very frugal living, opened his own photography shop.[15] M. Vaiguni of the village of Khups, also a graduate of Euphrates College, entered Michigan Agricultural College in 1898, then moved on to California to complete his PHD. After three years' study at Euphrates and some time spent teaching in Keghi, Khachatur Charchian of Tsermag village, migrated to Troy, New York, "where he spread the Protestant word."[16] For Keghetsis, Kharput was "the gateway to America." The movement of Keghetsis specifically to Canada did not get under way until the late 1880s and 1890s and consisted in large measure of the third group, i.e., yeomen, small-scale tenant farmers, artisans, and merchants from rural villages and from Keghi Kasaba.

Before 1908, migration out of Keghi seems to have been composed mainly of middle-aged, married, established men, frequently heads of households. Leaving their families behind under the protection of male relatives, who might take a turn later on, they sojourned for periods ranging up to twenty years in nearby places, perhaps visiting the village at intervals. Neither time nor distance changed their sojourner mentality, for their hearts and minds remained at home with their families. On the whole, these men were clear about their responsibilities, single-minded, and self-disciplined. They were tough but resilient enough to take blows yet keep on track, to cope with different cultures yet retain their language and religion, and to handle the vicissitudes of strange worlds yet remain loyal to family and village.

After the Young Turk revolution in 1908 and the deposition of Sultan Abdul Hamid II, the nature of migration began to change. The new regime removed many impediments to travel, allowing citizens to journey in and out of the country. The amnesty permitted men like Daniel Navoian to return to their families in Anatolia and the changes in travel conditions allowed more and more men, like Navoian's nephews, to sojourn in America. Working in North America, with comparatively substantial wages, could reduce their years of sojourn from fifteen or twenty to three or four. After 1908, Armenians emigrated in increasing numbers, especially after the massacre of their coreligionists in 1909 in the region of Adana. Following changes to the conscription laws, the increase in the military exemption tax, and Turkey's wars with Italy and the Balkans, more and more young men left their villages for America, expecting to return home when conditions improved. Aware, moreover, that temporary out-migration could be the first phase of losing a young son to permanent resettlement, parents often arranged the marriage of the young sojourner before he left, to insure his return.

Those who left, whether married or single, were not from the lowest economic and social strata of the population. Rather, they were the "stronger and the better element" of the people, since to embark on a voyage, particularly to distant North America, required strength, motive, vision, will, and means.[17] As travel to North America opened up and as men learned the routes, they disregarded the distances, costs, dangers, and hardships and crisscrossed the Atlantic. One such Keghetsi migrated to Pontiac, Michigan, on his first trip, to Erie, Pennsylvania, on his second crossing, and to Brantford, Ontario, on his third voyage.[18]

Men moved about not only as individuals, making solitary decisions, and as members of kinship or clan groups but also as parts of a village or regional migratory caravan. Sometimes they blazed new trails; sometimes, they retraced the steps of fathers, uncles, and older brothers:

In 1909 at the age of 16, I left the village [Chanakhchi] with my brother-in-law, Mardig Musheghian. In Bolis we were met by my uncle Nerses [his father's brother] who cared for us. We left Bolis for Marseilles where our cousin Giragos Zadurian ran a hotel. We passed the "bono" test and headed for Ellis Island.[19] My uncle Tosun [his father's brother] came from Troy and took me to his place. After a time, he went on to East St Louis and I went to Canada to join my uncle Krikor [his father's brother] in Canada. Leaving Hamilton after a short stay, I moved to Galt to join my other cousin Garabed Kaprielian ... After a while I returned to the United States, to East St Louis to be with my uncle Tosun.[20]

By means of such extensive networks men exchanged money and information about the obstacles and pitfalls ahead, government regulations and shipping agents, jobs and accommodation. Impelled into an unknown and intimidating world, far from the customs and social controls of home, men considered it a matter of family and village honour to take care of each other. They *expected* help from each other. Across land and sea the migration chain would clamour and reverberate with the shameful news of a man who had refused to aid a brother in need or who had denied "his own people." These informal networks and the unwritten code of mutual assistance, whether based on love, respect, or pragmatism, strengthened the cohesiveness among Keghetsis trying to cope with unfamiliar and changing worlds. Above all they enabled men to survive as members of families, as villagers, and as Armenians. As such, they were extensions of age-old traditions of mutual self-defence, mutual help, and solidarity.

The "caravans" they created spanned half the world: from Keghi to Constantinople, Alexandria, Varna, Sophia, Batum, Tiflis, Baku, Marseilles, Liverpool, Boston, East St Louis, Detroit, Troy/Watervliet, New York, Brantford, and back again. In turn, the caravan induced and enhanced mobility. As the scope of the migration expanded and as its prevalence intensified, Keghi society and economy ceased to be the geographic, administrative, and religious unit of Keghi but included also the many regional outposts around the globe. Introducing him to friends in East St Louis, Arakel Eghigian's father reflected the changes in the Keghetsi world when he remarked, "Keghi is here, my son."[21]

But the old land was not forgotten. Through their hard work, singlemindedness, and sacrifice, migrants restored a measure of economic stability to Keghi and provided an economic margin that facilitated greater migration to North America, especially after 1909, when travel conditions improved. The money Keghi men sent from abroad allowed their families to achieve not only economic stability but also a measure of upward social and economic mobility. A sense of the size of remittances is given in a report by an evangelical missionary in Brantford, Ontario, who was said to have arranged the transfer of eight hundred dollars at Christmas time to families in Turkey on behalf of Armenian workers (1909).[22] Outside capital enabled families to discharge debts and buy plots of land, make improvements to their farms and houses (for example, add a second story and install glass in their windows), build another house to ease family overcrowding, open shops, provide dowries, pay the military-exemption tax for a relative, build schools and churches in the village, and finance the emigration of other family members. Such developments changed the relative status of Armenian villagers. Already disliked by many Moslems for their religious persistence, their liberationist aspirations, their aptitude in trade and business, and their espousal of progress and modernity, some Armenians found themselves in a dangerously superior social, economic, and educational position compared to the local Kurds and Turks. In an impoverished countryside where cash was scarce, the inflow of money empowered the Armenians. In the face of famine they could afford to import food from other areas; in the face of theft of their sheep and crops, they could hire mercenaries to pursue the robbers. Such security made them less vulnerable and more confident, traits that aroused jealousy in their Moslem neighbours.[23]

Gradually, an economy that had relied almost exclusively on agriculture and trade and had functioned largely by means of barter shifted and emerged as a semicapitalist economy relying more and more on the transfer of cash from a far-off proletariat. While local agricultural productivity may have increased and regional trade and commerce may have progressed, villages became inextricably bound to a distant and impersonal labour market. A lay-off at the Pratt and Letchworth Malleable factory in Brantford, Ontario, for instance, could undermine the livelihood of Astghaberd village in Keghi. As foreign contributions became indispensable to the villagers' standard of living, the dependency on outside capital became self-generating. Once entrenched in the local economy, the cycle kept repeating itself.

As rural living standards improved, the option to emigrate and the act of emigrating – particularly to places as far afield as North America – became more viable. Distant points of the Keghi *spiurk* (diaspora) – Brantford, Hamilton, Detroit, Troy, East St Louis, Granite City, and Corey, Alabama – found their way into the villagers' everyday vocabulary and conjured up visions of hope and opportunity, as indicated in the following excerpt: "Is it worthwhile to stay in this dreary country where there is no liberty, no peace, no security, and no prospect ... I myself desire to breathe the air of that land of liberty and progress. I want to see all the wonderworks, and in that way improve the poor education that our school gave me."[24]

As links with North America expanded beyond letters and money, books and newspapers, the Westernization and Americanization of Keghi intensified. The new world surged into every aspect of Keghi society in both obvious and subtle ways. North America penetrated Keghi not just in the form of technological advances like sewing machines and better tools and equipment or in symbolic ways with dolls, posters of Roosevelt and Taft, or advertisements for Sunlight soap. American intrusion into Keghi, bringing with it new cultural and economic ways and values, was far more profound and inevitably transformed the people.[25]

In 1868–69, Consul Taylor had described abandoned villages, ruined churches, and deserted fields, and Armenian leaders had grieved over the increasing number of forced conversions. Now, forty years later, the depopulation of the countryside continued apace. With the emigration of ambitious and well-trained young men, Keghi began to suffer from a shortage of farmers, teachers, and artisans. The exodus inhibited village development efforts, not only by increasing the dependence on outside capital but also by increasing the proportion of the older, illiterate, and unprogressive elements of the population that stayed behind. As more young Keghetsis left after the outbreak of the Balkan wars and the call to arms, the region, like the rest of the country, "grew thin like a consumptive." Even though it had escaped the terrible massacres of 1909, when twenty-five to thirty thousand Armenians in the Adana region had been killed, Keghi was now suffering from a "white massacre," the drain of its young, strong, and virile youth.[26]

The decline in the number of work hands in Keghi meant that the burden of agriculture fell on the remnants of the population, mostly women and old men. It was up to the "white widows," the wives of sojourners, and the remaining male relatives to oversee the harvest, deal with tax collectors, and defend family honour and property. As women increasingly assumed control of household affairs, the social relationships in the village changed. "To an extent," noted a Keghetsi, "migrant workers lost their authority in the village and the women replaced them."[27] Some women thus gained status, as well as a measure of security from the cash inflow. But they were also vulnerable to robbery and rape; and the young, especially, suffered from loneliness and despair. Their pain was a persistent theme in contemporary literature. In his poem "The Keghetsi Wife's Letter," Setrag Shahen, from the village of Oror, captured the longing of the sojourner's mate:

Write, husband.
You've been sojourning for ten years.
The years fly by like the dance.
Find a way to come home.
My heart has turned to stone.[28]

The longing of wives was compounded by the worry and grief of aging parents whose last hope was to see their sons safe at home again. In an effort to encourage men to return, the *Armeno-American Letter Writer* echoed the deep-seated conflict in the hearts and minds of many families: "My dear, Father died longing for you and Mother is spending the days of her old age in tears which fill our hearts with sorrow. Why do you stay so long in that country ... Come and comfort Mother's last days and make us happy."[29] And in distant lands men pined for the warmth and love of their families. Their feelings are poignantly expressed in the beautiful, mournful song "Crane":

Where do you come from, crane?
I ache to hear your call,
to know you come from home.
Have you any news at all?

I bless your wings, your eyes.
My heart is torn in two.
The exile's soul, all sighs
waiting for bits of news.[30]

Armenian leaders in the Ottoman and Russian Empires and in North America feared for the future of their people in Anatolia. Repeatedly they reminded them that emigration from the Armenian provinces, forced conversion, resettlement of non-Armenians in Anatolia, and periodic massacre of Armenians all would eventually lead to national extinction. With his *depi gavar* (towards-the-province) movement, the catholicos Khrimian Hairik exhorted men to return to their home areas and there to work to improve the lot of the Armenian people. Other nationalists, like Edouard Aknuni (Khachatur Malumian), the Armenian Revolutionary Federation fieldworker, expanded the concept with a *depi yerkir* (towards-the-old-country) movement, denounced emigration, pointed to the dangers and pitfalls in North America, and called on Armenians to return to their families in the homeland:

> There is a house, but no one to tend it.
> There is a field, but no one to work it.
> There is a candle, but no one to light it.
> There are a people, but no one to inspire them.
> Everyone has left.
> One in protest.
> Another for money.
> Another for his ideals.

These various influences caused great turmoil in the émigrés, for they highlighted their dilemma: loyalty to land and religion on the one hand and physical survival on the other. The thought of losing their land and their identity made them heartsick, but what good were churches and schools, shops and farms when a hostile regime could destroy everything in one fell blow? In order to retain their ethnic and religious identity was it essential for them to tie themselves to the land, or could their identity be more effectively safeguarded in the diaspora, far from Turkish tyranny? Was it unpatriotic to take wife and children and leave for distant lands? Would they be able to cope with the guilt if they did so? In this manner each man struggled with his private anguish.

INTELLECTUAL AND POLITICAL FERMENT

The Armenian Apostolic Church, Protestant missionaries, and Armenian Catholic Mkhitarist monks in Venice and Vienna contributed to the great changes known as the *Zartonk*, the Armenian Renaissance, Reawakening, or Enlightenment of the nineteenth century. The intellectual and political renaissance of the Armenians, the spread of the vernacular language in written work, the increase in the number of classics translated into Armenian, and the proliferation of printed texts, especially newspapers, led to a large-scale drive towards popular literacy and mass education. Not only did the *Zartonk* affect all classes and regions of Armenian society, it also brought Armenians into contact with nineteenth-century European, Russian, and American currents of thought. More importantly, through these various forces Armenians were being transformed into a people conscious of themselves, aware of their history, proud of their religion, and determined to use their language – changes that did not endear them to the Turkish rulers.

At the same time, the restoration of constitutional government in 1908 and the deposition of Sultan Abdul Hamid II in 1909, followed by a series of reform measures, gave Christians and Moslems hope that the new regime was progressive enough and enlightened enough to establish law, order, peace, and harmony, to stabilize the crumbling regime, and to cure the Sick Man of Europe. Political developments, together with the influx of modern concepts from Europe, Russia, and the United States nurtured a generation of young men and women who were inspired by the ideals of democracy, liberalism, socialism, and nationalism.

In their own fashion, Keghi repatriates, returning from their sojourn in other worlds, became agents of modernization and politicization in the countryside. Their impact on the region was in keeping with a long tradition among Armenians. For centuries, diasporan Armenians had played a significant role in the economic and intellectual development of Armenians in the homeland. Indeed, the two most vital centres of Armenian cultural, economic, and political activity at the turn of the century, Tiflis and Constantinople, lay outside ancient Armenia. Small but prosperous colonies flourished also in Italy, Poland, Persia, India, Egypt, Holland, and the United States. Diasporan Armenians not only helped retain Armenian identity outside the homeland, where it was severely threatened, but they also established economic networks with their coreligionists on a global scale. Equally important, diasporan Armenians disseminated innovations to their confreres still in the native land. Whether one considers the printing of the Armenian Psalter in Venice in 1512 or of the Armenian Bible in Amsterdam in 1666, the literary pursuits of the Armenians in India, the very significant work of the Catholic Armenians in Venice and Vienna, or the establishment of Armenian schools in foreign lands, such as the Lazarian Institute in Moscow, diasporan Armenians created and maintained important links connecting Armenians with Western intellectual currents, on the one hand, and Eastern mysticism, on the other. Admittedly, the earliest and most dynamic recipients of these new offerings were the élites in the larger cities. More and more young people, both the children of the wealthy and bright young men hand-picked by the Armenian Church, went abroad to study. When these young people returned to their homeland they brought back with them the knowledge of different languages, cultures, and disciplines. By the last years of the nineteenth century, intellectual and political innovations were gradually permeating to the Armenian masses in the interior.

The history of the village of Chanakhchi, for example, reveals that the first Social Democratic cell in Constantinople was composed of Chanakhchi villagers. They carried their newly formed political affiliations back to the village, making Chanakhchi the "nest of Social Democracy in Keghi."[31] Other repatriates returned from Russia imbued with populist fervour.[32] Still others experienced labour disputes in Bulgaria, where Armenian labourers clashed with native workers. They had much in common with their brothers and cousins who had toiled in North American factories in industrial towns like Brantford, Ontario, Providence, Rhode Island, or Worcester, Massachusetts, and had returned with stories about the worker's struggle and with ideas about class conflict.

Repatriates displayed an unnerving self-confidence and propounded ideas about equality and liberty. Keghetsis learned not only about the chances for prosperity in America but also about the prospects for education and the progress of technology and industry. For a people perpetually on the verge of famine, the fabled abundance of North America was incredible. For those who struggled with old-fashioned tools and equipment, the vision of automobiles, movies, skyscrapers, bridges, and lighted streets was glorious. For men surrounded by illiteracy and despotism, the cleanliness, civilization, and freedom of North America were mesmerizing.

In North America men saw that a better way of life existed, and they were determined to use their earnings to give their children a chance for a better future. Like other Armenians abroad, Keghetsis formed village educational associations to raise money to educate the children still in the villages. Spurred on by the flow of money and ideas from abroad and encouraged by local initiatives, Keghetsis expanded and improved the educational facilities in their villages.[33] They set up schools, learning circles, literary clubs, reading rooms, and libraries, and more and more, they sent their young people outside the region for higher education.

One of these young men, Setrag Shahen, formerly a student at Euphrates College in Kharput, started the publication, *Veradsnund*

(Renaissance) in his home village of Oror in 1911. Through this newspaper, Shahen, a devout Social Democrat, informed the villagers in simple language how to cultivate vineyards, potatoes, and tobacco and how to reforest and graft trees. He denounced outdated educational practices and methods, criticized parochial schooling, and argued the advantages of modern curricula. The June 1912 issue was devoted entirely to the "Red Appeal." In it Shahen exposed the theft of the tithe farmers, showing that some were exacting eight times the government's portion. To undermine the power of those who exploited the poor people, the "Red Appeal" invited all Keghi villagers, Christians and Moslems alike, to muster their forces and present themselves at the auction of tithes. "The fruits of labour," advocated the newspaper in typical Social Democratic fashion, "are the rights of the worker." The five hundred copies of the "Red Appeal," which were distributed throughout the region, incited the villagers. On the day of the auction, Keghi Kasaba, the regional capital, was crowded with excited village leaders and anxious tithe farmers. Much to the chagrin of the tithe farmers, the villagers succeeded in winning half the tithes.[34]

Sending young people like Setrag Shahen out of the region to study was not a new practice, for wealthy families had frequently done so in the past. The Armenian church had also often recruited bright young men to study in seminaries and monasteries at home and universities abroad. In more recent times, Protestant missionaries had encouraged higher education. Their Euphrates College in Kharput became the most popular institution of higher learning for Keghetsi young people. Here Keghetsis were numerous enough to form their own educational club and to publish a newsletter. Keghi youth attending schools outside the area, whether in Kharput, Erzerum, Bolis, Russia, or North America, were exposed to new political and ideological currents. Many young people were inspired by the exhortations of such minority-rights activists and organizers as the beloved Kalust Antreasian (Hagop) and Hagop Tevekelian (Hapet): "Oppression and injustice create revolution," Hagop stated. "Revolution condemns injustice. Freeing oppressed people is a sacred undertaking." Hagop and Hapet were tried and executed for inciting revolution, but to Armenian young people they were heroes and martyrs. Many embraced the reform movement, and like the factions among Turks and Kurds, many saw hope only in revolutionary activity.[35]

Among the many liberal forces influencing Armenians in the Ottoman Empire were the North American Protestant missionaries. The American Board of Commissioners for Foreign Missions (ABCFM) was founded in Massachusetts in 1810 by Congregationalists and a smaller number of Presbyterians. By 1835 the missionaries had established a foothold in the Ottoman Empire. Because their original intention of proselytizing among Jews and Moslems was prohibited, they turned their attention to the Christian Armenians, who impressed them with their "piety and devotion to the Christian religion."[36] In 1846 a small group of Armenian men and women founded the Armenian Evangelical Church in Constantinople, and four years later the sultan granted the new church formal recognition as a separate millet, or religious community. Among the earliest proselytizers attached to the American Board in Turkey were at least thirty Canadian men and women, many of them Scottish Presbyterians.[37]

Not only did Armenian Church leaders oppose Protestantism, but the Armenian masses also initially rejected the new doctrine. By 1908 Protestants could claim scarcely sixteen thousand communicants and forty-two thousand adherents. The missionaries soon learned that an effective means of reaching Armenians was to emphasize educational, medical, and relief work. During the terrible famines of the 1880s and the massacres of the 1890s and 1909, Americans sent funds, food, seed, clothing, and machinery, and missionaries gave invaluable assistance in hospitals, orphanages, and schools.[38]

The eagerness of Armenians for education dovetailed with the missionaries' own program to spread literacy among the masses, in order to enable all men and women to read the Bible and thus move nearer to God. The Protestants translated the Bible into the vernacular Armenian, making the Scriptures more accessible. "The Protestants," writes Grabill, "converted Near Easterners to America's bookish culture and its individualistic and rational notion that the Bible must be widely available in the vernacular ... The printing press mentality of the United States ... became one of the most powerful implements the missionaries had in opening the minds of Armenians and Arabs."[39] In keeping with their educational agenda, missionaries established schools at their mission stations – small ones at first, leading gradually to more sophisticated and elaborate high schools and colleges which, like Euphrates College, offered bachelor of arts degrees. Statistics reveal the success of their contributions to education: in 1868 they operated 127 schools and sunday schools with over 4,700 students. By 1914, the numbers had escalated to 2,500 college students, 4,500 pupils in 50 high schools, and twenty thousand in four hundred elementary schools. And this for an Armenian population numbering just over 2 million.[40]

Missionary presence in Keghi started around the middle of the nineteenth century. According to oral testimony, Sarkis Menejenian brought Protestantism to Keghi Kasaba from Constantinople: "My mother's grandfather ... established Protestantism in Keghi. He and a friend ... had gone to Istanbul ... to a prayer meeting place ... The two of them ... covered their faces with their hats because they were laughing (in ridicule). As they were leaving the service, the minister shook their hands and gave them a Bible or prayer books. When they bring these home, they notice that they are written in Modern Armenian, not in Classical Armenian, which is what is used in (Apostolic) churches. They thought that the Modern Armenian was better so when they returned to Keghi they introduced Protestantism there ...they had very few followers. They were only about thirty families that became Protestant."[41]

From Keghi Kasaba, evangelicals gradually established a mission and a school in the large village of Tarman (Temron). During this early period, the most notable teacher was Melkon Jantamirian, whose school in Tarman shone as "a beacon to all the youth in the region." By the latter part of the nineteenth century, a number of Keghetsis were studying at the mission compound in Kharput. Around the turn of the century, Garabed Melkonian, a mission-trained teacher, was directing a highly respected school in Tarman where he reorganized and expanded the curriculum, used a number of new texts, and brought in men and women teachers from Euphrates College in Kharput. Not only did Melkonian's school attract students from the entire region, but it also served as a model for the Apostolic schools in other villages. Along with the Protestant school in Keghi Kasaba, Melkonian's school became a feeder to Euphrates College.[42]

Because Protestants opened their schools to both genders and all classes, more girls were exposed to schooling and indeed to higher education, as evidenced in the popularity of the Constantinople Women's College, founded in 1871. In 1913 girls outnumbered boys at Euphrates College. In a graded system of elementary and secondary schools, the missionaries introduced a varied and extensive curriculum that included Armenian language and history, mathematics, the sciences, trades, music, and physical education. They employed trained teachers, both American and Armenian, introduced progressive teaching and pedagogical methods from America, imported relatively modern equipment, and established libraries and prepared and published up-to-date texts in the vernacular language. Missionary endeavours fell on fertile ground, for Armenians not only hungered for education, they enthusiastically welcomed American innovations.

By such means, Protestants, many of whom had been influenced by the public school and Progressive movements in the United States, with their emphasis on child welfare, brought American ideas and concepts to the Armenians, living, as they were, in a backward and fundamentalist Islamic regime. Protestant educators also set an example for

Armenian Apostolic church and school authorities and spurred them to reexamine their standards and methods and to strive for basic reforms in their own institutions.[43]

Protestants influenced more than education and culture, for while they condemned rebellion and opposed the activities of political agitators, they, their instruction, and their history conveyed a different message. True, "missionaries never spoke of revolution. Just religion. God and Christ";[44] they exhorted their flock to refrain from violence and physical resistance and expelled young agitators from their schools.[45] Yet their teachings about democracy and liberty, their goals of self-sufficiency and self-reliance, their emphasis on freedom of conscience, their tradition of individualism, and their personal example of the dignity of the human being threw open new horizons for Armenians.

What is more, in the eyes of many Armenians, Protestantism represented a force championing reform and change. Many missionaries had been touched by the abolitionist movement, the post–Civil War efforts to educate former slaves, and the suffrage and temperance movements, and they carried these values and approaches to the Ottoman Empire. Protestants, whose beliefs represented a form of modern Western tradition and thought, inspired young people to make a conscious choice in favour of modernity, of social change, of the sanctity of law, and of the rights of man. Their presence and preaching opened new vistas and new possibilities for Armenians, who began to see that the status quo was not sacrosanct, that fatalism was not their only option, and that their cruel living conditions could and should be ameliorated.

Most significantly, the birth of Protestantism, based on protest and secession, and the birth of the United States, founded on revolution and independence – achieved through armed struggle – made a profound impression on Armenian young people and radically changed their mentality and expectations. "It was impossible to expose young men to western ideas and developments," writes Robert Mirak, "and still keep them chained to Turkish despotism." As role models and as symbols of liberty and democracy, American missionaries unwillingly served the Armenian nationalist movement and unintentionally fuelled public discontent among young Armenians.[46]

Missionaries did not have to be "disguised agents of republicanism" or subtle inculcators of the spirit of revolution. Their presence and preaching among the Armenians were enough to convey new possibilities for a people suffering oppression and persecution. For Keghi youth, as for many other young people in Anatolia, Euphrates College became the theatre of Armenian social consciousness and the fortress of Armenian patriotism in the heart of the country. The Protestants, whose beliefs, like socialism, were a variant of the Western modernist tradition, inspired many young people. Those who were influenced by the work and example of the Protestants served as a generation of progressive intelligentsia who played a role in the social, educational, and professional life of the Armenian people.

American and Canadian Protestants not only took modernity, Americanization, and Westernization into the heart of Anatolia, they also sent Armenia to North America. They facilitated, initially at least, the movement of young people to North America to study, particularly in the fields of science, technology, theology, and medicine, on the understanding that they would return to help their people. Andover, Yale, Princeton, Harvard, and Columbia all received Armenian young people, eager to further their education. Having lived and studied in the New World, some young people preferred to remain there. Others returned to their homes and families in Turkey but found the conditions bleak and the opportunities limited; many left again for North America.

The first Armenian cohort to come to the United States during the nineteenth century was composed of these pioneer students and clergy who came under the auspices of American missionaries. These early settlers, in turn, helped their kith and kin take up the migratory cane to the New World, and in this manner they paved the way to America for their compatriots. Many an immigrant claimed that Kharput and Euphrates College or Marsovan and Anatolia College opened the floodgates to America.

While some missionaries, like Armenian nationalists, were opposed to the exodus of young people, they were also aware of the difficulties they faced in the Ottoman Empire: "There is no trade in our ports and no facilities for improving matters," complained missionary Sophie Newnham in an effort to direct movement to Canada. "We try to instill into the minds of these boys an independent spirit and willingness to labour and they naturally ask us to show them where they can carry out these principles. Many are most anxious to get over to Canada and the States."[47] Some managed to migrate to the West. A few examples from Anatolia College in Marsovan prove the point. Garabed Nergararian, the first Armenian known to have emigrated to Canada, circa 1887, came from Marsovan, (outside Keghi) probably a Protestant student from Anatolia College; Hagop Isganian from the same college arrived in the United States in 1864 and set up an Oriental rug shop; Protestants from Marsovan were also the first Armenians to settle in Fresno, California (circa 1880–81); in the United Kingdom, Hovannes Kamberian, another graduate of Anatolia college helped found the Armenian Association of Manchester, which raised enormous funds for the Armenian war effort and relief of refugees; and Dr Garabed

Thoumaian, a professor of languages at Anatolia College, was instrumental in setting up and directing the Armenia orphanage for destitute Armenian boys in Chigwell, England.[48] All this is not to say that Armenians quit the Ottoman Empire because of the missionaries. Far from it. Armenians fled Turkey because of exploitation, forced conversion to Islam, insecurity of property, and, most serious of all, massacre, but the missionaries hastened the migratory waves to America.

Like most Armenians, Protestants were overjoyed at the prospect of a new dawn in the Ottoman Empire with the Young Turk Revolution in 1908 and its credo of liberty, equality, fraternity for all. But they were soon shocked by the massacre of Armenians in Adana the following year. And when the ultra-nationalist wing of the Young Turk party took power in 1911–12, a lightning rod even more terrible than the Red Sultan was unleashed, Turkification: "The right of the other nationalities to have their own organization must be denied – any form of de-centralization and self-administration is treason to the Turkish empire. The nationalities are a 'Quantité négligeable'; they may retain their religion, but not their language."[49]

The curtailment of school activities, the circumscription of the curriculum, surveillance of educators and students, the harassment and imprisonment of the intelligentsia on the mere suspicion of dissidence, discrimination in the courts against Christians, and unrelenting lawlessness in the countryside were fearful omens. Summing up widespread anxiety and expressing a sense of foreboding, an Armenian delegation headed by the patriarch presented a petition to Turkish authorities in 1913 on behalf of the Armenian National Assembly: "The constitutional regime ... has thus far been a disappointment to the Armenian community. While the vexatious oppression suffered by the Armenians has continued uninterruptedly and has even increased in the past four or five years, 'disquieting symptoms, precursors of a massacre, of a catastrophe capable of overshadowing, in its horror, the most fearful tragedies of the past' have become manifest more recently. ... The opinion is fostered among the Moslem masses that 'it will not be possible to preserve from European encroachments what still remains of Ottoman Territory, except by annihilating the Armenian element.'"[50]

Nationalism among the subject peoples of Europe, writes Carlton Hayes, was stimulated and intensified, rather than lessened, by repressive measures.[51] For Keghetsis like Garabed Melkonian, a member of the Armenian Revolutionary Federation, the national struggle was bound up with civil and human rights. They saw the Armenians as oppressed, because they were subjugated by an intolerant foreign power. Their efforts to learn their history, sing their patriotic songs, and revere their national heroes at the risk of detection and imprisonment were, first and foremost, a reaction to oppression, but they were also driven by the new spirit of nationalism and of liberalism.

Many Armenians took up arms to protect life, property, and honour. "Self-defence should be the order of the day," proclaimed the priest of Tsermag village in Keghi. "To deter the bandits we must show strength and to do so the Armenians must arm well."[52] In response to exploitation and murder, young Keghetsis – peasant heroes – organized secret guerrilla defence bands. In 1906, young men from several villages took up arms. Under the leadership of Boghos Seradarian, they joined up with a group of Moslems and forcibly put an end to the corvée in the village of Oror. By means of a court case against the Oror *beys*, they managed to restore some of the confiscated lands to the original owners. "The cooperation between the Armenians and Moslems destroyed the economic control of the Kurdish lords of Oror and their fate in turn had a mitigating effect on the other Keghi lords. Oppression was considerably reduced in the region."[53]

When the peasants petitioned, protested, revolted, and fought in self-defence, there was no continuity or coherence to their efforts, not even on a regional scale. Neither they nor their leaders were motivated by ideology. Their leaders were activists, not ideologists or prophets who formulated novel visions or plans of social and political organization.[54] But Erzerum had its ideologists in the Defenders of the Fatherland, as did Van in the Armenakan Party. Keghi, too, had ideologists and prophets. Men like Harutiun Ateian and Mamigon Varzhabedian (teachers deported from Bolis), Khachig Mateosian, and the young cleric Vardapet Nerses Kharaghanian set up local branches of the Hnchak Social Democratic Party. Rev. Der Suren (Hovannes Melkonian) of the village of Arek and Garabed Melkonian, in their turn, organized cells of the Armenian Revolutionary Federation in the region, probably before 1904.[55]

The Hnchak Social Democratic Party, or Hnchaks, and the Armenian Revolutionary Federation (ARF), or Dashnaks, were founded in the diaspora in response to the wretched condition of the Armenian minority in Turkey.[56] Both the Hnchaks, formed in Geneva in 1887, and the Dashnaks, organized in Tiflis in 1890, directed their efforts primarily at self-defence: they set up the local manufacture of guns and imported arms and ammunition from outside the region and trained Armenians in their use. The major consistent component of the Armenian political agenda in Keghi remained security of life and property, but political leaders also tried to bring the Keghetsis into the orbit of new intellectual currents. When the ARF journalist and fieldworker Simon Vratzian and the Hnchak propagandist Garegin Kozekian engaged in public lectures and debates in 1911 in Keghi, they placed the local problems within the larger framework of party ideology and national survival.[57]

During the early twentieth century, both parties were reappraising their goals and priorities. Both were absorbed in improving the state of the Armenian people. As the Dashnaks leaned more towards socialism and the Hnchaks towards social democracy, the party intelligentsia were, in effect, aligning themselves and their followers with advanced theories in Europe and Russia. In this way, the political parties acted as modernizing agents no less than the Protestants, the repatriates, and mass education, and like these other forces they too helped define Armenian identity.[58]

An agrarian and backward rural society opened up to the influences of modernity, industrialization, and urbanization. In the latter part of the nineteenth century, a British official remarked that Christians "never had justice, and though everyone complains as he suffers, he stoically resigns himself to what he seems to believe the ordinary condition of humanity, not to be remedied."[59] Farm boys could not help but be jolted by the experience of working in textile mills and leather factories in New England cities or of toiling in iron factories in Ontario towns. The impact of repatriates, the politicization by the Armenian political parties, the work of the Protestant missionaries, the influence of the British diplomatic corps, events in Russian Armenia, and far-reaching changes in the Ottoman Empire itself inevitably transformed the Armenians of Keghi, of Kharput, of Arabkir, of Van, and of Mush. They began to understand that what they had acquiesced in as a way of life and what they had stoically accepted as the natural destiny of Christians in Turkey was not their only choice. Conscious of a different quality of life, they became discontented with a society that condemned Armenians as sinners, subjected them to indignity and injustice, and in the long run tried to dehumanize them.

By the early twentieth century, a people whose identity had been defined by the state in religious terms as a millet had become the *Hai Azg* (the Armenian nation), aware and proud of its unique history and culture and unwilling to surrender its identity to foreign powers. For Armenians the concept of nation meant loyalty to land, religion, and language, and in political terms it embraced a measure of national autonomy.

Some Keghetsis remained on their ancestral soil and took up rifle or pen to right the wrongs. Others, unable to bear the intolerable conditions and seeing hope and opportunity across the Atlantic, left for the New World. Wherever they settled they took with them their deep-rooted attachment to their identity, religion, and language. By the outbreak of World War I, Armenian agriculturalists had travelled from ancient villages deep in the heart of Anatolia to young, industrial towns in Southern Ontario.

A list of pre-1914 Armenian and part-Armenian villages in the region of Keghi, indicating the names of the Armenian churches in each village. All churches were destroyed as Armenian places of worship. List compiled by Haigazn K. Ghazarian and published in *Hairenik Daily*, 9 January 1968

Portrait of mother and son, Makruhi and Kurken Migirdicyan, Van, pre-1914. During their flight from Van, the boy and his younger sister witnessed their mother's murder by Turkish Soldiers. Photo courtesy Migirdic Migirdicyan

Paul Courian, Toronto, ca 1900. Courian emigrated from Constantinople and was the first Armenian oriental-carpet merchant in Canada with stores in Montreal and Toronto. He imported rugs from agents in England and directly from ateliers in the East. Photo courtesy Paul Courian, grandson of the early pioneer, Archives of Ontario

PART TWO

Armenian Pioneers in Canada

3
The First Wave: To World War I

The day of leaving. July 26, 1910, the feast of Vartevar. The whole village [Chanakhchi] gathered on Karmir Kash mountain ... They had come to see the sojourners off. The village priest said Holy Mass. The women were weeping so much you'd think they were offering their children as a sacrifice to the pagan gods.

[We walked together] to the bridge of Alageoz ... They say this mountain is the last point where, through the mist we can get a last look at our village. We stopped, and longingly we strained our eyes for a final glimpse of our village. Before us was mist, heavy mist. Suddenly the mountain of Surb Luis [St Light] appeared ... as if to console us. It was as if the mountain appeared to say its farewell to us. If it had had a tongue, it would have asked us, "Where are you going? Why? You leave us here alone and you depart. Do you want me to be unloved, pining, with withered passions?"

With a kiss to Surb Luis, we departed.

Arakel Eghigian

PASSAGE

Men like Arakel Eghigian might have travelled by night, with the aid of Kurdish guides, either to Batoum or to Trebizond and hence to Marseilles via Constantinople. Along the way, they would have contacted relatives or village compatriots to lodge and help them along the next phase of travel. For Keghi travellers Le Havre and Cherbourg remained the most popular transoceanic ports of departure and Halifax, St John, and Quebec City the usual points of entry to Canada. As a rule, Keghetsis sailed in steerage on a trip that typically lasted seven to ten days.

The mounting pressures on Armenians to leave the Ottoman Empire and the attraction of North America, with its bounty, opportunity, freedom, and justice played on each other like a concerto. As Canadian industries and American branch plants opened their doors to European labour in the early years of the twentieth century, the movement to

Canada of Armenian agriculturalists like Arakel Eghigian gained momentum. They followed other Armenians who had migrated to Canada in the latter part of the nineteenth century. Mesrob Bagdasarian, from Kharput, was likely sent to Canada by Protestant teachers for advanced study.[1] In the 1890s Paul Courian, a Protestant rug merchant from Constantinople and California, immigrated to Canada with his family and eventually settled in Toronto.[2] In 1889 or the early 1890s, a member of the Cockshutt family, probably Colonel Harry Cockshutt (later Lieutenant Governor of Ontario), recruited ten Keghi migrants in Constantinople for the Cockshutt Plow Works in Brantford, Ontario. This recruitment represents the flutter of the butterfly wings of Keghi movement to Canada. The Cockshutt family may also have had links with Protestant missionaries in Turkey, possibly the Chambers family from Woodstock, Ontario. Harry's brother, Frank, president of the Cockshutt Plow Works from 1888–1911, was founder and president of the Evangelistic Union in Brantford (founded 1907).[3]

According to Canadian Immigration and Colonization Branch records, 62 Armenians entered Canada from 1 July 1900 to 30 June 1901. From 1 April 1907 to 31 March 1908, 563 Armenians landed in Canada. A year later, the number admitted at ocean ports dropped dramatically to 79. The fluctuations of Armenian entry to Canada reflected government regulations in both the Ottoman Empire and the Dominion of Canada.

Emigrating from Turkey

Leaving the empire before 1908 was costly, difficult, and dangerous. In order to exit Turkey temporarily before 1908, one was obliged to purchase a *teskereh*, or travel permit, from Turkish officials, who invariably demanded substantial bribes and subjected citizens to long and frustrating delays. Consequently Armenian émigrés often chose to risk surreptitious exit, to face possible imprisonment, forfeiture of Ottoman nationality, or exile. To emigrate from Turkey permanently was even more problematic: laws prohibited unauthorized emigration, and permission to leave required an exit visa (usually purchased through bribery), the renunciation of Ottoman citizenship and all property rights, and an oath never to return to the Ottoman Empire. So strict were the regulations that should Armenians have risked return carrying a foreign passport, their claims to foreign nationality would not have been respected by Turkish authorities, and those naturalized in Canada could not have expected British protection for themselves or their properties should they have travelled back to their place of birth.[4]

Leaving Turkey entailed other perils, for brigands ravaged the countryside, guides charged dearly to deliver fugitives to port safely, gendarmes scoured the borders and ports of Trebizond, Smyrna, and Constantinople, and charlatans preyed mercilessly on inexperienced travellers. In his memoirs Krikor Parseghian recounted some of the dangers he experienced particularly from a government informer who, posing as a travel guide, tried to lure him off the ship at Constantinople into the clutches of the Turkish police waiting to arrest him for illegal exit.[5]

After the Young Turk coup d'état in 1908, reforms eased travel restrictions, shipping increased, and fares declined. Road and rail services were improved and expanded; and major European shipping companies, such as Cunard, were allowed to operate in some of the imperial ports. The price of a voyage to the United States dropped: in 1900 a one-way passage in steerage from Constantinople to New York cost U.S.$34; by 1913 the price had fallen to U.S.$24. At the same time that the New World was becoming more accessible to Armenians, the Turkish government extended the draft to include Christians, raised the military exemption tax (*bedel*) to about U.S.$260, and assiduously enforced the more stringent conscription laws.[6] After the outbreak of war between Turkey and Italy in 1911 and the Balkans in 1912, growing numbers of young men left the country to evade the draft and payment of the *bedel*. After 1908 joining an uncle or father in Brantford or St Catharines, Ontario, became feasible, and after 1911, more than likely.

Travel Agents

Travellers invariably stopped off at Marseilles, a transoceanic port burgeoning with hopeful migrants and travel agents who were as vital to the migration process as the immigration officials who despised them.[7] Travel agents served as intelligence brokers, steamship agents, bankers, letter writers, and interpreters. Often they operated coffee houses or grocery stores on the side or ran boardinghouses for voyagers waiting for medical treatment, a ship's arrival, or private remittances from North America. Their reputation and income depended on their success in facilitating passage and entry of their customers. Some agents were honest, others disreputable. Some contrived to smuggle in "undesirable" immigrants to Canada and colluded with steamship company personnel and even government immigration authorities. Others swindled the immigrant of his savings, housed him in unsanitary and overcrowded "hotels," kept him ignorant and dependent, and exploited his fears of exclusion.[8]

To a degree the migrant accepted the agents as parasites and profiteers, because they were a necessary evil, a liaison between the home country and the destination, between the known past and the unknown and frightening future. The immigrant who used their services stoically acquiesced in a certain measure of dishonesty. Without the agents' knowledge and contacts, the inexperienced traveller, covering vast distances, unfamiliar with the languages en route, and unacquainted with customs and government regulations would have encountered even greater obstacles than he did, especially from immigration officials at ports of entry. As Canadian and American immigration rules and procedures grew more complex and restrictive, moreover, the services of such middlemen became even more indispensable. Indeed, the agents' role was all the more critical to the movement of Armenians to Canada, because this migration was individualistic. No padrone systems, no assisted migration schemes, and no emigration aid societies organized and planned resettlement or cushioned the hardships of the unknown. With little other recourse, save his own judgment and the support of kith and kin, the Armenian migrant was obliged to rely on the services of Armenian agents. The degree of dependency, the importance of the agent's role, and the extent of his influence were explicitly shown in 1907, when two Armenians smuggled on shipboard were caught and brought to trial. They steadfastly refused to testify against the Armenian agent in Liverpool who had made the arrangements.[9]

They were well aware that immigration officials who attacked agents for exploiting the bewildered and dislocated migrant were less concerned about protecting the victim and more about destroying the middleman, "the information broker," whose enterprising activities posed a threat to their efforts to control the population flow into their countries. Responding to an investigation of one of these agents, a steamship company representative pointedly observed that the question was not so much a case of the agent but rather whether the government wished to prohibit entirely the movement of Armenians and Syrians to Canada. If so, the government was obliged to "give each of the Canadian Lines prohibitory instruction to that effect ... but whilst there is no such class of passengers you cannot reasonably expect us to refuse such traffic which is legitimately handed to us."[10] Mindful of the attitude of immigration authorities towards Armenians, the agents were in the delicate and difficult position of trying to remain within the fine edge of the ever-changing law and of attempting to turn a profit by manipulating the passage and entry of an "undesirable" element. If their juggling among immigration officials, steamship companies, and countrymen became too unbalanced, they lost either their license or their customers, and if they were not careful, they might lose both.

As the routes to Canada opened up and more Armenians travelled the distances, they learned to be suspicious, wary, and outspoken. Forewarned by the Armenian press to be on the lookout for swindlers posing as kind-hearted and concerned compatriots and cautioned by relatives and friends who had been stung by "bloodsuckers," Armenian migrants were becoming audacious enough to complain to the police "if anything [was] stolen from, or lost by them." In one such case in Liverpool, an Armenian emigrant complained that the agent/boarding-house keeper had bought him a ticket to Philadelphia when he had specifically requested a ticket to Canada. "These Syrians and Armenians," concluded Detective Inspector Pierpoint, "are extremely mean in money matters, probably because they have great difficulty in saving anything among their poor surroundings in Turkey."[11]

As a precaution against corruption and also as a measure for facilitating entry into Canada, especially after 1908, settlers in Canada sent information, money, and tickets prepaid in Canada to their compatriots, waiting expectantly in Marseilles, Cherbourg, Le Havre, or Liverpool. An interviewee recalled that a former servant in his home in Keghi had migrated to St Catharines, Ontario: "When I reached Marseilles he sent me $25.00 so that I could buy some clothes. My friend had sent the steamship company $25.00 ... and on the specified day they came and picked me up and put me on the ship all the way to Quebec. On the Allan line."[12] And thus, their own informal networks and personal interventions lightened the misery of travel and acted as a counterbalance to the capriciousness and imponderables of passage.

THE CANADIAN IMMIGRATION PROGRAM

Before 1896 the Canadian Government exercised minimal control over those who sought entry. An open-door immigration policy, however, was evoking images among many Canadians of an influx of "Orientals," waves of "destitute derelicts," and "unassimilable misfits ... polluting a struggling young nation" with poverty, ignorance, disease, and crime. Weighing the balance between unrestricted immigration and the nation's economic and social needs, Prime Minister Wilfrid Laurier's minister of the interior, Clifford Sifton, adopted a selective immigration policy. First, he tightened health and morality laws. Physical, mental, and moral defectives, delinquents, beggars, vagrants, charity immigrants, and illiterates were excluded, regardless of country of origin. From 1903 to 1905 an estimated 80 to 90 percent of detentions and rejections were due to contagious "eye trouble, mostly trachoma among Continental people."[13]

The state of the immigrant's eyes was a source of constant anxiety to him and to the Canadian medical profession, which strongly opposed the admission of sick immigrants. Dr C.K. Clarke remarked that the "lack of proper facilities to inspect immigrants plays into the hands of selfish interests – shipping companies and profiteers."[14] Ironically, some of the profiteers belonged to Dr Clarke's own profession. In 1908 the *Ottawa Citizen* reported a scandal involving medical inspection in Halifax where "big money" was being made in the inspection process. Doctors were holding up "healthy immigrants as victims of disease when in reality the only trouble was they had not submitted to a 'holdup levy' for being passed unmolested." Doctors at the Trachoma Detention Centre in Halifax, "in whose interest it was to have many patients," managed to find many "victims." "Not only were men and women held up here on a charge of having trachoma ... but the alleged conspiracy spread to the other side of the ocean." " There," the *Citizen* report continued, "emigrants were asked for money and those who paid were given a pass word or sign." Men were instructed, for example, to touch their tie or to wear a previously agreed upon colour of tie, and this sign insured their passing through the medical lines at Halifax, regardless of their physical condition. For his part in these activities Dr Hugh L. Dickey, chief of the "trachoma hospital" (i.e., the detention hospital) in Halifax, was dismissed on 12 March 1908. Two years later, complaints were still expressed: "Money making pass and no pass, who has money is fit, who has none, not fit. The healthy ones suffer for unhealthy ones place."[15]

Robust and healthy when they left their native land, migrants were often subjected to deplorable shipboard conditions that brought on disease. While weather and seasickness could plague any passenger, steerage class travellers frequently faced overcrowding, filthy and unhygienic eating and sleeping facilities, dirty lavatories and grimy latrines, inadequate supplies of clean water, improper heating and ventilation, insufficient air space, noxious odors, and unsatisfactory care by the ship's medical officers. Dr Peter Bryce, chief medical officer (Department of the Interior) repeatedly complained about the poor accommodation for lower-class passengers that led to disease and rendered arrivals inadmissible by Canadian port authorities.[16] For Armenians who had to travel long distances and cope with filthy shipboard conditions, eye problems, usually trachoma, were the single most serious impediment to entry before 1908. However, as earlier Armenian settlers prospered in Canada, they arranged for better accommodation en route for friends and relatives and for medical treatment in England and Newfoundland for those suffering illness. Their efforts bore positive results, so that poor health gradually ceased to be a serious obstacle to Armenian entry into Canada.

A Westerner himself, Clifford Sifton gave priority to developing Western lands and meeting the needs of Western farmers. "We are in a position now," he commented, "to take our choice and we do not want anything but agricultural laborers and farmers or people who are coming for the purpose of engaging in agriculture, either as farmers or laborers."[17] Yet time and again, efforts by Armenian farmers to get Canadian government approval to settle in the West failed. Attempts by the Canadian Presbyterian missionaries in the Ottoman Empire, the brothers Rev. Dr Robert Chambers and Rev. Dr William Nesbitt Chambers, to garner support for government inducements to allow block settlements of Armenian farmers on prairie lands also proved unsuccessful. In 1896 James N. Chambers wrote to the editor of the *Montreal Daily Witness*: "Someone [W.N. Chambers] who has spent 16 years in Armenia and can judge them as colonists says, 'they are the most capable energetic, enterprising race in Western Asia, physically superior and intellectually acute and above all they are a race which can be raised in all respects to our own level [sic] neither religion, colour, customs, nor inferiority in intellect or force constituting any barrier between us ... It would be a good thing for Canada and a salvation to these people to get up an immigration movement.'"[18]

This letter was part of a lobby spearheaded by Rev. Dr Robert Chambers, who undertook to promote a scheme to establish an Armenian agricultural colony in Saskatchewan or in British Columbia during the 1894–97 massacres. Members of the Chambers family in Canada began a widespread campaign to win support from leading educators, lawyers, and clergymen. Among others, Principal Grant of Queen's University, Principal Craven of Knox College, and S.H. Blake wholeheartedly backed a plan that would save Armenians from pillage and massacre and populate the Canadian West with "bright, enterprising, industrious, adaptive" people who would make "good farmers and reliable citizens." The plight of the hapless Christians was carried in a number of eyewitness accounts in the Canadian press, especially in church periodicals, which enjoyed nationwide distribution. Canadians responded to the Armenian cause with money and support. In the *Daily Nor'Wester*, Harry H. Smith suggested that funds raised throughout the English-speaking world to feed, clothe, and house Armenians "together with an appropriation from parliament for transporting them to our North West" should be used in a scheme to settle Armenians in Canada.[19]

Responding to Rev. Chambers' original letter, immigration officials drew up a draft in April 1896 in which they outlined certain conditions and ended by stating that "every possible facility at the command of the Government of Canada will be afforded to any of the Armenians who may emigrate to Canada and establish themselves on homesteads." The final dispatch, however, sent two months after Laurier took office in 1896 recast the original. Deleting the above encouragement, it stated instead that the government entertained "grave doubts, in view of the difference which exists between the climate and conditions of life in Canada and those of their native country, whether it would be in the interests of Armenians themselves or in the interests of Canada that inducements should be held out to them to emigrate to this country." Undaunted by government rejection, Chambers tried again in 1904. James Smart, the deputy minister and Sifton's "alter ego," did not think Armenians were a people accustomed to such conditions as would make them successful farmers in the Canadian North West. Ironically, department officials were complaining that "very few persons of your nationality have taken up farms in Canada," at the same time that they discouraged farm settlement, refused inducements offered to other Europeans, and admitted that the department "does not look with favour upon the immigration to Canada of the classes above mentioned [Armenians] and those arriving are admitted only when they fully comply with all the laws and regulations restricting immigration and immigrants ... they are allowed in only when they cannot be legally kept out."[20]

Immigration department authorities successfully thwarted schemes to settle Armenian farmers in substantial numbers in the Canadian West. Their success gave them cause to protest, years later, that Armenians were not in the custom of taking up farming in Canada. But in fact, at the heart of the Canadian immigration program was a hierarchy of race. The superior races and preferred classes were British, Western and Northwestern Europeans, and naturalized Americans; the nonpreferred were other Europeans, who were allowed admission as need arose. At the bottom of the scale were the "undesirables" – Africans, Jews, and Asiatics, who were discouraged from settling in Canada. As people from Turkey, Armenians were classified as Asiatics and since "the Government of Canada does not encourage immigration from any part of Turkey," they were virtually barred from entering the Dominion.[21] Paradoxically, Armenians identified themselves not in racial terms but in religious terms and therefore did not expect to be denied by a Christian country. Aside from religious considerations, Armenians were racially Caucasian and spoke an Indo-European language. They therefore found it difficult to understand how they would threaten the racial purity of the country. But immigration officials disregarded their appeals. The convolutions of race and geography were to have far-reaching and unimagined consequences for Armenians following the Great War.

"Asia (except for Russia)," wrote William D. Scott, superintendent of immigration, "did not supply to this country a class of people who would become assimilated and form true Canadians in the best and widest meaning of the term." In order to curtail the immigration of "unassimilable" peoples, to control the racial composition of the Canadian population, and to limit the entry of cheap foreign labour, the government imposed "restrictions to prevent the Oriental from coming into Canada in numbers which my countrymen think undesirable." In 1908, the Canadian government passed regulations requiring every Asiatic man, woman, and child to have two hundred dollars in his or her possession on arrival at a Canadian port. Ostensibly authorities were checking immigrant pauperism. In fact, they had a ready means of excluding those people deemed "undesirable." Non-English-speaking Europeans found their fifty-dollar winter and twenty-five dollar summer requirements exorbitant. For Armenians, especially from the agricultural classes, two hundred dollars was prohibitive. It amounted to six times the cost of passage from Liverpool to Halifax![22]

In the meantime, Canadian industrialists, railway contractors, and labour agents were clamouring for able-bodied, cheap workers and regularly petitioning the government to waive the money qualification. Under such pressure, the government periodically, usually seasonally, relaxed the money qualification for Europeans, but steadfastly refused to show the same flexibility towards Asians. To caution border officials to apply this regulation with due vigilance, a departmental directive stated, "The Two Hundred Dollar regulation regarding Asiatics, applies to Armenians, Syrians, and Turks ... [and is to be] strictly enforced so far as these classes are concerned." As the immigration bureaucracy clamped down on Armenian entry, newcomers headed for the United States, where they fell under less stringent immigration regulations. With or without proper papers Armenians had travelled back and forth across the Canada–United States border almost at will until 1908. In that year, Canadian immigration regulations impeded entry by this route by forbidding the admission of anyone who did not come to Canada by means of a continuous journey from his country of birth or citizenship with a ticket purchased in that country or prepaid in Canada. Publicly, the government insisted that this regulation was applicable only when economic conditions rendered prohibition necessary. In fact, the terms were applied on a general and continual basis against Asiatics and were relaxed only when labour conditions warranted. In a circular issued to border authorities on 8 May 1908, the department emphasized that the continuous-journey ruling was intended "as a means of excluding those whom it is the policy of the government to exclude [i.e., Asians], but not to exclude those whom the policy is to admit."[23] The movement of Armenians coming to Canada via the United States was thus reduced to a trickle, though not entirely cut off.

Annual Armenian Immigration to Canada, 1 July 1900 to 31 March 1915

Year	Number	Year	Number
1900–1	62	1908–9	79
1901–2	112	1909–10	75
1902–3	113	1910–11	20
1903–4	81	1911–12	60
1904–5	78	1912–13	100
1905–6	82	1913–14	139
1906–7	208	1914–15	36
1907–8	563		
Total			1808

Sources: Immigration and Colonization, Annual Reports. See also Report of the Royal Commission on Bilingualism and Biculturalism, Book 4, The Cultural Contribution of the other Ethnic Groups, 1969, 238–9.

ARMENIAN ENTRY INTO CANADA

In spite of the many restrictions, slightly more than two thousand Armenians managed to enter Canada from 1890 to the outbreak of the war (for 1900–15, see table). In all likelihood at least half of them remained in Canada, for assuredly some returned home, while others moved to the United States. Some of the newcomers were recruited by Canadian industrialists in the United States or as far afield as Constantinople. The guarantee of jobs, however, did not always open the immigration gates. When twenty-one Armenian recruits holding employment cards of the Dominion Steel and Coal Company of Sydney, Cape Breton Island, attempted to enter the country, they were all turned back on the grounds that they did not each have two hundred dollars in their possession.[24] Industrialists, often desperate for tough, unskilled labour, sometimes sidestepped such rulings and took matters into their own hands. Dominion Steel of Sydney and Glace Bay, for example, smuggled in workers, including Armenians, from Newfoundland, either as crew on the steamers, as workers for the company, or simply as contraband. Since Canadian government officials needed a pass to enter the company grounds, this illegal traffic continued for some years, despite the government's attempts to block it. When the government imposed heavy fines on firms caught transporting illegal aliens into the country, the companies devised different ingenious means to circumvent the restrictions. On 30 December 1912, F.W. Hetherington complained that the Uranium Steamship Company was engaged in "subterfuge" in collusion with Dominion Steel and Coal. The shipping agent was apprehended while supplementing the cash immigrants possessed and the amount required by law to qualify for admission.[25]

Aside from recruits, Armenians were admitted to Canada by complying with all the immigration requirements. To do so, they invariably received assistance from friends and relatives in Canada who sent them funds, prepaid tickets, and advice in order to facilitate travel and admission. Other Armenians managed to enter Canada because at peak employment periods, port and border officials sometimes disregarded the money qualification and the continuous-journey ruling. If men were healthy and looked strong, had a few dollars and the promise of employment, they were occasionally admitted by officials who used their discretionary powers. Finally, some Armenians, usually women and children, were allowed in as sponsored relatives of Canadian residents/naturalized subjects who had promised to care for them.

These men and women were thinking and discreet individuals. To the extent that they chose to leave the Ottoman Empire either as sojourners or as permanent emigrants and to settle in Canada, they exercised a measure of control over the nature and composition of their diaspora. But Ottoman and Canadian government regulations played a monumental part in shaping the size and character of these early "outposts." Travel restrictions in Turkey prohibited the emigration of Armenians, at least to 1908–9, and their classification as Asiatics by Canadian immigration authorities circumscribed their admission to the Dominion. In 1908–9, when large-scale Armenian movement to Canada might have occurred following the relaxation of travel regulations in Turkey, the number of Armenians allowed in at Canadian ocean ports fell dramatically. In 1909–10, the year after the Adana massacres, the United States accepted 5,508 Armenians, while Canada took in only 75. Furthermore, by denying Armenian farmers inducements similar to those offered other Europeans and insisting on the two-hundred-dollar qualification, Canadian immigration officials effectively obstructed farm settlement, especially block farm settlement. At the same time, by their preference for farmers and farm labourers, immigration authorities discouraged the entry of the urban, educated, and well-off element that sought admission following the 1894–97 and 1909 massacres. Meanwhile, the growing availability of jobs in heavy industry and the intervention of Canadian manufacturers attracted young, able-bodied men. Turkish conscription laws and the *bedel* also spurred the emigration of young men. These laws had other ramifications, since families tended to use limited funds to facilitate the exit of men of military age, thereby delaying or altogether deterring the emigration of women and children. The money qualification in Canada added a further impediment to the migration of Armenian women and children and contributed to the creation and consolidation of a relatively small sojourner/male society. Thus the pioneer settlements in Canada were composed of permanent immigrants, exiles who may have returned to the homeland after 1908, sojourners seeking to improve their economic status, and young men fleeing conscription. A summary of passenger lists from Ellis Island further confirms the nature of Keghi migration to Canada. Of the 1,925 Keghetsis known to have entered the United States at Ellis Island from 1900 to 1914, slightly more than 11 percent (221) were destined to Canadian cities: 113 to Brantford, 74 to Hamilton, 19 to St Catharines, 10 to Dundas, 4 to Toronto, and 1 to Galt. All but 15 came to join a relative, emphasizing the family nature of the migration, but of a migration almost devoid of women, as only seven women travelled to Canada, and they came to join husbands, sons, or fathers. The overall age classifications included 5 children under twelve years of age, 31 teenagers, 48 in their thirties, 15 in their forties, and 1 in her fifties. By far the greatest number were in their twenties: 121, more than half the total of 221 immigrants destined for Canada. The pull of Canadian industry and its cultural inroads in the psyche of these newcomers needs no better proof than their practice of using the name of the iron company as the address of their kith and kin. Twenty heading for Brantford listed the Malleable Iron company (Pratt and Letchworth) while 8 of the 10 travelling to Dundas, a suburb of Hamilton, mentioned John Bertram's or the John B, as it was popularly known. (John Bertram and Sons was also known as the Canada Tool Works).[26]

SETTLEMENT

The destination of newcomers depended on knowledge of a worthwhile place to live, information about jobs, or incentives dispatched by relatives and friends already in Canada. Most who settled in southern Ontario were migrant workers who intended to return to their homeland as soon as they had accumulated sufficient capital or as soon as conditions had improved in the Ottoman Empire. Even so, a small core of settlers – some who had come to Canada as bona fide immigrants and others whose sojourn had convinced them to remain in this country – established a permanent foothold in the new land.

From the beginning of Armenian movement to Canada in the late nineteenth century to the outbreak of World War I, four distinct groups of Armenians settled in the Dominion. Three were small cohorts and included Armenian farmers from Russia (the Caucasus) who joined their Doukhobor neighbours in the Canadian West for a brief time before internal feuding split them up and led them to migrate to California.[27]

In 1902, Georges Nakashian, an Armenian Catholic from Mardin, came to Canada and settled in the Eastern Townships. His relative Aziz

Setlakwé (Sarafian), another Arabic-speaking Armenian Catholic originally from Mardin, brought his wife and two young children to Thetford Mines (1904). Like his Syrian coreligionists, Aziz peddled dry goods, including furs, to farms and rural communities in the area. His success ushered in the migration of other members of his family from Mardin and the Mardin diaspora. When the asbestos mines opened, another branch of the Mardin group migrated to Asbestos and Thetford Mines from Pittsburgh, Pennsylvania, where they had been working in the wire mills.[28]

Third, a contingent composed of perhaps thirty to forty students and merchants emigrated independently from Constantinople or other large urban centres in the Ottoman Empire and settled mainly in Toronto. The most prominent among them was Paul Courian, who with his family set down roots in the central core of Toronto. They were soon joined by others from Constantinople or its suburbs. Most had a Protestant background, came as members of nuclear families, and shortly after arrival started businesses with their own capital, favouring the import, sale, cleaning, and repairing of Oriental rugs. Together with a small group of unskilled migrant factory workers in the west end of the city, the Constantinople Armenians formed the nucleus of Armenian settlement in Toronto, numbering altogether fewer than fifty individuals before the Great War.[29]

The fourth cohort was by far the largest: small-scale farmers, small businessmen, and craftsmen from the interior of the Ottoman Empire. Travelling from European ports to Halifax, St John, Quebec City, or Montreal, they entered Canada as labourers, mechanics, farmers, clerks, and tradesmen. Some remained in Halifax, others moved on to Montreal, but most made their way to the industrial cities of Brantford, St Catharines, Hamilton, Galt, Guelph, Dundas, Preston, and Toronto, Ontario. Others joined them from the United States, crossing at Detroit, Erie, or Niagara Falls. Sarkis Arakelian, Mesag Dombalagian, and Melkon Janigian were among those who remained in the port city of Halifax. Here they carried on indispensable service to new arrivals, either as interpreters, travel agents, green grocers, or boardinghouse operators. Arakelian branched out into the increasingly popular field of photography.

Settlement started in Montreal in the 1890s. As early as 1896, for example, a group of Armenians who were naturalized as British subjects "both as to residence and by law" appealed for the protection of the British government to return to the Ottoman Empire "to pay a visit."[30] In this early period, it seems that Montreal was a jumping-off point to other parts of Canada or the United States. On the eve of the next wave, i.e., after 1918, perhaps as few as seventeen and certainly no more than fifty Armenians, largely men, remained in the city. By and large, they were villagers from Khochmat, near the town of Balu, or from the region of Keghi.

The majority of Armenian newcomers headed primarily to the four growing industrial towns of Brantford, St Catharines, Hamilton, and Galt. In the early years of the twentieth century, Brantford ranked as the third largest industrial centre in Canada and housed more foreigners per capita than any other Canadian city, including Toronto, Montreal, and Winnipeg. Alexander Graham Bell made his first long-distance telephone call from Brantford in 1876, and the city claimed the first Carnegie Library in Canada in 1902.[31] Opportunities beckoned the newcomers, and Armenian men flocked to the dynamic young city.

This movement can be divided between those who immigrated before 1908 and those who entered after that year. Settlers coming before 1908 were usually middle-aged married men with families still in the Ottoman Empire, and they were from similar educational, political, religious, and socioeconomic backgrounds. Many migrated to Canada from a place other than the home village – perhaps Constantinople, the Balkans, or the United States. Prohibited by Turkish law from returning home, some bought property and some took out Canadian naturalization papers. Describing the city's Armenian population, the *Brantford Daily Expositor* announced that Armenians were "permanent citizens ... the steadiest of the foreign class ... here to stay." Pointing to the Armenians as "the first of the foreigners to come in large numbers and settle here permanently," the newspaper account quotes an Armenian saying, "There is little hope of our wives ever coming over here. They cannot get out of the country. The government will not let them. When we came we had to bribe officials and soldiers to get out. Some women managed to escape, but they are comparatively few. In Brantford, for instance, there are only eight Armenian women. Some of us have wives in Armenia. We send them money, but we'll never see them again."

"Practically every Armenian in Brantford," the newspaper account continued, "has emigrated at the risk of his life. None, no matter how urgent the circumstances, is willing to return. Under these conditions, the Armenian, realizing that he must seek his fame and fortune in the land of his adoption is likely to settle permanently in whatever centre may offer opportunities, service, and the enjoyment of life."[32] Forty naturalized Armenians in Brantford had already appealed for British protection should they return to the Ottoman Empire to dispose of property or bring out their families. The reply from the British embassy in Constantinople confirmed the perils of repatriation.[33]

When Turkey lifted the travel barriers after the 1908 revolution, all

520 Armenians in Brantford rejoiced.[34] Some did, indeed, rejoin their families in the homeland, where their Canadian dollars provided a comfortable living if they could bear the oppression. Others, having walked the streets of Canada as free men, were loath to return to the Ottoman empire, despite the pleadings of family or the importuning of political activists. Changes in travel facilities and conscription laws also affected the nature of the migration to Canada after 1908–9, as more young, relatively better-educated men ventured directly from the village. But families in the old country were apprehensive about sending adolescents to North America for fear they would never return or would get "lost" or corrupted in the New World or stricken with venereal disease.

When they arrived, newcomers took lodgings close to the iron factories where they worked. When Cockshutt brought Keghi workers from Constantinople to Brantford, they probably found accommodation in houses rented from the factory. In 1900 the Pratt and Letchworth Malleable Iron Company of Buffalo took over the vacated buildings of the Grand Trunk Railway (Canadian National Railway) car shops on Wilkins Street in Brantford, where it started manufacturing castings for trains, eventually operating one of the largest iron foundries of its kind in Canada.[35] Armenians from Buffalo and Troy, New York – men like Khachig Haktsian, Khoren(?) Mushoian and fellow villagers from Tarman, Keghi – were recruited to man the factory and in all probability lived in company houses. Certainly, a positive correlation existed between initial residence and the location of the Pratt and Letchworth factory, the Malleable, or the "Mybil," as they more commonly called the P and L.

Similarly, in St Catharines the McKinnon Dash and Metal Works factory (later General Motors) offered new recruits lodgings on its premises (1904) and thereby established the first location of the Armenian colony on Ontario Street.[36] As more Armenians gravitated to St Catharines, settlement moved along Ontario Street, then along Carlton Street, but residence was always within walking distance of McKinnon's. Even when small groups branched out into other factories in the area, like the Welland Vale and the Warren Axe companies, St Catharines remained a one-factory town, and McKinnon's dominated both the workplace and the living space. In Galt a similar relationship existed between the Galt Malleable, where many Armenians worked, and the place of residence on Beverley Street. From their backyards the men had only to cross the train tracks to be at work.

The first Armenian listed in the *Brantford City Directory* (1901–2) lived at 29 Duke Street, across from the Malleable. To ensure that newcomers did not miss their boardinghouse, an operator located across from the railway station, probably on Wadsworth, painted it red. Every Armenian coming to Brantford knew the unmistakable instructions: "Get off the train and walk across to the red house." By 1913, the tax assessment rolls and the *Brantford City Directories* together reveal that Armenian settlement extended in an arc through the centre of the city from Terrace Hill south towards Dalhousie and across Queen to Peel Street south of Colborne. This arc of settlement reflected the location of a number of factories where Armenians were working: Buck Stove, Cockshutt Plow, P and L Malleable, Waterous Engine Works, Massey-Harris, and Verity Plow companies.[37]

While the workplace determined the initial residential pattern, access to facilities probably played the next most important role in shaping decisions about lodgings. In 1910 Harry, Mateos, Bedros, and Krikor Bozoian lived at 49–51 Queen Street in Brantford and worked respectively at Verity Plow, Buck Stove, P and L Malleable, and Massey-Harris, indicating clearly that factors in addition to the workplace dictated residential patterns. Brantford Armenians lived in the city core and thereby had access to all its amenities. Schools, churches, libraries, City Hall, the gas company, and the market were all within walking distance of their homes.

Within the Armenian enclave, family and village ties emerged as the most significant *internal* determinants of settlement. Such were the preferences of men from the village of Astghaberd (Keghi) that Brantford became known as "the capital of Astghaberd." Although the majority in southern Ontario were from Keghi, immigrants from other places also showed residential preferences. Men from the village of Urantz in the region of Van, for example, put down roots in Galt; and men from the area of Mush chose to settle in St Catharines and Hamilton.[38] Frequently, new arrivals from the same village congregated in one house: "The men from the village of Kharabeg bought a house in Hamilton," recalled an interviewee, "and from top to bottom they were Kharabegtsis." Newcomers from Jabaghjur (Bingol region) occupied a residence on Darling Street in Brantford, and those from the village of Oghnud near Mush rented one of the McKinnon houses in St Catharines.[39] Because clan ties often extended beyond village boundaries, neither the settlements nor the lodgings were "clear-cut one village." A young man, for instance, from Oghnud might join his mother's brother from Astghaberd in Brantford.

While family and village bonds led one man to choose certain lodgings, another, perhaps more politically committed, might opt to live with political comrades. The boardinghouse at 31 Duke Street in Brantford was occupied by men from at least five different Keghi villages, from the town of Keghi Kasaba, and from the region of Van.

Most were or became members of the Dashnak Party. Meanwhile, the boardinghouses run by Abraham Asadourian and by Mgrdich (John) Mouradian lodged mostly Social Democrat Hnchakians. Similarly, in St Catharines the two political groups preferred separate quarters, though on a somewhat informal basis. *Veri Tagh* [the Upper Quarter], around the "McKinnon's houses," on Ontario Street, was probably more heavily populated by members or sympathizers of the Dashnak Party, while *Vari Tagh* [the Lower Quarter], along Carlton Street, was more popular with Hnchaks.[40]

To a degree family and village were complemented by political affiliation; but partisan loyalty could also cut across clan and village ties, as could friendship. Two brothers who lived together might support two different political parties, while two friends from different villages, labouring side by side in the factory, might board in the same house.

Each of the Armenian quarters had distinguishable features. In Brantford, Armenians concentrated in the heart of the city, in a well-established area occupied by both working-class and upper-class Anglo-Saxon families and a growing number of "foreigners." For instance, Hagop Seferian's modest boardinghouse/barber shop/coffee house at 13 Sheridan was a stone's throw and a world away from the impressive mansion of Frank Cockshutt at 80 Sheridan. By contrast, Armenians in Hamilton settled in new housing developments of one- and two-story buildings in the midst of working-class people of various ethnicities on the fringes of settlement. The St Catharines Armenian quarter differed from that in Brantford by its proximity to farmland in Grantham Township, just north of the city, a geographic location that provided a regular supply of fresh food, as well as jobs during the slack summer periods at the factory. Gradually the St Catharines settlement developed into an amalgam of rural and urban living.

In 1905, about 150 Armenians resided in Brantford, of whom 40 were naturalized British subjects; by 1909, the number of residents had jumped to well over 500. A quantitative study of Brantford Armenians found that in the twenty years preceding World War I, at least 750 Armenian names were recorded.[41] Given that the population of Brantford was only 16,619 in 1901 and 23,132 in 1911, the number of Armenians entering this small Ontario town was comparatively large. The number and concentration of foreigners seemed to pose a threat to local Anglo-Saxons who complained about overcrowding, gambling, alcoholism, and labour competition. In Brantford, British Canadian residents grumbled about the depreciation of their property values and went so far as to demand segregated quarters for all foreigners.[42]

What emerges from an examination of Armenian residential patterns in this early period is a dense and complex web of mobility, networks, and loyalties. It reveals that Armenians seemed to favour occupying accommodations vacated by other Armenians. Thus, certain buildings housed Armenians for a long time, although tenancy and ownership changed hands. More significantly, such an examination shows that these southern Ontario settlements, in fact, made up a single community. Men travelled from the Armenian quarter in one city to another probably more quickly and certainly more safely than they had moved from one village to another in the old country. A Brantford Armenian, for example, would feel closer to a countryman in Galt than to a Pole or Italian who lived next door. A story about a Hamilton boardinghouse keeper serves to give a sense of these relationships. After providing breakfast and sending his boarders off to work, the keeper prepared his stew for the evening meal, took the "radial" to Brantford, played in a backgammon tournament with his friends, and returned to Hamilton to serve the men their evening meal. Ease of geographic mobility, bonds of intimacy, and commitments of mutual responsibility became as integral a part of the Armenian experience in Canada during this period as sojourning and to an extent offset the uncertainties of migrancy.

That Keghetsis dominated the settlements of Brantford, St Catharines, and Hamilton might have given them a regional character. The physical distance from mainstream Armenian life in the United States, moreover, might have isolated these communities and insulated them from outside influences. But these forces were counterbalanced by other dynamics. Letters and visits between relatives, village men, and political partisans residing in different cities, as well as articles in the Armenian press, kept the lines of communication alive and alert. Because they extended beyond the perimeters of the Niagara Peninsula, their associations and political parties also enhanced these internal mechanisms of solidarity. A Dashnak from Mush would feel at home among Dashnak Keghetsis in Brantford. A Hnchak from Detroit could travel to Brantford, visit the Hnchak *gradaran* (library/reading room), locate a friend, find lodgings, and secure a job, all on the strength that he was a comrade. Men would hear personal accounts or read articles in the Armenian press about events affecting their people in different parts of the United States, Europe, or the homeland. They would know about Armenian involvement in the Lawrence, Massachusetts, strike of 1912, the conditions of the iron foundries in East St Louis, Canadian immigration restrictions, or usurious agents in Marseilles. Through such a matrix, a variety of forces and lifestyles touched the newcomers and gave them a worldview with wider horizons than might have been expected from mountain peasants residing in small Victorian factory towns.

4
Family and Work

FAMILY

Of the 750 Armenians recorded in a reconstitution of the Brantford Armenian community, approximately 50 were married women and fifty were children. Whether the marriages had taken place in the old country or in Canada, they were almost all endogamous.[1] These families intended to stay in Canada; they bought houses and some opened businesses.[2] During the pre-1914 period, however, they represented a minority of Armenian settlers in Canada, for the majority were male sojourners, or at least they saw themselves as temporary migrants. Interestingly, the sojourner society itself was composed of family or clan units, as revealed by the interviewee who joined his uncles, his grandfather's brother with his two sons in St Louis, to "form one household."[3] That such households did not include many women does not negate the basically family nature of immigration and settlement. The Armenian sojourners may have been men without women, but they were definitely not men without family or friends. This fact is clearly borne out in the Brantford reconstitution project, as well as in a survey of Armenians in the Canadian Expeditionary Force, which confirmed the family nature of migration.[4]

The stories of several interviewees also give a sense of these sometimes complex interconnections. Harutiun Seraganian, born in 1908, related how his maternal grandfather, Kapriel Nubarian, from Astghaberd, immigrated with the Cockshutt recruits in the 1890s (perhaps even as early as 1889) and died in Brantford in 1903 at the age of forty-five. Within two years, perhaps sooner, two of Kapriel's nephews, Khazar and Sarkis Nubarian arrived "to place a marker on his grave." At least eight Nubarian men settled in Brantford and six are known to have been from Astghaberd (probably all were). Kapriel's widow, Altun, also saw her brother and her nephew, Hrant Humpartzumian, leave for Brantford, where he married Nevart Jamgochian. Many years before, Nevart's father, Toros, and uncle Mardiros had left Astghaberd and sojourned in Bulgaria before emigrating to Brantford with their families. Young Nevart's family and her husband's family had known each other in Astghaberd. By the marriage of Nevart and Hrant, the two families cemented their old-country bonds in the New World. Nevart's sister, Takouhi, born in Bulgaria in 1900, married Senekerim Chichakian of the village of Arek in Brantford in 1914, thus widening the kin circle beyond the village of Astghaberd. Senekerim had immigrated to Canada in 1907 with his mother, two sisters, and two brothers to join his father, who had come out earlier from Rumania. Kapriel and Altun Nubarian's daughter married Seragan Derderian, also of Astghaberd. Seragan's uncle, Krikor Derderian, was in Brantford along with at least eight other Derderian men from the same village. Seragan Derderian's sister, Eto, was married to Hovagim Donegian, who was also sojourning in Brantford. Together, these brief references from a few informants reveal the intimate connections among the Nubarian, Humpartzumian, Chichakian, Jamgochian, Derderian, and Donegian families.[5] They also address the links from the village of Astghaberd to the Balkans and finally to Brantford, Ontario.

BOARDINGHOUSES

By and large, the men who came without their wives or mothers preferred to live in Armenian-run boardinghouses.[6] While households with women invariably offered boarding or rooming facilities, usually to relatives, the most common phenomenon remained the all-male boardinghouse, whose flexibility facilitated the mobility of the men and their adaptation to an irregular job market. The malleability of these households underscored the importance of the boardinghouse as an institution that provided the framework for settlement and work, for communication linkages with the host society, and for intimacy and friendship. As such, boardinghouses were centres of stability.

Newcomers lived and functioned on a day-to-day basis in a foreign environment, but in the boardinghouses they recreated the atmosphere of the home country: they spoke its language and maintained its customs and values. Far from their beloved villages, cut off from familiar places, and without the constraints and controls of the Old World society, the new arrivals acknowledged their own vulnerability. Ever mindful of the pitfalls inherent in a relatively free and open society, older members acted in loco parentis to the younger men. "They watched each other when they were over here," remarked an interviewee, "to make sure you didn't do the wrong things. If you got sick they looked after you. They were like family."[7] For these men, conscious of shame and dishonour and eager to uphold their self-respect and reputation, boardinghouses provided the place to exercise control over each other and protect one another from the corruption of "painted women," the compulsion of gambling, and the lure of coffee houses, pool halls, and saloons.

By living together as kinsmen, village men, and comrades, settlers put themselves in touch with familiar faces, foods, dialects, customs, and ideas in a strange and new environment. The stability of the old-country *tun* (household) was transferred to the vibrant and intense kinship bonds they brought with them and to a powerful village allegiance that they formalized in the village educational associations. These family and village interconnections were tightly enmeshed in and crosscut by political and national loyalties, which, in turn, were strengthened by the society the newcomers were creating. This cohesive base enabled the settlers to find lodgings, secure jobs, receive assistance during illness or hard times, and still stay within an old-country frame of reference. Such strategies helped cushion the shock of a new culture, a foreign language, strange customs, unfamiliar rhythms of work, and different disciplines and protected them from the temptations and moral "looseness" lurking in Canadian society.[8]

ADJUSTING TO THE NEW WORLD

All this is not to say that accommodations and adjustment were flawless. As a rule, the sojourning men – bachelors and married men with wives and children still in the village – dominated Armenian community life in southern Ontario. This mostly male structure gave settlement a distinctly "undomesticated" flavour. Brantford newspaper accounts, for example, comment on the cleanliness and neatness of Armenian households run by women and, not unexpectedly, the shabbiness of houses run by men.[9] Conflicts, arguments, and even fistfights occurred among the men. Their political-party records reveal how, from time to time, internal fractiousness shook these young settlements. But what is striking is the resolve to keep a lid on their quarrels and to contain them within the community itself. Armenian leaders admonished men not to argue on the factory shop floor, not to take legal action against each other, and not to engage in public shouting and fighting under any circumstances. Just as H. Asman had apologized in the *Brantford Expositor* because Armenians had gone out on strike, so, too, was the community ashamed about any public display of discord. Such behavioural patterns reflect perhaps the legacy of Turkish repression and most definitely the desire to be law-abiding and respectable.

Consequently, the Armenian quarters in Brantford, St Catharines, and Hamilton were marked by an absence of violent crime and endemic pauperism. Court and jail records indicate that minor cases of drunkenness and illicit sale of liquor were the most serious and most common offenses. Occasionally, the residents' penny-ante card games resulted in gambling charges by overzealous local constables. The fear of deportation, the spectre of disease, the social control within the communities, and the threat of ostracism combined as effective mechanisms to keep men in line.

These pioneers were motivated by the realities and values of the world they knew and cared about. Coming from a despotic regime, they tried to minimize and counterbalance its debilitating effects on themselves and on those dear to them. The Anglo-Saxon factory worker who lived next door to the Armenians on Alfred Street in Brantford could send his children to the public elementary school a block away. By contrast, the Armenian worker had to save every penny – not even spend a few cents on a coke – to give his son the opportunity to learn basic reading and writing in the village. Accumulating a few dollars by living with nine others in a single-family house and taking shifts in a bed might mean a man could send his brother to high school or pay the cost of his transoceanic voyage or his military exemption tax. By living frugally and donating generously and unstintingly where it mattered to them, they could help a fellow villager in hospital, hire a teacher for their village school, or send money abroad to aid destitute and homeless Armenians.[10]

Adjusting to the new society was not easy, but Armenian pioneers, though unaccustomed to liberty, were learning about power bases, democracy, and representative government. They sought the assistance of factory owners to bring out their relatives. Concerned about returning to the Ottoman Empire, naturalized workers appealed to their members of Parliament and the Canadian government to ascertain the extent of danger.[11] When one of the Cockshutts became lieutenant-governor of Ontario, an Armenian was hired as an interpreter in the Legislative Assembly. Factory owners and politicians thus became their earliest liaisons with the receiving society.

Other links with the host community operated through their children in school. Usually, the public schools tried to help the newcomers assimilate to the new environment, but it was still often painful for Armenian youngsters, as Mona Chichakian's story indicates. The Chichakian youngsters heard from their schoolmates that Santa Claus was coming with gifts for all children. Mrs Chichakian baked all day, and then the family waited for this unknown visitor. Bearing in mind that Armenians celebrate the birth of Christ on 6 January and that it is a solemn occasion, it is not surprising that the idea of a jolly man sliding down the chimney with gifts never occurred to these newcomers. They waited, and when no one came, the children, quite disappointed, were sent off to bed. Their mother waited until four o'clock in the morning and was not pleased, because "that scoundrel fooled us and didn't come." When the teacher asked the children about Santa's gifts, little Mona had to admit that although her mother had baked pastries for him, Santa never showed up. The kind and thoughtful teacher replied that Santa did not know Mona's address and had left her gifts at the school. With this, she gave the delighted child an orange, shoes, candy, nuts, and a doll.[12]

As for most immigrants, transferring old-country customs and behavioural patterns to Canada could be less problematic with the help of older and more experienced immigrants. Andranik Donoian remembered his sponsors, an older cousin and his wife, who was "like a mother to me. When I drank water, I threw the rest on the floor, just like in the old country. 'Brother,' she said, 'they don't do that here. When you're finished, throw the rest in the sink, not on the floor.'"[13] Just as in the old country, misunderstandings and conflicts could occur within each family. In the past, traditionally, everyone worked for the benefit of the family, and the eldest took care of the entire lot. But this custom could not always be enforced in the New World, where mobility and freedom gave adolescent children, younger siblings, and even women avenues for independence undreamed of in the Ottoman Empire. For these urban settlers a frontier existed, different from the Western frontier, to be sure, but just as inviting and just as awesome.

WORK

The Factory

A contemporary account praised immigration on the grounds that it brings "a population of working age, unhampered by unproductive mouths to be fed ... their home countries have borne the expense of rearing them up to the industrial period of their lives and then America, without that heavy expense, reaps whatever profits there are on the investment." For the new and expanding heavy industries, profit rested in the strength and vitality of a cheap immigrant work force. In turn, newcomers – small scale farmers – found work and wages in the factory. Armenians "knew life was precarious for them," recounted an interviewee. "If you got a job – and where would you get a job if you didn't know the language and you're an agricultural person to begin with when you come here? You haven't money to buy a farm. To work on a farm you'd never be able to make a livelihood in those days. So where would they go? Naturally they'd go to the industries. Where else?" Aside from the factories mentioned in the previous chapter, Armenians worked at Deering (International Harvester) in Hamilton, Guelph Foundries (Guelph), Galt Malleable (Galt), Clare Brothers (Preston), John Bertram Foundries (Dundas), and Continental Twine and Cordage (Brantford).[14]

The usual picture portrayed by interviewees is of men with a clearly defined mission and motivated by allegiance to their families in a distant village, of workers able to adjust to the demands of heavy and dangerous industrial labour, of mobile immigrants willing to move from plant to plant, city to city, and country to country to find work. Initially, at least, the occupation network was the most reliable and effective means of finding employment, so it was not uncommon to find family and friends working in the same factory. They interceded for each other, "spoke to the bosses, even gave them bribes" to get their relatives a job. Experienced old-timers helped newcomers learn the skills and the shortcuts of the job and, whenever necessary, disciplined them. When sixteen-year-old Arakel Eghigian arrived in Galt, his uncle arranged to take him to "Galt College": "that's what they called it ... What college? What lecture hall? The tin department, next to the iron foundry ... [at the Galt Malleable] When I entered, from all four sides the boys came running, hugged and kissed me. There was our Mampré, Bezian, Mesag, Mardig and Nishan Mooradian, and Percho's Mihran. The foreman arrived and they introduced me to him. He handed me a tool, like theirs, gave me a demonstration on how to use it, and left. The boys, all experienced, didn't forsake me. They showed me how to do the job, helped me out, then left to do their own work."[15] In this way, young Eghigian became a "student" in the foundry, the school of hard knocks.

Invariably Armenians entered the labour market at the lowest rung of the ladder – unskilled labour – the most insecure work in the factory. As such, they earned ten to fifteen cents an hour, worked as long as ten hours a day, six days a week. As a rule, they aimed to be moulders, because of the status and relatively high wages; but it was strenuous work.[16] Commenting on foundry labour, an inspector noted: "there is no class of work more laborious and subject to such extreme temperatures as that of the moulder. And it is not surprising that each year the class of labour is becoming more scarce. The young men of today prefer to select an occupation that is easier."[17] The moulders ran the risk of disease, especially silicosis, and the danger of injury. An informant described the indelible physical marks of the moulder: "Their hands were so tough, so callused that you could stick a pin or knife in their hand and they couldn't feel it. And they couldn't close their hands. When they wrote, you'd wonder how, because their thumb and first finger were an inch apart. So full of calluses. They would walk to one side because the ladle they lifted was seventy-five to one hundred and twenty-five pounds. When they're doing that for two hours a day, they walked strange." Another interviewee recalled how hard her father worked: "Every Harvester tractor shipped out West had some of my father's sweat on it. Every plough shipped abroad was manufactured with some of his muscle power."[18]

At the plant they established their own behavioural patterns, stuck together, and neither mingled with other ethnic groups nor joined in the company's social and sports programs. In order to keep a job and earn a decent wage, it behooved them to work hard and to give at least the impression of docility. They did not quit every spring or drink away their wages or drift from town to town or return home every summer. Gradually they earned the reputation of steady, hard-working men. An informant whose father was a pioneer at McKinnon's describes their work ethic:

It's my opinion when the Armenians left their homeland, they came from Keghi, most of them, 90 percent were agricultural workers. Whatever they did was provincial, very provincial. Now they landed in this country. What did they do? Whatever job that came along was absolutely different than what they were doing in the old country. In the beginning, if they got a job in the factory, they stayed. Many of them learned all the trades in there. We had pattern-makers, coremakers, moulders ... And the stability was very important for them. They didn't want to be leaving one job and going to another. They stayed at that job ... Most of the foreign-born, who came to this country, particularly from backward, rural areas, naturally went in the work force, [they were] unskilled. But amongst that group, even in the factories they [Armenians] aspired to be moulders, coremakers, and patternmakers. And they worked at that. But whatever they took, they stuck to it. They didn't just jump from one place to another.[19]

Industrial wages in Canada, compared to their earnings in the Ottoman or Russian Empires, cut their sojourning period short. In Constantinople "a man might earn one gold piece a month, while in Canada, he earned one gold piece a week." Most Armenian guest workers intended to stay in Canada for about three or four years; and unless laid off, they usually worked in the same factory. Moses Der Manuelian (b. 1874 or 1875), for example, lived at 13 Sheridan Street in Brantford in 1905 and at 40 Chatham Street in 1906, all the while working at the Malleable (Pratt and Letchworth). His name appears again in 1911 as boarding at 85 Pearl Street and working in the same factory. Perhaps in the interval, he had returned to his village. In any case, Der Manuelian and men like him composed a relatively stable work force that contributed to the new, expanding industrial culture, itself undergoing great changes. In many respects, the needs of such migrant workers dovetailed with the priorities of industrialists who sought a steady but temporary labour force. [20]

For Armenian workers, the three greatest threats were industrial accident, disease, and unemployment. Diaries, memoirs, interviews, newspaper accounts, and the *Armeno-American Letter Writer* reveal anxieties associated with factory toil:

Finally I got a chance to work on the railroad ... There wasn't much money in it. The work day was nine and a half hours. By working three hours overtime, twelve and a half hours a day, I could make sixteen dollars a week. I worked a few months, cleared away my debts, and when we got through with the work I had about forty dollars left in my pocket. Now I am again without work.[21]

At that time we didn't know the language. We all worked in the factories, the iron factories ... I came to St Catharines in 1912 and in 1913 I went to America [to join my uncles]. There was no work. For three months I had no job. Nothing. I heard that the Utah Copper Company was looking for labourers ... I worked for over a year at the Utah Copper Company. Then I went to work for the Union Pacific Railroad.[22]

What to do? Live or die? Today again I feel abandoned ... I hate everything ... Friends and enemies, the laughing, the sad, the girl, the woman ... I hate my life, my love, my heart, my life and soul, my body and whole being ... I hate everything with all my heart. I hate, hate ...

Rest your head in your palms and think, contemplate to the point of losing your mind, or cry like a woman. That is how a man feels when he becomes unemployed, especially when he also owes a lot of money. To work? But where when there is no job ... You're a stranger. Ah, cursed is the foreigner. When you don't have even a cent. You're thrown out of your room and your acquaintances forsake you ... I contemplate and think that I have nothing now, the week will soon be over, and I can't pay for the room and board ... Your appearance gives the impression of a thief and the passerby looks at you with hatred and fear. What to do? There is no job. Absolutely no work. To live or to die?²³

Those who managed to find work were confronted by ever-present risks on the job. On 10 July 1912, Dragan Kalabian (probably Dikran Kalagian) was crushed to death in an elevator at Buck Stove company. The Brantford Trades and Labor Council protested to the provincial attorney general and passed a resolution expressing "regret and dissatisfaction that so many working men are killed in this Province and local authorities so easily come to the conclusion an investigation is unnecessary."²⁴ Like other working men, Armenians knew that each day in the factory their lives were at stake.

For these early pioneers, the factory was clearly not a way of life. Although the company dominated the work experience, controlled their periods and hours of employment and leisure, and imposed a new industrial discipline on them, it did not win their allegiance or their loyalty. As an informant observed, "It was a part of life they had to put up with. But it wasn't their real interest in life."²⁵ Their caring world was the young wife and little children they had left behind or the aging parents struggling to maintain the familial possessions or the brother desperate to evade conscription in the Turkish army: "Accustomed to excessive toil and fatiguing conditions, the Armenian labourer could tolerate very heavy work and conform to lower wages. He had on his shoulders the responsibility for the livelihood of a whole family, often pillaged and plundered."²⁶ Led by their own agendas, they resisted assimilation and did not readily participate as members of the Canadian working class.

But in time Armenian immigrants began to create a new set of work habits and disciplines and gradually became partly industrialized. In 1906, in Brantford, sixty Armenian workers joined a strike at the Malleable, demanding more than $.15 an hour. The strikers lost their jobs but were reinstated some time later. However, the event rankled in the community, for it was "a great moral injury." Responding to criticism of Armenians, H. Asman wrote, "It was an unusual thing for the Armenians to strike, and the citizens should not think that we are not an agreeable people. The Armenians are dutiful, patient and economical."²⁷ Be that as it may, Armenian moulders joined another strike at the same factory in 1911 for wages of $1.75 a day. The company brought in strikebreakers from Montreal and again defeated the strikers.²⁸

The following year a dispute in Hamilton showed a different side of Armenian workers and revealed the spirit of an age in which ethnic priorities interacted with work issues. Even if Armenians controlled the grey iron foundry at International Harvester, they were not a militant group, and they seldom put pressure on the company as a cohesive and organized force. In 1912, however, they reacted to the company's unfairness. One of their group, twenty-eight-year-old James [Hagop] Manoukian, who belonged to Harvester's Sick and Funeral Benefit Society, contacted tuberculosis and died in hospital. Harvester paid his funeral and burial costs but arranged for interment in a grave with another Armenian. When the mourners discovered this arrangement, they objected, halted the funeral service, returned to the factory, and walked off the job – an action that involved perhaps all 175 Armenians employed in the plant. Unable to tolerate the indignity to their friend, the Harvester workers used the only weapon they had, even at the risk of antagonizing company officials. The plant superintendent adjudicated in their favour, and Manoukian was buried in a single grave in Hamilton Cemetery.

In 1915, Armenian foundrymen at McKinnon's threw down their shovels in a somewhat similar protest. Since at that time most of the foundrymen were Armenian and McKinnon's manufacturing revolved around the foundry, the Armenians effectively brought operations to a standstill. Such militant behaviour at the work site went against all their instincts, which told them that obedience and invisibility were the best means of coping in Canadian industry. But the threat of losing their jobs or being deported could not deter them. Eventually, the company acquiesced in their demands, and Armenian workers returned to the foundry.

These incidents highlight contrasting views of Armenian migrant labourers in Canada before World War I. One paints them as obedient drudges in the flow of labour to capital, victimized by exploitation and socially isolated. Manoukian's cemetery and funeral-home records suggest that he had been alone and indigent: the funeral home provided his shroud, Harvester was listed as his next of kin, the City Hospital was given as his address, and he was buried in a simple grave with no tombstone. The *Armeno-American Letter Writer* portrays a somewhat similar view: "For three years such a current carried me, throwing me from one city to another, from one factory to another, from idleness to the disappointments of underpaid drudgery. I was almost lost" (17–19). "The days go by, one week succeeds another and I already count six months in this strange land. I am lonely among millions of people and live without comfort ... I returned with a bitterness which I cannot describe. On my way I saw men passing fast in automobiles;

I felt myself reduced to such insignificance that I thought I was a useless existence crawling around" (35–9).

But the other view of Armenian migrant labourers in Canada depicts them as enveloped in an intimate world in which the men, who were often connected as relatives, godparents, fellow villagers, or friends, joined together to cope and to protect one another in an unfamiliar and uncaring land. To the outside observer, James Manoukian was an inconsequential man whose life was undistinguished and who died a pauper, a nameless cog swallowed up like thousands of other lonely and lost souls by industrial capitalism. But Manoukian was neither alone nor destitute. If we peel away the layers and look at him from within, we see a thinking and diligent man: he had drawn up a will in which he entrusted his personal effects and $149 in savings to two friends to distribute, some in the New World and some in the Old: an "invalid chair" was to be bought for City Hospital; $60 was to go to his sister in the village of Oghnud, in the Mush region. And whatever property he had in Armenia he bequeathed to the family he had left behind: his wife Arousiag and their three-year-old daughter, Paratzem. Nor was he alone and ungrieved, as the entire Harvester Armenian workforce rallied on his behalf.[29] In the wider society, both the St Catharines and the Hamilton protests symbolized ethnic honour and ethnic solidarity; they superseded the boundaries of political affiliation and economic need and revealed the newcomers' commitment to each other and to their people.

Business

While Armenians took jobs as unskilled or semiskilled urban labourers in the small towns of southern Ontario, many were not altogether ignorant of city or factory life before coming to Canada. Some had sojourned in the multiracial metropolis of Constantinople or in Bulgarian or Rumanian cities, where they had encountered nativist resistance. Others had toiled in American factories, where they had experienced the workers' struggle, been exposed to industrial capitalism, and learned to function in a dollar economy. Moreover, men brought many skills from the old country, including knowledge of merchandising, cobbling, metal work, carpet weaving and repairing, and the production of foodstuffs such as *bulgur*. In the villages, men had apprenticed in trades as varied as stone masonry, barbering, and carpentry. So while factory jobs consumed the energies of some men, others – skilled tradesmen and entrepreneurs – were establishing an economic foothold outside the factory. Records in Brantford to 1915 list five grocers, four tailors, three barbers, three shoe shiners, two bakers, one varnisher/ painter, a waiter, a plumber/tinsmith, two interpreters, two confectioners and coffeehouse operators, and three other coffeehouse managers. Because of incomplete data, it cannot be stated categorically that a positive correlation existed between entrepreneurial work and bona fide immigrants. A factory worker could conceivably take up his old-country trade, such as barbering, while sojourning in Canada; or another might find factory work totally unsatisfactory, branch out into another field, and consider his success a good reason to remain in this country. From the available information, however, it is likely that those who engaged in business activity probably intended to stay in Canada. The reverse does not follow. All who intended to remain in Canada did not become businessmen; some toiled in heavy industry all their working lives.

The usual pattern for Armenian entrepreneurs was to start as industrial labourers, then branch off into business. Initially they operated their small businesses out of a room in their dwelling. For an assured income, family members sometimes ran the business in conjunction with other jobs, usually in a factory. Not only was the factory a stepping-stone to less dangerous work, but it also attracted entrepreneurial activity, as men established confectionery shops, little restaurants, coffee shops, and barber shops close to the factory to meet the needs of factory workers. While the factory too often exploited and abused the newcomers and used up their youth and vitality, they, in turn, used the factory to gain an economic foothold in Canada.[30]

Information about two Brantford families is illuminating because it brings these complexities into focus and suggests the significance of a commercial or urban background to enterprise in Canada. During the 1890s, Hagop Seferian, born in 1857 in Tarman village in Keghi, migrated to Bulgaria (probably via Bolis). Around the turn of the century he and his wife emigrated to Brantford with the intention of settling down if conditions were favourable. Shortly after he arrived, he bought the house at 13 Sheridan Avenue, and while he worked at the Brantford Box Company in 1906 and the Verity Plow Company in 1907, he converted his premises into a boardinghouse for Armenian workers. Probably around 1905 his two sons joined him from Bulgaria. Vahan, born in the Ottoman Empire, married in Brantford in 1905, lived at 13 Sheridan, and worked as a moulder at the Verity Plow Company (1907 and 1910). His brother Solomon brought his wife and child with him. They had two more children in Brantford, and in 1912 at the age of twenty-eight his wife died while trying to abort a fourth child. In the same year he married a widow and had another child. In the records he is first listed as a labourer at Massey Harris

(1907), and from 1911 to 1915 he is intermittently recorded as a barber and chef at 13 Sheridan. Oral interviews confirmed that he cooked for the boarders, ran a barbershop in one room of the house, and operated a small coffeehouse.[31]

Another family, the Mooradians, also provide an excellent example of the links between background, immigration, and business. As already mentioned, the Mooradians operated a textile importing and exporting business in the old country spanning the home village of Arek, the provincial capital of Erzerum, and the capital of the Ottoman Empire, Constantinople. Yeghishé Mooradian, who immigrated to Canada in 1905, brought out other members of his family. From 1907 to 1909, various family members resided at 40–42 Chatham Street and around 1910 a number of them moved to 36 Wadsworth Street. During this early period several of the men are recorded as labourers. By 1913 they all lived together at 182–84 Dalhousie Street, part of which had been converted to boarding accommodations. Yeghishé and his brother Nishan ran a grocery store; another married brother, Hagop (Jack), who had attended school in Brantford, ran a tailor shop in partnership with Dikran Khachadourian; and still another relative, Hagop, operated a barbershop on the premises. Meanwhile, an uncle, Garabed Mooradian, was listed as a moulder at Massey Harris.

The account of these two families reveals more than the nature of Keghetsi movement to Canada. The experience of life away from the village had given both families a taste of new worlds and exposed them to opportunities that did not exist in the village and that provided a livelihood above subsistence level: it enabled their talents to develop and opened the way for occupational mobility and a certain measure of independence. Indeed, these two families serve as a more pronounced example of a phenomenon common among the earliest settlers, for in a larger way they were like the men who brought their cooking expertise with them from the *khans* or inns of Constantinople or the experience of managing a coffeehouse in Trebizond or Varna. After initially working in the factory, they used the skills they carried with them to establish a measure of economic independence in the New World.

The Seferian and Mooradian families were different from the small number of students who preceded them and the large number of sojourners who almost submerged them. They cannot, of course, be classed in the same economic category as the wealthy Courian family, the Constantinople rug merchants who settled in Toronto. But in their background, their skills, their solvency, and their intention to remain here, they were different from the agriculturalists who came directly from the village as sojourners.

But even among the sojourners there were men who displayed initiative when they saw opportunities for social and occupational mobility. Harry Apegian of Keghi had been recruited as a labourer in Troy, New York, in the early 1900s. For approximately ten years he worked in at least two different factories in Brantford. Around 1912, six years after he married in Brantford, he joined in partnership with Baghdasar Bozoian, a coffeehouse operator, to take over the premises of 152–4 Market Street. The building housed a barbershop, Chinese laundry, boardinghouse, and grocery store and even an immigrant bank, all of which Apegian and Bozoian either ran or rented out to others. To survive in the old country men had engaged in a multitude of occupations. In the early years of settlement in Canada, Armenians displayed the same flexibility. Men like Apegian probably believed that self-sufficiency was the key to independence and economic mobility.

As the Armenian settlement was composed largely of men, it was inevitable that they would transplant the ubiquitous Armenian coffeehouse to the new world. The coffeehouse, or *srjaran*, was an informal, leisure-time meeting place for Armenian men, an integral part of their lives, and an important source of recreation. In a corner of a grocery store, in a room behind a barbershop, or in a big room devoted solely to that purpose, the men sat on bentwood chairs around wooden tables, smoked cigarettes, and played cards – scambile and pinochle – and backgammon, "and the loser bought a chocolate bar or a coke for the winner."[32] They drank Armenian coffee, tea, and soft drinks, read the newspapers and listened to the latest gossip. At least one coffeehouse in each town secretly carried on gambling "in the basement." If he were young, the operator probably ran the coffeehouse in conjunction with another job, while an older man might consider the coffeehouse a full-time occupation. The manager paid the rent, bought the fuel, tended the stove, kept the place clean, and derived his income from renting the playing cards or the backgammon boards and from the sale of beverages, cigarettes, and confections.

Probably the most common and popular form of entrepreneurial activity was running a boardinghouse. Communal living was a tradition that had been entrenched long before movement to Canada. Having lived together "en village" in the *khans*, or hotels, of Constantinople, Armenian men were familiar with a practice they considered necessary to a profitable sojourn, whether in Constantinople, the Caucasus, Varna, or Brantford. The *pandkht*, or sojourner, in any city lived *khumana* (communally). In Constantinople sojourners had lived in apartment-inns; in Canada they converted two-story single-family dwellings, some with running water and indoor toilets, all opulent and enormous by their standards, into communal living quarters. When the settlers arrived in St Catharines, McKinnon's provided the men with living quarters at minimal cost. In the beginning they lived collectively, appointing a cook who divided the costs equally, with a small payment for himself.[33]

Initially, men organized the boardinghouses as co-operative dwellings. Running a boardinghouse could offer considerable flexibility and require little financial investment. Under certain circumstances, a man could work in the factory and run a small boardinghouse on the side, or he could pack up and leave town altogether with no financial loss. But gradually, operating a boardinghouse evolved into a business and involved a complex network of informal trust, cash exchange, and careful accounting of food and services. The usual practice was that two men would jointly rent a house. While one ran the boardinghouse, the other worked elsewhere. When they had accumulated enough capital they would purchase a property as partners and eventually one would buy the other out. This circuitous route to property ownership nevertheless entailed hard work, careful planning, and astute management.

The early pioneers in Canada were mobile men who followed work opportunities from place to place, across oceans and international boundaries. Unlike Armenian workers in Glace Bay and Sydney, who left little trace of their sojourn – reflecting both the boom/bust history of Dominion Steel and their own preferences to move on – and unlike the Armenians in Montreal, who also relocated elsewhere, those who settled in southern Ontario laid and sustained the foundations of community life. The presence of a number of nuclear/extended families, the phenomenon of property ownership, often combined with commercial and trade/craft activities, and the naturalization of approximately three hundred Armenians before 1914 indicate that for some newcomers permanent resettlement in Canada remained a viable option. They showed an eagerness to formalize associational and institutional bonds. Together with the sojourners, those mobile men who intended "to die in the old country," they established the initial stages of community formation in the new land.

5

Community Development: The Formative Years

Permanent and temporary settlers and those with different political viewpoints established the foundations of community life in southern Ontario. Not only were those foundations rooted in the Old World culture, but they strengthened the informal networks of family and village. They were both secular and, like the immigrants they served, mobile.

Because the Armenian Church is autocephalous, no pre-existing church community awaited the Armenian immigrant upon arrival in the New World; for the Armenians there was nothing like the Roman Catholic Church, which offered a religious home to countless Europeans. If the newcomers wanted religious services – and many did – either they attended the Anglican Church, which was theologically close to their own but whose language they could scarcely comprehend, or they relied on the occasional visit by itinerant Armenian priests from the United States to perform the rites of passage.[1] Most found solace by praying in private, chanting their beautiful *sharakans* (hymns) and the ancient prayers that had sustained their people through centuries of turmoil. Like their forefathers banished by conquest, these expatriates sang their psalms and read the Scriptures: "Each was to himself a church, each a priest; their bodies served them for the sacred altars, and their souls were the offering."[2]

Spiritual yet practical, they knew that if they built a church, it would, of necessity, have to be based almost entirely on lay initiative. In 1910–12 the little community in Brantford was in an uproar between the permanent settlers who wanted a church and the sojourners who argued that buying and maintaining a church in the new land would be costly and deplete their meagre funds. As they already had a church in their village in Armenia, they said, available funds should be used to enhance the church there, not to build one in a place where most were "here today, home tomorrow." Even though Frank Cockshutt, president of the Cockshutt Plow Works and a leading Evangelical, offered his assistance to buy a church, the sojourners could not be convinced.[3] To emphasize the well-spring of their loyalty, they took up a collection and purchased a clock for their village church. The constraints on their lives are highlighted by the events that followed: a small group of men returned to the village of Astghaberd triumphantly carrying the clock, but the local warlord confiscated their treasure, imprisoned the men, and eventually had them killed.[4]

The futility of their actions did not diminish the importance of the Armenian Church, which embodied multiple facets of their lives. It represented not only their spirituality but also their religious nation, and hence, their Armenianness. Their religion had been as much a part of their world as had their mountains. Now, far from all that was dear to them – the music, litany, poetry, and incense and the solid yet graceful little churches – they tried to cope in a strange land, with a strange language and customs, to live in abnormal conditions without their mothers, wives, and children, and to work in filthy, dangerous, and noisy factories.

Because of the circumstances of migration, sojourners did not believe it feasible to build a church in Canada. To do so would be unpatriotic, for it implied abandoning their homeland. Rather, they established two types of secular associations that could easily be transplanted: village educational societies and political organizations with their ancillary groups. These forces emanated, like rays, from the nucleus of family and clan cohesion and increasingly symbolized their hope in reforming and uplifting their oppressed people.

THE VILLAGE EDUCATIONAL ASSOCIATIONS

Founding the Associations

As Armenian émigrés rallied in different countries, they began to focus on the needs of their home villages. When he left home, "The Armenian sojourner did not cut himself off from there," noted one account. "He was anxious about his home country ... The comfort and safe life in foreign lands, and the pleasures of living and working in freedom inspired in him dreams of making his homeland like that some day."[5] As men earned the "green dollars of America," their remittances to their families still in the old country transformed the home scene. Sojourners, "pouring out their sweat in the factories of North America," helped to revitalize the region; they also breathed new life into education in the village.[6] Aware of educational deficiencies in the village and anxious to improve the education of their children and siblings still at home, Armenian migrants in America, like their forefathers in Constantinople a few decades earlier, voluntarily created their own compatriotic fraternities, which evolved into educational associations or societies.

During the nineteenth-century *Zartonk*, or renaissance, Armenian educational activity centred primarily in Constantinople. In a vibrant intellectual and cultural milieu in the capital city, various groups – primarily the Armenian Apostolic Patriarchate, the American Board of Commissioners for Foreign Missions in Turkey, charitable foundations, societies, and wealthy benefactors – worked to spread popular education and to teach working-class adults, mainly provincial migrants, to read and write. In an effort to reach such people, men like Krisdosdur Ghazarosian and Harutiun Markarian organized the Andznver (Altruistic) Society in the 1860s, to offer free education to adults in Constantinople, much like the Mechanics Institutes in the Anglo-American world. For thirty years Ghazarosian lectured every Sunday to the poor and uneducated Armenians in "Bolis." Andranig Bey Gurjikian opened a Sunday school in 1864 to teach physical sciences to the working class.[7] When these migrants returned to their villages, they took their learning back with them and in this way acted as a conduit of literacy, disseminating knowledge to village youngsters. One of the most important consequences of this movement was convincing a generation of Armenians, especially in the cohort that had school-age children, that schooling was crucial to personal advancement and national progress (see chapter 2).

Although useful, this method was not as effective as properly organized schools. Towards this end, sojourners in Constantinople, led by better-educated compatriots, formed village educational associations with the express purpose of raising funds to subsidize a school in the village and to pay a teacher's salary. In the 1870s, for example, men living in Constantinople from the village of Khups (in Keghi) organized the Haigazian Educational Society of Khups to improve the education in their village.[8] In this way they hoped the village children could benefit from the absence of their fathers, uncles, and brothers. Dedicated though such men were to helping their villages, their efforts were hit and miss – lacking leadership, direction, and continuity.

In 1880 three major educational societies – Dprotsasirats Arevelian Enkerutiun (the Eastern Educational Association), Araratian Enkerutiun

Hayots (the Armenian Araratian Association), and Giligian Enkerutiun (the Cilician Association) – amalgamated to form the Hai Miatsial Enkerutiun (The United Armenian Association, or UAA), which took on responsibilities similar to a department of education: course and curriculum design, textbook preparation, teacher training and placement, and school construction and supervision.[9] In addition to the association, the Azganver Hayuhyats Enkerutiun (Patriotic Armenian Women's Organization) and the Dprotsaser Tiknants (Women's Educational Association) actively promoted the education of women and the training of women teachers. Led primarily by the Armenian intelligentsia, the middle class, and the urban élite, these various educational societies worked indefatigably for almost fifteen years to promote universal education.

With the decline of monastic schools, rudimentary popular schools were beginning to take shape in the district of Keghi well before the 1890s. The town of Keghi Kasaba and the wealthy village of Khups established their schools in 1878 and 1880, respectively, and were the first to work with the United Armenian Association.[10] Several villages, like Tarman, Arek, and Astghaberd, also organized schools in cooperation with the association. These early schools were generally for "children whose parents could afford the tuition." According to an interviewee, Astghaberd "had one hundred and fifty households ... We could have sent at least two hundred children to school ... but in that school, there were hardly twenty-five or thirty boys. Little boys. Like a kindergarten, three to five years of age."[11]

In retaliation against Armenian demonstrations and protests calling for reform in the 1890s, Sultan Abdul Hamid dissolved the UAA and disbanded its schools.[12] These school closures coincided with the expulsion of thousands of Armenian sojourners from Constantinople, either to exile in foreign lands or to retreat back to their villages. The villages, in turn, were pillaged and plundered and the Keghi countryside laid waste. Contending with economic ruin, families were obliged to concentrate on providing for their daily bread, reconstructing their houses, and rebuilding their farms. Under such conditions, villagers found it difficult to maintain their schools and pay their teachers. In 1899, Khups villagers reluctantly closed down their once highly respected school, and instead of attending school, children were out "roaming the streets."[13] School buildings throughout the region deteriorated into "dark and damp places," and local education suffered a major setback. The Hamidian school closures, like the closures of Armenian schools in the Caucasus under the czars, debilitated the education of a generation of school-age youngsters.

A villager from Osnag gives a sense of the abject conditions and the informal efforts of villagers to try to educate their children:

In the spring, about April, we no longer attended classes, but attended [*sic*] our goats, cows, and buffalo while they grazed. We did this all day, until November. In November we continued our education. The period of schooling was only four months a year. We were taught to read and write mainly, and to read some religious works, like the Psalms ... At this time, the village hired a teacher. The name of our first teacher was Mesrob Der Vartanian, who was elected to this office by the villagers. We also had a small school which was built on the ground with no floor and was very primitive. It was also damp and gloomy ... The teacher left after only six months' service and the school continued on the same basis as before – without a teacher but with the help of villagers who could read and write.[14]

Following the Young Turk revolt in 1908, Armenians revived the United Armenian Association. Once again, it endeavoured to reform and systematize education among Armenians. To administer to a population dispersed throughout the Ottoman Empire, the association leadership divided the country into regions, each under the direction of a superintendent. The association undertook to supervise the construction of schools, to train and to hire competent teachers and teaching assistants, to revise the curriculum to include the sciences, to restructure the grading system, and to prepare new textbooks. It also encouraged women to enter the teaching profession. Their services came at a crucial time, when large numbers of young men were emigrating either to work or study abroad or to escape conscription.

Although mass education was not universal among Armenians in the Ottoman Empire before 1915, literacy was becoming progressively more accessible to a growing number of Armenian girls and boys. According to the association's annual report for 1911, it supervised fourteen schools in Keghi with 1,179 students and 31 men and women teachers and teaching assistants.[15] An informant from Astghaberd recalled the changes in the village when the association took over operations:

The association entered Astghaberd in 1910 ... the [regional] headquarters [of the association] were in Erzerum. They sent us two men and two women teachers in 1910 ... The number of children increased when the association arrived. Part of the expenses were paid by the association and part by the parents. So with a very small monthly payment, you could send your children to school. Around 1910–11 there were approximately one hundred to one hundred and fifty students, both boys and girls, studying in our United Association school. We had a new school building and left the church building ... Some of the money came [to the association] from America and some from the children's parents. The Association would pay the salaries and whatever was left the villagers had to pay. Whoever had it and could, would pay. If they didn't have it, they would arrange to have the money sent from America.[16]

Not every village depended on the United Armenian Association to supervise its school. The village of Chanakhchi, for instance, was proud of its independence and of its close affiliation with Euphrates College in Kharput. On the other hand, Keghi Kasaba and the village of Tarman had, in addition to schools run by the association, schools operated by Armenian Protestants. Regardless of whether they participated in the association or not, almost all village schools relied on funds from abroad.

Educated Keghetsis in the United States, men like Markar Baidarian, Mampre Toroian, and Arsen Diran (Damkhajian) – a graduate of Euphrates College and correspondent to Mshag, Dzain Hairenyats, and Gotchnag newspapers – joined forces during the late 1890s to form the Keghi Educational Society in North America, in Boston, Massachusetts.[17] The expressed goal of the association was to mobilize Keghetsis in the United States, Canada, and Mexico to raise funds to develop schooling in Keghi.

Eventually, as more migrants travelled to America, the Keghi Educational Society gave way to separate village associations. The Khups Educational Union, one of the first village associations of Keghi, started in Providence, Rhode Island, in 1900.[18] The Tarman association followed in 1902, with headquarters in Troy, New York; Astghaberd in 1903, in Providence; Keghi Kasaba, in Boston in 1904; and in the same year, Osnag villagers founded their organization in Brantford, Ontario.[19]

Records indicate that emigrants of at least twelve Keghi villages created these independent associations, each with its own constitution, bylaws, accounts, and executive bodies.[20] If we accept that the district of Keghi had about 20,000 Armenian inhabitants in 1914, then each of the 12 associations represented 1,666 Armenian inhabitants in the region. If we further calculate the school age population – probably about 60 to 70 percent of the total – the number of village educational associations serving the Armenian children of Keghi was truly impressive.

Settlement in North America broadened the newcomers' vision of the potential. The determination to improve village education and the impetus to organize educational associations were no doubt affected by the quality and accessibility of public education in the New World. But the fundamental initiative and the drive for improvement did not grow out of the North American environment. Rather, the North American experience dovetailed with the Armenian enlightenment. Formation of educational associations in the New World represented continuity with an existing tradition that was already popular among Armenians in the old country. Rt Rev. Suren Papaghian, in his account of the Khups Union in America, asks the pointed question, "Is not the Haigazian Education Society of Khups, founded in Constantinople in 1870, the forerunner of the Khups Village Educational Union, founded in Providence, Rhode Island, in 1900?"[21] The commitment to establish educational societies when away from home was rooted in a precedent among Armenians in the Ottoman Empire long before the great migration to North America. The father had sojourned in Constantinople well before the son migrated to America.

Similarly, the diasporan commitment to promote universal and free schooling in the homeland was an extension of a legacy that had begun earlier in the Ottoman empire. In the mid–nineteenth century the Armenian Patriarchate in Constantinople declared in favour of popular education on a free basis. In a statement of general principles, the Patriarchate emphasized that "the nation resolves that all children of both sexes, of whatever condition, should, without exception receive the benefits of education and should at least be initiated in essential knowledge." To provide for this education, the Armenian nation, which already paid its share of state taxes, was obliged to inflict on the people an additional burden which was very heavy, since contributions also had to provide support for hospitals, orphanages, and other welfare institutions.[22]

Three major factors, then, propelled these educational societies: the growing demand for popular education among Armenians in Turkey, the need for outside capital to build and maintain the schools, and the heightened emigration of the Armenian rural population to North America.

Structure and Function of the Educational Associations in North America

Émigrés from each town or village, regardless of where they settled, participated in these associations and their activities. Neither religion nor politics nor length of stay entered the equation, at least not critically. Apostolics and Protestants, Dashnaks and Hnchaks, sojourners and permanent settlers generally cooperated for the benefit of the village, which remained the nucleus of their loyalty.

Each organization drew up its own constitution and bylaws, maintained its own accounts, and elected its own administration.[23] Members annually elected a central executive and established the practice of rotating headquarters to different cities. Headquarters changed according to the numerical strength of the branch or its willingness to assume additional responsibilities. For example, from 1904 to 1906, the Osnag headquarters were located in Brantford; the following year, members in East St Louis took charge of the central executive. The Khups central executive remained in Providence from 1904 to 1916, then moved to Granite City, Worcester, and Detroit.[24] The central executive received regular reports from the chapters outlining their activities and updating their accounts.

According to the Osnag Educational Association Constitution, three or more villagers could form a branch of the association. If there were fewer than three, they could participate by sending their dues directly to the central executive. In this way, all villagers, no matter where they lived, could belong to the organization. Before 1915 the Astghaberd village association had branches in Boston, Massachusetts; Brantford and St Catharines, Ontario; East St Louis, Illinois; Providence, Rhode Island; Batum, Georgia (in the Caucasus); Keghi Kasaba; and, of course, in the village itself. Osnag, a relatively small village, succeeded in setting up branches in Providence, Rhode Island; East St Louis, Illinois; and Brantford and St Catharines, Ontario. The establishment of branches and the movement of the executive among them not only reveal a desire to share power but also provide a map of village migratory patterns, the availability of jobs, and the high incidence of mobility among members. Under such circumstances, the international boundary between Canada and the United States virtually disappeared.

On the whole, the associations were limited to villagers from the home place. While the constitution of the Osnag association allowed nonvillagers to belong, it did not give them voting rights. Membership was open to both men and women, but most members were men, and young men at that, reflecting the newcomer society itself.[25] The growing number of Keghi men in America was particularly evident after 1912, when the Balkan wars stepped up conscription and led to a growing exodus of young Armenians. As the immigration of Keghetsi men intensified, membership increased. The Osnag records show fifteen members in 1905 (January to July), thirty-nine in 1912 (January to July), and sixty in 1914 in the same six-month period.[26] The mobility of migrant workers meant that each branch roster varied from month to month, since members could belong regardless of where they were living and working. In 1913 the St Catharines branch of the Osnag Educational Association claimed twenty-six members (January to June); all but six had shown up previously in the Brantford membership roster. The structure was democratic and egalitarian, since each dues-paying member had one vote. Old-country class distinctions vanished in industrial North America – the great leveller – where the son of the rich villager was on par with the son of the poorest peasant, especially if they worked side by side in the same factory.

An annual conference assembled members from different cities to elect a new central executive, to discuss important issues and fundraising programs, to plan future activities, and to negotiate among themselves about donating money to the village. According to the Osnag constitution, no decisions could be made either by the central executive or by the branch executive without majority agreement, a critical manifestation of the majoritarian underpinning of these grassroots organizations. This same emphasis was evident in the matter of accountability. The Osnag constitution stipulates that each branch executive, consisting of a president, secretary, and treasurer, had to be elected every six months and that the executive had to submit a detailed financial report to the members and to the central executive at the end of the six-month period. So that strict control of funds would be maintained, all financial transactions required majority approval by the membership at large; no funds, the Osnag constitution stated, could be withdrawn from the bank without the signatures of the president, secretary, and treasurer, and all three had to give regular financial accounting to the membership, which kept a careful eye on the accounts.

Each member was obliged to pay $.25 monthly dues – the price of a good meal in a restaurant; and anyone who did not pay his dues for a period of six months without just cause was ousted from the organization – a shameful punishment among men who knew each other's families. An interviewee gives a sense of what membership meant to these factory workers: "Fifty to sixty sojourners from Astghaberd undertook to form a branch of the Astghaberd Educational Association [in Canada, in 1910] in order to bring the association into the village ... Let's say that annually they [Canadian sojourners] could raise $100 or $150 here. At that time they worked really hard to earn $1 a day. Sometimes they would make $7 or $8 a week. So if there were fifty or sixty Astghaberdtsi members of the association, they would deduct a bit from their income and they would send that money to the United Association headquarters in Erzerum, earmarked for the village school."[27]

Dues were augmented by larger sums raised at concerts, dinners, raffles, and picnics. People also donated funds at funerals in lieu of flowers. In 1905 at the Astghaberdtsi association's first *hantes* (concert) in Canada, M. Zakarian spoke about the value of education and S. Khatchigian started the fundraising. In fifteen minutes, the local newspaper reporter proudly noted, the organization had collected about $223. Some members contributed as much as $15, and everyone present, even those who did not have much, made a donation, none less than $5!²⁸ In 1906 (January to June) the Brantford chapter of the Osnag association received $31 in dues from its twenty members; a year earlier, the group had raised $120 at a concert.²⁹

Money was constantly moving from North America to Keghi.³⁰ Funds sent or taken to the village were modest compared to the amounts the fraternities banked in North America. From 1902 to 1905 the Tarman association built up a treasury of $1,056 but sent only $315 to the village, albeit a substantial sum in Anatolia and probably enough to pay for the annual school costs.³¹ Since its inception in 1900, the Khups association sent the United Association $2,512 (covering the total school expenditures) but kept several thousand in its treasury in order to build a secondary school in the village.³² In 1907, East St Louis sent almost $117 to the old country, while it kept $806 in the treasury. In 1910 the Osnag association boasted about $1,227 in the regional coffers but sent about $100 to the village, despite a general appeal to fund a teacher-training course in Keghi Kasaba in the summer of 1911.³³

Still, the amounts they sent abroad were considerable by Anatolian standards. According to the Osnag records, from 1905 to 1911 inclusive, the branches sent almost $525 to the village. This amount was in addition to $1,000 sent to the village in 1908. By such donations members confirmed their commitment to the village, but they also strengthened the village's dependence on them – a fact that became more controversial as more young men came to America.

That the associations kept a tight rein on their funds in North America raises issues about the power of the purse and the collective control over the village school. Undoubtedly, tensions arose between the membership in North America, mostly young men earning relatively large sums in the factories and mills, and the board of trustees in the village, mostly older men embedded in preindustrial agrarianism. As the North American membership increased in numbers and as their treasuries swelled, members used the power of the purse – at first with hesitation, then with growing confidence – to control school policy in the village. They had something to say about the hiring of teachers and school construction and renovation. They even commented on the curriculum. Indeed, if the North American branches refused funds, the village elders found themselves hamstrung. In 1912, for instance, the Osnag members refused to send funds for the salary of a teacher they did not like.³⁴ If a total shift in power did not occur, at least the village hierarchy was forced to consult with members an ocean away before making major decisions. Not only that, they had to make certain their North American relatives remained satisfied and harmonious. In a letter from

Osnag in 1910, the trustees first expressed the home village's gratitude (probably for a donation) and then referred to "a misunderstanding." "Rich or poor," the letter emphasized, "whoever enters the threshold of our school is equal." Apparently discrimination in the village school had caused considerable dissatisfaction among members in the New World.[35]

Impact of the Educational Associations

Following the depredations of 1894–97, many schools in Keghi closed their doors. In 1901, according to the Armenian Patriarch in Constantinople, twenty-seven schools were operating in Keghi, with 1,703 students. In 1911, Psak Vardapet Der Khorenian, the Apostolic head of the region, reported that he had forty-eight schools under his jurisdiction in Keghi, including the association schools. In addition, at least two schools functioned under Protestant jurisdiction. Thus, in 1911–12, at least fifty schools were functioning in the region, or roughly one school for every 400 Armenians.[36] These statistics are noteworthy because they not only give an idea of the spread of education among the masses in the interior but also reflect the impact of outside involvement.

In some villages the number of teachers and the educational budgets doubled and even tripled before 1915. Astghaberd, for example, which had paid its one teacher twenty lira before its relationship with the association began, acquired three teachers and a budget of sixty-eight lira by 1910–11. Eventually, "one school became two and one teacher became four," and enrollment increased to eighty boys and fifty-two girls; this, in a village that in 1914 claimed only about 150 Armenian households.[37] On a broader scale, progressive Keghetsi leaders who were concerned that Keghi students had to travel outside the region for secondary education were working towards the construction of at least one and perhaps two high schools in the region of Keghi.

In spite of serious constraints imposed by the Turkish government, the educational ferment of the pre-Genocide period represented an explosion in rural schooling. Within a period of ten to twelve years this revolution managed to raise the literacy and numeracy level of the Keghi countryside. In these sweeping changes, the village educational associations in North America played a critical role. Their goal was to send money to the village in order to build, maintain, or refurbish the school, to pay for the teachers, and to subsidize the education of children from needy families. By this means every child could receive the best schooling the villagers could afford and would thus benefit from the absence of their male relatives. With their meagre but regular contributions, these men helped strengthen the grass-roots movement of rural education, in large and small, near and remote villages.[38]

In turn, these villages were drawn into the orbit of nascent bureaucracies that provided administrative, pedagogical, and technical assistance.[39] In a deep sense, to create schools with somewhat regular timetables, select teachers whenever possible by merit, and provide an increasingly efficient administration was to initiate the first modern and democratically controlled institution in Anatolia. This, too, was a profound revolution.

Villagers scattered about in foreign lands enlarged the village frame of reference. By 1914 the Khups village association boasted chapters in Providence, Rhode Island, Worcester, Woonsocket, Center Falls, Boston, New York, Watervliet, Whitinsville, Haverhill, Portland, Philadelphia, Chicago, Granite City, Detroit, and Bingham and, after 1908, in France and Constantinople.[40] Strewn like the villagers themselves from country to country, across mountains and oceans, these contact points inevitably expanded the village's vision of the world. The village social structure, with its far-flung kith-and-kin networks, annexed, in a psychological sense, cities in distant lands. This contact inevitably helped prepare village mentalities for new ideas from a modern, industrial, and urbanized world. More profoundly, it also prepared village mentalities for change and reform in a world where change and reform were suspect and feared.

The sojourners were aware of the acculturation they themselves were experiencing in North America and of the impact their American sojourn was having on them. As peasants from Anatolia came into contact with North American society, as they attended night school, studied English, participated in the struggle for workers' rights, and learned about democracy and republicanism, they were invariably transformed. Having experienced the fruits of liberty in North America, having viewed the potentialities of the industrial revolution, and having seen the opportunities for schooling in the New World, the villagers themselves changed. Their metamorphosis shook the home region, as villagers disseminated new ideas to their countrymen still in the native land and as they carried back to them scientific and technological methods and advances. In this way, young people still in the village knew about Brantford and the Mybil, about night school and labour strikes, about moulders and shake-out men, about the British king and queen and the American president. Keghi youngsters were exposed to North America long before it was their turn to emigrate (see chapter 2).

The elasticity between Old World and New had many dimensions. Western enlightenment had planted powerful roots in Turkey well before the migration of the Armenian rural population to Canada and the United States, as already seen in previous chapters. Except for those who settled in Quebec, the newcomers encountered a world governed by Anglo-Saxon Protestants. The interaction between the immigrant and the Anglo-Saxon Protestant environment played a critical role in the psychology of young Keghetsi men. North American values and attitudes inevitably influenced the newcomers, especially young people who attended local schools and colleges and became leaders in the fledgling diasporan communities.

Perhaps the most imperceptible characteristic of these associations was their secularism. The village educational societies were secular organizations, and they developed in a world where church and state were separate, where education was under public tutelage, and where science, rationalism, and the rule of law were eroding faith, revelation, and the Word of the Bible. [41] Had they had more time to develop and had the Genocide not overwhelmed and destroyed the Armenian presence in Turkey, the associations might eventually have brought a stronger secular dimension to a homeland where people still identified themselves primarily in religious terms.

The educational associations and the men who belonged to them contributed, then, to a massive reformation of the villages in three ways: they strengthened rural education by providing funds; they prepared the traditional rural mentality for the inflow of new ideas; and they transported elements of modernity and progress back to the countryside. As a result, the home villages were not the mythical, isolated, little hamlets on the Keghi mountainsides but they had evolved, rather, as an integral part of a vast and dynamic transoceanic movement of men, money, and ideas.

The village educational associations can be examined in another context. Men and women from Keghi saw themselves as Keghetsis. Their *yerkir* (homeland) was Keghi. No mode of discourse existed in the village whereby they saw themselves as Armenians, except in religious terms. While they may have been identified in America as Armenians, they still identified each other, among themselves, by their clan, their village, and their region. Since the educational associations were based on geography – on a specific place on the globe – they differed from political and religious affiliations. The political parties that upheld the concept of the larger nation, of pan-Armenianism, denounced such regionalism as an agent of internal fragmentation and divisiveness. But by cutting across political lines, the associations mitigated the stridency and eased the partisanship of opposing factions. By affirming loyalty to the home region, these associations were instruments of cultural maintenance, every bit as effective and profound as the political parties.

The village educational societies also represent a democratization, or at least a proletarianization, of two élitist traditions among Armenians: first, the tradition of charity and philanthropy. For centuries wealthy Armenians had assumed the responsibility for helping their less fortunate compatriots. They had built churches, schools, hospices, and orphanages.[42] During the twentieth century, a democratization of this honoured tradition evolved. The indigenous model of philanthropy percolated downwards, as ordinary peasants, unskilled laborers in Canadian factories who were imbued with a powerful sense of duty, collectively took up the challenge of communal self-help.

Secondly, wealthy Armenians in the Armenian diaspora had for generations donated great sums towards Armenian enlightenment. For centuries Armenians had left their homeland to study abroad, to build financial enterprises, or to flee persecution, and from foreign shores émigrés had enhanced learning and progress at home. Diasporan Armenians created and maintained important links connecting the Armenian millet (religious community) with Western intellectual currents, and they also contributed vast sums to schools and churches in the homeland. This diaspora/homeland relationship was expanded in the twentieth century when working-class villagers – none wealthy or famous – collected funds, penny by penny, dollar by dollar, in North America to remit back to the village to build and enhance its schools. Their emphasis on education attests to the widespread conviction that it was a vital mechanism not only of social mobility but, more importantly, of national development. In North America leaders of the educational associations were progressive men, and some were relatively well educated and had themselves benefited from the opportunities offered by the Armenian Apostolic Church, Protestant missionaries, or secular authorities. Now, the rank and file, humble men – literate and illiterate, skilled and unskilled – assumed the responsibility of bringing "civilization" and enlightenment to their home regions through these associations.

The educational associations also played a role in the lives of the newcomers themselves. Their organizational structure, for instance, gave villagers opportunities for leadership, for high-profile status, and for a measure of importance among their own people. Men who were simple factory workers during the week could assume executive roles on Sundays: run meetings, give regular written reports, or provide financial statements. Their annual gatherings, too, provided a venue for social activities, encounters with potential spouses, renewal of relationships, and the exchange of ideas and information about people, jobs, and events.

For the growing number of sojourners in North America, the associations reinforced the village networks in a formal manner and on an international scale. Wherever fate took the villagers, they knew that through these societies they could always keep contact with their confreres around the globe and with the village itself. Pinpointing their allegiance to one small place on the globe also nurtured their allegiance to the village, which was, in turn, continually nurtured by it.

For many, the years of sojourn may have blurred the vision of the home soil. Where, after all, was home? Was it Bulgaria, which had opened its doors to Armenian refugees in the 1890s? Was it Constantinople, where some had been born, or was it Erzerum, where others had attended school and prospered? Or was it the little mountain village where men had been born but which they had not seen in many years and before 1908, in any case, had little hope of ever seeing again? A young man born in Constantinople of parents from the village of Arek in Keghi perhaps best symbolizes the village bonds. When Krikor Der Krikorian arrived in Canada in 1911, he had never seen the village of Arek or the region of Keghi. But in the New World he joined the Arek village association and identified himself as an Arektsi, almost as if he were being relocalized.[43] In this way he strengthened his loyalty to the Old World and retained a measure of his heritage in a new environment. This re-rooting, multiplied hundreds of times for hundreds of immigrants, buttressed a collective solidarity among newcomers and helped them deal with the bewildering life in North America.

In the long run the educational associations acted as agents for kindling elements of a heritage under constant threat of annihilation. The constitution of the Osnag association states that if the organization had fewer than seven members, it would have to be disbanded and the funds sent to the village school. If there was no school, then the money would be sent to St Minas Church in Osnag. Little did members envision that in 1915 the school, the church, the farms, the homes, and the Armenians who lived in them would all be destroyed. It is to the credit of the survivors and their determination to write about their home villages that a fragment of a forgotten world has survived.[44]

POLITICS

Formation of Political Organizations

By 1907 both the Social Democrat Hnchaks and the Armenian Revolutionary Federation (ARF), or Dashnaks, had established branches in

Brantford, Hamilton, St Catharines, and Galt.[45] For Canadian members, the local political organizations represented first and foremost brotherhoods with nationalist goals, regardless of how fanatically Marxist some of the leaders might be, dispersed as they were in the United States, Europe, Russia, Egypt, and the Ottoman Empire. The primary concern of Canadian members was the fate of Armenia and of Armenians in the Ottoman and Russian Empires, not the future of the ethnic group in Canada. The contrast between the free environment in which they lived in Canada and the oppressive world in Turkey that they had left behind strengthened their resolve to bring about changes in the Old World. Local success, then, depended on the extent to which the parties worked for the cause of Armenian national interests. Towards this end, parties raised funds to send abroad, formed cells to train young men in the arts of self-defence, and mobilized them for the struggle at home.[46] In an effort to reinforce Armenian consciousness, they set up libraries and reading rooms to enlighten and politicize their members, encouraged self-improvement for men and women, and started Armenian reading and writing classes for children.

Of the 130 members listed in the Brantford Armenian Revolutionary Federation census (1907–9), only two had joined in the Ottoman Empire, one in Batum, and thirty-six in the Balkans, and of the remaining ninety-one who had joined in North America, eighty-four had taken the oath in Brantford.[47] This finding highlights both the degree of politicization of the men and the extent of repression in the homeland.

"Exile," stated Lord Acton, "is the nursery of nationality, as oppression is the school of liberalism."[48] The Hamidian massacres in Turkey, the confiscation of church property in Russia (1903), and the closure of Armenian schools and institutions stiffened the resolve of Armenians to confront such injustices and drove them to organize political and militant cadres. As a result of continued and intensified oppression and periodic pogroms, a liberation movement that had started with the purpose of attaining security of life and property and acquiring basic human rights for Armenians in the Ottoman and Russian Empires became politicized. Both the Social Democrat Hnchaks and the Socialist Dashnaks propounded an ideology of democracy and equality and shared the common aspiration of a free Armenia that represented a whole range of concepts from federated autonomy to an independent state. Both parties experienced somewhat similar intraparty conflicts between different socioeconomic classes, urban and rural elements, Eastern (Russian and Persian) and Western (Turkish) Armenian interests, pro- and antichurch factions, right and left wings, and nationalism and international socialism, and they experienced conflicts over radical or reformist tactics, as well as the tensions inherent in political parties with one foot in the diaspora and the other in the homeland.[49]

Functions of the Political Organizations

While it may be true that the rank and file in southern Ontario did not always understand the complexities of party ideology and ideological abstractions, it is also evident that a sense of duty to support the Armenian national cause through political mobilization was so powerful among the newcomers that as immigration of Armenians increased after 1910, membership in the political parties grew apace. In the years 1915–18, the Brantford Hnchak chapter boasted eighty-seven members, and the St Catharines chapter, seventy-five. The Dashnak branches in Brantford, St Catharines, Hamilton, Galt, and Guelph also showed a marked increase in membership. Such participation strengthened Armenian identity in the New World, even while rivalry between the two parties often generated dissension in the community.

New members learned proper procedure, appropriate behaviour at meetings, and party discipline, especially the requirement for regular attendance at the monthly meetings and punctual payment of dues. They learned the consequences of improper deportment: suspension for absenteeism without just cause or notification and for nonpayment of dues. Political parties operated not on authoritarian or hierarchical lines but on egalitarian and fraternal principles. As if to emphasize this structure, members referred to each other as comrade and brother and took great pride in the process of participatory democracy. Thus, in the small, crowded, and smoke-filled meeting rooms, these newcomers from a peasant background laid the foundations of a democratic political tradition in southern Ontario.

One of the most important functions that the political parties assumed in southern Ontario in this pioneer period was governing the communities, an especially important mandate of leadership in view of the absence of a church. As Josef Barton notes, such groups furnished a tangible organizational reality with which the newcomer could identify and by which he could declare his solidarity with his people.[50] By becoming involved in various aspects of immigrant life, the political parties assumed a role akin to the village councils, or, more appropriately, a role like councils of governance and culture rather than political parties as they are understood in Canada today.

On behalf of the good reputation of Armenia and the Armenians, the parties disciplined the men in their everyday life. Each branch held the threat of ignominious expulsion for drinking, gambling, and excessive swearing. Anxious to keep the peace among members, furthermore, the parties held their own internal courts. When a Brantford member who had been embroiled in a court case ran for the presidency of the local chapter, another member questioned his moral fortitude to stand as leader. Following this altercation, a special committee was set up to hold an enquiry. After hearing both sides, the committee fined each man ten dollars – the first for "bringing dishonour on us" by taking an Armenian to court and the second for making an unjust accusation against a comrade. As a minority in the old country, the Armenians had been sensitive about their image and wherever possible had regulated their own affairs. This same tradition was transplanted to their new environment. On 24 January 1915, for example, members of the Guelph chapter of the ARF were instructed by the local executive "not to argue with the Armenian opposition in the presence of Canadians, and to get along amicably with Canadians."[51]

Such counsel, however, did not prevent tempers from flaring in a brawl between the two political groups in St Catharines in the summer of 1915, at a time when the men were tense under the shadow of the Genocide.[52] Seven years earlier, a similar outbreak had occurred during a visit by Murat (Hambardzum Boyajian), one of the heroes of the Sasun uprising (1894) and later a member of the Armenian National Assembly and the Ottoman Parliament. According to Hnchak sources, the Dashnaks condemned him as a socialist-anarchist to border authorities who subjected him to a long and arduous interrogation before allowing him to enter the Dominion.[53]

While such visits may have precipitated the occasional quarrel, they were usually more constructive. The charisma of party fieldworkers like Murat, Aknuni (Khachatur Malumian), Siamonto (Atom Yarchanian), Nazareth Mankuni, Arsen Mikaelian, Pandkht, Petros Pontatsi, Stepan Sabah-Gulian, Setrag Shahen, and Y. Sirvart electrified their audiences and rallied them to support the national liberation struggle. When Aknuni travelled to southern Ontario in 1910–11, he explained the relationship of the ARF with international socialism, discussed the conscription issue in Turkey, exhorted men to return to their families, and appealed for funds to help Armenian prisoners in the Caucasus.

Aside from the regular membership dues, the party called for funds to carry on its work in the homeland. In Brantford, for example, Hnchaks contributed $480 in 1903 towards starting up the party organ *Yeritasard Hayastan* (Young Armenia). In Hamilton, Dashnaks raised $400 on 31 December 1905 to support Armenian self-defence and counterattacks against the Azeris, following the Azeri massacre of unarmed Armenians in Baku (February 1905) and successive attacks in other areas of the Caucasus.

Fundraising and propaganda were not the only purposes of these tours, for fieldworkers also strengthened links between the local chapters and party headquarters in the United States. When, for instance, the Hnchaks held a Canadian regional conference in Hamilton in 1918, with representatives from the five men's chapters and three women's branches, the chairman of the proceedings was Sabah-Gulian, editor of *Yeritasard Hayastan*.[54] A close relationship with headquarters was mutually beneficial, for it brought local chapters into a wider sphere of action, while it tightened discipline, consolidated party power, and spread political ideology.

Leaders not only dealt with old country issues but tried to bring Armenians into the orbit of North American political and socioeconomic developments. Ruben Khan-Azad (Nshan Karapetian), one of the founders of the Hnchak Party, travelled from city to city in an effort to enlighten and revolutionize the Armenian worker in America and to awaken class consciousness in him. Khan-Azad, on friendly terms with Russian and Jewish Communists, "did not speak of narrow issues of nationalism but combined the question of nationalism with class struggle and socialism ... His attacks on American capitalists antagonized Armenian intellectuals, merchants, and Protestant missionaries who feared his activities would alienate American employers."[55]

Aside from trying to involve Armenian settlers in new movements and ideas, the political parties also laid the foundations for Armenian-Canadian charitable, intellectual, and cultural traditions. Geographically distant from the large Armenian settlements in the United States and outside the cultural and political framework of the Canadian host society, the Ontario Dashnaks and Hnchaks formed ancillary organizations, such as the women's groups and the *gradaran*s, or reading rooms/libraries that bridged the distance between events in the homeland and North America and established the precedent of an Armenian intellectual, educational, and cultural tradition in the diaspora.

Both parties heralded the rights of women. Their press generally promoted the suffragette movement and gave full encouragement to the participation of women in the national struggle.[56] At the turn of the century, small groups of concerned Armenian women in North America founded local committees in association with the Hnchak and Dashnak branches, in order to serve the educational, health, relief, and social needs of their compatriots. As early as 1903, women's groups associated with the Dashnak Party became known unofficially as the Armenian Red Cross. Similar women's groups were also being formed in the old country, notably in Meziré, near Kharput, in Tigranakert, and in Constantinople. The massacres in and around the city of Adana in 1909 brought two outstanding women to the scene of the crisis,

Zabel Esayan and Arshaguhi Teodik. Both women, shaken by the tragic scenes, wrote about their experiences and thus gave a great impetus to the work of the women's committees in the United States. In January 1910 the New York committee adopted the name Armenian Association of the Red Cross.

In the same year the Armenian Revolutionary Federation fieldworker Aknuni undertook to amalgamate the Dashnak women's relief committees into a formal organization, to be known as the Armenian Revolutionary Federation Red Cross. It became the first voluntary pan–North American Armenian women's charitable organization.[57] Its priorities were to protect the physical and national existence of the Armenian people, especially in foreign lands, and to help Armenians in distress, wherever they might be and in whatever way was necessary.[58]

Aknuni's visit to southern Ontario in 1910–11 made a lasting impression on the local settlers. His passionate and fiery speeches describing the destitute condition of Armenians in Cilicia were a call to action. Brantford, the largest Armenian community at the time, rose to the occasion and its women's committee formed the first branch of the new organization in Canada, in 1910–11. In fact, the Brantford branch is listed as one of the seventeen founding branches of the ARF Red Cross in North America. With the outbreak of hostilities in 1914 and reports of renewed campaigns of murder and deportation of Armenians, women in Hamilton, St Catharines, and Galt joined the ranks in 1915.[59] The ARF Red Cross chapters and the three Canadian Hnchak women's groups raised money for unfortunate Armenians and undertook local endeavours for educating the young, helping the indigent, visiting the ill, and spearheading cultural pursuits.

Armenian newcomers brought with them an awareness of their heritage. In the old land they were part of a minority group, the Armenian millet. Yet on the eve of migration, they identified themselves first and foremost as members of a clan and of a village. Invariably, they introduced themselves first by family name, then by village. They came from a land of tyranny, and many stoically acquiesced in the condition of their lives. But in a country where they could enjoy full citizenship far from the repression and intolerance in the Ottoman and Russian Empires, men began to see a new kind of life with different values and priorities. Contact with the host society inevitably transformed the immigrants. The rights of man and liberty and equality were no longer words in books about the English, French, or American Revolutions or inscribed on banners touting the Young Turk revolt. Rather, the newcomers experienced freedom and began to understand the meaning of equality. They themselves fervently believed in enlightenment and self-improvement. They wanted to change even while they were determined to preserve their threatened culture. In such a fertile atmosphere, political leaders undertook to remould the thinking of their compatriots, to unite men from disparate regions and different socioeconomic backgrounds, and to mobilize them for the "sacred struggle." They took it upon themselves to define patriotism in terms of resistance against despotism, on the one hand, and in terms of nationality and nationhood on the other. In these currents of modernity, the *gradaran*s and the political press held a pivotal role.

THE *GRADARANS*/READING ROOMS

Conditions in the Ottoman Empire were not conducive to enlightenment and learning for Armenian Christians, whether they were rural agriculturalists or members of the urban élite, who were considered one of the most modern and progressive elements in the Ottoman Empire.[60] As a case in point, Rev. Cannon MacColl declared in 1892 that he could not find a copy of Dante or Shakespeare or a single issue of *Murray's Handbook* in Constantinople, because they were proscribed. It was forbidden, he complained, to publish or publicly utter such expressions as "the grace of God," or "the Gospel of Jesus Christ is good news," because it was not admitted that Christians had any relations with God, except those of condemnation and wrath. The teaching of Armenian history was banned in the schools, as was the teaching of sciences.[61] Even after the Young Turk revolt, the reinstitution of the Constitution of 1876, and the abdication of Sultan Abdul Hamid II in 1909, the call to freedom held sway only until the ultra-right-wing junta of the Committee of Union and Progress ascended to power. The Armenian press, the spoken language, and the schools suffered from stringent restrictions, censure, and closure, especially after 1912. By contrast, the liberal society that immigrants found in North America was a refreshing incentive to self-advancement. To be backward in the old country was understandable and perhaps even excusable; to be ignorant in the New World was a stain on a person's character.

Clerics like Khrimian Hairig, educators like Migirdich Portukalian, and writers like Raffi (Hagop Melik-Hagopian) tried to awaken their countrymen from "centuries of lethargy": "Years of slavery," mourned Portukalian, "have destroyed the soul of humanity among the Armenians ... In Europe men live; in Turkey they sprout." In his periodical, *Armenia*, he exhorted his countrymen: "Come brothers, let us join hands and weave a beautiful tapestry. Our enemy is ignorance; Let us not search for it in other places. Our enemy has reduced us to servitude ... let us conquer learning and expel ignorance from our midst."[62]

Armenians used their new-found opportunities in Canada effectively. An account from Hamilton published in the *Hairenik* newspaper reports how in the summer of 1904 a group of young people formed the Armenian Young Peoples' Educational Brotherhood. The eighteen Dashnak members dedicated themselves to helping people find work, setting up a *gradaran*, and teaching illiterate countrymen to read and write.

While the impetus for organizing a *gradaran* came from the political party as a service to members, the *gradaran*s were self-governing, and the members provided their own intellectual direction and administrative leadership.[63] They elected their own officers, raised their own funds, and decided on their own finances. Needless to add, their activities were always within the ideological framework of their political affiliation.

Because the southern Ontario communities were small and closely-knit, the Hnchak and Dashnak reading rooms were near one another in the midst of the Armenian quarter, and they shared many common features. In Brantford the first Hnchak club on Usher Street and the first Dashnak club on Chatham Street were a short distance from the Pratt and Letchworth Malleable Iron Company.[64] In St Catharines Armenians set up their reading rooms close to McKinnon's. In Hamilton the first *gradaran*, located on Princess Street east of Sherman, was run by Dashnaks. They later held their reading room "in the big room behind Nishan Mooradian's grocery store on Gibson Street." The Hnchak room was two blocks away on Earl Street and run by Garabed Zadurian from the village of Chanakhchi, which boasted a strong Hnchak cohort.[65]

Located in a large rented room in a boardinghouse or store, sparsely furnished with tables and bentwood chairs, the spartan reading room provided the milieu for people to read, study, and converse together. Income was derived largely from dues, lending and selling books, and special events, such as debates, lectures, and concerts. Dues for the Khrimian Library were 10¢ a month per member in 1910, raised to 15¢ in 1912 and to $1.00 a month in 1917. A Labour Day concert in 1910 in Brantford grossed $129, and an additional $44 was the profit for the sale of 270 tickets for a debate. The proceeds were spent on books, newspapers, and periodicals, since many of the men could ill afford to buy or subscribe on their own. Partly because of the small number of women in the community and partly because of their traditional role as homemakers, women were generally excluded from membership. Members ranged in age from fourteen to forty-three. Of the thirty-two names in the Khrimian membership list in 1910, the ages of twenty-seven were recorded, and of these, eighteen were between twenty-two and thirty-five years of age. These membership figures also attest to the popularity of *gradaran*s. In 1910 the roster shows thirty-two members; in 1916, membership rose to sixty-two and in 1919 to seventy-six.

Men of disparate educational backgrounds gathered in the *gradaran* and exchanged ideas and experiences. The better-educated taught illiterate comrades to read and write Armenian, familiarized them with Armenian history, politics, and literature, and helped them write letters to their loved ones in the old land. The men met regularly for informal study sessions. Volunteers read aloud, explained difficult vocabulary and passages, then initiated discussion.[66] The reading rooms were "a kind of school. One evening each week there were lecture groups, at which the educated comrades spoke on scientific, political and social questions ... Later the group turned into an educational hearth, which assisted the illiterate to be educated; we promoted the zeal for self-improvement."[67]

An examination of the Brantford Khrimian reading room book inventory (no date) mentions a number of translations of English, French, and Italian classics, notably Shakespeare. The underlying theme of the Armenian literature was the condition, suffering, and aspirations of the Armenian people in the Ottoman and Russian Empires; it included such books as *On the Road to Freedom*, *From Sasun to Yeldiz*, *Towards the Old Country*, *Concentration Camps*, *Turkish Jails*, *Armenian Sons in Turkish Prisons*, *Armenia and Europe: Armenian Suffering and Europe*, *The French Revolution*, *Socialism as the Right Path*, *The Workers' Condition*, *The Essence of Communism*, *Land and Capitalism*, *Towards Federation*, *The Government of Britain*, *Armenian Song Book*, *Armenian-English Conversation*, *The Armeno-American Letter Writer*, *Socialism and the Question of Nationality*, *General Hygiene*, and *Sexual Hygiene* (titles translated by the author).[68]

Lectures in Armenian on current political and nationalist issues, as well as economics and current affairs, were delivered by local members or by travelling party field-workers. "The [public] lectures were often rough and ready debates," notes Robert Mirak in his account of the American scene. "The typical, long-winded newly-minted Armenian intellectual was often forced to abide with interruptions from political opponents or by infants' cries."[69] Still, topics such as, "Will the Armenians of the Diaspora be more helpful to Armenia by preparing with arms or knowledge?" drew full houses and exposed immigrants to new currents of thought.

The *gradarans* were more than libraries and reading rooms, for they also doubled as coffeehouses.[70] Their humble surroundings belied their community importance. Men needed a gathering place where they could fraternize, drink tea or Armenian coffee – never alcoholic beverages – discuss the latest news, play cards and backgammon, retell their favourite jokes and stories, recite their poetry, sing their folk tunes, and rouse to their revolutionary songs.[71] The theme of exile, reflected in such poems as "The Wandering Armenian to the Cloud" dominated their thoughts and their emotions:

> O cloud thou hast no native land!
> Far happier thou than I.
> To north, to south thou floatest free,
> At home in all the sky.
> But I, at every step, shed tears
> In sorrow and in gloom.
> Each step away from mine own land
> Is nearer to my tomb.[72]

Talk of home buoyed the spirits of men far from their familiar world: "We gathered every evening and told stories, especially of life in the village and in this way we relieved our alienated emotions ... They'd go to the *gradaran* and read the books there or they'd borrow them. But they had no real home to take the books to. They were all men living in boardinghouses. They worked hard in the factories and then came to the *gradaran* to meet with each other, read, talk, and hear the latest news from the old country. You can imagine what it was like in there when they heard the news that their wives and children had been killed by the Turks and Kurds."[73]

At first the *gradaran* served a political and cultural focus, but eventually it became a community centre or club. Here the men held their political meetings, and the women carried on benevolent and charitable activities. Here they celebrated feasts, weddings, and baptisms and mourned together at their wakes. Here they formed choirs to sing their favourite patriotic and folk songs, staged concerts and plays, and held public lectures, poetry recitations, raffles, and fund-raising dinners. Cultural, social, and political theatrical productions drew crowds both from political groups and from neighbouring cities. Of particular interest was the Murat theatrical troupe, organized by the Hnchakians in St Catharines in 1917. Staging such sociopolitical works as *Les Misérables* and *Hagop-Hapet*, "the troupe made a great impression on the community."[74] Performances by travelling theatrical and operatic companies and visiting musicians also generated great excitement in the community and brought together compatriots from cities as far away as Niagara Falls, Detroit, Buffalo, and Troy, New York.

In the old country, men had regularly gathered together in someone's house, where they had drunk, smoked, played cards and backgammon, told stories, and discussed village events and current news. In the *oba* (living room) they had listened to travelling guests, political activists, or troubadours. Immigrants transplanted this male custom to Canada, where it evolved into a focus of community life. New traditions were being established in the new land as the foundations of Armenian cultural, intellectual, and political life took shape.

The new arrivals were trying to break out of the intellectual constraints of the Old World and the limitations imposed on a subject people. Men had come to Canada with various degrees of education and literacy and with various levels of worldly experience. They sought not to become coarse or insular in the New World but to become "civilized" and refined and to broaden their horizons during their Canadian sojourn.

In this vein Armenian newcomers endeavoured to learn English. They set up English-language classes in their reading rooms, attended night-school classes organized by the local school board, or gravitated to the social gospel of Protestant missions. As early as 1903, John Ajootian taught English to Armenians under the auspices of the Brantford Technical Board. In 1908 the *Brantford Expositor* reported that during a period of unemployment Armenians had requested permission from the local board to attend both day- and night-school classes. The Brantford Evangelistic Union (founded 1907) carried on special work among foreigners teaching the gospel and the English language. Because of the large number of Armenians interested in learning English, a special unit was created for them with Armenian teachers working in conjunction with the Brant Avenue Church.[75]

One of the few surviving testimonials to the importance placed on reading and self-improvement is a scrapbook prepared by Khazar Nubarian and presented to the Khrimian *Gradaran* in Brantford in 1911. The young man collected clippings and copied accounts by hand from a number of Armenian newspapers and periodicals (unfortunately he did not include the names of his sources). His scrapbook includes Armenian poetry and biographical sketches of Armenian theatrical, musical, literary and political figures, as well as articles on such topics as Haley's comet, Armenian revolutionary fighters, the Turkish constitution, and the Young Turks (the Committee of Union and Progress). The book ends with a poem and a short personal note apologizing for his errors and referring to the poor education he had received in his village. Probably the most telling part of the scrapbook is a proclamation of his joy in living in a free society where Armenians could read any books or newspapers they wished and where they could discuss their past and present condition without fear of police surveillance and intimidation, dread of arbitrary arrest, or the threat of imprisonment.[76]

THE ARMENIAN PRESS

The will to learn would have been thwarted, however, if the men had not had access to a literature that was both comprehensible and challenging. Commenting on the transition from the liturgical to the vernacular language in the press, Robert Park concluded that "it was through the medium of the national press that the literary and linguistic revivals took place. The growth of the vernacular press also brought the masses into contact with modern political ideas and ushered in a revival of the nationalist spirit among subject peoples."[77]

By reporting and responding to the turbulent events that beset the Armenian nation in the first twenty years of this century, the Armenian press in North America, particularly the political press, not only reflected the opinions of Armenians but also instructed them and directed their activities. Far from Turkish government censorship and violent suppression, the Armenian press blossomed in the fertile soil of the New World, and through the publication of newspapers, periodicals, and books it left an imprint on the small Ontario colonies lying on the periphery of Armenian settlement in the United States.

Unable to sustain their own local press, the Armenians of southern Ontario imported their books, periodicals, and newspapers from Armenian publishers in Boston, New York, Geneva, Constantinople, Tiflis, Venice, and Vienna. To stimulate learning in the community, the reading rooms bought and loaned books and subscribed to a number of newspapers and periodicals that for some newcomers became serialized textbooks. Armenian periodicals, starting with *Azdarar* (Monitor), published in Madras, India, as early as 1794 were vital agents in the Armenian Enlightenment and in the spread of mass literacy. "My newspaper," recalled a Hamilton resident almost two hundred years later, "was with me wherever I went."[78] The ARF *gradaran* in Brantford subscribed to at least seven Armenian newspapers and periodicals including *Hairenik* (Fatherland) and *Asbarez* (Arena), published in Fresno, California, *Ashkhatank* (Work), *Harach* (Forward), *Shepor* (Bugle), *Bzhishk* (Health, Doctor), and *Aravod* (Morning). *Hairenik* (founded, New York, 1899), mouthpiece of the Dashnak Party, and *Yeritasard Hayastan* (Young Armenia) (founded, Boston, 1903), voice of the Hnchak Party, were the two most commonly read newspapers in southern Ontario. Park notes that these papers had a combined circulation of 10,000 readers, while the entire circulation of the Armenian press was 19,400.[79] *Hairenik* and *Yeritasard Hayastan* devoted their pages to updating the far-flung North American Armenian pioneer settlements about news from home. On 23 January 1904, for example, *Hairenik* published news from Keghi describing the exorbitant taxes imposed on the region, especially the tax on windows. Other articles, dated 19 March 1904 and 14 May 1904, warned sojourners that moneychangers in the old country were forging signatures on cheques and stealing the sojourners' hard-earned money with impunity. It was estimated that at least eighty pounds sterling had been lost by "criminal circumstances" in the previous six months. Names of honest and dishonest moneylenders were published.

The papers also tried to familiarize North American Armenians with nationalist issues. The seeds of nationalism bore tangible fruit. Shortly after its inception in 1899 *Hairenik* called for men and money to defend the freedom fighters of Sasun, in Turkey. It became embroiled in the confiscation of Armenian Church properties by Russian forces and in the Armeno-Azeri wars (1905–6). With the Turkish Proclamation of 1908, *Hairenik* hailed the new dawn, only to see the dream of the Armenian people smashed by the massacre of Armenians in Adana (Cilicia) in 1909. By informing the immigrants and involving them in events in the old country the Armenian American political press bound them mentally and emotionally to their homeland and kept them conscious of their responsibilities. In 1910–11 Hamilton and Brantford Armenians rallied to send official statements to the Canadian government protesting the imprisonment of approximately five hundred Armenians in Russian jails and together with the Galt and the St Catharines communities, raised $680 for the political prisoners' defence.[80]

If nationalism was the spirit that guided the paper, politics provided the rationale that sustained it. As the official organ of the nationalist Dashnak (ARF) Party in North America, *Hairenik* and its Hnchak counterpart *Yeritasard Hayastan* explained party ideology and action, discussed the party's relationship with other Armenian organizations and institutions both in the United States and abroad, and published analytical editorials on Armenian, American, and international events. In 1916, for instance, *Hairenik* gave extensive coverage to the American presidential election and its position vis-à-vis Wilson's peace platform. The role of politicization was typified in the following editorial in *Yeritasard Hayastan*:

The laborer is a man, but without the rights of man, he is an agent of production, but not his, but for his boss ... [The wage-labor system] is productive of cunning, deceit has trampled underfoot the poor, robbed the laborer's reason, drained a large part of his sweaty-bloody wages, and made him a beast of burden ... That system has turned the boss into an unbridled tyrant, and the laborer into a slave, captive, will-less creature ... [That system] cuts life short, creates sicknesses, bereavement and crime. It disinherits mankind's great class and centralizes wealth into a few capitalist hands ... The state, state laws, state officials – they are all united against the laborer, they are ... forces to preserve the laborer in his semi-enslaved, semi-beast of burden condition. The church pulpit is on the boss's side, it preaches a fraudulent morality, it exhorts the laborer to submit to his station, and resign himself to his condition. The press, intoxicated with yellow gold, is a striker of the laborer, likewise the schools, the universities, those temples of science have corrupted the truths, preached the dogmas which are the product of partisan spirit. The courts, administrative institutions, do not distribute equal justice to the laborer and the boss. Wherever the eye turns, there are chains.[81]

The newspapers were also concerned with the nature and evolution of the fledgling Armenian communities in the diaspora. Recognizing the strong assimilative influence of the host society, the press sought to preserve Armenian language and culture and tried to encourage its development in the New World by publishing Armenian poems, folktales, and serials of novels, memoirs, and translations. For language maintenance *Hairenik* carried excerpts from such Armenian textbooks as Ruben Zardarian's *Meghraget* (River of Honey). The national language became an important symbol in the political/nationalist movement. The Armenian political press linked the use of the national language to patriotism, so that language loyalty became a highly charged, emotional and cultural issue and a political gesture. "The struggle," observed Park, "to maintain the national language and the national culture has always been a struggle to maintain a national press without which there could be no national schools or even national church."[82]

Hairenik devoted a column to American-Armenian life in which the activities of even the smallest and most isolated branches of the ARF were described by chapter "reporters." From these far-flung accounts we get a sense of the human story of pioneer settlement. Brantford, for example, in a major fund-raising drive in June 1905 raised approximately $450 for Armenian self-defence in the Caucasus. On 15 August 1915 the Dashnaks held a large public lecture in Hamilton, where Arsen Mikaelian, an ARF field worker, spoke on Armenian involvement in the Great War and its relevance to the Armenian people. The newspapers also linked up the new settlements by running announcements about meetings and special events in different towns and assisted chapters by printing tickets and flyers in Armenian for occasions like lotteries, plays, and concerts. Such information and such announcements were supplemented by the *tertiks*, or brief handwritten newsletters, that local members prepared and distributed among the community or sent to the political party "office" in nearby towns.

The American-Armenian newspapers also ran advertisements for such items as Armenian foods, books, newspapers, furniture, bicycles, cigars, wines, and patent medicines. They offered information about medical, dental, legal, and funeral services and carried want ads placed by both Armenian and non-Armenian firms. On 24 June 1905 the International Heater Company of Utica, New York, advertised in the *Hairenik* for moulders at $2.50 to $3.00 a day. The Great Northern and Northern Pacific Railroads offered jobs to two thousand workers in the same newspaper on 23 April 1918. *Hairenik* also carried advertisements for steamship companies, such as the Compagnie Générale Transatlantique, the Austro-America Line, and the Lloyd Line; published information about passage; and cautioned the unwary traveller about crooked agents along the route.[83]

At the same time the nationalist newspapers did not look with favour on Armenian villagers remaining in the New World, warned of "immigrants walking the streets" with "no work, no money,"[84] and echoed Aknuni's *depi yerkir* (towards the old country) appeal to return to the homeland:

> Let us return, refugee Armenians
> Let us return, émigré Armenians
> Let us return to the Homeland.[85]

LEADERSHIP

In these nascent communities and within these newly established organizations a form of leadership was beginning to take shape. Knowing English placed a man in a special category, for he could be the community's interpreter and liaison with the host society. He could speak to the factory foreman, the landlord, the courts, or the newspaper reporter. Immigrants needed the interpreter and translator and they respected him, but they also distrusted him, for he could be an exploiter. In the Grace Anglican Church (Brantford) marriage and baptismal records, Harry Gourjian is clearly the most popular godfather and sponsor. Canadian government records show the same Harry Gourjian interceding with bureaucracy, interpreting, arranging passage, and dealing with members of Parliament on behalf of his countrymen. In short, Gourjian was the typical "hinge man," the liaison between the ethnic community and the host society.[86] In an article about Armenians in the city, the *Brantford Expositor* ran a photo of the well-groomed, fashionably dressed, and elegant Gourjian, the spokesman and agent for the Armenian colony. The caption reads, "The Leading Armenian. First among foreigners to land in town has maintained his reputation as a leader during his 7 years of residence here." In the same year, however, he was subjected to an internal inquiry by the Armenian Revolutionary Federation and fined. Three years later, he was again interrogated by the ARF, but this time he was ousted from the party for immoral conduct and was virtually driven from the city.[87] One of his accusers was young Yeghishé Mooradian, who had recently immigrated to Canada. He eventually operated his own grocery store and became and remained a community leader for decades. Yeghishé's cousin, Alexander Mooradian (A.B. Davies), who migrated to Canada via Egypt, after the war, and Yeghishé's brother Hagop (Jack) were also to become prominent community leaders in later years.

Educated men like Mardig Apigian, Aghayeg Bedrosian, Migirdich Mkhitarian, Garabed Mooradian, and Levon Raician were factory workers. Their jobs in Canada serve to emphasize that a learned man had far greater difficulty transferring his skills to a new country than a merchant or craftsman. But within the Armenian milieu, these men played a leading role in teaching Armenian language and culture to children and adults alike and held a trusted and respected place in the hierarchy of community governance.

In the pioneer stage of Armenian settlement in Canada, the political parties – both local chapters and central headquarters – the press, and reading rooms structured and organized the far-flung Armenian communities, educated and uplifted the people, strengthened Armenian national consciousness, and garnered support for the Armenian liberation movement. Together with the educational and patriotic associations, the political parties and the political press helped form a collective response to an unfamiliar society. At the same time that they fragmented and divided the communities they gave comfort and support to the people, preserved and enhanced Armenian ethnic culture, and bound the Armenian settlements in North America to each other and to the homeland.

As important as these links were and as crucial as the role of leadership from outside Canada was, it can never be emphasized enough that the early development of Armenian community life depended on the individual dynamism of ordinary immigrant labourers and their willingness to contribute their time, energy, and resources. Like other immigrants, Armenians faced discrimination, exploitation, and marginality. But they also found a measure of freedom, equality, and tolerance. With remarkable suppleness, they started to weld together elements of the old and the new. They had found an English-speaking, civilized, Christian land that allowed their talents scope to develop, provided a reasonable livelihood and a degree of economic independence, and opened the way to occupational and social mobility. From a family/clan/village base they created an Armenian cultural, intellectual, and nationalist infrastructure that enabled them to cope with their new environment and retain a sense of their own identity. Like the moulds they formed in the factory, they began to mould a new type of order in the young Dominion. Little did they know that their old world would soon disappear and the humble foundations they were laying in Canada would be transformed by tragedy.

PART THREE

*Genocide, Survival,
and the Response of Canadians*

6
Genocide and Survival

"The old country is a cemetery for our elders and an orphanage for our children."

The Armenian experience in Canada from 1915 onwards is comprehensible only within the framework of the Genocide and its aftermath: the disappearance of hundreds of thousands of compatriots; the anguish of uprooted, dispersed, and destitute survivors who were prohibited from returning to their homeland; the military contribution of Armenian soldiers in the Caucasus and in Mesopotamia; the creation of the independent republic of Armenia, its treatment by the Allies, and its collapse; and Armenian resistance to Communism and the final sovietization of Armenia.

Armenian immigrants in Canada were transfixed by news from abroad. For them, the period of innocence was over. Gone were their villages, their homes, and their families in their homeland. Henceforth, they would seek their future in the New World. Even as the settlers looked to Canada with gratitude and hope, they never ceased to be tormented by the haunting tragedy of loss and by the overwhelming fear of national extinction. And, in a multitude of ways, their lives were changed by the refugees who found sanctuary in Canada after the war. Bringing with them all that they had suffered, the newcomers inextricably left their imprint on the young communities. As if the challenge of rehabilitation and reconstruction of Armenian community life after the Genocide was not formidable enough, Armenians were confronted by international political developments that sowed the seeds of future discord and conflict in Armenian group reformation in Canada and the United States.

This chapter gives a brief overview of events in the homeland from

1915 to 1923 and touches on the people's struggle for survival. The following chapter links the Old World with the New by discussing the response of Canadians to the plight of "the little ally" and the reaction of Armenian Canadians to the catastrophe of their people.

GENOCIDE

Factors Leading to the Genocide

The continuing downward spiral of the Ottoman Empire during the rule of Sultan Abdul Hamid II (1876–1908) generated widespread discontent and led to four distinct reactions on the part of Armenians: emigration, sojourning, attempts at peaceful resolution, and, finally, armed resistance to oppression. Those who remained in the Empire, especially in the countryside in the six Armenian provinces, grappled with banditry, forced conversion, exploitation by semi-feudal Turkish and Kurdish lords, and collusion and corruption by government officials, the military, and the police. Armenians appealed to the courts for justice, petitioned the Turkish government for basic security of life and property, and pleaded with the Sultan for relief from the demands of tribal chieftains, tax collectors, and government representatives. When these avenues failed to ameliorate conditions, Armenians solicited the support of the European powers, which had increasingly participated in the political, economic, military, religious, and social life of the Ottoman Empire. But the internationalization of the Armenian Question and the commitment of the European powers to supervise reforms promised by the Sublime Porte did little to improve the lot of the Armenian millet.[1] On the contrary, European intervention on behalf of Christian minorities antagonized the Turks, even though, ironically, the Turkish state, itself, was increasingly indebted to Western powers. Conditions continued to deteriorate, with ever fainter hope of improvement, even as Armenian self-awareness was spreading and acquiescence in the face of tyranny was waning.

As was evident in the Balkans and in Syria/Lebanon, the Turkish government reacted to discontent and the demand for reform not by negotiation and compromise but by confrontation and massacre. Armenians knew this "sub-culture of massacre" well; as life became intolerable, men took up arms in a desperate attempt to defend their families and homes. Sultan Abdul Hamid's retaliation was swift and brutal. From 1892 to 1897, approximately three hundred thousand Armenians were massacred, and inestimable property was stolen or destroyed.[2]

In a drive to salvage the remnants of the decaying empire, a revolutionary Turkish junta, the Committee of Union and Progress (CUP)

(Ittihad ve Terakki) took the reigns of power in 1908, forced the abdication of Sultan Abdul Hamid II the following year, and restored the constitution of 1876.[3] With its promise of liberty, equality, and fraternity for all, the Young Turk revolution was hailed by many throughout the realm as a refreshing wind sweeping across a dark and decadent empire. With renewed hope, Turks and Armenians embraced in the streets.

Turkey's military and territorial losses by 1913, particularly the humiliating defeat of the Turkish army by the Serbs and the subsequent secession of most of European Turkey, disgraced the struggling regime. Blaming the liberal wing of the CUP for weakness and ineptitude, a right-wing faction of the Ittihadists unseated the liberals in 1913, wrested control of the party, and embarked on a program of radical nationalism. To popularize their political ideologies, the new Ittihadist leaders and thinkers manipulated and exploited powerful and complex forces: Turkish nationalism, pan-Turanism, domestic racial and ethnic tensions and jealousies, religious differences, class struggles, and foreign intervention.[4]

Non-Turkish minorities, like the Armenians, were portrayed as impediments to a Turkish national consciousness. By their very existence in the Ottoman Empire, these "aliens" constituted an internal enemy. Rallying to the call of "Turkey for the Turks," Turkish nationalists set about trying to pound the "non-Turkish peoples into a Turkish mortar."[5] Fearful of losing their ancient identity, however, Armenians resisted assimilation. Their determination to keep their language, religion, and culture served only to entrench intolerance and suspicion against them.

Turkish nationalists, moreover, conjured up visions of revitalized Turkish military prowess. Having lost their European possessions, they now looked eastward to a mighty and glorious empire stretching from Constantinople to the far reaches of Asia. According to the racist pan-Turanism ideology, Armenians in Anatolia, together with their compatriots in the Russian Empire, were barriers to the dreams of Turkish expansionism into Asia.

Nationalists were not the only ones to denounce the Armenian minority. Many Ottomans wanted to preserve the prerevolutionary structure of society: the subordinate status of the conquered and colonized peoples and the inferior role of the non-Turk and non-Moslem. They held that their forefathers had paid the price of victory with their blood. In their view liberty, equality, and fraternity were treacherous and despicable concepts imported from Europe, and Armenians, with their espousal of reform, egalitarianism, and modernity, were corrupting the purity of the Turkish nation-state. Add to these factors the envy of Armenian economic progress and the greed for Armenian wealth, and the causes for disaster become evident.[6]

Moslem fundamentalists, too, abhorred secular reform and despised Christians as *gaiurs*, or unbelievers. Even though many CUP leaders were not religious, they grasped the opportunity to win the backing of fundamentalists. Portraying their actions against Armenians as a righteous religious struggle against the infidel, CUP leaders whipped up support not only among fundamentalists but also among the rank and file. They advocated vengeance against the unfaithful as a sign of religious piety and thus masked a basically political and economic issue in the powerful guise of religion.

Dispersed throughout the empire with no geographic concentration, no standing army, no trained officer corps, no centralized political leadership, no naval port, no cache of arms and ammunition, and no widespread incentive to revolution, the Armenian millet did not seek to revolt against the Ottoman government in a quest for independence – a criticism levelled by leading Young Turks. Nor was independence their principal goal; rather, they sought a measure of local autonomy and basic human rights: impartiality before the law; freedom of speech, press, and assembly; the right to bear arms; and the legitimization of the ownership of their properties.[7]

Infuriated by such demands, Ittihadists condemned Armenians as disloyal. They fomented contempt against the Armenian race and religion and incited public hostility against a vulnerable minority.[8] In the wake of war, they insisted that Armenian leaders in the Ottoman Empire instigate revolt among their compatriots in Russia. Faced with this impossible dilemma, the leaders refused to interfere with Russian Armenians but assured the CUP that in the event of war Armenians in Turkey would fight in the Turkish armies.[9] This response was unacceptable to the Ittihadists; they condemned Armenians as traitors and scapegoated them as a major threat to national security. The Russian government made the same demands and received the same answer from Armenians: those in Russia would fight for the Russian Empire but would not incite trouble among their compatriots in the Ottoman Empire. When war broke out, Armenians in Russia fought in the Russian army, and when Turkey declared war, Armenians fought in the Turkish army, as they had fought in the Italian and Balkan wars.

As they strengthened their grip on the capital, the CUP moved to wrest total command of the country by taking control of the government bureaucracy and the police, setting up secret party cells throughout the empire, extending their network of spies, co-opting or at least neutralizing careerists and businessmen, and creating the Special Organization. Formed by the Committee of Union and Progress outside the structure of government and equipped with specific funds and weapons, the Special Organization had clear instructions to destroy the Armenians. To do so, the CUP arranged the release of hardened convicts, "the most ferocious murderers" as instruments of carnage.[10]

Implementing a Policy of Genocide

Emboldened by the crisis of war and encouraged by their German allies, the Young Turks embarked on a well-planned and systematic scheme to put an end to the "Armenian Question" once and for all by clearing the empire of the Armenians.[11] The destruction was deliberate and premeditated.[12]

As a vital preliminary measure to render Armenians "easy prey," the CUP struck at Armenian men in the military. As already mentioned, reform measures after 1908 had allowed Armenians to enlist in the Turkish armed forces. In his memoirs, Galust Surmenian recounts how he and a number of Armenians were accepted at Turkish military colleges for officer training and how at the outbreak of war, thousands of young Armenians, numbering perhaps as many as 250,000, were either recruited or volunteered for the Turkish army.[13] In early 1915, government authorities disarmed them and dispatched them to slave labour camps, reduced them to pack animals, and tortured or shot them. Henry Morgenthau, American ambassador to the Sublime Porte, describes the fate of unarmed Armenian soldiers in the Turkish army:

Army supplies of all kinds were loaded on their backs, and stumbling under the burdens and driven by the whips and bayonets of the Turks, they were forced to drag their weary bodies into the mountains of the Caucasus ... They were given only scraps of food and if they fell sick they were left where they had dropped, their Turkish oppressors perhaps stopping long enough to rob them of all their possessions – even their clothes ... squads of 50 or 100 men would be taken, bound together in groups of four, and then marched out to a secluded spot a short distance from the village. Suddenly the sound of rifle shots would fill the air ... In cases that came to my attention, the murderers had added a refinement to their victims' sufferings by compelling them to dig their graves before being shot.[14]

Under the guise of requisitioning supplies, arms, and money for the war effort, Turkish authorities disarmed the civilian population and used the opportunity to intimidate the people. In a personal memoir a survivor recalls the searches: "Though a child of nine, I remembered the soldiers vividly. They were brutal men in rough khaki, heavily armed, heavily booted, coarse and vulgar in manner and speech. They entered our homes on the pretext of searching for guns and revolutionary books – things which were unknown in Bandirma [her village]. We children were terrified at the sight of the soldiers. With their gun handles and the sharp edges of their bayonets and sabres they ripped open wall, floors, cabinets, storage bins; they cut comforters and mattresses to shreds looking for things that were not there. With lustful looks at my mother and sister Nectar, they left, leaving behind them a trail of terror and destruction."[15]

The persecuted people," observed the American ambassador, "patiently obeyed the command." When Turkish officials found no arms, they seized the leaders and harassed them on grounds of noncooperation. When they did find rifles or ammunition, they confiscated them as evidence that a "revolution" was being planned and regularly threw their unsuspecting victims into prison on a charge of treason. "Nothing was sacred to the Turkish gendarmes," wrote Ambassador Morgenthau. They ransacked churches, pillaged altars, "held mock ceremonies in imitation of the Christian sacraments" and beat priests, accusing them of being instigators of sedition.[16]

Beginning on the night of 23–24 April 1915, the Turkish police arrested and jailed hundreds of Armenian political, religious, educational, and intellectual leaders, mainly in Constantinople and Smyrna – far from the Russian war zone.[17] Filthy, rat-infested hell holes, Turkish prisons turned into diabolic death chambers, where executioners "hew off their feet or else hammer nails into them just as they do in shoeing horses. This is all done at night time and in order that the people may not hear their screams and know of their agony, soldiers are stationed round the prisons, beating drums and blowing whistles."[18]

Left without leaders, without arms, and without young men to defend them, the Armenian civilian population now faced mass race murder. With the order for deportation, the Turkish government gave the signal for plunder and massacre. Assuring Armenians of "temporary" relocation from the war zone for their own safety, guaranteeing them protection of life and property, and promising shelter and food along the way, Turkish officials rounded up inhabitants from towns and villages throughout the empire, even those far from the Russian frontier.[19] First, Turkish authorities disposed of the male population, including teenage boys. Some they killed outright. Others they drove out with the rest of the people, and on the outskirts of town separated the men and boys from the women and children, took them to a convenient place, and murdered them, often after forcing them at gunpoint to dig their own graves.[20]

As the deportations got under way, the government issued orders to expropriate Armenian goods and property. This action went beyond the widespread extortion that had taken place in the fall of 1914, when the Turkish government made excessive demands on Armenians, especially merchants, to provide money and supplies for the war effort. By means of the Abandoned Properties Law, the Turkish government took possession of all "abandoned" Armenian goods and properties. Turkish authorities confiscated the personal and community properties that had not been looted, destroyed, burned, or handed over to Moslem refugees from Thrace or Bulgaria. Government officials seized Armenian churches, schools, and monasteries and disposed of these cultural symbols, either as a means of obliterating the presence of Armenians altogether or as a means of financial gain. Thousands of books and newspapers, priceless ancient manuscripts, and carefully collected and notated sheets of folk music were burned.[21] (Scholars are now using the term libricide to refer to the destruction of books, manuscripts, and libraries.) To give a sense of the scope of the destruction, two sets of statistics are useful. In an inventory carried out by the patriarchate in 1913–14, it was estimated there were 2,538 churches, 451 monasteries, and 1996 schools. In 1919 in a statement to the peace conference sitting in Paris, Avetis Aharonian and Boghos Nubar Pasha noted damage to or destruction of 1860 churches and chapels, 229 monasteries, 83 episcopal seats, 26 lycées and seminaries, 1439 schools, and 42 orphanages.[22] Land, buildings, commodities, and bank accounts were expropriated. By this "gigantic plundering scheme," members of the Ittihad party and their friends amassed great fortunes at the expense of their victims.[23]

The deportees, mostly women, children, and the elderly, faced terrible hardship. Driven over mountains, across rivers, and through deserts, they were dehumanized and decimated in a slow, agonizing death. Indeed, the Ittihadist leaders well knew that the majority of deportees would be robbed, beaten, or maimed; that they would die of thirst or starvation, exposure, exhaustion, disease, or torture; or that they would be violated, abducted into captivity, forced to renounce their religion, or murdered along the way. The Armenian people suffered all the perversities and depravities of humankind.[24] German consul von Scheubner-Richter reported that "such a transfer of population is tantamount to massacre ... One cannot justify these measures by military consideration, since it is not a question of a revolt among the Armenians of the region, and the people who are being deported are old men, women, and children."[25] In Trebizond the Italian consul-general, Giacomo Gorrini reported:

It was a real extermination and slaughter of the innocents ... The passing of the gangs of Armenian exiles beneath the window and before the door of the

Consulate ... the city in a state of siege, guarded at every point by 15,000 troops in complete war equipment, by thousands of police agents, by bands of volunteers and by the members of the 'Committee of Union and Progress'; the lamentations, the tears, the abandonments, the imprecations, the many suicides, the instantaneous deaths from sheer terror, the sudden unhinging of men's reason, the conflagrations, the shooting of victims in the city, the ruthless searches through the houses and in the countryside; the hundreds of corpses found every day along the exile road; the young women converted by force to Islam or exiled like the rest; the children torn away from their families or from the Christian schools, and handed over by force to Moslem families, or else placed by hundreds on board ship in nothing but their shirts, and then capsized and drowned in the Black Sea and the River Deyirmen Dere – these are my last ineffaceable memories of Trebizond, memories which still, at a month's distance, torment my soul and almost drive me frantic ... all Christian powers that are still neutral would be compelled to rise up against Turkey and cry anathema against her inhuman Government and her ferocious "Committee of Union and Progress," and they would extend the responsibility to Turkey's allies, who tolerate or even shield with their strong arm these execrable crimes, which have not their equal in history, either modern or ancient. Shame, horror, and disgrace![26]

Morgenthau, who initially believed the government was deporting Armenians as a measure of assimilating them in Turkish villages far from their homeland, confirmed that the real purpose of the deportation was robbery and annihilation. The deportations were the result of "prolonged and careful deliberations ... He [Talaat] told me that the Union and Progress Committee had carefully considered the matter in all its details and that the policy which was being pursued was that which they had officially adopted." For Morgethau, the deportations "represented a new method of massacre. When the Turkish authorities gave the orders for these deportations they were merely giving the death warrant to a whole race; they understood this well, and, in their conversations with me, they made no particular attempt to conceal the fact."[27] Such was the toll of human life, that Talaat Pasha, the minister of the interior could boast, "I have accomplished more towards solving the Armenian problem in three months than Abdul Hamid accomplished in thirty years."[28]

As the death marches began, Miss Alma Johannsen, a Swedish nurse working with the German League of Assistance in Mush, asked the *mutessarif* (local ruler) if she could take the Armenian children of the orphanage with her rather than leave them behind. "'You can take them along,' he replied, 'but being Armenians their heads may and will be cut off along the way.' I begged the Mutessarif to have mercy on the children, but in vain. He replied that the Armenian children must perish with their nation ... All these details," she wrote, "show that the massacre was planned."[29] Indeed, Enver Pasha, minister of war, insisted to Morgenthau that the treatment of Armenians was not the work of uncontrollable fanatics or wartime excesses. "We have this country absolutely under our control. I have no desire to shift the blame on to our underlings and I am entirely willing to accept the responsibility myself for everything that has taken place. The Cabinet itself has ordered the deportations ... no underling would dare proceed in a matter of this kind without our orders."[30]

Survivors, both in oral interviews and written accounts, give a sense of the weight of those orders. The first three of the following excerpts were selected to show how the destruction was organized in part of the Keghi region. A number of interviewees from different villages in the same general area recounted how they were taken, village by village, to the field of Kulekan, where they were attacked by Kurds and Turks.[31]

[After leaving the village of Djerman] at Koulakan we were attacked. Someone blew a horn and suddenly they fell on us. With swords and axes they killed us. My mother, cousin and I clung to each other. A Kurd was beating us. Ripped off our clothes. We were almost naked, all three of us. Still clinging to each other. He was beating us. What a beating! When he raised his arm to strike us with his sword, my mother let go of me. He abducted me. I was sixteen years old. They married me to a Kurd. Every day I said my prayers. "Dear God, I am a prisoner here. Have pity on me. Save me, dear God."[32]

In 1915 Armenian young men had been conscripted into the Turkish army and had been sent to far-off places. The nightmare fell on the elderly, the children, and the women. [During the war] Armenian women were knitting socks and gloves, were sewing clothes for the soldiers. On May 29, the police marched into Armenian villages and announced: "To protect you from Kurdish attacks and pillaging, you and your goods are to be moved to Turkish homes until further orders."

The seventy-five Armenian households of Oror village, with their belongings, moved into twenty-five Turkish homes. The next day, [the police] pounced on us with their rifle butts and their clubs. They beat us and drove us out of our village towards the river. We waited. At dawn, villagers arrived from Tarman, Aboghnag, Tsermag, and other villages. They drove that huge throng of people, whipping, thrashing, hitting us all the way to a village called Chan. The caravan grew as more and more Armenians were dragged out from their homes along the way. Terror and weeping overshadowed the heavens, but there was no one to hear. From Chan, they pushed us towards Balu until we reached a Kurdish village called Koulakan. The Kurdish-Turkish forces surrounded us ... Suddenly the sound to attack rang out. The Armenian caravan, numbering thousands of people plunged into hell ... we were swimming in blood. They plundered what we had left. They gathered up those of us who were hiding behind rocks or in bushes ... separated the children from us and drove them away. They gathered together the corpses and poured oil on them and burned them. They forced us to watch that vision of hell.[33]

When we were nearing Darmon [Tarman] village, they searched every single person, thoroughly, for small weapons, watches, anything of value. They disarmed everyone ... Our people were left unarmed, helpless ... The Turks and Kurds made a barricade like a fence and collected us and brought us to a deserted barren place called Koulakan ... Babies were crying, no milk, no food. Wounded. Lost children.

It was night again. The *khoojan* [mob] drew closer. The Armenians were in the middle and from all around they were coming at us. As it got darker, they got closer. They were armed. Suddenly, their leader must have given the order, they opened fire on us. They began killing people. People were trying to flee. No place to flee. They had surrounded us like a chain. How can you stand up against artillery? My grandmother had dressed me up like a little girl and put some money in my pocket. There was a moon, but it was dimmed by the smoke of the firing. They had emptied so many rifles. My grandmother took my hand, but I can't remember what happened. I must have fainted.[34]

The following accounts reveal the fate of women and children.

Group by group, they took us out to a valley and killed us. By a miracle I was not killed. I survived underneath the corpses. I must have been four or five years old. I was crying. A lady heard me and found me. There isn't a night that I go to bed and don't think about the events of those days. I am all alone in this world, completely alone. I relive everything.[35]

Water had been the worst of our problems. For the most part it was the rainwater in pools at the roadside that we had been compelled to drink for want of anything better ... the plaintive cries of little children, imploring their mothers to give them water to drink, wrenched one's heart. Old people sick and suffering groaned for it as they dragged themselves along with leaden feet. Water! Always water ... I looked down at myself – a human scarecrow! My hands lay limply in my lap. The wrists seemed nothing but sticks and the fingers, bones – no! claws, for I noticed with revulsion how long my finger nails had grown.[36]

I was struggling along with my mother, my aunt and her children. We had been driven from our home. My aunt had two children, a little boy who was holding her hand and a little girl, about two years old, in her arms. The baby's name was Keghouhi, which means beautiful and she was a real beauty. Suddenly a Kurdish woman dashed out and grabbed the baby girl and ran. My aunt chased her. From nowhere a Kurdish man on horseback appeared. With one stroke of his sword, he slashed my aunt.[37]

We arrived at the summit of a mountain. The chief of the escort had noticed a young girl in the caravan and desired her. She resisted. Later he appeared surrounded by a band of Kurds and said to us: "If you do not deliver her to me, you will all be massacred." This was the price of the safety of the caravan. We threw ourselves at the feet of the young girl pleading with her to consent to his demands. She was silent, she cried, she hid her face in her hands. Finally she gave in to our appeals. She begged me to go with her for she didn't dare go alone ... She returned the next day ... Then she disappeared towards evening. She had probably gone to throw herself in the river which we had just crossed.[38]

A girl about fourteen years old was given shelter by Herr Krause, depot manager for the Baghdad Railway at Aleppo. The girl had been so many times ravished by Turkish soldiers in one night that she had completely lost her reason. I saw her tossing on her pillow in delirium with burning lips and could hardly get water down her throat.[39]

Those deportees who survived the macabre convoys were driven towards the Syrian desert to extermination camps in Meskené, Rakka, Der el-Zor, and Ras-ul-Ain, where, it is estimated, the majority of the Armenian population of Turkey was killed or died from the unbearable conditions. Turkish officials forbade anyone to provide aid to the victims and arrested those who tried.

The Government would not allow any help in money, food, or medicine to be given; if they knew of anyone so doing, they stopped it ... As long as I live I can never forget the camp ... not far from Tarsus. Here there were 10,000 to 15,000 Armenians awaiting further deportation towards the desert. They were in the broiling sun, with no shade or shelter save the rudest arrangements – anything that came to hand thrown over poles or sticks. There were all kinds of people and families of all ages, crowded together within a certain radius, beyond which they might not go. They looked scorched by the sun, their clothes were fast wearing out and there were poor little children, boys and girls, taken from school, with simply nothing to do but await their fate ... There were no sanitary arrangements whatever, and the air was impregnated with foul odours.[40]

For another five days they [the deportees] did not receive a morsel of bread, neither a drop of water. They were scorched to death by thirst, hundreds upon hundreds fell dead along the way, their tongues turned to charcoal ... On the seventy-fifth day when they reached Halep [Aleppo] 150 women and children remained from the whole caravan of 18,000.[41]

What remains of the Armenian nation, scattered along the banks of the Euphrates, consists of old men, women and children. Men of middle age and younger people, as far as they have not been slain, are scattered over the roads of the country where they smash stones or do other labors for the Army in the name of the state ... Inside a tent measuring perhaps five or six meters square, I saw roughly four-hundred orphan-children – they were starving. These miserable children are supposed to receive 150 grams of bread per day. It happens often that they receive nothing for two or three days. Of course the mortality rate is fearfully high. As I was able to ascertain myself, the dysentery claimed seventy victims within eight days ... The entrance to these concentration camps could well bear the legend imprinted on the gates of Dante's hell "Ye who enter here, abandon all hope."[42]

They died all the deaths on the earth," wrote another witness of the horrors, "the deaths of all the ages."[43] Approximately six hundred thousand Armenians perished in the first year of the Genocide.[44] Hundreds of thousands were deported and driven to extermination camps. Others were herded into overcrowded and unsanitary refugee camps in Syria/Lebanon or in the fledgling Republic of Armenia, where war, poverty, disease, exposure, and famine continued to take their toll of human life. Of the 2 to 2.5 million Armenians in the Ottoman Empire in 1914, an estimated 1.5 million were either killed or died under disastrous conditions from 1915 to 1923. About 150,000 were Islamicized and never reclaimed, thus losing their ethnic identity. These figures do not include those who perished in the Caucasus, both indigenous Armenians and refugees from Turkey.[45]

CONTINUED TURMOIL

After the armistice between Turkey and its enemies, Turkish Armenia remained in a state of political and military turmoil. Russian advances deep into Turkish territory during the war, the Communist Revolution and the withdrawal of Russian troops, the success of Armenian regiments in holding the Caucasian front and the Baku oilfields, the treaty of Brest-Litovsk and the Russian surrender of the vital centres of Kars, Ardahan, and Batum to Turkey, and finally the Armistice of Mudros (30 October 1918) meant a constant change in political realities in the Ottoman Empire. Like storm-tossed vessels, Armenian survivors in

Turkey were in a state of constant upheaval, now fleeing enemy advances, now returning to their homes.

While 1918 saw the end of the war in Europe, hostilities continued in the Middle East and the Caucasus as Britain, France, the United States, Greece, and Italy vied for the spoils of war, notably oil, and jockeyed for spheres of influence. In the Caucasus, peace was far from a reality, regardless of Armenian victories over the numerically superior Turkish armies at Bash Aparan, Kara Kilisa, and Sardarabad in 1918 and the creation of an independent Armenian republic in the same year. From its very birth the new state was enmeshed in a life-and-death struggle to survive.[46] Conflicts with Georgia and Azerbaijan, continued warfare with Turks and Tatars, rail blockades, fuel shortages, famine, epidemics, internecine rivalries between pro- and anti-Communists, and the destitution of tens of thousands of refugees created havoc in the little republic.[47]

During the war and immediately following the armistice, the allies advocated war crimes trials and punishment for the perpetrators of the Genocide. On 23 May 1915, Britain, France, and Russia condemned Turkey for the massacre of Armenians and stated that the Allies would "hold all members of the Ottoman Government, as well as such of their agents as are implicated, personally responsible for such massacres." The Allies also upheld the concept of an independent homeland for Armenians. In his Fourteen Points, President Woodrow Wilson declared the right of self-determination for minorities, and he himself drew the boundaries of an independent Armenia with access to the sea.[48] In 1918, France and Britain issued a joint declaration calling for the "complete and final liberation of the peoples who have for so long been oppressed by the Turks, and the setting up of national governments and administrations that shall derive their authority from the free exercise of the initiative and choice of the indigenous populations." At the opening of the Paris Peace Conference in January 1919, Allied leaders agreed that Armenia must be "completely severed from the Turkish empire." They proclaimed the Armenian right to be free of the "blasting tyranny of the Turks" and guaranteed their "little ally" a national homeland. They spoke of the bravery of Armenian soldiers during the war and pledged reparations for Armenian losses.[49]

Mindful of these promises, Armenia looked expectantly to her former allies for assistance. "There was a general belief that suffering was at an end and the dawn was about to break," wrote Alexandre Khatissian, one of the Armenian prime ministers. "The sun of liberty and independence shone on Armenia. We were waiting for the Allies, like manna from Heaven, like saving angels."[50] No country responded to "the cry for existence." No government moved in to give meaningful aid to the new state. If anything, the Allied governments pursued a set of confused and contradictory policies towards the Armenian state, virtually paralyzing it. They withheld de facto recognition of the republic until January 1920, thereby subverting attempts to arrange international loans and lines of credit for essential noncombatant goods like blankets and medicines and equally essential items like arms and munitions. After putting pressure on Armenia to disarm and disband its wartime regiments, Britain withdrew its own infantry divisions from the Caucasus, leaving Armenian civilians at the mercy of Azeri violence in Baku.[51] Finally, in May 1920 the United States Congress, in a move towards "splendid isolationism," rejected the role of mandatory power over the republic of Armenia.

In August 1920 the Allies imposed the Treaty of Sèvres on the newly installed regime in Constantinople. By its terms Turkey was obliged to recognize the Armenian state, which finally received de jure recognition by the Allies, and to accept the frontiers between Armenia and Turkey established by the president of the United States. Neither the terms of the treaty nor President Woodrow Wilson's boundary demarcations (November 1920) were realistic unless backed by strong Allied support. Allied leaders knew that if they did not fulfill their commitments, the republic was doomed. But none of the powers stood up to enforce the terms. Sèvres was as meaningless as the paper it was written on; it blinded Armenians to the perfidy of their erstwhile Allies. Wilson's boundary decision came at the same time that Turkish armies, reorganized under Mustapha Kemal (later Ataturk) with the aid of Soviet gold and weapons, invaded the struggling Armenian republic, pillaging, burning, and massacring as they advanced. Communists, anxious to create a Soviet sphere in the Caucasus, attacked on another front. Strangled between Kemalist Turkey and Communist Russia and on the verge of total collapse, Armenia saw no alternative but to salvage what little territory it still possessed by opting for the Soviets (December 1920).

Meanwhile, Armenians who had managed to survive in the Middle East were struggling in overcrowded, poverty-stricken, and disease-infested refugee shanty towns. In 1919 France invited them to return to Cilicia, the residence of the Armenian Catholicosate of Sis and the seat of an ancient Armenian kingdom. At least one hundred and fifty thousand Armenians responded, and immediately began the daunting task of rebuilding their homes and communities.[52] Mobilizing his army against the French presence in the region, Kemal attacked the French garrison stationed outside the city of Marash. Just as the Turks thought themselves on the brink of defeat, the French unexpectedly retreated from the besieged city in February 1920, leaving the terrified Armenians unprotected. About three thousand trudged behind the French troops in a raging blizzard that claimed the lives of about a thousand refugees. A second column of about two thousand Armenians followed the first, but most were massacred before they could escape. Famine and starvation devastated the ten thousand who remained in the city. Then in March 1920, Turkish forces attacked Hadjin, another hill town in Cilicia. For seven months the Armenians defended their homes and families without the promised French reinforcements. A town of 30,000 Armenians in 1914 was decimated to 480 by 1920.[53]

In February 1921 in the siege of Aintab, French and Armenian forces succeeded in bringing about a Turkish capitulation. But in October, much to the horror of the Armenians, the French handed Aintab and the rest of Cilicia to the Turks and withdrew their protection from the same Armenian refugees that they themselves had invited to settle there only two years earlier. Not only did the French discourage the Armenians from leaving Cilicia, on the grounds that the Kemalists had guaranteed an amnesty and protection of minorities, but they also refused to facilitate the exodus of the incredulous population. General Henri J. E. Gouraud, the French high commissioner in Syria and Cilicia and the commander of the French troops in the Levant, admonished the inhabitants: "To leave is to run disastrous risks which will have unfortunate results. To remain, is to maintain the fruits of the labour of your ancestors, to live again in peace and prosperity in Cilicia, Kilis and Aintab."[54] He adamantly refused to provide any special arrangements for the evacuation of refugees, even women and children, and warned that no camps would be waiting for them in Syria. Fearing what lay in store for them if they fell into Turkish hands, most Armenians fled en masse, taking the risk of retreating with the French army on foot or boarding ships for unknown destinations. For weeks the vessels "wandered ... like phantom ships over the Mediterranean," attempting in vain to land in British-controlled Egypt, Cyprus, or Palestine. Eventually Greece accepted some refugees; others finally found asylum in the French protectorate of Syria/Lebanon.[55]

On the Aegean front, the Kemalists pursued the Greek army into the port city of Smyrna (Izmir) in September 1922. Smyrna, the second largest city in Turkey, was teeming with refugees, both Greek and Armenian, who had converged on the city in search of safety. Shortly after penetrating Smyrna, Turkish soldiers began "the most terrible looting, raping and killing." American teachers, missionaries, and consular officials "watched the soldiers kill civilians in the street in front of the school, enter homes and kill families and throw them out into the street, and then take loads of goods along with them." They set fire to the Armenian and Greek quarters of the city. As flames engulfed Smyrna, Turkish soldiers gunned down the panic-stricken people. Nearly half a million petrified inhabitants crushed each other on the quays in a frenzy to escape. Meanwhile, British, French, Italians, and Americans anchored in the harbour made little attempt to intervene in the carnage and only reluctantly allowed some of the fugitives to board ship. About 100,000 Greeks and Armenians died, and another 160,000 were deported to slave labour camps. Thousands of Armenians, perhaps as many as 100,000, found temporary sanctuary in Greece, itself experiencing grave hardship.[56]

In the same year, thousands of Armenian refugees, mostly children sheltered in European and American relief missions and orphanages in such cities as Kharput and Sivas, in Turkey, were forced to evacuate as Mustapha Kemal and his nationalist armies advanced.[57] Those who remained in the Ottoman Empire were never safe. Throughout the 1920s theft, extortion, banishment, and massacre continued to drive the remnants to the congestion and chaos of refugee camps in Syria, Lebanon, and Armenia. As late as 1929 the International Labour Organization reported on the extortion and expulsion of Armenians from Anatolia in spite of international agreements guaranteeing the rights of minorities. To acquire their passports, the people were required to pay "fantastic" taxes, such as the military-exemption tax for five-year-old children. Payment of these "duties" rendered the people penniless, and the passports they acquired at such great sacrifice *prohibited* them from returning to Turkey – a critical disadvantage for those who later wished to emigrate to Canada.[58]

The fate of the Armenian people was sealed with the final blow in the international game of promises. Unlike the Treaty of Sèvres, the Treaty of Lausanne, negotiated in 1923 between the Allies and Kemalist Turkey, did not mention Armenians at all. The final chapter was written as if no Armenians had ever existed in the Ottoman Empire; as if the Allies had not vowed to hold the perpetrators of the Genocide responsible for their actions (23 May 1915);[59] as if thousands of Armenian civilians and soldiers had not vanished in jails, forced labour battalions, and prisoner-of-war, concentration, and extermination camps; as if no Armenian men had died defending the Caucasian front, the rich Baku oil fields, and Mesopotamia. It was as if no Armenian state had ever been promised or created.[60]

The noninterventionist approach of Western powers in the face of uncontrolled state aggression by Turkey and the abandonment of the Armenian cause and of Armenia by its allies represented their acquiescence to the decision of any nation-state to consolidate its existence and affirm its supremacy by the annihilation or violent assimilation of its minorities. For Armenians, Allied inaction and duplicity heaped another trauma on a people already reeling from the catastrophe. Armenians everywhere were shattered by the final assault of Lausanne.

SURVIVAL

From 1915 to 1923, one and a half million Armenians perished, and with them, the beloved homeland in Western Armenia. A truncated Armenian state was incorporated into the Soviet Union. Hundreds of thousands of refugees, who were prohibited by Turkish authorities from returning to their homes, were dispersed in Greece, the Balkan states, Egypt, Palestine, Syria/Lebanon, and Europe. Yet even in the darkest days of agony, the spirit of survival did not die. It may have fluttered, but it did not die.

"The miracle," wrote one of the survivors, "was not how we managed to live, but how we managed not to die."[61] While a fortunate encounter or a stroke of luck could mean the difference between living and dying, the hand of fate was just as often guided by a child's resilience, a woman's resourcefulness, a man's strength of will. Recounting his survival, Kerop Bedoukian paid homage to his mother's ingenuity in saving the lives of four of her children and helping others.[62] An interviewee credited her father's presence of mind with saving their entire family. When the Turkish soldiers separated the men and boys from the women, children, and elderly, he waited for a moment of confusion to walk, unobserved, to the group of elderly. As the only surviving adult male of his family, he cared for the wives and children of his relatives.[63] Another informant – blond, blue-eyed, and still beautiful – praised her grandmother's ingenuity in shaving off her hair and covering her scalp with tar "to make me look ugly, so they wouldn't abduct me."[64] Exhausted and despondent, another interviewee's mother regained her strength and felt "tough like a lion" whenever she considered what her daughter's fate would be if she gave up. Converts to Islam had been obliged to formally renounce Christianity, and, often under surveillance, had to pray at the regular calls to prayer from the mosque. Many grasped the first chance to break out of their religious bondage and flee to freedom.

Survival took many forms. Thousands of Armenian women and children had been abducted by Turks, Kurds, and Arabs. In spite of directives from Talaat Pasha, minister of the interior, to dispatch all Armenians to the Syrian desert regardless of age and sex, countless numbers of Turks, Kurds and Arabs saved Armenian women and children, even at the risk of their own lives.[65] Oral interviews indicate every manner of motive and treatment. Some families, opposed to the government's crimes against one of the most skilled, industrious, and educated elements of the empire and unconvinced of Young Turk propaganda alleging treason, sheltered Armenians at the risk of their own lives. Some concealed Armenians purely on compassionate grounds and when a safe opportunity arose allowed them to leave to rejoin their own people. Some Moslems found the events abhorrent and intervened on behalf of the refugees. An interviewee credited a group of Turkish women with saving the lives of a decimated convoy: "There were a couple of hundred women and children left of that huge caravan of people. We were in rags. Hungry and thirsty. Full of sores and wounds. Ten or fifteen Turkish soldiers began harassing us. Suddenly a group of Turkish women walked between us and the soldiers. They were crying. They said, 'We can't stand the sight and smell of blood anymore. We can't stand seeing all these bodies. Leave these poor people alone.' The soldiers didn't attack us. The women gave us some clothing."[66] Such courage and moral fortitude existed among all levels and classes of society. Interviewees who had seen compassion and kindness praised those who "guaranteed the survival of the survivors."

On the other hand, malevolence motivated many abductions. Moslems took Armenian children into captivity and made them a part of their families, falsified the children's birth certificates, changed their names, and taught them the Koran. Some had women and children tattooed to obfuscate identification and prevent rescue. For Armenian women and girls tattoos were shameful scars of bondage. Taking Armenians into captivity enabled the abductors to build up their own nation and religion at the expense of their victims, a fact that was not missed either by the captives or the captors. Still others kidnapped Armenians in order to exploit them as concubines, prostitutes, or slaves and often used deliberate ill-treatment and violence to prevent escape. A special commission set up by the League of Nations to reclaim Armenian women and children found instances of brutality: a boy with a broken spine from beatings inflicted with an iron rod, a child with burns over a large part of his body, a woman with a dozen scars on her back from dagger wounds for each time she tried to run away.[67] An interviewee wept as he recounted his suffering as a nine-year-old shepherd boy. His captors enslaved him, starved and overworked him, and beat him mercilessly. Each time they whipped him, they cursed him as an infidel. "Dear God," he prayed, "as I care for these sheep, please take care of me." Luckily, one of his attempts to escape coincided with the armistice.[68]

The double-edged treatment of Armenians by Kurds is highlighted by the events in the Dersim Mountains, where the Turkish policy of pitting Kurds against Armenians did not always succeed. In his memoirs, Rev. Henry Riggs, an American Protestant missionary in Kharpert, describes how the missionaries engineered an underground railroad, spiriting Armenians into the mountains with the assistance of and payment to friendly Kurdish clansmen. Keghetsis also found hope among the friendly Dersim Kurds, even while pursued by other Kurdish tribes. According to a survivor's account, the Lolantsi clan offered refuge to Armenian villagers of Hertif. When Shefkhi, another Kurd who searched for and killed Armenians, confronted Kirva Haso, demanding he surrender the Armenians, Haso, the clan chieftain refused, and in the stand-off Shefkhi and his men retreated, burning one of Haso's houses as they took flight. In their turn, in appreciation for Kurdish generosity Armenians helped Kurdish villagers: they constructed a dam for irrigation, built a loom to weave cloth, used herbs and plants for medicinal cures, and rebuilt Haso's house, so that it was even more substantial than before. With the Russian advance to Erzinga, Kirva Haso arranged for the safe passage of his guests to the Russian army. "Today," wrote the survivor, "as we commemorate the fiftieth anniversary [of the Genocide], we do not forget the Lolantsi people of Dersim to whom we owe our lives. Some of them were later captured by Turkish authorities and hanged for having protected us."[69]

Saving the refugees took on monumental proportions with the creation of the National (Armenian) Central Committee for Refugee and Orphan Relief in Constantinople after the armistice.[70] One of its first and most important tasks centred on organizing searches to reclaim women and children sequestered in Moslem homes and orphanages. The Treaty of Sèvres (1920) confirmed the nullification of religious conversions and permitted the family or religious community of kidnapped persons to seek them out and claim them. Aside from formal efforts by Armenians to save their people, a special commission received authority from the League of Nations in 1922 to reclaim women and children.[71] In addition women and children escaped on their own as soon as they saw a way out. Such flight occurred particularly in Anatolia, where, as the Russians advanced in 1916, thousands fled from bondage and regrouped behind Russian lines. With an equal degree of single-mindedness, survivors themselves tried to locate and liberate their family members. They considered it a patriotic and moral obligation to rescue their people, and many interviewees pay tribute to the inventiveness of coreligionists who sought out and saved women and children sequestered in Moslem homes.

Among the heroic saviours were "the orphans' fathers," men like Garabed Donabedian, Ruben Herian, and Rev. Aharon Shirajian who braved danger and disease searching for abducted children. In his effort to save children taken by Moslem families, Donabedian met with stiff resistance from Turks and Kurds who submitted him to such torture that he died from his wounds. Shirajian, dressed like an Arab, regularly drove his wagon into the desert to gather up Armenian children. "He was talking to my mother," recounts an interviewee, "standing there under the blistering sun. That desert road to Der el-Zor was so unbearably hot. I was just a child, perhaps six or eight years old. My mother held me and kissed me. No tears. Just a tender embrace. She said she was going to care for the sick people in our group and would join me later. Then he picked me up and gently put me in the wagon. I did not take my eyes off my mother. She, too, just stood there and watched the wagon move further and further away. I never saw my dear mother again but I see her every day of my life, standing in that pitiless desert."[72]

The spirit of survival is nowhere more evident than in acts of heroism: the Armenian women of Baku fought with the men, stood their ground, and held Baku and the rich oil fields until the British garrison arrived (summer, 1918); the women of Urfa, women like Elizabeth Yotyeghparian, fought and died alongside their husbands and brothers in the defense of their homes. Resistance by villages like Khups and towns like Shabin Karahisar and Van have become national symbols of courage no less noteworthy than the daring of the defenders of Hadjin, Zeitun, and Musa Dagh.[73]

Most beloved are the volunteers, the freedom fighters who took up arms to defend their people in the face of more numerous and better-equipped adversaries. Armenian legionnaires in Mesopotamia and Armenian freedom fighters in the Caucasus fought with an indomitable will and won an honoured place in the hearts of the people. The feats and victories of their commanders, in spite of monumental odds, of men like Generals Nazarbekian, Njdé, Dro, Keri, Sebough, Murat of Sivas, and Yessai Yaghoubian and of the most revered, General Andranig Ozanian, formed the heroic stories cherished by the survivors and passed on to their children.

Others were notable for their endeavours to bring justice to the perpetrators of the Genocide. After the war, after Turkish courts had sentenced the triumvirate of Enver Pasha, Talaat Pasha, and Jemal Pasha and other leaders to death in absentia, since most had conveniently fled from Turkey, Armenians, who had expected the Allies to bring the war criminals to justice and mete out punishment, took matters into their own hands. Under the cover of Nemesis, which was organized by the Armenian Revolutionary Federation, Armenians tracked down and carried out the verdicts of the tribunals. One by one, Ittihadist war criminals were executed. Internationally, the most famous case was the execution of Talaat Pasha by Soghomon Tehlirian, who was tried and acquitted by a Berlin court (1921). Others also, like Arshavir Shiragian, Arshak Torlakian, and Aram Erganian enforced the verdict against war criminals, and searched out and executed the perpetrators.[74]

RELIEF AND REHABILITATION

In spite of acts of valour and daring, the remnants of the Armenian nation lay huddled in filthy, demoralizing shanty towns in Middle Eastern and Mediterranean countries, scarcely tolerated in their places of exile. They formed a separate nation – a disparate band of humanity, predominantly women and children who belonged nowhere.[75] Poor and unwanted, they had no place to go. They came from all parts of the Ottoman Empire, from both rural and urban areas and from every socioeconomic and educational background. Driven from their homes, forbidden to return, separated from their loved ones, dispossessed of their properties and wealth, they had been levelled to the status of refugees – homeless and stateless.[76] In particular, the children – neglected, hungry, orphaned waifs – were in desperate need of care. These ragged urchins came from a cross section of Armenian society. They were the sons and daughters of merchants, farmers, teachers, doctors, and tradesmen. "The unclean, wizened, emaciated, pathetic faces, pleading for bread, gave no hint of a forgotten happiness, an abandoned home."[77] Tens of thousands of these wandering young vagabonds were gathered up and placed in orphanages, which became hospitals and schools and training centres as well. One of the main goals of the orphanages was to teach the children to be independent and self-supporting. Accordingly, reading, writing, and learning a trade were as much a part of orphanage life as bread and medicine. Boys received training as cobblers, carpenters, silversmiths, or barbers; girls learned all types of fancywork, weaving, or domestic work. The fruits of their labour were ploughed back into the orphanage to help other needy children.

Many of the orphanages, whether in Turkey, Armenia, the Middle East, or Greece, received aid from abroad. Well into the 1920s, the plight of the poor Christian refugees moved the hearts of people in Europe and North America. The London Lord Mayor's Fund, Friends of Armenia and the Save the Children Fund (all in Britain), the Society of Friends, the Mennonites, the Jesuits, the International Red Cross, and the Armenian Relief Association of Canada (ARAC) organized orphanages or contributed to other measures for relief and rehabilitation. Working with them was the High Commission for Refugees, under the auspices of the League of Nations and Armenian institutions, notably the Armenian General Benevolent Union and the Armenian Red Cross. With a mandate to help repatriate and rehabilitate the refugees, to provide for the care of orphans and widows, and to promote the social, economic, and industrial welfare of the destitute, the American Near East Relief (NER) emerged as the biggest, most extensive, and most effective humanitarian agency.[78] The work of resettlement and reconstruction affected hundreds of thousands of adults and children in Armenia and in countries of exile. The rescuers took on the task of bringing in immediate relief and of helping the refugees rebuild their lives, a colossal undertaking considering the needs of each individual survivor and the dispersion and fragmentation of the Armenian people.

Just as massacre and disease decimated the people, so the opportunities for reconstruction and revival gave them hope and self-esteem. With a little outside help, for instance, orphans established an agricultural colony in the Sardarabad region and laid the groundwork for self-sufficiency. Before 1922 in Kharput the Americans started a woollen factory that employed at least sixty women in washing, carding, spinning, and weaving woollens. In Yerevan and Alexandropol the Near East Relief (NER) hired twenty-five hundred women to spin cotton and wool, to knit twenty-five thousand pairs of stockings for distribution, and to make six thousand quilts. The spinning wheels and looms were made by refugee carpenters, thus giving employment to two hundred men. "For two years," reported James L. Barton, "all the clothing and bedding which were given in large quantities to the refugees, were made by other refugee women in the industrial workshops."[79]

In Syria and Lebanon refugee women adept at all types of fancywork offered embroidery and laces for sale on the streets. In an effort to organize them and provide them with self-sustaining employment, the NER set up the Near East Industries (NEI). A workshop bureau supplied the women with designs and materials. The finished items – tablecloths, runners, doilies, and handkerchiefs – were sold by the NEI in local markets and in America. As rapidly as the fancywork was sold, the NEI employed more women. In the beginning the sale of goods covered the cost of the raw materials and part of the wage payments, but the work was so successful that it gradually became self-supporting. In a single season, rejoiced Barton, the NEI sold eighteen thousand dollars worth of these goods. Other workers unravelled woollen-knit articles, then washed, dyed, and reused the yarn in weaving carpets. By such means the native arts of dyeing, designing, weaving, and fancywork were preserved, stimulated, and passed on to younger people, at the same time that the refugees were gainfully employed. In other cases, refugees sorted, washed, and repaired clothing from America, then sold the refurbished items to the people at a nominal cost. In the professional spheres, young Armenian women were trained as teachers and nurses; they did yeoman's work in running orphanages, schools, and hospitals. These "work-for-food" undertakings gave refugees a means of support and a measure of self-respect.[80]

These projects of rehabilitation reflect once again the courage and determination of Armenian women. During the dark days when their husbands and sons were either killed or were away fighting, the women assumed the role of family head, protected their relatives, foraged for food and lodging, and struggled to keep the remnants of the family alive. Then, during the period of reconstruction, they worked at whatever jobs they could find and spared nothing to save the lives of the children, regardless of the risk to themselves. These women – these unsung heroines – saved a nation through their self-reliance, resourcefulness, and bravery.

The resilience and industry of Armenian refugees impressed both League personnel and French authorities, especially in the back-to-the-land movement in Syria and Lebanon. The projects that were part of the movement, even though they were small-scale considering the numbers in need, helped refugees establish agricultural colonies and revitalize abandoned settlements. One report, for instance, praised a group of thirty families who had occupied some unused land for only six weeks: "Stone houses grow out of the soil. Several are finished and thatched. Gardens invaded by pines are clean and neat. The fields of stone and weeds have been worked and the good black earth is ready to receive the fall planting."[81] In Syria and Lebanon, Armenian farmers were engaged in draining swamps, market gardening, cattle raising, planting vineyards and orchards, and starting sericulture. It was well known that instalment repayment of funds loaned to the settlers usually required seven to ten years. "Thanks, however, to the enterprise and industry of the colonists ... advances ... will be repaid in a much shorter period."[82]

Each survivor, even very young children, embarked on an odyssey to find family members. In their quest, every piece of evidence, such as a birthmark or a scar, played a role in identifying people and in reuniting families. As the orphanages disbanded during the 1920s, the names, ages, birthplaces, and any other distinguishing features of the children were publicized in local and international Armenian-language newspapers.

In their turn, older refugees advertised information about themselves or searched for news about their families in bulletins, notices, and newspapers: a woman from Marash in the refugee camp at Alexandretta searching for her sister; a man from Smyrna in Athens looking for his daughter; a woman from Mush in Marseilles trying to find her two children; a man in Galt, Ontario, seeking his wife and eleven-year-old son from the town of Van. People passed along all manner of information about each other: three sisters from the town of Berejik in the Port Said refugee camp; a boy in the Sabun Khan orphanage in Aleppo about seven years old who knew only his first name, Garo, and his sister's name Mariam; a child about eight years old with a brown birthmark on her forehead in the Bird's Nest orphanage near Beirut. Survivors searched everywhere for their relatives – in orphanages, in refugee camps, in hospitals, schools, inns, and Moslem homes. They searched in the Middle East, in Armenia, in Europe, and in America. Some searched all their lives. Thousands whose families had been destroyed found replacements: a widower who had lost his wife and two children married a widow and adopted her child; a mother "found" a boy who looked like the one she had lost; a child "found" a brother or sister to replace the one who had perished.[83] In a million ways survivors tried to piece together their broken families and to stabilize their personal worlds.

7

The Impact of Genocide

Political chaos in the state of Armenia, widespread dispersal and refugeeism of the Armenian people, and loss and desperation marked the period leading well into the 1920s. Armenian institutions and organizations reeled under the pressure of turbulent forces. As they struggled to come to grips with changing realities and as they endeavoured to rebuild the nation, usually in their own image, the Armenian Apostolic Church and the Armenian political parties reshaped the loyalties and lives of their compatriots in the diaspora. At the same time, Armenian and non-Armenian Canadians, moved by tragedy in the Ottoman Empire, took up the relief and rehabilitation mantle or took up arms to fight Turkey and her allies.

THE ARMENIAN APOSTOLIC CHURCH

Perhaps the Armenian Apostolic Church suffered more than any other institution during the Genocide. Over the centuries, as the state church it was shaken at each major cataclysm engulfing the Armenian nation – conquest, earthquake, pestilence, war, flight. The Genocide was no exception. The murder of about five thousand clergy and the confiscation and destruction of church wealth left only a trace of the church precisely at a time when it was called upon to help the strewn and sorry people.[1] The Catholicosate of Cilicia was eventually reestablished in Antelias, near Beirut. Following fast on the heels of the trauma in Turkey and before it could restore the damage, the church was struck by another crisis with the sovietization of Armenia. Like other religious institutions in the Soviet Union, the Armenian Church faced oppression and censure, particularly after the 1929 Soviet constitution prohibited the propagation of religion and forbade challenges to atheism. The confiscation of church property and the imposition of exorbitant taxes forced the clergy to live a miserable and penurious existence. Religious services and practices were curtailed, seminaries circumscribed, and churchmen placed under constant surveillance. Following the death of Catholicos Kevork Vshtali (the Despairing one) in 1930, communist authorities did not immediately allow the election of a new catholicos. In fact, from 1920 to 1945, communist leaders left the catholicosate vacant for at least nine years and for the rest of the period held the Catholicos under virtual house arrest.

Closure, confiscation, persecution, imprisonment, and murder threatened the very existence of the church. In order to retain a vestige of life, the church "finally succumbed." The "Soviet authorities once defied by the church hierarchy in the early twenties, now [in the late twenties and early thirties] were tolerated by these churchmen who even prayed in the churches for the regime. The church had finally adjusted itself to the new political and social order of Armenia."[2]

POLITICAL FACTIONS

Entangled in the church crisis and the sovietization of Armenia and embroiled in the quest for power in the diaspora, four political associations redefined their platforms and priorities. The Social Democratic Hnchakian Party officially proclaimed its unequivocal support for Soviet Armenia, which fulfilled the goals it had pursued since its founding in 1887.[3] But internecine strife, murders, and the hanging of the party's leaders by Turkish authorities had greatly weakened this faction. Rivalry between social democrats and communists further undermined the party. In an attempt to preserve ethnic autonomy and to support Armenian national interests in the face of communist centralization of power and internationalism, the Social Democratic Hnchaks did not affiliate with the Third International or Comintern, founded in 1919. The sharp division in the world labour movement between Marxist-Leninists (and later Stalinists) and social democrats, with respect both to ideology and to tactics was mitigated in 1921. In an effort to unite the two factions against right-wing parties, Hnchaks in the United States linked up with the Armenian Workers' Party (also known as Armenian Communists), but communists and social democrats soon had a falling out. The object of communist parties was to capture the masses, and in this struggle for power, until 1935 at least, the "real enemies" were not the right-wing parties but the socialists, who were competing with them for the loyalty and support of the workers (see chapter 12).⁴

Following the decision of the Comintern in 1924 to destroy or seize control of social-democratic forces for "temporizing with the bourgeois-capitalist order" and to "bolshevize" national movements, directives from the Soviet Union almost wiped out the Hnchak organization in North America. Virulent propaganda denounced the Hnchaks and urged members to join the HOG (HOK) or Hayastani Oknutian Gomide (Komite) (Relief Committee for Armenia) and, later, the Hai Banvorakan Kusaktsutiun (Armenian Workers' Party/Armenian Communist Party).⁵ In a state of disarray in the midtwenties, the Hnchaks struggled to continue publishing *Yeritasard Hayastan* (Young Armenia), their official organ.⁶ The party, under the leadership of Stepan Sabah-Gulian, remained loathe to surrender its autonomy and its ethnic loyalty. It never regained its former popularity in North America, not even after 1935, when the Seventh Congress of the Comintern moved in favour of the United Popular Front and encouraged collaboration with antifascist elements, including social democrats. The 1935 rapprochement between Communists and Hnchaks did not lead to a revival of the party. All along, party members remained steadfast in their support of Soviet Armenia. In spite of a number of pro-Marxists in the leadership, the rank and file could not be clearly seen as either Marxist or pro- or antireligion, but they were consistently pro–Soviet Armenia.⁷

In North America, Armenian Communists and their sympathizers rallied around the banner of the Banvorakans, or Armenian Workers' Party/Armenian Communist Party, which maintained close ties with the official party line in the Soviet Union. Among the Banvorakans were atheists who agitated for the annihilation of the church altogether or sought to render the church a tool of Bolshevik propaganda in America. On the other hand, some Banvorakan sympathizers were solicitous of the Armenian Church, not so much as a religious institution but as an agent of ethnocultural retention.

In 1938 the United States House Un-American Activities Committee investigated the Armenian Communist Party and its organ, *Banvor*. Soon afterwards *Banvor* ceased publication, and the ACP went underground. Members of the ACP and its sympathizers reorganized as the Amerikahai Harachdimakan Kusaktsutiun (Armenian-American Progressive Party), later called the Amerikahai Harachdimakan Miutiun (Armenian-American Progressive League). Its official organ, *Lraper* (Reporter), was considered "the most important Armenian-language newspaper in New York City prior to the Cold War."⁸

Armenian Communists also operated procommunist front associations, the most significant being the HOG. Founded in Soviet Armenia in 1921, the HOG was too loosely constituted to be a political party, but it enjoyed popular and widespread grass-roots appeal, with chapters throughout the world. The leadership in the United States was Communist, but the rank and file represented communist and noncommunist friends of Soviet Armenia who were eager to help reconstruct what remained of the homeland. Indeed, the HOG raised funds for industrial, agricultural, and hydroelectric development, for rebuilding Leninakan after an earthquake, for refugee repatriation, and for cultural development.[9]

The Ramgavar Azatakan Kusaktsutiun (Armenian Democratic Liberal Organization, or ADL), founded in 1921, represented an amalgamation of the Armenakans (founded 1885), the Verakazmial Hnchaks (Reformed Hnchaks, or Liberals), who had seceded from the Social Democratic Hnchak Party in 1896, and the Sahmanadir Ramgavar Party (Constitutional Democratic Party), founded in Cairo in 1908.[10] Among its first leaders the party could claim fighters against Turkish oppression like Mihran Damadian, poets like Vahan Tekeyan, and men closely associated with the Armenian General Benevolent Union (AGBU). Composed of the middle class and supported by wealthy businessmen, the Ramgavars represented a conservative, proChurch, antirevolutionary, and antisocialist element. Responding to both geographical and political realities, the Ramgavars and their press, *Baikar* (Struggle), insisted that without Russian protection Armenia would be swallowed up by Turkey. Because of their fears for the survival of the Armenian church and nation and in spite of major ideological differences, they adopted an accommodating attitude towards Soviet Armenia. "Everything I believe," confided a Ramgavar leader, "is against Communism. But as an Armenian, I am pro-Armenia. As a small nation we have got to be tied to the Soviet Union. If the Soviet Union were to become democratic, Armenia has got to be democratic. If she wants to become a monarchy, Armenia has to be part of that monarchy. We cannot turn our back against the Soviet Union."[11]

Although the Hai Heghapokhakan Dashnaktsutiun (Armenian Revolutionary Federation), or Dashnak Party had joined the Second International in 1907, it saw itself primarily as a nationalist party. Dashnaks had dominated the creation and governance of the Armenian republic. When it was crushed between Russian and Turkish armies and partitioned, Soviet authorities drove out Dashnak leaders, murdered Dashnak supporters, destroyed the western liberties they had instituted, engaged in cultural suppression, surrendered hard-won parts of the republic, notably Kars and Ardahan to Turkey, and handed over Karabagh and Nakhechevan to Azerbaijan.[12] By 1921 the Dashnak Party, which had been founded in the Caucasus, which had derived great strength from Eastern Armenia, and which had worked on behalf of its people in Western Armenia before the war, became a party of the diaspora. In its ideology and aims, the federation remained straightforward and single-minded: a free, independent, and united Armenia.

With its North American centre in Boston, the Dashnak organization operated a thriving press: the well-established *Hairenik* (Fatherland) one of the most important Armenian-language newspapers in the United States, and the *Hairenik Amsagir* (Fatherland Monthly) (1922–69). [13] Regularly, the party sent out field-workers to visit, encourage, and revitalize branches throughout North America. By such means, the party kept members and sympathizers in far-flung places informed about important developments and in regular contact with the central executive and with each other.

The accommodation of the Armenian Church to the Soviet regime and the displacement of the Cilician See to Lebanon together with the struggle for power by the four political organizations and the complexity of the relationships with each other, the West, and Soviet Armenia, would have far-reaching ramifications in North America during the 1920s and 1930s.

CANADIAN HUMANITARIANS

In the meantime, others were involved in the Armenian cause. Canadian humanitarians, led by Protestant missionaries, tried both to educate the Canadian public about events in the Middle East and to influence government and nongovernment action in favour of Armenians and Armenia. News of the expulsions, tortures, and murders captured the attention and compassion of the Canadian public. Already during the 1894–97 massacres, the persecution of the Christian minority had aroused "widespread indignation." Canadian Protestant missionaries in Turkey reported back to their friends and congregations that "Murder and pillage have run riot in almost every part of Turkish Armenia ... Wholesale massacres have occurred at Trebizond, Guran, Erzerum, Bitlis, Sivas, Sassoun, Zeitoun and Kharpourt ... Streets were littered with corpses, churches filled with the slain, families despatched in their houses, pits filled with victims ... Tens of thousands probably have been slain."[14] In a passionate letter to Principal George Grant of Queen's University at Kingston, Ontario, William Nesbitt Chambers poured out his frustrations and anguish at the sight of the devastation and murder of Armenians in the Erzerum region: "The fact is this whole country is a horrible Burmese prison. A few escape, a few are dismissed, the great bulk of the prisoners (Christians) are retained for torture and slaughter ... One official told them the road to hell was open they could go there. They might have answered they were there already. ... The destitution is complete and indescribable. It is a most terrible thing to see thousands and thousands of people in this appalling condition. When will this black blot of the East be removed and justice done to these people?"[15]

Responding to the destruction in Turkey, humanitarians in Britain and North America formed Armenian relief associations. Congregations observed Armenian Sundays, listened to sermons about the condition of their Christian brothers and sisters in Armenia, and listened to lectures about the suicidal "laissez-faire policy" of the powers of Europe. The events in Turkey had blunted "the edge of feeling," turned back "the clock of progress," and threatened "the very foundations of civilization." Sympathizers took up special collections in churches, Sunday schools, colleges, societies, and mass meetings and sent the funds abroad, where Protestant missionaries and relief workers aided the unfortunate Armenians.[16] Among those engaged in relief work were such notable women as Frances E. Willard, president of the Women's Christian Temperance Union in the United States, and Clara Barton, guiding light of the Red Cross.

As accounts of the 1894-97 massacres received widespread attention, more missionaries from Canada, especially from the Toronto Bible College, felt compelled to go to the aid of their fellow Christians. Among Canadian missionaries assigned to Turkey by the American Board of Commissioners for Foreign Missions (ABCFM) were a good number of Scots and Scotch-Irish, mostly Presbyterians and a smaller number of Congregationalists: the Chambers family, Alexander MacLachlan, Miss Emily MacCallum, Frederick William MacCallum and his son Frank Lyman MacCallum, James P. McNaughton, and Mrs Mary Cameron Martin.[17]

"Our people," writes W.N. Chambers, "were North of Ireland stock in comfortable positions. My father's family possessed estates of considerable extent in Co. Tyrone ... While my parents were still young the families sought better conditions in Canada."[18] Rev. Dr Robert C. Chambers (1849-1917) was born in Oxford County, Ontario, educated at Queen's University and the Princeton Theological Seminary and ordained in 1870 in the Presbyterian Church. Nine years later, under the auspices of the ABCFM, he was assigned to Erzerum, where he carried out educational and evangelical work. In 1888 he furloughed in North America, where he lectured and wrote about mission work in Turkey. Returning to the field in 1891, he took up the post of principal of the American high school in Bardizag and of supervisor of the Bithynia district. After the 1894-97 massacres, Robert Chambers founded an orphanage for Armenian children and tried, unsuccessfully, to gain Canadian government support for an agricultural colony of Armenians in the Canadian West. His reports and letters, those of his brother, Rev. Dr William Nesbitt Chambers, and those of his sons, Dr Robert Chambers Jr and Rev. Lawson Powers Chambers, as well as those of other missionaries like Edward Carruthers Woodley in Marash and Ada (Moyer) and Thomas Ford Barker in Hadjin, sustained the sympathy and interest of their friends and congregations back home in Canada.

In 1915 their writings, sermons, and lectures took on renewed vigour as they continued to inform Canadians of the tragic upheavals in the Middle East. In 1916, Lawson Chambers explained to Canadians how religion was being manipulated to turn the Moslem population against the Christians. While Turkish rulers appealed to religious fanaticism, the real cause of the Genocide was economic and political:

The Armenians, by their genius for commerce and superior integrity and foresight in the conduct of affairs entrusted to them, readily acquire such positions of wealth and influence in Turkey as to arouse the jealousy and hatred of the Turkish officials ... The reason why the Young Turks now in power at Constantinople are not content to prune but desire to exterminate the Armenians is to be found partly in their belief that so long as there are Armenians left in the land the Powers of Europe will continue to make of the presence of Christians under Moslem rule a pretext for interference in Turkey's internal affairs. But while the interference of Europe has seldom if ever been single-minded, nevertheless it is not the presence of Christians in Turkey which has supplied Europe with occasions for interference, but the palpable inability of the Turk to manage his own affairs of which inability the gross misrule of his Christian subjects has been the most patent indication. In massacring the Armenians the Turk is not solving any problem but is merely killing off the most progressive element in the community.[19]

The Genocide was widely publicized in Canada and the United States.[20] Church periodicals and bulletins condemned the killings and sensitized readers to the crisis in Armenia. The *Canadian Churchman*, published by the Anglican Church of Canada, spoke of the Turkish government's "careful plan for extirpating Christianity all over Asia Minor and Armenia." [21]

Under the heading "L'extermination des Arméniens," *L'Action Catholique* described how Russian soldiers found 850 decapitated Armenian corpses in pits and wells. Canadians read regular accounts of such atrocities. The *Montreal Daily Star* reported that in every case orders for the massacres came directly from Constantinople. "In some instances local governors being humane, pious men, refused to carry out the orders and at least two governors were summarily dismissed for this reason." In addition to religion, observed the *Berlin (Ontario) Daily Telegraph* under the headline "Greatest Massacre of Modern Times," Turks hate Armenians because they are the real businessmen in the empire. "They are the most prosperous and progressive people in the country, and naturally the Turks envy them." The *Toronto Globe* published accounts of the Italian consul in Trebizond who, as we have seen, witnessed "thousands of innocent women and children placed on boats which were capsized in the Black Sea." In Montreal, *La Patrie*, under the headline "Le Martyre d'une race," wrote that "Les Turcs poursuivent avec un esprit diabolique la destruction de la famille arménienne en détruisant ses villages." "The Armenian slaughter," noted an editorial in the *Manitoba Free Press*, "makes the massacre of the Albigenses and Alva's cruelties in the Netherlands mere performances in the kindergarten."[22]

In May 1917 the Anglican Primate of Canada issued a letter asking the churches to organize relief drives for Armenians. Quoting the Archbishop of Canterbury, he said that the anxieties and sorrows in England "are dwarfed in comparison with the unutterable misery and devastation which has been wrought in the lives and homes of the Armenians." In the *Halifax Herald*, Canadians read a cablegram from Clive Marshall that, perhaps more than any other, captured the general attitude of Canadians regarding the political and religious underpinnings of the terrible events: the "definite occupation of Constantinople by the allied forces shows that the Beast of Turkish lust and cruelty, which the Germans loosed in 1915 against the Christian peoples of the Near East, has at last been brought to bay. The Gorilla is at bay, but not yet chained. Its hands are still dripping with the blood of new victims, and the Armenian massacres go on despite the fact that death penalties are being pronounced upon the Turkish officials who originally carried out the secret instructions of Berlin." Dan Smith's graphic drawing accompanying the caption shows a young woman being dragged off by a Turk, brandishing a sword. In the same year, news arrived of the military tribunals. The *Gazette* announced that Kemal Bey, the former Turkish minister of food, had been publicly hanged in Constantinople for his part in the Armenian deportations and massacres in the Yozgat region. The trial prosecutor summed up the view of many, saying "it was necessary to punish the authors of the massacres, which had filled the whole world with a feeling of horror."[23]

To co-ordinate the numerous relief efforts throughout the country, Canadian churchmen joined ranks in 1917 with businessmen and politicians to form the Armenian Relief Fund. The fund garnered an enthusiastic response from Canadians to raise money to meet the needs of survivors abroad. The fund was renamed the Armenian Relief Association of Canada (ARAC) in the 1920s, when it undertook to facilitate the entry of Armenian refugee orphans to Canada.[24] Headquartered in Toronto, the ARAC had branches in Kingston, Ontario, and Victoria, British Columbia, and enjoyed the patronage of His Excellency Lord Julian Byng, governor-general of Canada, the Most Reverend Neil McNeil, archbishop of Toronto, Venerable Archdeacon H.J. Cody, the Honourable Sir William Mulock, and Colonel Sir Henry Pellatt, and it enjoyed the official involvement of Mayor T.L. Church and Donald A. Cameron, manager of the Toronto branch of the Canadian Bank of Commerce. The Armenian Relief Association of Canada was the first public interdenominational, interethnic nongovernmental organization in Canada to assist refugees abroad and to help them migrate to Canada.

Taking up the cause in 1920, the *Toronto Globe* placed all the influence it could command at the disposal of the association in a campaign to raise funds to save the "far-away women and little ones from the tragic and terrible fate which is daily befalling them."[25] Other newspapers, such as the *Halifax Chronicle*, joined in the campaign, calling on "the rich and poor of all denominations and creeds." Appeals by prominent Canadians like Sir Robert Falconer, president of the University of Toronto, went out in support of the starving masses, wracked with disease and suffering from exposure, particularly during the severe winter in Armenia in 1919–20.

Each day for almost two months in 1920 in a column entitled "The Call from Armenia," the *Globe* published news from the stricken land where the remnant of the nation, "chiefly women and children, are surrounded by hostile Turks, Kurds, and Tartars, and face almost certain extermination this winter unless help on a large scale comes." With great emotion, the *Globe* appealed for aid:

Remember the Armenians. Save the Armenian children. Civilisation failed to save the Armenians from massacre. It should save the remnant from starvation ... The remnant of the race must be fed and saved. Christian powers dare not again stand idly by ... And the babies! What weak, pitiful cries they give! Is there no milk to be had, no way of saving even them?

There is one cry that touches the hardest heart and never fails to bring a response. It is the hunger-cry of little children. And nowhere in the world is it sounding louder to-day than among the cold, rugged mountains and on the bleak city streets of poor, stricken Armenia. Here is a nation that has fallen among thieves. Its people have been left stripped and bleeding by the wayside. The question therefore arises: Will it be possible for Canadians, like the priest and the Levite to pass by on the other side? Can they do otherwise than bind the wounds, clothe the naked body, and supply the life-giving food? How can they help acting the part of the good Samaritan toward this sister nation? The widows and orphans of a martyred people await their visitation.

The "despair of hundreds of thousands of hard-pressed women and children" whose "fathers, husbands and brothers died for the Allied cause ... touched the sympathy of a generous people. Where there is great suffering, great distress, the men and women of Canada are not passing by on the other side." Church groups, secular organizations, and individuals across the country responded to the "The Call from Armenia": the Woman's Institute of the Whitby Methodist Tabernacle sent $12.50; St Mary's Sodality (Roman Catholic) sent $50; Tom Mulcahy and his two little sisters sent $2 out of their banks; Mrs Hendrie from Hamilton contributed $100; the children and staff of the Home for Incurable Children in Toronto contributed $12.75; and N. Thompson of Huntsville sent $1. The response was widespread, disinterested, and spontaneous. Never before had Canadians responded so generously and so willingly to a call for help from abroad. They contributed over $300,000.[26]

Zaven, patriarch of Constantinople thanked Canadians for helping thousands of orphans and spreading hope to the "broken hearts" of the people. In their turn, Armenian Canadians, "with sincere and loving thankfulness," expressed their gratitude to "the noble response of our Canadian friends to the urgent call of the unfortunate and bleeding Armenia." The funds were forwarded to Turkey, where Canadians Dr Frederick W. MacCallum in Constantinople, Dr William Nesbitt Chambers in Cilicia, and Dr James P. McNaughton in Smyrna supervised the relief work in the field in cooperation with the Lord Mayor's Fund and the Near East Relief. The issue of relief from Canadians to the Armenian republic raises some questions, for although newspaper accounts described conditions in Armenia and although funds were raised ostensibly for the destitute in the struggling country, the money was instead sent to relief officers in Turkey, presumably to help refugees, both Christians and Moslems, in Constantinople, Smyrna, and Cilicia.[27]

Not only did Canadians raise funds for overseas relief, they also tried to bring pressure to bear on the government. As early as 1895, the *Presbyterian Review* exhorted its readers to seek justice for the persecuted brethren of Armenia. In an editorial, the *Review* reminded readers that to the church was entrusted "the weighty responsibility of holding the nations to their moral duty, and of arousing the public conscience when iniquity flares in the face of Heaven." The editorial bemoaned the inaction of the church in Britain. "There have been remonstrances [in Britain], but they were feeble; petitions, resolutions and an occasional demonstration there have been, but where has been the mighty voice of awakened British Protestantism? Where have been the burning eloquence, the public indignation, the marshalling of the moral forces which would have made the strongest government which Britain has ever seen tremble for its fate and which would have made trifling and vacillation impossible?"[28] In 1896, Robert Chambers, writing from Bardizag (Ismit) derided the "Great Weaknesses." "Christian sentiment," he lamented, "seems dead and buried in the gov't offices of the Christian Powers," where people seem to be "the slaves" of their political masters.[29]

Twenty years later Canadians were again reminded of "the bonds of humanity." They read about the services rendered by the Armenian forces in the Caucasian and Mesopotamian campaigns. In 1918, Lord Robert Cecil praised the Armenians for holding the Caucasian front (over two hundred miles long) after the defeat and withdrawal of the Russian army, for fighting the Turks for five months, and for rendering very important service to the British army in Mesopotamia. Armenians, he noted, also captured Baku from the Turko-Tatars and held it from March to July 1918, until the arrival of the British. "They have served alike to the British, French and American armies, and have borne their part in General Allenby's victory in Palestine. The services rendered by the Armenians to the common cause can never be forgotten." James Gerard, chairman of the American Committee for the Independence of Armenia estimated that approximately two hundred thousand Armenians had fought in the ranks of the Allied and Associated armies.[30]

Canadians were informed about the Allied promises to help create and sustain an independent homeland. In an editorial entitled, "Forlorn Armenia," the *Canadian Churchman* admonished Western powers for disposing of the Armenian question by "a disposal of the Armenian people." The Allies had pledged to deliver the Armenians from "Turkish misrule," but the promises were never kept.[31] From the press, the pulpit, and in public lectures, Canadians were reminded that the Allies had supplied Armenian volunteers with guns and ammunition after the Genocide began and encouraged them to fight, giving them assurances of a national homeland. Now, after a hard-won victory, to allow Turks to rule Armenians "would be to doom [them] for loyalty to our cause." Canadians protested against any move that might re-establish Turkish control over non-Turkish populations. Canadian newspapers called for an end to "this defiance of justice and inhumanity, this deliberate war of annihilation waged by the Turks against their own unarmed and helpless subjects ... Surely our young men have died in vain if such a Government is to be confirmed by the sanction of the Peace Treaty." Rev. Dr S. Dwight Chown, superintendent of the Methodist Church in Canada, issued a letter to Methodist congregations requesting that on 15 February 1920 formal protests against Turkish rule over Armenians be made in every congregation throughout the land and that an official report of this action be sent to imperial authorities in London. He urged other religious groups, universities, the Empire and Canadian Clubs, boards of trade, the Imperial Order of the Daughters of the Empire, and other organizations to "unite in a similar protest" in support of an independent Armenian state.

The governor general wrote about the strong sympathy in Canada for the Armenian people and the wish "to secure the maximum possible independence and protection for Armenians." In Turkey, Canadian missionary Lawson P. Chambers advocated that the Allied powers establish an Armenian state. His uncle, Rev. W.N. Chambers, who had saved many Armenians in Adana during the 1909 massacres and who was now Near East Relief director in Cilicia, recommended to successive American commissions the creation of a new Armenian state and the inclusion of Cilicia within that state. Responding to public feeling, the Canadian government passed an order-in-council opposing "the continuance of Ottoman sovereignty over the Armenian provinces" and expressed "the hope that in the negotiations for the treaty with Turkey, provision may be made for the emancipation of Armenia from Turkish rule" (PC 400, 20 February 1920). Canadians concerned about the future of Armenia read in the *Toronto Globe* that their government had informed the Allied Powers of "the intense feeling of Canadians that the Armenian Provinces should not be restored to Turkish rule ... there is no doubt that the Government feels its influence should be cast whole-heartedly in favor of Armenia."[32]

In 1920, even before the United States had rejected mandatory power over Armenia, a suggestion was put to Canada to undertake responsibility over Armenia "if financial and military guarantees were given by other nations of the League." Canada's commitment would be to set up an administration for Armenian affairs that was similar to the one established for the Saar Valley. In November 1920 another proposal was placed before Canada by the League Council: either on its own or jointly with other states to attempt to stop hostilities between Armenia and the Kemalists. The Canadian government declined these responsibilities. But in December 1920 Canada voted in the Assembly in favour of admitting Armenia to the League, one of only eight states to do so.[33]

As late as the summer of 1922, Canadians were still protesting against "the stain" on "our Empire's honour" for "having tolerated so long the injustice and vengeance of the Turk upon Christian minorities." In letters to the government and to the king, Canadians, perhaps naively, given the record of Armenia's wartime allies, urged "a speedy and fearless stand" against "the hand of destruction of the Turk." "Armenians are not receiving the protection which was pledged to them by Great Britain while they were fighting as her ally. This systematized savagery remains unchecked under the apathy of Christian governments." Congregations voiced "Canada's desire for the freedom of our heroic allies" and urgently requested "that the Government of Canada ... demands the fulfillment of our pledges to these victims of Turkish misrule, and of our inertia."[34]

The massacred Armenians, the needs of the starving remnant, the cause of "our little ally" so "shamefully betrayed" by her Allies aroused Canadian public opinion. Regardless of how sincere the appeals and impassioned the protests, the churches and other humanitarian groups were powerless. The Treaty of Lausanne was beyond their control. "An amazing tragedy," wrote Oliver Baldwin, was "taking place under the eyes of the League of Nations and rewarded by British recognition in the Treaty of Lausanne."[35]

ARMENIAN CANADIANS

Events in the homeland sent a chill through the hearts of Armenian Canadians. Not a single settler was spared the pain of losing loved ones or the agony of unmitigated helplessness and frustration. Harutiun Srabian, a young sojourner himself, recalled how "these men, these strong men, who were doing such heavy work [in the factories] started to weep like babies" when they first heard about the fate of their people.[36] Men "went crazy," "got drunk," despaired, mourned, yearned for death. By virtue of the fact that they were in Canada, some of the settlers were the only surviving members of their entire clan, often numbering seventy to eighty people. In the fury of a lightning bolt, they had lost the independent republic, their ancestral land in Western Armenia, their homes and their families – everything that was dear to them.

Gripped by tension and anxiety, the communities joined in Armenian fund raising campaigns to supply the freedom fighters with weapons. Individual men who earned twenty-five cents an hour in the hot and perilous foundries generously contributed one hundred dollars. In 1915 a campaign organized by the Hnchak chapters raised at least twenty-one hundred dollars in Canada for the war effort in the Caucasus.[37] Armenian Canadians held dinners and lotteries, staged plays and concerts, sold homemade fancywork, and in co-operation with non-Armenians organized Armenian Tag Days to collect money for refugee relief and rehabilitation. They listened to the news on the radio, assiduously read their Armenian-language newspapers, and sent protest letters to their members of Parliament.

They also fought for the cause of freedom. During hostilities, young men volunteered for Armenian regiments in the Caucasus, the Armenian Legion in Mesopotamia, or the Greek army in the Aegean campaign. Hnchak and Dashnak field-workers recruited volunteers throughout the diaspora. In St Catharines Armenians gathered in Setrag Mooradian's coffeehouse to hear the inspired field-worker [Pandkht] announce that the man who volunteered first would receive a pair of field binoculars. Parsegh [Percy] Mooradian proudly joined up first, followed by Mardig Der Varanian, Arshak Topoian, Nshan Dunoian, and Nshan Der Zakarian. After initial training in the United States, most of the Canadian recruits were shipped to the Caucasian front, often via Murmansk. Manoog Muradian and Parsegh Der Vartanian were two recruits who saw action in Cilicia and the Aegean. Meanwhile, 400 Armenians, about 10 percent of the Armenian community of France, joined another 1,172 volunteers from the United States to enlist in the Légion d'Orient in Palestine, set up with the assistance of Boghos Nubar Pasha in 1918.[38]

When war broke out, Armenian citizens of Turkey residing in Britain and in Canada were viewed as enemy aliens, but this classification was removed in 1915. A contemporary account estimated that about 100 Armenians enlisted in the Canadian Expeditionary Force.[39] In fact, at least 150 names were identified as Armenian in the CEF records, a number considerably more than 10 percent of the adult male population if we calculate the *total* Armenian population at that time to be approximately 1,500. If volunteers in Armenian regiments are included, the percentage of Canadian Armenians in allied forces is much greater. Of these 150 recruits, I examined a sample of 38 files, selected randomly. The files render such information as marital status, date and place of birth, name and address of next of kin, occupation, religion, weight, height, distinguishing marks, status (volunteer or draftee), health, gas and shell shock, pay, will, overseas or domestic duty, medals and badges, rank, battalion, illegal absences, desertion, and discharge.

The findings appear typical of any military cohort, including information about gas attack, shell shock, venereal disease, accidents, wounds, and illnesses like tuberculosis. A unique feature of the Armenian recruits, however, was their place of birth. Of the thirty-eight men whose files were studied, only one was born in North America, and he was a sixteen-year-old who was discharged as a minor. Of the remainder, one was born in Bulgaria, three were born in Russia, and the rest in the Ottoman Empire, primarily in the province of Erzerum, probably mostly in Keghi. Six of the thirty-eight were drafted and remained in Canada for the duration of the war, while thirty-one volunteered. Most saw active duty in England, France, or Siberia. Of the thirty-eight, one was a widower, six were married, and the remainder were single men. The majority gave their last address in Canada, specifically in southern Ontario (Brantford, St Catharines, or Hamilton). Approximately seventeen were likely Armenians from the United States who had volunteered for duty with the Canadian forces, reflecting once more, the fluidity of the Canada–United States border – for Armenians at least. Twenty-six men gave the name and address of a relative in North America as next of kin; the relatives were mostly, but not always, male, highlighting the predominantly family nature of migration. Two soldiers were killed in action overseas, while at least two died in battle-related illnesses. After discharge, four reenlisted in the British army, probably, as one volunteer put it, "for the purpose of fighting on the Eastern Front," i.e. against Turkey.

Among the first to enlist in the CEF were Bagharsak Baronian (14 August 1914) and Ohanas Vartanian (31 August 1914). Both men joined the first Canadian overseas contingent and both were killed in action in France in early 1915. Samuel Harry Chickegian (Sempad Harutiun Chichakian) also volunteered. Born in the village of Arek, Keghi, in 1899, Sam, and his mother and siblings migrated to Brantford in 1907 to join his father, who had immigrated via Rumania. A slight youth, weighing scarcely 115 pounds and under 5'4" in height, Sam enlisted on 5 June 1917. On 2 September 1918, roughly two months before the Armistice, young Sam was killed in action and buried in France. He was awarded the Memorial Cross.

Meanwhile, in Keghi, another eighteen-year-old youth who eventually made his way to Canada saw action of a different kind. When the villagers were being deported, his uncle pleaded with young Hagop (Jack) Kaprielian to flee to the mountains. The uncle, whose brother was sojourning in Canada, felt obliged to remain with the family to take care of the women and children. Escaping on his own, Hagop was apprehended by Turkish police and passing himself off as a Kurd, was commandeered into the Turkish army. After initial training, he was sent to the Russian front, and as soon as he could, he fled to the Russian lines. Unable to speak Russian, he kept crossing himself until a Russian officer brought an Armenian recruit to question him. "When I heard him speak Armenian, I started to cry. I thought I would never see an Armenian again. I cried so hard, I couldn't control myself." Hagop volunteered under Pandkht on the Caucasian front and later fought under General Andranik in Armenia.[40]

Such men and their armed struggles were intertwined with the fate of mothers and fathers, sisters and brothers, wives and children. As hostilities came to an end, each settler in Canada tried to save his surviving relatives by bringing them to Canada, far from the horrors of death marches, the poverty and despair of refugee camps, and the spectre of hunger and disease.

The killing fields of Keghi, near the villages of Koulakan and Chan. The Dersim Mountains are in the background. In 1948, the United Nations enacted the Convention on the Prevention and Punishment of the Crime of Genocide. The Genocide Convention defines genocide as "any of the following acts committed with intent to destroy, in whole or in part, a national, ethnical, racial or religious group": (a) killing members of a group; (b) causing serious bodily or mental harm to members of the group; (c) deliberately inflicting on the group conditions of life calculated to bring about its physical destruction in whole or in part; (d) imposing measures intended to prevent births within the group; (e) forcibly transferring children of the group. Photographer, Stacy Churchill, 2004

1st DEPOT BATTALION
1st C.O.R.

Killed in action

ORIGINAL

THIS MAN HOLDS NATURALIZATION PAPERS IN ORDER: ARMENIAN.

ATTESTATION PAPER.
48th Highlanders, C.E.F.

No. 2393367

Folio.

CANADIAN OVER-SEAS EXPEDITIONARY FORCE.

QUESTIONS TO BE PUT BEFORE ATTESTATION.
(ANSWER)

1. What is your surname? .... **CHICKEGIAN**
1a. What are your Christian names? .... **Samuel Harry**
1b. What is your present address? .... **128 Alfred St., Toronto, Canada**
2. In what Town, Township or Parish, and in what Country were you born? .... **Arek, Armenia**
3. What is the name of your next-of-kin? .... **Lucille Chickegian** 2 Carlton St
4. What is the address of your next-of-kin? .... **128 Alfred St., Toronto, Canada** St Catherines
4a. What is the relationship of your next-of-kin? .... **Mother**
5. What is the date of your birth? .... **April 15th, 1899**
6. What is your Trade or Calling? .... **Soda Dispenser**
7. Are you married? .... **Single**
8. Are you willing to be vaccinated or re-vaccinated and inoculated? .... **Yes**
9. Do you now belong to the Active Militia? .... **No**
10. Have you ever served in any Military Force? .... **No**
    If so, state particulars of former service?
11. Do you understand the nature and terms of your engagement? .... **Yes**
12. Are you willing to be attested to serve in the CANADIAN OVER-SEAS EXPEDITIONARY FORCE? .... **Yes**
13. Have you ever been discharged from any Branch of His Majesty's Forces as medically unfit? .... **No**
14. If so, what was the nature of the disability?
15. Have you ever offered to serve in any Branch of His Majesty's Forces and been rejected? .... **No**
16. If so, what was the reason?

DECLARATION TO BE MADE BY MAN ON ATTESTATION.

I, **Samuel Harry Chickegian**, do solemnly declare that the above are answers made by me to the above questions and that they are true, and that I am willing to fulfil the engagements by me now made, and I hereby engage and agree to serve in the Canadian Over-Seas Expeditionary Force, and to be attached to any arm of the service therein, for the term of one year, or during the war now existing between Great Britain and Germany should that war last longer than one year, and for six months after the termination of that war provided His Majesty should so long require my services, or until legally discharged.

Date **June, 5th, 1917** 191 .... (Signature of Recruit)
.... (Signature of Witness)

OATH TO BE TAKEN BY MAN ON ATTESTATION.

I, **Samuel Harry Chickegian**, do make Oath, that I will be faithful and bear true Allegiance to His Majesty King George the Fifth, His Heirs and Successors, and that I will as in duty bound honestly and faithfully defend His Majesty, His Heirs and Successors, in Person, Crown and Dignity, against all enemies, and will observe and obey all orders of His Majesty, His Heirs and Successors, and of all the Generals and Officers set over me. So help me God.

Date **June, 5th, 1917** 191 .... (Signature of Recruit)
.... (Signature of Witness)

CERTIFICATE OF MAGISTRATE.

The Recruit above-named was cautioned by me that if he made any false answer to any of the above questions he would be liable to be punished as provided in the Army Act.
The above questions were then read to the Recruit in my presence.
I have taken care that he understands each question, and that his answer to each question has been duly entered as replied to, and the said Recruit has made and signed the declaration and taken the oath before me, at **Toronto Canada** this **5th** day of **June, 1917** 191
.... (Signature of Justice)

N.B.—ATTENTION IS DRAWN TO THE FACT THAT ANY PERSON MAKING A FALSE ANSWER TO ANY OF THE ABOVE QUESTIONS IS LIABLE TO A PENALTY OF SIX MONTHS' IMPRISONMENT.

Attestation paper of Samuel Harry Chickegian (Chichakian). Shortly after he turned eighteen, Sam volunteered for active duty and was killed in action in France. Courtesy National Archives of Canada

Discharge paper of volunteer Hagop (Jack) Kaprielian from the first Cavalry Company of Armenian Special Forces in the Caucasus, dated 10 March 1919. His age is listed as twenty-six in this document, but he was actually twenty-two. Courtesy Hagop Kaprielian

Young Armenian survivors in an orphanage in Aleppo, early 1920s. Such photographs were sent abroad to prospective suitors in an effort to reestablish family life after the Genocide. The girls usually corresponded with the prospective groom, and when an agreement had been reached, the man paid for the passage to North America. Kaprielian Collection

Courtship photo of Kapriel Kaprielian sent to his bride-to-be in Aleppo, Syria, ca 1920s

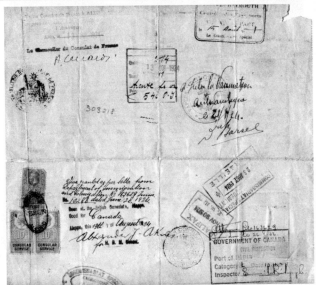

Front and back of a passport issued by French authorities in Aleppo, Syria, for a young refugee girl to travel to Canada to her betrothed. The reverse side shows the routes taken by refugees on their way to Canada. (Her name has been withheld according to her children's wishes).

Young picture brides with their first-born children, Hamilton, ca 1926. Like many couples, they had a child within a year or two after marriage.

Excerpt from an article about the founding and early endeavours of the Hamilton chapter of the Armenian Relief Society. *Hai Sird* (Armenian Heart), July 1960

The Georgetown boys express their appreciation to the Canadian people, ca 1925. For some of the children, Georgetown represented the first time they had a roof over their heads, proper clothes on their backs, and food in their stomachs. Their delight is revealed in the following excerpt from an interview: "Then on the second of July, 1926, about 6 o'clock, we got on the boat ... eight Armenian boys going to Canada ... We landed in Toronto on the second of August. Then they put us on a street car [radial]. Went right to the farm. Stop 69. We landed in Georgetown around 9:30. The minute we stopped we heard the band; music going. Oh we were happy! We wondered where we were! The rest of the Armenian boys met us at Stop 69. The Georgetown Armenian boys! Then they took us down to the farm building and they gave us a big feast ... I loved Georgetown. That was a better life than I ever had." Oral interview of Levon Vassoyan, taped by Jack Apramian, July 1979, Multicultural History Society of Ontario

QUESTIONNAIRE

8/21/33
C.W.

Name of Claimant ......
Occupation ....Labourer.............
Address Birch Beach Ave., (178)
City Hamilton, Province of Ontario.

QUESTION	ANSWER
1. Date and place of birth.	1884, in the Village of Charman, in the County of Kughey, in the Province of Erzerum.
2. British Subject by birth; if by naturalization give date and place and number.	Naturalized British subject, Jan.25, 1924------ No. 28595 Series "A" in the Town of Sandwich, Ontario.
3. Names, occupation and residence of parents or outbreak of war or date of death if prior to August 1914.	
4. Give full details of claim.	My father, mother, my wife Maro and my two sons my one brother Sarkis, his wife Annah and their one son. Two sisters both married and had several children--Mayram and Parus were all killed by the Turks. Property destroyed and valuables confiscated.
5. On a separate page give the following details of the property which is the subject of claim and state in what vilayet (Province) situated and name of nearest Village or Town.	Our property was situated in the Village of Charman, in the County of Kughey, in the Province of Erzerum.
(a) Land confiscated.	
(b) Total area in acres.	2 Houses, barns, stables, etc. and 200 acres of land.
(c) Area in cultivation in acres.	201 Acres.
(d) Area under timber in acres.	100 "
(e) Area of vineyards in acres.	10 "
(f) Area of orchards in acres.	
(g) Area of mulberry groves in acres.	
(h) Area of pasture in acres.	90 "
(i) Area of bush or scrub in acres.	
(j) Give the situation and area in acres of each piece of land and the names of: The registered owners of the adjoining land on all sides.	Names of the registered owners of the adjoining lands were: Megerditchian; Injaian; Navaian; Sarkisian; Markar Megerditchian.
6. In case of real property (buildings, land, etc.), how did you become owner?	By inheritance.
7. If inherited, from whom and when?	From my parents in 1915.

Questionnaire submitted in pursuit of reparations. This request for reparations was denied on the grounds that the applicant had not been a Canadian citizen before World War I. Such questionnaires are useful not only for the questions asked but, more specifically, for the information about the ownership of property and chattels in the old country by early Armenian immigrants to Canada. Name withheld to preserve privacy

PART FOUR

Refugee Entry into Canada, Rehabilitation, and Reparations

8

A Drop in the Bucket: Armenian Refugees and Their Entry into Canada

After the war Armenian Canadians tried to locate their dispersed surviving relatives and friends and to bring them to Canada, but their attempts were systematically and effectively thwarted by the Canadian immigration program. Engaged in developing and enforcing immigration policy and regulations, government officials compounded the racial, cultural, geographic origin, and work-related bases for exclusion prevalent in the prewar period by adding refugee status as grounds for barring entry. Statistics reveal the consequences of this multiple jeopardy. From 1920 to 1929 the following were admitted via ocean ports: 50,740 Germans, 40,676 Poles, 38,329 Jews, 29,960 Finns, 26,419 Italians, 13,997 Russians, 5,568 Chinese (before 1923), 4,140 Japanese, 3,148 Greeks, and 1,662 Syrians. From 1919 to 1930, when the Armenians were desperately seeking sanctuary, the Dominion allowed the entry of about 1,250 Armenians, considerably fewer than it had accepted from 1900 to 1914 and negligible by comparison with 80,000 taken in by France and almost 23,000 granted asylum in the United States, which had severely restricted entry from 1921 onwards.[1] As in the prewar period, Canadian exclusionist regulations played a fundamental role in controlling the entry of Armenians and consequently affecting the composition and size of the Armenian community in Canada.

The postwar immigration differed from earlier cohorts because it took place in a dramatically different global order. World leaders were obliged to wrestle with the thorny issues of the displacement and statelessness of millions of civilians, the sovereignty of nation-states, the rights of minorities and the rights of individuals, war crimes and crimes against humanity, and international humanitarian intervention. The movement of Armenians to Canada must be seen against the backdrop of human rights, Canada's treatment of stateless individuals, and the tensions between Canada's initiatives towards greater international participation and recognition, on the one hand, and national policy and isolation, on the other.

In the postwar period, Canada was extremely cautious about being drawn into spheres of international responsibility that might embroil the country in collective military action or entail heavy financial cost, and it was just as ill-disposed to international obligations that might in any measure diminish control over its borders. Prime Minister Mackenzie King's promise of "whole-hearted support to the League of Nations and particularly to its work of conciliation, cooperation, and publicity" may have included attempts to protect minorities abroad, to halt the traffic in women and children, and to curtail the international trade in drugs. It may well have included a willingness to assume the presidency of the League Assembly, to sit in the League Council, and to make financial contributions to the High Commissioner for Refugees. But it did not include cooperation with the League and its affiliates in the permanent resettlement of refugees. They were considered Europe's problems and Europe's responsibilities. Without going as far as the United States, which had rejected membership in the League and established a strict quota system for immigration, the Canadian government adopted an international stance and pursued immigration practices that rested on similar premises. All along, the Canadian government rejected the principle of individual rights and freedoms, specifically the individual's right to safety and security. "It is not," emphasized Mackenzie King, "a fundamental human right of any alien to enter Canada. It is a privilege."[2]

REFUGEES

Most Canadians were touched by the depth of human suffering, as shown in the numerous humanitarian efforts to help the refugees abroad. But public reaction to Armenian refugees also revealed a complex and ambivalent attitude towards refugees in general, an attitude combining pity with anxiety and compassion with suspicion. Some Canadians were hardened to the view that suffering reflected divine punishment, in effect another way of blaming the victim that was summed up in the words of an Ontario farm wife: "If the Armenians had been really God fearing as well as God worshipping, I do not think they would be in their present circumstance."[3] Ironically, just a few years before, Armenian women had thrown themselves into the Euphrates River for the sake of their faith and honour and Canadian newspapers had regularly reported starvation and murder.

As recipients of international charity, moreover, refugees were often viewed as the beggars of the world, the poorest of the poor. Frederick C. Blair, superintendent of immigration, underscored the economic condition of refugees whose "lack of ability to finance themselves either for passage or settlement" involved "an advance of funds on the part of the Canadian Government" in "any scheme of assistance." Disregarding government assistance to British emigrants, adjustment difficulties of thousands of voluntary immigrants, and help offered by Armenian Canadians, Blair discouraged the admission of refugees, contending that "A refugee coming to our shores naturally would have to be housed, fed and found employment [by the Government] or become permanently a public charge." Those, like Blair, who viewed refugees as burdensome drains on resources failed to appreciate their varied background, their spirit of survival, their talents, skills, and potential contributions. True enough, refugees were impoverished victims of circumstances; but under normal conditions many could and would again become carpenters, farmers, lawyers, doctors, and teachers. But, like his colleagues in the Immigration Branch, Blair doubted whether refugees would be other than "a permanent problem to Canada if their admission could be arranged."[4] During the 1920s Blair and his colleagues did everything in their power, considerable by any measure, to block the admission of Armenian refugees.

To Arthur Turner, a Hamilton barrister working on behalf of refugees, Blair revealed his unwillingness or at the least his inability to understand the mentality of an uprooted nation. Worse still he disseminated a totally false concept of the Armenian case: "Canada cannot possibly offer a solution to Armenia's troubles and anything we have done or could do, is but a drop in the bucket. Tens of thousands of Armenians are in distress. If Canada offered an open door, we would have all who have money to move, and our cities would be literally overrun with these unfortunates."[5]

This reasoning amounted to refusing help to a starving man on the grounds that such assistance would be unfair to others suffering the same fate. It was also misleading to imply that Armenians expected Canada to carry the burden of "Armenia's troubles" or that Armenians sought "an open door" to Canada. While it is true that some refugees wished to join family in Canada, the main aim of many survivors was voluntary patriation to an independent homeland. In the uncertainties of the postwar period, Armenian leaders were hopeful that the international political situation would stabilize according to

Allied promises made to them during the war. They encouraged the survivors to stay together in the Middle East in the cherished hope of imminent patriation to a free state protected by their allies. Even after Armenia's allies abandoned her to the double onslaught of Russian and Turkish aggression and even after the Treaty of Lausanne, Armenian leaders continued to oppose large-scale dispersal, especially of orphan children. Scattering the people, they believed, would inevitably lead to the extinction of the Armenian nation, thereby completing the scheme of the Young Turks.

Following the war, many Canadians believed that immigration should be controlled.[6] The prospect of the world's needy, the misfits of devastated Europe, political malcontents, and racially undesirable aliens flocking to Canadian shores evoked images of contamination and race suicide. Although Canada did not establish a quota system like the one operating in the United States, the government, nevertheless, effectively barred "undesirables" by promulgating laws that were "framed and applied with the object of making easy the entry of those classes and races suited to, and required for, the settlement and development of Canada, and preventing the admission of those mentally, morally, industrially or otherwise unfit." The ideal classes and races were farmers, farm labourers, and domestics from the "preferred" countries: Britain, the United States, and northwestern Europe. As a second choice, Canada filled her immigration needs from "nonpreferred countries," i.e., from southern, southeastern, and eastern Europe. On the bottom rung were the "undesirable races," specifically, non-Europeans. In addition, the unfit classes included urban dwellers, paupers, criminals, anarchists, and mental and physical defectives.[7]

As for refugees, no specific Canadian laws governed their entry during the 1920s. No concept of a shared responsibility to help the downtrodden overrode exclusionist immigration policy and practice. Authorities recognized the "humanitarian reasons" that called "loudly for help" but steadfastly held that Canada was not in a position to offer a home to the distressed of the Near East, whether adults or orphan children. Accordingly, Armenian refugees were admitted only if they complied "in the fullest possible way" with existing regulations governing all immigrants, notably the passport regulation, the Asiatic classification, the money qualification, the continuous journey ruling, labour qualification, and family reunification. As an additional precaution, instructions from the departmental deputy minister, William John Egan, forbade "any special privileges for the refugees."[8] In other words, officials were not to relax any of the regulations. In their turn, politicians generally sanctioned the activities of senior civil servants but tempered the harshness of exclusionist policy with a tinge of compassion.

PASSPORTS

For Armenian refugees one of the most exacting regulations was the passport ruling. In the early part of this century, more and more states were extending control over their borders by issuing national passports. By this means, governments could regulate entry, transit, and exit and could coordinate the national labour market. Inevitably, the passport became indispensable for travellers. In addition to easy and certain proof of identity and nationality, it gave the holder diplomatic protection and assistance. The passport facilitated establishing a domicile in the country of immigration and drawing up official documents, such as birth certificates, for the immigrant and his family; it enabled the holder to enter into labour or other contracts and to qualify for social, economic, and medical assistance. Finally, the passport allowed the holder to return to the state that had originally issued the document.

The impetus for the requirement that travellers to Canada carry passports appears to have come initially from a wish to use such documents as a means of exclusion. Well before World War I, Canada recognized the growing importance of the passport and passed legislation requiring immigrants, especially those classified as "undesirables," like Asians, to show bona fide passports.[9] Control over the entry of "undesirables" was gradually extended to others. In 1923 the government passed Order-in-Council 1885, which stipulated that immigrants were to be "in possession of a valid passport issued in and by the Government of the country of which such person is a subject or citizen, such passport to be presented within one year of the date of its issue." As an additional safeguard intended "to weed out as far as possible the unfit at port of embarkation," immigrants from countries other than the British Isles and the United States were obliged to have their passports visaed abroad either by a Canadian consular officer or by a British officer in countries without Canadian diplomatic representatives.[10]

An important reason for insisting on a bona fide passport was the right of returnability or deportability. The Canadian government reserved the right to return or deport any immigrant classified by Canadian officials as undesirable. Political activists, especially those involved in left-wing movements, criminals, or public welfare recipients – the ill and the indigent – were subject to deportation and could be returned to the country of citizenship as indicated on the passport. Insisting on the possession of a bona fide passport for voluntary immigrants could be justified on many grounds, but requiring a refugee, stateless by definition, to carry a bona fide passport seemed deliberately exclusionist. Promises by Armenian Canadians to sponsor and support the refugees so that they would not become public charges met with the response that "this is a very uncertain quantity because the relative may die or lose his money or move away and if he does any of these, the security disappears." An interviewee well understood the grounds for rejection in the 1920s: "We were refugees. We were children without a homeland ... we were stateless. Without a country. I received a letter from Ottawa turning me down. As refugees we were forbidden from entering Canada." He was one of the fortunate ones who eventually received permission to rejoin his surviving siblings in Canada – thirty years later.[11]

For Armenian refugees seeking entry to Canada, acquiring a passport was a problem aggravated by the stipulation that it should be issued by the country of citizenship. Although some Armenian refugees came from Persia or Russia, the majority were originally from the Ottoman Empire. To comply with Canadian regulations, they were obliged to arrange for passports from the very Turkish authorities from whom they sought escape. Return to Turkey was extremely dangerous; survivors still in that country were being murdered or driven out throughout the 1920s.[12] After the Soviet Union and Turkey gobbled up the Armenian republic, thousands of Armenian survivors of the 1915 massacres found themselves once again under the hostile authority of Turkish rule and were obliged to evacuate their domiciles once again. Throughout 1922 columns of refugees were trekking towards the congested refugee receiving centres in Syria, Lebanon, and Russian-occupied Armenia. In keeping with the policy of ridding the country of minorities, the Turkish government under Mustapha Kemal prohibited their return to their homes. Turkish authorities confiscated Armenian property and bank accounts and proscribed the return of those with Turkish passports by stamping these documents with "Il ne peut pas retourner," thus complicating even further the question of returnability.[13]

Syria/Lebanon had taken in approximately one hundred thousand Armenian refugees. By the terms of the Treaty of Lausanne (1923) and by decrees issued by the French High Commission in the Levant in 1924 and 1925, Armenians who had established themselves in the mandated territories before 30 August 1924 acquired nationality as an absolute right upon relinquishing their Turkish citizenship. It was reported that in 1925 alone, by application of the Treaty of Lausanne and Decree 2825, thirteen thousand Armenian refugees had opted for Lebanese nationality.[14] Armenian refugees also acquired passports issued by Persia and, for a time, by the independent Republic of Armenia. Year after year, more and more Armenians complied with the passport ruling but Canadian officials found still other grounds for obstructing their entry.[15]

NANSEN PASSPORT

Legal problems surrounding passports assumed a new international dimension after 1918, when millions of refugees were roaming Europe and Asia. In order to deal with this crisis, the League of Nations convened an intergovernmental conference in July 1922 that under the leadership of Dr Fridtjof Nansen, established international travel documents, first, for refugees from Russia (1922), then, for Armenian refugees (1924). The identity certificate was issued annually and not only stated the holder's identity, nationality, and race but also provided him/her with some freedom of movement. With this document, known as the Nansen passport, the holder could move from one country to another to work or to rejoin family members. Regardless of its efficacy, however, the Nansen passport did not replace a national passport, because it did not give the holder the right to return to the country that issued the document without a special provision to that effect approved by the issuing state.[16]

An intergovernmental conference held in 1926 defined an Armenian refugee as "any person of Armenian origin, formerly a subject of the Ottoman Empire who did not enjoy or who no longer enjoyed the protection of the Government of the Turkish Republic and who had not acquired another nationality." The principal elements of definition were statelessness (apatride) and the deprivation of protection, with the additional proviso that the person must be outside his country of origin or citizenship. Individuals in such circumstances were an anomaly in an international order where issues of rights, nationality, and protection were becoming more stringently defined and more regularly enforced.

Canada steadfastly refused to recognize the Nansen passport for all refugees on the grounds that although it established race and nationality, it did "not allow the return of the refugees to the state which issued the certificate." If European states wanted Canada to offer relief by taking some of the refugees," officials argued, "they in turn must be prepared to assume responsibility for the return of the misfits."[17] Such a position may have seemed "unassailable," but events showed that it was little more than a pretext to bar refugees.

During the 1920s and early 1930s, the problem of returnability was being resolved as more and more issuing states recognized the right of return. T.F. Johnston, assistant high commissioner for refugees, emphasized that in Greece, Nansen passports were issued only to those

Armenian refugees who were mentally and physically fit, who complied with the agricultural or domestic work regulations, and who had obtained a five-year return visa from the Greek government.[18] Considering that Greece had given asylum to at least forty thousand Armenian refugees and perhaps as many as one hundred thousand, League officials hoped that Canada would cooperate in giving sanctuary to specially hand-picked survivors. These expectations were unfulfilled, and Armenian refugees, struggling to survive in impoverished Greece, continued to face obstructions. As a case in point, a boy who had escaped to Greece under the protection of the Near East Relief Mission and who had obtained a prepaid ticket from his uncle in Canada and a "laissez-passer" (Nansen passport) from the Greek government on the approval of the League of Nations Representative faced rejection on the grounds that he carried an invalid passport.[19] Time and again Johnson assured the Department of External Affairs that all refugees recommended by the Refugee Service for transfer to Canada were qualified with practical agricultural experience and were in possession of visas granting returnability for a period of five years. No applications, he emphasized, regardless of country of domicile, were submitted on behalf of refugees who wanted to proceed to Canada "unless they have obtained not only the return visa in question, but one valid for five years."[20]

As more and more states indicated their willingness to affix a five-year visa to the Nansen passport and thereby to accept *within* five years the return of a refugee classified as undesirable in Canada, government officials shifted their ground by insisting that if the cause of deportation occurred *within five years of entry*, refugees could be deported later on. "The Nansen Passport," insisted Blair, "must be valid for the return of prohibited immigrants the cause of whose deportation arises within five years after entry." Thus, if a refugee became a public charge or a political radical or was otherwise deemed undesirable any time after acquiring Canadian naturalization, he would be liable to deportation if it was found that the cause of his undesirability had arisen during the first five years of his residence in Canada. The right of return was being twisted to place unlimited responsibility for refugees on countries of first asylum, on charitable organizations like the Near East Relief, and on international agencies like the League of Nations, even if Canada supported these organizations financially and morally. Equally serious, the right of return was being perverted to impose different values on Canadian naturalization. It placed naturalization granted to refugees in a category inferior to and more stringent than that granted voluntary immigrants.

MONEY QUALIFICATIONS

In 1923, the Canadian Government passed Order-in-Council, Privy Council Order 182, which prohibited the entry of any immigrant of the Asian race except bona fide farmers, farm labourers, or domestics and the wife or child under the age of eighteen of any person legally admitted to and resident in Canada who was in a position to receive and care for his dependents. All Asiatics who could not comply "in the fullest possible way" with these immigration regulations were to be barred from Canada. As with exclusionist laws passed before the war, the main intent was to keep out Orientals from the Far East. In the prewar period, civil bureaucrats had classified Armenians as Asians. Despite vigorous and persistent Armenian objections to and arguments against the racial classification, immigration authorities steadfastly held their course.

Before 1914, all Asians – men, women and children – were obliged to show $200 landing money at the port of entry, supposedly as a means of guaranteeing against immigrant "public charges." In fact, the regulation provided "a ready means of excluding those who are clearly undesirable." After the war the amount was raised to $250, a formidable, if not an impossible, sum for refugees.[21] The amount required for their entry is best understood in the context of information then available to Canadians. The *Toronto Globe* described how two hundred thousand Armenians were in famine's grip in Kars and Alexandropol. Conditions in the refugee camps were so severe, the report continued, that starvation and disease would destroy the surviving remnants of the Armenian nation. In Syria, refugee orphanages were under armed attack, and orphanage personnel were unable to protect the children. Neither the conditions of the refugees nor appeals on their behalf succeeded in having the money qualification waived. On the contrary, it was a source of some satisfaction that rigid application of this law would contain the movement to only "the few wives and children" of legal residents.[22]

FAMILY REUNIFICATION

Family reunification was a basic principle of Canadian immigration policy. Armenian Canadians, classified as Asiatics, were legally permitted to bring in only their wives and children under eighteen. The separation from loved ones – mostly women and children – who were in dire straits in refugee camps, receiving centres, and orphanages caused immeasurable suffering for Armenian Canadians. A young woman, for example, tried in vain to bring in her younger sister whose subsequent death from pneumonia at the age of twenty-five left her with a gnawing guilt for the rest of her life: had she tried hard enough to help her sister? Her attempts, no matter how determined, had been pitted against a bureaucracy that, on the one hand, upheld the principle of family reunification and, on the other, refused to "offer relief to many whose relatives are in Canada."[23] Departmental records indicate how another applicant was obliged to seek the assistance of a lawyer and member of Parliament to enable his wife and orphaned seven-year-old niece to join him in Canada. When government officials resisted the efforts of this naturalized Canadian subject, William Elliott, a member of parliament, vented his anger and frustration: "It seems to me that the Department is doing everything in its power to hunt up excuses to keep these people out of Canada, but for the Department to refuse the entry of the wife and child of a naturalized Canadian subject is beyond my comprehension."[24]

Aware of the ramifications of family reunification, officials opposed the entry of unaccompanied minors who might act as "anchors" for surviving relatives. In 1923 the Armenian Relief Association of Canada concluded negotiations with the government to facilitate the movement of one hundred Armenian orphan boys to live and work on a farm/home/school in Georgetown, Ontario, before being sent out as foster children or indentured workers on Ontario farms. Some of the boys managed to locate surviving family members, and when they tried to arrange for their admission to Canada, the ARAC was compelled, in response to bureaucratic pressure, to limit all further movement to orphans who had no other family members "whose admission to Canada [might] be applied for later."[25]

One such boy, who tried to bring in his mother, was Kegham Babigian (George Mooradian), who in 1926, at the age of twelve, was sent out as a labourer to an Ontario farm. "The dear little man," wrote his foster mother, "is quite intent in having his mother and taking care of her." After visiting the boy in his foster home, G. Bogue Smart, superintendent of juvenile immigration, reported that Kegham was "a very tender hearted lad" who cried when he spoke about his mother and asked whether his mother could come to Canada. Kegham's mother, meanwhile, was in Istanbul in good health, with savings of about three hundred dollars and anxious to come to Canada to join her son. She was prepared to work hard, and she looked forward to the day when they would "have a little house of our own, under the Union Jack and be happy." Rev. Ira Pierce, the liaison between the boy and the ARAC and, subsequently, the United

Church of Canada, promised to do "everything in my power to bring your mother to Canada, and I think perhaps it will be possible. Certainly I would like to see her given back to you. May God bring your mother to you, is my sincerest wish." Hopeful that she would join her son soon, Kegham's mother wrote, "At last my son our prayers were heard so now we are drawing near to the great day when we shall meet again and be happy and serve God as He hath served us." Kegham continued to beseech Pierce "not to disappoint my mother, my dear mother who is anxious to hear that few words (Come over to Great Canada to this great country, for the way is open to you)." In early 1930 he was anxiously waiting for the "precious words" and stressed that his mother was "willing to come and work hard and do her duty well." In 1931, in response to continued appeals, Frederick C. Blair, superintendent of immigration advised that if the boy wanted to reunite with his mother, "he should join [her] overseas." At the age of twenty, Kegham died of tuberculosis in Canada, still pining for his mother.[26]

THE CONTINUOUS-JOURNEY REGULATION

The continuous-journey regulation, another constraining law, had been on the statute books since 1908, and after a stormy beginning, particularly with respect to East Indians, had remained an effective barrier to the entry of unwelcome classes and races. Lacking even a pretense of any justification for the welfare of the state, the continuous-journey regulation conveniently provided authorities with the discretionary means of rejecting "all classes of people who on general principles may be considered undesirable." Under its terms, immigrants were obliged to come to Canada by continuous journey from the country of which they were natives or naturalized citizens using a through ticket purchased in that country or prepaid in Canada. Driven from their homes, Armenians had taken refuge in any country that would grant them asylum. They had fled to Egypt and Ethiopia, to Palestine, Syria and Persia, to Greece and the Balkan states. For them to comply with the continuous-journey regulation entailed a return to Turkey, with all its attendant dangers. But to attempt movement to Canada from a country of refuge meant outright disqualification and rejection. In 1921, when Armenian Canadians appealed for a one-year reprieve from this regulation because of the "present distress" of their people, the minister rejected their petition because it would then be "impossible to defend the application of the same regulation to other races and nationalities."[27]

LABOUR REQUIREMENTS

In his report of 1923, the deputy minister of labour underscored the government's policy of linking immigration with the country's labour requirements – in particular with the need for farmers, farm labourers, and domestics. In cooperation with the two national railways, the Department of Immigration and Colonization expanded the areas of recruitment for agricultural families to countries previously designated as "nonpreferred," i.e. the countries of eastern and southeastern Europe. The department's efforts, however, regardless of the extent of government assistance and concessions, did not produce the desired effects. Prospects did not indicate that the agricultural labour requirements would be fulfilled, for "it was found that these immigrants were not staying on the land but were drifting to the cities and were interfering with the Labor market."[28] So serious was the shortage that farmers and farm labourers of the "Asiatic race" were legally permitted admission provided they could comply with the other regulations stipulated in the Immigration Act. If they were agriculturalists or domestics coming to follow one of those occupations in Canada and holding either proper evidence of employment or sufficient capital with which to farm for themselves, Asians would be allowed to enter the Dominion. Under such conditions the government could "offer much more considerate treatment" than it had "on account of unemployment conditions prevailing here."[29] Thus heartened, Armenian Canadians arranged for jobs as farm hands and domestics for their relatives and friends abroad.

They were discouraged to learn, however, that officials became increasingly more preoccupied with the work they themselves were doing than with the type of work the newcomers would be undertaking. Armenian Canadians were reproached because they had not shown "any disposition to engage in agricultural pursuits," "even against their own personal inclinations." If they would farm, government officials might be encouraged to admit labour "to assist them," and to "arrange for a reasonable number of ... relatives from Armenia to assist ... on the land." It is uncertain whether these terms, stated in a departmental memo, were ever offered to the Armenian community. If they were, the initial date, recipient, and terms are unknown. The failure of the old-timers to settle on the land demonstrated to Blair and his officials, either that they were "not disposed to engage in farming in this country" or that they were "not particularly anxious to help their fellow countrymen in a practical way."[30]

Granting Armenian refugees permission to enter the country on condition that the earlier cohort take up farming had serious implications, for authorities were usurping their role as civil servants. The position taken by bureaucrats implied that they were assuming the right to dictate the employment of naturalized Canadian citizens or at least residents of long-standing on the basis of their ethnic origin and employment. Such a role was an abuse of power that would presumably never have been tolerated or attempted for any group of citizens who had immigrated in the "preferred" class.

Because the majority of Armenian Canadians clustered in urban centres, worked in factories, or operated stores, officials predicted that the newcomers would undoubtedly migrate to the same places, engage in the same endeavours, and inevitably add to the congestion and unemployment in the cities. On such grounds, officials denied a request to facilitate the entry of Armenian farm workers: "Judging from our past experience it would mean that at the end of six months they would all be in the cities looking for something to do for the winter."[31] Past experience, however, did not substantiate such views. As far back as the turn of the century, as we have already seen, groups of Armenian farmers had been denied admission to Canada. The precedent having been set, the response was the same in 1923 when a group of young Armenian men, with education, agricultural training, money, and a knowledge of English requested guidance in purchasing farm land: "We have never strongly encouraged the immigration of people from the Near East in the belief that they will farm in Canada. The style of farming to which they are accustomed is so different to the farming in this country that they cannot be looked upon as having any experience of much value to them."[32] With these words the bureaucrats hit on the lack of Canadian farming experience as still another means of rejection. They scoffed at the success of Armenian agricultural colonists in Syria and Lebanon. As a further insult, they credited the success of Armenian farmers in the San Joaquin Valley in California to the favourable climate, omitting to mention the problems of early frost or unseasonal rains and the difficulties of irrigation. Farming in Canada, they insisted, was as different from farming in Turkey as night was from day and, indeed, as Armenian was from English. "Whatever experience they [might] have had in farming in their own country," they argued, "would be little or no use to them in farming in Canada." Officials went so far as to claim that farming was "an absolutely foreign field" to Armenians.[33]

An Ontario farmer pleaded with the government that he "would accept an Armenian if you can't send us any better as we are completely tied up for help and will have to sell if we don't get more hired help. We would be glad to get anyone who could even clean out stables and do a few chores and could teach him more as we went along."

Blair responded by cautioning that Armenians "have no experience in Canadian methods of farming" and are unacquainted with English. Because "their fellow countrymen in Canada do not farm, we have hesitated to encourage this movement in the belief that it would be better to get farm help from other countries, such as the Mother Country, Holland, Belgium, France and Scandinavian countries, where farming is carried on much as it is in Canada." In an attempt to quash a scheme to supply Ontario farmers with Armenian farm workers, Blair offered the farmers "help before spring." The following month he was obliged to write: "I cannot at the moment get you the kind of man you want at $200."[34]

Aware of the government's priorities and desperate to help their families abroad, some Armenians and their friends took to the land at considerable financial risk. When Rev. Movses Der Stepanian bought a hundred-acre farm near St Catharines and requested the admission of his family to help him work the property, he did not receive "favourable action," because his adult children could not comply with the passport regulation. Men like Rev. Der Stepanian had acted in good faith and found themselves criticized by a senior official who objected "to making Canada a sort of third rate prison and forcing people who have no desire or intention of farming, to make a pretense at that occupation solely with the object of being allowed to enter our gates."[35]

Although the majority of the pre-1914 cohort of Armenians worked in factories, many created a complex strategy for survival by combining factory work with farm work, just as they had combined farming with other forms of business in the old land. Oral interviews indicate how foolhardy and impractical it would have been to jeopardize seniority at the factory for poorly paid and seasonal farm work. But if they were laid off at the factory, they frequently took up farm labour as a means of staying off the dole. In general the men could not afford to buy large tracts of land. But some, particularly in Brantford and in the Niagara Peninsula – around Grimsby, Vineland, and St Catharines – lived frugally and saved their factory wages for several years to buy farmland, parcel by parcel, acre by acre, without government assistance and without the benefit of an organized land scheme. In an effort to hold on to their land or to purchase more, some men worked on their farm from spring to fall and in the factory during the winter, while others used the farmhouse as a boardinghouse or converted a front room into a small shop. Such initiatives were dismissed by a division commissioner who mocked "the few acres of ground" that were being cultivated.[36]

The same disdainful attitude was applied to a group of about seven families from the region of Van who had settled in Galt, established a colony in the Owen Sound area in Ontario, and carried on farming during the 1920s until the Depression forced them off their farms and back to Galt.[37] None of these endeavours could convince bureaucrats that Armenians did in fact engage in farm work, nor could the indentured and paid agricultural labour of the Fegan's boys and of the boys from the Georgetown farm/home/school in Ontario demonstrate that Armenians were contributing to the country's agricultural development. Officials continued to cast a blind eye and an unwilling hand on Armenian entry.

RACE

For Armenians the most incomprehensible policy remained obstruction on the grounds of Asiatic classification. Even though they admitted that Armenians were not, strictly speaking, of the Asian race, government officials argued that the category of race was a geographical rather than a racial or ethnological term. Since most Armenians came from Asia Minor, they were required to be classified as Asiatics.[38] Yet the question of geography and race took on a different perspective for others, as indicated in the assistant deputy minister's comments: "The difficulty of making a Regulation apply without naming the people to whom it applies was sought to be overcome by the use of the term 'Asiatic race.' Had we used the term 'Asiatic countries,' then it might have excluded persons of British race, so-called, born in Asiatic countries." Ten years later, his views had not changed: "Canada, in accordance with generally accepted practice, places greater emphasis upon race than upon citizenship."[39]

To be identified in either geographic or racial terms seemed bizarre to Armenians, for they had always been identified in religious terms. They were proud to have been the defenders of Christianity since AD 301. For centuries they had faced persecution because of their religion. Now, at a critical juncture in their history, they were being discriminated against because of a racial categorization – and by a Christian country, at that. Armenian Canadians considered their Asiatic classification to be a mistake and could not understand why the Canadian government – benevolent and civilized – considered them Asians, "like the Turks."[40]

It is baffling that Armenians did not challenge the Canadian categorization in the courts, considering the landmark victory of Tateos Cartozian in the United States in 1925, which touched on the controversial issues of genetics, race, and social Darwinism. In *United States v. Cartozian*, the American government attempted to cancel Cartozian's certificate of naturalization on the grounds that he was not entitled to naturalization, since he was not "a free white person." In dismissing the case, Judge Wolverton emphasized that Armenians were of Alpine stock and of European persuasion and had migrated to Asia Minor, that they were "white persons," and that they "amalgamate readily with the white races, including the white people of the United States."[41]

To those classified as Europeans, the Canadian government offered more favourable terms with respect to the money qualification, to occupation, and to family reunification. Europeans, for example, were allowed to bring in their parents, unmarried children of any age, and unmarried brothers and sisters. European Canadians could also participate in the "nomination scheme," which allowed them to sponsor a relative in the old country provided they gave a guarantee of agricultural work, accommodation, and support. Senior civil servants opposed reclassifying Armenians as Europeans, claiming it would mean the repeal of Privy Council Order (P.C.) 182 – the regulation curtailing the entry of Asians – would signify a change in immigration policy, and would open the door to a "fairly generous" immigration of other "undesirable" elements. Armenians repeatedly emphasized that they did not seek the abolition of P.C. Order 182, simply a reclassification of Armenians as Europeans under P.C. Order 183.[42]

When Minister of Immigration and Colonization Robert Forke seriously considered relaxing some of the restrictions, senior departmental officials "immediately raised the question as to what we would do about Syrians and others," and further worried, with good reason, that reclassifying Armenians as Europeans "would open the door to the charge that many of the rejections of the past under P.C. 182 had been illegal" – arguments they were to use again twenty years later (see chapter 17). Using his prerogative as minister, Forke instructed his staff to allow Armenians to bring in relatives under P.C. 183, provided the applicants were Canadian citizens and the intending immigrants carried proper passports and could comply with the relationship arrangements under P.C. 183. Apparently Armenians were not notified of this concession, for there appears no evidence that at this time Armenians knew about the change of intent.[43] Only fourteen Armenians were admitted from 1929 to 1930.

As early as January 1928 the minister had expressed the view "that we might change our minds about the Armenians being of Asiatic race and hold that he comes under P.C. 183." It took a further two and a half years of advocacy to override departmental objections. On 3 September 1930, under the newly formed Conservative government of Prime Minister Richard Bedford Bennett, a circular was forwarded to immigration inspectors noting the instructions of the immigration minister, Wesley Ashton Gordon, that Armenians and Syrians were no longer to be classified as Asiatics and were to be dealt with under the provisions of P.C. 183. It was a typical case of too little, too late. By this time, in view of the economic conditions in Canada stricter controls had been imposed on European immigration as well. Stricken from P.C. 183 were clauses allowing the admission of bona fide farm labourers, female domestics, fathers, mothers, unmarried sons or daughters eighteen and over, and unmarried brothers or sisters of Canadians, as well as persons satisfying the minister that their labour was needed. Therefore, the reclassification of Armenians, desirable as it may have seemed, did not effectively relax the criteria for entry of Armenian refugees at that time. On the contrary, because of the discontinuation of the special permits issued by the minister, it could be argued that Armenians were in a worse position than before. Such permits had introduced the practice of lobbying on behalf of individual immigrants and had encouraged applying pressure on the minister through members of Parliament, business interests, lawyers, and various immigrant aid organizations. The use of such permits had provided a slim shaft of hope for Armenian Canadians intent on saving their relatives and friends.[44]

On 16 September 1930, the government passed P.C. 2115, which excluded all Asiatics from entering Canada, except for the wife and unmarried children under eighteen years of age of a Canadian citizen legally admitted to and resident in Canada. This regulation replaced P.C. 182 (1923), which had given some occupational leeway to people of Asian race by allowing the entry of farmers, farm labourers, and domestics. By 28 October 1930, Armenians were again classified as Asians and fell under the narrow constraints of P.C. 2115. During the two crucial months when they were classified as Europeans, only two Armenians entered by ocean ports.[45]

The rescue of Armenian refugees had been blocked at a time when the Canadian economy was enjoying periodic healthy surges (1924–29), when farmers were begging for farm hands, when the Canadian government was actively recruiting immigrants, when continental European immigration increased from 394,378 during the first decade of the century to 429,086 from 1920 to 1929, and when Armenian refugees were desperate to escape from refugee camps and rejoin their family and friends in Canada.[46] To keep out Armenian survivors, senior bureaucrats like Blair and Egan demanded meticulous adherence to the rules, arguing that "We are safe in administering the regulations, but not in ignoring them." Conceding that Armenians had suffered "as no other race in the present century," government officials confessed that they "do not rigidly enforce the regulations for any other class unless for Chinese." So effective were senior officials in thwarting the admission of Armenian refugees that they could deplore the "more than a few" who had slipped in despite "the precautions taken by the Department." Summing up the department's position, J. Obed Smith, superintendent of emigration for Canada in London, England, highlighted the "unassimilability" of some classes. Certain types and nationalities "do not succeed in Canada," he wrote, and are not considered desirable immigrants. "By this it is not exclusively meant that the people themselves are undesirable, but that their conditions of life, their training, and their ability preclude their finding employment of a satisfactory character in Canada, and this is why there has been no attempt to propagandize in Russia, Greece, or Asia Minor, and indeed all approaching Canada from these countries must necessarily submit to the stringent regulations that are in existence."[47]

ARMENIAN REFUGEES

Labelled "unassimilable" and "undesirable," i.e., culturally unassimilable, Armenian refugees were further disadvantaged because they did not have a powerful organization working on their behalf in Canada, notwithstanding the efforts of the Armenian Relief Association of Canada. Most Armenian Canadians were factory workers and not well off, especially since many had been remitting money to their families in the old country before the outbreak of war and to survivors long after the war was over in Europe. Comparatively recent arrivals, they were inexperienced in and unfamiliar with Canadian ways and lacked the sense of security, language skills, and solidarity that was required to deal effectively with the federal government. As sojourners, the settlers had not built a church, the one institution that might have provided the leadership necessary to raise funds, rally the small and dispersed communities, and win widespread Canadian support. Their organizations, too, were ineffective as lobbying agents in Canada, because they were oriented to the turbulent events in the old country: the punishment of Turkish war criminals responsible for the Genocide, compensation for confiscated property and bank deposits, the rehabilitation of refugees, the restructuring of Armenian community life in countries of refuge, the peace treaty deliberations, and, most notably, the creation and fall of the independent Armenian republic. Nor did Armenian Canadians create an effective and representative organization specifically designed to intervene with the government on behalf of potential immigrants and to assist in their resettlement. While it is true that the Armenian Immigration Association in Galt and the Canadian Armenian Union, founded in Toronto, tried to bring about change, these associations were too small and too powerless to bring heavy pressure on Canadian authorities.[48] Seen from an international perspective, furthermore, the Armenians could not rely on a single state, not even a parent-state, to mediate through diplomatic channels for the refugees. Even Britain, to whom Armenians had looked as an ally, turned its back on its former partner. In short, Armenian Canadians possessed no negotiating strengths in their dealings with federal authorities. Senior officials did not miss the weakness of the Armenian lobby and brushed aside individual Armenian attempts to help beleaguered compatriots: "As practically all the agitation comes from one source, viz. from Mr. Amirkhanian, there is no sufficient ground for changing the regulations."[49]

As an additional precaution to keep out Asians and refugees, officials often pushed their powers beyond "administering the regulations." Too often they pursued their mandate as civil servants in a manner that strained the limits of the exclusionist intent of both policies and regulations. When, for instance, Armen Amirkhanian, the young spokesman, referred to the French government's willingness to issue passports to Armenian refugees in Syria and Lebanon, the assistant deputy minister's response was as subtle as it was inaccurate: "It is apparently hopeless to have Mr. Amirkhanian realize that we have gone to the source of the rumours that the French Government is giving valid passports to Armenians and we know it to be false. There are many thousands of Armenians in France. They are regarded there as refugees and are living there on sufferance, having no claim to French nationality."[50] Blair cleverly obfuscated the issue of refugees in France and those in French mandated territories, even though he well knew that Armenians in Syria and Lebanon were receiving bona fide passports issued by France. In her study of the Immigration Department's handling of deportees, Barbara Roberts found that senior bureaucrats stretched and ignored the department's own rules. They "violated the letter and the spirit of the law, routinely concealed their activities behind bureaucratic reporting procedures, sometimes falsified statistics, and, when necessary, deliberately and systematically lied to the public and the politicians."[51]

Unquestionably, senior administrators used their extensive discretionary and day-to-day operational powers effectively to influence policy, to formulate and enforce laws, and to twist rules and regulations to suit their private prejudices. Their entrenched position was all the more powerful because they could sustain their role over long periods of time and bring considerable knowledge, experience, continuity, and pressure to bear on successive ministers and politicians. Yet without a fundamental understanding and agreement on priorities and values between politicians and senior civil servants, their power might have been curtailed. As a case in point, the decision by bureaucrats in 1908–9 to classify Armenians as people of Asiatic race received tacit consent from successive ministers. In the last analysis, it was the politicians who governed the country, and even though Blair and his colleagues were powerful, they were civil servants accountable to the elected representatives. In a democracy like Canada, the prime minister and his cabinet are ultimately accountable to the people for government policy, and in the end, they must shoulder the responsibility for the treatment of Armenian refugees.

Politicians could, if they chose, override bureaucratic opposition, as the following case demonstrates. A seventeen-year-old refugee girl stranded in France faced rejection because there was "some doubt" whether she was the child of the applicant, because she did not possess a bona fide passport, and because her father was unable to raise the one thousand dollars that had been requested as a bond. In his memorandum Blair elaborated on his exchange with the minister, who believed the man, a naturalized Canadian, should be given "the benefit of the doubt as to relationship and allow the girl to come in." Concerned about setting a precedent, Blair continued to argue against the girl's entry. But the minister decided that "the girl being a daughter, in good health coming to join her father ... should be allowed to come in on compassionate grounds ... even if some difficulty arose later he thought we would still be forgiven for having allowed a refugee child in good health to join her father, a naturalized citizen of Canada." Denying sanctuary to Armenian refugees was a political decision and fell into the same category as changing the racial classification by a stroke of Minister Gordon's pen.[52]

ARMENIAN ENTRY INTO CANADA

During this period, no regulations facilitated the entry of refugees qua refugees. No separately formulated policy governed decisions concerning refugees. No differential immigration standard existed to deal with compelling humanitarian need. Rather, a pervasively discriminatory attitude towards refugees linked together decisions taken either at the bureaucratic or at the government level. For Armenians, past events had already shown that refugeeism was tantamount to rejection. I have already noted how, after both the 1894–96 and the 1909 pogroms in the Ottoman Empire, the number of Armenians allowed admission to the Dominion declined dramatically.

About 1,250 Armenians received permission to enter Canada from 1920 to 1930. Many were obliged to fulfill every legal requirement for

Armenians Entering Canada via Ocean Ports

Year	Number	Year	Number
1920–21	85	1926–27	65
1921–22	70	1927–28	44
1922–23	59	1928–29	17
1923–24	486	1929–30	14
1924–25	304	1930–31	21
1925–26	85		
Total			1,250

Note: See also *The Report of the Royal Commission on Bilingualism and Biculturalism*, book 4, *The Cultural Contribution of the other Ethnic Groups*, 1969, 240.

immigrants. But other refugees who were unable to comply with the stringent laws were admitted to Canada on compassionate grounds. They were allowed to land with special permission by the minister, acting within his powers to grant concessions to meritorious individuals incapable of meeting the provisions. The most notable instance of ministerial prerogative was invoked in 1923, when the government waived regulations pertaining to passports, money qualifications, and the continuous-journey requirement for one hundred Armenian orphan boys.

The experience of Armenian refugees demonstrates, on the one hand, the complex relationship between political clout and admission on compassionate grounds, and, on the other hand, it focuses on an important initial step, albeit a small one, in the adoption of the principle of humanitarianism in immigration/refugee policy. The government's humanitarianism was sufficient to grant asylum to 1,250 survivors of a genocide that left hundreds of thousands of Armenians homeless and at least 1.5 million lost.[53] Still, by setting aside the regulations and accepting Armenian refugees on compassionate grounds, the government went a step further than it had gone at the beginning of the decade when it donated twenty-five thousand dollars to the League of Nations for Armenian relief *overseas*.[54]

The postwar refugees may be divided into two major groupings. The first was a contingent of about 165 orphan boys and girls sponsored by non-Armenian associations and admitted under the agricultural or domestic labour category. At the forefront of these organizations stood the Armenian Relief Association of Canada, the organization that arranged for the immigration of Armenian orphan boys to a farm/home/school near Georgetown, Ontario, and of Armenian girls as domestics in Toronto.

In a letter to the ARAC in 1922, Prime Minister William Lyon

Mackenzie King clearly set forth his government's priorities. Responding to a request for subsidized passage from the port of sailing to temporary homes in Canada for two thousand Armenian orphan children, the prime minister stated the government's position. Immigration policy aims to encourage movement to Canada from the British Isles, northern Europe, and the United States, he said, since they are "the countries whose peoples are likely to be the best adapted to our country and most readily assimilated with our own." The Canadian government contemplates bringing to Canada "numbers of young boys and girls [from Britain] between the ages of eight and fourteen to work in rural districts in different parts of Canada." Canada, he continued, owes her first obligation "to the children of English, Scotch, and Irish parentage who have been rendered parentless or destitute as a consequence of the late war. There can be no question as to the character of the contribution to our population which these children are certain to make."[55] The government turned down the request for subsidized passage for the Armenian orphans. In case there might be any question about priorities, the number of Armenian orphan children finally permitted admission plunged from the requested two thousand to a token one hundred orphan boys.

Among the supporters of the ARAC and its work were Canadian missionaries in the Ottoman Empire. In 1922, shortly after the conflagration in Smyrna, Lawson P. Chambers sought British cooperation in arranging for the movement to the British dominions of Armenian refugees in imminent danger in Constantinople. Writing to the British high commissioner in Constantinople, Chambers pleaded on behalf of the refugees, who "are by no means all of the poorer or the undesirable classes. Many were wealthy and educated and are refugees through force of circumstances. With Asia Minor practically closed to Armenians and Greeks and with Europe crowded with refugees, threatened with epidemics, and a prey to a disturbed economic situation, it would be a welcome act of humanity for the British Dominions to offer their hospitality to these unfortunate refugees, the majority of whom would be most desirable immigrants."[56] His attempts to organize such an immigration plan, like the attempts of his father, were thwarted time and again, but his persistent efforts on behalf of Armenians, which were similar to the efforts of other Protestant missionaries, no doubt carried some weight in convincing Canadian government officials to allow the movement of the orphan children.

The second group of refugees included all others and consisted of sponsored relatives or friends of Armenian Canadians immigrating either as family members or fiancées of the old-timers or as farm labourers or domestic workers sponsored by the prewar settlers.

Armenian refugees who were accepted complied with the rules pertaining to mental and physical health, morality, criminality, and literacy, and all were politically acceptable, since Armenians had fought alongside the Allies during the war. The refugees came from all parts of the Ottoman Empire, and although they were originally from every socioeconomic class, they were now reduced to poverty and destitution. According to Immigration Department statistics the two most active years were 1923–24 and 1924–25, probably reflecting the stringent quota system imposed in the United States, as well as some success by relatives and friends in helping refugees comply with Canadian immigration requirements. The immigrants were mostly young and largely women and children. Of 304 arrivals in 1924–25, 159 were women, 61 were men, and 84 were children. Of 90 women who entered from 1925 to 1928, 53 were between the ages of eighteen and twenty-nine. Newcomers were destined mainly to central Canada; 249 of the 304 who entered in 1924–25 headed for Ontario. One hundred and eighty-four of the 486 who entered in 1923–24 came in under the farming category and 120 came in as female domestic workers. Of the 61 men who entered in 1924–25, 46 entered as farmers and 4 as labourers. None of the 21 arrivals in 1930–31 were classified as illiterate.[57]

Naturally enough, the government's policy of restricting Armenian immigration had an impact on the Armenian Canadian community. Because such a small number were allowed to enter, the size of the Armenian community in Canada remained minuscule. The government's preference for farmers, farm workers, and domestics limited the number of Armenian entrepreneurs and professionals entering the Dominion. As a result, community development occurred without the talents, expertise, and leadership of the merchant and professional classes. Most tragically, family formation and structure were distorted for generations. Families that had been fragmented by the Genocide were further fragmented by Canadian immigration policies and regulations and by their implementation.

In the end, the small pre-1914 Armenian cohort carried the heaviest responsibilities in helping their needy countrymen and women. Despite the absence of a powerful lobby to plead their case with officials and politicians, despite the absence of regulations to facilitate entry, and despite tough opposition among civil servants, a small group of Armenian Canadians – about 1,500, managed to bring in and care for roughly an equal number of kith and kin. The extent of their success represented a testimonial not only to their personal commitment, determination, and sacrifice but also to their industry, generosity, and sobriety.[58] They sent funds abroad for the upkeep of their relatives in countries of asylum, helped finance their passage to Canada, provided them with the required $250 landing money and put up bonds for them, sometimes as much as three thousand dollars. In keeping with a tradition of mutual assistance, they helped the newcomers find jobs and lodgings and assisted them in adjusting to Canadian life. It is to their credit that in his prodigious correspondence, Frederick Charles Blair, superintendent of immigration and later director of the Immigration Branch, was never able to gloat over a single case of an Armenian public charge. In their turn, the refugees who entered Canada considered themselves saved. For them the Dominion represented a haven of liberty, progress, peace, and civilization – the exact antithesis to the brutality and violence that had tormented them in Turkey.

9

Refugee Resettlement in Canada: The Early Years

"When I put my foot on Canadian soil, when I saw that pure white snow, I fell in love. I loved Canada then and I still love this country."

V. Lalazarian[1]

In the lightning stroke of a lifetime, the Genocide had left a nation and a people wounded and dispersed. Men, women, and children who had once belonged to a family, a clan, a congregation, a town were now homeless and stateless. Their trauma could not but affect their psyche and their collective strength. What triumphs could they possibly achieve that would comfort their suffering? What happiness could dim their losses? What joys could allay their fears? Those fortunate enough to be admitted to Canada during the 1920s felt saved. Newcomers formed a heterogeneous group from various walks of life and from diverse parts of the Ottoman Empire. They differed in age, education, socioeconomic background, and geographical origin from the prewar settlers they joined. Reflecting the pattern of survival, the majority were women and children.[2] Of a total of 1,277 Armenians who entered via ocean ports and via the United States, 309 were men, 310 were children, and 658 were women.[3]

Like many other newcomers, the refugees arrived with limited means. They set about trying to meet their basic needs: to find a job, seek out shelter, establish a stable lifestyle. Like other immigrants they encountered problems with a new language and strange customs. They had to learn to deal with an unfamiliar way of life that was itself changing rapidly: industrial development, movement from farms to cities, a growing and diverse population, and increasing urbanization. Unlike most voluntary immigrants, however, the refugees were obliged to build everything up again from nothing, for they had lost much of what was dear and meaningful to them. No contact was easy for them, either in their private life, within the Armenian community, or in the Canadian environment. Everything had to be resurrected from nothing.[4] For people who had been reduced to "nothing," renewing life and reestablishing order required strength and perseverance, all the more so since they often had to cope with poverty and prejudice as well.

Displacement, flight, loss, and incarceration in concentration and extermination camps, refugee camps, or orphanages – all characteristics of the genocide/refugee experience – had a profound impact on how the newcomers coped with life in the new society. Gender, age, and point in the life course at the time of the tragedy and at the time of arrival played a critical role in refugee rehabilitation: the normal development of adolescence might be disrupted, perhaps irreparably; a young woman might become sterile because of an unsanitary miscarriage during flight; an older woman might lose her children and be past the child-bearing stage in her life; a man who lost his fortune might feel too old, too tired, or too intimidated to start over again in a new society; another might be unable to cope with his wife's or daughter's rape.[5]

As the initial excitement of entering Canada wore off and as the fear of deportation or return vanished, other issues began to churn in their hearts and minds. All immigrants must cope with disruption in their life course. Even newcomers who are motivated and well prepared and who encounter the most receptive circumstances experience a measure of distress initially. For the refugees, the usual stresses of transition were heightened by the harrowing circumstances of their expulsion, the years of deprivation, and the double-pronged process of rehabilitation and adaptation. For survivors, the heaviest burden was loss: loss of home, culture, religion, country, and, most devastating of all, loss of family. Mourning lingered on for years, especially for those who had been unable to bury their dead, who had been separated inadvertently from a sister or brother left in their care, or who had witnessed violence against a family member. Many agonized at not knowing where their loved ones were or if they were alive at all.[6] A "survival guilt" haunted many refugees, particularly those who had been unable to protect and defend their kin. Day after day, night after night, they were tormented by the gnawing questions, Why me? Why was I saved? Is my anguish punishment for the effrontery of having survived? Some found it hard to enjoy the blessings of a new land and suffered a lifetime of anhedonia, or an inability to enjoy life.

Each survivor grieved in a different way. Some steadfastly suppressed the memory of the atrocities, while others never stopped talking about them. Some survivors were filled with the desire for revenge while others were burdened with guilt. With bitterness, some questioned their faith: What did our people do to deserve such treatment? How could God do this to us? Are we so cursed? Or they would cry out, God has given us this tragedy, why does He not give us the solace and strength to bear it? Some resigned themselves to destiny: Such is the will of God; such is the fate of the Armenian people. Others, perhaps more militant, might never lose a sense of anger and indignity and might pass on to their children a commitment to change the course of political realities.

All Armenians, both refugees and old-timers, were conscious of a lost homeland and a culture in disarray.[7] They were afraid of losing themselves as a people and a nation. For some, the Armenian Soviet Socialist Republic became the centre of national revival. Others could see Soviet power only in the light of the occupation of the land and the suppression of the language, church, and culture. Regardless of their views, they believed that all survivors, as remnants of a persecuted people, were the crucible and the well-spring of national rebirth and revival. To them fell the enormous responsibility to sustain the spirit of patriotism, to nurture Armenian culture, and to pass on their legacy to their children, lest it disappear altogether.

What were the foundations on which they could build? For many refugees, perhaps for most, the only knowledge of their language, customs, and culture were learned not in family and community surroundings but in orphanages. Their role models had not been mothers and fathers, aunts and uncles, but orphanage helpers, teachers, doctors, nurses, missionaries, and clergymen. Most of the young refugees carried, at best, a disrupted and disjointed culture. Brutally cut off from the conventions and traditions of their homeland, the survivors treasured the fragments of their culture and refused to allow their ethnic and religious identity to slip away.

Most Armenian refugees were young and looked with hope to the new challenge in a new land. They had learned survival skills in a world torn asunder, and they were anxious to start again in a land of peace. They had come, moreover, from a society where the only predictable thing was life's unpredictability. Even before the Genocide, Armenians had lived in a world of insecurity and instability, for who could predict what pogrom, what violence, what exploitation would strike on the morrow?

Fortunately, they could face the new challenges in a safe environment. Gradually their fears were replaced by a sense of security and eventually by a profound feeling of loyalty and gratitude to Canada. In their new-found paradise, they tried to learn English and to familiarize themselves with Canadian ways. They pledged allegiance to the Union Jack and tried to learn the national anthem, "God Save the King." The new arrivals also found comfort and support in the fledgling Armenian community. Those who had immigrated before the Great War had already established the framework of a pioneer society and had begun to adjust to Canadian life. They cushioned the shock for the refugees who were thrown up against the unfamiliar conditions of the urban working class in Canada. The old-timers embraced the refugees, assisted them, wept with them, married them, taught them their Keghi traditions, values, and customs, and shared with them their "Canadian expertise." The old-timers and the refugees – wounded and scarred by events in the old country – joined forces to conquer adversity and to fashion a new place in a new land.

A large number of refugees were sponsored by the prewar settlers as relatives, friends, domestics, farm labourers, or picture brides. The second major group was sponsored by nongovernmental organizations and included just over one hundred young boys who entered under the auspices of the Armenian Relief Association of Canada (ARAC). The children were settled on a farm/home/school near Georgetown, Ontario, and later sent out to Ontario farms as foster children, or indentured or paid farm labourers. The association also brought in about forty young women as domestics in Toronto homes. In addition, Mr Fegan's Homes sponsored as farm help about fifteen teenage Armenian boys who had originally been sent to England for farm work.

The remainder of this chapter will examine the early adjustment of the picture brides and will finish with a very brief account of the unaccompanied boys, popularly known as the Georgetown Boys.

THE PICTURE BRIDES

With the destruction of the social and cultural bulwarks that had sustained the Armenian nation, survivors found themselves in unstable and chaotic circumstances. They met these challenges by calling up pre-Genocide practices and traditions or by creating totally innovative responses. Like other forms of social behavior during and immediately following the Genocide, marriage patterns wavered in a state of flux. Arranged marriages, including long-distance arranged marriages, which had largely been a response to male migration, were rooted in tradition. Such practices took on new relevance under drastic new conditions as they became entangled in the pragmatic need for a dispersed people to reestablish family life.

Armenian and non-Armenian newspapers and tracing agencies and a far-flung informal network served to reunite families and to bring together eligible men and women. The story of Haiganush Ergatian, one of the fortunate ones, reveals how convoluted the process of family unification could be. Driven from her native Keghi, Haiganoush struggled to eke out an existence as a weaver in the city of Mardin for seven and a half years. Fortunately, a relative in Aleppo, Syria, saw an advertisement about her submitted by missionaries to a newspaper. He contacted a fellow villager in Detroit, Michigan, who in turn brought the information to her husband at his restaurant in Guelph, Ontario. Immediately, her husband sent a cheque for five hundred dollars to the relative in Aleppo and instructed him to take all necessary measures for his wife's immigration to Canada. The relative arranged with the Red Cross to bring her to Aleppo, where she spent another seven months with a village acquaintance until her papers were in order and she could emigrate to Canada.[8]

Bachelors and widowers in North America and survivors in the Mediterranean, the Middle East, and the Caucasus sought each other out. Their motives were as varied as the actors and actresses themselves: a man might not search for his pre-Genocide wife, preferring, instead, a young survivor; a refugee girl might marry a Canadian just to get out of the orphanage or to get to North America, regardless of the social and emotional cost; another might marry in the hope of bringing her surviving family members to Canada "to save them."[9] However diverse their motives, marriage was their immediate goal. Marriage was also on the minds of orphanage personnel, for as the orphanages began winding down in the 1920s, administrators were anxious to ensure that the girls had someone "to look after us." Their practical concerns led them to encourage orphan girls to marry strange men in distant lands. As for criteria, it seems that men selected girls who were pretty, healthy, young, and docile.[10] Then, they might consider family background and genocide experiences, particularly abduction and rape. Girls, on the other hand, seemed to prefer men who were well-off, had a good job, and could provide for them. Naturally, it was crucial to be certain each was single. Because of the disruption in Armenian society, the Armenian church insisted on an oath from both partners, above and beyond the normal vows, that they were not married or that as far as they knew, their spouse was dead. Such was the extent of the upheaval that even this precaution did not prevent cases of bigamy.

Through the auspices of intermediaries – usually friends, relatives, or acquaintances – men and women in places as distant as Brantford, Ontario, and Aleppo, Syria, were linked up. In the pre-Genocide society, individuals, usually women, had acted as matchmakers, but in the post-Genocide period everyone became a potential matchmaker: a woman chose a mate for her son and brought the girl to Canada with her; a man selected a bride for his village compatriot; a girl arranged for a friend to marry her brother; a man travelled to Marseilles to choose his prospective wife picked out by the cousin of a friend from a shipload of refugees who had landed in this French port city the previous day.

Before the Genocide, marriages arranged between families had not been unusual. After the Genocide, the prospective groom or his proxy requested the girl's hand in marriage from an older surviving relative, preferably, but not always, a male. Often the arrangement was finalized without the girl's consent or at best with her reluctant approval. Female compliance in arranged marriages, already a well-established tradition among Armenians, was intensified by the desperate situation of these young women in orphanages and refugee camps. Poet and novelist David Kherdian, writing about his mother's engagement, describes how as a fifteen-year-old, his mother was asked by her aunt whether she wanted to get married. She did not know what to reply, for it "wasn't my place to approve, or disapprove … I found myself blushing, not knowing what to say, or even understanding what it was I was feeling … I was speechless … terrified!" Her "suitor" was in the United States but his mother, like her a refugee in Greece, had entered into negotiations with her aunt: "Nothing was said at first, and by the time I had gone out, made Turkish coffee and returned, it [the engagement] was already settled. Of course, I couldn't speak, nor did anyone speak to me. It was all very official and proper, and I wasn't included in the negotiations."[11] Another interviewee confirmed the submissive role of the young girl. When asked whether she had been consulted regarding her marriage, she replied, rather ruefully, "Who would ask me? I had a photo taken. Sent it to him. There was no exchange of letters. Just an agreement. I was engaged at nineteen."[12]

More usually in such long-distance arrangements, the couple corresponded, exchanged photographs, and made preparations for the girl's travel. The following excerpts from letters give a sense of the delicacy of some of these relationships; the first is a letter from Canada to a young survivor in Aleppo, Syria, and the second is her reply. The man, a labourer in a factory, had written to his sister-in-law's aunt in Aleppo to choose a suitable mate for him, "an old-fashioned girl with traditional values." He wrote:

Although this is my first letter to you, it will not be considered out of order. Naturally we do not know each other personally, but through my friends and the picture you sent, we know each other a little. Based on that fact I dare to write this letter to you. Of course the matter is clear, that is why I write unabashedly. I believe you have received my photo and you have also given your consent to be my life's companion – faithful and obedient. Is that right? I have received your photo consenting to be my fiancée. I love you and I am keeping your photo in my right pocket. We are joining our fate and destiny to each other, and as our pure hearts are joined together, we must know each other well. I am sure I will find in you all the qualities that I have hoped for. I know that you are an unattached person; as for me, I was married in my homeland but during the devastating world war, my family was all killed. Naturally, my friends have talked to you about me, and told you all the details.

She replied:

You have expressed your intentions, and now I would like to write about my wishes. Like you, I too do not value riches but I do value love. So far, I have not been through much suffering and I hope I will not be in the future but if I do experience difficult times, I will consider it my fate and I am ready to accept whatever is God's will. I ask for love only. You understand that I value love a great deal ... I must also tell you that I am not so experienced in these matters. I have written this much so that you would not worry. My family urged me to write this letter. Do not fret, I am not like other girls, I will keep my promise [to marry you] ... By the time I read your letter [to his friend requesting the name of a suitable girl for him to marry] my father and mother had already given you their consent, so I accept their decision and I hope with God's will we will not regret the decision and our wishes will be fulfilled ... Forgive my poor writing. I wrote it in the dark, secretly. You too must write secretly. It is shameful. You know, in the past I used to jeer at others saying that they got engaged by writing letters to each other. Dear, if I have written anything improper please forgive me, because I am not experienced in such matters.[13]

Such tenderness in courtship letters resonates again and again. In another set of letters, the girl and man start with very formal salutations, Highly Respected Miss _____. Over the period of a year, while they are making preparations for her transoceanic travel, the salutations evolve to Dear Miss _____ and then to the more endearing My dearest sweetheart. The contents of the letters change too and reveal a growing affection, perhaps even a fine thread of passion, as their destinies become more entwined.

Both men and women faced risks in such transoceanic relationships, but the perils were especially great for young, inexperienced girls, whose vulnerability was highlighted by the general absence of family protection, community guideposts, and the social controls of the pre-Genocide period. People tried to find a safeguard in the extensive networks to vouch for the intended spouse and to pass along pertinent information, but this strategy was not always effective or even possible. Thus, a poorly educated or illiterate person might seek out the services of an articulate acquaintance to write his or her letters or refer to an *Armenian Letter-Writer* guide book.[14] In such cases, the contents and style would not be a true reflection of the individual himself or herself. At the same time, both men and women were known to cheat about their ages, their experiences, and their wealth and/or to send outdated or touched-up photos. H.H. Kelekian, in his short story "Crossroads in Wasteland," describes how wealthy Baron Hagop sent an old picture of himself to the orphanage and the administrators convinced beautiful young Anna to marry him. The only "advantage" for her was that some day she would be a rich, young widow, for Hagop had contracted venereal disease as a young man in America. Unfortunate Anna not only married a sick old man but was deprived of having children, the one bright light in the lives of many picture brides.[15]

Once the couple had agreed to marry, the prospective groom was obliged to obtain permission from government officials for his fiancée's entry into Canada. Government decisions regarding fiancées were inconsistent and arbitrary. If Canadian authorities admitted the girl, the prospective groom paid for his fiancée's passage to Canada and sent her money for clothes and maintenance en route and for the $250 landing money. Once the preparations were made, the young woman would embark on a journey that would seal her fate forever. If the groom-to-be was unsuccessful in arranging her entry, he might try a number of other strategies. One man might gather up all his savings and borrow from friends to make the long voyage to the Middle East, marry in the country of first asylum, and return to Canada with his wife. Another might meet his betrothed in Marseilles, Lyons, or Paris, important refugee centres, and, using the services of representatives of the Armenian republic and the Armenian church, arrange for a hasty wedding abroad and the necessary papers for her admission to Canada.

For the picture bride, the trip itself could be fraught with danger. Swindlers were lying in wait for unwary travellers. In one such case, a dishonest travel agent asked a young refugee "to wet the paper." His demand for money under the table was totally misunderstood by the unsuspecting girl, so she failed to negotiate her passage to North America. Bribes and long waits could double the cost of the trip; and fraud in accommodation arrangements could make travel insufferable.

The voyage to freedom, moreover, could take a refugee far afield, as in the case of a woman who, having survived the attacks on Bitlis, fled with her son, travelled for months across Asia, and finally reached Japan. In Yokohama, Diana Agabeg Apcar, the philanthropist who had established a colony for Armenian refugees at her own expense, helped the woman and her son arrange passage to Oregon, New York City, and eventually to Hamilton, Ontario, and her husband.[16]

Aside from the vagaries of the journey, most young women were filled with a mixture of relief and trepidation for what lay ahead, as the following account reveals:

After the Genocide, my aunt and I went to Marseilles. My mother and father had been killed. We had no relatives. We had no one. I was 18 or 20 years old. I worked in a biscuit factory and my aunt found a job somewhere else. There was a big hotel in Marseilles; we were all refugees there. Hotel de Lyons. The owner was not Armenian but there were Armenian agents who helped the refugees. Another refugee woman was coming to Canada to join her husband in _____. She lived in the same hotel and she saw me. She told me she was going to take me to America and asked for my picture. Then my husband-to-be saw my picture and sent me money and said he was arranging my passage. Well, this is my luck. I decided to come. When you are alone and when you have no choice and there is someone who will look after you, what can you do? And he was Armenian. You say, "this is my luck and you throw yourself in." There were several of his country people who knew him and they told me he was a fine man and came from a good family. I came from Le Havre on an English ship. First class. One thing I was afraid of – that there might be cheating. It happened that the man would send a picture of himself taken years ago. I left myself in the hands of God. When I came, I saw the house; it was old but clean. The store was clean and all the fruit were set out in a neat and clean fashion. I saw him and his family and I said, "Thank God."[17]

Another interviewee who travelled to Halifax to meet his prospective bride remembered that "When my wife [his betrothed] arrived in

Halifax, I met her at the boat. She was so pretty and petite and she looked much younger than her nineteen years. I was, at the time, thirty-nine years old. I said to myself, how can I marry this child? To her, I said, 'Someday I'm going to be an old man walking around with a cane like this,' and I showed her and 'you will be in your prime. Do you really want to marry me?' We were married in Hamilton by the Armenian priest. My nephew also married a young woman. We had a real kindergarten in our house."[18]

Creative strategies brought the couples together. A groom-to-be spoke to his minister at St Barnabas Anglican Church in St Catharines, who in turn contacted an Anglican priest in Halifax. When the young woman arrived, the priest and her fiancé were waiting in the receiving centre in Halifax, where the marriage was solemnized. He later confided that if she had refused to marry him, he would have forfeited the $250 bond demanded by the Canadian government. Often such hurried marriages were followed by festivities in the groom's home city and by official photographs, in which the bride would wear a white wedding gown, usually borrowed from another girl.

The betrothed did not always marry. An interviewee recalled that because her intended mate considered her too young for him, he arranged for her to meet a younger man. Her husband-to-be, scrupulous to a fault, came dressed in dirty work clothes because he refused to deceive her by wearing "fancy clothes" at their first meeting: "He wanted me to see what he would look like for the rest of his life."[19]

Not every young woman was as fortunate. Deception about age, background, and wealth was a recurring problem as indicated by another respondent. Her fiancé had written that he was twenty-seven years old, a barber who owned his own house. When she arrived in Quebec as a sixteen-year-old, he quickly married her on the ship, trying to calm her misgivings by arguing that Ottawa would deport her, that he would lose the thousand-dollar bond he had put up for her, and that if she did not like him, she was free to leave him after the marriage. He brought her to _____ , where she learned the truth: he was actually thirty-five years old, worked as an unskilled labouer in a local factory, and owned a house in partnership with another man. In retelling the story, she bristled with indignation: "My husband tricked me. I was crying so much. Just crying. He should have married my sister; she was closer to him in age. But the go-between said she wasn't pretty enough." "Still," she added, "I bore him four children and lived with him until his death forty years later. He looked after me well and I cared for him in his old age."[20]

Stories circulated about misrepresentation and unsuitability. A woman, already married, agreed to marry a man who paid for her passage, but as soon as she arrived in New York, she vanished with her husband. Another story, highlighting mismatches, has a young woman from a good background married to a boor. The morning after their wedding, she gently asks, "What woke you this morning, my dear husband? Was it the song of the birds, the warm rays of the sun?" "Na," he replies, "I hadda go to the toilet." As a point of interest, this same story is also told in reverse, with a husband speaking gently to his wife who responds using coarse language.

While each individual had the final choice of whether to marry or not, for many women, it was a choiceless choice. If she refused to marry, what could she do in a strange country? Where could she go? Who would look after her? How could she bear the shame? Besides, the girl felt a strong sense of obligation, since a promise had been made and money had been spent. It became a question of honour. How could she break her family's word, particularly if the man had assisted her family and/or supported her en route while she waited for her travel papers? What would be her lot if she returned to Europe or the Middle East? Working in foreign lands, especially for refugees, was complicated by bureaucratic red tape, as we have already seen with respect to the Nansen passport. And if she found work as a domestic or in a factory, what would be her fate?

In the September 1929 issue of *Yergounk: Revue Littéraire Arménienne*, the following statistics confirm the movement of adolescent girls to France: in 1923-24, 600 orphans immigrated to France; in 1926, 300, and in 1929, 71. Among the 471 girls, none was as old as 20; 180 were 19; 162 were 18; and 129 were 17 years of age.[21] Repeated articles describe the "commercialization" and exploitation of such young Armenian girls. "They are beguiled by unconscionable administrators who pack them off to different countries, alone and inexperienced (as house workers) ... Who knows their story? How they marry? How they die? How they are buried?"[22] Finding a suitable young man among the refugees in countries of sanctuary, moreover, especially one who could support a family, was equally daunting. Women outnumbered men in the refugee communities, since many men had been killed by the Turks or had taken up arms in self-defense. At the same time, the orphanages, particularly those of the Near East Relief, were winding down their operations after 1923, and as the children reached adolescence, they were sent out on their own. Orphanage supervisors often dispatched girls as domestics and boys as farm workers to countries as far apart as England and Egypt.

Not only, then, were gender ratios imbalanced in different refugee communities, but eligible women and men were dispersed to distant parts of the world. A woman might reasonably examine her options: it would be better to marry an Armenian – albeit a stranger and an older one at that – in a far-off land who could take care of her than to be exploited and enslaved as young, docile labour in foreign places or to miss altogether the chance to marry and to spend her life in spinsterhood.

In the predominantly male communities in Canada, women arrivals were seldom rejected, or if they were, the man could easily find another suitor and redeem his costs.[23] Rather, men were so anxious to marry, they often took the precaution of keeping their fiancées sequestered in a room until after the wedding, for fear they might be spurned for another man.[24] The old-time settlers in Canada were all the more worried because in age, education, socioeconomic background, and geographical origin they differed from the women they hoped to marry. Most were peasants from Keghi who by the 1920s had spent their youth in the iron factories of southern Ontario. By contrast, the newcomers were from all parts of the Ottoman Empire and from every socioeconomic and educational background. By the 1920s, they were in their late teens, their twenties, or early thirties, considerably younger than the middle-aged men they married.

It was said that the women refugees who came to North America were saved. Yet life in the new world could be difficult for them. As young immigrant women from a conservative and backward society they were attempting to adjust to a modern, urban, industrial, and foreign environment. Most did not know English or Canadian customs and habits. They were ignorant of Canadian foods and cooking methods and unfamiliar with Canadian machines and technology. One did not know how to flush a toilet; another scorched the clothes whenever she ironed; still another had trouble using the washboard. In facing the strangeness of the new world they were like many other immigrant women.

Unlike voluntary immigrants, however, they were refugees. They had not planned to come to Canada. Nor had they saved and prepared to live in North America. They had been unwillingly uprooted from their homes, torn from their loved ones, reduced to stateless vagabonds. For some, the warmth and love of family life was a vague memory overshadowed by pain and anguish. An informant's recollection gives a sense of the loss: "I was very young. I had no idea about marriage or family. I knew nothing about home life. Because I never knew my father. My mother, with what hardship she saved our lives and looked after us! Here, there. Conversion. Flight. Poverty. Orphanages, one after another. Refugee camps. Poverty. Hard toil."[25] Some women suffered physically for many years because of their past experiences. Many had been stricken with malaria, cholera, or Mediterranean (Armenian) fever; more commonly, the lack of clean water had affected their eyes.

Other afflictions were less visible: anxiety, fear, sadness, the inability to enjoy life, feelings of worthlessness and helplessness, and depression.[26] Their suffering ran deeply and subtly into the subconscious. Almost eighty years after the event, an interviewee told the story of beautiful, young Zivart who knocked at the door of the house she and her family were occupying after the war. The house had belonged to Zivart and her doctor husband before the war, and she had come to request some belongings that had no monetary value but were precious to her. Eventually, in tears, Zivart revealed her pathetic story. When the Genocide started, the mayor of the town took her captive, admitting that he had lusted for her for some time. The young woman pleaded for her husband's life, so the Turkish mayor had him imprisoned for the duration of the war. Each day, Zivart took food to her husband in jail. At the end of the war, when the couple was to be reunited, the doctor husband found his wife "repulsive."[27]

The question of how to deal with rape victims troubled the people. In an article in the Armenian language newspaper *Hairenik*, G.H. Karageulian broached the painful topic of victims of rape and abduction. To the question, "How do we treat children born of Armenian women who were taken captive," Karageulian replied, "We can neither recognize nor accept those children. Those children have no place in Armenian life." To the question, "Should the Armenian young man, who wishes to marry a virgin, refrain from marrying women who have been taken captive?" Karageulian replied, "The Armenian youth should have no qualms about marrying women taken captive, because it was not their fault and so they are not morally responsible for what has happened to them."[28] Karageulian's answers reflect the general attitude of Armenians. Although rape victims were more or less accepted in the community, they faced their own silent purgatory. Whatever the circumstances of the rape, victims were plagued by severe repercussions, especially a sense of sinfulness and debasement.

For some who had undergone unbearable pain, living itself was hell. An interviewee remembers that "When we were kids, we all used to make fun of Mrs _____. She was a bit 'light.' " But later on, her mother told her the unfortunate woman's story: The Turks had killed her husband. Then, during the deportations she hid her two little children under her skirts, for two days. On the third day, the Turks found them, took the boys and right in front of their mother's eyes, they poured gasoline on them and burned them. Then they carried her off.[29]

Even if people connected symptoms and causes of illness, many other factors combined to make mental health a complicated issue: the language barrier, Armenian distrust and fear of hospitals, their ignorance about mental health disorders and treatment, their tradition of looking after their own people, and their general reaction to mental illness as a sign of weakness, an inability "to stand on one's own two feet." On the other hand, by today's standards, the state of mental health care in Canada was rudimentary. The medical profession did not understand, and perhaps did not try to understand, post-traumatic stress, especially among a small group of working-class foreigners. Consequently, the two or three severe cases were incarcerated for a lifetime in institutions for the mentally ill.

The Genocide had other domino effects, particularly with respect to broken families. "For years," recounted an interviewee, "he tried to find his wife and children through newspaper tracing services and word of mouth. No luck. Then he remarried and he was getting along fine with his new wife when all of a sudden who should appear on the scene but his first wife and son? So he left his second wife and took his first one but they never got along, always fighting." In another case, a woman's first husband suddenly showed up. "She hadn't heard from him in years. Thought he was dead. He wasn't dead but he was almost blind. So she left her second husband to look after the first."[30] Such occurrences highlight not only the strong sense of duty but also the ensuing heartache.

For these refugee women, recovery from trauma was intrinsically enmeshed in adjustment to life in Canada, in the transition to womanhood, and in unusual marriage patterns. In the old land, before the Genocide, traditional structures like family, clan, village, and church supported people on a day-to-day basis. People assisted each other during life crises – the birth of a child, choice of a mate, marriage preparations and adjustment, the death of a family member, financial difficulties, marital conflicts, generational tensions, and other family problems, like troublesome in-laws. A reciprocal mutual assistance allowed people the pleasure of enjoying with one another the goodness of life and the backing necessary to combat the evils and cope with the sorrows. In the process of the Genocide, these age-old mechanisms were destroyed, and men, women, and children were left to their own devices and resources, defenseless against sinister forces and unprotected by ancient custom and practice.

For many young survivors, the knowledge of pre-Genocide patterns of behaviour, customs, and relationships was obliterated by the rawness of life in the convoys of deportees, in concentration camps, and refugee shelters. What they knew about how to behave they learned in refugee camps and orphanages, not in homes and families. For them the warmth and happiness of family life and the love and tenderness of father and mother were at best a slim memory over-shadowed by pain.

Many young women found that their lives had been irreparably disrupted by the Genocide. For them, the normal flow of childhood to adolescence had been shattered. The physical and emotional changes of adolescence had not been allowed to run their natural and normal course with the help and support of family and community.[31] Instead of dealing with issues of blossoming female sexuality, they had struggled to find a morsel of bread, a drop of water, a place of rest.

"You shrank before you grew," whispered the grandmother of Kherdian's heroine, Veron, upon seeing her again after a separation of four years. Young Veron, just fifteen, wanted more than anything "to be a young girl" again and to go to school. But she had grown up quickly – too quickly – and she knew that "my time for being a young girl had passed."[32] This theme of lost childhood is ever-present in the stories of survivors. Oghda Haroutounian, for example, was married at thirteen and had her first child at fifteen. When the children played outside, she would cry because she too wanted to go out to play.[33] Embarking on the next stage of life's adventure, young women like Veron and Oghda had come to North America alone, without family and without money. Pitched into a strange new land, they were obliged to make a quantum leap from refugee child to wife and mother.

Differences in age, background, and temperament and initial unfamiliarity with each other cast a joyless aura on the early years of marriage. A cultured and educated woman ended up with a man who was "loud, boisterous, crude, and rude. Everything a cultured lady wouldn't be." "What did we know?" recalled another respondent, "Laid down, got up, had children."[34] Another, already bruised by life's blows by the age of seventeen, commented: "I was not happy. Married to a strange man. I hadn't spoken two words to him [before the marriage]. We had no idea of each other's opinions. What was love? There was no love in those days. No. The man needed the woman and the woman needed the man. That's why they married. They were old; the women were young. But we were old-country women. We were obedient to our men. Every home had troubles. There isn't one family who could say we had it easy."[35]

Indeed, neither women nor men found it easy to live with a total stranger, chosen by Chance, "like a lottery," "like a grab-bag." A song popular in the 1930s and 1940s in North America recounts, with a touch of humour, the woeful tale of a young man married to a refugee girl who had found sanctuary in Cuba:

> I worked for seven years, and saved $1000.
> I decided to get married.
> So I went to Cuba looking for a wife.
> There were many pretty Armenian girls in Cuba,
> but one of them won my heart.
> She smiled and assured me she didn't care for riches.
> She just wanted to make me happy.
> She loved me, she said.
> So I married her and brought her to America.
> A year later, she said she wanted a diamond ring.
> So I bought her a diamond ring.
> Then she wanted a fur coat.
> So I bought her a fur coat.
> Then she wanted an automobile.
> So I bought her an automobile.
> Then, she said, she didn't like my pillow.[36]

This critical genre of song could also be found in the Middle East. A favourite song chastises young girls, who, eager to marry an American, take the path of corruption by "painting themselves red, bobbing their hair, and deceiving the groom."[37]

Vulnerability, dependency, unfamiliarity with acceptable societal behaviour, and uncertainty about respective roles complicated already complex relationships. A perspicacious woman who had a good understanding of the situation explained that her husband of fifty years had been deeply in love with his first wife. Theirs had not been an arranged marriage. They had fallen in love and chosen each other. "She was the dream of his youth, and, as he never forgot his youth, he never forgot her or their children who had been killed during the Genocide. But as time went on, that world in Keghi became a shadow, fell into a distant perspective." When asked about *her* marriage, she said that times were different then. Armenians were trying to recreate family life; they were trying to rebuild a nation that had almost vanished in the mountains of Anatolia and the deserts of Syria. Her marriage was one of necessity.

"My husband and I cared greatly for each other and respected each other; our destinies had merged." Sometimes, she explained, the role of husband/father blurred with wife/daughter. "I was just a few years older than his daughter and, in the early years, he sometimes treated me like his child. And I didn't like that very much."[38]

Armenian guidebooks and newspapers often gave instructions on how husband and wife should behave. "Women," instructed one such book published before the Genocide, should

be clean and neat, and dress modestly, never ostentatiously – in such a way as not to embarrass your husband. Do not spend any money without his knowledge. Behave in a well-bred manner, always with patience and good cheer. Be forgiving even if you are right and never bear a grudge. Tend to his needs first, then your own and always spare him the problems of the house. Make the home comfortable and prepare his favourite meals. If you want your husband to stay home, take care of your kitchen. Carry out his wishes, respect his authority and discuss important matters with him. Train your children to be obedient to his will also. Strangers should never see any conflict or disagreement between husband and wife. Never talk about his shortcomings or mistakes to others. To complain to others only opens the door to unfaithfulness. Keep no secrets from him, do not open his letters or look into his pockets or his papers. Believe that you are happy and you will be happy. Make him proud of you and of your home.

Directions to the husband were equally revealing:

Do not forget that your wife is your better half. Never abuse your position of authority, nor remain indifferent, strict or coarse with your wife. Do not wound her by word or deed. Do not enslave her to such a degree that she shudders in your presence. Do not bring the cares of your work into your home. Keep your appearance clean and neat. Keep your wife happy by indulging in her little fancies. Remember your wedding anniversary and your wife's birthday. Understand her wishes before she reveals them and carry them out. Trust her with your financial affairs, discuss your business affairs with her – your successes and failures. Give her the required money on time; recognize how belittling it is for her to ask for money for a pair of gloves. If she works, let her use some of her earnings for her own needs. Do not ridicule your wife's inclinations, nor criticize her work in the presence of others; train your children to respect their mother. As you do for strange women, bend down and pick up an item dropped by your wife, stand to acknowledge her, show her the best place, help her on with her coat, request her permission to smoke. By becoming her slave, rule over her.[39]

Events of the Genocide changed such attitudes and perceptions, especially among mature women. Those who had conquered the ordeal of starvation, disease, and poverty could not easily be dominated. Young girls, however, were a different matter, for their lives had been disrupted at a critical stage of development.

With slight variation, the women hoped for good providers, faithful husbands, men who did not drink or gamble. There were "unbearable things," noted an interviewee. "For instance, if the husband is lazy and doesn't bring money home. Or if he is a drinker. Or runs after women." As for the women, they wanted to build their own "nest," to be efficient homemakers, chaste wives, and good mothers. It was a question of honour to act in such a way as to bring credit to their husband's name. The women knew their role and their place: "He is my husband. I am his wife. I must be obedient. Cook, wash, sew and rear the children. He must work outside and bring money home. That's the tradition."[40] Especially in the first years of marriage, when women were almost totally dependent on men, old-country models of the husband's authority were barely questioned, whatever the demands: to remove his shoes and wash his feet at night, to leave the room when other men were present, to keep her arms and head covered when she went out, to refrain from wearing makeup or having hair permanents. She was not to be "silly," or to speak or laugh out loud. Above all, she was to be good to her husband; after all, "he was the breadwinner."

Although rare, family violence did occur; such abuse was often occasioned by the beginnings of wifely rebellion against an old-country order that was increasingly out of pace with Canadian society. In the following excerpt, an informant describes her early experiences while married to a strict man in a strange country:

I used to do my washing by hand, in the washtub – the galvanized washtubs and scrub boards. No machines. The men had long underwear. I couldn't even wring it. I used to go up and down like this to squeeze the water out to hang it to dry. Then bring it in to iron. We didn't have those electric irons. We had those coal irons. We used to burn some coal in them. At night I used to sew, crochet, knit. Needlework. If we had the paper, we sat down and read the Armenian paper. Letters, I used to write a lot of letters to my sister and my cousins ...

I knew I couldn't afford a lot of children. I like children but it was so hard to look after them, to dress them and send them to school. But there was nothing we could do. Even if we went to the doctor, he wouldn't give us anything. Just had to be careful. I had them one after the other. That used to worry me. What I'm going to be if I have one every year. I used to nurse them a long time – eighteen months. So I didn't get my period. Then I had an operation.

I wanted my husband to help me around the house. I didn't know what it was – the family life. He should have told me. He knew more than I did, but he never told me anything. He should have been more tender with me. I was so young. He used to leave the house early in the morning, come home late at night. He used to stay in the store late to earn a few more cents.

He used to treat me like a slave. Anything he said I had to do. We were never to use the word, No. We didn't even call them by their first names. We were far too formal for that. Because he wasn't home, I had to look after everything. We had two Quebec stoves. I used to bring up the coal from the basement and take out the ashes. That was the man's job. It was too heavy for me. He didn't do anything around the house. At first he used to do the shopping. Didn't want me to go out alone. I was too young and inexperienced. He'd bring the food home and I'd cook it. I didn't know what to cook. He used to say, do this, do that. I didn't know how to cook. After a while I started doing the shopping myself and from here and there, I learned how to cook.

He didn't want me going out much. There was a wedding, but he said I was too young to go. Here I was married. I wasn't too young. But to go to a wedding I was too young! Maybe he didn't want me to meet someone else or to learn too much. We all got married so quickly after we came. And quickly had children. So we'd be stuck with the kids. Stay in the house. Sometimes when a girl came, the men wouldn't let anyone else see her. Kept her in the room until they were married. But it didn't happen that women ran off with other men. We were old-country women. The first visitor I had, was 6–7 months after I was married. Two women came to see me. Even now, one of them remarks about how young I was in that big house, all alone. Then my sister-in-law came and we became like sisters. Even ate out of the same dish.[41]

When asked how she had felt at the time, since her comments were made fifty years after the fact, the interviewee quickly replied that she had been satisfied with her lot. Her life had been no different from the condition of other Armenian women. Like them she worked hard and so did her husband. He was "a good provider" and "a decent man." Initially, at least, the women relied on their husbands. The strength of the marriage often depended on how adroitly, diplomatically, and kindly the husband educated, nurtured, and assisted his young wife to cope on her own.

As they gained more experience, acquired more skills, and understood the comparatively less subordinate role of Canadian women, their power and authority in the family increased. Publicly the man was still "the king"; privately, the woman was "the crown." In time, the women considered themselves the backbone of the family and of the household. The home was their domain, and it was up to them to run it and to maintain harmony. "It is the mother," noted an informant, " who makes the home; it is the mother who destroys it." "The woman sees," she continued, "but she does not see. She hears but she does not hear." "In her place, in her home, the woman had respect," added another.[42]

The preoccupation with carving out a new life and the struggle to make ends meet usually ruled out marital separation, desertion, and divorce. More significantly, for people who had lost their loved ones, the family was sacrosanct; deserting spouse and children was unthinkable. As an informant who had spent his childhood and adolescence in orphanages so aptly said, "I had never known the tenderness of mother or father; when I had my own family, I treasured my wife and children more than my own life." During inevitable periods of tension, misunderstanding, and conflict relatives, friends, and community and religious leaders intervened to try to keep the family together. For a small number, to be sure, the mismatch was so intolerable that separation might occur. While passion and love, adultery and infidelity are threaded through their stories, most men and women simply regarded their marriage as part of their fate, accepted it, and tried to make the best of it. Some were even fortunate enough to look back years later and say with conviction: "those who fall in love before marriage, waste their love. We married, and our love came after; and we remained happy."[43]

Because of deaths and abductions, miscarriages, abortions, unsanitary birth conditions, and the breakdown of the menstrual cycle, the Armenian population plunged during and shortly after the Genocide. Partly to resurrect the Armenian family and nation and partly to take the place of lost loved ones, each couple considered child bearing and child rearing a vital priority. Most couples had a child within a year or two of marriage. More than that, interviewees revealed the powerfully cathartic role of children. Men were anxious to replace the family they had lost, but for women children represented more than replacement. All women interviewees spoke lovingly about their children: "When I had children, I gave them all my love. I was happier"; "I used to tell my children, 'you're all I have on earth.'" "No," said another informant, "I never loved my husband and never will. I tolerate him because of my children." "I was a child; I missed my mother. I had no one. No one to help me. And I wasn't a Keghetsi, so they made me feel like an outsider. When I had children, I found comfort and joy. Praise God.

His help was near." "We were orphaned so young. All we could do was think about our mothers. We looked everywhere for them. Later, when we had children of our own, it was as if all that longing was poured into them. We craved their well-being more than life." Thus, by creating their own families, the women gradually managed to suppress their grief and sense of loss, relive their own lost childhood and adolescence, and find fulfillment.[44]

Informants indicated that the young brides were naive about pregnancy, birth control and contraception, abortion, and child birth: "no one told us about those things in the orphanage." An orphan from the Bird's Nest orphanage in Lebanon recalled that when she started menstruating, she thought she was dying. Explaining that it was normal, one of her girlfriends gave her a piece of cloth but no pins. She flushed as she remembered her embarrassment when she was skipping and the soiled pad fell on the ground for all to see. Another, with a measure of modesty, recounted a conversation with her husband:

I didn't know about pregnancy. About five months after I was married, I said to my husband that something was happening in my stomach. What could it be?
"You're pregnant. The child is inspirited."
"What does that mean?"
"It means the baby is alive. It's breathing."
"Then it's going to die because it can't breathe. It's going to drown."
"No, it won't die. If you breathe, so will the baby."[45]

Still another turned to an older woman for information and advice: "She told me I was pregnant. I was so innocent. I was only seventeen. She explained to me how I was going to have that baby. She looked after me like a mother. She took the child. When the baby was born, she rubbed it with salt according to our old-country custom. I knew nothing. When the baby cried, so did I. I didn't know how to bathe the baby. But I was young and I learned."[46]

Other strategies to create normal family life also helped to bring equilibrium to the communities. People realigned themselves in such a way that remarriages, adoptions, half- and stepsisters and stepbrothers were not unusual phenomena among survivors seeking stability above all else. Another distinguishing feature of some families was the wide age gap – sometimes as much as 20 years – between siblings or half siblings born in the old country before the Genocide and those born in Canada.[47]

As the newcomer women became acquainted with each other, they began to share their knowledge and experiences. Gradually they found replacements for relatives lost in the Genocide and slowly reestablished guideposts of social behaviour. Those from different origins and socioeconomic backgrounds lived next door to one another and became bound by their common sorrow, their mutual need, their ethnic identity, and their humanity. The women created a female collectivism that permeated their daily lives. They shared their hardships and their triumphs, encompassing all facets of life: homemaking, birth control, child rearing. They exchanged outgrown children's clothing, shared information about the wonder formula, Pablum, and about well-baby clinics, and loaned each other books like the (Armenian Mothers' Guide) (1923) and (Practical Hygiene) (1911).[48] They wept and rejoiced together, rallied in times of distress, helped in household chores and the care of children, interpreted with doctors and school teachers, worked, learned, and played together. In the long run their interdependence created a true sisterhood.

In their families and communities, the women found support to cope with the trauma of the Genocide, to deal with the adjustments of marriage, and to withstand the pressures of functioning in a new environment. Without a working knowledge of English, lacking the degree of sophistication needed to function effectively in an urban industrial environment, ignorant of the city beyond the few blocks of the Armenian neighborhood, and limited, to an extent, by the cultural constraints of the Armenian community, the women looked inward to their families and community members for the framework of continuity and stability. With hard work, humour, imagination, and patience, they brought vitality and domesticity to a group of heart-broken men. In turn, they derived strength from the new world they helped to build.

The strong links among the women reverberated in the community and in a way reflected the relationship among the men in the pre-Genocide communities. Friends, godparents, distant relatives, village people, and political confreres were treated as intimate relatives. The bonding of fictive kin solidified the community and acted as an anchor for the next generation.

THE GEORGETOWN BOYS

The same could not be said about 109 boys who were brought to Canada by the Armenian Relief Association of Canada (ARAC) to settle on a farm/home/school near Georgetown, Ontario. Initially, at least, they were not part of the Armenian community. They had no choice but to cope with the recovery from their traumatic past, the normal stresses of adolescence, and the anxieties of adjusting to a new culture largely on their own and with each other. Because the boys had been very young when the Genocide started, their memories of the prewar period revealed only tiny glimpses, treasured vignettes, of the warmth and affection of family life: an uncle's laughter, a mother's lentil soup, a father's loving embrace, a grandmother's solemn blessing. Their images of the deportations were also scant, though far from insubstantial: the excruciating pain of an infected hand; terror from constant shelling; a sister carrying one of them on her back along a hot, desert road to nowhere; going berserk at a mother's mysterious disappearance.

With the fall of the Armenian Republic and with deteriorating conditions in the Middle East in the early 1920s, ARAC decided to move approximately two thousand Armenian refugee children to Canada and to establish a house of passage until arrangements could be made to send the youngsters out to foster homes.[49] The Canadian government, however, rejected requests both for the entry of a large contingent of children and for financial concessions for the small number to be admitted. Eventually the government allowed the admission of 100 healthy refugee boys between the ages of eight and twelve, and, on humanitarian grounds, relaxed passport and continuous-journey restrictions. The ARAC, in its turn, agreed to provide a suitable children's home that would become, as far as possible, "self-sustaining" through public subscription. Here the boys would be kept "for several years"; they would be given "opportunities to secure an education up to the end of the fifteenth year as any other boys will have in our country." They would be "trained in agricultural and horticultural work" in preparation for being "hired out to farmers and fruit growers under our personal supervision until such time as they are of age." The association agreed that after proper training in the receiving and distributing farm/home/school the Armenian children would be sent out to foster homes and "situations" selected for them "under a legal form of indenture." "Whenever necessary" the children would be able to return to the home. The ARAC promised to assume full responsibility for their wards until they reached the age of sixteen – and possibly eighteen – to make personal visits to them on the farms, and to ensure compliance with the Provincial School Attendance Act.[50] The association's aim was to develop the boys "into good citizens under the very best possible influences here in Canada," to make them into "permanent and industrious citizens," and "to build up the very highest type of Canadian citizen." "Our purpose," stated the association, "is not only to rescue these homeless, defenceless children from the hand of the Turks, but to help the building up of Canada."[51] The vision was both philanthropic and patriotic, and the generosity of Canadians, so evident in raising funds to send abroad to the "starving Armenians," was confirmed in the successful general appeal on behalf of the refugee children. Enough money was collected or pledged to pay for their transportation to Canada, for the purchase of a farm/home near Georgetown, Ontario, and for the children's initial care while at the home.

The first group of 50 boys ranging in age from eight to twelve – on the threshold of puberty – left the island of Corfu in the summer of 1923. They reached their farm/home at Georgetown in a state of euphoria: "They said that we're going to Canada where money grows on trees. The funny part of the whole thing was, when we came off the train ... We noticed that there were a lot of trees – green apple trees. Everybody climbed the trees looking for money!"[52] The boys did not find any money in the apple trees; they found something much more precious. Awakened by his friends from a nightmare about the bloody murder of his parents by Turkish attackers, young Onnig Shangaian is relieved to find himself safe in Canada and cries out, "O Canada, how do I love thy freedom and beauty."[53]

The boys' little corner of paradise was a 135-acre farm (later increased to 200 acres) situated about thirty miles west of Toronto. It had a thriving apple orchard, tillable land, a number of farm buildings, including the main house and a barn. Additional structures, like dormitories and a dining room, were constructed to accommodate the youngsters. Here, as the culture shock wore off, the boys gradually settled down. For the first time in their young lives they had shoes, enough food, and a fine set of clothing. At the Georgetown farm/home, the boys attended school, worked on the farm, and enjoyed leisure-time activities such as sledding, skating, baseball, and stamp collecting. Slowly, they began to adjust to the new environment, and as they did so, they built up strong bonds with each other. George Bogue Smart, superintendent of juvenile immigration, noted with satisfaction that "The deep personal interest which is being taken in the highest welfare of these children, together with their training and discipline, is of such a nature as should result in their becoming good, industrious and patriotic citizens of Canada."[54] So impressed was Smart that he recommended the entry of more Armenian children under the auspices of the association. Forty more boys were brought over in 1924 and 19 in 1926 and 1927.

In late 1924, Dr A. J. Vining, a very popular figure among the children, resigned as secretary of the ARAC. One of the boys recalled Vining's great faith in their future: "Vining said some of our boys would be members of Parliament and maybe become the prime minister of this country. And we were going to be educated until manhood ... We were going to leave Georgetown with a trade or profession in our hands. And we were happy with what Vining said and it registered in our minds."[55] Vining's replacement, Rev. Ira Pierce, had been sent out to do mission work among the Armenians in Kharput just before the outbreak of the war and had lived through "the dark tragedy of 1915."[56] He could never forget the experience. Eloquent, cautious, articulate, diligent, strict, and inflexible, Pierce gradually became one of the most powerful figures in the ARAC in defining and implementing policy regarding the Armenian children.

However, in spite of good intentions, acute problems began to surface. Part of the difficulty lay in an element of confusion and imprecision about the role of the farm/home, the length of stay, the age at leaving, and the type and length of education. These issues were not resolved; instead, the ARAC administration revised its original commitment. In his reminiscences, Rev. Andrew Lane, a former superintendent of the farm/home, confirmed that "the original intention of the Association was to shelter, support, and educate the boys at the farm until they had reached the age of sixteen." But in 1925 a new policy was adopted in order to give the lads "a fine home atmosphere" and "the opportunity for public schooling."[57] The boys were to be sent out to farmers in southern Ontario on a work contract that required the younger ones to attend school and permitted the older ones to work full time. Bearing in mind the history of the children and their remarkable progress at the farm/home, the new policy was ill-conceived. Just as unfortunate for the boys, it was poorly implemented and led to exploitation, hardship, and even death.

In January 1928, in another reversal of policy, the ARAC sold the Georgetown farm/home to the United Church of Canada. Before the takeover, the Sub-Executive Committee of the Board of Evangelism and Social Service of the United Church of Canada resolved that the board would conduct the Georgetown farm/home "in such a way as to meet the responsibilities which it accepted for the proper care of the Armenian boys" and that it would "further establish and conduct" on the farm "Christian work for needy classes of people in Canada."[58] The board's intentions became somewhat more obvious in January at the official ceremony of sale, when Rev. Dr Webb stated that the United Church proposed "later to set up a home and training center for delinquent girls."[59] On 18 May 1928, the Armenian boys' farm/home at Georgetown formally ceased to exist and was replaced by a home for delinquent girls with a monthly grant of $500, commencing 1 July 1928.[60]

From that point on the Board of Evangelism and Social Service of the United Church undertook to supervise the boys, now located in different places, until the age of eighteen. The service helped them in finding jobs and advised them when they were unemployed or ill. Even after they turned eighteen, the United Church of Canada office became the point of orientation for many desperate young men facing the tribulations of the Depression. The boys struck out on their own and made for all parts of the globe, often to search for or join surviving family. Some headed for Canadian cities and different work experiences; some enlisted in the Canadian armed forces; others gravitated to Armenian enclaves, themselves undergoing great changes.

Older immigrants who had left the homeland with a past already entrenched and young refugees with a slim past together began to reconstruct a new world in Canada. Imperceptibly, gradually, they refashioned defeat into victory and remoulded their lives. They looked to Canada with thanksgiving. Just as loss had been the overriding force that plunged them to the depths of hell in the old land, so hope personified their future in the "paradise" of the young dominion.

10

The Quest for Reparations

The quest by Armenian Canadians for compensation for lost relatives and property can be understood most effectively within the framework of the Treaty of Versailles (ratified 10 January 1920) and the Treaty of Lausanne (24 July 1923, ratified 6 August 1924). From the records, it appears that Armenian Canadians became enmeshed in a complicated international legal morass in which concepts of international crime and of humanitarianism were only gradually being formulated and international jurisprudence regarding war crimes, crimes against humanity, and refugeeism were in the early stages of systematization. Ignorant of international law and the various perambulations following the war, they were at the mercy of lawyers, politicians, and civil servants and the general postwar confusion of regulations and laws. They were bounced from one committee to another, from one commission to another, from one country to another – too often without their knowledge. In the end, their persistence led to frustration, disappointment, anger, and a feeling of injustice.

BACKGROUND

The process for compensation can be viewed within several jurisdictions: the Canadian Reparation Commission; the Royal Commission on Compensation for Suffering and Damage by Enemy Action (15 August 1921), also known as the Sumner Commission; the Mixed Arbitral Tribunal between Britain and Turkey; the Inter-Allied Commission for the Assessment of Damage Suffered in Turkey, also known as the Paris Commission (23 November 1923); the Special Commission on Armenian Claims, also known as the McDougall Special Report upon Armenian Claims (9 May 1931); Charles H. Cahan's confidential Report to Council on the Armenian Claims (20 January 1932); and Order-in-Council 571 (12 March 1932).[1]

In 1920–21, Armenians naturalized as British subjects before 1914 sent a petition to the Canadian government, through the secretary of state, seeking reparations under the terms of the Treaty of Versailles for loss of family and property suffered during World War I. These claims were eventually submitted to the Canadian Reparation Commission upon its formation in March 1923 but, inexplicably, were not heard by the commissioner. On 24 July 1923 the Allies signed the Treaty of Peace with Turkey at Lausanne.[2] Four months later, Britain and the other contracting powers signed a convention, or agreement, to set up the Paris Commission, which consisted of three members, one each nominated by France, Britain, and Italy, to assess and provide compensation for claims by Allied civilians for damage occurring "as the result of any act or negligence of the Turkish Government, including damage resulting from measures of requisition, sequestration or confiscation and also direct damage."[3]

The Armenian Canadian claims had already been lodged by Canadian authorities with the Paris Commission by February 1925, when in August 1925 Governor-General Lord Byng of Vimy requested that the Armenian claims be forwarded to Constantinople for consideration by the Anglo-Turkish Mixed Arbitral Tribunal. This body had been set up according to articles 66–70 of the Lausanne Treaty, articles that were designed specifically to deal with confiscation of property, restoration of property, and payment of proceeds of sale of property. Lord Byng was assured that the claims would be presented to the tribunal, which presumably had appropriate jurisdiction to hear them. It appears, however, that the Tribunal did not receive the Armenian petitions, or if it did receive them, it did not adjudicate them.[4] Similarly, thirty-four Armenian claims were dispatched to Constantinople by lawyer James A. Keyes of St Catharines but it seems the tribunal did not assess them either.[5]

THE PARIS COMMISSION

The Paris Commission, then, was left to consider the Armenian Canadian claims for reparations from Turkey. What reparations was the Turkish Government to pay? Originally, Allied delegates fixed Turkish reparations at £15 million in Turkish gold, then reduced this amount to

£12 million, and eventually to nothing.⁶ In short, the Allies abandoned the expenses of occupation as well as reparations arising out of Turkey's declaration of war against them. Instead, Allied delegates at Lausanne claimed only a forfeitary payment of £T5 million to indemnify their nationals. Turkish leaders had transferred these funds in the form of bank deposits from Constantinople to Berlin in 1916, as security for a War Measures Loan floated in Germany and also probably as a precaution against Allied conquest of their capital city.⁷ When the Allies entered Berlin, they confiscated these deposits at the time of the armistice, and Turkey renounced them under the terms of the Lausanne Treaty (see articles 58, 65, 66, 69). The commission also had at its disposal Turkish government treasury bills that the British government had purchased from the holders in 1914 and that were valued at about £846,100.⁸

On 11 February 1925, Canadian officials dispatched approximately 201 Armenian Canadian claims via the high commissioner for Canada in London to the British delegate, under whose auspices the Canadian claims were to be presented to the Inter-Allied Commission for the Assessment of Damage Suffered in Turkey, sitting in Paris. About 73 additional claims were also sent but reached Paris too late for consideration.⁹ In a list of 163 names giving the claimants' villages, approximately 150 were villages known to be of Keghi. In another list, 20 of 29 villages of origin are of Keghi, 4 of Van, 3 of Balu, 1 of Mush, and 1 of Bitlis.¹⁰ There appears to be some doubt whether the Armenian claimants were informed about the many peregrinations of their claims and whether or not they actually gave their permission to have them sent on to Paris.¹¹

The commission began its work in Paris in the summer of 1925 and completed its findings on 15 March 1930, adjudicating approximately 16,000 claims.¹² Recognizing the complexity of their case, a number of Armenians engaged Grace Brown, of Detroit, Michigan, to act on their behalf and to assume power of attorney.¹³ When Brown travelled to Paris to ascertain the situation, she found the commission about to conclude its inquiries without having dealt with the Armenian Canadian claims. A proposal, possibly advocated by Brown to the British delegate, suggested that a subcommission be sent to Turkey to carry out necessary investigations and a subcommission be sent to Canada for an examination of witnesses or, alternatively, that the Canadian government conduct such an inquiry. These recommendations were not accepted by the commission.¹⁴ To salvage the claims, in 1928 Brown engaged Captain David Windrum Carlisle to represent her clients in Paris, to obtain an extension of time, and to help gather the required evidence. Carlisle was a barrister at the Inns of Court, Northern Ireland, specializing in laws dealing with international claims. He had previously acted as British delegate at Constantinople for the Paris Commission, and seemed highly qualified to act on behalf of the Armenian Canadian claimants.[15]

According to Sir Eliot Colvin, president of the Paris Commission, the assessment of the Armenian Canadian claims "provided one of the most difficult tasks with which the Commission had to deal." The commission was presented with certain irrefutable and uncontroversial facts:

1 Claimants were naturalized Canadians before 1914.
2 They were originally from the Ottoman Empire.
3 They had family, in many cases wives and children, in the Ottoman Empire at the outbreak of war.
4 Turkish government officials drove their families from their homes, shops, and farms by official decree.
5 Most family members were massacred by Turks, Kurds, or Circassians or died as a result of the hardships of the forced death marches authorized by the Turkish government.
6 The homes, shops, and farms of the Armenians were damaged, destroyed, or confiscated by Turks, Kurds, or Circassians.
7 Much of their personal property in the form of jewellery, rugs, books, and objets d'art had also been stolen or ruined by Turks, Kurds, or Circassians.

The petitioners had emigrated to Canada before 1914 and, not surprisingly, had left their property deeds and other certificates with their families in the home villages. These documents had either been destroyed or confiscated by Turkish authorities or by others who had seized Armenian belongings or abducted Armenian women and children to claim their families' properties. So thorough and so extensive had been the destruction of life and property that it was as impossible for Armenian survivors to provide specific documents and deeds as it was to redeem their lost possessions and resurrect their lost relatives.

To arrive at a reasonable assessment of claims in general, the commission was mandated to collect evidence. Delegates themselves visited Constantinople, sent a subcommission to Palestine, and established a permanent subcommission in Constantinople and another in Smyrna with representatives from Britain, France, and Italy engaged in examining claims on the spot. But the Paris Commission did not investigate the Armenian Canadian claims. Nor did it take effective "steps to collect evidence of damage suffered in Armenia" or call on the claimants themselves for evidence.[16]

Its half-hearted attempt to gather evidence ended up a total fiasco. In January 1928, almost three years after the Armenian claims had been submitted to the Paris Commission, the French delegate to the commission offered to entrust the inquiry into the Armenian Canadian case to a French consular officer in Turkey, M. Malzac, who was travelling to Erzerum on other business. The Canadian dossier was forwarded to Malzac in preparation for his trip to the interior. In April 1928 the British Embassy in Constantinople, which had previously said it was unable to conduct an inquiry into these cases, informed the British delegate that it might be possible to send a British officer to Erzerum to carry out the investigation of the Armenian Canadian cases. Since, however, it was understood that Malzac had already begun his investigation, the British delegate to the Paris Commission turned down the Constantinople offer. On 16 November, however, the British delegate learned that Malzac had not yet started for Erzerum, because of the difficulties of the journey and the fear of Kurdish bandits in the area. The French government had, therefore, abandoned the idea of the Erzerum voyage.

The British delegate to the Paris Commission then decided to prepare the Armenian Canadian case for the commission on whatever evidence he could obtain and to appeal to the commission to be indulgent in the matter of "strict proof." He underscored the futility of insisting on the production of official proof of ownership. "It is literally impossible to produce either original or duplicate Deeds ... The fact that the whole population of the district was deported and massacred in 1915 is of common knowledge."[17] In the absence of strict evidence, however, his evaluation, did not "commend itself to the majority of the Commission."[18] Indeed, as early as August 1925, the then British delegate, H.E. Garle, had reported differences among the various national delegations in arriving at a uniform system of judging the claims. The British practice, used by the Board of Trade and the Royal Commission in somewhat similar deliberations, required every claim to be supported by a statutory declaration, but not necessarily by sworn or declared corroborative evidence. The Italian system, by contrast, was to send the original statement to the local consul, requiring him to obtain corroborative evidence under the solemnity of an *acte de notoriété*. In view of the different elements of evidence, the obstacles before the Armenian Canadian claims become readily obvious.[19]

Carlisle suggested that the petitioners "do for themselves what the Commission had done for all other allied claimants," i.e., carry out their own investigation in Turkey. While this may have seemed appropriate, it was unrealistic, considering the distances, the costs, and the unwillingness of Turkish authorities to allow travel into the interior for all but officials with diplomatic privileges and protection. In late 1928 the commission warned Carlisle that his clients' claims would be judged on 15 January 1929, with or without the evidence. Only after repeated and energetic representations was Carlisle able to postpone the hearings until 15 August 1929. In order to expedite the general distribution of funds to other claimants, the Paris Commission set aside twenty thousand Turkish pounds (£T) for the "satisfaction of these Armenian Canadian claims."[20]

In the meantime, Brown made every effort in North America to collect information, have questionnaires filled out, and prepare affidavits, while Carlisle, it seems, travelled to Constantinople to gather data and to hire experts to investigate the claims. It is unclear whether or not the experts he engaged managed to visit the region, since travel in the interior was, typically, unsafe and since the Turkish government "would not permit the entry of any foreigners into this part of their territory." Even if the investigators had managed to reach the Erzerum region, Turkish authorities would not have been likely to provide extracts from the old registers, still less extracts to prove damage or confiscation for which they themselves were responsible. Indeed, it was widely reported that the Turks had deliberately destroyed the old land registers.[21]

On 15 August 1929, Carlisle presented his evidence to the commission. "It was," he later confided, "exactly similar to evidence submitted in the case of other Allied subjects of Armenian origin whose claims were admitted by the Commission." In particular, this applied to the evidence of land registers: "It had been admitted by the Commission that the production of copies of those non-existent registers was not necessary." (Pour la preuve de la propriété immobilière, la production du titre de propriété n'est pas indispensable, mais le reclamant doit être avisé que faute de cette production, des difficultés et retards en résulteront qui lui seront préjudiciables: Decision 99).[20] In many other cases where petitioners could not produce property deeds, the commission accepted the evidence of witnesses regarding property ownership and paid awards accordingly. The Paris Commission did not provide the Armenian Canadian petitioners with proper investigation of their case in Turkey, did not consider the evidence of the approximate state of Armenian losses presented by the Armenian delegation to the Paris Peace Conference, and did not accept "Secondary Evidence" submitted by the victims, which, "according to the Law of Evidence would in the circumstances have been acceptable in any British Court of Justice."[22]

With no deeds and no land registers, what secondary evidence could the Armenian Canadian claimants muster? They relied, first, on historical evidence of the events in Turkey during World War I, including, but not only, the detailed report by Viscount Bryce.[23] Carlisle also had the evidence, the experience, and the report by experts who had previously worked in Turkey for the Paris Commission itself.[24] The report (15 August 1929), which was prepared by Griscti and Deroin, architectural and agricultural experts, outlined the conditions and mode of life in Armenia at the outbreak of war, the different types of property and the minimum values of real and personal property.[25] The experts divided agricultural properties into three categories: small, average, and large; gave details of the structures that would be necessary and would be certain to have existed on each type of farm; and set out the relative quantities of stock, implements, and personal property in each case.[26]

The third category of evidence that the claimants furnished was testimony in the form of affidavits. Some of the witnesses were themselves claimants; others were survivors who had been in the villages until 1915 and were very familiar with the possessions of each family. As an additional point of interest, many of the claimants had come to Canada before 1914 and, having decided to stay, had taken out naturalization. However, many had left their families in the old country and regularly remitted funds to them. These Armenian Canadians, who earned their wages at heavy and dangerous work, would have had a very precise idea of how much money they had sent to their families and how that money had been spent. After 1909, when travel restrictions were lifted in Turkey, some had returned to the old country and personally confirmed their holdings and those of other villagers. There seems no doubt that claimants would have had a reasonably good idea of the extent and value of their own and their neighbour's farms and possessions.

In addition, they had filled out detailed questionnaires that requested specific information: date and place of birth; British subject by birth or naturalization; date, place, and number of their naturalization certificate; family members lost; *vilayet* (province) and nearest village or town of property; lands confiscated (in acreage), cultivated land, timber, vineyards, orchards, mulberry groves, pasture and scrub; exact location of property; how claimant became owner of real property; if inherited, from whom and when; whether sole or part owner; names and addresses of other part owners and their respective shares; dimensions of buildings and construction material; income from farm property (manufacturing or commercial), rents; number of stories, number of rooms and a description of its situation (so that the individual's representative may be able to find it); name of registered owner and place of registration; date last seen by claimant; date of damage; condition and value of property on 6 August 1924 (date of ratification of the Lausanne Treaty); condition and value of buildings before 6 August 1924; residents of the property prior to or on the date of damage; nature of damage and cause; details of personal property (ownership, location, inheritance). In addition, questions 32 to 37 included the following:

32 Give full details of any other facts which will assist in the collection of evidence in support of your claim and give names and addresses of witnesses stating in each case what information they can give.
33 All values should be given in Turkish Gold Pounds and should be those on the date of loss or damage.
34 Can you produce documents of title of land and buildings? If not, please state why you cannot do so: whether such documents exist and if so in whose custody.
35 Who can give evidence as to your ownership or the property damage or loss and state briefly what evidence they can give.
36 Who can corroborate your statements as to description and value of such property and state their means of knowledge.
37 In case of inheritance, can you produce any documents in proof of succession? If so, state their nature. If you cannot do so, give the names and addresses of witnesses who can give evidence as to your relationship with the person from whom you inherited and state briefly the facts within their knowledge.[27]

Finally, for each individual claim Carlisle prepared and presented a special *mémoire* giving the general circumstances and the legal arguments in support of it. He also sent a copy of his *mémoire* to the Canadian government for information and approval and throughout the negotiations consulted with Canadian diplomats in Paris, who gave him "valuable and sympathetic support."[28]

All this evidence was not considered proof of relationship, of ownership, of inheritance, and/or of extent of damage or loss. Sir Eliot Colvin, writing in his confidential report, noted that "it was extremely probable that many of the claimants had suffered real and direct damage to their rights in Armenia, though it was impossible to establish the exact nature of the rights or the extent of the damage." He was convinced, he said, that the rejection of such a large body of claims, which were "no doubt in many cases substantially justified, though not legally proved, would reflect unfavorably on the Commission's general sense of equity." In the end he recommended that an award based on the experts' report be paid by the commission to the Canadian claimants.[29]

The terms of the convention of 1923, however, provided for a decision by majority vote. When the Armenian Canadian claims were put forward with the British delegate's recommendation, the French and Italian delegates rejected them. This vote came at a time when the British delegate had lost all leverage, since the claims of French and Italian nationals had already been settled. Because the British delegate refused to acknowledge the ruling of the commission and because the French and Italian delegates remained adamant, a deadlock ensued, followed eventually by a compromise.[30] On 5 October 1929 the commission rendered its decision to disallow the claims regarding property, on the grounds of insufficient evidence, i.e., on the ground that no claimants could produce the title deeds destroyed by Turkish authorities. This decision applied both to outright owners and to heirs. Delegates who had discussed the sticky problem of inheritance at some length sought to ascertain when the damage had occurred, when family members had died, and whether the property had devolved to heirs before or after those dates. To save face, the commissioners agreed to compensate the claimants for loss of wives and children. They reasoned that leaving his family in the old country represented a strong enough sign that the claimant still maintained a link with his country of origin. For this purpose the commission set up a solatium of £19,440 out of the £20,000 earmarked for the Armenian Canadian claims. The funds were to be disbursed on a fixed scale of compensation whereby every claimant who had lost a wife was awarded £100 (approximately Can$436) and £20 for the loss of each child.[31] The commission reduced this sum when it *actually* awarded only 55 percent of the specified amount, i.e., £55 for the loss of a wife, or £47 sterling, equalling about Can$240 and about Can$48 for the loss of each child. In no case did the commission make allowance for more than three children in one family. According to commission documents, it received 267 Armenian Canadian claims and granted reparations to approximately 75 claimants. Before reduction the grants averaged about £140, for a wife and two children, or about Can$336 after reduction.[32]

In a later decision, commissioners also awarded a sum for *property loss* to a group of only 33 claimants on the grounds that they were heirs or partial heirs because their fathers had died before 1915. Thus Artin Terzian, of the village of Arek (Keghi), who was naturalized in Canada in 1907 and a veteran of the CEF, made claim to reparations for a small farm of twenty-six acres with a house and a flour mill. Terzian's father had died in 1901, and his mother, three brothers, and a sister were killed during the Genocide, leaving him sole heir to his family's property. Considering the comparatively large number of people living on the farm and based on the scale established by the commission, Terzian was entitled to $2/9$ of the value after a deduction of $1/8$ for his mother and a portion for his siblings, who would have been entitled to part of the inheritance. In total he was to receive $2/9$ of £T300, or about Can$325.[33]

The commission's decision, wrote Grace Brown, was "unprecedented," the "injustice ... too glaring." The "paltry amount awarded could only be regarded as an insult to the memory of those who had been lost."[34] Carlisle, in his turn, protested vigorously to the British government, arguing that the Armenian Canadian claims had not received the same attention that had been given to other claims. In other cases, he noted, the commission had sent subcommissions to the devastated areas in Turkey to collect evidence, but in the case of the Armenian Canadians, the commission had failed to take similar effective action. He complained that the commission had shown discrimination in rejecting the demands for compensation for loss of property for the Armenian Canadians, since it had previously admitted other claims where title deeds could not be produced. In fact, Sir Eliot G. Colvin, the British delegate at the time, indignant at the position taken by the other commissioners, had drawn attention to "similar cases from out-of-the-way places" for which the commission had been "generous" and had "not insisted upon proof of loss or ownership." He listed the names of three Italians for whom there was "absolutely nothing on the files to prove" they had "suffered the losses for which they claimed" but for which they had received reparations.[35] Carlisle, too, bristled that the commission had failed to deal with these claims at the same time and in the same manner as other claims and had disregarded its own precedent in cases where other British, French, and Italian subjects of Armenian origin were awarded compensation for losses arising out of the same occurrences and supported by similar evidence.[36]

For Armenian Canadians, the Paris Commission's decision was a bitter blow, for it flew in the face of history. They denounced the commission's ruling as a black mark against the principles of equity and humanity and a shameful display of injustice among former allies who could muster no more than a token gesture in reparations. For these humble people, the decision confirmed yet again their impotence, their powerlessness.

Armenians were well aware that the £T5 million transfer that the commission had been mandated to disburse was largely in the form of gold bank deposits and that without any doubt some of it, if not a major part of it, had belonged to Armenians. In a 1924 petition addressed to Ramsay MacDonald, then British prime minister, Herbert Asquith and Stanley Baldwin refer to the £T5 million that had been transferred by the Turkish government to the Reichsbank in Berlin in 1916 and seized by the Allies after the armistice. This money, their petition stated, "was in large part (perhaps wholly) Armenian money which the Turkish Government had had transferred to the State Treasury in Constantinople."[37] As a corroboration of this fact, in November 1923 Husri Bey (who had been Turkish governor-general of Erzerum in 1915) wrote in the daily Turkish newspaper *Jumhuriet*, published in Constantinople, that "in the Autumn of 1915 he received orders from his Government to collect all Armenian properties in the bank and transfer them to the Treasury at Constantinople."[38]

Viscount Bryce's Report gives further insight into the theft of and damage to Armenian property, both real and personal. In Erzerum, Armenians, who were justifiably suspicious and worried about the "relocations," deposited nine hundred "bales" of various goods with Rev. Robert Stapleton, the American missionary and another five hundred bundles with Dr Case, his colleague, for safekeeping. The bundles, which were carefully identified, contained such items as gold, silver, paper rubles, jewellery, insurance policies, deeds to houses and lands, promissory notes and other valuable papers. Stapleton accepted the valuables but gave no receipts and assumed no responsibility. Of the gold Armenians had left with him, Stapleton dispatched by telegram through the Imperial Ottoman Bank in Erzerum approximately £T5,000 to Constantinople to Mr W.W. Peet, Business Agent and Treasurer of the four Turkish missions of the American Board of Commissioners for Foreign Missions. The paper rubles and jewellery were packed into tin boxes and sealed with the mission seal and deposited in the Imperial Ottoman Bank in Mr Stapleton's name for safekeeping. [39] In August 1915 the Turkish government appointed a commission from Constantinople, ostensibly to protect the property of the deported Armenians. This commission appropriated and sold this property, including the valuables left with Dr Case.[40]

The Turkish government, or more specifically, high-ranking officials in the Committee of Union and Progress took possession of valuables left with other missionaries. In describing her father's work, Ida Alamuddin recounted how Jacob Kuenzler was ordered by Turkish dignitaries to send the personal items left by Armenians in his safekeeping in Urfa to Turkish central authorities in Constantinople.[41] By means of the Abandoned Properties Law (Law Concerning Property, Debts and

Assets Left Behind by Deported Persons, also referred to as the Temporary Law on Expropriation and Confiscation, 13 September 1915), the Turkish government took possession of all "abandoned" Armenian goods and properties.[42] Government officials seized land, buildings, commodities, and bank accounts and confiscated personal and community properties that had not been looted, destroyed, or handed over to Moslems. After the Committee of Abandoned Goods, for example, had confiscated hundreds of thousands of dollars in the Kharput region, "it conveniently lost its books and explained that, as all the money received had been used up for expenses and there were no funds on hand, there was no necessity anyway of rendering any account!"[43]

The Turkish government also tried to take possession of Armenian insurance policies with Swiss and American life insurance companies, notably the New York Life Insurance Company and the Metropolitan Life Insurance Company. United States Ambassador Henry Morgenthau recounts how the interior minister, Talaat Pasha, demanded the names of all Armenian policyholders. Since Armenians, Talaat argued, "are practically all dead now and have left no heirs to collect the money, it of course, all escheats to the State. The Government is the beneficiary now." Morgenthau's firm refusal did not deter Talaat from making the same demands on Swiss insurance companies holding Armenian policies or on other insurance companies operating in Turkey.[44]

In the end, the Paris Commission rejected all such evidence, Carlisle's protests, and Armenian appeals. The commission's decision was to stand. But Carlisle, as determined as ever, requested compensation from Reparations Receipts of Britain and from the German government, and he sought the intervention of the Canadian government with British authorities. Advised to place the claims before the Canadian Commission for Reparations, Carlisle then brought the matter to the attention of the Canadian secretary of state, Charles Hazlitt Cahan, emphasizing the shoddy treatment given the Armenian Canadians in Paris. In a letter to Cahan, Carlisle wrote that the Armenian Canadian claimants felt convinced that "a universal antagonism" prejudiced their rights and interests. They believed they could hope neither for sympathy from the Canadian government nor for the unprejudiced consideration of their claims by the commission now sitting in Canada. So discouraged were the claimants that they were prepared to abandon further efforts to seek compensation. Carlisle pleaded for the "sympathetic consideration" of the secretary of state and of the prime minister. He added that his clients would accept the Canadian Commission's judgment of their cases if they could receive "unprejudiced consideration on their own merits."[45]

The Quest for Reparations 217

THE McDOUGALL COMMISSION

Although the closing date for the presentation of the claims before the Canadian Commission was 1 November 1930, Cahan accepted Carlisle's previous correspondence with the department as "notification of these claims," and offered him until 1 January 1931 to present the Armenian Canadian petitions. The Canadian Commission for Reparation was to decide whether it had jurisdiction to assess compensation claims of Armenian Canadians, based on the reparations articles of the Treaty of Versailles, specifically articles 231 and 232 and annex 1, notably clause 9.[46]

The commissioner, Errol Malcolm McDougall, King's Counsel, from Montreal, was a respected judge. He diligently reviewed the Armenian claims and offered the claimants the opportunity to present their case in person at sittings held in St Catharines in March 1931. Based on an agreement between Carlisle and Cahan, the commissioner, it seems, treated the claims as a group rather than considering each case on its own merits, for in his report, McDougall refers to his request to deal with "typical cases" and the lawyer's acquiescence. Carlisle chose to present the case of Charles Artinian, to provide a thorough explanation of the nature of his client's case, and to bring in testimony from several witnesses.[47]

There were basically two different groups of claimants: those who were registered owners of real and personal property (approximately 133 claimants) and those who inherited the property from relatives who had died during the course of the war (approximately 141 claimants).[48]

McDougall based parts of his investigation on the report by Viscount Bryce, which was not – nor was it intended to be – a legal document giving judicial evidence. The Bryce Report, however, was an exemplary historical document, consisting of a long introduction, a summary of Armenian history, a geographical study, an examination of the events in 1915, reports and eye-witness accounts pertaining to those events, and a general conclusion. The book covers the beginning of the Genocide but does not go beyond events in mid–1916, even though a great number lost their lives during the forced death marches and/or as a result of attacks by Turks and Kurds at desert concentration/extermination camps, notably at Ras-ul-Ain, Rakka, and Der el-Zor. Bryce's account was published *before* the massacres in Cilicia, the burning of Smyrna, and the invasion of the newly created Republic of Armenia – events that occurred after 1918 and further brought the plight of the Armenians to the attention of the Western world.[49]

In his report, dated 9 May 1931, McDougall rejected the Armenian claims for judgment on two main grounds: 1 the claims had been submitted to and dealt with by the Paris Commission and claimants were, therefore, precluded from presenting them anew to the Canadian Commission; 2 claimants failed to show that their claims fell within the specified reparation provisions of the Treaty of Versailles. McDougall also stated that even if he were to have jurisdiction, he would dismiss all claims because the evidence submitted did not and could not constitute proof of the demands made. Let us review his arguments in more detail.

First, rejecting the Armenian Canadian claims on the grounds that because claimants had sought reparations from the Paris Commission they were precluded from applying anew to the Canadian Commission seems strange, bearing in mind the facts: the claimants had originally lodged their petition with the Canadian government (1920–21), and through various maneuvers Canadian and British authorities had sent the claims on to Paris without, it appears, the prior permission of or consultation with the petitioners. If the fact that the petitions were heard in Paris precluded them from being heard anew in Canada, why would the Canadian secretary of state have allowed them to be submitted to the Canadian Commission in the first place – at considerable cost, time, and effort? And on what grounds were the claimants precluded from petitioning anew? Furthermore, the Paris Commission had been governed by terms of the Treaty of Lausanne, while the Canadian Commission acquired its mandate under the terms of the Treaty of Versailles. According to the petitioners' lawyers, the instructions in McDougall's commission did not authorize him to apply the Paris proceedings to his judgment in these cases.[50] Even if the Paris Commission findings should have been considered, the issue still remains that it had awarded meagre compensation for property damage or loss, and the reparations for loss of wife and children had been for so few claimants as to be an outright insult. Ultimately and significantly, the petitioners never regarded the Paris judgment as final.

Second, Errol McDougall's most fundamental statement pertained to whether or not the claimants fell under the jurisdiction of the Treaty of Versailles. The pertinent sections read as follows:

Article 231: The Allied and Associated governments affirm and Germany accepts the responsibility of Germany and her allies for causing all the loss and damage to which the Allied and Associated Governments and their nationals have been subjected as a consequence of the war imposed upon them by the aggression of Germany and her allies.

Article 232 (first two paragraphs): The Allied and Associated Governments recognize that the resources of Germany are not adequate after taking into account permanent diminutions of such resources which will result from other provisions of the present Treaty, to make complete reparation for all such loss and damage. The Allied and Associated Governments, however, require, and Germany undertakes, that she will make compensation for all damage done to the civilian population of the Allied and Associated Powers and to their property during the period of Belligerency of each as an Allied or Associated Power against Germany by such aggression by land, by sea, and from the air, and in general all damage as defined in the Annex I hereto.

Annex 1: "Compensation may be claimed from Germany under Article 232 above in respect of the total damage under the following categories ... (9) Damage in respect of all property wherever situated belonging to any of the Allied or Associated states or their nationals, with the exception of naval and military works or materials, which has been carried off, seized, injured or destroyed by the acts of Germany or her allies on land, on sea or from the air, or damage directly in consequence of hostilities or of any operations of war.

The Canadian Commission was mandated to deal with damages "directly in consequence of hostilities or of any operations of war." The term "hostilities," McDougall wrote, implies and involves "enemy activities" and cannot be construed to mean the action of "a power in quelling an insurrection of its own people, or, as in this case, a wholesale slaughter of its own subjects." The losses sustained by Armenians, McDougall judged, were not the result of an act of war. The destruction wrought upon the Armenians, immense though it was, did "not raise the act to the dignity of either a 'hostility' or an 'operation of war.'" He concluded that "the war was merely a cloak for the depredations committed." "History," he wrote, "records no such tragic fate as that which overtook the Armenian population of Turkey in the year 1915 ... the Turkish Government inaugurated and pursued a policy of extermination of these people which was carried out with the utmost ferocity and brutality." The massacres, deportations, confiscations, and destruction were "the consummation of traditional Turkish policy, which could be and was perpetrated with impunity due to the preoccupation of civilized nations in the world war." Despite Turkish and German insistence that the treatment of Armenians was generated by the exigencies of war, McDougall, in his turn, insisted that the events starting in 1915 were part of an ongoing Turkish policy to annihilate the Armenians and that this policy was already evident *before* the outbreak of World War I. Therefore, based on a "strict application" of the treaty sections that fell within the terms of his commission, he felt bound to rule that he had no jurisdiction over the Armenian Canadian claims.[51]

The interpretation of annex 1, paragraph 9, is also contentious. It states in part that compensation would be based on damage of all property belonging to any of the Allied or Associated states or their nationals that had been "carried off, seized, injured or destroyed by the acts of Germany or her allies on land, on sea or from the air, *or* damage directly in consequence of hostilities or of any operations of war" (italics mine). In a letter to the Board of Trade in London, Carlisle sought British precedent in administering paragraph 9, particularly with respect to the Royal Commission on Compensation for Suffering and Damage by Enemy Action (15 August 1921), otherwise known as the Sumner Commission. He referred to the "absurd decision" to reject the Armenian Canadian claims because they did not fall within the term "damage directly in consequence of hostilities or of any operation of war," and he protested that the commissioner had refused to recognize damage in respect of property "carried off, seized, injured or destroyed."[52]

Months after the McDougall Report, Canadian officials once again sought British precedent from the Board of Trade in interpreting paragraph 9. In a telegram dated 1 December 1931, Canadian authorities requested to know whether the words "damage directly ... operations of war" referred to damage to property "caused by war operations or not." The reply stated that the Sumner Commission did not make a decision to interpret paragraph 9, but that it was "accepted" that the words "damage directly ... war" "did not in any way qualify the preceding passage [i.e., carried off, seized, injured, or destroyed] but rather tended to its *amplification*" (italics mine).[53]

The Sumner Commission dealt with cases involving *moral claims* by British nationals for compensation for suffering or damage within the terms of the Treaty of Versailles.[54] In his first report, Baron Sumner elaborated on the circumstances, noting that the inclusion of the phrase *moral claim* in the terms of reference authorized the commission to depart from the procedure and arrangements of a court of law and to bend, to some extent, strict legal rules, sometimes in favour of allowing claims and sometimes in favour of disallowing them.[55] While it may be true that the Sumner Commission's recommendations for compassionate allowance in certain cases could not be held as defining particular clauses of the Treaty of Versailles, it is also true that the flexibility that the Sumner Commission exercised once again highlighted the narrowness of the Canadian approach.

This is particularly true since the Sumner Commission made "*many hundred[s] of awards* to British subjects of Armenian origin, who suffered damage to and loss of property arising out of the Armenian Massacres of 1915 in Turkey ... claims similar in every respect and arising out of the same set of circumstances" as those that the Canadian Reparation Commission was adjudicating (italics mine). It was not only in Britain that awards had been based on the Versailles Treaty. Previous reparation commissioners in Canada had also ruled in favour of Armenian claimants under the terms of the Treaty of Versailles.[56]

Third, having decided that petitioners were precluded from applying anew to the Canadian Commission, since their claims had already been heard in Paris, and having determined that he had no jurisdiction over the claims, since they did not fall under the specified terms of the Versailles Treaty, McDougall then proceeded to rule on the validity of evidence provided by the petitioners: "Even were I to accept these claims for consideration and assessment," he asked, "have these claimants proven or can they prove a loss suffered ... susceptible of being measured with reasonable exactness by pecuniary standards?"

He explained that the lawyer for the claimants had submitted evidence upon the following points: 1 Canadian nationality prior to the beginning of the war, 2 cause of damage or appropriation, 3 ownership of property seized or destroyed, and 4 amount of loss. No problem regarding nationality existed, since citizenship could easily be verified by naturalization certificates. Similarly, the cause of damage or of confiscation was clear. The main issues remained proof of ownership and amount of pecuniary loss. Since the "best evidence," i.e., deeds, could not be obtained for proof of ownership, the claimants' lawyers, noted McDougall, relied on "secondary evidence," i.e., sworn testimony of witnesses and of claimants themselves. McDougall judged that "these witnesses could not know of the state of the title at the time it was expropriated," since the owner might have "transferred, mortgaged or otherwise dealt with his property." Venturing thus into the realm of "possibilities," McDougall concluded that it would be "manifestly improper" to make an award for damage or loss that "quite conceivably, never arose, due to possible mutations in the title of the original holder." Thus, while he himself pursued the realm of "possibilities," he required "conclusive" evidence from the claimants.

Let us consider the right of inheritance. Vesting title in these claimants was based on the presumed death of all relatives who might have had an interest in the property. "While this may, in general, having regard to the immensity and completeness of the massacres, be regarded as a reasonable presumption," wrote McDougall, "yet it is by no means '*conclusive*' since tens of thousands of Armenians survived" (italics mine). Claimants, he argued, could not prove beyond doubt that they and they alone were the true heirs. Even if they might have been true heirs, the adjudicator ruled, claimants could not prove that the destruction of the property had occurred *after* they had inherited it, i.e., after the death of their relatives in Anatolia. In other words, he argued that the property probably belonged to Turkish nationals at the precise moment of destruction and not to the claimants as Canadian citizens. McDougall, it seems, treated the entire question of inheritance as if the property were at hand and he was engaged in a lawsuit to prove exactly who should inherit it. As for those who were registered owners, about 133 claimants, McDougall had equally stern words: "They were not living on the properties at the time and it would be the scantiest hearsay for witnesses to declare that such claimants were the owners of such and such properties." He declared that the sworn evidence of the registered owners and of other villagers fell "far short of legal proof and would not be accepted by a court of law."[57] Stated bluntly, he distrusted the veracity of the sworn statements by registered owners, heirs, and other witnesses.

Responding to the argument that these claimants should not be penalized because of their inability to furnish more substantial proof through the destruction of their deeds and the land registry records by the Turks, he discounted the sworn testimonies and the secondary evidence which would have stood up in any Court of Justice in Britain, and declared, "*Inability to furnish proof*, however distressing and difficult may be the circumstances, cannot by that fact create a *legal* claim"[58] (italics mine). As to testimony regarding the precise amount of damage or of theft, McDougall, having already rejected the evidence of Armenians, commented on the report provided by the architectural and agricultural specialists to the Paris Commission (referred to above): "Admirable as may be this report, it forms an insecure foundation upon which to assess damages, particularly having regard to the dubiety of the claims themselves."[58]

In short, no proof offered by the claimants was accepted by the commissioner. It was as if Armenians had left their wives and children and their parents and grandparents in a state of destitution in the old country and had migrated to Canada where they had squandered their earnings. It followed, then, that their claims were presumed to be false. The claims to ownership of land and houses, it was implied, were simply fabrications, engineered to extract money from the Canadian government under false pretenses.

In fact, the reverse was true. Those who came to North America from Keghi were not only men with vision but also men with some means to make the transatlantic journey. By local standards some had come from well-off families. As already shown, about 300 Armenians had become naturalized British subjects before 1914. Presumably they did not intend to return permanently to the old country. The remainder, perhaps 700 to 1,200 people, mostly men, were probably intending to return home at some future time. Whatever the immigration status of the newcomers, it is clear that many remitted funds to their families still in the old country.

The money remitted to the village by Keghi sons, including those who were naturalized British subjects, made a monumental impact on the economic status of the Armenians.[59] With this outside capital, Armenian families were able to restore their homes and farms, which had been devastated by the pogroms of 1894–97. They were able to buy more land, to build new houses in order to ameliorate overcrowded living arrangements, and to add a second floor to existing houses. In some cases they added glass to their windows, the height of local luxury. But McDougall turned a deaf ear to their testimonies.

While he said he was "not bound by rules of law" and would decide these cases upon principles of equity, justice, and good faith, in fact he disregarded the principles he claimed to espouse and proved unwilling to accord the "widest latitude." Rather he acted in favour of "strict legality."[60] In his view claimants were unable to provide real "proof," and the evidence offered as to ownership and loss was "conjectural and speculative." In short, the claims were "inchoate." The adjudicator applied the criterion not of proof beyond a reasonable doubt but of proof beyond all measure of doubt. He dealt with the loss of property not on the basis of equity and justice but on the fine points of law. Time and again he referred to the legalities of the case, insisting that the claims be based on contract law, certified property ownership, and paper proof. If he had been equitable and just, he would have understood that had the destruction not been so total, perhaps then the victims would have been able to salvage some deeds and papers. Lord Sumner, the British commissioner, recognized the extent of loss when he emphasized the "complete destruction of property making local investigation fruitless," particularly "in parts of Turkey where massacres of Armenians and pillage of their property are known to have taken place."[61]

Not only does McDougall fail to deal equitably and justly with dispossession of *property* sustained by the claimants, but he rigorously avoids mentioning the far more morally binding basis for equity and justice: the loss of human life. Nowhere does he deal with the loss of wife and children, of sisters and brothers, of mothers and fathers. By excluding the loss of family and confining his judgment to the loss of property, McDougall rejects the consequences of mass murder and, in the process, reveals his biased and dogmatic approach.

McDougall's rejection struck Armenian Canadians like a thunderbolt. Not only did he rule that their petition was outside his jurisdiction, but he also determined that if he had had jurisdiction, he would have dismissed all 274 claims on the grounds of lack of evidence. In effect, he doubted the word of the claimants and their witnesses about their losses and ruled that they, as a group of naturalized British subjects, were not entitled to reparations. McDougall's position was all the more galling because Armenian men had died fighting in the trenches of France and at least eleven claimants were veterans of the Canadian Expeditionary Force, either as volunteers or draftees, and had seen active duty in Europe and Siberia.[62] In other words, Armenian Canadians had been called upon and had tried to fulfill *their* obligations as British subjects. While these facts may not have been *legally* relevant, they carried considerable *moral* weight among Armenian Canadians.

In general, McDougall's views echoed those of another commissioner who conceded that naturalization gave one the rights of "a British subject in Canada" but added, "why should our country be called upon to protect the property and interest of naturalized immigrants in the countries of their origin when they see fit to return?"[63] Was naturalization to be a one-way process that involved only responsibility or obligation by the naturalized subject himself but no corresponding responsibility by the state to protect him, his family, or his interests outside Canada? In fact, one of the rights of a British subject was the right to protection by his government of his person and property against enemy aggression.[64] These naturalized Armenian Canadian claimants should have been regarded in the same light as natural-born British subjects who were owners of real and personal property in Turkey at the outbreak of the war.[65]

In spite of the lawyers' protests, the Privy Council and the governor-general accepted McDougall's report on 13 May 1931.[66] On 30 June 1931, angry and frustrated, the Armenian claimants took an unusual and unprecedented step; they petitioned and set their case before the governor-general of Canada. Using McDougall's statement that the claimants may be entitled to "consideration upon another basis and from another authority," the Armenians requested a second commission to examine and assess the 274 claims. Through their lawyers, Carlisle and Coté, they also agreed to a fixed sum in cash or bonds to be allocated for payment and compensation. The original claims amounted to $4,953,955 and with interest had risen to $8,917,199. The petitioners, however, were prepared to accept the lower sum of $4,043,179, based on the *minimum* estimates of the official experts of the Paris Commission in Turkey.[67]

In a lengthy, strongly worded document, Carlisle and Coté examined the history of the Armenian claims from the time they were submitted to the Canadian government in 1920 to the McDougall Commission.

In particular, they condemned McDougall in no unmistakable terms for giving "judgment on the facts, although Counsel had not been notified that the claims were *at trial*" ("Petition," annex 4, 1; italics mine). "Out of the obvious confusion of issues arises the anomaly of a Tribunal holding that it had no Jurisdiction to hear a case and then giving Judgment in the Case, admitting in fact, either that it had jurisdiction to try the case or that it tried it without having jurisdiction and without notice to the applicant" ("Petition," annex 4, 18). They berated the commissioner for having "misread" and misinterpreted the pertinent sections of the Treaty of Versailles (annex 4, 4, 12) and for making decisions that were "bad in law" (annex 4, 14). They drew attention to the claimants' triple jeopardy: not only had Germany's ally destroyed their property and destroyed the evidence of their ownership, but the Canadian commissioner had refused to grant them compensation for these losses: "So that a claim for compensation made against Germany should not fail for non-production of evidence destroyed by her or by her ally – so in fact that the responsibility of the enemy should not be lessened in respect of one set of damage, by another act of damage committed by that enemy."[68] "To his Government," they concluded, "he [McDougall] justifies a shameful sacrifice of these claimants' rights and the infliction of a grave injustice" ("Petition," annex 4, 21).

CAHAN'S REPORT

Enter Charles Hazlitt Cahan, the secretary of state. Like McDougall, he was a lawyer from Montreal of Scotch-Irish background. Born in 1861 in Nova Scotia, Cahan received his law degree at Dalhousie in 1890. While a student, he worked for the *Halifax Herald and Mail*, an experience that almost cost him admission to the bar. In Nova Scotia at that time, each law graduate had to take an oath that he had not been employed while a student. Cahan refused to take the oath and was, accordingly, refused admission. For the next two years he campaigned in the pages of the *Herald* to have this rule repealed, on the grounds that it favoured the sons of the wealthy and placed prohibitions on impecunious students working their way through university. The rule was in fact repealed, and Cahan was called to the bar in 1893. During the 1890s he reorganized the provincial Conservative Party and ran against Hon. W.S. Fielding and the secessionist movement in Nova Scotia. He opposed legislation relating to the Dominion Coal Company on the grounds it would create a monopoly that would be prejudicial to the interests of Nova Scotia and of Canada. Hired by Sir

William Van Horne, Sir George Drummond, and Sir Edward Clouston he carried out legal and administrative work in organizing tramway and light-and-power undertakings in British Guiana, Trinidad, and Mexico.[69] In 1908 he returned to Canada to practise law in Montreal, where he entered federal politics in 1925. Cahan, a specialist in Canadian constitutional law, was a member of the House of Commons from 1925 to 1940 and acted as secretary of state and custodian of enemy property during R.B. Bennet's tenure. A tall, big man, Cahan was regarded as spokesman for big-business interests and was also known for his "ardent and active sympathy for minorities," most notably in defending the rights of the French in the Manitoba School Question. He often took up the cudgels in defence of those he believed to be "labouring under disability of some description."[70]

On 20 January 1932 Cahan brought down a lengthy confidential report in which he recounted the history of the Armenian claims. Rebutting many of Carlisle's arguments, he went a step further by responding to Carlisle's references to the rights of the petitioners under the Treaty of Versailles. In the petition, Carlisle had argued that the petitioners were "entitled to claim compensation from Germany" according to the terms of the Treaty of Versailles, articles 231, 232, and annex 1 (see above). Cahan took the opportunity to discuss the relationship between the state and the individual with respect to reparations. Citing a memorandum from the secretary of state for the colonies to the governor-general of Canada (27 April 1920), Cahan declared that Canadian nationals "*as individuals*" had no rights to compensation under the terms of the Treaty of Versailles (italics mine). Outlining the decision of the British government regarding payment to individuals for loss or damage, Cahan quoted from the above-mentioned memo, emphasizing that "claims to be made are claims by Government in respect to wrongs done to the State and not claims by individuals in respect of private wrongs." The government was not an agent for an individual to put forward his claim. "*Therefore any payments received from Germany are property of the Nation and no individual will have any claim in law for any sum which His Majesty's Government may receive from Germany in respect of Reparation*" (italics Cahan's). Again citing British precedent, he stated that any payments that had been made to individuals had been "*an act of grace on the part of His Majesty's Government*" (italics Cahan's). In Canada, he added, *all payments of reparations* had been made "*purely as a matter of grace,*" and no petitioner had any "*legal* right whatever to any such payments" (italics mine).[71]

Accordingly, Cahan recommended in his report that a second commission be denied on the grounds that such an undertaking would prove "expensive, unnecessary and utterly futile," since no evidence had been submitted that would "enable the Commissioner, under the terms of his Commission, to make a favorable report" on the claims. However, departing from McDougall, he made the important point that there were "probably" naturalized Canadians who were relatives of those who had been massacred during the war and whose property had been pillaged and destroyed. It was impossible, he continued, to prove conclusively the identity of those who had been massacred and those who had survived and to establish by any known legal evidence the identity of the relatives of those massacred, who "were entitled by law to inherit their property." On this basis, then, he recommended that as a matter of grace – typical in all reparations cases – Parliament make the "appropriation of a gratuity, limited in amount, which might be distributed on an equitable basis as a solatium" among the Armenian Canadian claimants who were naturalized British subjects.[72]

On 27 January 1932, Cahan recommended to Prime Minister Bennett that $350,000 be placed in the estimates as a compassionate allowance in final compensation for the 274 claims. He suggested that the distribution be based on the rules established by the Paris Commission in assessing the claims with respect both to loss of life and loss of property. For the sake of an equitable distribution, Cahan recommended that the 73 claims for loss of life, which had reached the Paris Commission too late for consideration, be given "first charge" on the appropriation. The secretary of state assured the prime minister that in his discussions with the claimants' lawyers they had agreed to his proposed disposition of $350,000 and had stated that the claimants would accept the distribution "with gratitude and satisfaction." He added that he did not concur with the lawyers' request that only $325,000 be distributed among the claimants and that the remaining $25,000 be granted to them to cover legal charges and expenses in collecting evidence. On 1 February, Carlisle and Coté wrote to Cahan that on behalf of their clients, they would accept $300,000 for immediate distribution "without the necessity of further production of evidence."[73]

Thereupon ensued a flurry of correspondence involving the Department of the Secretary of State, the auditor-general, and the Department of Justice. Cahan asked the auditor-general, Georges Gonthier, if the amounts for the Armenian claims could be taken from item 484 of Appropriation Act No. 5 (Reparations from Germany) of the last session of Parliament, in which $3.2 million had been voted "To provide for the payment of claims for compensation for loss sustained by the civil population and prisoners of war of Canada during the late War, interest thereon, and cost of administration."[74] Gonthier replied in the negative, stating that the word "claims" must be "construed" to mean "claims properly adjudicated upon." Citing Hansard, he noted that the discussion in the House of Commons "appears to imply that amounts paid from this Vote were to be for claims on which the Commissioner had made awards. No such awards were made in regard to the Armenian claims."[75] Thomas Mulvey, the under-secretary of state shot back: "I scarcely agree with the view you take. I do not see any reason why you should read into the Estimate any words whatever which are not there. I would point out to you that the Estimate itself used the word 'claim,' although there cannot be any doubt that there is no legal right to the claim." In qualifying the word "claim" by adding "claims properly adjudicated upon," Mulvey complained, the auditor-general was giving the term "claim" a connotation of legal liability.[76] This exchange brought in the Department of Justice.

In a seven-page memo, C.P. Plaxton, the deputy minister of justice, reviewed the history of the Armenian claims, emphasizing the statements made by the secretary of state in his Report to Council pertaining to the legal rights of claimants: "any payments received from Germany [under the terms of the Treaty of Versailles] are property of the Nation and no individual will have any claim in law for any sum which His Majesty's Government may receive from Germany in respect of reparation ... His Majesty's Government recognize that while there is no legal claim, private individuals may have strong moral claim for compensation for sufferings and damage ... payments can be made to individuals as an act of grace on the part of His Majesty's Government."[77]

Plaxton then proceeded to split hairs, distinguishing between payment as an act of grace and as a gratuity. Payments of compensation, he stated, were granted ex gratia out of funds provided by Parliament for that purpose, but the funds were not to be regarded as an eleemosynary (charitable) fund. The secretary of state had recommended "a gratuity ... as a solatium." "In law," noted the deputy minister of justice, "a solatium is a sum of money paid, over or above the actual damages as a solace for injured feelings ... a compensation as a soothing to the affections or wounded feelings." He did not think that the proposed payment of a gratuity as a solatium could be regarded as payment of claims for compensation under Vote 484.[78] Before replying to the auditor-general's request for clarification, however, Plaxton sent a draft of his negative opinion to the minister of justice for his personal consideration. A much shorter statement, it was, nevertheless, just as marked by nitpicking: "The terms of the Vote [484] ... [are] for payment of 'claims for compensation for loss' ... presumably only such claims as might be found to be based upon strong moral or equitable grounds ... The payments which the Secretary of State has recommended are payments of a gratuity of limited amount, as a solatium, to the claimants. Payments of that character appear to me to be entirely heterogeneous to payments of claims for compensation for loss sustained."[79]

The logic for denying the Armenian claims was collapsing into tatters. As seen above, McDougall had taken considerable pains to adjudicate the Armenian claims in purely legal terms and had refused to adjudicate them in moral or equitable terms. Now the deputy minister of justice was arguing that claims were to be considered in moral or equitable terms, but not as a gratuity.

Whether either Plaxton's memo or his draft opinion fell into Cahan's hands is uncertain, but on 7 March, in a letter to the minister of justice, Cahan emphatically and straightforwardly stated his case:

My contention is that the Governor in Council has discretion to authorize, by order in council, the payment of $300,000 in final settlement of those claims.

The policy of making such a compromise is not now under consideration; that is a matter of policy for the Governor in Council to decide.

I contend that a favorable report of Commissioner McDougall is not a necessary condition precedent to the exercise of the discretion of the Governor in Council: as the Commissioner was appointed by Council to procure information on which the Council might act.

The Council, nevertheless, is not bound by the Commissioner's Report, but can exercise its own discretion in ordering payments out of this vote of $3,200,000."[80]

Simply stated, total discretion to grant reparations lay with the Sovereign or his/her representative.

On 8 March the minister of justice agreed with Cahan, declaring that Item 484 of the Appropriation Act No. 5 (Reparations payment) constituted "sufficient parliamentary authority" for the settlement of the Armenian claims and that the governor in council had "discretion to determine whether and to what extent the moneys as appropriated" should be expended in settlement of these claims.[81]

THE SOLATIUM

On 12 March 1932 the Canadian government passed Order in Council P.C. 571 authorizing the sum of $300,000 to be set aside for the Armenian claims, based on Item 484, which provided for the "payment of claims for compensation for loss sustained by the civil population and prisoners of war of Canada during the war," including interest.[82] The money was to be taken from the funds which Canada received annually as its quota of reparations from Germany.[83] The specific amount of each claim was to be calculated on a sliding scale according to the formula established by the Paris Commission.

By 29 August 1932, 257 Armenian Canadians had received a total of $299,191.71, including interest. About 23 of the recipients were women, most frequently widows; the rest were men. The amounts for each claimant varied from between $400 to $5,000. Recipients signed receipts upon accepting the specified sums. Only Nishon Fustukian of St Catharines, who was to receive approximately $808, refused to accept the cheque and returned it to the government, presumably on a point of principle,[84] possibly on the grounds that his brother, Mamigon Fustukian, a veteran of the Canadian Expeditionary Force, had been wounded in action in France and that he considered the sum of $808 an insult, particularly in the light of legal fees[85]

The claims fell into three categories: loss of life of wife and/or children; loss of farms, assessed in acreage; and loss of other property. The award used the Paris Commission's scale of values, setting aside £47 sterling, or approximately Can$240, for the loss of a wife and £9 sterling, or Can$48, for the loss of each child.[86] Based on these calculations, the grant awarded $17,627 in total for loss of life. The remaining $282,373 was assigned to loss of property, again on a sliding scale. Farms were calculated on the basis of acreage, the minimum being fifty acres and the maximum being five hundred acres. For the loss of other property, such as shops and factories, an assessment was made directly in Turkish pounds.[87] The final rate for property losses amounted to Can$.803 per £T, or about 18 percent of the *original* claim.

It appears that the attorneys, including Grace Brown, Windrum Carlisle, and Louis Coté, of Ottawa, received perhaps as much as 40 percent, or approximately $120,000, of the award on a contingency basis for their fees and disbursements.[88] The Canadian government issued cheques in the names of the claimants and forwarded them to their attorneys who, having power of attorney, endorsed the cheques, took their share, and deposited the remainder in special accounts, usually in the Canadian Bank of Commerce in Ottawa. The lawyers then sent drafts and receipt forms to the claimants, who were obliged to sign the receipt before receiving the payment.[89]

After twelve years of negotiations and many setbacks along the way, the Armenian Canadians received but a token amount. Most were disappointed with the financial arrangements. Several of the original petitioners had died, some intestate, and their heirs were obliged to seek further legal assistance at further cost to receive the prescribed amounts.[90] In the end, though, even the small amount these mostly humble factory workers received proved useful. During the early 1930s, when many labourers were often unemployed, the money from the Canadian government could mean the difference between being evicted and paying down a mortgage.

Apart from the fact that Armenian Canadians received a sum of money, this episode of reparations has other, significant ramifications. McDougall made a peculiar decision with respect to the claimants as naturalized British subjects. He ruled that the Turkish government's confiscation and destruction of Armenian Canadian, and hence British, property in Turkey during the war was not reparable under the terms of the Treaty of Versailles. When Turkey committed those deliberate depredations upon British property, he insisted, it was *actually* carrying out a general seizure of the property of its *own* subjects, regardless of whether or not they had been naturalized elsewhere. Accordingly, Armenian Canadian claimants fell outside the terms of the Treaty of Versailles. In other words, he treated Armenians naturalized in Canada not as British subjects but as subjects of the Ottoman Empire, a position that is steeped in racism.

There were no provisions in Canadian or British law under which a naturalized British subject was obliged to abandon or surrender his property or interests in his country of origin. In a memo entitled "Rights of War Claimants of Armenian Origin through Naturalization in Canada under the Peace Treaties," McDougall's ruling is seen as introducing "a novel – not to say quite unheard of – principle into international law, namely, that the responsibility of a state for physical and direct damage that it has caused to the property of the nationals of a belligerent state in time of war, *would depend, not upon the fact and the nature of the act of damage and upon its results, but upon the motive behind the act*" (emphasis in the original).[91] Armenians naturalized in Canada, like all other naturalized Canadians, fell under the aegis of the international rule of law that property follows nationality. They were subject to the same obligations and liabilities and entitled to the same rights and privileges – including rights of property in foreign states – as all natural-born British subjects.

Both McDougall and Cahan underscored that the events starting in 1915 were an internal matter in the Ottoman Empire and that the Armenian tragedy was not a consequence of the war but rather of the ongoing Turkish policy of annihilating the Armenians. In their appraisal of Turkish policy, they were absolutely right. Since the 1880s Turkish policy had been set to destroy the Armenian minority, a goal that became evident during the pogroms of the 1890s. The obvious question is whether or not killings and depredations would have occurred had there been no world war. The answer is in the positive, though clearly the war provided the Young Turk party leaders with an adequate cloak for extensive and severe operations against Armenians.

One need only recall that massacres and confiscations started *before* the Great War and continued in Cilicia, Smyrna, and the Caucasus *after* the armistice in 1918 (see chapter 6).[92]

The Canadian position is in stark contrast to that taken by successive Turkish governments which have claimed that the massacres were the consequences of the war. To the Armenians at the time, Turkish authorities gave assurances that they were being "relocated" from the war zones for their own "safety," even though authorities were also deporting Armenians far from the battlefields. To the world, Turkish governments have argued that the treatment of the Armenians was necessary because of an imminent Armenian insurrection. In fact, developments before the outbreak of war were very favourable for the Armenians because a special European Commission was on its way into the Anatolian interior to institute a measure of law and order, to bring about peace and security, and to provide a measure of local autonomy for the Armenian minority. Armenians, moreover, provided the Turkish war effort with arms, money, military billeting, and soldiers. The Armenian *millet* hardly appears to be a people engaged in civil war, as some Turkish apologists have since argued.

The issue of naturalization and its attendant rights placed Armenians in a tangled web. During the war, Britain and Canada did not view Armenians in Canada as enemy aliens and did not incarcerate them. Armenians in Canada, in turn, assumed their obligations by raising funds and supplies for the Canadian war effort and by enlisting in the Canadian Expeditionary Force for overseas service. Yet when it came down to a question of their rights after the war, they were being treated, in effect, as Ottoman subjects – even those naturalized in Canada. This placed Armenians in double jeopardy, for during the war, Turkish authorities demanded that Armenians fulfill the obligations of citizenship and contribute to the war effort. Thousands of Armenian men, both civilian and military personnel, were called upon to work in labour battalions (they are not to be confused with prisoners of war); Armenian doctors were relegated to work in Turkish hospitals; and countless numbers of Armenian women and girls were ordered to work in Turkish hospitals and Moslem homes and institutions: all unpaid labour – slave labour, to be exact, since the Turkish government had already abrogated the rights and privileges of citizenship from these same Armenians.

The question of Armenian reparations is also important because, in effect, it drew out a distinction between war crimes and crimes against humanity. On 24 May 1915, in view of the massacres by the Ottoman government and its agents, the Allies issued a joint declaration, in which they declared they would hold "personally responsible ... all members of the Ottoman Government ... as are implicated ... *in such massacres*" (italics mine). Vahakn Dadrian emphasizes that this statement was similar "to the nineteenth-century tradition of proclaiming the doctrine of humanitarian intervention on behalf of oppressed nationalities and minorities," that it ushered in the use of the term "crimes against humanity," and that it became the forerunner of the principle of crimes against humanity eventually adopted by the United Nations Convention on Genocide.[93] But in the post–World War I period, the Allied powers did not carry out Nuremberg-type trials. Such was the sanctity and inviolability of state sovereignty that Turkey's criminal abuse of sovereignty went almost unchallenged. If the Ottoman government had mistreated its own citizens and had massacred one of its minorities, it was an internal matter, not a war crime.[94]

Although both McDougall and Cahan argued that the massacres did not result from the "operations of war," they described the events in the Ottoman Empire as "brutal," "cruel," "inhuman." Cahan wrote that "these massacres were inexpressible, brutal and inhuman, and undoubtedly great suffering and loss were thereby sustained by the Armenian population of Turkey."[95] Their use of words like "annihilate" and "eradicate" are significant. By implication, they conclude that these massacres were crimes against humanity. Eleven years later the world was to hear another synonym for the same overwhelming destruction of a people: Genocide. Already, then, in the early 1930s Canadian jurists and senior officials held concepts that would crystallize in the post–World War II period.

John Maynard Keynes was correct when he remarked that major changes on the international scene took place during and after World War I. Concepts of refugees, war crimes, international intervention, crimes against humanity, and the relationship of the state to the individual were in the process of being formulated after World War I. International jurisprudence was only just beginning to come to terms with definitions, rules, and regulations. It would take another war and another holocaust to induce the international community to set up guidelines, standards, and definitions.

It is unfortunate that the Armenian claims were buffeted from one country to another and from one commission to another. Perhaps if they had been heard by the first Canadian Commission, as they might have been, or by the Sumner Commission in Britain, the Armenian Canadians would have fared better. Disappointed though they were, the Armenian Canadians, in the end, appreciated the symbolism of the Canadian government's action. It was called a solatium. It was called an act of grace. It was called reparations. Clearly written at the top of each receipt were the words, "Department of the Secretary of State of Canada, Reparation Payment." For Armenian Canadians the act of grace was proof that their government recognized their losses and acknowledged their grief. For Armenians generally, the Canadian government's action represented one of a small number of reparations payments that the survivors of the Genocide received – anywhere in the world.

Postcard of the Armenian General Benevolent Union, with a photo of one of its founders, Boghos Nubar Pasha, ca 1920. Kaprielian collection

Crotcheted and needleworked handkerchiefs, the work of Armenian women in southern Ontario. Photographer, Albert Kaprielian. Kaprielian collection

Book cover of revolutionary and patriotic songs. Published by the Armenian Revolutionary Federation, Beirut, Lebanon, 1977. Kaprielian collection

Group photo of a picnic in Hamilton, ca 1936–37. Growing up in Ontario provided a fusion of Canadian and Armenian heritages. "During the day, we'd go to public school. Talk and play in English. Learn about Champlain and Sir John A. Macdonald, get caught up in the exploits of the Royal Canadian Air Force, about the war and Stalingrad. We'd sing 'British Grenadiers,' 'Rule Britannia,' and 'The Maple Leaf.' Then in the evenings we'd go to Armenian school and learn about General Antranig and the Armenian volunteers and sing 'Lusin Chigar' and 'Iprev Artsiv.' We'd learn about our ancient Armenian civilization and Christianity, and about 'Mesrob Mashtots.'" Z. Zakarian, Hamilton. Photo in Kaprielian collection

Tombstone, Brantford. The Armenian lettering gives the birthplace of both husband and wife. Murad Gergosian was born in the village of Astghaberd, Keghi, and his wife Saten was born in the city of Erzerum. The birth dates reveal the age differences between husband and wife. Photographer, Canon Harold Nahabedian, Toronto

We Believe

We Believe:-

That the building of a nation is somewhat analogous to building of a family unit. Whether a child is born of the parents or adopted by them, that child should deserve the same measure of care and affection.

In return, the highest sense of appreciation must be developed within the children in order to harmonize the life of that family with sincerity of purpose.

We Believe:-

That in this glorious country of ours regardless of differences of race or creed everyone is enjoying liberties in abundance on equal terms, therefore, we must also discharge our citizenship responsibilities with utmost loyalty and sense of belonging.

We Believe:-

That the destiny of Canada is ordained and the guiding hand of the Almighty has brought together from all corners of the world a variety of builders to create a beautiful tapestry of citizenship. Though somewhat different in their mode of building nevertheless the faith and understanding of each one is to build a nation to symbolize peace and harmony for the rest of the world to follow.

This We Believe!

A statement of goals expressed by Armenian community leaders, Ontario, 1960s. Kaprielian collection

Paul and Norman Kaprielian, 1931. "I remember one year in public school the teacher would read us from *The Secret Garden* every Friday afternoon, and in the evening at Armenian school, Varjabed would tell us about the great Armenian victory at Sardarabad, when the bells of every Armenian church tolled for days and every Armenian farm boy left his plough and every city boy left his home to go and fight to save the nation." Taped interview, Z. Zakarian, Hamilton. Photo in Kaprielian collection

PART FIVE

Reconstructing New Worlds

11

Foundations of Material Life: St Catharines

The Armenian became an immigrant when he viewed his future in Canada rather than in the homeland.

The Genocide, followed by the postwar traumas, made a profound impression on the Armenians and confirmed once again that they would survive only by relying on their own resources. The will to survive ran deep. Each person sought to rebuild his life, his family, and his nation. In the annals of history, expulsion has been a deliberate act of destruction. Exile has been synonymous with uprootedness and death. But for those who survive such traumas, exile has also signified a new beginning, a new life with new sorrows and new joys. With an indomitable spirit, with patience and tenderness, tears and laughter, love and hatred, refugees and oldtimers together set about to create their own new world.

The small, tight, pre-1914 neighbourhoods close to the factories attracted the postwar immigrants. A list from 1928 of 274 Armenians who had taken out Canadian naturalization before 1914 reveals that 251 lived in the old Armenian settlements of Brantford, St Catharines, Galt, and Hamilton, with the rest living in Guelph, Preston, Windsor, Sandwich, and Toronto, Ontario. The pre-1914 neighbourhoods remained stable, as Ontario and Carlton Streets in St Catharines; Buffalo, Darling, Market, Marlboro, Grey, Wellington, and Park Streets in Brantford; Beverley and Cameron Streets in Galt; and Princess, Gibson, and Earl Streets in Hamilton remained centres of settlement.[1] A glance at *Vernon's St Catharines City Directory* for 1941 confirms the existence of an Armenian "village." Of 22 names listed on the north side of Carlton Street running two blocks east of McKinnon's factory, 18 were Armenian, 1 was the Armenian church, and 1 was the Armenian club. Of 16 names listed in the same year on Ontario Street – directly opposite the factory – 10 were Armenian.[2]

A certain homogeneity had prevailed before the entry of the second wave. The great majority of early settlers were born in Keghi, and they dominated settlement in southern Ontario. In smaller numbers immigrants from other areas also came to the province: men from Jabaghjour settled in Brantford; migrants from the region of Van gravitated to Galt and Guelph; and newcomers from Daron/Mush chose St Catharines and Hamilton.[3] In spite of different origins, the pioneers had much in common, for they were all small farmers from the Armenian provinces and spoke and thought in similar ways. And, as already shown, most were sojourners; only 10 families, for instance, had settled in St Catharines before the war.[4] By contrast, the refugees who arrived after the war came from different parts of the Ottoman Empire and from different backgrounds, some from well-off, educated urban families. This fact enriched the texture of community life and enlivened its spirit at the same time that it generated tensions and feelings of superiority, for some could never forget their former wealth and comfort.

In these settlements the Armenian churches and community centres were constructed after the formation of a neighbourhood. In St Catharines the church, built in 1930, was on Carlton Street a couple of blocks from the factory, and the Armenian "club," bought in 1934, was on the corner of Ontario and Carlton Streets, directly across from McKinnon's. Similarly, in Hamilton clubhouses and, finally, the community centre, built in 1951, were located on Princess and Gibson Streets, in the heart of the Armenian neighbourhood. These structures served not only to confirm the configurations of Armenian settlement but also to entrench these areas as Armenian *taghs,* or quarters.

Armenians entered Canada as farmers or farm labourers. Contrary to repeated denials by immigration officials, some actually took up farming, initially as farm help, then as farm owners, specifically in the Niagara Peninsula – in St Catharines, Stoney Creek, and Grimsby. By Prairie standards, their farms were miniscule, between five and thirty acres, mainly orchards and market gardens. Before they could afford to buy their own farmland, however, newcomers were obliged to work elsewhere to save enough money to invest in such a major purchase.[5]

Most Armenians in St Catharines worked at McKinnon Dash, later a subsidiary of General Motors. At the turn of the century, McKinnon's built a new plant in St Catharines and recruited Armenian labourers from the United States, who settled in the factory's shadow. The new factory was located at the northern limits of town, where St Catharines touched the farming region of Grantham Township. Thus, urban growth gradually encroached on the countryside. Agriculture and industry merged. Rural and urban, farm and factory, meshed in the community's economic life. In winter farmers worked in the factory to supplement their farm income, and when the factory was slack, moulders and coremakers took to the fields to make ends meet. But it was the factory, more than the farm, that dominated the community's economic development. In a hundred ways the factory took, but it also gave; in a hundred ways the men gave, but they also took.

Brantford had been the biggest Armenian settlement in Canada before World War I, but after the war, depression and unemployment drove many workers away.[6] Armenians set off to find jobs elsewhere, to join relatives and friends in other cities. A cousin in East St Louis, Illinois, might beckon a young labourer, or a friend might invite an unemployed compatriot to the Hood Rubber company in Watertown, Massachusetts. Brantford settlers moved off to Windsor, Granite City, Niagara Falls, Boston. With his promise of a five-dollar day, Henry Ford lured many to Detroit.[7] McKinnon Industries also offered employment. Converting from wartime production to the manufacture of automotive parts, the company rebounded quickly from the 1920–21 postwar depression. Gradually the settlement in St Catharines replaced the one in Brantford as the largest Armenian community, claiming between four and five hundred settlers during the 1920s, when the population of the city was edging up to twenty-four thousand.[8]

MEN AND THE FACTORY: 1920 TO 1950

By 1920 the pre-1914 settlers had been living in America for a minimum of six years. They had acquired a little English and some knowledge of North American ways and culture. Those who were working at McKinnon's had earned good wages during the war and had built up a relationship with their bosses. They had learned the moulder's craft and the art of survival on the shop floor. For these aging men, the plant had offered a measure of security, a crucial factor for immigrants who had lost everything in the homeland. The tragedy in the old country shook these settlers and made stability and rootedness all the more crucial.

Men who had worked hard in the factories during the war and who had accumulated some capital spent their savings after the war on finding and helping relatives, on facilitating their entry into Canada, and on buying houses. For them the 1920s were marked by family reconstruction and home purchase. *Vernon's City Directory* for 1931 reveals that of fifty-eight men's names mentioned in the Ontario-Carlton Street area, forty-two owned their own homes, four owned their own farms, and only twelve were tenants, probably newcomers who hoped to buy their own house as soon as possible.[9] Except for a slump in the mid-twenties, the men had more or less regular work during the decade and believed they could afford to buy property. One man might acquire a six-and-one-half-acre farm and house on Ontario Street in 1919 for just under ten thousand dollars. Another might purchase a six-room frame house on a small lot on Carlton Street in 1925 for four to five thousand dollars.

Property ownership, with its attendant debt, bound the men to the factory and, in a way, bound the factory to the workers. It gave the relationship between worker and factory an underlying sense of permanence. The factory was far from obliged to respond to the needs and requirements of transient labourers. But if the factory believed in the efficacy of a stable work force and demanded the loyalty of its employees, it could still ignore the workers' call for better wages and improved working conditions, but not as arrogantly.[10]

McKinnon Dash and Metal Works and the Warren Pink, Warren Axe, McKinnon Columbus Chain, Foster-Wheeler, and Welland Vale Companies all enabled relatively unskilled Armenian agriculturalists to establish an economic foothold in St Catharines before and during World War I. Most of the plants were located around Ontario and Carlton Streets, at the northern city limits on the edge of rural Grantham township. Oral testimony reveals that from the 1920s to the 1940s approximately 90 percent of Armenian factory workers in St Catharines worked at McKinnon's, including both oldtimers and newcomer refugees. *Vernon's City Directory* verifies this preference: Of thirty-nine Armenian men in the Carlton/Ontario Street area whose place of work is mentioned in 1931 (for 1930), thirty-five are listed as working at the plant.[11]

Lachlan Ebenezer McKinnon started a hardware store and backyard manufacturer of carriage parts in St Catharines around 1878. In 1901 he built a new plant at Ontario and Carlton streets, employed 95 men in the new malleable foundry, and renamed his company McKinnon Dash and Metal Works. Four years later, McKinnon Dash erected a drop forge and introduced the first electric welded chain to North America. When war broke out, the company expanded its work force to 750 to meet the wartime demand for saddlery and constructed a new building for the manufacture of shells and fuses. In the meantime, McKinnon recognized that the automobile was crowding out the horse drawn carriage as a means of travel. After the war McKinnon Industries Ltd. (the company had a new name) diversified production and engaged in the manufacture of automotive radiators, transmission gears, rear axles, differentials and other such components for a number of automobile manufacturers. The auto industry's relatively speedy recovery from the postwar slump is reflected in the number of employees: 750 during the war, 1,200 in 1922. In 1929 McKinnon's sold to General Motors, its biggest customer, and became a totally owned subsidiary of the American conglomerate but retained its own name, with its own president and general manager and board of directors. The Depression hit the company, but it bounced back and erected new buildings, including the Delco plant in 1930 (Dayton Engineering Laboratories Company, of Dayton, Ohio).

In 1936, the old foundry was dismantled and an overhead crane system installed for a forge and a new foundry, which produced both grey iron and malleable iron. The manufacture of automotive parts continued until World War II. From 1939 to 1945 McKinnon's doubled its floor space, in order to manufacture army truck components and other wartime essentials. Employment during the war fluctuated to a peak of 5,100 at the 43-acre Ontario St site. Seven years after the return to peacetime production, the company opened the largest and most modern malleable and grey iron foundry in the British Commonwealth on 140 acres in Grantham Township.[12]

As at International Harvester in Hamilton, at Massey Harris, Cockshutt's, Waterous, and the Malleable in Brantford, at Clare Brothers in Preston, at Bertram's in Dundas, at the Sandwich Foundry in Sandwich/Windsor, at the Galt Malleable, and at the Guelph Malleable, most Armenians worked in the foundries as unskilled labourers and as moulders, coremakers, shake-out men, stokers, and pattern makers. Before World War I they were earning about 10¢ an hour at McKinnon's, working ten hours a day, sometimes six or seven days a week. By the late 1920s they were earning about 25 to 28¢ an hour, moulders perhaps as high as 40¢ an hour.[13] The situation changed during the Depression, when the company cut back operations. Those who were lucky enough to work a day or two a week at McKinnon's "kept their heads down, tried to stay in the good books of their foremen, and looked to personal strategies of survival."[14] Wartime demands boosted the wages once again, this time to as high as $1.50 to $2.00 an hour.[15]

No extensive or organized padrone tradition existed among Armenians, as each man fended for himself within an informal network of mutual help. The experienced men considered it an obligation to assist newcomers to find jobs in the factories and to teach them the tricks of the trade. When he settled in Preston as a young refugee, an interviewee recalled how his uncle, a moulder at Clare Brothers foundries, took him around to various "shoe factories" to help him find a job. Eventually he landed a job at the Buffalo Sled Company, and when he had gained some experience, his uncle arranged a job for him at Clare Brothers. He taught him first how to "shake out" the sand for impurities and to mix the sand in preparation for the moulders' pouring. Gradually, the uncle taught the nephew how to be a moulder. In time, the roles were reversed; the young man helped his aging uncle at his job.[16]

Like all foundrymen, Armenians worked long hours doing "dirty work." They justifiably feared industrial accidents, for safeguards were few; each man could well remember a friend or relative who had died or had been maimed on the job. In 1930, for example, a forty-two-year-old foundry worker, an Armenian war veteran and the father of young children, was blinded by sparks at the Brantford Malleable (Pratt and Letchworth Malleable). He was never able to work again. He received $1,400 compensation.[17] Boghos Halagian, who was swooped into the furnace at McKinnon's and burned from the waist up, also received little help from the factory. Men ached from body deformations brought on by the weight of the hot ladles they lugged and suffered from diseases like silicosis induced by industrial pollution in the plant.[18]

They had no job security, they were under constant threat of layoff, and they were always at the mercy of the foreman, who ruled the floor with an iron whip. "It was a personal thing. It all depended on how good a worker you were, and Armenians were steady and reliable workers. It also depended on how well the boss liked you."[19] Special favours for the foreman: the bottle of scotch, the Christmas dinner, and cutting grass and clearing snow were all part of the accepted shop-floor tradition. This was especially true if a man wanted to arrange a job for a friend or relative or if he wanted better pay and conditions for himself. "Workers," summed up a respondent, "were competing with each other to see who could treat the boss better. That's the way it was. Just part of the job."[20]

Many stayed in the factory and accepted the work as their destiny, their only reality. They felt they had no other option but to work in the factory to support their family and pay their mortgage. In the final analysis, it was much better than their lot in the Ottoman Empire. "My father and his group," recalled an interviewee, "knew that they had to eat in a foreign country. So they plugged along and worked ... They had to hold on to what they had." Like many other Canadian factory workers, Armenians accepted management's role. As a rule, they "showed a very low profile. They said, 'We want to work. We want to raise our children. We don't want to get into any trouble with the government or the police or any *odars* (non-Armenians). We want to raise our kids.' That's really what it was. They didn't want to be involved in anything that might cause problems. If they had a job, they stayed with it and didn't make trouble."[21]

Even if they dominated the foundry at McKinnon's to the point that it was known as Little Armenia, even if they controlled the malleable iron foundry at International Harvester in Hamilton and for a time made up a major portion of foundry workers at Galt Malleable,[22] Armenians were not an organized force and seldom brought pressure to bear on the company as a unified power. For most Armenians, as for thousands of other workers during this period, "management was management; their authority was unquestioned."[23]

Yet there were internal compulsions that unified the men and made the company recognize Armenians as a distinct group, one that moved to its own rhythm.[24] Thomas Rice, former assistant superintendent of works at the Harvester remarked that Armenians did not mix much with other groups: "They kept to themselves." He went on to reveal another telling characteristic. Starting in the winter of 1931–32, Harvester provided a measure of relief for workers with service of five years or more. Based on the size of the family, the company gave food vouchers, provided clothing for children, and supplied families with coal and coke. None of the Armenians registered for relief. When he questioned their absence in the list of registrants, Rice was told by the foremen that the Armenians refused to accept relief. Thereupon he arranged to meet with the Armenian men in their own "club" to determine how they were living and why they had turned down company assistance. They told him they were buying some of their food on credit; they were struggling but managing. Only after Rice insisted that they apply for relief, did some reluctantly agree to accept aid.[25] Another interviewee describes further their adamancy: "One day my husband's foreman came to our house. He said to him, 'Your name isn't on the list.' 'No, I don't want relief. No relief. I want to work. I want to earn my money with my own sweat.' 'But there is no work,' the foreman insisted. He asked me for my children's sizes. A couple days later, a big box arrived with clothing for the children: coats, shoes, sweaters and pants, and a box of food – rice, flour, and such. My husband was furious. I pleaded with him. Gradually I convinced him. The whole country was out of work; it was not a shame or a dishonour to accept help. They considered it beggary."[26] For such able-bodied and hard-working men to be reduced to relief handouts was humiliating. They wanted "real work at real wages." "Boondoggling" was also hard to swallow but in desperation reluctantly accepted. Recalling the pick-and-shovel work in the quarries he was obliged to do in return for municipal rations, a St Catharines interviewee shuddered at the memory: "they degraded us with convict labour."[27]

Armenians were highly sensitive to oppression, exploitation, and privation, having suffered all three in the Ottoman Empire. As they became more entrenched as Canadian workers, they gradually began to be "more labour-action conscious," especially as a consequence of the Depression. Some became convinced that only through collective action and collective pressure could they challenge factory owners and make them respect the needs and rights of workers. "Organization," insisted an early union activist, "was the only way the working man could get anywhere."[28] In the early 1930s union activists began agitating at General Motors in St Catharines to create a union. By 1936–37 union activities centred on the United Auto Workers and the Committee for Industrial Organization (later the Congress of Industrial Organizations, or CIO). Four of the charter members of the UAW at GM in St Catharines were Armenian, and one of them, Hygus Torosian, recounts his experiences.[29]

During the period of the craft unions some Armenian moulders had joined the International Moulders Union. They paid their dues, but most were "not knowledgeable about unions, workers' rights, collective bargaining, or wage positions." "The company," recalls Torosian, "paid what it wanted; put us on the group bonus scheme, which we hated. There was no time and a half for overtime, no paid holidays, no hospitalization, no seniority, no social security whatsoever, just favouritism." Torosian began working at General Motors around 1930. "I was a product of my work. My real schooling was in industry. I became conscious of what was going on around me ... I'd be getting, say, thirty-four cents an hour. Another guy might get thirty-six or forty for doing the same work. We weren't satisfied with that."

When John L. Lewis and his supporters organized the CIO (1935), workers began to see that

> only by uniting, by joining the one union, would you get more, no matter what your craft was ... Whether you were a labourer or a moulder or a craftsman, it didn't matter. What mattered is that you were a producer. One of the things that put the death knell to craft unions was modern industrial techniques, the assembly line. You no longer were the proud maker of a full chair; you didn't make the whole chair. This is what finished the craft unions. [We wanted] men to get a little more for their productivity.

During lunch periods, we had discussions about shop conditions and the CIO and what benefits we could get if we were organized. These talks were enriched by the *Daily Clarion,* which was the organ of the Communist Party of Canada.[30] It was introduced to some of us by the local leader of the Communist Party in St Catharines, John K. Smith, who was the father of Local Union United Auto Workers 199. He was a worker in the factory, not an outside agitator. He was Polish/Ukrainian and dedicated to the working man.[31] Three Armenians, Mateos Korkigian, Mateos Bedrosian, and I were among the founding members of the UAW in St Catharines in 1935. The others were John K. Smith, Jack Haslam, George Campbell, Charlie Williamson, Jack Crozier, Joe Smith, Ernest Wheatley, and Alec Milne. We were helped by Frank Haslam, who was a member of the Communist Party, and he guided us in the beginning, then when we got on our own, he pulled out ... I don't know where he got his education but John Smith was a Communist. Joe Smith was an Englishman, and he was very anti-Socialist. On the charter, there were all political shades. I daresay there might've been a Fascist or two.

Before we got our charter, the company heard we were organizing and said, "You don't need an outside organization, we'll give you a company union ... And we'll give you the opportunity of electing amongst yourselves a representative." I was one of the sixteen representatives of the Works Council, represented the foundry [McKinnon Employee Council]. Even though we were organizing the other union, we felt if the company could give us what we wanted, why should we belong to something outside? We weren't anxious to belong to an organization in the States ... All we wanted was a fairer distribution. We wanted higher wages, better working conditions.

At our company union meetings we'd discuss what was bothering us, but we didn't give up on the outside union. The first thing we brought up was to standardize the days we got paid.[32] The company said they couldn't do that, they'd have to hire more girls to prepare payroll. It was going to cost too much. Every idea we had, they threw it out ... All we got was the right to express our issues to them. They didn't give much; and therefore we decided they were in business for the benefit of the company and not for its employees.

On 15 December 1936, eighteen men signed the charter forming Local 199 of the United Auto Workers, General Motors, in St Catharines. While the majority of the signatories were British, some "foreigners" also signed, including John Bulanda, Metek Micowski, Walter Taras, Vid Vucic, and the three Armenians mentioned above, as well as Arshag Krikorian.[33] On 1 May 1937 the first ratification vote took place, with a vote of 1,190 for and 12 against. Following ratification, management entered into "an agreement to accept a Committee selected by employees who are members of the local Automobile

Workers' Union as their representatives for collective bargaining purposes." [34]

Divisions along ethnic and class lines or according to occupation and skill were superceded by concern over wages and working conditions: "People who were working at McKinnon's in the early times [pre–World War I] hated the foreigners. That all vanished. Still, the union was an Anglo-Saxon thing. The leadership. In the beginning. We didn't care what nationality, what political party people belonged to. We wanted them in the union. Because people organized for their immediate conditions. They didn't worry about Poland or Russia or Armenia. Right now there was an issue. The issue was better wages."

"We were forced to have a strike in 1941 when the war was on ... For better wages. Everything was peaceful. We weren't out for any violence." The General Motors strike was viewed by Labour Minister Norman McLarty as "a deliberate attempt to undermine the wage policy of the Dominion government," i.e., P.C. 7440. In rejecting the conciliation board's recommendation of the payment of the maximum wartime cost-of-living bonus (i.e. $1.50 a week), he said, the workers – four thousand of them – were challenging the government's war wages policy, and by striking during wartime, they were showing themselves to be disloyal. To intimidate the picketers, Munitions Minister C.D. Howe sent in two hundred RCMP. The union stood its ground, seeking the right to negotiation and demanding parity with GM workers in Windsor and Oshawa – a ten-cents-an-hour increase for day workers and a 15 percent raise for piece workers.[35] Strikers countered the criticism of disloyalty by arguing that many GM workers had bought war bonds and had volunteered for the front. Members rallied, singing

> We shall not ..
> We shall not be moved.
> Just like a tree
> We shall not be moved.
> (Name of union member in armed forces) is fighting for us
> We shall not be moved.

To show their sympathy with the strike, about sixty volunteers who were attending the Canadian Congress of Labour convention in Hamilton, joined the picketers, and a large number of women working in the Delco Division of GM joined the UAW union for the first time.[36] On 22 September the *St Catharines Standard* quoted Robert

Stacey, UAW international representative, as saying that separate meetings of Polish, Ukrainian, and Armenian workers had "unanimously reaffirmed their decision to remain on strike until negotiations for wage increases were achieved." When GM plants in Windsor and Oshawa were seriously affected by the strike, the company capitulated. After a strike of seventeen days, negotiations were resumed.37 The eventual agreement of 29 September 1941 reaffirmed the union as the sole collective bargaining agent, forbade disciplinary action either by the firm or the union, and allowed for the reinstatement of workers under conditions existing before the strike. Because each side had maintained its position with respect to wages, to settle this dispute the agreement called for further company-union negotiations to be completed within a month and to be retroactive to 29 September 1941. Torosian remembers the victory: "The union was recognized and we got concessions we never had before. Eventually the pay was increased."38

As a group Armenian labourers did not take the initiative in union agitation. "The Armenians," Torosian recalled, "felt they couldn't do anything about conditions. That was up to the native people [Anglo-Saxons]. So whenever the native people led the front, Armenians followed, but they didn't initiate disputes or action." For example, Armenians at International Harvester in Hamilton, who also recognized the need for change, cooperated with the company system. They initiated a change to improved safety shoes and leather aprons for the moulders and supported workers' demands for accident insurance and unemployment relief through the company union. They were not in the forefront of union formation, even though they might have sympathized with union goals, agreed with the labour politics of their member of Parliament, Sam Lawrence, and supported the newly created Co-operative Commonwealth Federation. When union agitators took up the call at the Harvester, it was in the forge shop, which was run by British old-timers, not in the foundries, which the foreigners dominated and where most of the Armenians worked.39 Perhaps, also, recognition of the corporate welfare system at the Harvester, fears about company retaliation, concerns about their precarious job tenure and their political abhorrence of Communist infiltration in the union led them to tread warily.40

Yet not all Armenians were followers; some were in the vanguard of union organization: Seth (Setrag) Bejian in Brantford, Garo Raician in Galt/Preston, and Hygus Torosian in St Catharines, to name but three front-runners. Intelligent, humane, and dedicated to the cause of social justice, all three were totally convinced that industrial unionism was the most effective way to achieve workers' rights. Seth Bejian, a colourful union organizer, was probably educated at Euphrates College in Kharput at a time when the school was seething with the call for reform and progress. A native of Keghi, he immigrated to Canada before 1914 and worked at the Galt Malleable for a time before moving to the United States. He later returned to Canada and took a job as a coremaker at the Brantford Malleable (Canadian Car and Foundry).[41] Actively involved in Armenian life, Bejian taught English to newcomers, as well as Armenian to both newcomers and children. He wrote for the Armenian left-wing press, notably for *Yeritasard Hayastan*, mouthpiece of the Hnchak party, and later for *Lraper* (Reporter), the voice of the Armenian-American Progressive Party/League in the United States. At the same time, he threw himself into the workers' struggle in Brantford, helped organize and strengthen the UAW-CIO in the plant, and eventually became chairman of the shop committee. "He was a fiery speaker. When he got on the stage, he held his audiences spellbound, in English, let alone Armenian." "He was a short man, but when he spoke, he was dynamite."[42] His efforts to help working people were dashed when the company refused to renew the union contract in 1952, closed down operations, and moved to Montreal. Bejian was heartbroken to see coworkers who had for decades used up their vitality at hard labour receive no pension and no recognition.[43]

Garo Raician was a survivor of the Genocide. The grandson of the head man of Astghaberd village in Keghi, Raician survived the ordeals of genocide by sheer wit. As a twenty-one-year-old in Preston, Ontario, he worked a full day's shift at the Buffalo Sled company, then ran to the foundry at Clare Brothers to "shake out" three floors for fifty cents a floor and prepare the sand for the moulders' morning work. He learned the moulder's craft and in time became one of the best moulders in Preston/Galt. Raician believed the union was an effective way of ending the injustices of management. In 1943 the Galt Malleable Iron company penalized him for agitating for a union and tried to dismiss him on wrongful grounds:

The foreman, timekeeper and superintendent were like dictators. The foreman and timekeeper were corrupt. Went to moulders' homes to drink. Men couldn't open their mouths. Boss gave you a job. It's ten cents a mould but if you didn't buy him a bottle, he would give you five cents. It was during the war. We were trying to get the union [the CIO] ... sixty-five men signed. The next day at the plant, my job was gone. A huge job in its place. I had to pour twenty-two hundred pounds of hot iron in the morning and twenty-two hundred pounds of hot iron in the afternoon. And that was in addition to all the preparation. I asked the foreman for help. He refused. I asked to work close to the fire. He refused. It was inhumanly heavy work. The foreman marked six cents a mould on my card. That was not fair. All that iron! All that heavy work! A hundred moulds for six dollars! ... The foreman said it was office orders. I went to the superintendent ... He said, "you better give us seven days notice." I said, "you give me notice." He wrote on my card that I was being dismissed because I was not used to working in the malleable![44]

Eventually Raician, with other like-minded workers, succeeded in bringing the United Steelworkers of America–CIO, Local 2899, to the Galt Malleable under the guidance of Arthur Williams of the Canadian Congress of Labour. After a prolonged strike in 1943 and a hearing by the Industrial Disputes Investigation Act board, management recognized the union as a collective bargaining unit in the plant.[45]

Hygus Torosian was also a Keghetsi, born just before the Great War. After leaving high school, he started working at General Motors, where he became exposed to injustices inflicted on working people and to ways of helping them improve their lot. He was one of the founding members of UAW 199 in 1936 and was elected to the district council of the St Catharines, Windsor, and Oshawa locals. In 1938–39 he won a scholarship awarded by the York Educational Trust, the Workers Educational Association, to study at Harlech College in Wales and at Ruskin College, Oxford, where he specialized in history and economic theory from "a strictly nonpartisan standpoint." He returned to Canada and became engrossed in union activities and the subsequent 1941 strike for recognition and increased wages. As a private in the war, he was selected to take further courses at Balliol College, Oxford, in 1944. On his return home as a four-year veteran, he followed in his father's footsteps and took up full-time farming but remained involved in the workers' struggle and in community activities.[46]

During the 1920s and 1930s and for some, during the 1940s, rank-and-file Armenian labourers did not relate union participation to activism in the *Canadian* political arena. Their small numbers, language limitations, and sense of insecurity acted as constraining factors. Perhaps, also, because they were Genocide survivors, their political interests lay within the Armenian, rather than the Canadian, political field. In this respect, Torosian steadfastly rejects any suggestion of a spillover from Armenian political sympathies to the Canadian Labour movement: "Armenian political thinking had nothing to do with the forming of the unions in St Catharines ... [or] with the workers joining together to get better working conditions ... Their political thinking stayed home. They didn't take it with them to the factory."[47] Torosian insists that union *membership* was motivated by economics and pragmatism: men and women joined the union in response to unfair wages, poor working conditions, and immoral treatment by bosses. Based on this perspective, Armenian factory workers did not interweave the Armenian warp with the Canadian weft. According to this outlook, during the interwar years, at least, the mentality of Armenian labourers was marked by a double dimension, struck on parallel lines: on the one hand, their Armenian political consciousness, revolving around Soviet Armenia and Armenian communities throughout the world and on the other hand, their Canadian affiliations, bound up in the dignity, worth, and rights of working people.

It is true that the Armenian Canadian labour union movement was born in Canadian factories and nurtured on the hardships and dehumanization of the Depression. It signified a protest of working people against exploitation, corruption, and injustice. But not all Armenian labourers responded to trade unions in the same way. In Hamilton, for instance, with its strong Dashnak population, not a single Armenian stood in the forefront of the union struggle. Could their reticence be attributed to a weak union movement at the Harvester compared to a better-organized and militant one at GM in St Catharines, with its connections to sister unions in the United States? Whatever the case, even in St Catharines Armenian reaction to unions differed dramatically. Considering that Armenian men were doing the same work, under the same conditions and in the same factory and considering that they were all politically to the left, why did some at General Motors in St Catharines jump into the trade union movement from the beginning, while others held back, at least initially?

No doubt some feared or distrusted the government, the police, the management – in short, the power élite. Those who had lost all that was dear to them were leery about taking risks, and in the 1930s union involvement was risky business. It could lead to dismissal, imprisonment, or deportation.[48] Explaining why his father was suspicious of the union, an interviewee explained: "My father was a great believer in job security. Honest work for an honest wage. He didn't want to owe anything to anyone. He was not a gambler. He preferred to keep his own shirt on his back, even if it was torn, than take a risk for a new one." Others simply "didn't believe in the union ... In the initial period, some kept out of it. If it had to do with working conditions or an international organization, they didn't have any opposition, they just didn't think it would do them any good. ... They felt they could accomplish as much individually [in the plant]." Be that as it may, many reacted to the trade union movement on the basis of their political beliefs. It seems plausible that this politicization, embedded in an *Armenian* political culture, motivated their involvement in or resistance to the *Canadian* union movement. [49]

Although most Armenians in North America came from the Ottoman Empire, they could not help but react to Soviet Armenia, a remnant of the former Armenian province in the Russian Empire, and the only political entity to survive the Armenian republic. The conflict between the pro- and anti-Soviet Armenia factions simmered in North America until it boiled over in 1933, culminating in an enduring and acrimonious break between the opposing camps: those who upheld Soviet Armenia and the Soviet Union and those who clung to the hope of a free political homeland, rid of Communism. During the 1930s most Armenian trade unionists belonged to the pro-Soviet Armenia faction. They saw in the Soviet Union not only support for an Armenian political reality but also promise for working people. They were inspired by fundamental changes in the general strategy of the Communist Party when it moved to action in North American factories and instructed each follower to "turn his face to the factory."[50] As the Communist Party penetrated the Canadian labour movement by organizing the Workers' Unity League (1930), setting up unemployment councils, and trying to seize the leadership of strikes, these leftist Armenian workers were stirred, and they hailed such actions as signs of hope for working men and women.[51]

The relationship was even stronger. An examination of their background shows a political culture with a history of sympathy for the Social Democrat Hnchakian party, the Relief Committee for Armenia (HOG), the Worker's Friend (i.e., the Armenian Workers' Party), and the Armenian Progressive Party/League – all pro-Soviet Armenia and pro-Communist. They read the Armenian leftist press from the United States: *Yeritasard Hayastan* (Young Armenia), *Banvor* (Worker), and, later, *Lraper* (Reporter), and they kept abreast of major "radical" events such as the trials and execution of Sacco and Vanzetti; the imprisonment of Canadian Communists in 1931 and the attempted murder of Tim Buck in Kingston Penitentiary; the Ford Hunger March in Detroit in 1932; the sit-down strike at the GM plant in Flint, Michigan, in 1937 and the victory of the UAW; and the strike at GM in Oshawa in the same year. When John L. Lewis formed the Committee for Industrial Organization in 1935, leftist Armenian workers were on the ground floor of union activity.

Among the Dashnaks, too, were politicized workers, socialists sensitive to the sufferings and exploitation of working people. They, too, were convinced they could be the agents of change.[52] Through the press, notably, *Hairenik*, they, too, kept informed about labour struggles, the New Deal, the Wagner Act (the National Labor Relations Act, 1935) in the United States (which guaranteed labour's right to organize and bargain collectively), and the formation of the United Popular Front by Moscow. They, too, heard about the workers' attempts to organize in Canada, the outlawing of the Communist Party in 1931, the Trek to Ottawa, and the Dominion Day Riots in Regina in 1935. They knew about Prime Minister R.B. Bennett's tough stand against unions and Communists, Ontario premier Howard Ferguson's recalcitrance, and Premier Mitchell Hepburn's "implacable hostility" to the CIO. They, too, attended mass demonstrations of the unemployed, like the notorious protest rally in Hamilton's Woodlands Park in the summer of 1935.

Like their confreres, committed Dashnaks defined their union stand within the framework of their Armenian political culture. For them the Communist regime in Armenia was a sham: brutal and vicious, a totalitarian regime that was weakening the Armenian language, religion, and culture and destroying the liberties they so cherished. Not only were Communists strangling Armenian life in the homeland, but in the diaspora Communists were trying to undermine the Armenian nationalist movement and the struggle for Armenian independence. Pointing to the 1933–34 conflict between pro- and anti-Soviet Armenia sympathizers in North America, Dashnaks held that Communists were manipulating Armenian patriotism to win support for Soviet tyrants. They vehemently repudiated any movement associated with Bolshevism.

During the 1930s, politicized Dashnaks saw the union movement as an invidious "Red" plot to control working people in North America and correctly concluded that Communists were involved in the UAW-CIO at General Motors. Local Communist activity was following instructions of the Sixth Congress of the Comintern (1928) to intensify the class war, to extend the class struggle under Communist leadership to the factories, and to mobilize workers against capitalists.[53] After the Workers' Unity League was dissolved, as part of the move towards the popular fronts ordered by the Seventh Congress of the Comintern (1935), many Communists threw their energies into building up the CIO in Canada. Dashnaks denounced this affiliation and rejected the union as Communist propaganda, interference from Moscow, and a mark of disloyalty to Canada.[54]

These different political perspectives existed, but during the major General Motors strike in St Catharines in 1941 almost all Armenians, including Dashnaks, backed the union. No doubt the most convincing reason for workers in both factions was the union's justified position. For the more politicized Dashnaks, the wartime alliance between the Soviet Union and the West lessened their resistance to the union movement. The creation in 1939–40 of the Canadian Congress of Labour, moreover, revealed the growing power of the anti-Communist, socialist forces in the Canadian labour movement.[55] No doubt Dashnaks were also aware that critical changes were afoot in the United States, as John L. Lewis and Walter Reuther were purging the CIO and UAW leadership of Communists. In later big strikes against General Motors in St Catharines, like the three-and-a-half month strike in 1948 and the 149-day strike in 1955, the participation of the Dashnaks was unequivocal; they offered their hall at the corner of Carlton and Ontario streets as strike headquarters.[56] Still, some Dashnaks clung to a symbolic denial. Simon Merakian, for example, paid his union dues when General Motors moved to a closed shop, but he adamantly refused to *belong* to the union.

At the turn of the century, McKinnon Dash and Metal recruited immigrant Armenian labourers from the United States to work in its new plant at the corner of Ontario and Carlton Streets. The men came as sojourner labourers and brought with them strong bodies and a willingness to use them. Among the first to work in the new plant, the pre-1914 men felt insecure, for they needed the work to help families constantly facing attack by gangs of thugs and exploitation by corrupt government officials in the Ottoman Empire. On the other hand, because of their lack of skills and the absence of job security, they were flexible and mobile and could move from place to place in search of work. They operated within a complex and extensive Armenian network pinpointing most of the major cities in southern Ontario and the northeastern and midwestern United States. At a time when the factory system in North America was undergoing a technological transformation of great magnitude and when capitalism and industrial production were forging headlong into changing patterns of work and labour relations, these foreigners – preindustrial farmers – inserted themselves into the North American labour force and eventually settled in southern Ontario.[57]

Thirty-five years after the first cohort of Armenians arrived in St Catharines and after cataclysmic events in the old land, a reappraisal of their place in North America, and the hardships of the Great Depression, Armenians were in the vanguard of union organization.

For Armenian labourers, both non-Dashnaks and Dashnaks, the union came to represent practical issues like better pay and better working conditions. But they also saw the union as a symbol: their way of assuming a measure of control over their lives and livelihood inside the factory gates.

Their work in the foundries was dangerous and heavy; but many made the choice to remain, though it was more often than not a choiceless choice. It was a decision for the benefit of their children. After working in the foundries for almost forty years, an interviewee, bent and deformed, could say his life had paid dividends, not because he relished the dreary conditions of the moulder's lot, which often left him in such pain he could not undress himself, but because he and his work had enabled his children to attend university. "I once saw his pay cheque in 1947 or '48," remembered one of his sons. "It was eighty dollars with just a little bit of overtime. It was good money. People in 1967 were earning eighty dollars a week and my father was earning that ... in 1947."[58]

The men had migrated to St Catharines in search of jobs. Initially the company provided them with cheap rental accommodation in nearby houses, known as "the McKinnon's houses," just south of the factory. From this point of initial settlement, Armenians gradually pushed a few blocks northward to Carlton street and the factory gates: those enormous jaws, opening and closing to the rhythm of industrial time. With marriage and property ownership the die was cast. The neighbourhood and the factory became entwined. The factory and its milieu emerged as the agents of change for a better life for Armenian families. A key ingredient in the interaction between the factory and the Armenian community was the multifaceted role of women's work, which complemented the work of the men.

WOMEN AND WORK

"From my friends I heard that she was studying hard, taking a nurses' training course. She was popular everywhere and young Armenians clustered around her. More than one had asked her to marry him, but she said that she did not want to marry; she wanted to work, like American women."[59] This reference to an Armenian refugee girl in the United States by an American woman doctor who had practised among survivors in the Middle East provides an interesting insight into the belief that, unlike American women, Armenian women did not work outside the home. Interviewees, however, have revealed a totally different experience.

Even in the homeland before the Genocide, Armenian women and girls worked as domestics, teachers, and nurses. In some areas, where a measure of industrialization had taken root, they found jobs in factories, notably in silk and rug weaving, as seasonal and permanent employees. They were, moreover, becoming attuned to issues of injustice, dignity, and self-worth, as attested to by periodic strikes for better wages and conditions.[60] During the years of upheaval after 1915, thousands of women, as we have seen, struggled to eke out a living. They laboured as domestic servants, agricultural labourers, seamstresses, fancyworkers, cooks, bakers, laundresses, nurses, nurse's aids, teachers, or teaching assistants. Others tried their hand at entrepreneurial activities, usually buying goods and selling them from door to door. Testimony reveals that surviving women in the Middle East worked in such places as cigarette factories and took jobs in nontraditional employment, such as road and building construction.

In North America their situation varied, depending to an extent on available opportunities in the location of settlement. Generally, if Armenians lived where major industries traditionally hired men, few Armenian women worked in plants, initially at least. By contrast, if they settled in regions where factories hired women, as in the textile industry in Troy, New York, and Lyons, France, Armenian women found and took jobs.[61] Those who came to St Catharines, Hamilton, and Brantford as picture brides and married shortly after arrival did not find industrial work opportunities near the Armenian neighbourhood. Other factors, furthermore, militated against outside work: the men's comparatively well-paying and steady jobs in the iron factories; the women's ignorance of the language and the new culture; the fear of being "corrupted" by Canadian society; and finally and most significantly, the desire to have children and "build a nest." Since for both men and women, family reconstruction took top priority, almost all the newcomers were staying home and having children during the early years of marriage, i.e., in the 1920s. The recollection of an interviewee gives a sense of their initial isolation in Canada: "For two years I didn't go out shopping. It was not our custom for a woman to go out shopping. My husband and his uncle made all the purchases. I was only seventeen when I came. I was inexperienced. I had no one. No family. No one to give me advice except my husband."[62]

As they adjusted to Canadian life, their labour in the home was as necessary to the survival of the family as their husband's work outside the home.[63] By running the house, the women made it possible for their husbands to make a living in a factory, on a farm, in a small business, or in a trade like barbering or tailoring. They kept the house clean, procured and prepared nutritious food, made and maintained much of the family's clothing, reared the children, and nursed ill or elderly relatives and friends. Their ability to bargain at the farmer's market in spite of their faltering English, to judge the quality of foods for sale, to garden, cook, and bake, use up leftovers carefully, and preserve produce meant the difference between the family eating decently and poorly. Every family planted a vegetable garden. In the fall they harvested the produce and, together with bushels of fruit the women bought at market they canned and dried food for winter use. Aside from sewing household needs like curtains, sheets, and pillowcases, they also designed and sewed clothing, knitted and crocheted a variety of items, and made over used clothing to ease the family's budget. They did all their own washing and ironing; seldom was an article, even a shirt, taken to the laundry. Some bought wool fleece from a farmer and washed and combed it to make *vermaks*, i.e., Armenian duvets. A few spun and dyed the wool and most of the women knit sweaters, scarves, socks, and gloves. By their toil, inventiveness, talents, and frugality these young newcomers contributed to their family's economic stability without earning a penny.

Some women, however, did bring in outside income. A number of families converted a portion of their homes to boarding facilities.[64] An already-established precedent in the pre-1914 period, boarding took on new significance after the war, as women assumed the job of providing accommodation for the unattached men – both old-timers and refugees. While their husbands worked outside the home, women ran boardinghouses. Boardinghouses were not the desperate recourse of widows and troubled families; they were business enterprises in which women were clear about the exchange of money and the services rendered, as indicated in the following account: "My mother would go out and do all the groceries and butchering and she'd bring it in and total it. She'd get $1.50 a week. That was her wages. And I wasn't charged. I got my food for nothing and she got her food for nothing. The rest was divided up among the number of boarders that were there. My father had to pay too. And I think they paid $1.00 each a month for their rent."[65]

In this way, women who ran boardinghouses contributed to the family's income within acceptable boundaries – without wandering from the woman's traditional place, the home. The custom of running boardinghouses enabled families to use the house to pay off mortgages. An examination of tax assessment rolls in Hamilton, St Catharines, and Brantford shows that some families rented a house, occupied a small portion for themselves, and converted the rest to a boarding-house or rented a portion to tenants. A few years later, these same families bought their own homes and used the same approach to pay off the mortgage. As their children grew up, as the family grew in size, and as they whittled down the mortgage, less of the house was relegated to boarders or tenants.

Women found different ways to help the family economy. Farmers' wives, for example, spent every Saturday in the open air market with their husbands and/or children selling their farm produce. Many of the young refugee women, moreover, who had learned "the art of the needle" in the orphanages where they had taken refuge used this expertise to do dressmaking in the home or to earn money by needlework, knitting, and crocheting: "I used to do handwork and sell it. There was a missionary [in Hamilton] who gave us the thread and fabric and we crocheted and needleworked handkerchiefs. We sold them, two for twenty-five cents. And I figured I could buy two pairs of stockings for the children with that money."[66] Such income should not be regarded as pin money for the women but as a contribution to the family's finances. Without stepping beyond the confines of her home or of the Armenian community, she engaged in simple "cottage industry" and brought in some income to ease the family budget.[67]

With changing economic conditions during the Depression, the role of many Armenian women was transformed.[68] With their husbands out of work or on reduced time, with mortgages still outstanding and families to feed and clothe, women ventured out of the home to work – in spite of initial disappproval on the part of their husbands and the community at large. It was a clear case of financial need. Just as they had laboured during the times of refugeeism, women went out to work to help their families survive. As long as the house and children were properly cared for, Armenian men gradually came to accept their wives and daughters working outside the home. By the 1930s, moreover, the women felt more comfortable in Canadian society; they were older, more mature, and more confident. Most of them had learned some English, either through their own initiative in studying Armenian-English self-help books or by attending day- or night-school classes organized by the local public school. Some women had learned English and the Canadian way through mothers' groups coordinated by Canadian women, like the "mothers' meetings" at All Peoples' Mission in Hamilton, the Imperial Order of the Daughters of the Empire in St Catharines, or the Armenian women's group at First United Church in Galt.[69]

Thus prepared, many women responded to need and circumstance and embarked on new ventures. They worked seasonally as farm help, as domestic cooks and cafeteria workers, and gradually as factory labourers. A respondent recalled that when the Depression hit, her husband lost his job at McKinnon's. "He wasn't an outdoor man. He stayed home and looked after our son. I could earn more than him doing farm work – picking, sorting, and packing fruits and vegetables. Even selling fruits and vegetables at market. My girl friend and I used to walk four miles to the farm and four miles back each day. They'd pay twelve cents a quart for beans and one cent a quart for strawberries. I ended up working at the Robertson farm for twenty-three years."[70] Another described how in Hamilton the farmer used to drive his truck and pick up women of all nationalities – Poles, Ukrainians, Hungarians, Slovaks, Italians, and Armenians. "What could our husbands do? We *had* to go to work. So we went to the farms. We could eat all day, earn a little money, and bring some fruits and vegetables home for our families to eat and for us to preserve."[71]

A few young, single Armenian women were hired by General Motors during the late 1930s. An interviewee with a high school diploma in commerce was sent to a job in the plant: "No Armenian women were hired as clerical help," she recalled. "It was hard for foreign women to get in the office at McKinnon's. A man by the name of McCarthy ran the office and he didn't like foreigners ... I also applied for a job in Fleming's [law firm] office but I knew they wouldn't hire us because we were Armenian. So I worked in the factory and then got married. I'm sure my qualifications were fine. This was back in 1936."[72]

The hard times of the Depression were followed by the demands of the Canadian economy during World War II.[73] Recognizing the labour shortages, Armenian women, both young and middle-aged, single and married, responded to the recruitment drive for female factory workers. While their brothers and sons fought in the Canadian armed forces, they "rolled up their sleeves for victory" and moved into the factories, motivated both by patriotism and high wages. They ventured, hesitantly at first, then more easily, into canning factories like Canadian Canners Company in St Catharines and Stafford's and Wagstaff's in Hamilton; into textile mills like Empire Rug Mills in St Catharines, Eaton Knitting Mills, Niagara Cotton Mills, Cosmos Mills, Chipman-Holton, and Moodie's in Hamilton and Slingsby's and Watson's in Brantford; into men's tailoring firms like Cornell Tailors and tobacco companies like Tuckett's Tobacco in Hamilton; and into heavy industry, especially for war production, like General Motors in St Catharines, Wallace Barnes in Hamilton, and Waterous,

Massey Harris, Verity, and Cockshutt in Brantford. ""We were working seven days a week at the Waterous plant," remembered an interviewee. "About forty or so Armenians, mostly women, even older women about fifty-five or sixty years of age. They desperately needed workers. When the men left for the war, we younger ones took over as machine operators, manufacturing heavy shells. I started at 35c an hour, then 45 cents. Later they put me on piece work and paid me about eighty cents to a dollar an hour. Seven days a week! I worked just like a man – very heavy work, but the country needed us and so we went. And when I came home, I still had to do all my housework. I worked at Waterous for two years and for almost two years at Massey Harris."[74]

Factory work was not easy for married women, because whether they were on full- or part-time work, or on seasonal employment, they still remained the backbone of the home. Usually they could rely on help from their husbands and children and on domestic labour exchanges with relatives and friends. Aside from the long hours, heavy work, and family responsibilities, Armenian women encountered other problems in the factory. "Most Armenian women," explained an interviewee, "knew some but not a lot of English. They asked me to translate for them. But the floor lady didn't like to hear us talking our language at all. She told me that we shouldn't talk Armenian because we were working in a war factory. I told her we weren't the enemy. We were just speaking our mother tongue. She was also giving some Hungarian men the same treatment. One day, they'd had enough. They and the other foreign men came to the plant but refused to work. The whole plant came to a stop. The boss was shocked. The men told him that if they couldn't speak their mother tongue, they wouldn't work. Either she left or they left. She was fired on the spot."[75]

Prejudice against "foreign" women working in the office continued during the war. An interviewee recalled that her sister, who had graduated as one of the top students in the local commercial high school, was told during the war to anglicize her surname if she wanted clerical work. "None of us could get jobs in the office at General Motors," recalled another informant. "But we wanted to help the war effort, so many women worked the Victory shift – 4 to 11."[76] It was hard enough for Armenian men to secure a clerical position, so when a young woman, a university student whose father worked at the Harvester, managed to land a summer job in the office during the 1950s, it was viewed by the community as a sign of "progress".

After the war a few women, especially the childless and the needy, continued to work in factories. A childless informant who had started work in 1935 laboured continually in different factories for the next forty-three years; another, who was widowed at the young age of forty with four young children, worked for twenty years in a candy factory until her last child finished university. These examples, however, were not the norm. Most women saw factory work in temporary terms and left industry soon after the war: their husbands were back to work, their mortgages were paid off or almost so, most of their children had grown up, jobs became less plentiful with the return of veterans, the company showed a preference for hiring men, and they themselves were looking at other ways of earning a living. Single unmarried women, too, gradually left the factory, preferring instead to get married and start their own families.

THE FACTORY AND THE NEIGHBOURHOOD

The factory held an important place in the lives of Armenian families, for it provided other outlets for work. During the late 1930s, GM gave permission to an Armenian "caterer," Depan Bedrosian, to take a hand cart with hot meat pies, soft drinks, chocolate bars, and cigarettes around the factory twice a day to provide the workers with snacks. A few years later, during the war, GM brought in workers from Quebec, housed them in apartments close by the factory, and hired women – including Armenian women – as charwomen, chambermaids, and cafeteria workers.

For other Armenians the factory offered a different kind of flexibility. Men who despised industrial work, who disliked the favouritism and bribery, or who had ambitions for other employment understood, even as early as the pre-Genocide period, that the factory could be a stepping stone to other work. Hairabed Mooradian, for example, started working in the factory and then opened a shoe-shine parlour and hat-cleaning establishment. The factory, despised though it might be, provided a point of insertion for men who had arrived in Canada without money, without English-language skills, and without the expertise of North American business practice. In his discussion of Armenians in the United States, Robert Mirak refers to the "painful initiation into the new industrial order as the mandatory first step" that permitted many to pass on to "the broader opportunities of the promised land."[77]

One of the most popular routes from the factory was to barber school. Barbering was a clean, respectable, white-collar job that did not require a profound knowledge of English. As men always needed a haircut, a barber was seldom out of work. His trade was mobile; he could easily move from one city to another, and during hard times he could cut hair in his own home. An interviewee expressed her pride that the family had not gone on the dole during the 1930s: "Even during the worst of the Depression we didn't starve and we didn't go on relief. If my husband's customers had no money to pay for the haircut, they would barter with a basket of fruit or a dozen eggs."[78] The strategies were limitless. For most of his working life, Setrag Serabian, in Brantford, shifted back and forth between the factory and the barbershop. In the Depression, he converted one of the rooms in his house to a barbershop and for four or five years held down two jobs. He cut hair until one or two o'clock and then went off to the factory on the evening shift if there was work. During the war he worked in the factory, and in the 1950s he took up full-time barbering once again.

Buying farmland was another popular venture, particularly in the Niagara Peninsula. Men struggled for as many as ten years in the factory and lived frugally to save enough money to pay for their own farms. In the immediate area around the Armenian neighbourhood in St Catharines, in Grantham Township, there were at different times at least six Armenian farms and others in the Grimsby, Stoney Creek, Dundas, and Brantford areas.[79] While one man worked an eight-hour shift in the foundries and then came home and worked on the farm, another might augment farm earnings by alternating between winter work in a factory and farm labour in the spring, summer, and fall. An informant recalled that when work was slack at GM, his father, along with other Armenians, travelled as far as Jamestown, New York, for factory work in winter.[80] By such endeavours, often spanning perhaps twenty years, families could pay off their farm mortgages and increase their acreage. Such practices not only repeated the old-country sojourner tradition of returning to the family farm from work in urban centres but also contributed to the stability of the community itself by keeping families permanently settled in one place.

As early as World War I, Armenian men were opening little shops to service not only their own community but also the workers at McKinnon's.[81] In almost all cases men combined commercial enterprise like boardinghouses or coffee houses with factory labour. The postwar period is marked by an expansion of such enterprises and by manifold variations of creative coping strategies, frequently utilizing the help of family members. The Bedrosian brothers in St Catharines built a substantial building on Ontario Street across from General Motors. While one brother worked in the factory, the other two used the building for business – one operating a barber shop and the other a confectionery store. During and after World War II, when GM was expanding production, the number of little businesses depending on factory clientele proliferated. Families often converted a room or two of their house for a business. Those who prospered sold their property – usually to another Armenian[82] – and bought or had built in the same general vicinity a larger structure that included a store in front, living quarters for themselves in the rear, and an apartment on the second floor to rent out.[83] Such was their spirit of entrepreneurship that by the late 1940s and early 1950s a number of Armenian-owned shops were competing with each other for business in the Ontario-Carlton Street area.

The GM factory gates, at the point where Carlton Street intersects with Ontario Street, linked the neighbourhood to the plant. The gates had a certain magical quality about them. When the whistle blew, the gates were flung open, and the men rushed out for lunch. It was an exciting moment – friends greeted each other; they exchanged news and information; they smoked, talked, laughed, argued. It was all hustle and bustle. The little shops were primed for business. After lunch the shopkeepers cleaned up and prepared for the final whistle. Like a dragon, the gates then spewed forth the workers and gobbled up the next shift of men.

The workers had an hour for lunch and found easy access to the luncheon counters, coffee shops, grocery stores, fish and chips stores, and confectioneries lining Ontario and Carlton streets and the little side streets. To make purchasing easier, shopkeepers often gave credit until payday. Each business seemed to be noted for something – coffee, sandwiches, soups, hamburgers, or baked goods. Some entrepreneurs introduced Armenian foods, like *shinuk shakar*, "pulled candy," to their non-Armenian clientele. On their way in and out of the company gate, workers could cash their cheques for the price of the change and have a cup of coffee at Cappy Ashukian's Lunch. They could buy cigarettes at Jack Mooradian's variety store on Carlton Street, home-made candy at Hagop Malkonian's shop, or a quart of milk and a loaf of bread at Avak Mooradian's grocery. They could pick up meat pies and "honeymoons" (chocolate covered toffee) at Rose Bedrosian's shop on Beech Street, hamburgers at Verkin Papazian's lunch counter on Ontario Street, buns at Zarouhi Aloian's confectionery, or sandwiches in Andy Shakarjian's restaurant. To have their hair cut, they had a choice of Berj Aloian's, Krikor Der Krikorian's, or George Sahagian's barbershops. If they wanted fresh fruit, they could walk north to Alex Moukperian's or Ohannes Torosian's farm. And after a hard day's work they could drop in for a beer in Balig Saroughanian's Golden Pheasant hotel or shoot pool in John Anegian's coffee house.[84]

Some of these businesses were run as full-time careers, as were other shops far from the factory, like Nerses Avakian's and Edward Krekorian's shoe repair shops, Annie Krekorian's Campus Coffee Shop across from the St Catharines Collegiate, and Kirkor (George) Andonian's Lion shoe shine parlour in downtown St Catharines. Most of the ventures near the factory, however, were combination factory/business enterprises. While some men courted danger every day for decades, many viewed factory labour as a means to an end. As soon as they could, men like Ohannes Torosian left the factory and devoted their energies to the family business full-time. They may have started off as factory workers, but they embarked on new endeavours in cooperation with family members, usually their wives.

The numbers and the role of women in these enterprises cannot be underplayed. By the 1940s women who had entered Canada as young picture brides fifteen and twenty years earlier were reaching their prime and were in striking contrast to their husbands, who were nearing retirement age. The women were able and ready to work for a better life for themselves and their families. Like their husbands, they were eager to see that the mortgage was paid off and were determined to enable their children to continue their education beyond high school. One or two women ran the business on their own, but most enterprises were run as cooperative family undertakings, calling on the resources of wife, husband, and children.[85] Men minded the store when they were not working in the factory, ordered merchandise, or planted fruits and vegetables, which the women prepared for later use – preserving, drying, and preparing sauces. Children, in their turn, ran errands, babysat, served customers, and generally acted as interpreters for their parents. As soon as they were old enough, some young people ran the business themselves, like the Derderian children who ran the family confectionary on Ontario Street. The contribution of children in family-run enterprises served as a means of keeping young people closely integrated into the community. This meant, in turn, that the younger generation was likely to retain its sense of community identity.

As the men were working in the factory, the day-to-day operation of the business was often in the hands of the women. The store was housed in the same structure as the home. This proximity enabled women to move back and forth easily from public space to private space, but it also meant that if they were to make the home run smoothly and the business function profitably, the demands placed on women were enormous. Keeping the house clean and neat now included keeping the store tidy and presentable; providing meals for husband and children now included a concern for customers' needs;

dealing with baker and milkman now involved dealing with supplier and delivery or pick-up; maintaining household accounts now meant business bookkeeping. "You had to be pretty smart and a good worker if you wanted your store to run a profit," recalled one of the businesswomen.

Women who were thus engaged in family businesses were functioning within controllable boundaries and within permitted behavioural patterns; they were presumed to be safe from harm and the corrupting clutches of the larger society; and they could continue doing what they and their husbands considered to be their most important work – caring for their home and their families.[86] The situation in St Catharines was a typical one in which outside observers might be tempted to view the role of women in stereotypical terms, assuming that their staying at home meant a perpetuation of Old World patterns of subservience. In fact, the location of business activity in the home merely disguised the reality that they were adopting distinctively New World patterns of relationships with their spouses and were moving into roles of progressively greater initiative, responsibility, and autonomy within both the family and the community.[87] In this transformation, the physical space of the house and garden played a critical role. More than a place of residence, they became, for almost every family, the locus for generating income. This fact is true whether the family had boarders or rented a portion of the house to another family or whether family members engaged in cottage industries or in small-scale enterprises. Building or buying larger premises that included a store was simply a step towards more concentrated commercial activity.

For more than sixty years St Catharines Armenians provided a cohort of strong, steady workers for McKinnon's – a cohort that included three generations in some families. The adaptation of Armenians to the industrial system in St Catharines was constrained neither by an industrial tradition that they brought with them nor by a tradition that they found entrenched in the factory. They entered heavy manufacturing at a time when it was undergoing monumental changes. Like thousands of other immigrant labourers of the period, they became part of a working class that was just learning to cope with the demands on it and to deal with the economic and industrial giants trying to dominate it. In time these agriculturalists adjusted to the factory as surely as they adjusted to Canadian society; and in turn the factory and the society adjusted to them and their families. Some worked in the factory for thirty and even forty years and felt a strong loyalty to the company and pride in themselves and in their skills. Perhaps one of the most symbolic comments was Andoon Kalagian's: he refused to celebrate the coming of the new year until he heard McKinnon's whistle blow in the joyful occasion.[88]

Armenians did not view the plant as the enemy of communal life.[89] Rather, the factory environment became, in some respects, the backdrop of community institutions: family and kinship were useful to help individuals find jobs and get ahead in the factory; businesses clustered around the factory and sometimes penetrated it. Even though the factory bosses were distant and even though Armenians of the first generation did not, either individually or as a group, achieve positions of power in the plant,[90] industrial employment furnished inputs of revenue that sustained the underpinnings of community life – family, farm, small business, church, and community centre. The shop floor itself, played a vital role in community stability. Men who worked in the factory, who were members of the UAW and who manned the pickets together, found common cause. Whether they respected or despised one another, they were compelled to work together and were bound to each other on the shop floor. By the mid-1930s some men had worked side by side on a day-to-day basis for as long as twenty years. Loyalties and hatreds lingered on and often cut across kin, village, and political affiliation. Bonds of the workplace, accordingly, emerge as important factors during periods of community political strife, notably in the 1930s and during the Cold War.

Using myriad strategies, with relatively little capital but with hard work and ingenuity, St Catharines Armenians also provided a multitude of services and access to a number of commodities for the workers at GM, not the least of which was the use of the Dashnak club as union headquarters during strikes. The activity in and around the club and the coffee and snacks sent to the strikers by Armenian businesses and Armenian families were a natural outcome of the ebb and flow of the interaction between factory workers and community members. As a matter of interest, a somewhat similar situation occurred in Galt. When workers at the Galt Malleable went out on strike (1943), eighty Ontario Provincial Police were called in to disperse the picketers. Nora Garabedian, who, with her husband, owned a restaurant located across the street from the factory, recounts how, pregnant with her fourth child, she confronted the police and in no uncertain terms told them to get off her property and to stop molesting the strikers who were demonstrating on her private property. "Why don't you go fight in the war?" she angrily demanded of the police. "What do you want with these poor people?"

The interrelationship between factory and community was possible partly because of the conditions in St Catharines itself. McKinnon's was built on the outskirts of town, on the doorstep of the countryside in an area that was emerging from rural hinterland at the time of the arrival of Armenian settlers. As one of the first groups to move into the area, Armenians established their quarter tucked in between the factory and the farmland. The new settlers put their own stamp on the region. They set their own pace and created their own peculiar pattern of activity – in effect, their own jobs – in response to the factory and particularly in response to the factory gates. Early on, Armenians recognized the importance of the gates and used them as a point of orientation for housing, work, and enterprise. Thus, when the factory was booming, as in the 1940s, Armenian businesses prospered. In the 1950s, when the factory allowed only a half hour for lunch and provided its own canteen and in the 1960s, when the Ontario Street shopping strip began to develop, the impact on the community was no less remarkable, since these changes coincided with major events in the family cycle itself. Remarked a respondent, "When my husband died and my son graduated from university and got married I closed down the store. Then K-Mart opened up in the late '60s [along Ontario Street]; that was the final blow. Most of the little businesses closed down after that."[91] Nothing could more clearly address the interaction of the family and neighbourhood with the immediate environment.

Armenian entrepreneurship in St Catharines not only facilitated the flow of money within the community but also brought in outside capital. Thus, without risking whatever security the factory had to offer, Armenians endeavoured to stabilize their economic situation and to neutralize the control of the factory in their lives.[92] Commercial enterprises outside the gates, along with union activity inside the gates, helped reduce their dependency on the factory and mitigate the fear, so prevalent among iron-factory workers in the early twentieth century, of unemployment, industrial accident, illness, and the dole. Commercial venture was more than grasping an opportunity, for it was frequently motivated by a strong determination to give children a professional education. Unfortunately, these creative efforts in St Catharines have not been recognized, not even in Armenian sources that consistently refer to St Catharines Armenians as factory workers or farmers – and overlook the crucial dimension of budding capitalism. Intriguingly, among these merchant families, this petty bourgeoisie, were unionists and socialists who would justify their commercial activities on the grounds that they were not engaged in exploitation.[93]

An overview of Armenian work experience in St Catharines reveals the transition of old-country peasants to semiskilled and skilled labourers and to union members and commercial entrepreneurs. This development is partially explicable if, as Edna Bonacich states, "the culture of origin is an important contributory factor." Villagers from Keghi had often combined farming with other craft and commercial activities – milling, carpentry, spinning, weaving, and tinsmithing. They also provided way-stations with food and lodgings for caravaneers travelling through the district of Keghi, and engaged in various entrepreneurial endeavours outside their home territory. The mentality and experience that they brought with them, accordingly, affected the way they reacted to new conditions in a strange land.

The will to "make it" in Canada reveals the ravelling of yet another strong thread in the daily lives of the immigrants. In the old land, in order to survive, Armenians had relied on the collective. Family, clan, village, church, political party, and nation bonded Armenians to one another. Such interdependence has been a major theme in this study, for the newcomers continued this deep-rooted tradition in the New World. In North America, another equally important dimension was empowering the people. Just as the Armenians were learning to wear different clothing and to speak an unfamiliar language, they were also learning to adapt to new values. They were in a country that encouraged individualism and free enterprise, and each grasped these concepts in his or her own personal and innovative way, according to each person's intelligence, resourcefulness, and potential. A simple, yet significant, example is the woman who had no formal education, who could neither read nor write English, but who had a keen eye for business. She managed to buy and sell real estate to such an extent that she provided each of her five children with their own homes. Another telling example is Moushegh Buzbuzian of Guelph, who, finding conditions at the Guelph Malleable unbearable, opened his own foundry, Standard Brass and Aluminum. These examples shed light on how a group of newcomers manoeuvered, strategized, and adjusted the often conflicting forces of collectivism and individualism.

Such an option was open to them because life in Canada was peaceful and civilized, people were law-abiding, and justice was comparatively impartial, a far cry from the insecurity and instability that had bedeviled them in the Ottoman Empire. Without the support and protection of his family, clan, and village, a man, let alone a woman, would have found individual free enterprise in Keghi an impossibility. As the forces of individualism and self-reliance took hold in Canada, the tradition of dependency on the collective and, in turn, loyalty to the collective, was shaken – a fact more evident among the second generation. Nothing was unchanging. Nothing remained static. Depending on family circumstances at a particular time and depending on available opportunities, Armenians in St Catharines worked in the factories, on farms, in small businesses, and in homes. Their strategies were malleable and flexible, sometimes overlapping and always responsive to conditions. In the final analysis, people managed not simply to survive but to improve their standard of living: indoor toilets replaced outhouses; furnaces replaced stoves; refrigerators replaced ice boxes; and children were given unimagined opportunities to further their education.

12

The Church and Politics: Background, 1914–1930

> Religious or political, the two questions are deeply, inextricably intermingled at their roots. Confounded in the past, they will appear tomorrow as they really are, one and identical.
>
> Jules Michelet, *Histoire de la révolution française*

Newcomers were inextricably bound to the destiny of Mother Armenia, whose picture, weeping among the ruins of her ancient cities, hung on a thousand walls and reminded the uprooted people of their devastated heritage and broken dreams. Always, the fate of the beloved and tormented homeland, whether in Turkey or Russia, remained the linchpin of their loyalties. In the United States these bonds became the battleground of divisive ideological warfare. The Apostolic Church, as the principal national institution among Armenians, fell into the crossfire of conflicting political and social forces. The interaction of church and politics emerged as the focus of internecine community strife in a country where democracy, freedom, and enlightenment could not control the passions of men and drove them, instead, to commit murder. In 1933 events in North America that were intimately and intricately enmeshed in the old land touched off such a storm of conflict that the communities reeled from the shock for decades.

Long before the Genocide, Armenian socialists and conservatives, revolutionaries and antirevolutionaries, and clerics and anticlerics had locked horns in the old land and the new. At the same time, the power of the church hierarchy and its strong ally, the wealthy merchant, or *amira*, class, was being eroded by the increasingly better-educated lower classes. The peace treaty negotiations, too, had been a struggle between strong adversaries: the Dashnaks (the Armenian Revolutionary Federation), representing the Republic of Armenia, on the one hand, and Boghos Nubar Pasha, the president of the Armenian General Benevolent Union, representing the refugees from the Ottoman

Empire, on the other. The struggle for status continued in North America, where the factions were less clearly marked between a rich merchant class and a poor peasantry, between urban and rural, and between educated and ignorant and where the old power structures could not easily reestablish their ascendancy in a country where liberalism and representational government gave voice to common folk.[1]

Political organizations that before the Great War had concentrated on liberating their people from Ottoman and Russian tyranny directed their attention after 1918 to the Republic of Armenia and to Soviet Armenia.[2] In the postwar period, four political groupings in the diaspora aligned themselves into two rival camps, based to an extent on their approach to Soviet Armenia, which was the propeller, churning and whipping up the vortex. While Hnchaks, Communists, and Ramgavars differed fundamentally in ideology, the three groups, strange bedfellows to be sure, often spoke with one voice in common opposition to the Dashnaks. Because of their divergent political ideologies, it is difficult to assign a defining label to the three parties when they combined forces and took a concerted stand. Writers have referred to them in negative terms such as anti-Dashnak or non-Dashnak, but it seems that a descriptive term might be more useful. For want of a better term, I have chosen the phrase conservative/left, which, being an anomaly, perhaps appropriately describes their incongruous affiliation.

In its turn, the Dashnak organization denounced pro-Soviet and pro-Soviet Armenia organizations and accused them of conspiring to divert the attention of Armenian immigrants from the struggle for Armenian independence, of leading the unwary to accept Communist/Russian control of the homeland and eventual russification, of deflecting attention from Armenia irredenta, and of crushing the nationalist movement. They held that the communist front camouflaged its true goal of serving the Soviet Union under the guise of Armenian patriotism and loyalty to the Armenian Church.

Dashnaks and their sympathizers condemned the victimization of the Armenian Church, which, they believed, had been forced to capitulate to the communist regime and was being used to further Soviet objectives at the expense of Armenian interests.[3] "The unholy matrimony between the Armenian Church and Communism," comments Sarkis Atamian, "is not only the annihilation of Armenian religious and national values, it is the negation of Christianity."[4] Underscoring the Dashnak nationalist agenda, one of the party leaders emphasized that the party had never been inclined, and was not inclined then, to sacrifice the Armenian fatherland to the triumph of any aim or goal, be it world revolution, socialism, or the workers' paradise. The federation (the Dashnaks) did not accept socialism in order to sacrifice the fatherland to certain remote aims, but it espoused socialism in the firm belief that in a socialist setting the fatherland would grow stronger and more prosperous. As the federation viewed it, regimes come and go; so it would be with the socialist regime, which would stand as only a milepost in the history of mankind, whereas the fatherland would remain endless and eternal.[5]

While their concept and definition of nationalism or patriotism varied, the one consistent and common theme among the political groupings in North America, even among some Armenian Communists, was their avowed loyalty to the concept of a homeland and to an identity that had almost been annihilated. Each organization judged itself the epitome of patriotism and cursed the opposition as the archetype of apostasy, the enemy of the Armenian nation.

Since the creation of an American Diocese in the United States in 1898, the Armenian Church in North America had been wracked with political turmoil. For church leaders, transplanting the Armenian Church to North America was, in itself, a complex challenge. Like other ethnic churches that played a pivotal role in the survival of a group as an identifiable entity, the Armenian Church faced the arduous task of maintaining traditional culture on foreign soil.[6] As Armenian immigrants increasingly perceived America to be their permanent home, this role of the church became contentious, for in order to survive and to lead, the church was obliged to adjust to a new language and to a set of different values, needs, and demands. Well-established old-country administrative and authoritarian traditions and clearly delineated class distinctions could not always function smoothly in a new society where democracy, individualism, and freedom of speech were sanctified. If it responded to the concerns of the North American-born and met the exigencies of the present and future, how could the church reconcile liberal reforms with the customs and structures of its long and revered history? If it changed, how could the church in North America be reconciled with the Armenian Church serving communities throughout the world and with the Mother Church in Echmiadzin, since the Apostolic Church was the national church of Armenians and the church and the people, regardless of where they might be living – in Persia, India, Russia, Canada, or the United States – constituted an indivisible whole? How, under new constraints, could this autocephalic church maintain its unique and predominant position as a national church in Protestant North America and not submit to being simply another competing Christian church? The Armenian church in North America, moreover, had to minister to people from diverse origins and experiences who spoke not only different dialects but also different languages, including Arabic or Turkish. The church, further, had to reconcile high-ranking clergy from "Russian" Armenia with a far-flung congregation in America composed largely of immigrants from Turkey.

The questions of power and governance also needed to be addressed. As the Armenian Church administration had a very strong lay constituency, who should exercise ultimate power? The primate, as head of the church in North America, or the Central Executive Committee, which traditionally assisted him and was composed of both clergy and elected lay representatives? Closely associated with the issue of governance was whether the Armenian Church should stand as the Armenian nation in exile or whether a separation of church and state – in effect, a separation of religion and politics – should be the anchor of ethnocultural survival? At a time, moreover, when many local churches in the New World saw themselves as almost autonomous institutions, how much decentralization could the Church sustain and still remain a viable force? And finally, there was the issue of money. During the 1920s and 1930s, when the church was in dire financial need, in order to establish a sound foundation on foreign soil and to meet the enormous demands on it, thousands of newly arrived immigrants were straining to help their refugee family members abroad, to establish themselves in the New World, to aid in the reconstruction of Armenia, and to survive the difficulties of the Great Depression.

Meanwhile, the relationship between Echmiadzin, the Mother See, and the communist leadership had repercussions not only on the church in Soviet Armenia but also on the most distant and isolated Armenian communities in the world. The bulk of Armenian Church members and nearly three-quarters of all active Armenian churches were outside Soviet Armenia.[7] Binding together this "church of the diaspora" was the Catholicos, the spiritual head of the Church and a highly respected and influential national symbol. Thus, if a secular political power controlled Echmiadzin, the seat of the Catholicos, it held a potent weapon to manipulate Armenian communities around the world.[8]

The fragile survival of the Church in Armenia, its subservience to communist power, and its influence on the hearts and minds of diasporan Armenians generated heated debate in North America especially when Echmiadzin dispatched controversial directives: the Supreme Council of Echmiadzin, for example, announced in a circular that the Holy See had "no political affiliation or partisanship," and, in the same document, underscored its loyalty and solicitousness to the Soviet regime. The circular aroused hostility among anti-Communists in the diaspora, when it exhorted "Primates and spiritual servants throughout all Sees to similarly remain loyal to the Soviet regime, and not allow speeches against the Soviet state."[9] Such directives highlighted not only the struggle between the pro- and anti-Communist camps but also the tensions between a faction that favoured power in the hands of Echmiadzin and another that sought to grasp administrative and financial control in North America. Interconnected with these complexities was a power struggle among the diasporan political factions, whose leaders and press used the church as an arena for partisan disputes and, conversely, accused the church of interfering in political affairs "almost to the exclusion of her spiritual ministry" (see chapter 7).[10]

In such an environment, the responsibility fell to the primate, as head of the North American diocese, to devise a workable framework for operations among various political factions in the United States and to "negotiate" the demands of the Holy See if they conflicted with the needs and aspirations of the American constituency.[11] From 1922 to 1928, Archbishop Tirayr Der Hovannesian, who had spent many years in Echmiadzin before coming to the United States, managed to channel the Diocese through precarious waters. With diplomacy and compromise he guided religious and administrative reforms, notably in the promulgation of a constitution. Firmly believing that the church was the moral and spiritual mainstay of the Armenian people, he called for renewal and expansion of parish churches and church organizations, and he encouraged the establishment of Armenian Sunday schools and supplementary language schools "to stem the tide of assimilation and to preserve our national heritage." By the end of 1930, Der Hovannesian had consecrated ten churches, bringing the total in North America to twenty.[12] This flurry of activity reflected not only the efforts of the church but also the determination of survivors to meet the needs of a growing population in North America and to pass on Armenian language and culture to the increasing number of children. One of the churches that Der Hovannesian consecrated was St Gregory the Illuminator in St Catharines, Ontario. The first Armenian church in Canada had started unpretentiously with the newcomers' efforts to build an Armenian community school.

THE RAFFI ARMENIAN COMMUNITY SCHOOL

After the Genocide, the main focus of the prewar immigrants centred on assisting family and friends in dire straits abroad, helping struggling survivors in Armenia and in countries of asylum, and rebuilding the fledgling political state of Armenia. While these preoccupations continued during the 1920s, other concerns jockeyed for attention as the number of children increased in Canada and as the settlements developed a sense of themselves as permanent communities with a spirit, history, and life of their own. Expressing a growing dissatisfaction with the Old World/New World tug-of-war and showing concern for the education of diasporan children, a mother castigated Armenian American leaders for being asleep and indifferent to the danger of assimilation. "Our children," she complained, "are denied the means of receiving religious and moral education in the spirit of our church and are gradually being lost." She feared the "foreignization" of Armenian children and the "bastardization of our national language and traditions." In one city alone, she pointed out, "we spend nearly $30,000 for religious purposes, but barely $300 for Armenian language and national education. We also send $30,000 to orphans and refugees in Armenia and other countries but we don't think of our children right here before our eyes."[13]

Aware that their culture hovered on the brink of extinction, St Catharines Armenians sought to take action on behalf of their children: "to keep them Armenian," to teach them the language, and to transmit a vestige of an ancient heritage. A group of thirty-four people, largely, but not all, Hnchak or HOG (Hayastani Oknutian Komite, or Relief Committee for Armenia) sympathizers, came together in December 1924 to discuss the creation of an Armenian community school, something more formal and more permanent than the front room of a boardinghouse or a space set aside in a coffee house. In honour of Raffi, the pen-name of the famous Armenian writer Hagop Melik-Hagopian, they called their supplementary school Raffi *varzharan* (school).[14] It opened its doors in January 1925 to thirty-five students in Setrag (Seth) Mooradian's coffee house, on the corner of Carlton and Ontario Streets, directly across from McKinnon's. All children in the community were encouraged to attend the school, which ran classes three evenings a week, from 6:30 to 8:30 P.M. Tuesdays and Thursdays were reserved for adult English classes.

The focus on the education of Canadian-born children and on the retention of their cultural heritage encouraged men and women to set aside their political differences and to work together as teachers, as executive members of the school council, and on various school committees.[15] The Raffi school does not rank as the first Armenian school in St Catharines, since each political group had, in previous times, operated its own school, nor did it provide the only occasion when children from both factions attended the same school. But this undertaking marked the first time since the series of national tragedies had shaken the communities that settlers joined forces for an official, local, community project. Raffi school was also the first step towards a more ambitious goal.

THE CANADIAN ARMENIAN UNION

During 1926 the Raffi school group evolved into the St Catharines branch of the Canadian Armenian Union (CAU), which had been founded in Toronto a year earlier.[16] The thirty members of the St Catharines cohort represented many components of the community: bachelor and household head, young and old, villager and townsman, factory worker and entrepreneur, Hnchak, HOG, and Dashnak. Although women participated in the activities, women's names are notably absent from the membership roster. This fact may be partly explained by the existence of two women's organizations: the Armenian Relief Society and the Armenian National Red Cross. But it is more likely that families were represented by male household heads. A good working relationship existed among the various factions and the CAU, as evidenced by their joint ventures, including, for example, the memorial service for General Andranik, the Armenian war hero, who died near Fresno, California, in 1927.

The CAU reconfirmed the educational emphasis of the Raffi school group for both children and adults. A library for adults provided a variety of books for loan and different political newspapers, including *Hairenik* (Fatherland), with Dashnak leanings; *Yeritasard Hayastan* (Young Armenia), the Hnchak mouthpiece; and *Baikar* (Struggle) the Ramgavar organ. The CAU organized plays and concerts and held raffles and banquets to raise funds for its various endeavours. As an indication of its broad scope and interest in the welfare of local Armenians, the CAU sent two hundred dollars in support of the Armenian orphan boys at Georgetown, Ontario.

Unlike the Raffi school, which was a local endeavour, the CAU was part of a larger entity with connections to the more sophisticated, more highly educated, wealthier, and urbane Armenians in Toronto. Throughout the minutes, references are made to "headquarters in Toronto," to visits by Toronto members such as Levon Babayan, Mesrob Bagdasarian, and Paul Sevagian, and to conferences and meetings with the Toronto group, as well as with other chapters in southern Ontario, such as the Ararat group in Hamilton, to which young newcomers like Aris Alexanian and Frank Avedis Ozanian belonged.

As an organization, the CAU formalized the structure of the Raffi school executive committee. Meetings were held on a regular basis, a prescribed agenda became more standardized, and minutes and accounts were kept in a much more orderly manner than before, with a treasurer's report at every meeting and regular auditing.

The CAU housed the school/library in several facilities in the vicinity, renting space at different times from Setrag Mooradian, Hagop Mooradian, and Mateos Korkigian. A small coffee house in the school/library enabled men to read books and newspapers, play cards, discuss issues, debate, and gossip. The rented quarters thus evolved as a school, library, meeting room, clubhouse, and rehearsal hall. By 1928 the growing community recognized the need for a permanent structure to house a school/library/meeting place. With full community support at a public meeting on 24 February 1929, the CAU executive dispatched a letter to headquarters in Toronto stating its intention to buy land to build a school and clubhouse. When headquarters responded positively, the executive formed two committees: one to look into the purchase of land and the other to visit various Armenian communities to raise money. When the St Catharines CAU bought two house lots on Carlton Street about two blocks from General Motors in the heart of the Armenian neighbourhood, the fundraising campaign began in earnest. Usually, two members travelled to different cities, lodged with relatives or friends, and canvassed every Armenian household in the area. In Troy, New York, they collected almost $100; in Erie and Meadville, Pennsylvania, $106. Galt, Preston, and Guelph donated over $60 altogether, and Niagara Falls, Buffalo, and Lockport, New York, contributed $170.

That the minutes of the CAU in St Catharines do not mention an interest in building a church is noteworthy, considering that even before World War I, Armenians had invited priests from the diocese in New York to make regular pastoral visits. Canadian communities elected religious councils, which collected a monthly fee, perhaps 25¢, from each community member, to bring a priest, to say mass, or to perform the rites of passage. Fathers Vagharshag Arshagouni, Seropé Nershabu, and Mateos Manigian and later Atig Dzotsikian, Movses Der Stepanian, and Zkon Charkhougian used the premises of local Anglican churches for Armenian services. As early as 1918 St Catharines had an elected religious council that functioned throughout the 1920s.[17] Starting around 1923, the itinerant priest Rev. Movses Der Stepanian, working from his farm near St Catharines, served the southern Ontario communities for marriages, funerals, baptisms, house blessings, and mass. When he heard about the intention to build a school, he suggested to Arshag Krikorian, chairman of the religious council, that a church be considered. Der Stepanian, Krikorian, and Senekerim Chichakian, the school teacher, contacted Levon Babayan, chairman of the CAU in Toronto and Der Stepanian proceeded to Toronto to discuss the matter.

At a public meeting in Hagop Mooradian's coffee house, probably in June or July of 1929, Der Stepanian, Babayan, and Mesrob Bagdasarian from Toronto urged the settlers to construct a church with a hall in the basement. Some secular voices, however, expressed disapproval of such a venture, arguing that a church was unnecessary. After considerable debate and after Babayan pledged his financial and moral support, the majority voted in favour of a church with a hall in the basement.[18]

It was a monumental decision for this small group, numbering at most 100 to 120 families, or about 400 to 500 people, but they were confident that with commitment and diligence they could realize an unimaginable dream.[19]

By 1929, perhaps encouraged by events in St Catharines, the religious councils of St Catharines, Toronto, Hamilton, Brantford, and Galt came together under the wing of the newly created Central Board of Trustees of the Armenian Apostolic Church of Canada, the first attempt by Armenians in Canada to establish a Canadian regional religious authority. Under the chairmanship of Levon Babayan, the board was to oversee the activities of the elected religious councils in each city. The religious councillors arranged the visits of itinerant priests and organized their lodgings, meals, and payment. Within their own limits, these laymen were responsible for the spiritual life of their own community and for maintaining ties with the Central Board in Toronto and through it, with the diocese in New York city.

In Toronto on 8 March 1930, Ontario Armenians held what was perhaps the first regional religious convention in Canada; it was chaired by Alexander Mooradian (A.B. Davies) of Hamilton, presided over by Father Zkon Charkhougian, and represented by delegates from the five parish councils in Canada.[20] The main topic on the agenda was the construction of the St Catharines church. Other items discussed at the Toronto convention focused on finances, including the salary of itinerant priests, the request for quotas by the Central Board and by the diocese in New York, and the annual donation by the Anglican Synod.

The Canadian Central Board maintained good relations with the Anglican Church, which was theologically very close to the Armenian church. Around 1930, the Anglican Church donated the sizeable sum of $2,500 a year for a period of two years to the Armenians in Canada for religious and educational purposes, provided that the Armenians matched the amount. Because of difficult financial times, the Anglican Synod lowered the sum to $650 in the third year and stopped support altogether in the fourth year. Whatever the contribution, it proved to be vital assistance at a time when Armenians were trying to establish their own church in Canada.[21]

BUILDING THE CHURCH

St Catharines had about $800 in its treasury, hardly enough to construct a church that would cost approximately $13,000.[22] Members launched a concerted fund-raising campaign. Community members worked sedulously at raffles, bake sales, teas, and concerts, and they organized an Armenian tag day. Members travelled to different cities and visited individual Armenian households to raise funds. Bedros Ghazarian, of Niagara Falls, donated the large sum of $1,000. The Gulbenkians of New York donated $500 and the Karageuzians, also of New York, contributed $300.[23] Der Stepanian collected about $1,000 from Granite City, Racine, and Chicago. By the time the church was consecrated, the community had raised about $9,000. Babayan promised to pay the interest on the mortgage of $4,000, which he, in turn, arranged. More significantly, men and women who were struggling to make ends meet during a period of unemployment contributed in other ways. Men excavated and helped in the construction work; women cooked meals and made fancywork items for fund-raising raffles and dinners. Building the church involved the whole community.

Situated on Carlton Street on about three-quarters of an acre of land, the church was constructed of red brick and measured approximately sixty feet by thirty-five, with a usable basement of equal size and seating for a congregation of about 150. Externally it had no distinguishing Armenian architectural features and resembled a Canadian Protestant church; the interior, however, was typically Armenian.

For months the community had been actively preparing for the consecration. Women were feverishly sewing garments and fine laces for the altar. Some were busy baking *Maas*, the unleavened bread given to each parishioner to symbolize his or her participation in the Divine Liturgy.[24] Others were cooking the meal that would follow the consecration ceremony. Until the last minute, men were hammering and polishing, adding the finishing touches to the building. Young people and older immigrants were diligently rehearsing the music of the Armenian service.

On the last day of November 1930, a crisp, sunny fall day, full of hope and excitement, Archbishop Tirayr Der Hovannesian, from New York, assisted by the Reverends Movses Der Stepanian, Zkon Charkhougian, and Atig Dzotsigian consecrated the first Armenian church in Canada, with Levon Babayan as the godfather.[25] The parishioners of St Gregory the Illuminator could well be proud of the magnificent sight. The clergy in their resplendent robes, the altar decked with flowers, the crosses shimmering in the light, and the heavy aroma of incense enveloping the pretty little church. Armenian worshippers from near and far, members of the Canadian clergy, St Catharines city councillors, and other Canadian dignitaries joined to celebrate this auspicious day. The beautiful sounds of the Armenian liturgy rang out, as the choir, its numbers swelled with participants from Toronto and Detroit, joyfully and solemnly led the congregation in chant. As the Archbishop blessed each cross with the holy chrism, the parishioners must have rejoiced, for the day marked the fulfillment of a cherished dream of having their own church where they would worship according to their own rites in their own language. Here they would witness their children's marriages and their grandchildren's baptisms, and from here they, themselves, would some day be buried.

Like many other Armenian churches built in North America during the 1920s and early 1930s, St Gregory embodied the expectations of immigrants who sought stability and peace away from a traumatic past. But before the church could flourish, it was engulfed in the Depression and then cast in a drama of international proportions. Events in the United States were to rock the very foundations of the church and almost wreck the community.

VIOLENCE IN THE UNITED STATES

Following Primate Tirayr Der Hovannesian's resignation in 1928, an interregnum of three years, with only a Locum Tenens at the head, ushered in a period of uncertainty, a sense of diocesan ineffectiveness, and further attempts to solidify local autonomy. And while the diocese was weakened by a leadership vacuum, it was hamstrung by financial hardship that was aggravated by the Great Depression.

Finally, a new primate was elected, and in June 1931 Bishop, later Archbishop (1932), Ghevont Tourian, from Manchester, England, began his tenure. Born of humble family in 1881 in Scutari, near Constantinople, Tourian had studied under two outstanding scholars and administrators, the Armenian patriarch of Constantinople, Malachia [Maghakia] Ormanian, and the Armenian patriarch of Jerusalem, Eghishé Tourian. Described by contemporaries as a dynamic reformer and devout man, totally dedicated to the Mother Church in Echmiadzin, Tourian was faced with complexities, anxieties, and fears that were inextricably bound up with the tragedies of the preceding sixteen years. The responsibility for stabilizing this quarrelsome community and reconciling the rancorous factions was a Herculean challenge for any leader, especially considering the vulnerability of the church in Soviet Armenia.

Even before assuming his post in New York, the bishop had spoken in defence of Soviet action. He had published two articles declaring that the confiscation of church property by communist authorities provided the church with an opportunity "to free itself from the chains of commerce" and enabled it to embrace once again its true, spiritual function.[26] Less than a year after taking office, Tourian provoked anti-Communist parishioners further by inserting the word "Soviet" in the customary prayer for Armenia in a newly published book of the Divine Liturgy. At the same time, while he allowed the clergy to hold memorial services for Genocide martyrs in their churches, he forbade them to preside over commemoration exercises outside the church, on the grounds that these observances might degenerate into anti-Soviet mass demonstrations. Rumblings preceding his primacy grew into outspoken dissatisfaction as the primate steered the helm of power into the raging storm. The *Hairenik*, mouthpiece of the Dashnak group, denounced the primate as the willing tool of the Soviet Union in North America. The pro-Tourian faction, on the other hand, considered such allegations totally unjust and rallied to the bishop's defence.

Soviet Armenia and the Armenian Republic emerged as the double-edged sword of identity. The conflict centred more and more on the flag as the mark of loyalty. Dashnaks revered the Tricolour of the Armenian Republic – the red, blue, and orange – as the symbol of a free and independent Armenian people. The conservative/left, by contrast, condemned this flag as a symbol of Dashnak power in the Armenian Republic and of the Dashnak government in exile. By repudiating the flag, the conservative/left rendered it synonymous with the Dashnak party and with Dashnak sympathy. Thus, a flag that had represented the yearnings and aspirations of the Armenian people came to stand for only one segment of it. The Tri-colour, which had been the proud rallying symbol for all Armenians, became the source of bitter slander and violence in every Armenian community.

In 1933, in the depths of the Depression, when churches were heavily in debt, families were struggling with unemployment, and nerves were raw, tensions between the two factions escalated. Tourian travelled to Chicago to speak on Armenian Day, 1 July 1933, at the Century of Progress International Exposition. There, a group of Dashnaks placed the Tricolour on the podium alongside the American flag, a common practice at official functions. The archbishop refused to speak until the Armenian flag had been removed, on the grounds that if he proceeded with the program under the Tricolour, it would appear that he was taking political sides and endorsing all that the flag symbolized. This action, he argued, would create dissension in America and could result in reprisals against Armenians in the Soviet Union. Since this was a meeting in America, he would continue only under the American flag, in order not to implicate the church in any political controversy. The ensuing shouting and fighting was quelled only by police intervention. The Archbishop concluded his speech without the Tricolour.

News of the event reverberated throughout North America, for in the eyes of many, the archbishop had in fact "taken sides." Accusations and counteraccusations in the press, in churches and halls, and at picnics charged the air with impending doom. The *Banvor* (Worker), ever anxious to stoke the fire, "quoted" the archbishop as saying that the Tricolour was "a manifestation of revolt and disdain against the state organization of Present Armenia." The *Hairenik* fired back, charging those "who defile our flag" with treason.²⁷ In such a strained atmosphere, fifty-seven delegates met at the annual Diocesan Representative Convention, the governing body of the diocese, held in St Gregory the Illuminator (Holy Illuminator) Mother Cathedral in New York City on 2 September 1933. Before the meeting convened, during the process of electing lay representatives, the political forces had vied for voice everywhere, and in some cities rivalry broke out into violence. When the meeting convened in the church, the relationship between the two factions was already tense and embittered. Excusing himself because of illness, the primate assigned Bishop Hovsep Garabedian, chairman of the Diocesan Central Committee, to preside over the meeting as his representative. From the moment the public meeting opened, the two factions were seething about the events in Chicago. The pro-Tourian group withdrew to the Hotel Martinique, creating, in effect, two conventions. Both claimed legitimacy. The Holy Illuminator group, composed largely of Dashnaks and their sympathizers, on the grounds that it held a legitimate majority, passed a vote of nonconfidence in the archbishop and called for his resignation. The pro-Tourian group, largely Ramgavars and their supporters, also claiming a legitimate majority, expressed confidence in the primate. In this deadlock, both conventions appealed to Echmiadzin for confirmation.²⁸

In the meantime, uncertainty and intrigue rankled every Armenian community in North America. In New York, Ramgavars, Hnchaks, Communists, and the HOG established a united front in a war against the Dashnaks and the Tricolour. On 25 October 1933, the Supreme Spiritual Council in Echmiadzin passed a resolution in which it recognized the Hotel Martinique group, condemned the decision of the Holy Illuminator group to depose the primate, sanctioned the Primate's actions at the Chicago Exposition, called for peace and unity, and directed the archbishop to convene a new diocesan convention in which both sides would participate.²⁹

During the fall, the wedge deepened. If anyone needed proof of the archbishop's communist sympathies, the Dashnaks argued, he need only note the Maxim Litvinoff affair: Archbishop Tourian was the only clergyman from Communist-dominated countries to attend a dinner in honour of Litvinoff, the new Soviet ambassador to the United States.³⁰

Calls for unity went unheeded as tempers flared. Before a new convention was called, tragedy struck. After months of wrangling, events reached a climax on Sunday, 24 December 1933. As he proceeded to the altar of the Church of the Holy Cross in New York City to say Divine Liturgy, in a church overflowing with parishioners during the festive season, Archbishop Ghevont Tourian was stabbed to death.

Pandemonium broke out in every Armenian community in North America. The trial hit national newspapers. Nine pro-Dashnaks were convicted of the crime. Seven received sentences ranging from ten years to life imprisonment, and two men received the death sentence, but these were later commuted to life imprisonment. The Dashnak Party, meanwhile, vehemently and steadfastly denied any official role in or responsibility for the crime.

Following the primate's assassination, civil strife ripped apart Armenian communities in North America. A people so sensitive to their good reputation hurtled into a mad spiral of mass protests, riots, allegations, fighting, and bloodshed. Vituperative name-calling besmirched the Armenian name. Like "a festering harvest," Armenian community life turned "putrid" and "ugly." Armenian businesses were picketed, boycotted, and sabotaged, property was damaged, people were attacked and beaten. Each church split, sometimes fighting for possession in ugly court proceedings, further weakening these institutions that were struggling to survive during hard economic times. "Church lovers," recalled an interviewee from St Catharines, "even if they were anti-Communist, refused to accept this heinous act."[31] Families broke up: brother turned against sister, father against son, mother against daughter. Not a single aspect of Armenian life escaped the turmoil.

The Hotel Martinique group clung to control of the New York diocese and strengthened its position with support of the Holy See in Echmiadzin. In response, Dashnak sympathizers, still very strong, held the Cathedral of St Gregory the Illuminator and formed the Prelacy of the Armenian Apostolic Church, which in October 1934 organized its own convention, with clerical and lay delegates.[32] In effect, two separate institutions emerged, institutions based on the same theology but each with its own church buildings, priests, and parishioners.

The disaster that took Tourian's life occurred beyond Canadian borders, but it clamoured with as much fury in Canada as in the United States. St Catharines, Ontario, provides an example of how a group of good people seeking stability and revitalization attempted to cope with conflicting agendas in their community and how they tried to come to grips with large, global events beyond their control.

13

The Church and Politics: Crisis in St Catharines, 1930–1933

We have kept the feasts, heard the masses,
We have brewed beer and cyder,
Gathered wood against the winter,
Talked at the corner of the fire,
Talked at the corners of streets,
Talked not always in whispers,
Living and partly living.
....
We have all had our private terrors,
Our particular shadows, our secret fears.
But now a great fear is upon us, a fear not of one but of many,
A fear like birth and death, when we see birth and death alone
In a void apart. We
Are afraid in a fear which we cannot know, which we cannot face, which none understands,
And our hearts are torn from us, our brains unskinned like the layers of an onion, our selves are lost lost
In a final fear which none understands.

T.S. Eliot, *Murder in the Cathedral*[1]

In April 1932, less than a year after taking office, Primate Ghevont Tourian paid a pastoral visit to Canada to celebrate Easter and hold memorial services for martyrs of the Genocide. Wherever he travelled, the tall, cultured, and erudite theologian was visited by the local mayor and city councillors, leading Anglican clergy, and newspaper reporters. In Galt, the primate held services in Holy Trinity Anglican Church and in Hamilton at St Philip's. He placed a wreath on the cenotaph in front of the Toronto City Hall in the company of Mayor Stewart and called his coreligionists to prayer at St Stephen's Anglican Church. In Brantford he held services in Grace Anglican Church where he urged his flock "to become real citizens of Canada, not only law-abiding, but intensely loyal to their new home, in which they had every liberty of worship which had been denied to them in their homeland." Only in St Catharines, at St Gregory the Illuminator, did the primate say Divine Liturgy in an Armenian church.[2]

It was the church that was very close to the heart of Levon Babayan, Tourian's intimate friend. Their relationship went back long before Tourian came to North America. In fact, Babayan had voted for Tourian's tenure as primate and paid for his trip from Manchester, England, to New York. As a member of the Diocesan Central Executive and as a delegate to diocesan conventions, he steadfastly supported Tourian and, needless to add, was part of the Hotel Martinique group, elected as second chairman.[3] The primate returned the respect and admiration, bestowing on Babayan the newly created Cross of St Margaret and dedicating a book of his sermons to Babayan's mother. Years later, Babayan dedicated his biography to the memory of his dear friend Archbishop Tourian.[4]

In the spring of 1932, when the terrible events of 1933 had not yet taken place, Babayan must have been proud to invite the primate to St Gregory's in St Catharines. But Babayan's role in St Gregory's, important to be sure, went hand in hand with the work of the parish council, which ran the day-to-day affairs of the church.

THE PARISH COUNCIL: 1930–33

In its own way the St Catharines Armenians transferred the functions of a typical Keghi village parish council to Canada, where it exercised religious, social, educational, and moral authority in the community. Since the parish council was elected by church members, it represented the whole community, including people from various walks of life, bachelors and heads of households, old-timers and refugees, people of different ages, backgrounds, and places of origin. The first parish council, all foreign born, was composed of men from both political groups: the president, Nishan Krekorian, and the recording secretary, Hagop Melkonian, were pro-Dashnak, while the treasurer, Ohannes Torosian, and the keeper of the seal, Krikor Der Krikorian, were pro-Hnchak/HOG. Election to these offices depended not on political affiliations but on the qualities, talents, and skills the men had to offer.

In the Canadian milieu these men would have been seen as uneducated, unskilled foreigners doing the filthiest and lowliest jobs in the factory or as small tradesmen and shopkeepers. The parish council minutes, however, reveal a group of men who not only worked sedulously and devoted time and energy for the benefit of the community but who set high standards for order and propriety and directed the affairs of the settlement with intelligence, kindness, and common sense.

The parish council, or board of trustees, guided the daily management of the church and school and became the internal religious and moral authority of the community. Because they were the first parish councillors, without precedents to depend on, the councillors tried to create a strong and durable framework and to entrench rules and regulations for the smooth operation of affairs, always with a long-term view in sight. The council held its meetings in an orderly fashion, with a consistent agenda, appointing committees on a regular basis to investigate issues or problems and make recommendations. Full membership meetings were called annually and periodically, whenever important decisions had to be made. Meeting frequently, perhaps two or three times a week, the parish council elected a choir master, appointed a caretaker, decided on maintenance and renewal, arranged for heating and lighting, supervised the church finances, paid the mortgage, made decisions about land acquisition, and arranged for the rental of the church and the church hall.

The council's most important responsibility was the appointment of and relationship with the priest. Initially the councillors, with Babayan's approval, hired Rev. Movses Der Stepanian, a pro-Dashnak newcomer from the region of Mush in Western Armenia as their part-time priest. In 1931, the St Catharines council invited Father Zkon Charkhougian. Like Babayan, Father Zkon was a conservative from Constantinople. In 1929, through Babayan's intervention, he and his family had immigrated to Canada. Settling in Montreal, he held services in St John the Evangelist Anglican church for the small Armenian community. A year later, the family moved to Toronto, and Father Zkon was officially hired by the St Catharines community on a part-time basis. Although he lived in Toronto, he held services in Hamilton, St Catharines, Galt, Toronto, and Brantford, customarily on a five-week schedule. Whether saying divine liturgy, performing the sacraments and rites of the Church, ministering to the distressed, sick, and dying, or blessing the homes, the itinerant priest became a familiar figure in the Armenian settlements of southern Ontario.[5]

Anyone in the community could be a member of St Gregory's for a two-dollar initial membership fee and an additional charge of twenty-five cents a month for bachelors (giving them one vote each) and fifty cents a month for married couples (giving them two votes). Church membership of 68 households in the first year rose to 110 by December 1932, and church attendance varied from 20 to 30 to full capacity for mass and for feast days.[6] The parish council invited Armenians from nearby towns, especially for the high holy days, Armenian Christmas, on 6 January, and Easter. For Armenians throughout southern Ontario and upper New York, the church became a favourite place for the rites of passage. Thirty-three children born between 1925 and 1931 in St Catharines, Hamilton, Brantford, Galt, Preston, Niagara Falls, and Buffalo were baptized in the first year of the church's existence.

The parish council also operated the supplementary school, which it ran like trustees and administrators of a board of education. It hired teachers and decided on their salaries, ordered texts, discussed curriculum, dealt with discipline, provided regular inspections of the school, formed committees to examine the children at the end of the year, and held school concerts and parties. The spirit of voluntarism was particularly evident in the school, as men and women often taught free of charge or acted as teacher's assistants to help maintain discipline. Like the Raffi and CAU schools, it was open to all children, free for church members' children and at a minimal cost for nonmembers' children. To meet the needs of adults, the parish council provided a library with newspapers, loaned books for a small fee, and organized a theatrical group and a church choir.[7]

Before the church was built, Armenians in Canada had undertaken measures at self-regulation, either in an informal way or under the auspices of the political organizations. On 27 July 1920, for instance, Dashnak members passed a resolution expelling from their ranks anyone who gambled.[8] With the construction of the church in St Catharines, the parish council took on the responsibility of a communal tribunal. Since the council, or board, was composed of the rank and file, it was in constant touch with the people, with local events, and with the daily functioning of the community. If an altercation occurred in the factory, at school, between neighbours, or in a coffeehouse, the councillors would hear about it immediately. Since election to the council was considered an honour, councillors commanded a great measure of respect, and their decisions – always made and taken very seriously – carried considerable weight in the community.

The council regularly received letters of complaint from community members seeking arbitration. It tried to settle disputes among family members and feuds between neighbours, assisted indigent individuals and families, and made judgments in quarrels dealing with money, debt, and the use of "bad" language. In each case the council endeavoured to negotiate a compromise between the complainants. It is impressive to note the extent to which people who had made a fuss about an issue offered public apologies to each other and shook hands after the council had become involved. "The parish council," notes Torosian, "was the conscience of the tight little community which had a clear-cut conception of what was acceptable behaviour and what was not. This code of behaviour was based both on religious teaching and on practical considerations ... Those who were unprepared to live by the community's moral and social code were either ostracized or held up to ridicule."9 Since neither exclusion nor ridicule was palatable and since the parish council decisions were viewed with respect, the community functioned relatively peacefully. This type of self-regulation contributed to maintaining communal harmony, reducing ill-will, and defusing tension before it got out of hand. "The police hardly ever came into our community," recalled an interviewee. "They didn't have to, because we policed ourselves."10

The minutes and interviewees alike stress that successive parish councils made determined efforts to maintain fraternal and amicable community relations, not only between individuals and families, but also between generations and between the political factions. In order to keep peace, for instance, the board allowed any local group, political or otherwise, to use the hall for meetings free of charge. It insisted on its neutrality in other ways: when the Hai Petakan Karmir Khach (Armenian National Red Cross) invited the parish council to celebrate the tenth anniversary of the creation of Soviet Armenia, the council declined to attend as an official body, because it viewed its neutrality as inviolable, although members were allowed to participate as private individuals.

In its first few years of existence the parish council achieved a remarkable measure of internal harmony and peace. It symbolized the expression of group loyalty, of morality, and of right and wrong. These uprooted immigrants took a moral code that emanated from experiences in a distant land and passed it on to future generations in Canada. In this way they established a point of orientation for themselves in a new and changing world and gave their children a sense of "Armenian values."

Self-regulation reveals another dimension of their mentality. As an ethnic group, Armenians felt that they had no one to look after them, no great power, no ambassador, no strong church presence. They were a small community made up of many refugees, and they were on their own. It was crucial to their survival as Armenians and as an Armenian community to live in harmony with each other. It was also vitally important to establish a reputation in Canada as being hard-working, law-abiding, loyal, and peaceful members of society.

EXTERNAL RELATIONS

The church was functioning within three religious spheres: Echmiadzin, located in Soviet Armenia; the Diocese of the Armenian

Apostolic Church, in New York City; and the Central Board of Trustees in Toronto. For Armenian immigrants in Canada, Echmiadzin, which was under Communist authority in Soviet Armenia, continued to be revered as the sacred fountainhead of their faith. But neither Echmiadzin nor the Catholicos were active participants in their lives. The Mother See was far away, in another world. No mention is made of Echmiadzin, either in the minutes of the St Catharines church to 1932 or in the accounts of the regional religious conference cited in the previous chapter.

By contrast, the St Catharines parish council communicated with the diocese in New York City with which it was affiliated and with the primate who presided over the Church's Central Executive Committee, either directly or through the central board in Toronto. Long before the Genocide, a relationship existed between the diocese and the Armenians in southern Ontario, for they had often requested the diocese to arrange for itinerant priests. One of them, Rev. Mateos Manigian actually resided in Toronto for a time in the late 1920s. During the early 1930s, Canada as a whole was treated as a separate region under the aegis of the central board in Toronto. On a regular basis, St Catharines and other Armenian communities were represented at the diocesan assemblies in New York.

The importance of the central board in Toronto cannot be overemphasized, because it reflects an attempt, at this early stage, to create a separate Canadian regional religious authority, and because, at its helm, stood the formidable Levon Babayan. Combining his personal stature as a wealthy businessman with his official roles as chairman of the central board and the CAU, Babayan was for the working people of southern Ontario a prosperous merchant, a member of the Toronto élite, the crucial contact with Armenian religious and financial leaders abroad, and the unofficial but highly visible spokesperson, or ambassador, as he himself phrased it, for the Armenian community among political and media leaders in Canada.

Babayan was consulted on major church decisions. "He was overseeing our church," recalled a member, "therefore a lot of people [outside St Catharines] did things for our church. It was an incentive." When the parish council negotiated with Der Stepanian in November 1930 for his salary, he requested fifteen dollars a week, ten dollars to come from the central board in Toronto and five dollars from the St Catharines community, which would in turn receive the income from divine liturgy, marriages, funerals, and baptisms. The council waited for the central board's consent, that is, Babayan's approval, before agreeing with Der Stepanian's terms. Through his supporters and "lieutenants," Babayan kept a watchful eye on affairs in St Catharines and in the other communities. And for good reason. If we consider the interrelationships from a different perspective, it may be that St Gregory's and the central board sustained Levon Babayan's image and prestige with Tourian and the New York diocese. From 1931 to 1933, five to six lay and clerical delegates annually represented Canada at the diocesan assemblies.[11]

In addition to the three Armenian constituencies, St Gregory's was also operating within the Canadian milieu, where Armenian religious culture was accepted and recognized, particularly by the Church of England. In the process of building and maintaining their church, parishioners experienced a sense of communal pride and a feeling of empowerment. Most importantly, as Christians and Armenian Church members in Canada, they had freed themselves from the hated epithet of the *gaiur*, the unbeliever.

LAY INITIATIVE AND LOCAL AUTONOMY

The St Catharines church was the epitome of lay initiative. Although the idea to build a church had been suggested by Father Movses and supported by Babayan, both of whom were not an integral part of the community, the final decision rested with the St Catharines people. These men and women who had migrated to Canada and had regrouped themselves in the New World did not have to be told that it was they who would have to make the sacrifices and reap the benefits of their own church. And indeed, while money was donated by people outside the community, it was the small donations, the voluntarism, the work, and the dedication of the local group that built and sustained the church.

Just as crucial in these early years was the transplantation of the Old World custom of local autonomy. From time to time Fathers Movses and Zkon presided over council meetings as ex officio members of the board, and Babayan was consulted on important matters. Undeniably, his presence, authority, and leadership loomed large. But the daily administration and financial operations were the duties of a freely elected parish council. The initiatives came from the rank and file, from a group of working class men, who had had no previous extensive experience in running a church. The minutes reveal the extent of a democratic modus operandi. Major issues were put to a council vote and often to a general membership vote. Even the question of sending a "quota" to the Toronto board was argued interminably. St Catharines members were not pleased, for instance, to learn that they were expected to send a fifty-dollar quota, or tithe, to Toronto for the diocese in New York. On 4 October 1931 they decided that because of financial constraints, they could not pay at that time.¹²

Nowhere is there greater evidence that St Gregory's was a "people's church" than in the tradition of church services conducted by lay members. Both Fathers Movses and Zkon were part-time priests who also served the other Armenian communities. Although St Catharines could not afford a full-time priest, parishioners could say morning prayers in the church every Sunday with the choir master, Krikor Der Krikorian, a barber by trade who was vested as deacon in 1932, and with the assistance of Senekerim Chichakian, a coremaker at General Motors and the local Armenian schoolteacher. Laymen shared a measure of spiritual authority with the part-time priest, but they never vied to replace him or to undermine his spiritual leadership. Their staying power in the community depended not on introducing innovations but on retaining the old forms of worship.

The dynamics of the community itself, its old-country traditions and geographic distance from the centres of power in the United States, also contributed significantly to the development of local lay autonomy and allowed the St Catharines congregation to tend its own affairs.¹³ As final proof of their autonomy, parishioners insisted that the deed for the church be in the name of the St Catharines community and not in the name of the diocese in New York, under whose jurisdiction they operated.

THE CHURCH

The parishioners of St Gregory's came from an empire where they represented a colonized minority for whom religion and language had defined identity. Bringing this fusion with them from the old land, they continued to identify themselves and to define their ethnic boundaries within this context. The church gave these immigrants a point of orientation in a new land and strengthened group identity in a pluralist society. For all, but particularly for the refugees, whose lives since 1915 had been marked by dislocation, the church represented stability and continuity with their past.

For members of the congregation the church provided a frame of reference for their battered heritage. The classical Armenian language of the services, the rites and rituals, and the prayers and hymns that nurtured them were the same things that had sustained their parents and grandparents in churches now destroyed. The feast of *bagharch* celebrating the birth of Christ; the fires of *Diaruntarach*, commemorating the presentation of Christ at the Temple; the terra-cotta coloured eggs at Easter, remembering His Death and Resurrection; the water of *vijak*, marking the Feast of Ascension; the Blessing of the Grapes and the church picnic, rejoicing in the Feast of St Mary, Mother of God; and, always, the sacrificial lamb linked their Christian faith with their long and tumultuous history.[14]

For the pious the church was a place of worship in fellowship with one another, and it was a house of prayer that brought them into communion with God. Here, amid incense and hymn, the drawn curtain before the altar, separating the holy from the profane, reminded them of their humanity and of God's omnipotence. Here, in their own language, in rites familiar and loved, they experienced the mysteries of their faith. And here, in the church, the rituals, marking time, marking years, marking life itself, gave them hope and strength.

For young and old, women and men, believer and nonbeliever, the church also offered a structure for community activities. It channelled peoples' energies in productive ways. Religious, educational, cultural, intellectual, organizational, and social life centred in and around the church. For these newcomers, the church became a haven and a refuge where they could share tragedies and join in communal thanksgiving. As their church, courthouse, school, and library, the little brick building solidified the community.

The church also forged a new form of communal authority far beyond anything associated with the Canadian Armenian Union. For the first time a religious institution existed that had won the allegiance of various local groupings and brought together settlers with different political and regional perspectives. Thus, the church formed a communal assembly through which the general popular voice could be heard, and it prevailed as the forum for the interaction of community power. From the moment the first parish council was elected, the church represented the focus of community leadership and the means of recognizing that power. It gave birth to a new stratum of authority and evolved as the mechanism for expressing communal aspirations. On the other hand, while the church may have imperceptibly drawn into its foyer men and women who had opposed constructing a temple in the first place, the church's progressively important role in the community may have displaced earlier bases of power and antagonized secular, antichurch, anticlerical, or atheist members of the community.

CRISIS IN ST CATHARINES

If Armenians in St Catharines took politics at all seriously, they belonged to one of the two organized political factions – Dashnak or Hnchak, at least before the Communist/Hnchak faction split. Their socialist leanings are not surprising, considering that they were working-class men operating on the lowest rung of the socioeconomic ladder and the constant target of discrimination, exploitation, and unemployment. They were linked to each other in background and education, and many in the community, both pre- and post-Genocide immigrants, were bound to each other, either by blood, marriage, or god-parenthood. They lived in the same neighbourhood, worked in the same factories, sent their children to the same schools, shopped in the same stores, and spoke the same language. Inevitably they established intimate friendships with each other, both as individuals and as families. Under normal conditions it is unlikely that their political differences would have erupted into division and bitterness. But a fierce tempest blew in from the south and swept them into the maelstrom raging in the United States.

The Dashnaks formed a relatively well-organized, well-disciplined, and stable substructure of Armenian community life. In 1917–18, while McKinnon's was operating at wartime capacity, the Dashnak organization in St Catharines had about 70 members. In a 1918 census, 44 of the 68 members were born in Keghi and approximately a third of the remainder were born in Mush, a neighbouring region of Keghi. Membership plummeted to 22 in 1924, reflecting the exodus of Armenians from the city, but with the influx of refugees during the 1920s, the party was revitalized, expanding its roster to 31 in 1927.[15] The Dashnak group thus had many components, including old-timers and newcomers, young men and old, Keghetsis and Mushetsis.

The Dashnaks remained the only viable political organization in Canada. With its women's wing, the Armenian Relief Society, the Dashnaks maintained an active political, social, and educational life.[16] Always, they gave pride of place to a free Armenia, the Tricolour flag, the coat of arms, and the anthem. For them, symbolism and affiliation were fused with identity. Ethnicity merged with patriotism and became the anchor and bond of Dashnak families. Typically, they viewed Russian Soviet control over Armenia as the antithesis to their vision of a free, independent, and united Armenia. A diehard member emphasized the Armenian Revolutionary Federation (ARF) point of view: "Even if Armenians were forced to accept Communism inside Armenia, they didn't have to accept it in the diaspora."[17]

The imprisonment and hanging of 140 Hnchak leaders from 1913 to 1915 by the Young Turks irreparably weakened the larger Hnchak organization. In Canada most Hnchaks were Keghetsis and had emigrated from Western Armenia before the Genocide; the leadership was composed almost exclusively of older pre-1914 immigrants. The Hnchaks operated branches in Galt, Brantford, Hamilton, St

Catharines, and Guelph. It is estimated St Catharines alone had 75 Hnchak members during World War I.[18] The Winnipeg General Strike, the Red Scare and fear of anarchy in Canada led to a witch hunt of the left. Hnchaks were accused of being Bolsheviks, revolutionaries, and anarchists. The Royal Canadian Mounted Police seized Hnchak records, closed down clubs, blocked its newspaper, *Yeritasard Hayastan* (Young Armenia), at the border, and arrested a few local Hnchak members. While these persecutions were temporary, they were insidious enough to demoralize members, some of whom fled from Canada, usually to the United States; and some quit the party altogether.[19] Exodus, old age, and death of the early members led to further attrition during the 1920s and 1930s, but, unlike the Dashnaks, the organization was unable to rejuvenate itself during the twenties.

According to Hnchak historians, antagonistic forces from the right undermined the party further. "Most of our members [in St Catharines]," notes Kitur, "joined the Canadian Armenian Union ... It was difficult to get our people to understand that the protector Babayan in order to prepare the ground for the Armenian General Benevolent Union was destroying the revolutionary organization." The severest blow, however, was a volley from the left. After their rapprochement in 1921, the Social Democrats and the Communists broke in an acrimonious struggle for power, which inevitably had an impact on Armenian political groups. According to Hnchak sources, the party in the United States initially welcomed the HOG organizers from Armenia, at least until it realized they intended to smash the party. Procommunist former Hnchaks in the United States tried unsuccessfully to wrest control of *Yeritasard Hayastan* and rushed to various branches and exhorted Hnchakian members to quit the organization. Only through *Banvor* (Worker) and the HOG (the Relief Committee for Armenia), they proclaimed, could the people support their reborn motherland. Two field workers, Soghomon Kaprielian and Mampre Amirkhanian, went so far as to burn the Hnchak party archives in Hamilton. Such was the devastation by the HOG that the Detroit chapter of 320 members was reduced to 35; St Louis plunged from 70 to 6, Racine from 110 to 16 and chapters in Canada gradually disintegrated.[20] Even though other Hnchak field-workers tried to keep the party alive and some die-hards remained faithful to the Hnchakian cause till their dying day, the organization never regained its former strength in Canada. Not even the beloved writer Setrag Shahen, a Hnchak son of Keghi, an honoured relative of some local Hnchaks, and an editor of *Yeritasard Hayastan*, could invigorate the party. "We had what we wanted," explained an interviewee, "a socialist state for Armenia. There was no longer any need to continue with the Hnchak organization." "As Hnchaks," recalled another, "we couldn't help Armenia. Only as members of HOG, the Progressives, and the church could we help the homeland."[21]

Organized in St Catharines around 1925, the HOG continued operations until 1937, when directives from Soviet Armenia dissolved the international movement. In St Catharines, the HOG had about thirteen members, but its women's wing, Hai Petakanan Karmir Khach (Armenian National Red Cross), which started in 1926, was very active and in the early thirties claimed a membership of twenty-five to thirty, mostly women.[22]

Thus, on the eve of the crisis, the pro-Soviet, pro-Church faction in St Catharines was composed of Hnchakians and members of the Communist front organizations, the HOG and the Armenian National Red Cross. Among them were anticlerics and nonbelievers who supported the church because of their conviction that it was an effective agent in maintaining Armenian cultural identity in Canada and a countervailing force to assimilation. As in other places, the left joined forces with conservatives, but the conservative strength in the community emanated not from St Catharines but from Toronto: from Levon Babayan and his friends.

Already as early as 1931 trouble had started in St Catharines between pro- and anti-Soviet groups, but the parish council had immediately stepped in to prevent tempers from getting out of hand. Throughout 1932 the newspapers from the United States were seething with articles about Tourian, the Mother See in Echmiadzin, Soviet Armenia, the Republic of Armenia, and the Tricolour. Because of the high level of literacy in St Catharines and because the newspapers of the various political factions were readily available, the people were relatively well informed about developments in the United States. They could not fail to be affected by the political and religious cauldron brewing south of the border.

On the primate's visit to St Catharines in the spring of 1932, an altercation erupted between him and a number of parishioners who were angry because he had publicly insulted Rev. Movses Der Stepanian, their priest, political confrere, fellow Mushetsi, and former freedom fighter. They resented, too, Babayan's interference in displacing Rev. Movses with Rev. Zkon Charkhougian, who, like Babayan and Tourian, was a conservative from Constantinople. Before the squabble could get out of hand, Babayan hurriedly escorted the primate out of the church.

A year later, on 21 or 22 May 1933, as they had done every year, the Dashnaks held a meeting in the church basement to commemorate the anniversary of the founding of the Armenian Republic. It was a public meeting with an invited speaker. Outside, over the church door, in keeping with past tradition, Dashnaks raised the Tricolour and the Union Jack. Under the existing tense conditions, however, the pro–Soviet Armenia group considered the Dashnak action provocation. Fearing trouble, the council hurriedly met in the church to ward off direct confrontation between the two groups. But before it could take action and before the speaker, Kopernik Tandurjian, a Dashnak field-worker from the United States, could utter a word, some of the pro-Tourian group rushed out to tear down the Tricolour. A fistfight ensued, and the police were summoned.

The parish council intervened to bring a measure of calm to the community. Its efforts were clearly self-regulatory, since five of the seven members of the council had been involved in the scuffle. In the end, people apologized, shook hands, and carried on the business of running a community. The incident was set aside but not forgotten. With trouble in Chicago on 1 July 1933 and the ill-fated Diocesan Convention in New York in September, St Catharines, like other Armenian communities, erupted into total anarchy.

The two adversaries were deadlocked. Community business came to a halt; the church, the school, and the parish council were barely functioning. Everyone was "wound up." Each rival group was conspiring with "outside" advisors. Directives from Babayan in Toronto and from the Tourian and the Hotel Martinique group in New York were counteracted by equally fervent appeals from Dashnak headquarters in Boston. Amid accusations and counteraccusations, the beleaguered church council tried to keep a lid on emotions until the two councils in New York could resolve their differences. In the meantime, the church was in dire financial trouble, because parishioners refused to pay their dues to the church or the school.

Tension mounted as the date for the annual election of the council approached. To ward off total breakdown, the councillors called a special meeting on 27 October, two days before election day. The council invited eighteen leading members of the community, with partisans from both factions, to come together to discuss how to keep the peace and maintain harmonious coexistence "considering that hostilities in the United States were leading to a destruction of the community." About twenty-five men gathered together on 27 October 1933 in the church basement to decide the fate of the church, the school, and the community. After impassioned debate, twenty-three signed the following resolution:

Mindful of the conflicts which are outside our community and our authority; the creation of two Diocesan councils, unprecedented in the life of the Armenian community; the conflicts in the Armenian-American church; the split in two camps in the United States and the damaging impact on the Armenian communities in the United States and Canada; the character of our community which is different from others; and fearing the negative effect on the peace and well-being of our community, we resolve to exercise wisdom and vigilance and to work towards a goal of peaceful co-existence. In this spirit we agree

1 to allow the present councillors to continue for a period of three more months [i.e., to 27 January 1934] and to keep relations open with the Central Board of Trustees in Toronto;
2 to break off relations with both executives in New York (i.e., the St Illuminator group and the Hotel Martinique group), as long as they, by their actions, are splitting the communities and causing conflict;
3 to refuse to obey any directives from either executive which might destroy the peace of our community; and
4 to do so until such time as the Catholicos has spoken his last word regarding which council is the legitimate one.
5 During mass, remembrances in prayers for Tourian to continue as before until an official directive comes from Echmiadzin.[23]

All members of the council, including three Dashnaks and four pro-Soviet Armenia leftists, voted in favour of the resolution. Of the twenty-three who signed, nine were pro-Dashnak and fourteen were not. The agreement of the Dashnaks seems somewhat puzzling, but perhaps, like most people, they expected an imminent compromise between the two warring diocesan councils. Two Dashnaks abstained. They adamantly refused to recognize Echmiadzin in administrative matters, rejected Tourian as their spiritual leader, and opposed the mention of his name in the "special intermission" prayers during mass. Still trying to hold the community together, the council organized a children's Christmas party. In retrospect, their efforts seem so futile, for what could safeguard the community from the tragedy of 24 December? What peace could be found between the hammer and the anvil?

Tourian's assassination brought everything to a head. People were afraid to go near the church. The house of God was bolted. When a wreath and flowers were placed on the church door after the murder, they were just as quickly removed. Name calling, threats, beatings, fights, resignations, walk-outs, police intervention: the St Catharines community, the epitome of harmony and cooperation, was pitched in battle. The pro-Tourian faction argued that the archbishop, in trying to strengthen the Mother See, had been "the greatest Armenian of his time" and that the remnant Armenian state would be gobbled up by hostile Turkey were it not for the Russians. The Dashnaks, in their turn, upheld the Tricolour as the national flag of Armenia and charged anyone debasing it with casting insults against the Armenian nation. They denounced Tourian and his supporters as puppets of the Communist regime, which was destroying Armenian culture and identity and the Armenian liberation movement. So deep, so intense were feelings that one man jumped up in front of the Tricolour shouting that he would defend it with his life. Another vowed to tear it to shreds. One man swore he would gladly have slain the archbishop himself. Another praised him as a saint. The combatants did what in normal times would have been unthinkable and shameful. They brought their conflict out into the open and voiced their grievances publicly.

STRUGGLE FOR THE CHURCH

By mid-January, St Catharines had, in effect, three parish councils: the remnant of the old council; a new, "pro-Soviet council," secretly elected; and a new Dashnak council, also secretly elected. [24] The left/conservative council was in possession of the church and the books and held its first meeting in the church on 15 January, at which time it made the ominous announcement that the doors to the church and school were open to all, on condition of obedience to the New York diocese and to Echmiadzin.

A 4 February memorial meeting in the church hall following requiem mass for the murdered primate brought together Babayan and supporters from the surrounding Armenian communities. In his speech Babayan referred to the "beloved Archbishop" as "a martyr for the Church" who would be "honoured for centuries to come." He concluded his remarks by welcoming members of the Dashnak Party, provided that "they left their political controversies outside."[25] The pro–Soviet Armenia group, with Babayan's backing, had possession of the church and made it clear that the price of church membership for Dashnak parishioners was renunciation of their political ideals. While the two rivals were locked in battle, evidence reveals that beneath the anger and recrimination, people expected the leaders in New York to resolve their differences, since it was inconceivable that such a state of affairs would continue for long.

The Dashnak group, meanwhile, demanded a full public meeting with the election of a new parish council, voted on by the entire community. When the opposition refused, the Dashnaks entered into legal proceedings. Led by Mihran Akazarian, plaintiff, the Dashnaks brought suit on 9 February 1934 against the Canadian Bank of Commerce and Ohannes Torosian, Krikor Der Vartanian, Paravon Kalajian, Mardig Der Vartanian, Hagop Torosian, Garabed Artinian, and

Ro(u)pen Sankimian. The grounds for action: the defendants had not called a public meeting for the election of the parish council, had carried out their election contrary to the constitution and by-laws of the Armenian Apostolic Church of America, and had barred the plaintiff and other regularly and duly qualified members of St Gregory's from admission to the church and from all proceedings conducted in it. He claimed that they had "wrongfully, illegally and without colour of right, usurped the offices of trustees to the detriment of, and against the wishes of, the majority of the members of the [Armenian Apostolic] church or parish." The defendants, he declared, were not entitled to exercise the function of the parish council. He requested an injunction restraining the defendants from exercising the function of a board of trustees, insisted that the 1932 parish council (composed of both Dashnaks and pro-Tourian men) was the legal council and should exercise the duties of their office until a new board had been duly elected, and requested an order restraining the defendants from access to the church's bank accounts.

The solicitor for the plaintiff, Stuart H. Fleming, of the St Catharines firm Trapnell and Fleming, endeavoured to show that the election of the parish council had been secret and illegal: the defendants had failed to issue a public notice and had excluded one group in the community from voting. He also showed that many of those who voted for the pro–Soviet Armenia council, including some of the council members themselves, had not paid their dues in full at the time of the election, thus nullifying the results of the vote.

The defendants, represented by Fred H. Barlow of the Toronto firm of Jones and Barlow, brought in by Babayan, denied all allegations and stated that the defendant had resigned as chairman of the board in September 1933 and that his resignation had been accepted and another person had been elected as a member of the board. Subsequently, the defendant "ceased to be a member of the ... Church ... was not at the time of the bringing of this action a member of the Church ... [therefore] had no status to prosecute this action." The defendants also stated that of the remaining seven on the former parish council, five had resigned and two had been duly dismissed as councillors by the Central Executive Committee in New York. The defendants maintained that they had been elected as councillors and that their election had been confirmed by the diocese. No mention was made of the secret election.

In the proceedings, which started in St Catharines and were later transferred to Toronto at the defendants' request, the local Dashnak parishioners, who had had nothing to do with the slaying, were implicated by association with those accused of the archbishop's assassination. The insinuation comparing the murder of Tourian with the murder of Thomas Beckett, archbishop of Canterbury, was driven home by effective reference to the friendship between Tourian and the current archbishop of Canterbury. The defence also made an issue of loyalty: while the defendants upheld only the Union Jack, the Dashnaks revered, as well, a flag of a foreign state, albeit a nonexistent one. The innuendo of possible Dashnak disloyalty to Canada ran through the proceedings.

The conservative/left held the church, the keys, and the books; with the support of Babayan and the diocese, they were operating from a position of relative strength. On 26 November 1934 the action, heard in the Supreme Court of Ontario, was dismissed with costs ($283). The church remained in the hands of the pro–Soviet Armenia faction. Thus, four years, almost to the day, after the church had been consecrated the community was irreconcilably divided and the Dashnaks were outside the church they had worked so hard to build.

As in New York and throughout North America, the adversaries in Canada did not break because of theological or doctrinal differences but, rather, as the consequence of political conflict. As in New York and throughout North America, the split caused a deep and festering wound in Armenian community life.

14

Aftermath of the Church Crisis: 1933–1950

Such was the break in the Armenian Church that people who were sensible in every other walk of life acted irrationally and by their words and deeds caused deep bitterness and lasting hostility. One group ridiculed the colour red and the other mocked the Tricolour. Neighbours, friends, and family members cut off relations and refused to speak to each another. An already small community was split into two separate camps, each with its own buildings, its own auxiliary organizations, and its own functions. Each developed its own customs and priorities, each treasured its own experiences and its own history, and each struggled to maintain itself during a time fraught with economic hardship. In some ways the conflict strengthened the community, as each faction tried to outdo the other, but in many other ways the split weakened the community, divided its forces, and dissipated its energy, especially in St Catharines where the greatest polarization had occurred.

Before the crisis, people could have remained nonpartisan, but afterwards neither camp would tolerate neutrality; both demanded total fidelity. For some parishioners the choice was straightforward, but for others the decision was wrought with great soul-searching. Senekerim Chichakian, for example, an intelligent and reasonable man, a staunch Dashnak, and a devout church member found himself in a dilemma of conscience. On 10 January 1934 the Dashnak branch received his letter of resignation. Members not only accepted it but voted unanimously to bar him from future membership in their ranks. The pro-Tourian faction was no less severe. In the parish council meeting of 15

January 1934, he was voted in as a teacher with the proviso that if he ever "so much as whispered a word of support for the Dashnaks, he would be driven out of the church."

Because of his attachment to the church, Chichakian opted for St Gregory's, but in his own way he stuck to his political beliefs. Although he became a church leader, a teacher, a deacon, and a union shop steward at General Motors, he never joined the political organizations supported by other church members. To the contrary, he joined the pro-Dashnak Compatriotic Society of Keghi. His exclusion from the Dashnak party, however, caused him great heartache, but a painful and brave choice based on conscience had been made and the consequences had to be borne.

The intensity and acrimony of the struggle varied in each place, depending on the size of the community. In Montreal, for instance, the settlement was too small to split; the people clung to their Armenian-ness, rather than to their political and religious differences. The comparative strength of each faction also played a role in the drama. In Hamilton the Dashnaks were far more numerous and better organized than the Progressives, who kept a low profile. Neighbourliness and family relations therefore continued; but the left, comprising fewer than ten families, did not participate in official events, both by choice and in response to an inhospitable atmosphere. In Brantford, where the cohorts were more evenly matched, the battle left abiding wounds. But the greatest belligerence occurred in St Catharines, where the two forces had vied for possession of the church structure.

THE CHURCH

Because numbers had fallen drastically and local resources had been cut back, St Gregory's experienced many years of financial hardship. From a membership of 110 in 1932, the church roster fell to about 50 in 1937. To keep the church functioning, the 30 to 35 active member families were called upon to make immense sacrifices. One woman recalled that after the split, "we each did what we could. Donated 5¢, 20¢, whatever we could afford. There was unemployment. We organized fund-raising activities like plays and teas. Each of us made and brought something. All of us cooked, cleaned ... Whenever we had a dinner [at the church], we had to bring our own dishes and our own pots and pans from home. My roaster spent more time at the church than in my own house."[1]

To maintain the church, parishioners were more than ever dependent on outside financial contributions. Babayan paid the interest on the mortgage and, later, the little that was left of the outstanding principal, leaving the building clear by 1940. His patronage confirmed his confidence in the church and in the parishioners' allegiance to it, at the same time that it strengthened his authority.[2]

Babayan's leadership as chairman of the Canadian Armenian Union and of the Central Parish Council is difficult to separate from his role as benefactor of the church, and these two roles are hard to distinguish from his personal authority. This bond between St Catharines and Babayan continued from the mid-1920s until his death in 1951. When asked whether Babayan "controlled" the parish council, an interviewee chuckled, "Nobody controls the St Catharines board of trustees," while another quickly added, "we wouldn't cross him." Yet others believed, perhaps rather harshly, that the wealthy outsider manipulated important decisions in St Catharines and that his intervention, or "intrusion," irreparably damaged the community as a whole.

Church Governance

Local autonomy, which had characterized the first years of the church, became more entrenched after 1933. Continued confusion and strife in Soviet Armenia and uncertainty in New York allowed the congregation in St Catharines to run its affairs without a great deal of outside interference, notwithstanding the communication between St Gregory's and Babayan and the New York diocese. As for the Canadian Central Parish Council in Toronto, it no longer had a region to represent and dissolved into anonymity. Over the years, the absence of hierarchical authority gave the parishioners – high-spirited as they were – a vested interest in the church they had built and contributed to the development of a mind-set both introverted and localized.

The absence of strong and consistent leadership from above was reflected at the local level: for almost two decades the congregation was unable to support a full- or part-time priest and was obliged to rely, once again, on the services of a number of itinerant priests, usually for special occasions like Christmas and Easter. Not only did the absence of a permanent priest make for irregularity of *patarak* (mass), but after Father Zkon took up a position in Providence, Rhode Island, in 1934 some sacraments and rites of passage were curtailed, perhaps for years. Church records, for instance, show no baptisms from 17 December 1933 to 28 January 1936 and from 11 September 1938 to 4 December 1946.[3]

Being without a priest for a long period of time encouraged lay participation in the church within both liturgical and nonliturgical spheres. From the moment the split occurred, it was evident that the remaining congregation would be compelled to work exceedingly hard for the church's continued survival. Service to the church went hand in hand with authority in the church. Every member had a say in how the church was run, and every member exercised this right in articulate terms. The arrival later on of a permanent priest with his own ideas of progress, change, and religiosity would inevitably lead to tensions. Always deferential to ecclesiastical authority, parishioners were, nevertheless, clear about what was right for their community and what was unacceptable.

A good part of the parish's strength evolved from the determination and ability to keep the church doors open, even under adverse financial conditions. To an extent, credit must go to the dedication of three deacons, Krikor Der Krikorian, Senekerim Chichakian, and Migirdich Krikorian. Led by the deacons, the people clung to their ancient forms of worship, treasured rituals, and Old World festivals. Considering any digressions from the old ways a dilution of the Armenian heritage, the deacons followed the old traditions "to the letter." Still, there were signs of gradual adaptation to Canada. Sacrificing a lamb, seen by some as cruelty to animals, and the fires of *Diaruntarach*, considered a hazard, were two rituals that gradually fell into disuse.[4] The parishioners also introduced innovations and relaxed some Old World constraints. For instance, people no longer rigorously refrained from eating grapes *before* they had been blessed at the Feast of St Mary in August. Notwithstanding some outward changes, the essence of their religious forms was retained, as they continued to look to the church for their religious sustenance and as the mainstay of their Armenian heritage.

The deacons' spiritual authority coincided with other forms of responsibility. If one regards the parish council as a reflection of local power, then an examination of the membership of the council would indicate who emerged from the 1933 conflict as leaders.[5] From 1934 to 1965, one or more of the deacons was also on the parish council every year except in 1959 and 1960. The leadership of the deacons thus went beyond spirituality into the realm of governing the church and the church community.

Women and the Church

Membership on the parish council was not the only manifestation of communal authority. If it was, one would date the acquisition of power by women from 1957, when the first woman was elected to the council as assistant secretary.[6] In fact, the split in the 1930s coincided with the maturing of young women refugees who had immigrated during the 1920s. By the 1930s and 1940s they were reaching middle age, venturing out into Canadian society, and learning about Canadian behavioural patterns. Their participation in the Canadian labour force and in their small businesses gave them a measure of autonomy and authority. Women's contributions as members of the choir, teachers in Sunday school, and workers in the ladies auxiliary was crucial to the church's continued existence, a fact recognized on the church's fiftieth anniversary: "In its fifty years of service the Armenian Church of St Gregory can well be proud of its women – every banquet, every tea, every social, and wherever their service was needed they responded both physically and with their intellect ... It can truly be said – without them the church would not have survived these fifty years."[7]

There were more than teas and banquets to women's involvement in the church; there was also more than the private and considerable influence on husbands and brothers who represented them on the parish council, for women were attached to religion. For them, as for all the faithful, religion was connected not just to their Armenian identity but to life itself. Their spirituality breathed life into the church, and their religiosity added a texture of faith and gentleness to the community, particularly among the young.

The Church as a Left-Wing Force

As the church and the conservative/left became more and more intimately identified, the leftists were accused of using the church as a smokescreen for Communist activities, since some members supported the Progressive movement in the United States and subscribed to *Lraper* (Reporter), its mouthpiece. It would be appropriate, then, to examine what the so-called Bolsheviks did or thought that made them "Reds." As a *group*, they did not agitate for the abolition of private property or for the abolition of religion; they did not propound anarchism or the destruction of capitalism; they did not espouse free love; and they did not brandish the hammer and sickle. Certainly they followed the adventures of Tim Buck, leader of the Canadian Communist Party, but they neither formed an Armenian wing of the CCP nor joined the party. With great interest they watched the creation of the Co-operative Commonwealth Federation (CCF) (Farmer, Labour, Socialist) and voted for the new party, as well as the older Liberal Party of Canada. They kept abreast of events in the Spanish Civil War, but like other Armenian Canadians, except for a young refugee from Toronto, they did not volunteer for active duty.[8] With great enthusiasm they championed social programs in Canada, hailed Roosevelt and the New Deal in the United States, and denounced exploitation everywhere. As a group they embraced two "leftist" causes with unmitigated fervour: workers' rights through participation in the trade union movement in Canada and Soviet Armenia as their homeland and as the workers' paradise.

For many of these immigrants, both women and men, involvement in left-wing or revolutionary causes had preceded the church controversy. Many had sympathized with the Social Democratic movement even before the creation of Soviet Armenia in November 1921. Some had taken a stand against oppression before coming to Canada, having experienced the cruel treatment of minorities in the Ottoman Empire. For them "revolution" embraced the rights of ethnic and religious minorities as much as the class struggle; it combined economics and politics with culture. Others took up the leftist cause in North America. They read the left-wing Armenian press from the United States, experienced the discrimination against foreigners, suffered the hardship of working people, and considered the capitalist system corrupt, industrialists exploitative and immoral, and the Great Depression a call to action. Their militancy, however, had limits, for while they struggled to bring about change, they did so *within* the capitalist system and *within* the framework of Canadian democracy and liberalism.

Despite the fact that the large majority had been born in Western Armenia in Turkey, the leftists viewed Soviet Armenia as their homeland. While North America was crippled by the Depression, unemployment, and breadlines, Stalin had forged ahead with his first five-year plan. The vitality and promise of the Soviet system, the conviction that the Soviet Union was the bulwark against fascism, and the rise of the Armenian worker confirmed their left-wing beliefs and entrenched their support of the Russian giant. These uprooted Armenians, cut off from their place of origin and deprived of an independent state, turned their attention to an inaccessible and distant political entity and pinned their hopes on a land whose recent history and language differed from their own. They set their sights on a regime that promised peace, progress, justice, and national viability. Such was their espousal of Soviet Armenia and the Soviet Union that they turned a blind eye to the purges, the artificial famines, the Moscow trials (1936–38), and the pathetic condition of the Armenian Church in their homeland.[9]

Parishioners faced other contradictions. The relationship between the Mother See in Echmiadzin and the New York diocese and the conflicts between the church and the Communist Armenian American leadership were sometimes so intense that parishioners of St Gregory's, like their confreres in other places in North America, were obliged to try to reconcile often opposing ideologies within the framework of their political and religious convictions.[10]

The Church as a Conservative Force.

In his relationship with the church, Babayan, no doubt, had his own motives. As a conservative man of the wealthy merchant class, as a supporter of the diocese and the conservative Armenian General Benevolent Union, and as an opponent of left-wing, revolutionary politics, Babayan sought to extend his personal influence and that of the organizations and the mentality he represented. He was a conduit and proponent of right-wing, conservative forces to the Armenian proletariat in Canada. The break in St Catharines, Brantford, Hamilton, Toronto, and Galt had been among working-class people with socialist leanings who had more in common with each other in socioeconomic and ideological terms than they had with the well-to-do like Babayan. Regardless of their differences, however, an understanding bound together one segment of this proletariat with the rich entrepreneur, ensconced in his magnificent mansion, Armavir, overlooking the city of Toronto.

The ideologies of self-educated, working-class/agrarian settlers of St Catharines, while perhaps not as sophisticated as those of their leaders in far-off places, might have taken them along the path of radicalism, but they did not. Seldom did they draw a clear-cut line between economic, ethnic, political and/or religious cleavages. Krikor Der Krikorian, for instance, had been born in Constantinople, but his parents were from Arek village in Keghi. All his life he identified himself as an Arektsi, rather than a Bolsetsi. Der Krikorian had been a member of the Hnchak party, and then was a member of the Armenian National Red Cross, the HOG, the Armenian-American Progressive League, and the conservative Armenian General Benevolent Union; he was both choirmaster and deacon in the church. *Lraper* and *Yeritasard Hayastan*, both left-wing newspapers, carried his obituary and the primate of the diocese eulogized him for his many years of dedicated service to the church.

Yet, there is more to their conservatism than the church or Babayan, for their worldview did not spring forth in 1930, when St Gregory's was built. What marks the St Catharines community and indeed the early Armenian settlers in southern Ontario is a strict code of moral and social behaviour. That is not to say that every individual was above reproach. But as a group they were morally and socially conventional. It would perhaps be more accurate to say, then, that the church, its conservatism, and its conservative supporters reinforced an inherent conservatism of this group of largely agrarian, mountain immigrants, who nevertheless preferred left-wing organizations to right-wing ones. Try as he might, Babayan could not sustain a branch of the Armenian General Benevolent Union (AGBU) in St Catharines. As indication of its political flexibility and confidence, the church subscribed to *Yeritasard Hayastan, Banvor*, and *Lraper*, in addition to the conservative *Baikar* (Struggle). Eventually, the leftist faction, or at least a major part of it, was absorbed and neutralized by the church and became known no longer as Red or Bolshevik, but as "the church." Social Democrats who had condemned Levon Babayan for undermining the leftist cause by leading the people down "the garden path" of religion may have had a point after all.

For St Gregory's the Toronto connection remained significant, and the association that had started in the mid-1920s continued after the break and continues even to the present. Baptisms, ordinations, and marriages of Torontonians took place in the St Catharines church, especially before Toronto built its own church in 1953. For *patarak*, banquets, and picnics, people travelled from Toronto to St Catharines. In their turn St Gregory's parishioners supported Torontonians in their efforts to build and maintain their church and contributed to Toronto AGBU campaigns to raise funds for Soviet Armenia during the 1930s and 1940s. The St Catharines – Toronto connection perhaps reached its most symbolically important point in the 1990s, when Rev. Shenork Souin, whose grandfather from Toronto had attended the church and whose father had been baptised in the church, became the first Canadian-born priest at St Gregory's.

BRANTFORD PROGRESSIVES

Although there were adherents to *Banvor, Lraper,* and the Progressive movement in St Catharines, the Progressives had their biggest following and a measure of official organization in Brantford, where they constituted a viable opposition to the Dashnaks. The Armenian Progressive Cultural Hall on Market street, bought around 1940, was the scene of their political, social, cultural, educational, and athletic activities.

A study of the Brantford leftists reveals the same complexities that were evident in St Catharines, even though the Brantford group operated within a secular structure, the hall. An interviewee whose father was a Hnchakian revealed that she knew the *sharakans*, or hymns, of the Armenian church service before she had ever set foot in an Armenian church, because her father had taught her. Every Sunday he used to "go through the whole Armenian church service. He knew the liturgy.

Had been a deacon in the old country."¹¹ When a revolutionary, atheist, anticlerical Armenian school teacher and staunch supporter of the *Banvor* and Progressive organizations was dying, he insisted on a secular burial. His wishes and his wife's courageous decision to carry them out after his death sent the Armenians into a state of shock. Another Progressive recalled the incident many years later: "I never heard of such a thing! How could you have a funeral without a priest? It was the first time in our community!"¹²

Through their various activities, through their contacts with the St Catharines church, and through reading *Banvor* and its successor *Lraper*, as well as the English-language *Armenian Tribune* (later the *Armenian Herald*), leftists in Brantford kept abreast of developments in the homeland, stayed informed about the workers' struggle around the world, and refined their understanding of the works of Marx, Trotsky, Lenin, and Stalin. Like hundreds of thousands of other Armenians, the left was troubled by the fear of ethnic cultural extinction. For them a fundamental contradiction played off their nationalism – the condition and status of Armenia – against international socialism and the propaganda about the brotherhood of workers. For them, participation in leftist organizations was underscored by their perfervid allegiance to Armenia and to their Armenian identity. As an interviewee remarked, "if they had believed in the international brotherhood of workers, then they would have wanted to include Turkish workers. I never heard of such a thing."¹³

In a way an incident in Brantford illustrates the priorities of the left. A group of Armenian children from leftist families joined the Brantford Mandolin Ensemble, which had been organized by Ukrainian leftists and included Ukrainian children and a Ukrainian director. When the Ukrainians decided to change the name of the ensemble to the Ukrainian Mandolin Ensemble, the Armenians protested. Since they made up about 40 percent of the group, the Armenians believed they had a legitimate complaint. When the leadership disregarded their wishes and changed the name regardless, the Armenian children quit en masse.

THE CONSERVATIVES

Because of their loyalty to the Armenian Church, the conservatives supported Soviet Armenia and assailed the Dashnaks. Conservatives in various cities maintained a bond with each other. For those engaged in the carpet trade, it was strengthened by their business affairs with Babayan. Predominant in Toronto among the élite and the developing entrepreneurial class, conservatives formed a small but influential cohort. With the leadership of men like Hmayeg Papazian, Oksen Teghtsoonian, and Set Adourian they established the foundations of the Armenian General Benevolent Union in Canada (see chapter 19).

THE DASHNAKS

Dashnaks stayed away from the St Catharines church not only because they felt unwelcome but also because they considered the conditions of church membership unacceptable. Excluded from St Gregory's and at the same time rejecting Communist infiltration and aggression in Armenian church affairs, Dashnaks in St Catharines found themselves outside the formal structure of the Armenian Church. Unlike the universalistic Roman Catholic Church, the Armenian Church is autocephalic. Thus, if Armenians were outside their own church, they could not simply attend another church of the same denomination. A sense of Dashnak isolation is revealed in the St Catharines court case in which a Dashnak witness described how they were compelled to have their children baptised in their homes, rather than in the church they had built. On the other hand, a respondent recalled that some Dashnaks "would not step foot in the church ... They said the church was Communist." "A former board member," said another, "was so angry at the way things had been done, that he ... would not enter the church for a funeral but would wait outside, then go to the graveside."[14]

After the events in 1933, St Catharines Dashnaks elected a new religious council. The president, Nishan Krekorian, had come to Canada from Keghi before 1914, and after working in Brantford for a few years had found a job in the foundries at General Motors. Although he had lost family during the Genocide, he had not experienced the death marches and deprivations personally. But Krekorian had his own cross to bear. As a twenty-five-year-old he had sailed for North America with several friends on the Titanic. When the accident occurred, he managed to scramble into a half-empty lifeboat and together with a sailor, rowed furiously to save the small craft from the strong undertow of the sinking vessel. All night long they rowed in the icy waters of the North Atlantic, until the next day, when the passengers, mostly women and children, were picked up by the Carpathia. Krekorian lost all his friends, and he himself suffered from pneumonia and wavered between life and death in hospital. For the rest of his life, he was haunted by the terrifying experience. Now in St Catharines, Krekorian, the same man who had so adroitly led the first parish council of St Gregory's in 1930, tried to stabilize the new religious council. With a membership ranging between forty and fifty, the council raised money for the prelacy's quota, arranged for delegates to the annual conventions, operated an Armenian school, and organized periodic church services in their newly purchased clubhouse with Rev. Loat of St Thomas Anglican church officiating. From time to time, they held *patarak* (Mass) in the hall or at an Anglican church with a visiting Armenian priest, usually Father Mateos Manigian or Father Movses Der Stepanian.[15]

Without a church structure, however, and with the uncertainties in New York and Echmiadzin, these religious initiatives were overshadowed by the secular/political organization. The Dashnak agenda emphasized the separation of politics and church. For Dashnaks outside the church in St Catharines and those in other communities, religious belief and faith became a matter of personal choice, almost separate from political ideology.

Nor did religion become part of their cultural ethos. They spoke of Armenian religious history, but for them and their families it was no longer a living group religion, familiar and ancient, in their own language. They were without regular sermons, the strength and redemption of Holy Communion, the salvation of the *hogehangist* (the rest of souls). They did not interact with each other in a church society or interpret their family and their world in the matrix of the Armenian Church, even though they may have been devoutly religious.

During the fractious days of 1934, while the St Catharines court case dragged on and the more virulent case of Tourian's murderers in New York fired the fuels of animosity throughout North America, Dashnaks regrouped themselves in a secular, rather than a religious, fashion. The St Catharines chapter consolidated its forces, strengthened its ties with other branches in Canada, and continued to meet with them at regional conferences organized by the ARF Canadian Regional Committee, founded in 1937. This type of collaboration created a united front, consolidated the Dashnak movement, and made it the strongest Armenian political force in Canada.

As before Tourian, the Dashnaks formed a subculture of the Armenian community. In St Catharines the Dashnaks bought the building on the corner of Carlton and Ontario Streets, across from General Motors and a couple of blocks away from the church. In the fall of 1934 they inaugurated their hall, naming it after the Armenian hero, Andranik. Thenceforth, they focused their efforts, time, energy, and money on their new "home," which for the local chapter saw the culmination of a twenty-year dream.

In Hamilton the Dashnaks first rented clubhouse quarters at the corner of Gibson and Princess Streets. In 1950 the ARF Vramian chapter built its community centre on Princess Street, in the middle of the Armenian neighbourhood. The Brantford Keri chapter bought the Pentecostal church building on Queen Street in 1946, and in Galt the Aram chapter bought a building on Imperial Lane in 1949, rented out a portion, and converted the rest into a clubhouse.[16] In the meantime, members of the Soghomon Tehlirian chapter in Toronto held meetings in each others' homes and for special occasions rented space in the YMCA on College Street. Under the leadership of men like Vahan Eloian, Levon Raician, Kapriel Kaprielian, Mihran Kasoian, Arsen Assadourian, and Jack Mooradian in Hamilton; Yeghishé Mooradian and George Der Stepanian in Brantford; Mihran Akazarian, Hagop Melkonian, Eddie Saroughanian, and Simon Merakian in St Catharines; Arsen Pargamian, Krikor Parseghian, and Moushegh Der Simonian in Galt; and Yeghishé Kostigian and Kirk Magarian in Toronto members endeavoured to keep the community intact and cohesive, to entrench the political organization and its platform in the hearts and minds of the people, and to transmit the language, culture, and history to the next generation, primarily through the auspices of the women's wing, the Armenian Relief Society (ARS), the youth group, the Armenian Youth Federation (AYF), and the Armenian supplementary schools.

THE INTIMATE WORLD OF FAITH

For some survivors the Genocide had stretched the limits of faith; feeling abandoned and disinherited, they forsook church and religion altogether. Others viewed religion only as a symbol of their ethnic heritage and an agent for the preservation of their Armenian identity. For still others, the Tourian conflict left them with a distaste for Armenian religious and political affiliations. But for many Armenians, religiosity was carried beyond their identity into the very depths of their worldview and of their place in it. When asked why they supported the church, a group of St Catharines interviewees replied, almost in unison, "It's God's house."[17] In God's house believers were in touch with the spiritual and the divine. Here, their faith found concrete expression in emblems and symbols, in the aroma of incense, in the emotional appeal of the music, in ceremonies, repeated year after year, and in prayers, honed by centuries of use. In the church, they participated in the rites of passage – the age-linked cycles of human development. They held up their new-born children to be baptized, rejoiced as their offspring embarked on the road of marriage, took bread and wine, and knew that one day they would be buried from the altar, which, week after week, heard their prayers. In the church they joined together in rituals and in feasts, beloved traditions of the past. Each event brought the parishioners together – working, dancing, singing, praying, grieving, and even arguing with one another. In these many ways, the church endowed vigour to spirituality; and piety infused energy and excitement into the church.

But what of the faithful outside the church in St Catharines and in other places? Where or how were they to find spiritual solace? The majority of Armenians, adhering to the Armenian Apostolic Church, attended the Church of England, or Anglican Church. For most foreign-born among them, regular attendance was unlikely, because they could not understand English well and because in some places they were only "barely tolerated" by the Anglo-Saxon congregation. Most waited for Armenian clergymen to visit the communities. But these visits could be irregular, even rare; Montreal, for instance, had no visitation from 1941 to 1948.[18] Those who could afford it might pay a priest from the United States to come for special rites, such as a wedding or a funeral. Invariably services were held in an Anglican church or in the Armenian club.

Some Armenian Protestants joined Canadian Protestant churches, for they were too few and too dispersed to form their own congregation. Some had brought Protestantism with them from the old land, either because their families had been Protestants or because they themselves had been converted in Protestant orphanages. Some, including a number of the Georgetown children, had adopted Protestantism in Canada, not a surprising development considering the role of Protestants in the Armenian Relief Association of Canada and their work in facilitating the movement and resettlement of Armenian refugee youngsters to Canada during the 1920s. After the war, Protestant missionaries from the old country kept in close contact with their former charges. The Chambers family of Woodstock and Ganonoque, Ontario, continued their friendship among Armenians in Canada, as did missionaries Rev. Thomas Barker and Mrs Ada Barker in Hamilton and Rev. Ira Pierce in Toronto. Protestant Armenians also held prayer meetings in Armenian in their homes, under the leadership of men like Michael Posigian in Brantford and Walter Merkle, a non-Armenian, in Hamilton. Except for such prayer meetings, Protestant Armenians experienced their religious life outside the framework of their Armenian heritage and as a rule did not become entangled in Armenian political debate.

Many Armenian faithful expressed the particularities of language and belief in private communion with God. Women and men, including those from the left, said their prayers and *sharakans* (hymns and chants) at home. An interviewee recalled how, as a child, she would stand by her father's side as he prayed every day before leaving for work. "My mother was a very pious woman too," she continued.

Every day, without fail, she would read the Bible, say her prayers, and sing hymns. Every night she would stand by our bedside and say a prayer. Naturally, she would have preferred to attend an Armenian church, for the sake of the language and the traditions, but in our city there was no Armenian church. She disregarded the divisions of religious denomination. In Turkey there were constraints on religious practice, but in Canada my mother could go to any church she wanted, and she did. She went to the Anglican Church on special occasions, like Easter, to the United Church for the Mother's meetings, and without fail, every Good Friday, she attended the Roman Catholic church for the Stations of the Cross. She went to Protestant prayer meetings [in Armenian] at the home of Mrs Esther Charkoian and welcomed the Protestant preachers, Mr Merkle and Mr Posigian, to our home, as well as Father Movses and Father Zkon."[19]

The faithful also engaged in collective religious expression. Aside from the more formal *patarak* arranged by the religious councils, the people performed their own, informal religious rites. On the feast of Ascension, forty days after Easter, women often gathered together to commemorate the festival of *vijak*, a ritual associated with the rites of spring and the divining powers of water.[20] In Hamilton, Loussaper Kaprielian, who owned a book of handwritten poems, considered it her *religious* duty to prepare the *vijak*. The evening before Ascension, seven glasses of water and seven different flowers from seven different homes (i.e., springs or wells) were collected in a large pitcher. Mrs Kaprielian poured the contents of the pitcher into a large, pretty bowl, covered it with an embroidered cloth, and said a prayer over the entire contents. The following day, the women gathered together and each placed a personal token into the bowl, such as a ring, an earring, or a button. After saying the Lord's Prayer, a selected woman – the bride – wearing an embroidered veil, drew the items, one by one, out of the bowl of water. As she did so, another woman read a quattrain, "a charm song," from the book. The owner of the token considered the poem her "fortune." She did not take the predictions seriously, or at least not too seriously.

The poems dealt with love, hatred, jealousy, success, failure, friendship, marriage, children, and death. Zabelle Boyajian provides two examples of *vijak* poems:

Like a star whose brightness grows
On the earth my beauty shows;

> Thou shalt long for yet, and seek
> My dark eyes and arching brows.

Another stanza, still on the theme of love:

> Eden's smile my vineyard wore,
> Flowers bloomed a goodly store;
> Handsome youth and ugly maid —
> This was never seen before.[21]

The poems reflect the concerns of Armenian women in past and contemporary times. For example, the loneliness of the woman whose husband is sojourning in distant lands is poignantly expressed:

> I picked roses on Vartavar Sunday.
> I can't bear the fire of my love.
> Mountains tumble; waters dry up.
> My love is sojourning and I must join him.[22]

The ritual clearly has pagan roots, but chanting traditional prayers in fellowship constituted a religious experience for the participants. After the *vijak*, the hostess prepared a meal, and the women enjoyed the remainder of the afternoon in each other's company.[23]

Settlers also practised the ritual of the sacrificial lamb, *madagh*, and though it might be viewed as typically pagan, it was invariably accompanied by symbols of their ancient Christian faith. In Brantford a family vowed to sacrifice a lamb if their son returned safely from the war. By the time he was discharged, the family had moved to Windsor, but they had not forgotten their vow. They returned to Brantford, purchased a lamb, and, because there was no Armenian church in Brantford, slew it in the basement of the Hnchak Club on Market Street. With the lamb's blood a layman drew the sign of the cross on the boy's forehead. The ceremony was followed by a dinner with lamb shish kebab and pilaf to which the entire Brantford Armenian community was invited. In these many ways, piety and faith found private and collective expression.

IMPACT OF THE SPLIT ON THE YOUNG

Children of the Parishioners

Adults who had devoted great energy to trying to pass on their endangered ethnocultural heritage to their children and had sacrificed time and money for Armenian-language schools allowed their hostilities to override their good judgment and cloud their vision. The youngsters, in whom Genocide survivors had found such comfort and such catharsis and in whom they had placed great hope for the perpetuation of their heritage, grew up separated by different traditions.

In St Catharines, where Armenians prospered along with General Motors, the church managed to keep the young people together and to expose them to its rites and rituals. They attended and later taught in Sunday school, sang in the choir, and as they matured, were elected to the parish council. In the late 1940s they organized a branch of the Armenian Church Youth Organization of America (ACYOA). Initially youngsters had more *official* contact with like-minded sympathizers in other cities than with youngsters "from the other side," who lived a few blocks away. By the 1950s, however, most young people chose their friends without serious consideration of their parents' political affiliation. An interviewee who was a member of the ACYOA, the daughter of one of the founders of St Gregory, a charter member of Local 199, and a diehard Progressive was the best friend of a member of the Armenian Youth Federation whose family were staunch Dashnaks. Regardless of their parents' political affinities, the first-generation young people also married each other.

Children of the Progressives

Children of the left were weaned on the workers' struggle. Their Armenian school, community, and home cultures, moreover, brought them into contact with Soviet Armenia, its history, its arts, and its progress, but these associations often had confusing connotations in a North American environment: "Our kids went to school and they were taught that the Soviet Union is our enemy. Then they would come home and we would try to tell them that Soviet Armenia is our motherland. They didn't know what to think"[24]

As the parents aged and lost some of their momentum, the children, becoming more aware of acceptable practice and behaviour in Canadian society, resented epithets like "Bolshevik" and "Red," bristled about name-calling at school, and feared for their jobs and careers. The stigma of communism was threatening: "they begged us not to get involved in politics," noted an old-timer.[25] Progressive organizations struggled to survive, but the Cold War took its toll. Natural attrition through old age and death and out-migration reduced the numbers of the committed even further. "As more of us died off," opined an elderly Progressive, "our left-wing organizations died with us." In Brantford, where they did not identify as "the church," young Progressives continued for a number of years as members of the Armenian Youth Association (AYA), under the political umbrella but in a social and athletic context. As a political force the Progressive movement was doomed. By 1960 the end was near.[26]

Children of the Dashnaks

Dashnak children also had to contend with derision, particularly during the war, when they, like their parents, were vilified as fascists. Dashnak children, and indeed children other than the St Catharines church group, grew up outside the milieu of the Armenian Church, which did not became a vital force in their lives, either as a religious institution or as an agent of ethnicity. Some had been taught the *sharakans* and prayers by their parents or Armenian school teachers, but even such limited exposure was rare, bearing in mind that many parents had been children at the time of the Genocide and that they themselves were not knowledgeable about the meanings and subtleties of church liturgy. Their children's relationship with the church was further complicated by language. Canadian-born young people had difficulty learning to read and write the vulgar Armenian; for them the liturgical language – the *grabar*, or classical Armenian – beautiful as it was, was almost incomprehensible.

Nor did the Armenian Church become part of their national heritage. Other than the church group in St Catharines and their coreligionists from Toronto, most Armenian young people remained unfamiliar with the rituals, feasts, and customs connected with the church. They learned about ancient saints and martyrs, about Armenian heroes of the resistance movement, revolutionary songs, poems, and plays, and the tragedy of the Genocide. If they learned about Armenian Church music, architecture, art, saints, and saint days, it was only as "history." For them ethnicity and religion were separate. For them ethnicity was secularized, a strange development for a people who had been identified by and, indeed, persecuted for their religion. Young Dashnaks were exposed to Soviet Armenia and to Echmiadzin, but only within the context of history, not in a living and vibrant way. Their hope of a free country, furthermore, while it remained an anchor, was not bound to the political state that existed in the Soviet Union. Rather, their vision of a free homeland was linked to the birthplace of their parents in western Armenia. They spoke more of Van, Sivas, Kharput, Erzerum, Keghi, and Mush than they did of Yerevan.

CANADIAN CHURCHES

Armenian young people, other than those associated with St Gregory's, were obliged to find their religious affiliation outside the Armenian

Church. While their parents may have found their most profound religious expression in their Armenian prayers, religious customs, and traditions, the children found their religious affiliations outside the framework of their Armenianness, if they found them at all. Their religious experience was usually in an Anglican church, for it was in this institution that they were baptized and confirmed, took communion, and were married and buried. They sang in the Anglican choir, attended Anglican Sunday school, played sports in the church hall, and belonged to the Anglican Young Peoples' Association. For many the Anglican Church provided an element of acceptance and perhaps even a measure of social mobility. As an interviewee recounted: "In school, whenever I had to fill out 'nationality' in a questionnaire, I would write 'Armenian,' knowing that foreigners were regarded as inferior. When the form asked for religious denomination, I was pretty proud to write 'Anglican.' It made me feel more accepted. Part of the Canadian world."[27]

The connection between the Armenian community and the Anglican Church had historical antecedents. Not only did the Anglican and Armenian Churches have theological common ground, but the churches had a long history of mutual association. British government documents, for example, record the intervention of the Archbishop of Canterbury and other Anglican clergymen on behalf of Armenian clergy who were persecuted by the Turks, most notably the renowned musician Father Komitas, who was imprisoned and tortured during the Genocide.

In Canada the Armenian and Anglican churches had a good working relationship, as indicated by the willingness of Anglican churches to allow Armenians to use their facilities for Armenian services, by the number of Armenians attending Anglican churches, and by the generosity of the Anglican Synod in making financial contributions to Armenian efforts to establish their own religious structures in the Dominion.

The ties between the Anglican Church and the Armenians reached an unprecedented level in Hamilton during the 1950s. The link between Armenian immigrants and St Philip's Anglican Church, located in the Armenian neighborhood, had always been excellent; and the priest, Father Brewer, was loved and respected by the Armenian settlers, particularly by the Armenian young people. Father Brewer's death in 1949 coincided with demographic changes, as many Anglo-Saxon church members were moving away from the north end and the church was beginning to decline. But it was revitalized with the pastorship of three young clergymen, Rev. James Hooton, Rev. Robert Rolls, and Rev. Roy Wakelin. During the tenure of Father Wakelin, the church undertook a major fund-raising campaign for badly needed repairs and renovations. The Armenians, concerned about the state of the building, pitched in to help. They spearheaded the drive and raised enough funds to keep the church open. For Armenians, participation and donations were a way of showing their appreciation to the church that had met their religious needs for half a century.[28]

Such was the bond with the Anglican Church that those who later moved to a city where an Armenian church existed, if they retained any affinity with a church at all, found it difficult to attend the Armenian church, mainly because of the language and the general unfamiliarity with protocol, ritual, and liturgy, though they may have been enthralled with the beautiful service and the exquisite music. At best they combined Armenian and Anglican traditions, particularly in the rites of passage, by having an Armenian and Anglican priest say portions of both services for weddings, baptisms, and funerals. In an effort to deal with the language issue, the Armenian Church provided the Order of Services in both Armenian and English, and for those who were serious about church attendance, these translated texts proved exceedingly useful.

WORLD WAR II

Nowhere is the interplay between local and international, between Old World and New World more evident than during World War II. Since Soviet Armenia embodied the last vestige of an Armenian homeland, Armenians in North America, regardless of their political affiliations, were inextricably drawn into the relations between Canada and the United States and the USSR.

During World War II their detente affected the dynamics of the Armenian community in North America. With the signing of the Ribbentrop-Molotov Treaty of nonaggression between Germany and the Soviet Union, with its secret protocol partitioning Eastern Europe between them, and with Hitler's invasion of Poland, its subsequent partition, and the Soviet invasion of the Baltic states, Armenian leftists, bristling from accusations of Bolshevism, now had to ward off innuendoes of disloyalty to the West. After Hitler attacked the Soviet Union in June 1941, the roles were reversed; leftists turned on the Dashnaks and charged them with fascism. Indeed, many Dashnaks hoped the war would weaken the Soviet Union enough to allow for the creation of an independent Armenian Republic, just as thousands of displaced persons after World War II hoped for the demise of the Soviet state. As a party, however, the Dashnaks, though anti-Communist, did not endorse fascism.[29]

The war and the improved relations between the West and the Soviet Union eased the conditions of the church in Armenia and in America. The Soviets allowed the revival of the official publication of Echmiadzin, the convening of the National Ecclesiastical Assembly, the reopening of the theological seminary at Echmiadzin, the recovery of a number of churches, and most importantly, the election, in 1945, of a catholicos to fill the vacancy left after the death of Khoren I in 1938, himself a victim of the purges.[30]

These developments were not entirely surprising, given the relationship between the diaspora and the homeland. Through moral and financial support of Echmiadzin and of Soviet Armenia, diasporan Armenians, both of the right and of the left, influenced Communist authorities to temporize their treatment of Echmiadzin, especially since another faction of the diaspora, the Dashnaks, was ever vigilant and critical of Soviet activities and used its powerful press to keep the Armenian North American public well informed.

From a political perspective, even before the outbreak of World War II, the Dashnaks and Ramgavars, who were regularly condemned by the communist press as "the two segments of the Armenian bourgeoisie," met in Cairo (in 1938) to establish common goals and to draw out different spheres of interest. They agreed that Armenia as it was constituted at that time was the nucleus of Armenian existence, regardless of the regime in power. The Dashnaks promised not to participate in any acts leading to the dismemberment of the USSR – upon which the safety of Armenia depended – to give due respect to Echmiadzin, and to refrain from fighting over church administration outside Armenia. "By this agreement," concludes Christopher Walker, "a dangerous collision was averted.[31]

During the war the various political and religious factions raised funds for the Allied cause, sometimes on their own, sometimes in a united effort.[32] They also organized campaigns for Soviet Armenia and for other Armenian victims of the war in the Middle East and Europe. The primate's Armenian War Relief Committee spearheaded two campaigns in North America (1941 and 1943). Of particular interest was the drive to raise money for the David of Sasun Tank Column for the Red Army (1943). Over one hundred thousand dollars was contributed from the United States and Canada. "Altogether," comments Walker, "it was a remarkable display of patriotic fervor, and of loyalty to the reality of Armenia both as part of the USSR, and as one of the components of the anti-Nazi alliance."[33]

In July 1944, according to a United States State Department Intelligence Report, the Dashnaks reversed their anti-Soviet policy in an attempt "to help the USSR in its efforts to rebuild Armenia." While the party did not reconcile itself to Soviet hegemony in Armenia, it held that "it would be unpatriotic to block the efforts that are being made for the progress and territorial aggrandizement of Armenia."[34] This reference clearly touched on Soviet attempts to pressure Turkey, which had remained neutral until the final days of World War II, to return Armenian lands ceded by Lenin and Stalin after World War I.[35] Regardless of political affiliation or place of settlement, Armenians lobbied, petitioned, and raised money to support the campaign for the return of Kars and Ardahan to Soviet Armenia.[36]

At the same time, Soviet Armenia called on Armenians in the diaspora to return to rebuild the homeland after the destruction of war. In this endeavour, various groups collaborated, initially, at least, to support emigration to the homeland (1946–48). By 1948 the repatriation movement had dissolved, but not before eighty to one hundred thousand Armenians from all parts of the world had rerooted themselves in the homeland.[37] The Canadian response to the repatriation movement was remarkable for its lack of participation. According to oral interviews, only four Armenian Canadian families signed up and "packed to join the repatriates." But plans were aborted from abroad, and not a single Armenian family from Canada joined the movement to Soviet Armenia.

In Canada, all groups showed their allegiance to the Allied war effort. They bought Canadian war bonds, worked in war munitions factories, contributed to war charities, and prepared food and clothing packages for men at the front. In St Catharines, the community raised $650 in twenty-four hours as part of its "quota" towards the Canadian government's war effort.[38] Armenians in Canada also enlisted in the Canadian armed forces. An informal survey reveals that the proportion of enlisted men, including the young men of the Georgetown farm/home/school, was outstanding, considering the small number of Armenians in Canada at the time.[39] Part of this contribution can be ascribed to demographics. The large number of marriages during the 1920s meant newly created families. The average number of children was, as a guesstimate, about three per family. Many of these children, along with the boys at Georgetown, reached maturity during World War II, at an age to enlist in the Canadian armed forces.

International events continued to influence local communities. Officially the two "sides" went their separate ways. When St Gregory's held Christmas Mass and the traditional Keghi feast of *bagharch* afterwards, the Dashnaks normally did not attend. When the Dashnaks celebrated the founding of the Armenian Republic (1918–20) on 28 May, the parishioners stayed away. In time however, a softening occurred. To a noticeable extent the war brought the political opponents together. In 1941, Armenian workers of both factions, recognizing their common interests, joined the crucial strike at General Motors in St Catharines. Similarly, at the end of the war, St Gregory's organized a dinner for all Armenian Canadian veterans, regardless of political affiliation.

Officially the two factions remained separate – their differences irreconcilable – but individual Dashnaks held weddings, baptisms, and funerals at St Gregory's, while parishioners attended Dashnak social and cultural functions. In their own way, even fanatics communicated with people "on the other side." Individuals cared for and respected each other as relatives, friends, or village compatriots. They worked side by side in the same place, drank coffee and played cards in the same coffeehouses, and belonged to the same village associations, which cut across political lines. But when they left the workplace or the coffeehouse, they each went their separate ways. Women, too, were friends and neighbours. They chatted with each other over the fence, exchanged recipes, looked after each other's children. Then they, too, went their separate ways. Children attended the same public school and played with each other on the street, and then they attended their own Armenian school. The physical proximity, the bonds of blood and god-parenting, and the memory of friendship and mutual help brought people more and more into touch with each other. In their own fashion, individuals made compromises. An interviewee elaborated: "When the split occurred, one of [my uncles] sided with the church. But the families continued their relationships ... We just don't talk politics. I don't discuss with him what goes on here at the Armenian Community Centre and he doesn't talk to us about what goes on at the church."[40] Even more telling was the compromise in death. "She was," recalled an interviewee, "a devout member of the Armenian Relief Society, a committed Dashnak, and a tough anti-Communist. In her later years, she moved away from St Catharines to live with one of her children. But when she died, she was buried from St Gregory's and the wake was held in the Dashnak club."[41]

Later, much later, when Tourian was all but forgotten, St Gregory's church hall, named in memory of the ill-fated archbishop, would be renamed Babayan Hall and the Tricolour would be hung in a place of honour in the church where it had been reviled decades before.

15

Family and Community in Hamilton: From Being Armenian to Being Armenian-Canadian

Welcome and blessings on your coming
In this world of wounded hearts your words are balm
and cheer. How often in days to come
will we sigh for this day that we are in one place.
    Hovannes Ersengatsi Blouze (1230–93)
    Translated by Diana Der Hovanessian and Marzbed Margossian

The acrimonious struggle for the church and the split in the ranks weakened the Armenian community of St Catharines. By the mid-1940s, Hamilton emerged as the principal Armenian settlement in Canada, mainly because it had not been shaken by the church crisis to the same extent, because work opportunities were plentiful, and because the local Dashnaks provided stable leadership. Hamilton, with a small Armenian population of no more than five hundred people in 1945, provides the forum for discussion of family and community at midcentury.

FAMILY LIFE

In the period after World War I, refugee women formed an important component of family and community life. Within each family they were expected to be obedient, respectful, and formal. So formal was the relationship that women usually referred to their husbands as "man" or "husband," seldom by their first names. And when they spoke of their husbands to others, they usually gave his name preceded by "Mister," as in Mr Sarkis. Initially, the women were almost totally dependent on their husbands, who were older and more familiar with

Canadian society. Men generally dealt with the "outside world"; at home they were authoritarian and patriarchal. During the 1920s they earned enough at the factory or in their little shops to allow their wives to remain at home with the children. As we have seen, the situation changed dramatically during the Depression and the war years.

As women grew older and more confident, they stepped out into Canadian society. They enrolled in English-language classes and learned the language by studying dictionaries, crotchet and knitting instructions, and Armenian-English guidebooks. The *Armenian-English Conversation* was particularly popular, for it provided commonly used vocabulary and conversation phrases in Armenian, in English and in English with Armenian letters.[1] Women also enhanced their learning by participating in non-Armenian groups such as social programs at mothers' meetings sponsored by the United Church of Canada, the women's and altar guilds of different churches, and the outreach programs of the Imperial Order of the Daughters of the Empire. They learned about North American mores from movies and from their children, who brought Canadian values and attitudes into the home. By the 1940s and 1950s women assumed greater responsibility for family affairs. The power dynamics in families changed as the aging men deferred to their younger wives, now in their prime.

The disgrace attached to marriage break-up, the loss of family during the Genocide, and the demands to establish new roots usually ruled out marital separation, desertion, and divorce. The incidence of alcoholism, crime, and juvenile delinquency was low among Armenians. In a community with a strong sense of propriety and shame, the penalty for deviating from acceptable behaviour was derision and, worse still, ostracism. These behavioural patterns were not missed by local non-Armenian neighbours:

They said we Armenians were savages. I couldn't understand how these Canadians thought. Why were we savages? Because we were foreigners? Because we were dark? In the old country my family had been very cultured people. I can remember how beautifully my mother dressed, our gardens and orchards, our servants. We had been savagely treated, but we were not savages. We were poor refugees but we weren't savages ... But life is strange. Those women who called us savages later came to respect us. One's husband was an alcoholic, another's was a gambler, another ran off with a younger woman. They'd talk to me and say, "How come your family's so quiet? We never hear arguments or fights from your house. How come your husband works hard at the factory and then goes to market on Saturdays and then works in your garden? How come he never goes to the saloon?"[2]

The moral conservatism of the adults, who were firm about what was right and wrong, was passed on to the children. In such small communities, where scandal and gossip could destroy a reputation and, indeed, a whole family, adults impressed on their children the issue of honour and *amot*, or shame. The traditional mores, values, and behavioural patterns of family life were clear: respect for elders, deferential treatment of men, sober clothing for women, no public display of affection or emotion, no loud laughter or speech, and no pampering of children. Adults did not approve of girls crossing their legs; as a rule, parents did not kiss children on the lips, usually only on the forehead; and children lowered their eyes in conversation with adults, lest they be considered defiant.

The "eye" entered into various aspects of Armenian folklore and language: "light in your eye" as a congratulatory comment, "blind his eye" as a curse, "the good eye" as a good omen, and the "evil eye" as an evil omen.³ Most mothers gave their children a turquoise bead with a white dot to ward off evil or jealousy. Some mothers combined a turquoise bead with a cross and a clove of garlic sewn into a little cloth bag pinned to children's undershirts. Adults spoke of *jakatagir*, literally, the writing on the forehead, i.e., one's destiny. Bread was sacrosanct, both because of its symbolism in Christianity and because of its scarcity during the Genocide. Settlers considered it a sin to throw bread in the garbage. Women either used stale bread in their cooking or threw it out for birds. Children were also taught not to throw bread away; if a piece fell on the ground, they were instructed to say a prayer over it before giving it to the birds.

As a group, Armenian families treated their children with great devotion. When asked what distinguished Armenians from others, an interviewee, half-Armenian himself, quickly replied, "Armenians always place their children first."⁴ "Our parents protected and shielded us from the outside world," remembered another respondent. "They expected us to achieve in school; and they expected us to be obedient. At all times they demanded proper behaviour because whatever we did reflected on our father's name. My father used few words to keep us in line. A look was usually enough or a reminder of his shaving strap in the bathroom. Whenever we thought he was unreasonably severe, our mother would assume the role of mediator. She never undermined his authority; she just managed to win compromises from both sides. He was particularly strict about boys, especially non-Armenian boys. If he heard that I had been seen talking to a non-Armenian boy, he'd make it pretty clear he was not pleased. They wanted us to marry Armenians."⁵

Traditionally, Armenians indulged their sons more than their daughters. As future breadwinners, boys were given opportunities for education and training that were too often withheld from girls, who were sheltered and scrupulously disciplined. Daughters were required to help with household chores and until the 1950s were expected to marry before the age of twenty or twenty-one; otherwise they would be regarded as *tunmnah*, stay-at-homes, or old maids. A few young women broke away from the mould, took postsecondary education, and entered teaching, nursing, or medicine.

In the industrial cities almost all Armenians were on a similar socioeconomic level; no one was rich; everyone had been levelled by the Genocide. "In the old days, we Armenians were clannish. We leaned on each other; that was our world. We didn't have outside interests. Everyone was a *khnami* [relative]."[6] Men at work, children at school, and the community as a whole were introverted. They might have worked and lived next to Hungarians, Italians, Jews, Poles, and Ukrainians, but their real associations were with other Armenians.

Because of loss and dispersal and because of restrictive immigration regulations, extended families were rare. Children grew up without many "blood" relatives. Almost none had grandfathers, and few had grandmothers, two important sources of power, influence, and unqualified love.[7] Yet everyone in the neighbourhood was "aunt" or "uncle," and every Armenian house was a second home. This "replacement capacity," which was similar in many respects to the post-Genocide phenomenon of replacing lost family members, played a fundamental role in binding the people together and giving families a sense of kinship and mutuality. "All my mother's friends," recalled an interviewee. "were like aunts to me, but there were two who were special. Zarouhi Yakmalian was an angel of mercy. My mother was often sick and Zarouhi used to look after her. She would shop and cook for us. She was kind and generous with others as well. A selfless lady. The other was Arevaluis Mooradian. Her name means sunlight and she was just that. A ray of sunlight in our lives. She treated me like her real niece. In fact, my mother used to call her 'sister' and I always thought they were sisters. Actually she wasn't related at all. Whenever she went away on a trip she would bring something back just for me; when I visited her she would ask me what I wanted her to cook and she'd prepare anything I asked for, usually chips. She was very dear to me. As I look back now, we were lucky. We had all those wonderful people who really cared for us."[8] "I had no *real* aunt or uncle," recalled another informant. "But as a child I didn't know that, because every Armenian woman was my *aunt* and every Armenian man was my *uncle.* Only as an adult did I realize I had no *blood* relatives. Except for my father's brother in Detroit, all my mother's and father's immediate family had been murdered in 1915. My parents' friends became our relatives."9

Names held a special place in the Armenian world and reflected the many changes Armenians had experienced. Following the Genocide, families named their children after their lost relatives. The names were typically Armenian, like Anoush, Ara, Vartouhi, Haig, and Yeghishé. Parents also named their children after heroes of the resistance, with names such as Antranig, Murad, Paramaz, and Sebough.[10] Invariably, children had two names: one for the home and the Armenian community and another for school. Garabed might be known in public school as Charles, Ashot as Arnold, Vartouhi as Rose, Zabel as Isabel, and Takouhi as Queenie. Sometimes families chose double-duty names which were similar in both languages, names like Mary, Alice, Alexander, Victoria, or Gloria. Even so, everyone actually possessed two names, for not only were the double-duty names pronounced differently in English and Armenian, but each name carried with it a distinguishable behavioural pattern: the culture of the home and the culture of the school and Canadian society. The two cultures, and hence the two behavioural patterns, did not always reconcile with each other.

Surnames, too, reflected the peoples' experiences. In the early period of settlement, newcomers changed their Turkish names. In Turkish, for instance, Demirjioghlou means son of the ironmonger. One Armenian might choose to change his name to Demirjian, while another might Armenianize the name altogether and take the name Yergatian. Similarly, the name K(h)ahfedjioghlou, which in Turkish means son of the coffee maker, might be revised by one Armenian to Kafejian, while another might take the name Surjian, *surj* being the Armenian word for coffee and the suffix "ian" meaning "son of."

In the early years of settlement, Armenian surnames were not standardized. Vartkes, son of Vartan of the clan Simonian might, in North America, take the name Vartkes Simonian, while his brother Zaven might prefer to use his father's first name followed by "ian" and become known as Zaven Vartanian. A family name like Hovannesian, i.e., son of John, might have multiple variations or diminutives: Hovannesian, Ohannesian, Ohanian, Onesian, Hovigian, Ovigian, Ovoian, or Onnigian. Or settlers might try to anglicize their name to O'Hanian, Ohaneson, O'Hanson, or Johnson. Anglicization became more common with second- and third-generation Armenians, especially for business and professional reasons. Thus, they changed Khachigian to Hachigan or Hatch, Atamian to Adams, Tosoian to Task, Haktsian to

Hawk, Mooradian to Moore, Bedrosian to Peters, Hagopian to James, and Mateosian to Matthews.

Armenian names could be Canadianized in other, typical ways. An interviewee relates how in elementary school she was Shoushanig Tatoulian, but her Sunday school teacher, unable or unwilling to pronounce Shoushanig, called her Jean. "I was Shoushanig at school and Jean at Sunday school. When I started high school, I decided to use "Jean" to simplify matters."[11]

NEIGHBOURHOOD AND COMMUNITY

As already indicated, most Armenian pioneers in Brantford, Hamilton, St Catharines, and Galt clustered near their workplaces, fashioning the beginnings of an Armenian quarter. When an influx of immigration occurred after World War I, newcomers, naturally enough, were drawn to the established settlement areas. Here they found family, friends, jobs, and hometown compatriots. Here they found a measure of mutual assistance and security. Armenians from different home places learned to live and work together and redefine their Armenianness in a new world that did not distinguish between a Kharputsi and a Bolsetsi (from Constantinople), a Balvetsi (from Balu) and an Erzerumtsi.

Each Armenian neighbourhood was different in its composition, its architecture, its flair and rhythm, even in its smells and sounds. Each was unlike the mainstream world in which it existed, unlike other ethnic enclaves in the same city, and unlike the Armenian quarters in the old land, in such cities as Van or Kharput, Constantinople, or Smyrna. Each Armenian neighbourhood was a segregated geographic space with a history of its own, affected by its environment every bit as much as by its own internal dynamics. Yet each Armenian neighbourhood had many similar physical characteristics: boardinghouses, coffeehouses, *gradarans* (reading rooms), church halls or community centres, houses with verandas, and streets and alleyways. More importantly, each neighbourhood was dominated by the same overarching sense of Armenianness.

The high degree of activity in the neighborhoods created an environment that helped transfer to the next generation the Armenian ethnocultural heritage, so precious to a people who had looked extinction in the eye and won. Armenian was spoken in the coffeehouses, at meetings, in church, on the streets. Children sang Armenian songs and listened to Armenian stories. Armenian voices rang everywhere in the neighbourhood. In their own fashion Armenian neighbourhoods played a critical role in moulding and strengthening Armenian identity in the diaspora.

In the early years of the twentieth century, Armenians in Hamilton had congregated along Sherman, Princess, Case, Clinton, and Ruth Streets in the vicinity of the Hamilton Foundries, where many of the men worked. At the same time (1904), the Deering (later renamed the International Harvester and then the Case Company) started operations in a new plant at Sherman and Burlington Streets. Immigrants hastened to take advantage of new opportunities, and eventually International Harvester became the major employer of Armenian men, some of whom rented houses from the company on Princess Street. In response to the workplace, Armenian settlement moved westward, stretching roughly from Sherman and along Gibson Street to Fullerton Avenue and from the Canadian National railway tracks to Barton Street. Within this span of about ten square blocks, Armenians had access to their own reading rooms and coffeehouses, to St Philip's Anglican Church, St Anne's Roman Catholic Church, the Mission to All Peoples, Gibson Avenue elementary public school, the Playhouse movie theatre, the police station, the public library, the post office, a large variety of shops and services on Barton Street, and the Beltline streetcar to uptown Hamilton, with its department stores, fresh fruit and vegetable market, and City Hall.

When Armenians began working at the Harvester in the early years of the century, the area near the plant was undeveloped. Following the construction of houses across from the factory around 1913–14, Armenians set up boardinghouses on Alpha and Beta Streets, but they found the living environment too close to the factory noise, soot, and smells. They preferred the old settlement area about a mile south, with its relative cleanliness and proximity to amenities.[12] It was situated in the heart of an industrial, mid-density inner city space with two-story houses, both detached and semidetached, occupied by Anglo-Saxons and a growing number of European newcomers. From this beginning, Princess and Gibson remained the hub of Armenian life in Hamilton for the next eighty years.

In the 1940s Hamilton Armenians operated only a few shops in their quarter, most of which catered largely to an Armenian clientele: two grocery stores, a barber shop, a shoe repair shop, several boardinghouses, and two coffeehouses that also sold confectionary items. A number of local peddlers ran their little businesses from the neighbourhood, selling cut wood or popcorn and peanuts outside the area. The need for a variety of services in the community itself was minimal, since every Armenian man was a carpenter and a cobbler of sorts and an electrician and plumber, and every Armenian woman was adept at cooking, sewing, knitting, and crotcheting.

More importantly, Princess, Gibson, and Earl Streets were close to

Sherman Avenue and Barton Street, two hubs of commercial activity. Here the stores were owned and operated by well-entrenched Anglo-Saxons who provided adequate services. Gradually, Armenians, along with other "foreigners," opened barber shops, shoe repair and shoe shine shops, confectionaries, and a restaurant on Barton Street, and in time they expanded their horizons to uptown Hamilton, where the rug businesses operated, catering to both Armenian and non-Armenian clientele. Interestingly, "Armenian town" was close to the Westinghouse, Brown Boggs, Otis Fensom Elevator, and Frost Steel and Wire factories. But in contrast to St Catharines, Hamilton Armenians did not operate stores in the vicinity servicing the workers.

In the neighbourhoods, the Armenian intelligentsia met the artisan class, and together they voiced their Armenianness with the illiterate villager who had never had the opportunity for an education in the old land. Along Gibson and Princess Streets, newcomers from agrarian and urban backgrounds consolidated the bonds of language, religion, and nation and shared the tragedy of violence. In their neighbourhoods Armenians could ease the sense of separation experienced by most newcomers. They could help each other cope with prejudice in the new society and deal with feelings of alienation in a land with a different language, different values, different political structures, different work patterns, and different school systems for their children. For Armenians, furthermore, exile was heightened by tragic events in the homeland. They suffered loss of family and of home and were banished forever from their native land. Reconstituting Armenian life in the neighbourhood or the Armenian *tagh* gave them a new place to call home, a place where they found not only solace and comfort but a point of orientation for innovation, creativity, and challenge.

For newcomers, these little Armenian "homelands" were points of insertion in the new land. They acted as a buffer to the unknown world and enabled immigrants to adjust to their new environment at their own pace, under their own control. From the known, comfortable world of the Armenian quarter, immigrants could sally forth into the larger society, attend school, take jobs, open shops, and always return to home base, where they understood their surroundings and where they knew they could count on safety and security. Because the neighbourhoods embraced the ethnic community, they acted as a bridge between Armenians and the New World and as a link with mainstream society.

The Armenian neighbourhoods were like telephone poles of a vast circuit of people, ideas, and money moving around from place to place in a far-flung Armenian diaspora. Newspapers and letters were not the only means of communication between coreligionists in different parts of North America and throughout the world. Face-to-face visits also helped Armenians keep in contact with each other. The churches, clubs, and coffeehouses acted as magnets in the core of the neighbourhood. They were the heartbeat of the community, and every visitor knew that through them he might find lodgings, a job, perhaps even a spouse. In the neighbourhood, people knew each other well, knew who was trustworthy, who was competent, who was frugal, who had a wandering eye, who had a questionable past. They knew where each family had migrated from in Armenia: from Bitlis, Kharput, Erzerum, or Keghi. They knew who would welcome a morning visit for a cup of coffee, who would lend money to a needy neighbour, who would act as interpreter for the doctor or teacher, and who could keep a secret.

For women the neighbourhood was a consequential space. Men often worked outside the neighbourhood and interacted between two worlds. They had a place both in the neighbourhood and in mainstream society, where they were known as barbers or factory workers, as tailors or shoemakers. By contrast, the women were simply "foreigners" in the mainstream world. They had no status in the host society, even if, at times, they worked in the factories or on farms. But in the Armenian neighbourhood, each woman did have a place; she was a somebody. Each woman could wield considerable power: perhaps through her husband, sons, or brothers or through her own abilities as a leader in women's organizations. Perhaps she could manipulate people and events through her words. Some of the most feared individuals in the Armenian neighborhoods were women gossipmongers. With their verbal twists they could plant the seed of suspicion, make or break an engagement, destroy a reputation. By the same token, some of the most respected individuals in the neighbourhood were the wise women who could, by the skilful use of words, give encouragement and generate self-esteem. Alongside them were the healing women, those sages who knew enough folk medicine to cure minor ailments.

The women had a special camaraderie with each other. They held regular bees to sew the *vermaks*, duvets filled with wool fleece. In the fall they would help each other with canning, and the smells of tomatoes, peppers, and peaches permeated every house. From grapes they would make grape juice and *bastegh* (grape-paste candy). An interviewee recalled the women's social get-togethers: "They used to meet every week at different houses to play cards [scambil]. And along with the cards was gossip and stories, jokes, and complaints ... Cards were popular, but nothing like bingo. They used to play with six or seven cards each, a penny a card. For hours. Very serious they were too .... They had good times with each other."[13] The women would then put away the cards or the bingo, and while the hostess prepared a tea table, the others would take out their hand work.

As already pointed out, crocheting, needlework, embroidery, and knitting were frequently used as commodities for sale. Armenian women survivors of the Genocide – both adults and young girls in orphanages – often referred to the needle arts as the "bread of the black day," for during hard times the needle often provided them with a means of subsistence. As well, during the Depression in Canada, women's fancy handwork helped the family budget. But beyond the economic contribution of the fabric arts lay a far more profound aspect of this work – women's self-expression. Each woman had her own specialty and her unique style. "Needlework," writes Anush Sharambeyan, "can be seen as giving women a kind of 'voice': stitches, instead of words, becoming a language through which she might speak." Aside from the actual execution of the work – and these Armenian women did exquisite work – the women also created their own designs. They shared their designs with each other and taught each other how to execute the intricate patterns. The women used these needle laces and embroideries to beautify their homes and their wardrobes – as collars, on blouses, towels, sheets, and pillow cases, handkerchiefs, doilies, runners, macassars, table cloths, and bedspreads. For these immigrant Armenian women, the needle arts were also an expression of their identity, as important to them as the church linens, vestments, and curtains they also fashioned.[14]

In these Armenian enclaves, sidewalks and alleyways, verandas and backyards were arteries of contact. Street life flourished. Women met on the street and exchanged bits of gossip. Teenage boys "hung around their corner." Children played with each other on porches, in backyards, on the streets. In the Armenian neighbourhood, children felt free and safe. They could roam the streets and alleyways, ride their tricycles and bicycles up and down, or roller-skate or scooter around the block. They knew that if anything untoward happened – if a stranger accosted them or if they had an accident and hurt themselves, someone would be watching, would see, and would come out to help.

Children could walk to the home of their relatives or friends and walk home again after a visit. If their mother was not home after school, they knew she would be visiting an "auntie." An interviewee recalled how he was often drawn to Mrs ——— house. As a hungry youngster on the way home from school, he would smell wonderful aromas and, unable to resist, would knock on her door and ask if his mother was there. "No," would come the knowing reply, "but come in, I have something tasty for you." The same interviewee remembered how, oftentimes, he would see her carrying heavy parcels on her way home from shopping and would run to her and relieve her of her bundles.[15]

Children also knew that if they misbehaved, someone would tell their mother before they reached home. They understood that in Armenian town, they had to behave, because many eyes were watching. This fact kept children in line, made the streets extensions of Armenian homes and gardens, and kept the degree of delinquency remarkably low. Just as the children regarded adults as part of their family, they also looked to each other as part of an "in-group." The relationship among Armenian young people was warmer than among other friends at school, for they regarded each other as "cousins." Group activities dominated their lives. Not only did they attend Armenian school together, but they also went together to the circus, the carnival, and the Saturday movies. They laughed, played, argued, and fought with each other.

The world of childhood in Hamilton is captured in oral interviews revealing games, imaginative story-telling, and adventure. In winter Armenian youngsters would go sledding down Nutcracker Hill, along Birch Avenue north of Princess Street, or ice skating on the rink at Woodlands Park, and they also played ice hockey. In summer, they would go in a group to the Harvester playground, which the company provided and maintained. During summer evenings children played for hours in front of "the club," while their mothers sat on verandas and their fathers played cards in the *srjaran* (coffeehouse) on the corner of Gibson and Princess. Men and women whose own childhoods had been swept away in the rushing waters of the Euphrates River or had been lost in the unrelenting sands of the Syrian desert watched as their children played – watched, disciplined, protected, and loved.

The children's play area comprised the four corners where the two streets intersected. The lamp pole on one corner was inevitably "home." Children played such games as stinker, lay-low, blind-man's bluff, British bulldog, red rover, London Bridge, kick the stick, kick the can, hide and seek, freeze tag, cowboys and Indians and war. Across from the coffeehouse/club/hall was a field the children called the sand pile; it belonged to a transport company. Here they played hide and seek among the huge transport trucks, and here young teenagers played baseball. The girls played skipping and jumping-rope games, hopscotch, or ball games, like 1–2–3 kiss Maggie, 1–2–3 elora, or ordinary movsies, laughsies, talksies. Sometimes the children played quiet games like I spy, true or false, jacks, hangman, checkers, Chinese checkers, snakes and ladders, agates (marbles) or pick-up-sticks. Every summer, the children's population in Hamilton swelled as youngsters visited their relatives from out of town: "we'd sit on verandas and for hours we'd tell stories, ghost stories, adventure stories, you name it."[16]

On Saturday afternoons, Armenian children gathered together for the Playhouse movie theatre on Sherman Avenue, next to All Peoples Church and across from the police station. During the 1940s, for six cents they saw a double feature, a cartoon, a serial, and the news, *The Eyes of the World*. "We used to call the Playhouse the 'garlic opera,'" chortled a respondent, "because all us foreigners used to go there and the place'd reek of garlic." At the Playhouse the children knew that when the door to one of the exits opened, someone would be sneaking in, and before the usher could take hold of the youngster, he would be hidden in and by the crowd. The children learned to shout out their discontent with the movie or with the film operator if there was a halt to the reel. They became quite skilful at finding a spot under their wooden seats to stick on their chewing gum and at blowing up and exploding their popcorn bags – the noisier the better. Not only did the place smell of garlic, it was usually bedlam, with children chattering and laughing and running up and down the aisles and with apple cores and scrunched-up bags flying through the air. If the situation got out of hand, the owner, a long-suffering Pole, would stop the movie, march on stage, and threaten to send everyone home without finishing the film. He would be met with an immediate response of boos, howls, and whistles. And when it was all over, the children, exhilarated and happy, "would act out what we'd seen." "I guess we took the name Playhouse quite literally," laughed an interviewee. "You can imagine how much fun we had playacting 'The Mummy' and the Jesse James movies."[17]

Somewhat like the practice of composing their own ghost and adventure stories, the movies fired their imaginations, especially the playacting the children inevitably carried out afterwards, and for many, Saturday afternoon at the cinema left a lasting appreciation for the movie medium. Like group trips to the playground and the carnival, the Saturday afternoon jaunts consolidated relationships among the children as much as the factory and the coffeehouses did for their fathers and the needle arts and bingo did for their mothers. For children the Saturday matinee was as much a part of their growing-up rhythm as the public and Armenian schools. Along with the public school, the movies gave them a perspective on North American society, culture, and mores that was much broader than they could possibly have found in their Armenian urban village.

The church hall and community centres or clubs that were situated in the heart of the neighbourhood brought together men, women, and children of all ages for a variety of different activities: social, political, cultural, educational, and intellectual. In these halls, Armenians created their own culture of exile.[18] These small "clubs" served at different times of the day or week as a coffeehouse/reading room for the men; a schoolhouse for the children; a place for meetings, wedding receptions, funeral wakes, banquets, and dances; and a concert hall for the community. Men were obliged to vacate the premises whenever the organizations needed the space for other activities, but when they were using the space as an all-male coffeehouse/reading room, women and children were discouraged from entering. If they wanted to buy a chocolate bar, a coke, or an ice cream cone, they entered with due reticence, lest they disturb the all-male ambiance of the smoke-filled room, and they hurried out, lest they overheard a "bad word."

In their halls, Armenians celebrated Christmas with Kaghand Papa (Santa Claus), and true to Keghetsi custom they prepared – and still do – the traditional dish, the *bagharch* (baked whole wheat flour with yogurt, garlic, and hot clarified butter). Here they rejoiced at Easter with their ancient custom of breaking terra-cotta-coloured eggs, the magnificent colour derived from boiling eggs in onion skins. In their hall, the community held the *khnjuik* (feast), a typically Armenian function combining speeches, musical entertainment, skits, and poetry recitations (which they adored), followed by feasting and dancing. After the formal program, they pushed the chairs alongside the walls for the older people, children had the run of the room, and young people danced the *shurdj bar* (circle dance), with baby fingers entwined, to the accompaniment of the local violinist and accordionist, Nubar Robert Melkonian. "We danced," recalled an informant with great glee, "until the floors shook!"

Most immigrants inevitably lose part of their cultural heritage in the transoceanic crossing, and they lose more in their adjustment to the New World. For Armenians an additional cultural loss had occurred during the Genocide, when the link with the past had been cut. Not only had the infrastructure of their culture been destroyed (churches and schools), not only were the transmitters of the culture dead (parents and grandparents), but the creators of the culture (writers, artists, and architects) had also been killed. Those who had survived often had little knowledge of the literature, the arts, architecture, and church traditions. At best, Armenian refugees brought with them a slim fragment of their rich and ancient culture, a fact that made them all the more determined to preserve and pass on to their children the precious shards of their heritage.

One of the most vital agents linking past to present remained the Armenian press, notably the political press. As discussed in previous chapters, political organizations used their presses to politicize their readers, but the presses also provided a cultural bulwark. Not only did they circulate newspapers, but they also published books of plays, poetry, songs, short stories, school texts, and histories. The contribution of the Armenian press to cultural preservation, particularly in resurrecting a devastated literature, cannot be overemphasized, nor can its popularity among immigrants and their children.

Plays were an important means of communication and entertainment, especially since some newcomers did not prefer or could not afford regular movies. Armenian immigrants loved the theatre and welcomed travelling troupes that staged pre-Genocide favourites, such as the works of Hagop Baronian and Yervant Odian and translated pieces like the operetta *Arshin Mal Alan* and Shakespearian plays. Immigrants also organized their own theatrical groups and often chose plays with a political or nationalist edge. In St Catharines in 1929 the Dashnak group performed *Sev Hogher* (The Black Earth), which was about the devastation wrought by Tamerlane. The Hnchaks put on *The Twenty Hanged Men*, by Setrag Shahen, which was about the execution of Hnchak leaders by the Turkish regime in 1915. In Hamilton in 1958 local residents felt confident enough to stage *Othello*, directed by Zarouhi Kaloustian, with Paul Kaprielian in the lead role, Vartevar Olmesian as Iago, and Ms Gubekjian as Desdemona.

Intermingled with formal plays were their own skits and amateur one-act plays depicting the immigrant experience. Alexander Davies (Alexander Mooradian) and his sister Parantzem, of Hamilton, wrote and directed the comic skit *Sara Khatun*, which portrayed the antics of a confused elderly Armenian lady who confounded her dentist with her garlic breath.[19] They also wrote and produced longer plays, such as Alexander Mooradian's *Gagosig*. In Brantford, Seth Bejian and Manoog Muradian staged the works of the Keghi expatriate, writer, and playwright Setrag Shahen, one of the editors of the Hnchak newspaper *Yeritasard Hayastan*.

Armenians in Canada also wrote poetry and short stories, many extolling the beauty of their beloved homeland or declaring their aspirations and yearning for a homeland. Probably the most poignant expression of exile was the movement to write village and regional histories. Realizing that they would never again return to their homes, survivors began an earnest effort to gather documents, photographs, memoirs, poetry, and stories about the world they had lost and to publish these accounts for posterity, largely, but not always under the direction of the compatriotic associations. These books included a history and geography of the region; a history of its churches and monasteries; accounts of notable individuals from the area; a description of the local foods; memoirs, poems, songs, sayings, and myths; and the history of the destruction of the region during the Genocide and the efforts at self-defence and survival. Individual Armenians also wrote their memoirs, painstakingly by hand, in order to leave evidence of a world destroyed.[20] One cannot underestimate the powerful role of regional loyalties among early Armenian Canadians. Typical foods, proverbs, dialects, folkways, and dances strengthened this link with the old land. Even their children, who identified themselves as Armenians in Canadian society, identified themselves in the Armenian environment according to their parents' village or region of origin. While it may seem anachronistic that young people born in Canada would take possession of their parents' home village, such were the bonds of the past and the depth of the tragedy of loss.

In the musical sphere the peoples' repertoire once again included their pre-Genocide favorites: hymns and troubadour, folk, patriotic, revolutionary, émigré, rural and urban love songs and song-dances. Armenians were particularly enthralled with the music of the famous monk Komitas, the musician so cruelly tortured by the Turks. Turkish authorities burned his large and rare collection of music, which he had gathered through years of painstaking research among Armenian villages. Armenians in Canada were also taken with the music of the troubadour Sayat Nova. They were entranced by the recordings of Armenag Shahmouradian, the orphan from Mush who rose to great heights of fame as a tenor of the Paris Opera. Armenians especially treasured his recording of "Hayasdan" (Armenia) and "Giligia" (Cilicia), the record he made with Komitas before the beloved priest's incarceration. In her turn Zabel Panosian, soprano, recorded such favourites as "Krunk" (Crane), and Oudi Hrant performed "Sirun Yar" (Sweet Love) on the oud.[21] Songs of exile, like the ever mournful Komitas song "Antuni" (The Homeless One) usually brought tears to listeners and singers alike. While they composed stories, plays, and poems about the tragic experiences of massacre and loss, their musical repertoire in particular reflected their sorrow, dominated as it was by dirges.

Armenians, both in the United States and Canada, also composed songs of the immigrant experience, such as the "Cuba" song, mentioned in chapter 9. Other immigrant songs recounted, with a touch of humour, the woebegone life of the husband/father, reflecting the complaint of a settler that "America is a woman's country":

For the daughter, an automobile
For the mother, a carriage
For the father a lame ass without a saddle.
For the daughter, rice pilaf

For the mother, bulgur
For the father, conchelli soup with no garlic.

By the 1940s and 1950s, as the children and grandchildren of the early settlers were reaching maturity, a North American-Armenian musical culture began to emerge. Popular music, for example, was a mixture of traditional Armenian, Turkish, and American influences. If people listened to recordings of Armenian music, it was usually of Armenian-American bands that were mainly from the United States East Coast, like the Vosbikian brothers, Artie Barsamian, the Nor-ikes (with Souren Baronian on clarinet and vocals by Charles Ganimian or Alice Arabian), the Aramite band, Y. Boghosian, and oudist George Mgrdichian.[22] From Detroit came Simon Javizian and the Ardziv orchestra, playing under the Ardziv label, and later came the "exciting sounds" of clarinetist Hachig Kazarian. Gradually, music from California filtered north: Hratch Yaboubian (under the Notable label), the M. Takakjian orchestra (under the Kevorkian label), oudist Richard Hagopian, and Reuben Sarkisian (under his own label). These Armenian American bands performed traditional Armenian melodies and songs, including "Tamzara," "Naz Bar," "Yar Vor Jan Im," and "Deliaman." Reflecting the musical baggage of the immigrants themselves, they recorded traditional Turkish melodies like "Chifte Telli" and "Oghlan, Oghlan." The bands broadened out into Armenian-American compositions, such as "Catskillin Jampan" (On the Catskill road), "Aghvor Aghchig" (Pretty Girl), "Miserloo," and "Sud é, Sud é" (It's a Lie). Guy Chookoorian and his Moosh Mountaineers or his Anoti Four (Lightning label) recorded such popular hits as "Mule Train" and "Come Ona My House," translated into Armenian.[23] Gradually performing artists included in their repertoire songs about Soviet Armenia such as "Golghozi Aghchig" (Girl of the Golghoz) and "Hay Jan Yerevan."

Local bands were either from Galt (with Cory Tosoian and Johnny Kostigian) or from St Catharines (with Ralph Markarian, Peter Markarian, and Billy Karres). Usually these bands consisted of four or five musicians with a clarinet, saxophone, or trumpet; dumbeg (drums); tambourine; and perhaps a violin, oud, mandolin, or accordion. As there was no sheet music for most of the old Armenian songs, musicians played the tunes by ear and added their own innovations and variations.[24] With the growing popularity of Armenian American and Armenian Canadian bands and the appeal of the recording industry, group singing, formerly a favourite pastime began to decline. At the same time, young Armenian Canadian musicians moved into the

Canadian sphere. John Nubarian, pianist, and Mary Ohanian, soprano, for instance, were noted for their classical work, while Johnny Kostigian enjoyed fame with his thirteen-piece band at Leisure Lodge.

A survey conducted in southern Ontario (1987–89) revealed that most children born in Canada remembered primarily patriotic songs, songs of resistance, and songs of daring and heroism of Armenian freedom fighters: "Krvetsek tghek" (Let Us Fight, Men), "Ibrev Ardsiv" (Like an Eagle, the song of the hero Andranik), "Bamb Vorotan" (Thunder Struck), "Lusin Chikar" (There Was No Moon), "Talvoriktsi" (Dalvorigtsi), "Verkerov Li" (Full of Wounds), "Dzain me Hnchets Erzerumi Hayots Lerneren" (A Sound Rang Out from the Armenian Mountains of Erzerum), and the Armenian national anthem, which included the lines "Everywhere death is the same / Man dies but once / Lucky is he who gives his life / For the freedom of his nation)." Ranking second were folk songs such as "Anush Garun" (Sweet Spring), "Mi lar Mayram" (Don't Cry, Mariam), "Zharum" (wedding song), "Zampur" (song dance), "Garnan Gutan Hanetsi" (I Took Out the Plough in Spring), "Kelé Kelé," and the ever-popular "Alakiaz" (Alakiaz Mountain).[25]

Armenian choirs, a more formal expression of the Armenian musical tradition, started in Toronto under the direction of Yervant Selyan. In 1928 the choir gave a public concert at Jarvis Collegiate, drawing an audience of several hundred people. On a regular weekly basis, the choir sang on CFRB, a Toronto radio station, and from 1928 to 1934 performed in St Catharines, Hamilton, Galt, and Brantford. Selyan taught the group patriotic and folk songs like those collected by Komitas, including the doleful émigré favourite, "Grung" (The Crane).

To the traditional Armenian *shurdj par* (circle dance) and the *tek par* (solo dance) settlers added specific favourites, like the *Tamzara* and the *Kochari* or regional dances like the Sebastatsi dance (*Vy Nishan*). The circle dances proved to be perfect community dances, as everyone – young and old, men and women – could participate; even little children trailed at the end. Indeed, early settlers were horrified at the Canadian practice of couples dancing with each other, considering such intimacy promiscuous.

Picnics were very popular summer events held in a local park or just outside the city limits. Invariably, the community hired a bus, and the trip to the picnic site started the festivities as people sang to the accompaniment of a mandolin or a clarinet. The picnics were somewhat reminiscent of monastic festivals in the old land, when people would gather at the monasteries for two or three days, celebrating various events. Once at the grounds, picnickers visited friends from other cities, ate traditional Armenian foods like rice *pilaf* and *shish kebab* (barbequed lamb), *beorag* (cheese or spinach in phyllo pastry), *gata* (coffee cake), *kifté* (stuffed meatballs), *paghlava* and *burma* (nuts wrapped in phyllo pastry), and *herisa* (chicken or veal with hulled whole wheat).

Whether they were held in the garden of St Gregory's after the celebration of the Blessing of the Grapes for the feast of the Assumption of St Mary, at Henley Park in St Catharines, at Sage's farm in Galt, at Hidden Valley in Hamilton, or at Humber Bay Park in Toronto, picnics were happy events. It was a joyful sight to see the lead dancer merrily waving a white handkerchief in one hand and energetically leading the circle with the other or to see two young people dancing the solo dance opposite each other, with picnickers leaping forward and slapping dollar bills on their foreheads, the money being a donation to the group organizing the picnic.[26] People enjoyed the aroma of barbecued lamb cooked on spits, the delicious traditional tastes, the sounds of the music, the chatter and laughter, men playing cards or engrossed in backgammon tournaments, dancers in their brightly coloured summer attire, races and tugs-of-war, young people flirting – but not too ostentatiously – and the elderly sitting on blankets and chairs under the shade of a tree, watching the whole scene with obvious pleasure.

Armenians also commemorated national days, such as *Vardanants* (February), remembering the battle of *Avarayr* and the bravery of the Armenian General Vardan; the founding of the Armenian republic (May) or the establishment of Soviet Armenia (November), depending on their political loyalties; the founding of various organizations; Mother's Day; the closing exercises of Armenian school.

None of these events could compare with the solemn services for the martyrs of the Genocide. Each year on 24 April, Armenians joined together – often all factions – to mourn their lost families, villages, culture, and nation in communal grieving. The impact of their grief on their children was not always readily recognized: the fear of authority; the reluctance "to make waves"; the depression of parents, especially of mothers; their overprotective instincts; and the burden of the murder of aunts and uncles, grandmothers, and grandfathers. The tragedy of a nation and the sorrows of a people fell on their young shoulders. A genocide complex – a legacy of Genocide – troubled many young people. Too often an incomprehensible insecurity disturbed them. "As a youngster," confided a Hamiltonian, "I was mesmerized by the picture in our club of Mother Armenia, among the ruins of her ancient cities like Ani and Van ... I can remember a play, *The Wounded Soldier*, with Norman Kaprielian as the soldier and Siranoush Aslanian as the nurse. The audience was silent. All you could hear was the sound of sobbing."[27] Another recalled that her mother and friends would gather together and tell and retell their stories in hushed voices and weep. When they saw their mothers crying, the children would cry too, " but we didn't know why."[28] Still another informant gave a sense of her mother's experience: "My mother was a survivor, but she didn't talk about the Genocide to me. Once, as a teenager, I'd been reading about hometowns. So I told her that when I grew up I was going to be rich and I would take her on a trip to visit her hometown. Her eyes filled with tears and she said quietly, 'My child, the house where I grew up has been destroyed; my hometown is a heap of rubble; all my playmates are dead. Hamilton is my hometown and I love this country. All my loved ones are here.'"[29]

But there was a deeper dimension to past events. Armenians were proud of what they, as a small nation, had achieved. Their literature, music, and architecture were outstanding, and their military competence had been proven at Bash Abaran, Kara Kilisa, and Sardarabad, where against great odds, they had defeated Turkish armies. Armenians had fought for and won their independence. Armenians in Canada and throughout the world commemorated these victories. But the Genocide would not and could not be forgotten. For decades, Armenians joined together and remembered their loved ones, wept on each other's shoulders, shared their suffering. The mourning was intimate and internal. Armenians would not forget. Gradually, they took their grief public. They wanted the world to acknowledge and remember events that had inspired an outpouring of sympathy for their people during and following World War I but that now, after World War II, had all but disappeared from public memory.[30] In 1955, the fortieth anniversary of the beginning of the Genocide, Armenians in Canada joined forces and organized a major march in Toronto. With the Union Jack and the Armenian flag at the helm, they felt secure enough as Canadian citizens to express their sorrow in the larger Canadian context. Who could ever imagine that anyone would or could deny the Genocide?

ARMENIANS MOVE INTO THE CANADIAN ARENA

Events in the homeland, Protestant writers, and the Canadian media had already brought Armenians, their tragedy, their cause, and their contributions to the war effort to the attention of the Canadian public.[31] Gradually Armenians themselves began to move into the Canadian scene and to display clear evidence of their intrepid spirit and resourceful nature. To show they were not of Asiatic stock, the Canadian Armenian Young Peoples' Association commissioned a book on genetics, using scientific data to disprove arguments classifying them as Asians.[32] Mesrob Bagdasarian published (1930) *The Sunny Side of the Armenian People: Its Past and Present*.[33] In his introduction he bemoans the fact that in the past thirty-five years the Canadian press and Canadian lecturers have so focused on the massacres and tragedies of the Armenian people that "this nation has come to stand in the popular mind as not much more than a helpless and suffering people." Armenians, he noted, are therefore regarded largely "as objects of charity." His aim was to remove such misconceptions and to "give a true insight into the character of these people" who have "shown marvelous vitality in preserving their national identity, their language, religion and traditions through age long persecutions and fiery trials." "Here is a nation," he writes, that "like an ancient oak still stands defying all the desolation and wreck of time." Today Armenia is poised on the threshold of the twentieth century, with wounds partially healed and eyes still dim with tears, "yet with a stout heart still throbbing with faith and hope in her destiny!"

In his brief account, Bagdasarian covers a great swatch of topics, speaking about geography, history, physical and moral characteristics, political history, the Genocide, the Soviet Republic of Armenia, the Armenian Church, Armenian culture, Armenian contributions during the Great War, testimonials, and, finally, an appeal to Canadians. In his summary of Armenian moral characteristics, Bagdasarian refers to the strong love for family life, marriage as the most sacred bond in life, and the Armenian woman's "deep sense of the sanctity of her sex." The author extols the virtues of Soviet Armenia, noting the reconstruction of villages and towns, irrigation and canal projects, repair of bridges and roads, extension of railway lines, building of hydroelectric power stations, the construction of schools and hospitals, and the creation of the University of Yerevan. All these things, he states, "have been made possible by the material assistance given by the Russian government and by the vast sums of money amounting to hundreds of thousands of dollars contributed by the Armenian colonies throughout the world." He makes special note of the intention to build a new town, Nubarashen, after Boghos Nubar Pasha, the founder of the Armenian General Benevolent Union, who pledged one hundred thousand dollars for this undertaking. Finally, Bagdasarian appeals to Canadians to remember the contributions made by Armenians during the war, to take into account their high "levels of culture," and to allow the admission to Canada of "a limited number of these deserving people." "If placed under the incomparably more favourable conditions of life in Canada, this glorious land of liberty with its great opportunities ... they would be able to rise even higher and make immeasurably greater contributions to her material and intellectual development." He calls for a "more kindly policy" based on the principles of "self-interest, justice and humanity."

Participation in public events reached a peak in 1946, when the Hamilton Armenian Choir, under the direction of Yervant Selyan, gave a stunning performance for the Hamilton Centennial. At the same time, Armenians organized a display of Armenian artifacts for an exhibition honouring the different ethnic groups living in Hamilton, and they entered a young Armenian girl, Jean Georgian, as Miss Armenia in the pageant. Armenians were showing greater public pride in their heritage. They were also proud to be Canadian citizens and took their Canadian naturalization very seriously. A respondent recalled that her father treasured his naturalization certificate. Whenever he mentioned Canada, he would invariably add a phrase like "God bless this peaceful land," "thank God, we're living in this civilized country," or "this beautiful and just land."[34]

As a group, Armenians actively exercised their voting privileges. Highly sensitive to the world of politics, they joined, worked for, and financially supported various Canadian political parties and maintained good relations with their elected representatives at all levels of government. They sought the assistance of their representatives and petitioned the federal government for intervention, for support of their compatriots abroad, for an Armenian homeland, for entry of their relatives to Canada, for reparations, and later on, for official recognition of the Genocide. Generally, they voted for the Liberal Party or the Cooperative Commonwealth Federation (CCF). During the Cold War staunch anti-Communists, most notably members of the Dashnak Party, moved to the right to the Progressive Conservative Party.

Armenians were not inclined to run for political office in Canada, perhaps because they were convinced a "foreign" name could not win votes or perhaps because they lacked the necessary connections in the established parties, due to their small numbers, working-class backgrounds, or immigrant status. More likely their reluctance to enter the Canadian political arena can be traced to the impact of trauma, uprooting, and loss: refugees and their children were obliged to devote their energies to physical survival and to the preservation of a threatened heritage.

Initially, their entry into politics was through ethnic/multicultural organizations. For example, John H. Mooradian of Hamilton (b. Arek, Keghi, 1892 – 1969) was founder and first president of the Canadian National Unity Council, which was established in Hamilton in 1947 and which was one of the first multicultural organizations in Canada. As the community matured, more Armenians ran for public office in mainstream Canadian politics. The first Armenian to hold elected office was Martin Avedisian, a rug merchant in Galt, who was elected city alderman in the late 1940s and early 1950s. Dr Ara Mooradian, son of John H. Mooradian was the first mayor of Deep River (1958).

Armenian youngsters were also being Canadianized: at the public school and the Anglican Sunday school and at the movies and through their friendship with non-Armenians. They were, in addition, moving into the Canadian world through work. In Hamilton teenagers delivered newspapers or fruits and vegetables for Wineberg's grocery story, caddied at the golf course, babysat, worked as part-time sales clerks, peddled home-grown fruits and vegetables, helped sell peanuts and popcorn at baseball games, and shined shoes. The following account is taken from an interview with a former shoe-shine boy, a representative of a cohort of youngsters who not only helped their families but expanded their own horizons beyond the public school and the Armenian neighbourhood at an early age.[35]

The boy began shining shoes at the age of eleven, in 1940, working Fridays after school until 9 o'clock and all day Saturday from 8:30 A.M. to midnight. When he started high school, he quit work until he "got used to high school." He had found the transition to high school difficult, because he attended a commercial school and "none of the friends I grew up with or I went to school with went to the same high school." Most of his non-Armenian friends attended the collegiate and most of the Armenian boys attended the technical school. For this young man and his family, attending a commercial school was considered an entree to white-collar work and therefore a step up from technical education.

Like a number of other Armenian boys, he worked for an Armenian-speaking Greek, Nick Almas, who ran a shoe-shine shop and a hat-cleaning and blocking business. From 1943 to 1946 he worked after school, from 4:30 to 8:30 on Mondays, Tuesdays, and Thursdays, and on Fridays until 9. On Saturdays he worked from 8:30 A.M. until midnight. The shoe-shine shop was located on Barton Street, across from the Hamilton Arena, which frequently held Saturday events. "On Saturdays, there'd be three of us, plus Nick, the boss. Six or eight customers on the stand and three or four waiting. So we were going full blast. In one hour's time, we'd shine maybe twenty or thirty-five customers."

It was wartime. Everybody was away and every able-bodied man who wasn't of military age was working and making lots of money in the factories. They were short of labour – because all the healthy men were in the armed forces.

On Saturdays if we were busy, we'd make a fortune. Saturdays I'd make about ten dollars in tips alone because the soldiers were home for the weekend and they'd give a quarter and I'd make fifteen cents tip.

The navy and air force boots had regular good leather. The patent leather was a nice soft quality. The navy boots, the half Wellingtons, and the air force boots were easy to shine. You could do them very quickly. But it was a real job shining army boots because they had oil in the leather. If they were new, it was hard to get a shine on them If they were old boots, the polish was caked up so you were actually polishing the polish, not the leather.

As in any job, there was a certain routine and there were certain rules of the trade. Whoever came to work first was up first, and so on. The boys kept a very close watch on each other to ensure that the order was maintained all day, but they devised their own ways to profit:

Say I'm shining a customer's shoes and he's an average tipper. Another man comes in and the second kid gets him. So I have to finish first, since I started my customer first. Then a customer walks in, he's a good tipper. Maybe tips twenty-five cents. Now he'd be my customer. So what does the other shoeshine kid do? He speeds up and gives his customer a fast "shuffle" job, snaps the rag and pretends he's giving the guy a good shine and finishes first, before I do. Deliberately speeding up or even putting on only one coat of polish – so he'd get the heavy tipper. Then an argument and fight develops. We were always arguing and even fist-fighting – never in front of the customer or in front of Nick. Once I tore a kid's shirt, I was so mad. Stalling is the reverse tactic to speeding. Seeing a poor tipper next in line, the kid would stall, take his time, work slowly so someone else would get the poor tipper ...

We knew all the customers. If a strange new guy comes in, we'd give him a good shine, and if he didn't tip good, then the next time he comes in we'd give him a lousy shine. We'd never forget him. He wouldn't know the difference. We wouldn't put on a half pound of polish. We'd pretend we were working hard when we weren't.

The informant, a good student, did his homework while customers were few during school nights, but as he got older he resented being unable to attend school dances. "I'd go to one dance out of four. Every Saturday night they had Teens Canteen at the Y[MCA]. I rarely went to one of those, we were working till midnight on Saturdays."

I was an altar boy at St Philip's Anglican church. By the time I came home Saturday night, had a bath, I'd go to bed around 2 o'clock then I'd have to get up the next morning at 8:30 or 9:00 to get to church on time for the 11 o'clock service ... I was in the army cadets, a drummer, during the war.

Nick was a good boss. From the old school. A distinguished gentleman. No gambling or card playing in the back of his store ... Before midnight we'd start cleaning and polishing the stand ... put all the polishes together, all the brushes together and clean the brass stands where you put your feet. We had to clean the marble base of the stand right across the whole front because polish and dye would drop on it ... I had to use naphtha gas to take the polish out of my hands ... After we finished work, cleaned up, and washed up, Nick would make nice toast, butter and feta cheese and olives and coffee.

Saturday night we'd go in the back and Nick'd give us our pay. All week, I'd make about twenty bucks in tips and he'd pay me ten dollars. So I'd make thirty dollars a week. I made my thirty dollars, which is what grown men were making working in the factories ... At that time, my father was earning forty-five or fifty dollars as a moulder at the Harvester.

I worked all summer too. We kids made good money during the war and helped our families a lot. I'd give all my money to my mother. She'd roll it up in nickels, dimes, and quarters and take it to the bank on Monday morning. She gave me a dollar a week.[36]

For this adolescent attending high school during the 1940s, the world of nickels and dimes meant the difference between having a new pair of trousers and wearing the same old tweed jodhpurs all year long. His mother carefully saved his tips and added them to whatever could be set aside from his father's earnings to buy a house of their own in the late 1940s.

His father, like most of the early pioneers in Hamilton, came from a peasant background in rural Turkey. These men had been the most adventurous and ambitious of their village and possibly the most progressive, for they had emigrated to better themselves and their families. They had risked the unknown to work in urban centres in the Ottoman Empire, in the Balkans, and eventually in North America. Wherever they settled they had found jobs at the lowest rung of the economic ladder – as porters in Constantinople, as delivery men in Varna, or as unskilled factory workers in Canadian industry. As such, they had entered the ranks of the urban poor, but they had had the awareness to recognize that self-employment and education were agents of independence and upward mobility. Many of the refugees, moreover, had themselves come from educated families from different parts of the Ottoman Empire and had suffered in the poverty of orphanages and refugee camps. They, too, recognized the importance of self-employment and education.

Men who had seen Tom Rice, works superintendent at the International Harvester, "do nothing but walk around the plant all day long with his hands in his pockets," men who identified work in terms of physical labour, wanted a better life for their children. Men who had strained and distorted their bodies and used up their lives in the foundries – immigrants for whom a high school education had been unattainable – were proud that, with the sweat of their brow, with their honest work, they could die knowing their children had had the opportunity to finish high school and in growing numbers to acquire post-secondary education.

To get a sense of the emphasis families placed on education, let us look at a few examples. Alice Jaraian's father walked seven miles daily to work and seven miles back to earn a dollar a day, and out of these meagre resources, her mother paid for her piano lessons, which cost thirty-five cents a week. As an adult, she earned her livelihood by giving piano lessons. Hovannes Hagopian mortgaged his house to send his son to university, and today he is a university professor. Eto Arakelian, already a middle-aged woman when she immigrated to Canada after the Genocide, worked in a restaurant to enable her nephew's sons to attend university. As a refugee Sadie Tateosian had been deprived of an education: "I was fifteen when my mother arranged for my marriage. I pleaded with her to let me go to school, but no one listened to me. In those days, that's how things were done. When I had children, I vowed I'd make sure they had an education. So I worked hard in different factories, in running my own little grocery story. All three have had a good education." When Vart Chaligian was reproached by her employer for sending her son to university ("the factory was good enough for his father, why isn't it good enough for him?") – Vart shot back: "That's why I'm here, working for you (cleaning house), so my son can have a university education."[37]

Being either agriculturalists or refugees, very few immigrants established themselves in the professions. A.B. Davies (Alexander Baptist (Mgrdich) Mooradian) is an interesting exception. Born in Keghi in the village of Arek and reared in Cairo, Davies immigrated to Canada as a young man shortly after World War I. He was a pioneer in chiropractic medicine and an outstanding naturopath who researched techniques of electromagnetic healing. A summary of his thought, a six-hundred-page study entitled *The Book of Life*, examines the major problems of human life from a scientific, political, physical, and spiritual perspective. Davies discusses the causes of human misery and suggests remedial measures for human beings to bring their lives to peace, harmony, and happiness. Anticipating public health concerns of a half century later, Davies was advocating a meatless diet and publicizing the health hazards of cigarettes and the dangers of prescription drugs as early as the 1920s. Bucking both the medical establishment and industrialists in

Hamilton, he fearlessly denounced industrial pollution of the environment, vaccinations, and the side effects of chlorinated water and second-hand tobacco smoke. A devout Christian, Davies propounded the efficacy of prayer and condemned money as a major source of society's anguish. To this day, he has not been recognized as the avant-garde healer, spiritual teacher, and profound thinker that he was.[38]

For children born to pre-1914 settlers, consisting by rough estimate of no more than one hundred families, mathematics and the sciences offered the most accessible route to a professional career, especially medicine. Arthur Haktsian of Brantford was the first Armenian doctor trained in Canada (possibly the first Armenian child born in Canada, in 1899). Anaid Kiernan-Mooradian (Hamilton and Winnipeg), the first Armenian woman doctor, and John V. Basmajian (Brantford and Hamilton), pioneer of electromyography and biomechanics, were also among the medical doctors from this pioneer cohort. In addition several individuals distinguished themselves in other fields, including Edward Safarian, an economist and former president of the Canadian Economics Association and dean of graduate studies at the University of Toronto, and Ara Mooradian, a nuclear physicist, former executive vice-president for research and development at Atomic Energy of Canada, president of the Chemical Institute of Canada, and appointee to the Science Advisory Committee to the director general of the International Atomic Energy Agency.

The importance of education and the pursuit of professional careers is indicated by an informal survey of those born in Hamilton between 1930 and 1939, which reveals that about one-third of these Depression children pursued postsecondary education.[39] In addition to medicine, these young people took up careers in nursing, engineering, economics, pharmacy, accounting, law, and education – including elementary school, secondary school, and university teaching.

Many of those who excelled in sports or in the arts as painters, singers, musicians, and actors moved to the United States to further their careers, notably Stan Giragosian (Greg Roman) in acting, and Harry Mooradian in baseball. Some, like Mary Ohanian, the outstanding soprano from Hamilton, stayed and carved out a career in Canada.

Traditionally, photography has held a prominent place among Armenians. Armenian photographers were in great demand in Constantinople before the Genocide and in Cairo and Alexandria after the Genocide. During the 1920s in Aleppo, Syria, almost all photographers were Armenian.[40] In Canada, Manuel Mgrublian's name appears as a photographer in St John, New Brunswick; Sherbrooke, Quebec; and Sydney, Nova Scotia – all before 1920. In that year, Sarkis Ar(a)kelian, who had studied photography in Boston, is listed as the proprietor of the Victoria Photo Studio, located at 51 Sackville Street in Halifax, with branches in St John and Moncton.[41] Malak (Malak Karsh), born in Mardin (in the Ottoman Empire) in 1915, specialized in landscape photography. He became famous for his photographs of tulips and for his "Paper and Politics" photo of logs in the Ottawa River alongside the Parliament Buildings, which appeared on the Canadian one-dollar bill before it was replaced by the "loonie" in 1987. The photograph of Queen Elizabeth II on the front of the bill was taken by his brother, Yousuf, the outstanding Armenian-Canadian portrait photographer. Born in Mardin in 1903, Karsh survived the Genocide and, as a young refugee, immigrated to Canada in 1924. He trained first with his photographer uncle, Georges Nakash(ian), in Sherbrooke, Quebec, then with Mgrdich Garo of Boston. Eventually he settled in Ottawa, where he honed his art, mastering particularly the use of light. Karsh was an internationally famous black-and-white portrait photographer, his portrait of Winston Churchill being one of his most celebrated photographs.

By the 1960s the life cycle of these early Armenian communities was drawing to a close.[42] A dedicated and diligent core group continued to sustain the community, but given the growing distance from the immigrant generation, the small and dispersed nature of settlement, the sometimes stifling nature of the community, the fractiousness of the political/religious segments, increased rates of exogamy, and the call of career opportunities, the early settlements were slowly fading away. Had Armenian settlements remained without further immigration flows, Armenian culture in Canada might have vanished altogether.

Photo of the Pasdermajian brothers standing in front of Yervant's Oriental Rugs on Sherbrooke St in Montreal, ca 1960s. *Left to right*: Hrant, Yervant, and Hagop. Photo courtesy of Yervant Pasdermajian

Interior of a rug store in Toronto, with Georges Yeremian and Stacy Churchill, ca 1980s. Kaprielian collection

Marriage ceremony, Toronto. Photographer, Danny Pivato. Kaprielian collection

Celebrating Easter by cracking traditional coloured eggs. Eggs are cooked in a pot of onion skins to give them a rich terra cotta colour. The young man is preparing to "hit" the egg held by the young woman. Photographer Stacy Churchill, Kaprielian collection

Growing up Armenian Canadian – the fourth generation, 2004.
Photographer, Lance Kaprielian. Kaprielian collection

Hnchak poster of Armenian heroes with Mother Armenia weeping among her ruined ci

Modern statue of Mother Armenia, Republic of Armenia. Note the contrast of this portrayal of a strong woman with the preceding depiction of loss and devastation. Photographer Aris Babikian

Armenian church architecture in Toronto: Holy Trinity Armenian Apostolic Church. Courtesy Holy Trinity Armenian Apostolic Church

Armenian church architecture in Toronto: St Mary's Armenian Apostolic Church. Photographer Albert Kaprielian

Armenian church architecture in Toronto: St Gregory the Illuminator Armenian Catholic Church. Courtesy of St Gregory the Illuminator Church

Armenian church architecture in Toronto: Armenian Evangelical Church. Coutesy of the Armenian Evangelical Church

Cover of *Sovetakan Hayastan* (Soviet Armenia), Yerevan, 1987. This illustrated monthly, published by the Committee for Cultural Relations with Overseas Armenians, focused on literature, art, and public affairs in Soviet Armenia. By such means, Soviet Armenian Communist leaders kept the diaspora informed about cultural developments in Soviet Armenia and strengthened the links between the homeland and the diaspora. The cover shows the great monument of mother and father. Located in mountainous Karabagh, the statue remains a symbol of the spirit of independence

Poster of David of Sasun marking the earthquake in Armenia in 1988, which took at least twenty-five thousand lives and left thousands more homeless. By permission of the artist, Paul Safarian

PART SIX

Old Foundations, New Communities

16

Old Foundations: Montreal and Toronto to 1950

The third wave preferred to settle in Montreal and Toronto, where they built on the foundations already established before their arrival. These communities differed dramatically from those in the industrial towns of Hamilton, St Catharines, and Brantford, notably with respect to size, composition, patterns of settlement, and means of livelihood.

In both Toronto and Montreal, the post-Genocide flow outnumbered the earlier settlers, even though leadership initially remained in the hands of prewar settlers. Since the refugees came from different backgrounds, the communities they built up did not have a strong single-origin base, and they were, consequently, far more heterogeneous in character and composition than places like Hamilton or Brantford. A list of Armenians in Montreal from 1930 to 1944 giving names of settlers with their town of origin confirms this heterogeneity. Settlers came from Adabazar, Amassia, Ankara, Arabkir, Balu, Ceasarea, Tigranakert, Marsovan, Istanbul, Keghi, Kharput, Malatia, Marash, Mardin, Sivas, and Van.[1] Differences also existed in levels of education, language, religious denomination, and socioeconomic background – differences people seldom overlooked or forgot: "Even as orphans," recalled an interviewee, "background distinctions remained."[2] As if to confirm this statement, one of the Toronto "élite" remarked: "They were nice people, and we often went to visit them and they came here, but they were not like us. They had a different background."[3]

Nor did the patterns of settlement in Montreal and Toronto mirror those in Brantford, St Catharines, and Hamilton. Rather, settlement assumed a character of its own. No single factory dominated the work culture, and no clear Armenian neighbourhood delineated the boundaries of settlement. Armenians dispersed throughout the urban area, motivated primarily by the location of the workplace.

MONTREAL

By 1907 it was estimated that approximately three hundred Armenians resided in Montreal, primarily in the southeast area near the docks; they included shoemakers, restaurant operators, wholesale/dry goods dealers, fruit vendors, tobacco importers, boardinghouse landlords, and factory workers.[4] Carnig Ateshian, for example, was manufacturing Café Noir cigars on St Gabriel Street as early as 1903–04, and by 1911–12 he was living on Park Avenue, one of the first Armenians to do so. Around 1908–9 Leon Hagopian ran a shoemaker shop at 122 Duluth, and D. Zarikian operated a wholesale dry goods business at 1657 Esplanade Avenue around 1912.[5] Many of the early settlers in Montreal migrated in family or kin clusters, but not as nuclear families, and included Harutiun, Vartan, and Vahan Deradourian; Setrak and Dikran Hazarian; Bedros, Khachig, and Ohannes Tatigian; and Khosrov and Mampre Melkonian.[6] They entered the work force as unskilled labour in the "iron factories": Montreal Locomotive Works, Canadian Car and Foundry, or the Steel company of Canada, and they resided near such factories, along Notre Dame Street (east and west), Parthenais, Poupart, and Park Streets. Interviewees indicate that both Dashnak and Hnchak political parties probably set up branches in Montreal before World War I, but with the exodus of Armenians from the city, these organizations soon folded.

By the end of the war fewer than fifty married and single men without women remained in Montreal. Following the Genocide, a number of refugees joined the old-timers, some as picture brides, others as relatives and village compatriots. From 1930 to 1945, an estimated forty-nine Armenian families totalling almost two hundred people and an additional twenty-seven single men and women lived in this important industrial centre. After World War II some Montreal Armenians quit the city, principally for the United States, leaving, once again, a reduced population of perhaps one hundred Armenians in the late 1940s.[7] Those who remained lived along Park Avenue (avenue du Parc), Hutchinson, Jeanne-Mance Street, St-Laurent north of Sherbrooke, along Park Extension, rue de l'Esplanade to St Zotique, up to Jean-Talon, and as far north as Cremazie.[8]

A particular category of business generally dominated enterprise in each city where Armenians settled. Such concentration might be attributed to demography, accessibility, preference, or geographic location. In St Catharines, proximity to the factory rendered the confectionery/grocery shop a viable endeavour. The few Armenians who remained in Halifax operated grocery stores near the harbour.[9] Montreal Armenians showed a preference for ice cream parlours and restaurants, one of the first being Bedros Hovaganian's (Hovagimian?) restaurant on Notre Dame East.[10] Nahabed Stepanian's adventures are typical of the geographic and employment mobility of these early immigrants. Leaving his native Van, he worked in Constantinople as a baker's helper. After the Armenian massacres in 1894–96, he found himself in serious trouble, both as a Hnchakian and as a migrant labourer in the capital city. With a group of friends he fled to Bulgaria, where he worked for a time, married an Armenian woman, and started a family. When discrimination and unemployment menaced him, he immigrated to Brantford (1910), because he had heard there were "plenty of jobs" in Canada. Eventually he moved to Montreal where, in partnership with another Armenian, he opened an ice cream shop.[11]

Before 1950 some of the Armenian run restaurants, coffee shops, and confectionaries in Montreal included Archie's Coffee Shoppe at 387 Bernard, near Hutchinson (Archie Shiroyan); the Splendide Confectionary at 352 Bernard, near Park (Mesag Janigian/Djanegian); the Delico restaurant on St Denis (Isidore Kalpakjian); the Victory restaurant close to McGill University and the Almar restaurant on Park Avenue (Albert and Martin Kojoian); Covena Lunch at 3886 Berri (John Kojoian); a grocery store/restaurant at 1101 Bleury run by Setrak Hazarian, later Marty and Johnny's Coffee Shoppe (Marty and Johnny Hazarian); restaurants on Rachel and Wellington Streets operated by the Dirado(u)rian family; and restaurants, ice cream parlours, pastry shops, and confectionaries in the St-Laurent, St Zotique, Park Avenue, and Montreal Boulevard areas, and on Ontario St East run by the Tatigian brothers over a period of some years.[12]

In the late 1920s, Dickran (Richard) Karibian, who had married Yevnigé Fermanian, started the Karibian Fruit Company with Vahram and Torkom Fermanian. From selling fruits and vegetables in Montreal, they expanded to exporting fruits and vegetables from Montreal to Ste Adèle in the Laurentian Mountains. Around 1935, Vahram Fermanian started a movie business in the area, travelling from village to village showing his films, frequently at the local Roman Catholic church. While this practice helped pay off the church debt, it was frowned upon by church leaders. In 1947–48, when he was not allowed to show films at the church any longer, he built his own movie theatre in Ste Adèle, a business that is still thriving in the family today.[13]

The Mardin group in the Eastern Townships also expanded after the Genocide, as settlers brought in their surviving relatives. Eventually, it included the Basmajian, Karsh, Nakashian, Sabiyan, Saine, Setlakwé, and Sheitoyan families, to name but some. Georges Nakash(ian) set up a photography studio in Sherbrooke and was to be the catalyst for his nephew, the world famous photographer Yousuf Karsh. The Setlakwé family opened a general store in Thetford Mines and eventually established a department store in Sherbrooke.[14] (For more on the Mardin group, see chapter 3).

TORONTO

By the end of World War I fewer than fifty Armenians had settled in Toronto – scarcely a dozen families and some single men. But by the midthirties, the influx of refugees increased the number of Armenians to between 250 and 300 individuals.[15] Many of the newcomers were single young people brought over either by the Fegan's organization or the Armenian Relief Association of Canada (ARAC). They had started their working lives in Canada in the two occupations preferred by Canadian immigration authorities: agricultural labour, mostly in southern Ontario, and domestic service, almost exclusively in Toronto.

Generally, Toronto Armenians settled in three areas, roughly reflecting their background, endeavours, and interests. During the 1920s, Armenians who worked in west-end factories lived in the Junction in the western part of the city. Others operated little shops in the centre and east end of Toronto and lived in the back of their stores. Still others owned lucrative downtown businesses and lived in relatively expensive homes in Rosedale or in the north end of the city.

Factory Workers and the Élite

Toronto Armenians can be divided into four distinct groups: the factory workers, the "élite," female domestics, and small-scale tradesmen, artisans, and businessmen. The factory labourers, relatively few in number, were generally older men, largely agriculturalists from the Armenian provinces in the Ottoman Empire. Some had immigrated to America before 1914 and resembled the settlers in Hamilton, Brantford, and St Catharines and, indeed, may have initially entered the work force in one of those cities before moving to Toronto. They were employed at Canada Meat Packers, General Electric, or Massey-Harris and lived primarily in west Toronto, in or near the Junction, not far from the plants.

The "élite," also a small group, was composed of prosperous, well-educated, multilingual, and cosmopolitan families that included the Courian, Babayan, and Utudjian families and, after World War I, the Papazian, Dervish, and Gumush families. Largely from Constantinople and its environs, they came from families of wealth and prestige, families that had distinguished themselves in the Ottoman Empire. Mrs Nevart Utudjian, for instance, was the daughter of Dr Mat(e)ossian, the personal surgeon of the sultan and a doctor in the American Civil War. Her sister, Zabel, was married to Hrant Gumush (Gumushgardian), son of the royal tailor and himself an accomplished cellist. Mrs Utudjian's uncle introduced Levon Babayan to Perouz Benlian, the future Mrs Babayan, whose father was a well-off rug importer in London, England. Juliet Rustigian, from Manchester, had an English nanny, attended a private girl's school in England, and like her father, knew several languages fluently. One of her aunts married a Gulbenkian. Her maternal grandfather, Dikran Djiladjian, had been the court jeweller in the Ottoman Empire, and her father, Hmayak Rustigian and his family had operated an extensive import/export business from Manchester, England. Like every Armenian, this group had lost family and property during the Genocide, but unlike others, they had not been throttled by events in the Ottoman Empire. They were men and women who had lived, studied, and operated businesses in different countries. Because of their international holdings and their domiciles in a number of countries, they managed to salvage some of their assets. Elegant and refined, they formed part of a vast personal, business, and political network that extended from Toronto to New York, London, and Paris. They travelled the world, stayed at the best hotels, dined with the rich and powerful. From time to time their activities, which were frequently deemed exotic, were reported in Toronto newspapers: on 23 April 1926, for example, the *Toronto Daily Star* noted that Levon Babayan had returned from Egypt with many rare treasures of art, including a mummy of a royal baby, which he donated to the Royal Ontario Museum. This small but influential group of people gave Toronto a special, sophisticated aura. "Toronto," quipped an interviewee, "had more class" than the other Armenian settlements.

Between the factory workers and the "élite" were sandwiched two other groups: female domestics and small entrepreneurs. While a number of individual Armenian women entered as domestics, only the records of the group of domestics sponsored by the ARAC and, later, the United Church of Canada have survived, and it is to this group that we now turn.[16]

Domestics

Until the beginning of World War II the demand for maids in Canada almost always exceeded the supply. The size of middle-class houses, the multitude of people residing in them, the primitive nature of domestic technology, and the production of a variety of necessities in the home contributed to the continued need for domestic servants. At the same time, middle-class women engaged more and more in voluntary and charitable work outside the home, and their working-class sisters, whose labour had facilitated such activity, found new opportunities, better wages, and improved conditions in factories and offices.[17]

Scarcity of the preferred British maids, "well-trained, respectful, and respectable," prompted concerned individuals and institutions to look to other countries for strong, healthy, and willing women workers. In order to meet this need and, at the same time, to perform a humanitarian act, the ARAC and its successor, the United Church of Canada, brought out about fifty Armenian women refugees to Toronto as domestic servants.[18] The women ranged in age from fourteen to thirty-eight, and came from diverse backgrounds and from different places of asylum including the Middle East, Greece, France, Bulgaria, and Austria. The ARAC usually arranged joint sponsorship with a relative, a friend, or another Canadian organization. Rev. Ira Pierce, coordinator of the program until he retired in 1930, maintained very strict supervision over the girls and steadfastly insisted they fulfil their labour contracts, which normally ran for a period of two years. These young women complied with the prerequisites of a good maid: they were "clean, celibate, obedient, respectable, hard-working." From all accounts, the Canadian employers were satisfied with their Armenian maids as indicated by the following praise: "Having had long, and often trying, experience with maids and nurses, I feel qualified to judge and may tell you, gratefully, that I have not had so great satisfaction with any young girl ... her happy disposition and dependable qualities of character make her a desirable companion for our children. It is a good deal to expect an outsider in a home to cook good meals, take an intelligent interest in the well-being of the family, and to conduct herself like a lady, but [she] does just so.[19]

An examination of domestic service in general reveals the frequently intolerable working conditions – long hours, sometimes fourteen to sixteen hours a day, with a half day off per week and the odd Sunday; the drudgery of what was euphemistically termed "the high art of scrubbing"; unsatisfactory sleeping accommodations in cold and dreary attics or basements; inadequate supplies of food; and a sense of inferiority that was imposed on them. On the whole, Armenian girls did not encounter such abominable conditions, or at least if they did, they did not vociferously complain. Their most common criticism, however, centred on food. Not surprisingly, food was a major issue for Genocide survivors, who had for so long suffered from malnutrition and severe shortages. They found it incomprehensible that well-off people would be so parsimonious about food. An informant recalled that her mistress bought a single loaf of bread for five people every three days and instructed her to drink water instead of milk because "water is good for you." Another resented her mistress's stinginess for criticizing the amount of butter she used. Eventually, she purchased her own supply.

A small number of the girls were overworked and exploited: "I was miserable and unhappy and often said to myself, 'whoever wants to marry me, I'm ready' ... I used to begin work at eight in the morning and work [straight] till six at night, cleaning and waxing, doing dishes and other chores. I was paid twelve dollars a month and had one half day off each week, when I went to see my sister. From this sum, I sent money to my mother in the old country, knowing that she was more in need than I was."[20] Aside from a few such complaints, the Armenian domestics echoed the satisfaction of their Canadian matrons. The following excerpt from another interview was, more or less, typical:

When I was 14 [1926], I finished my public schooling [in the orphanage] and they put me in with the girls who did embroidery ... We made beautiful tablecloths. Ten girls working on this side and ten on the other. Miss Jacobsen would send them to Denmark to raise money to provide for our school.

Mr Pierce, who worked for the United Church, had been a missionary in Kharput and knew my family there. When my aunt heard that the United Church was sponsoring girls to come in to Canada as domestics she appealed to him to bring me out. My uncle sent my passage money. Altogether, twelve girls from Miss Jacobsen's orphanage [Bird's Nest Orphanage in Lebanon] came to Canada; we all had relatives who paid for our passage.

I was so happy when I heard I was going to Canada. I didn't know anything about Canada. No idea. Cold, snow. But I wanted to get away from the orphanage. My aunt and uncle were in America [the United States] and I wanted to be near them. I felt lonely in the orphanage. I was beginning to feel like an orphan. I didn't know what a domestic was or what she did.

My first job was as a mother's helper with a family with a seven-year-old boy and a thirteen-year-old girl. I got up at seven, dressed in my black and white uniform and did the chores. She [mistress] did the laundry and cooking; I cleaned, waxed and dusted, set the table, and did the dishes. After lunch, I had a bath and put on my white and yellow uniform. I hated wearing the cap, made me feel like a slave. So she said it was okay not to wear it.

I had a couple of hours break in the afternoons; I read or crocheted. Then I helped her prepare dinner. I gradually started learning to cook; she taught me. At first I was a little nervous with the vacuum cleaner, but after I learned the buttons, it was fine, but I never did the wash. I was afraid of the wringer. By 7:30, the work was done, and I spent my evenings reading or doing crochet. Basically, I did whatever I was told.

I had my own room upstairs, opposite her daughter's room. It was a beautiful room. Well furnished. I ate whatever they ate, never went hungry. I just watched and copied them to learn how Canadians act. Whatever they did, I did. I saved my three-dollar-a-week salary. They were very kind people and I stayed with them for fifteen months. The only problem was that she was too strict about the curfew, said I had to be in by ten. I wanted to go out with my friends sometimes. So Mr Pierce placed me in another fine home.

He put us girls in respectable homes, very good people. Except for one case where my friend had to look after four children and the mistress was out all the time. My friend was overworked. But I was lucky; my second family was even more cultured than the first. I am still friends with them. During the three years that I worked for them I was very happy. She was motherly, never treated me like a maid, but like a daughter. Paid me forty dollars a month – of course I was more experienced by this time and I could cook rather well. I saved two hundred dollars in three years. They taught me about Canada and Canadian customs. Took me to concerts and plays. I watched and copied to learn Canadian ways. Whatever they did, I did.[21]

The young domestic had Thursday afternoons and Sundays off. On Thursdays she would join her Armenian girl friends, and they would go shopping downtown to Eaton's and Simpson's: "We were young. We wanted to dress and look like other young women. Sometimes we'd go to the movies. Loews. Romance movies mostly. It was cheaper to go in the afternoon." On Sunday afternoons some of the girls, numbering about twenty-five to thirty, attended Sunday school in the United Church, at first with an English teacher, then with an Armenian one. Afterwards, they enjoyed a light snack of sandwiches that they brought with them. In the evening, they attended church service again, and then "we talked about our lives, our troubles, our mistresses and misters, work, overwork, salaries, girlfriends, boyfriends. We had to be home by ten; they didn't want young girls out alone at night."[22]

The news of the presence of young women spread like wildfire in the Armenian community. Men travelled to Toronto from as far away as Detroit, St Louis, and Boston "to look us over and pick a bride. They would come to the church. You'd think we were up for sale."[23] Within a short period, usually after completing their contracts, the women left domestic service to marry.

On the whole, the experiment with the girls proved mutually beneficial. They were delivered from the loneliness and poverty of the orphanages and were admitted to Canada at a time when their refugee status and their classification as Asiatics would have obstructed their entry. Lacking specialized job skills outside of housework and fancywork and unable to speak English well, the Armenian women found that domestic labour provided them with a respectable job and an independent source of income, at least until they were married. It enabled many to sponsor other relatives, fulfil responsibilities to family members, and contribute to building up and maintaining community activities. While domestic labour may have been viewed as a low-status job by Canadian women, the Armenian girls were content to have a job in such refined surroundings. Being alone in an English-speaking household, furthermore, gave these young women a crash course in English. Through contact with their Canadian employers, they learned about Canada and Canadian attitudes, values, and culture. When, for example, one of the girls came home wearing lipstick, her employer discretely counselled her that she was too young, too pretty, and too refined to be a "painted woman." In such small but important ways, the girls managed to adjust relatively painlessly to Canadian society, a tribute to Rev. Pierce's choice of placement and to the employers themselves, particularly the women. At the same time the girls performed an essential service in Canadian society.

Young Businessmen

The fourth group under discussion in Toronto involves a growing entrepreneurial class composed of small shopkeepers and tradesmen. Newcomer refugees, like the Georgetown young men and Fegan's young men, joined old-timers in branching out into commercial activity. Most of these newcomers started off in low-paying jobs in central or east-end Toronto, and when they moved into self-employment, they preferred to remain in the downtown core.

Noting that most Armenians were moulders or iron workers, a report by the Immigration Department in 1923 complained that "not a few of them are engaged as store-keepers and they are getting into that line as fast as they can." For newcomers, starting a business offered a way of coping with discrimination, lack of skills, faulty English, and unemployment or dead-end jobs, especially during the Depression. It was a viable means of upward mobility, and it required little initial capital outlay, enabled family members to contribute their energies, and paid good dividends for hard work and long hours. If the newcomers had any doubt about the potential for business in this new land of opportunity, they had only to tread into the stately home of Levon Babayan, called Armavir, and situated atop the York Mills hill, overlooking the city of Toronto.[24]

An analysis of the Toronto experience reveals the complex process of business development. Often two men – sometimes brothers, sometimes friends – put together their meagre savings and either bought a business or started their own. Some of these fledgling businesses succumbed to bankruptcy; others prospered. In time the men dissolved the partnership, perhaps amicably, perhaps inimically; then each man established his own business. The partnership structure enabled men to be masters of their own affairs in the long run. It was an effective mechanism for newcomers to make inroads into the commercial pulse of Canadian society. Nevertheless, not everyone relished partnerships and some found other ways of engaging in business: here a man lived frugally for a number of years and put together his savings, and instead of buying a house, as was the main preoccupation in the older settlements, he opened a little shop; there another might start an enterprise in his living quarters and gradually expand it into a store. These initial attempts inevitably reflected a form of apprenticeship in Canadian business practice, and they were, initially, often marked by failure. Indeed, the general pattern invariably included a number of attempts, often in different types of businesses. Just as the sojourners changed jobs until they found relatively secure employment, so these young newcomers moved from job to job and from business to business until they hit on the right formula. As they picked up the language and "learned the ropes" some succeeded admirably.

The following account by one of the Georgetown young men provides a glimpse of early beginnings: the struggle to get on one's feet, the sacrifices required to start a business, failures and setbacks, successful ventures, perseverence, the conditions of work, and the contributions of man and wife. After he left the farm, Yeprem Kerbekian worked at Kneider's dairy in Dunnville and then for Sarvis, an Englishman, who made and sold candy. Kerbekian arrived in Toronto in 1936 with his motorcycle, which he promptly sold for $125. This he added to about $75 he had saved from his Dunnville earnings of $5 a week. In Toronto he stayed in a cheap room on Church Street for $1.50 a week and after three months found a job at Basil's restaurant at Yonge and Gerrard Streets washing dishes for $11 a week and all the food he could eat. He worked there for six months and systematically gave the wife of Percy Kalagian, one of his friends, $5 one week and $10 the next, to bank for him, as he was on shift work.

Yeprem wanted to work for himself, "to be independent." He reasoned that if he could run the shop for Sarvis successfully, he could do it for myself. By summer he had enough money saved up to buy a business. At that time, Mampré Shirinian (another Georgetowner) was in the process of buying Gregory Kasparian's fruit store (Rosedale Fruit Market) at Bloor and Sherbourne. Yeprem bought Mampré's grocery business, located at 207 Wellesley (near Sherbourne), for $500 cash and $25 a month for five months. "I used to get up at six. Go to the food terminal by street car. The wholesale fruit market was at the foot of Yonge Street, at Front. I put fruit on the sidewalk in front of the store."

Yeprem used to "hang around Nakashian's Ideal Cleaners on Church street." Nakashian, a World War I veteran, and his wife introduced Yeprem to one of the young domestics, Dikranouhi Khazarosian, who had come in 1930 from the Lazeer orphanage in Lebanon. They were married in 1938 and lived in a room at the back of the store. "I had no lease. Didn't know what lease meant. I just bought the business. My first business ... When I got married, the landlord jacked the rent up from $40 to $60. A few months later we had to get out. It was a miserable time. My wife was pregnant. I closed the business. Who would buy it? Not that easy to sell it. We were living in a dump on Church Street. A cheap rooming house. I couldn't apply for welfare. My wife wouldn't accept welfare. All I had in the bank was $2!" "I never borrowed money. From Babayan? I would know better than to ask him for money. I never entertained an idea like that! In those days you had to do it on your own. Sink or swim. My friends couldn't loan me any money. What they had they needed for themselves. They were struggling like me."

As luck would have it, Kerbekian discovered another suitable store for rent on Bleeker Street (in Toronto's Cabbagetown) and immediately set about recommencing business, selling the little stock remaining from his first store. For the shop and a small apartment he paid $40 a month rent. Gradually his bare-shelved confectionery began to sparkle with a variety of items: soft drinks, chocolate bars, chewing gum, pins and needles, thread, bobby pins, and the ever-popular meat pies. Yeprem and his wife worked hard from 8 A.M. to 1 A.M., and "the cash register was jingling all day long." For the first four years they were just breaking even, but from 1943 to 1944, they made enough profit to buy a brand new house in Leaside. Thus, twenty years after immigrating to Canada, and after several years in farm labour, in low paying jobs, and in his own business, Yeprem Kerbekian could risk buying his own house. In 1945 Yeprem sold his business for twenty-eight hundred dollars.[25]

The interaction between young survivors like Kerbekian, Kasparian, and Shirinian and the interweaving of their lives reflects the creation of kith-and-kin networks similar to those already discussed among the Keghi Armenians and, in its own fashion, to the far-flung international channels of the Toronto "élite." As the Georgetown and Fegan young men put together some money, they sponsored their sisters' and brothers' emigration to Canada, usually through the auspices of the Armenian Relief Association and then the United Church. The bonds of fraternity already shaped by the national tragedy and their common experiences in orphanages were cemented by marrying each other's sisters, acting as each other's best men, and pledging as godfather for each other's children. These links extended into business as well. They hired one another and sold business and real estate to each other, bearing in mind practicality and profit, along with friendship and loyalty.[26] Buying and selling each other's businesses was a common feature of entrepreneurial expedience among these young people, who were anxious to plant roots in the new land. Such activity not only reflected their initial insecurities in the Canadian commercial milieu but also expressed and solidified their reciprocal dependencies.

To get an idea of the variegated pattern of enterprise, let us examine the experience of a small group of these young people. Their ambition and optimism led them into commercial ventures that crisscrossed a key geographic area in downtown Toronto during the 1930s and 1940s.

After working at Ryan's Antiques in Toronto, Gregory Kasparian, a young orphan, tried his hand, unsuccessfully, at a small business. He returned to Ryan's and in 1931 he and another orphan, Vahé Alexanian, pooled one hundred dollars each and plunged into a grocery business, the Sherbourne Fruit Market on Howard Street near Wellesley and Sherbourne. The following year, when Alexanian bought him out, Kasparian borrowed two hundred dollars to open a grocery store at Bloor and Sherbourne, the Rosedale Fruit Market. Here, he and his wife worked diligently and enjoyed six years of success catering to the wealthy clientele of Rosedale. The business relied heavily on a telephone delivery service, for which Kasparian hired young Armenian newcomers to deliver groceries on their bicycles. In 1938 he sold his grocery store to Mampré Shirinian, one of the Georgetown men, who, in turn, disposed of his grocery shop on Wellesley Street to Yeprem Kerbekian (who was discussed above). In the meantime, Kasparian joined up with Percy Kalagian, who sold his rug cleaning business, Orient Rugs, to Varteres Nahabedian, one of the Fegan's boys, for nine hundred dollars. In 1938, Kasparian and Kalagian each put up five thousand dollars and bought the Turco-Persian Rug company from Mrs Utudjian. The deal included the business, the building, and the equipment and truck. Mrs Utudjian's husband had died a few years earlier, and running the business, even with the help of family, proved too burdensome for her. After eleven years Kalagian sold his share of Turco-Persian to Kasparian and moved to Grimsby, where he started his own shop; Kasparian continued to run Turco-Persian. Meanwhile, Alexanian sold his fruit business on Howard Street to Hagop Souin, whose first store had been on Wellesley and Sherbourne, not far from Mgrdich Khashmanian's shoe repair and shoe shine store. Alexanian decided to emigrate to the United States, where he created a fancy line of designer clothing under the Count Alexander label.

Inevitably, exploitation and cheating occurred in these transactions, but in such an environment, kith-and-kin connections imposed serious limitations on the maxim of Business is business. A person's honour and future relationship in the community constrained an unbridled market approach. By the same token, some interviewees refused to deal with their co-ethnics, either to work for them, hire them, or buy from and sell to them. They felt that no matter how they behaved, they would be open to criticism.

The variety of enterprises among Armenian newcomers runs the full gamut of endeavours: boardinghouses, barber shops, dry cleaning establishments, restaurants and coffee shops, fish and chip stores, ice cream parlours, grocery stores, shoe repair shops, shoe shine parlours, tailor and dressmaking shops, confectioneries, photography shops. Notwithstanding such variety, the rug trade, a traditional Armenian industry, emerged as the principal business enterprise.

THE RUG BUSINESS

The single most popular entrepreneurial activity in Toronto was the rug business. For Armenians the creation and possession of an oriental carpet carries special significance. In the old land, people used rugs on floors and walls, in doorways, as throws on sofas, as covers over horses and as suitcases. The role of the carpet determined its size, the choice of yarn, the colour range, and the artistic design. When a young couple married, their most important nuptial possessions were carpets, for rugs combined practicality with aesthetic beauty. The exquisite designs, the richness and subtlety of colours, and the lustre and sheen of the wool or silk gave the hearth warmth and vivacity and "held before the possessors a constant reminder of their hopes, beliefs, and prayers."[27]

Even before the Christian era, Armenians took meticulous care to express their art, culture, history, and traditions in the carpets they created. The process began with spinning the wool fleece into yarn or spinning silk cocoons into silk thread. Then dyers, who were considered highly specialized artisans, concocted a host of colours, notably the cochineal red, and created myriad ways to render the dyes more colour-fast. After the yarn had been dyed several times and left in the sun to dry, it was ready to be woven. Intricate and often stylized designs – the dragon, turtle, pomegranate, rose, phoenix, eagle, and serpent and the tree of life – symbolized elements of Armenian values, religion, folk tales, folk beliefs, and legends. Once the yarn was prepared and the design created, the painstaking job of weaving the carpet began. In urban centres rugs were often woven in ateliers; they were also woven by members of a single village or by a single family. Men, women, and children all contributed their energies to the creation of a carpet. At the turn of the twentieth century, the estimated number of looms in the towns of Sivas and Caesarea alone exceeded ten thousand, and probably more than twelve thousand Armenian carpet weavers were working in the same regions.[28]

As Armenians migrated to different countries, they took their art of rug weaving with them and established workshops in the Middle East, Iran, India, and Europe, sometimes essentially establishing the industry. Armenian merchants also traded in rugs, and they are credited with introducing the Oriental carpet to Italy, France, and the Netherlands. Rugs seen in Renaissance paintings may be the product of Armenian weaving, and the compositions "may have connections with earlier Armenian examples found in Armenian churches in the early 14th century."[29] In his magnificent volume on the Christian Oriental rug, Volkmar Gantzhorn confirms that these Renaissance rugs "are non-figurative icons, religious objects of the Oriental Christian churches, and along with [certain] other textiles, [they are] the greatest contribution of Armenian art to the history of world art ... the authorship of these works having been attributed subsequently to [Turkish] invaders, either through ignorance or manipulation. The heritage of oriental rug motifs is an important element of Armenian identity and must be treated as such."[30]

Around 1894, Paul Courian, his wife Pauline, their two sons (William and Nubar), and Mrs Courian's brothers, Pierre and Levon Babayan, fled Constantinople and immigrated via Constanza to Canada. Earlier, Courian had spent some years in the United States, probably in the rug business in San Francisco. His connections with rug importers and exporters in England, his contacts with weavers in Persia and Turkey, and his own considerable capital were essential assets in setting up a retail rug business in Montreal by the turn of the century, with his brother-in-law Levon Babayan as store manager.

Babayan, born in 1875, was just embarking on a career when insecurity and brutality compelled him to leave Constantinople.[31] The story is rather hazy, but judging from the *Toronto City Directories*,

Babayan had established Levon Babayan and Company Rugs and Carpets at 9 King Street East by 1900. By 1905, Courian had left Montreal, and the two men had formed a partnership, Courian Babayan and Company, Oriental Rugs, at 40–42 King Street East in Toronto. By 1915, Babayan had parted ways with his brother-in-law, probably inimically. Paul Courian and Sons continued at 40–42 King Street East and Babayan opened his own operations at 77 Bay Street.[32] By the 1920s, then, two Armenian Oriental rug stores were operating in Toronto's downtown core.[33] Socrates Utudjian, like Courian, a Protestant from Constantinople, initially worked for the Courian Babayan firm, then opened his own Turco-Persian Rug company, cleaning and repairing carpets.[34]

This small group of pre-1914 pioneers set very important precedents in Toronto, not only by showing the potential of entrepreneurial activity but also, more specifically, by serving as living proof of the commercial potential of the rug business. Just as the factory provided initial insertion into the labour force for newcomers in Brantford, Galt, or Preston, so the carpet industry provided jobs for newcomers in Toronto and later in Montreal, Hamilton, and Windsor. Not only did immigrants find jobs in the carpet trade, but aspiring young people also learned the skills necessary to open their own businesses. Arsen Baronian and his wife Satenig, for instance, worked on a farm near Winona, then for Turco-Persian, before opening their own Anglo-Persian Rug Cleaning company as a family enterprise on the first floor of their home on Jarvis Street in Toronto.

Some men, like George Der Stepanian and, later, Georges Yeremian, brought their knowledge of carpets with them from the old land. As a child in school in the old country, Der Stepanian first wove with paper and then darned socks, and finally, in an orphanage, he learned to weave rugs.[35] In Canada, Der Stepanian worked for a time for Turco-Persian, then moved to Brantford to clean and repair rugs for the Brantford Laundry. In 1946–47, he opened his own rug cleaning and sales operations in Brantford.

Unlike Der Stepanian, most young men learned the Oriental carpet business in North America. During the early years of the Depression, for example, two young refugees took the chance of opening their own rug cleaning and repairing store in Vancouver. Kevork Cachazn, one of the Fegan's boys, and Kerop Bedoukian, born in Sivas in 1907, had both survived the horrors of the Genocide and were anxious to start afresh in Canada.[36] They rented a reasonably priced single-story building on Thirteenth Avenue, just off Granville Street, the main artery. Fixing the place up, advertising for business, and then purchasing a second-hand car depleted their meagre resources in the first month. For the sake of economy, they moved into the store, where "we slept, cooked, ate and got on each other's nerves until we could hardly stand each other." Eventually, Bedoukian sold his share to Cachazn and returned to Toronto, where his widowed mother, Serpouhi "Mama" Bedoukian, ran a boarding house, primarily for the young orphan men. Soon afterwards, Bedoukian tried his luck in Montreal (1933): "I had to create a job. I decided to canvass stores, offering to do repairs on Oriental rugs. So I bought a cardboard suitcase for $1.98, filled it with needles and balls of wool in a variety of colours, and considered myself in business. For three days I forced myself to go to department stores and rug dealers, but I did not find work ... On the third day, H. Lalonde and Frères on Park Ave gave me a rug to repair (Lalonde sold oriental carpets) ... During this time, Eaton's hired me to repair a pile of damaged rugs. People could watch me while I sat in the rug department, working. Whenever someone asked me a question, I handed him my card ... there was also quite a demand for rug cleaning."

An enterprising young man, he soon rented a large building at a reasonable cost. The space offered plenty of room to repair, wash, and hang the rugs up to dry. Using his skills as a tailor – skills learned in the orphanage overseas – Bedoukian repaired rugs himself and washed them "with the care of a mother washing her baby." The myth preceded him: "People accepted me as an expert simply because I was Armenian." Eventually he saved enough money to buy a brand new truck and had ARARAT, his company name, painted on it. Satisfied with his achievements, he had his picture taken in front of his new vehicle and sent the photo to his mother as proof that he was fully "in business for himself." [37]

Mike Ounjian also learned his craft in America. Originally from Aintab, Ounjian fled to the United States before the war, and after a stint in the United States Army he took a job with the Nahigian Brothers rug company in Chicago. Here he learned the special chemical-wash formula for new Persian rugs. In 1924 he started his own business in Toronto, the Eastern Rug Cleaning company on Croft Street. The long hours, the heavy work of lifting carpets, and a growing clientele encouraged him to invite his two brothers, Charlie and Dick, also employed by the Nahigian's, as well as his brother-in-law, John Poladian to join him. Charlie's expertise in repairing carpets enabled the family to expand in this line of work.

After working for Babayan for seven years, another young man, Oksen Teghtsoonian, ventured out on his own by cleaning rugs in the basement of his home and repairing them in his kitchen with the help of his sister. When this arrangement proved unsatisfactory because of his growing family, he organized a little business in 1932 selling and repairing rugs in a section of Ridpath's fine furniture store on Yonge Street in Toronto.

I suggested a space about twelve feet by eighteen, near the Oak room ... instead of a fixed monthly rental for the space, perhaps it would be better to charge me a rate of commission on sales. If we made big sales, Ridpath's would make good profit for their space with no investment at all. On the other hand, if we didn't make enough sales to satisfy us both, the plan could come to an end ... the sales were to be made under Ridpath's name ... I was the sole proprietor of the stock, and I was to fix the prices of the carpets, to be competitive. I was willing to accept Mr Ridpath's suggested commission of 15 percent on sale prices.

This much accomplished, I rushed downtown to see Mr Babayan to sell him on the idea of giving me a stock of rugs. He was interested and wanted to know where this store was and wanted to see the place ... He was impressed with the display of fine furniture and agreed to give me a very limited number of rugs – fifteen – on a trial basis ...

I fixed the place nicely and waited for my first customer. Believe it or not, I made a sale the very first day ... I took a cheque for $270 of my own money and went to Babayan's to pay for the carpet. Mr Babayan was surprised and impressed by such a quick sale and prompt payment and told me that I could have another batch of rugs, say fifteen or twenty more pieces ... In 1936 [4 years after he started] I had over three hundred pieces of rugs in my store worth perhaps, with today's valuation, over $300,000. All this size of business with no capital of my own, purely on consignment, trust, and credit, was no small achievement.[38]

Courian and Babayan not only sold rugs, they also imported them, primarily from England, Turkey, and Persia. On a regular basis they made buying trips abroad, trips that lasted several months and took them to several countries. Their knowledge and skill in purchasing carpets, in building up stock, in working in the local languages, in networking in different parts of the world, and in possessing the financial resources to buy at the right time and in the right place were requisites for a successful endeavour.

As in the old country, the carpet business in Canada involved both men and women. Men were solely responsible for importing and selling rugs and for the heavy work of washing and drying them. They were often hired to combine selling rugs and working in the office. But as more and more women acquired the language and commercial training, they took on jobs in the office.[39] In addition, women shared the task of repairing rugs with men. Almost every Armenian carpet repair shop employed Armenian women at one time or another. The women, moreover, were working in "Armenian" surroundings; hence they were deemed safe from outside corruption. Women who had learned to crochet, embroider, knit, and do needlework in orphanages used these skills to repair and renew carpets. Lucy Postalian described how she carved out her own business refurbishing rugs. "Nobody taught me about rugs. If you know how to knit or crochet, repairing a carpet is easy." She would unravel the carpet to figure out the stitch, seek out wool that was compatible in weight and colour, or dye the yarn for a good colour match: "There are many ways of dyeing the wool so that it is an exact match with the rug. Especially with old rugs."[40] With her skills, ingenuity, and imagination, Postalian became an expert at repairing rugs and was recognized in Toronto as one of the best professionals in this line of work. As a measure of her expertise, the Royal Ontario Museum often consulted her about carpet renewal.

In his autobiography, Oksen Teghtsoonian notes that Babayan had plans for a coast-to-coast carpet-store chain. The elderly merchant established promising young employees in stores in cities that could sustain such a business and loaned them his rugs on consignment. Aris Alexanian, in Hamilton, and Paul Postian, in London were initially backed by Babayan, somewhat in the manner of a franchise. Paul Sivadjian, in Windsor, and Yervant Pasdermajian, in Montreal, opened branch stores. Babayan's hopes for a national chain, however, were dashed by the stock market crash, but his efforts had given enough impetus to young, ambitious, and diligent men to encourage them to try their own luck. Gradually men opened Oriental rug businesses in other parts of the country: in Montreal, Windsor, Oakville, Grimsby, Ottawa, Vancouver, Winnipeg, London, St Catharines, Brantford, Montreal, Galt (Cambridge), and Hamilton.

On one of their frequent visits to Paris, the Babayans met Yervant Pasdermajian, a relative of Mrs Babayan, and agreed to sponsor his admission to Canada. Pasdermajian, born in Ceasarea in 1906, had survived the Genocide and the nightmare of the burning and evacuation of Smyrna. He landed in Salonika with nothing but the rags he was wearing but thankful that he and his brothers were still alive. Eventually he made his way to France, where he learned the art of rug restoration in an Armenian firm. Babayan employed Pasdermajian in his Toronto store from 1925 to 1928. During the prosperous years of the late 1920s Babayan opened a branch store in Montreal, and Pasdermajian, whose knowledge of rugs and of the French language were decided assets, was transferred there with a senior non-Armenian employee in charge. The business, situated on St Catharines Street West, was badly hit during the Depression and Babayan closed the store in 1934. In the following year, Pasdermajian opened his own store in Westmount – Yervant's Oriental Rugs – selling and servicing carpets. Initially he brought in his stock on consignment from Babayan, or he bought directly from the bonded warehouses in London, England, where Armenian merchants had established themselves during the nineteenth century, and later on he himself travelled on buying trips to the East.[41] Pasdermajian's brothers, Hrant and Hagop, emigrated from France to join him in the business. In the beginning Yervant Pasdermajian cleaned and repaired rugs himself, but with prosperity he opened a factory that specialized in cleaning and repairing. When broadloom became fashionable and popular after the war, he realized they "could not fight the trend, so we joined it. For a while, oriental rugs were only a very small percentage of our business ... We opened a second store which specialized in broadloom on Côtes des Neiges."[42]

The rug industry allowed a man to be his own master and to do so in a way that linked him to the Armenian past and the Armenian homeland, and gave him a measure of prestige and respect in Canadian society. For some of the newcomers, like Pasdermajian in Montreal and Alexanian in Hamilton, the rug trade meant considerable wealth. Their diligence, hard work, astute business sense, and scrupulous integrity enabled them to build renowned establishments.[43] For a small number, selling and servicing rugs was the road to wealth, but the rug trade should not be regarded as a panacea – an easy road to comfort and riches. The business involved more than elegant shops with exotic furnishings and exquisite rugs. Like factory work the rug trade could be hard, dirty, and heavy. It took big, strong men to lift and roll the rugs, to wash, dry, carry, and deliver them. Men had to be careful not to rupture themselves when they were moving wet eight-by-ten and nine-by-twelve-foot rugs. As a critic of the rug business muttered, "To get involved in carpets, you had to be strong in the back and weak in the mind."[44]

Nevertheless, the rug business provided an outlet for labour for both men and women and thus fulfilled an important function in the community, a function somewhat similar to the role of the iron factory in the older settlements. More significantly, rug merchants like Kerop Bedoukian and Yervant Pasdermajian, in Montreal, and Gregory Kasparian, in Toronto, often sponsored immigrants and provided them with jobs. Pasdermajian and Bedoukian, who were heavily immersed in the work of the Canadian Armenian Congress, also provided lodgings for newcomers.

The rug trade generated spin-offs for many industrious, ambitious, and creative young people: Set Adourian, Archie Ajemian, Aris Alexanian, Sarkis Alexanian, Jack Apramian, Martin Avedisian, Arsen

Baronian, Paul Postian, George Der Stepanian, Yervant Selyan, Kevork Semerjian, Paul Sivadjian John Sohigian, the Tamakian family, and Setrag Tatarian, to name a small number in southern Ontario towns, could work for someone else, acquire some experience, then start their own business in selling and servicing Oriental rugs and later, broadloom as well. An informal survey of sixty-five Armenian families in Toronto during the interwar period revealed that members of at least forty-one, including both women and men, had worked in the carpet business at one time or another in their lives – importing, selling, cleaning, repairing, dyeing, delivering, or clerking in the office. For some, like the Tamakian family, the rug business developed into a family enterprise (the Indo-Persian company) and enabled men and women, young and old, to contribute their talents and their time to a family venture and to pass on their contacts and expertise to their relatives.

To a few the rug trade brought wealth and fame. For some it represented the chance to be one's own boss, to make use of family labour, and to be financially independent. For the rank and file, the rug industry offered a simple and decent living. Armenian employees were prepared to work long hours at low pay with the tacit understanding of a measure of job security. At the same time, such business practices enabled the owners to get a firm grip on the rug trade, particularly in Toronto. Armenian concentration in the carpet business and the tradition of mutual assistance enabled the owners to dominate the Oriental rug trade in Canada by the 1940s.[45] What is even more significant, this concentration was part of a far-flung network of Armenian rug merchants and traders that stretched halfway around the globe.

Aside from its role among Armenians, the carpet industry also had an impact on the larger Canadian society. Armenians contributed their knowledge, skills, and contacts. Through their networks, they imported some of the finest examples of Oriental rugs to Canada. By sales and auctions in different towns, the rug merchants made their wares accessible to Canadians who might otherwise have had little opportunity to buy such treasures. Their contribution in importing and selling rugs was matched by their skill in repairing and renewing old and damaged carpets.

Not only did the rug merchants sell and service oriental carpets, but they also taught their customers about the artistic value of these gems. Oksen Teghtsoonian, for example, gave regular lectures at Ridpath's and in small Ontario towns like Barrie. He elaborated on the various motifs, types, and characteristics, the proper care, and the role of the Oriental carpet in home decoration. Pasdermajian gave slide presentations of the different types and origins of Oriental rugs and showed movies depicting how they are made. In his turn Babayan wrote a book describing Oriental rugs and their care. The Sacred Tree motif, he explained, "is the symbol ... of hope itself. The tree indicates life everlasting ... The Tree of Life is usually represented by a Cypress, because that variety best suggests unending life; Cypress wood is almost indestructible and is seemingly little affected by the corrupting influences of time."[46] Such lectures and books were excellent marketing devices, on the one hand, and a means of enlightening Canadians about the precious and expensive items they were purchasing, on the other. Thus, by their activities and acumen, Armenians encouraged an appreciation for this art form while they pursued and developed a trade that was almost nonexistent in Canada before their arrival.

During the interwar period, furthermore, Armenian rug merchants introduced a totally new concept of merchandising with branch stores and buying on consignment. They established a type of franchise marketing long before such entrepreneurial practices were common in the Dominion. After World War II, new arrivals found the rug business already well entrenched among their co-ethnics, and they could more readily move into the trade. When broadloom became popular, Armenians were able to diversify and expand their operations to include the sale and installation of broadloom as well, and this, in turn, led to such enterprises as the Alexanian family chain of stores.

In Toronto and Montreal, the post–World War I newcomers – relatively poor refugees, but young and energetic – were anxious to excel in the new land. Just as the young refugees revitalized the aging communities in St Catharines, Hamilton, and Brantford, so also, the refugees brought their enthusiasm and vigour to Toronto and Montreal. Unlike the older settlements, however, where the refugees adopted many of the ways of the old-timers, the Toronto and Montreal newcomers, with a whole host of different background experiences, dominated the Armenian community. When they migrated to the big city, these young people found no existing Armenian neighbourhood that might welcome them, no single plant that might employ them, and no political organization or religious institution that might embrace them. On the other hand, they did not find a social, economic, religious, or political milieu that would limit and restrict them. They had been levelled by the Genocide, and now they were all carving a niche in a great land of opportunity.

For the young newcomers, the élite served as a role model, an important model that dispelled the debilitating sense that Armenians were impoverished, downtrodden, and oppressed. The élite were living examples of Armenians who had prospered and were respected in both Armenian and Canadian circles. The precedent was set; the young refugees took it with growing self-confidence. They "took off," and in the process they demonstrated that a lack of education neither constrained enterprise nor stifled intelligence.

In dealing with their new environment Armenians relied on an age-old tradition of mutual help. They supported each other not in an organized way but in an informal manner, not based on cash but on friendship, mutuality, and reciprocity. They helped one another get started, loaned money if they could, offered training, credit, information, and easier terms of purchase. Those who could gave jobs to their countrymen, sometimes in an exploitative way. Mutual help was not without ill will and discord. Tensions between people were inevitable, and internally this type of fractiousness and feuding occurred and was compounded by political differences. Interviewee reaction to the Babayans is a prime example of this dichotomy. Some who worked for them in the store, plant, or home complained that they were stingy taskmasters. Others appreciated Babayan for his business acumen and his willingness to hire newcomers.

Overall, the impression of the new society Armenian immigrants were creating is one of mutual assistance and a complex web of interdependency. The exuberance of these young men and women found fertile ground in Montreal and Toronto. Newcomers were attracted to the city by the availability of jobs, inexpensive rental accommodation, and readily accessible and cheap transportation. Some immigrants managed to put enough money together to buy into a business, especially if they found a willing partner. In the process, they manifested a spirit of individualism, like their confreres in St Catharines, as they came to terms with the conflicting values of the Old World and the New. The big city offered good scope for commercial enterprise, and these young men and women were eager to grasp opportunities and make the best of them. Little did they know they were the forerunners of Armenian communities that would flourish as the century advanced.

17

New Communities: The Third Wave, 1950–1988

As in the period before and after World War I, the Canadian immigration program, including immigration policy, laws, and their implementation, played a key role in the movement of Armenians to Canada and hence in the size, structure, and composition of the Armenian community. Changes in the Canadian immigration program in the 1960s and 1970s, coinciding with upheaval and instability in the Middle East, where Armenian refugees had found asylum after the Genocide, helped to rejuvenate and redirect Armenian community life in Canada.

With the inclusion of Armenians under the restrictive terms of P.C. 2115 (16 September 1930) and the general decline of immigration during the Depression and World War II, Armenian movement to Canada effectively came to a halt. In May 1947, Prime Minister Mackenzie King announced that Canada would again open the immigration doors, at least to the extent that newcomers could be absorbed into the Canadian economy. The Dominion was also prepared to give refuge to some of those displaced by the war, but only to the point where the composition of the Canadian population would not change. "The people of Canada," emphasized the prime minister, "do not wish to make a fundamental alteration in the character of our population," and he added, "large-scale immigration from the orient would change the fundamental composition of the Canadian population." The government would open its doors to immigration for population growth and economic development, but it had no intention of removing the existing regulations curtailing Asiatic immigration "unless and until alternative measures of effective control have been worked out."[1]

In the same month, Canada repealed the restrictive Chinese Immigration Act, which had virtually blocked Chinese immigration to Canada since 1923. The initiative gave Armenians a shaft of hope that they, in turn, would be treated with greater leniency. However, because they were designated as Asiatics, Armenians continued to be virtually excluded from entry. After many years of waiting, Armenian Canadians continued to feel frustrated in their attempts to bring in surviving relatives.

THE CANADIAN ARMENIAN CONGRESS

Formation of the Congress

Two issues pressed Armenian leaders in Canada to focus on immigration: the Asiatic designation and the fate of about thirty-five hundred Armenian displaced persons in refugee camps in Europe. In 1948, George Mardikian and Suren Saroyan of San Francisco, founders of the Armenian National Committee to aid Homeless Armenians (ANCHA) visited Canada in a fund-raising drive to provide emergency aid to these Armenian war victims and to arrange their movement to the United States. Taking the lead from ANCHA, on 3 April 1948 a small group of Armenian leaders established the Canadian Armenian Congress (CAC) as an independent, voluntary, nonprofit, nonpolitical, and nondenominational organization to deal with the immigration issue – initially for the displaced persons.

Possessing almost no funds, the CAC nevertheless undertook the ambitious task of facilitating the immigration of "desirable" Armenians to Canada, assisting in their resettlement, and promoting an "appreciation of the Canadian way of life."[2] So reasonable was the congress in its dealings with government authorities, so even-handed with Armenian factions and institutions, and so effective in helping newcomers, that the flow of Armenians to Canada in the postwar period – first from Europe, then from the Middle East – cannot be considered without reference to the congress and its work. Members, advisors, and the executive came from all parts of the country. They included John (Jack) H. Mooradian (Hamilton), the first president; Dr. Joseph Saine (Montreal) vice-president; Martin Avedisian (Galt), secretary; Yervant Pasdermajian (Montreal), assistant secretary; John Kostigian (Galt), vice-chairman; Kevork Semerjian (Toronto), treasurer; Tom Apegian (Brantford), counselor; Kerop Bedoukian (Montreal), counsellor and later corresponding secretary; and the noted photographer Yousuf Karsh (Ottawa), honorary chairman. By 1952 the major centre of operations had shifted from Hamilton to Montreal, under the able presidency of Yervant Pasdermajian.

Immediately upon its formation, the CAC applied to the Canadian government to rescind the Asiatic designation. It made this initial move because it was an incorrect racial and cultural designation of Armenians and because the categorization virtually prohibited the immigration of Armenians to Canada. Government officials, however, claimed that the designation of "Asiatic race" was not from an "ethnological," i.e., racial, perspective but from a "geographic" one.[3]

Canadian Immigration Regulations

On 22 March 1949, Hugh L. Keenleyside, deputy minister of mines and resources, sent a confidential note to F.P. Varcoe, deputy minister of justice, stating that the minister (Colin Gibson) had asked him to prepare for Cabinet approval recommendations that would modify existing regulations regarding the admission of Asiatics, to the extent of admitting Armenians, Lebanese, and Syrians who complied with requirements applicable to European immigrants. The goal, it seems, was to rescind P.C. 2115, which limited all Asian immigration, and replace it with a regulation restricting the admission of Asians *except* Armenians, Lebanese, and Syrians. These three groups would still be classified as Asians, but provisions of entry would be broader, and similar to those governing European immigration (P.C. 4849).[4] This recommendation generated prolonged discussion and correspondence about entry regulations of the three groups and about the wisdom of repealing or revising regulations. For instance, at one point, it was suggested not to rescind P.C. 2115 but to amend it to exclude immigrants of Armenian, Lebanese, or Syrian origin.[5] But on 12 May 1949, a memo for file from Arthur L. Jolliffe, director of the Immigration Branch, noted that Cabinet had decided *not* to make any changes in the regulations governing the admission of the three groups.[6]

On 20 May 1949, Jolliffe wrote that the minister had decided (May 19) that the government *would* admit to Canada by order-in-council Armenians, Lebanese, and Syrians who came within a broader class of relatives such as were defined in P.C. 4849, subject to compliance with the usual requirements (i.e., health, security). Where settlement conditions were satisfactory, the cases were to be recommended to Cabinet for the waiving of P.C. 2115. In other words, on paper the three groups were to continue to be dealt with under the terms of P.C. 2115, but the restrictions were to be circumvented somewhat, because, in fact, their cases were to be heard by Council under the broader provisions of P.C. 4849. The minister's decision gave Armenians a ray of hope for family reunification.

Then in July, Colin Gibson recommended that P.C. 2115 be revised to exclude immigrants of Armenian, Lebanese, or Syrian origin and that they should fall under the provisions of P.C. 2743 (of 2 June 1949), which controlled European immigration. In short, the regulations would be revised so as to maintain the designation of Armenians as Asiatics but to treat them as Europeans for immigration purposes. Accordingly, the regulations governing their entry would be relaxed to allow the movement of first-degree relatives of legal residents in Canada, including husband, wife, son, daughter, brother, sister, father, mother, orphan nephews and nieces under twenty-one years of age, and fiancé(e)s.[7]

However, on 29 September, Cabinet decided *not* to revise P.C. 2115 but to consider applications from the three groups for first-degree relatives. The three groups were to continue to fall under the terms of 2115, but they were not to be "absolutely barred by the provisions" of this regulation. "Meritorious individual cases" of first degree relatives of Canadian residents might be dealt with by an appeal to the discretionary powers of the minister. The usual procedure – cumbersome and time-consuming – adhered to the following pattern: after a review of appeals submitted by those who did not come within any of the admissible classes as defined by the current immigration regulations, the minister would or would not give consent. If the minister approved, the potential immigrant's dossier would be forwarded to Cabinet for endorsement. No clear definition was forthcoming regarding "merit," which could be based on humanitarian factors, benefit to Canadian society, or any other criteria deemed meritorious by the minister. The permit issued by the minister was similar to the ministerial prerogative that applied to Armenians during the 1920s.[8]

As Armenians, Lebanese, and Syrians continued to press the government to ease the restrictions against immigration of their relatives, the deputy minister reviewed the situation again in February 1950. In a lengthy memo to the minister, he summarized the reasons for and against the general exemption of the three groups from P.C. 2115. In favour of the exemption, he noted that the three groups were unable to bring their first-degree relatives to Canada. They claimed their culture was like that of Europeans and that they were not Asians in the true sense, i.e., Orientals. Against exemption, he stated – without elaboration – that the three groups were not readily assimilable in Canada and that their activities in Canada, with regard both to "occupation and business" were "extremely limited." He noted also that exempting them would result in "discrimination" in the application of the law. The government of India and East Indians in Canada had also been requesting exemption on the grounds that they were British subjects, members of the Commonwealth, and of Aryan stock. Should the Middle Eastern people be exempted, argued the deputy minister, the Indians would insist ever more vigorously for relaxation for their people as well. Reasoning that any changes to P.C. 2115 would open up immigration from the Middle East and would raise questions about racial discrimination in immigration regulations, he advocated that no changes be made to the current regulations. He recommended that the current procedure whereby Cabinet heard the "meritorious cases ... would to a large extent accomplish what the Near Eastern people desire, namely, the admission of their relatives." In other words, little had changed since 1930. As proof, the department informed a correspondent in April 1951 that the Canadian government could *not* accept Armenians unless they could comply with P.C. 2115, passed 16 September 1930.[9]

Resistance to changing the designation and the regulations was reflected in the movement of Armenian displaced persons to Canada. In 1948, in view of the government's intention to facilitate the entry of about twenty thousand displaced persons, the Canadian Armenian Congress appealed to authorities to allow the admission of five hundred displaced personss from camps in Germany, Austria, and Italy. To enhance their chances, since Canada clearly favoured contract labour, the congress secured assurances of employment for the newcomers from several firms in Hamilton, Ontario, including the International Harvester Company, Glendale Spinning Mills, and the Chipman-Holton Knitting Company. Efforts to bring Armenians in as factory workers, domestics, or farm workers proved as ineffective in the late 1940s as they had during the 1920s. The Cabinet Committee on Immigration took no decision regarding this movement, since Armenians were still classified as Asiatics. Nor did the Immigration Labour Committee look with favour on the "admission of any bulk movement of Armenians for general employment in Canada." In his report, Jolliffe, director of the Immigration Branch, considered it "inadvisable to move Armenian labour to Canada at the present time [1950] due to the unemployment situation," but recommended in rather vague terms that the Immigration Labour Committee "give some serious consideration to the possible employment of Armenians as soon as employment conditions have improved."[10]

A full year later, John Mooradian, then president of the Canadian Armenian Congress, appealed to Walter Harris, minister of the newly formed Department of Citizenship and Immigration. Mooradian expressed his disappointment at the discrimination against Armenians. Congress had been "led to believe by authorities in charge at the time that the Armenian DPs would receive the same consideration as other races under the I.R.O. Constitution [International Refugee Organization, founded in 1946], but the fact proved otherwise because many immigrants have been allowed to enter of many other races with the exception of the Armenians." He was, of course, absolutely right since immigration to Canada after World War II reached unprecedented levels, but initially only a miniscule number of Armenians were allowed admission.[11]

By the end of 1951, Kerop Bedoukian, a Montreal businessman, was able to write about a slight relaxation in the treatment of Armenians. Although the regulations had not changed, a "few people" had entered on "humanitarian" grounds through the minister's permit.[12] This permit, he noted, was based on a wider category of relationships than the more restrictive Asiatic regulations but still required the sponsorship of a legal resident of Canada who was obliged to guarantee a job and lodgings for one year. Bedoukian concluded his letter by emphasizing that the immigration regulations pertaining to Armenians had not changed and that unless the prospective immigrant had an immediate relative in Canada, he would have no hope of admission.[13]

Finally, by regulations passed on 4 July 1952, the provisions of P.C. 2115 were no longer to apply to Armenians. When asked specifically whether the department "no longer classifies the Armenians as Asiatic race," the reply was ambiguous: "The provision[s] of P.C. 2215 [read 2115] which govern the admissibility of persons of Asiatic race are no longer applied to Armenians."[14] The decision to include Armenians and others from the Middle East under the terms of this order-in-council marked an early step towards discontinuing racial categorization as a fundamental bulwark of the Canadian immigration program. For Armenians, too, it was vitally significant. After more than half a century they were no longer to be barred by racial classification. And some, at least, were to be treated like other Europeans. Specifically those born or naturalized in the British Commonwealth or those born in the United States or in France and coming directly from their country of birth were permitted to enter the Dominion if they were sponsored by a legal resident of Canada or if they could prove they had a job or sufficient means to maintain themselves for a reasonable period of time after their arrival. In other words, they could enter with or without sponsorship from the countries mentioned above if they could maintain themselves for a reasonable time after entry. To a degree, the change in policy thus mitigated racial discrimination and expedited family reunification. That is, legal Canadian residents could bring in a husband or wife, son or daughter, brother or sister, together with a father or mother, grandparents, an orphan nephew or niece under twenty-one years of age, and a fiancé/e.[15]

However, Armenians who were in countries other than those listed above and who were *without* family sponsors in Canada were to be dealt with according to their citizenship or country of residence. These terms were confirmed by Departmental Directive No. 46, pertaining to the "Armenian race," which also reiterated the government's willingness to continue to consider "meritorious cases," which would include a wider range of relatives than were usually considered when applying the regulations to Asians. No clear definition was forthcoming for the interchangeable terms "exceptional merit" and "meritorious cases." Such cases were based on the minister's discretion; consideration could be warranted on humanitarian grounds or for public benefit.[16]

With the new Immigration Act and Regulations (1 June 1953) admission to Canada was to be governed by section 20 of the regulations.[17] A numerical accounting indicates the impact of the new regulations as well as the efforts of Armenian Canadians to facilitate immigration: from 1944 to 31 December 1949 inclusive, 47 Armenians entered Canada;[18] from 1 January 1950 to 31 October 1953 inclusive, 259 were admitted; and from 1955 to 1958 inclusive, 815 immigrants of Armenian ethnic origin entered Canada.[19]

To sum up, Armenian Canadians were allowed to sponsor a wider range of family members, as indicated above. On the other hand, the new terms meant that *unsponsored* individuals from Middle Eastern countries (where Canadian inspectorial services were limited)[20] – exactly those states where Armenian survivors had found sanctuary after the Genocide – were largely excluded from entering the dominion.

Sponsorship

The issue of sponsorship played an increasingly important role during the late 1950s and the 1960s. In March 1956, immigration authorities informed the Canadian Armenian Congress that they would allow the organization to sponsor "a limited group of Armenians who, though not within the admissible classes of close relatives, are otherwise able to comply fully with Canadian Immigration requirements," i.e., particularly regarding employment in Canada, health, and security.[21] Again in 1959–60, the government established annual quotas and allowed the congress initially to sponsor fifty applications (not fifty persons) for immigrants of Armenian origin *"who have no close relatives in Canada who could sponsor them"* (italics mine).

For those who were stateless and inadmissible under regulation 20 *because they were not refugees from a European country* and for those who were not in possession of a travel document acceptable under regulation 18(2), the officer in charge was to request the necessary order-in-council authority to waive the regulation after medical and civil examinations had been satisfactorily completed.[22] The issue of nationality was a major problem, since Armenians were not always citizens of the country of domicile. In most cases, wrote W.R. Baskerville, director of immigration, Armenians were not nationals. "In Greece, for example, even Armenians born in Greece cannot acquire the citizenship of the country. In France these persons are refugees. In Lebanon nationality may be obtained so easily that the status is meaningless." Based on these realities, the department stated that Armenians applying for admission "need not be nationals (i.e., citizens) of the countries in which they reside."[23]

In 1961 the government agreed to accept another 100 applications "for the admission of families of Armenian origin who have no close relatives in Canada who could sponsor them." The CAC agreed to provide co-sponsors who were acceptable to the department and who could produce evidence of their ability to guarantee homes, jobs, and maintenance for the immigrants. The congress further agreed to carry the responsibility for transportation of the immigrants to and in Canada and for any further help or care that the immigrants might require.[24] From 1 October 1964 to 29 February 1968, for example, the congress submitted 478 applications to the government on behalf of Armenians from Turkey. Only 72 had co-sponsoring family in Canada; the remaining 406 were sponsored solely by the congress and nonfamily sponsors. Mindful of its responsibilities, the congress was particularly careful to select immigrants who would reflect well on the Canadian-Armenian community.[25]

In dealing with special movements of specific ethnic or religious groups, government authorities preferred to conduct negotiations through a representative organization in Canada, wherever possible.[26] Government officials recognized the work of the CAC and the intelligent leadership of Pasdermajian, and they looked with favour on the record of the new settlers. In a 1959 memo to the minister, Laval Fortier, the deputy minister, confirmed that the government had always given "sympathetic consideration" to the Armenians who are "mainly self-supporting," generally "self-employed as traders" or professionals.[27] Three years later, the director of immigration noted that "Our overall experience with Armenians has been good – at least they have given us no trouble and we are not aware of any problems of integration or economic establishment." In 1962 the same director of immigration reported to the deputy minister that "This [movement of Armenians to Canada] seems to be a particularly well organized scheme and the Canadian-Armenian Congress is obviously seeing to it that persons who come forward are looked after immediately." The deputy minister, Claude M. Isbister, wrote in a confidential memo to the minister that "The Congress has scrupulously honoured its obligations and there are no known cases where the immigrants have not settled in satisfactorily." He reminded the minister that the congress had had two problematic cases and, that rather than jeopardize the movement, it had arranged for the return of these persons to the countries of origin, without reference to the Immigration Department.[28]

To get a sense of the immigrant cohort, let us look at a random selection of the records of a group shortly after their arrival from Egypt in 1962. Their exodus had been prompted by President Gamal Abdul Nasser's nationalization scheme, which was causing immeasurable financial loss to members of the Armenian minority. In all cases the immigrants were married men with children under eighteen, clearly indicating a young cohort:

_____ arrived with two young children, worked as an engraver/printer earning $75–$80 a week.

_____ arrived with two children, worked as an office machines repairman earning about $75 a week.

_____ arrived with two children, worked as a diamond setter.

_____ arrived with two children, had a job as a lathe operator earning $80 a week.

_____ arrived with two children, worked as a die maker/toolmaker, earning $81 weekly.

_____ was a chemist earning $90 a week.

_____ arrived with one child, was an engraver earning $95 weekly.

_____ arrived with three children, was a photographer.

_____ arrived with two young children, worked as a salesman on a commission basis and wrote a typical comment: "It is a privilege to enjoy and share life in Canada."

The Canadian Armenian Congress was grateful for the co-operation of the Department of Immigration. In a general meeting, the CAC expressed its "deep appreciation" to the department, noting that Armenians in different countries were faced with political turmoil and were anxious to emigrate. The CAC firmly believed that Canada was "their hope of [the] promised land." It also believed "that Armenian immigrants, with grateful hearts, [would] wholeheartedly contribute to the development of Canada."[29] In a letter to Pierre Berton, following a television show critical of the Canadian immigration program, Yervant Pasdermajian defended Canadian immigration officials in Cairo against the criticism of painting far too rosy a picture of Canada to prospective immigrants. He praised the placement section of the Immigration Department for their "most sympathetic, helpful, and successful" efforts in finding employment for newcomers commensurate with their ability. He concluded his letter by noting that the main concern of the immigrants was to be able "to bring their relatives and friends to Canada ... they have all taken into consideration that starting a new life in a new country is not the easiest thing in the world, and they were prepared to make certain sacrifices which they are doing willingly."[30]

So successful was the congress in the eyes of both immigrants and Canadian government authorities that the Immigration Department reviewed the status of Armenians in North Africa and the Levant and agreed to allow congress to sponsor Armenian immigrants from those countries or immigrants from those countries now residing in Europe *"without numerical limit"* (italics mine). The department agreed to accept applications from immigrants sponsored by the CAC who

a were desirable persons who did not meet in full the normal occupational requirements;
b were socially or physically handicapped;
c were admissible as sponsored relatives, except for the fact that the financial or economic position of the potential sponsor was not yet secure enough to warrant approval under current immigration procedures; or
d were from Algeria, Egypt, Greece, Iran, Iraq, Israel, Jordan, Kuwait, Lebanon, Libya, Morocco, Syria, Tunisia, or Turkey.

In all cases the congress had to assume *full responsibility* and had to be the formal sponsor, even though the proposed immigrant might have a co-sponsor in Canada. The congress's responsibility was to extend for a period of five years or until the sponsored person became eligible for Canadian citizenship.[31] The congress accepted the terms of the proposal and indicated how greatly the organization valued the department's confidence. It promised to "do everything in [its] power to justify" that confidence.[32] In November 1964, a Revised Operating Memo indicated that the department would accept applications submitted by the congress or *"by individual sponsors, regardless of their relationship to the immigrant,"* for the admission of families of Armenian origin from certain countries, without numerical limit (italics mine). In all cases, the congress was still to be regarded as the official sponsor, since the department considered co-sponsorship a private arrangement between the congress and the person completing the application.[33]

Despite the special arrangements, the "numbers without limit" did not generate a huge movement of Armenian immigrants compared to other ethnic groups, such as Italians or Germans, but the numbers were appreciably greater than they had been before this special arrangement. As indicated above, the CAC rigorously screened for "quality" immigrants. The carte blanche arrangement lasted from 1964 to 1967–68 and facilitated the movement of between forty-five hundred and five thousand people.

Changes in the Canadian Immigration Program

During the 1960s major changes were introduced in the Canadian immigration program. As Freda Hawkins points out, there was dissatisfaction with the racial categorization and the sponsorship procedures. There was a growing demand for "quality migration" in the form of skilled manpower and for a more stable and coordinated immigration program.[34] Because the labour supply was insufficient to meet the needs of the booming economy, the government took steps to update the program and introduce reforms. Towards this end, it published the discussion paper *Canadian Immigration Policy*, otherwise known as the *White Paper* (1966), which emphasized Canada's continued need for immigrants: "Immigration has made a major contribution to the national objectives of maintaining a high rate of population and economic growth." Among other recommendations, the *White Paper* called for an end to ethnic and racial discrimination in the selection of immigrants and stressed a more active interface between immigration and the manpower requirements of the country. "The number of immigrants who can be absorbed depends on the level of their qualifications and how adaptable [they are] to Canadian society."[35] Reflecting this emphasis, the Department of Citizenship and Immigration was restructured as the Department of Manpower and Immigration in 1966. The following year, the Government brought down new regulations that formalized a 1962 initiative replacing the selection of immigrants on the basis of race or nationality with selection on the basis of education, skills, and adaptability. Accordingly, the regulations set up an "ethnic blind" points system that was to be based on education, training, adaptability, language facility, age, arranged employment, presence of relatives in Canada, and area of destination. The weighting was to be flexible and to be tied to the country's changing needs.

A principal impact of these regulations was a shift in source countries. Although the uneven distribution of Canadian immigration offices abroad remained an indirect basis of racial discrimination (as pointed out above regarding the Middle East), the absolute and proportionate number of immigrants from countries formerly designated "undesirable" or nonpreferred increased dramatically. Before 1967 Asian immigration had averaged less than 4 percent but jumped to 23 percent of those "landed" in 1973 and 1974.[36]

As a matter of interest, even before the publication of the *White Paper* and the promulgation of the 1967 regulations, the CAC had established its own system of choosing prospective immigrants based on their qualifications, their potential for easy adaptation to Canadian society, and their ability to be contributing citizens of Canada. But as early as November 1965, departmental officers were expressing dissatisfaction with the practice of private organizations "controlling" a segment of the immigrant flow.[37] Departmental objections to special movements and to organizations as sponsors continued to mount during 1965–66. The fundamental questions were, who should determine entry and how should refugees or quasi-refugees be treated? In a sternly worded memo, B.A. Gorman, chief, Admissions Control Division, probably expressed the dissatisfaction among other officers in the Immigration Branch. He preferred to eliminate all "special movements," notably, Jews under quasi-refugee status and Armenians under the CAC, ironically the same groups that had faced severe immigration restrictions in the past. Failing outright elimination, he recommended a greater measure of control by imposing annual numerical and geographical limitations. "I have heretofore," he emphasized, " and do now object to such concession to particular racial or religious groups. Further, I object strongly to the department soliciting representations from individual racial and religious organizations." He complained about these organizations exercising too much control over immigrants. Their involvement in the immigration and resettlement process, he argued, tended to direct the interests of immigrants inward, toward the racial or religious group, and prevented, or at least deterred, assimilation into the wider Canadian community. Moving then into the area of refugeeism, he maintained that Canadian Jews and Armenians were treated more favourably vis-à-vis other religious or racial groups "whose members are similarly discriminated against and persecuted in some foreign countries." Finally, he recommended that the department terminate all existing "private" arrangements with separate organizations and instead consider representations from organizations and other interested parties on behalf of specific groups whose way of life was incompatible with the customs in the foreign countries in which they resided. The foreign groups most deserving of special consideration would be accepted in numbers representing *a percentage of the total immigration for the previous year*. Selected immigrants would then become the responsibility of the department, rather than of private organizations. He argued that such an arrangement could be "played up as a humanitarian gesture on the part of the government." It would provide a predictable annual flow of such cases, enable the department to regulate distribution across the country and reduce the possibility of establishing "pockets" of racial and religious groups, eliminate the interference of private organizations in the immigration process, and eliminate discrimination in favour of some racial and religious groups in Canada. And it might include refugees as part of this "humanitarian" movement.[38]

In 1968, in an effort to tighten control over immigration, the government withdrew blanket sponsorships from all nongovernment organizations and reconsidered the whole concept of co-sponsorship. On 27 November 1967, R.B. Curry, director of the Immigration branch, notified the congress that "it is neither necessary nor desirable to continue the special sponsorship arrangements made with your Congress. The arrangements will, therefore, be terminated effective February 29, 1968."[39] When points rather than race dominated the selection of immigrants, when organizational sponsorship was discouraged, and when the carte blanche was removed, CAC leaders believed the organization's work was done.

The Canadian immigration program continued to spark public debate. Seeking to deal with immigration issues by possibly bringing down a new Immigration Act, the government published a series of discussion documents in 1975 collectively known as the *Green Paper on Immigration*. Like its predecessor, this discussion paper raised several explosive issues, such as the question of unskilled workers, the racial and cultural composition of the current immigration program, the advisability of bringing in temporary workers, and concerns about urban congestion.

Finally, after public and parliamentary debate about the immigration program, in 1976 the government tabled a new immigration act that brought a measure of stability to many regulations and directives (the act received royal assent in 1978). This major piece of legislation was based on such fundamental principles as nondiscrimination, family reunion, humanitarian concern for refugees, and the promotion of Canada's social, economic, demographic, and cultural goals. The Immigration Act of 1978 linked the immigration program to Canada's population and labour market needs, allowed Canadian citizens or permanent residents to sponsor close relatives, required immigrants and visitors to obtain visas or authorization abroad, prohibited visitors from changing their status from within Canada, and introduced security measures to protect Canada from international terrorism and organized crime.[40]

The Work of the CAC

Although members of the CAC were untrained volunteers with their own work and family responsibilities, the amount and type of work they carried on for the congress was staggering: they dealt with individuals, organizations, various governments, and changes in immigration policy and regulations in Canada and abroad. They held public meetings to familiarize Armenians in Canada with their work and with immigration possibilities, and they circulated government regulations in Canada and abroad. They met with officials, lobbied on behalf of Armenians, and helped arrange visas or passports, medical and security examinations, transportation, and loans. And once the newcomers arrived in Canada, the congress and other members of the Armenian community conscientiously assisted them with finding lodgings and jobs, provided other social and medical needs, and made every effort to keep them off the welfare rolls.

Yervant Pasdermajian, the driving force behind the CAC; Sarkis Hanemian; and Kerop Bedoukian, whose independent work (see below) was incorporated into the CAC at the government's suggestion and who became its corresponding secretary, each received and reviewed the extensive correspondence. They scrupulously read and replied to the enormous number of letters requesting information and direction and examined the equally high number of applications with accompanying questionnaires (sometimes with as many as 120 questions and detailed family histories). They met on a regular basis once every week or every two weeks to consider each dossier and screen all applicants. They took into consideration the applicant's possibilities in Canada, his/her trade, language/s, age, and absorptive capacity and employability in Canada. "We had to make sure they'd be self-sufficient. We had to be careful. We had established certain criteria, certain prestige vis-à-vis the immigration department, and we were very anxious to maintain that."[41]

They issued circulars explaining immigration regulations and their assistance program for prospective immigrants and providing a description of living and working conditions in Canada. Shortly after the 1952 ruling, for example, Bedoukian sent circulars to Greece explaining the situation in Canada: the sponsorship structure, i.e., the fact that Canadian residents, both permanent residents and newcomers, could sponsor their first-degree relatives; the role of the Canadian Council of Churches in sponsoring stateless and poor individuals; the provisions for travel loans and their repayment; the responsibilities of the sponsor; and the difficulties involved in settling in a new country, including the language problems. Bedoukian ended his circulars by noting that in Montreal there was no Armenian church and no Armenian "home," that newcomers lived like sojourners and orphans for the first two or three years, and that anyone contemplating coming to Canada had to give the matter very scrupulous consideration.[42] The response to the circulars was overwhelming. Bedoukian's personal records reveal that from 1958 to 1962 he received and answered thirty-six hundred letters (in English, French, and Armenian), almost all of them from total strangers.

The CAC also received correspondence from Armenians who had settled in Canada seeking advice and assistance for their friends and acquaintances still abroad. In 1968, for example, a group from Egypt wrote to the CAC thanking the organization for helping them fulfill their dream of starting a new life in a free, democratic, and Christian country and expressing their gratitude to the Armenian community in Montreal for their moral and financial support. They drew attention to the unfavourable living conditions of their compatriots still in Egypt and pointed to the real possibility of Egypt closing its doors to emigration. "Thousands of applications," they wrote, "have been turned down by Canadian authorities, including applications from professionals and non-professionals, young and old, married and single, educated and uneducated, speakers of French or English. Had they been nationals of other countries, many would have been accepted by Canada, but because they are from Egypt, Canada is reluctant to accept them." The writers appealed to the congress to help facilitate their entry to Canada.[43]

As word of the congress' work spread, the organization was inundated with applications, largely from the Middle East, which was in a state of turmoil as one country after another became destabilized: military/Socialist rule in Syria in the 1950s, tightening of regulations in Greece, anti-Armenian riots in Turkey in 1955, economic constraints in Egypt, the Greek-Turkish conflict in Cyprus in 1974, the Arab-Israeli war, civil war in Lebanon in the mid–1970s, the Iran-Iraq war, and the revolution in Iran (1978–79). The events devastated the Armenian communities in these countries and compelled this Christian minority to seek safety elsewhere.

Even after the CAC had brought its operations to an end, letters from desperate people continued to arrive. In 1977 an appeal from a group of Armenians from Iraq with temporary residence in a European state, gave an idea of the persecution they faced in Iraq. Political and religious discrimination had led to the nationalization of all Christian private schools, including the Armenian school. The authorities "closed our sport clubs, they take off the Holy Christ picture and the cross, instead of them they fixed the signs and pictures of the Baath Party's leaders. Also instead of praying in the morning, they forced the students to sing Baath songs." They interfered in the election of the Armenian National Committee Board, insisting that most of the elected members must be members of the Baath Party. Commemoration of the Genocide was forbidden on 24 April, and the church doors were closed. Anyone entering the church on that day would have been arrested and jailed. In addition to engaging in religious persecution, the political authorities insisted that private businessmen would not receive materials or goods unless they were registered in one of the Baath organizations. As for military service, they complained, the normal requirement of eighteen months had been extended for many Armenians, sometimes to periods up to four and even six years.[44]

The congress had no financial means at its disposal but saw to it that when selected immigrants came to Canada

> they were met, they were given guidance, they were introduced to someone who could find jobs for them ... it was all voluntary ... we did *everything* possible so they wouldn't go to welfare ... I used to tell my friends ... when you see this man here, twenty years from now ... some of these people ... will be big businessmen. Some will be big professional men. That is a prediction I made which has come true. We have some Armenians, wherever you go, you [will] find in good positions – girls and men. I think the name of the Canadian Armenian Congress was always treated with respect ... [the Immigration Branch] knew that we had very clean operations ... Our relationship was cordial with everyone of [the Armenian organizations, churches, political parties]. We didn't bring any politics into the matter ... nobody has been able, [to] blame us [for] being partisan ... And to the credit of my colleagues in the organization, who were mostly ARF [Armenian Revolutionary Federation, i.e., Dashnak] men, I must say that they were ... non-partisan. All they were interested in was that they had a job to do and that's got to be done for everybody that deserves it, for every Armenian ... they said whoever merits, let him come.[45]

Ever conscious about its mandate to bring in immigrants who could not otherwise be sponsored, the congress limited its selection to those who had no other sponsors and who would reflect favourably on the Armenian Canadian community.

KEROP BEDOUKIAN

Independently of the CAC, Kerop Bedoukian began sponsoring Armenian immigrants after World War II, at first on his own and later (1962), as a member of the CAC. Initially working in conjunction with the Society of Armenians from Istanbul, he spearheaded the immigration of about 750 Armenians from Turkey in the 1950s and 1960s.⁴⁶ Under the auspices of the Canadian Council of Churches and the World Council of Churches, he facilitated the movement of immigrants from Greece in the late 1950s and 1960s.⁴⁷ According to Bedoukian's own report in 1962, he had sponsored 182 families from Greece. In addition, he had acted as guarantor to several hundred more who had arrived as parents or close relatives of the earlier immigrants. He had further given 65 letters of support or guarantee to those who wished to bring in their relatives but were not in a position financially to be accepted as sponsors by the Immigration Department.⁴⁸

The immigration from Greece was quite unlike any other. As noted in a previous chapter, war-torn Greece had given sanctuary to thousands of Armenian refugees in 1922. At the same time, Greece received approximately 1.4 million Christian refugees from Turkey (including Armenian refugees) in the exchange of populations under the terms of the Lausanne Treaty (1923). To ease the overwhelming refugee explosion, Greece granted Armenians Nansen identity or travel certificates. Canada, for one, refused to accept these certificates on the grounds that without bona fide passports the stateless persons could not be deported should they become public charges (see chapter eight). During the 1920s, thousands of Armenians left the makeshift refugee camps in Greece, for Soviet Armenia, France, Egypt, or other Middle Eastern countries. It was estimated that between twenty-five and forty thousand Armenians remained in Greece; almost all of them had been born in Turkey.

After World War II, about fifteen thousand Armenians from Greece emigrated to Soviet Armenia, leaving at least ten thousand Armenians from Turkey still in Greece by the late 1950s. Of this group, approximately five thousand had been granted naturalization by the Greek government, but the remaining five thousand, along with two thousand children born in Greece, had not been granted Greek citizenship. These Armenians were designated by the Greek government as "stateless" and given Nansen status rights in Greece, i.e., the Greek government gave them asylum and allowed them to work, but they were obliged to apply for residence and work permits (sometimes on an annual basis) and did not enjoy full civic rights or the privileges of Greek citizenship. Indeed, Greek authorities urged them to leave the country to seek work and settlement elsewhere. Although there were among them tradesmen and artisans, most had been so constrained by their legal status that they were "hand-to-mouth wage earners" and had "acute lodging problems."⁴⁹

In 1951 the Greek government began to describe them on their identity cards as "Turkish" nationals, on the grounds that that had been their true legal status all along but that the Greek government had not described it that way, in order not to upset them. Thus Armenians in Greece, as a rule, were considered Turkish nationals, and their children, born in Greece, were also regarded as Turkish nationals, having acquired their father's nationality.[50] Attempts to test the Turkish Government's willingness to accept any of these Armenians as "Turkish nationals" was met with "absolute silence" from Turkey.

The Greek refusal to grant them citizenship was regarded as an "international anomaly," since by Turkish law Armenians had been prohibited from returning to Turkey and obtaining Turkish passports. The Turkish Decree on the Withdrawal of Nationality (23 May 1927) was viewed internationally as a decree of "mass denationalization." The United Nations High Commissioner for Refugees took up their status and ruled that these Armenians in Greece, including the children born there, were stateless, international refugees, who therefore fell under its mandate.[51]

The status of Armenians in Greece raised certain policy issues in Canada in the 1950s and early 1960s. Canadian authorities, still hazy about the designation of refugee, decided that these Armenians could not be defined as "bona fide refugees." Instead, they classed them as "stateless" persons who did not fall within any of the admissible classes of the immigration regulations. Accordingly, these "stateless" Armenians in Greece, who fell under the jurisdiction of the United Nations High Commissioner for Refugees but who were not defined by Canadian officials as refugees, were to be dealt with by special orders-in-council.[52]

Bedoukian started acting on behalf of these stateless Armenians around 1951; his efforts became more effective as he worked with the Canadian and World Council of Churches, which were focusing primarily on assisting refugees and stateless persons to immigrate to Canada. Like the congress, Bedoukian was recognized by the department in very favourable terms. In an internal memo to the deputy minister, the director of immigration referred to Bedoukian's record of three hundred persons who all "became established in a relatively short time after arrival, entirely through the efforts and assistance of Mr. Bedoukian and his wife, who, incidentally, is a professional social worker ... his previous movements have been successful and his guarantee seems to be trustworthy."[53]

As an additional measure, Bedoukian often arranged travel loans to prospective immigrants, mostly but not all from Greece, often through the Canadian Council of Churches (CCC), which paid two-thirds of the ticket costs, while he himself paid the remaining one-third. It was always a satisfying occasion when a newly arrived immigrant had repaid his loan, as the following letter verifies. Writing to Alexander Maclaren, director of settlement for the Canadian Council of Churches, a young immigrant enclosed a money order for fifteen dollars as his final payment on the travel loan. After thanking Maclaren and the CCC for their help in his immigration to Canada, he then gave an account of himself: he had a very satisfactory job at the Canadair plant; his wife worked, and their eight-year-old son "already speaks English like a Canadian ... My mother, who is with us, does the cooking and does not miss an opportunity to pray for those who were instrumental for the blessing bestowed upon us."[54]

Bedoukian was also involved in the work of the Armenian General Benevolent Union and the Cathedral of St Gregory the Illuminator (Montreal) in assisting newcomers, especially refugees, in their movement to and settlement in Canada. During his twenty years as president of the Montreal chapter of the AGBU and his fifteen years as a member of the AGBU Central Committee of America he galvanized the support of this organization for immigration work.[55] In 1955 the AGBU set up a revolving fund of two thousand dollars and added another five thousand dollars in 1962 for loans to needy newcomers. It is to the credit of Bedoukian's leadership that these funds were loaned on the basis of need rather than of political affiliation. In addition to the settlement services provided by the CAC, largely in terms of lodgings and jobs for sponsored newcomers, Bedoukian spearheaded immigrant social services, largely counselling, as early as 1956. At times he worked under the auspices of the Armenian General Benevolent Union and at other times on his own. His contributions in this field and that of his wife, the former Marjorie Clark, are largely unrecognized, yet they played a vital role in assisting newcomers to cope with adjustment and family-related problems.

OTHER VOLUNTARY IMMIGRATION

Not all Armenians who entered Canada were sponsored by the CAC, by Bedoukian, or by their relatives. Many came through sponsorship by Canadian industry or as independent immigrants. The following gives a profile of two such families, showing, in addition, their migratory path over a number of decades.

In the early 1900s, Migirdic Migirdicyan was a well-to-do community leader in Van. In 1903, his wife Makruhi gave birth to their first child, a son named Kurken, followed four years later by the birth of a daughter, Hushursh. In 1915, at the start of the Genocide, Migirdic was killed during the Armenian defence of Van; Makruhi and her two children fled the city with the surviving inhabitants.[56] Two days into their march Turkish forces attacked the column of refugees, robbed Makruhi, and murdered her in front of her children. Thus traumatized, twelve-year old Kurken and eight-year-old Hushursh were driven through the mountains towards Yerevan and relative safety. During the last days of the trek, the two children were inadvertently separated in the chaos of throngs of disoriented, starving, and exhausted refugees. Seeing the terrible plight of Armenian children, the poet Hovannes Toumanian, his daughter Nevart, and her friends searched for destitute children along the roadside and placed them in a hurriedly organized orphanage in Echmiadzin. Kurken and Hushursh eventually found each other in this orphanage.

After years of political and military upheaval, Armenia, now under Soviet domination, finally found a measure of peace. A music teacher from the Moscow Conservatory visited Yerevan seeking talent among the orphan population for further study in Moscow. Kurken, who had a beautiful voice, was selected, but before he and his sister moved to Moscow, Kurken decided to visit relatives who had managed to escape from Van to Istanbul during the Genocide. A week after his arrival in Istanbul, the Soviet Union closed its borders, leaving Kurken in Istanbul and Hushursh in Yerevan. They never saw each other again.

In 1940 Kurken married Luiz Husyan, whose family had left Van for Constantinople in 1913 when Luiz was a year old. Six months after his marriage, Kurken, who operated a little sandwich shop, was conscripted into the Turkish army. Their son, Migirdic, graduated from the Armenian Mkhitarist (Armenian Catholic) high school in Istanbul in 1962 and later received his engineering degree from the American University of Istanbul (formerly Robert College, founded in 1863, the first American university established outside the United States). "My parents," he confided, "didn't talk about the Genocide, for fear of reprisals should Turkish authorities find out." But he could not forget the violence in Istanbul on 6 September 1955, when the government "organized gangs of Turks to plunder and smash stores and workplaces belonging to its citizens of Armenian and Greek descent."

Following his two-year stint in the Turkish army, he joined Burroughs Corporation in Istanbul as a computer-systems engineer. In 1970, Migirdic married Ani Hanimyan, and a year later he was transferred to Germany to work with the Burroughs subsidiary in Frankfurt. While in Germany he learned more about the Genocide and about Turkey's denial. Feelings of frustration and shame deepened at the thought of carrying a Turkish passport. With the guarantee of a job at Burroughs Canada in Ottawa, Migirdic emigrated to Canada in 1975 with Ani and Anoush, their six-month-old daughter. A week after the Parti Québécois came to power in 1976, Migirdic was promoted to a key management position in Montreal. During a house-hunting trip to Montreal, a French truck driver, seeing their Ontario license plates shouted at them, "Go back to your own country." They felt confused. Which country? Canada? Germany? Turkey? They were shocked and upset.

About a year later Migirdic was promoted to a position in Toronto, where his sister and Ani's brother had immigrated with their respective families. Migirdic heard the news: the Canadian government had reduced the five-year citizenship waiting period to three. "It was a happy day for me. I couldn't wait for the three years to pass. I desperately wanted to be a Canadian." Three years and a day after their arrival in Canada, the Migirdicyans applied for and shortly thereafter, were granted Canadian citizenship.[57]

Another equally revealing story depicts the movements of a family from Caesarea. During the Genocide, Haig Seferian, born in 1899 and the eldest of four children, escaped to the Sanjak of Alexandretta (Iskenderun), later a "special administrative" region under French protection.[58] After the war, Haig and a small band of young men made regular clandestine expeditions into Turkey to rescue Armenian women and children abducted during the Genocide. The men would bring the survivors to the Armenian church and the priest would help the refugees find work, adoptive parents, or spouses. Among the group was young Nazeli, born in Sivas in 1910. Haig married her in 1933, and they settled down in a small town outside Alexandretta and began family life. He operated large agricultural equipment for an Armenian contractor, who hired out operators and equipment to local farmers.

In 1936, Kemalist Turkey agitated for annexation of the territory, even though Turks made up approximately one-third of the population and were outnumbered by the combined total of the Arabic-speaking people. About twenty-three thousand Armenians, who formed about 11 percent of the population, lived in the region. In 1938 Kemalist forces occupied the Sanjak, and France handed over the area to the Turks in what Christopher Walker terms "an action which recalls Hitler's occupation of the Rhineland two years before." Once again the Armenian population, in a state of turmoil, was forced to flee; some escaped to Lebanon, like Haig's three siblings; others, including Haig and his family, found safe haven in Syria. In a single week during the summer of 1939, fourteen thousand Armenians fled from the Sanjak. Once again reduced to poverty and refugeeism, thousands squatted in a huge field, later called New Village, just outside Aleppo. They set up corrugated tin shacks and under extremely primitive conditions tried to eke out their daily bread. Nazeli, who, in the chaos, had been separated from her husband, took work at a licorice-root farm, "working for almost nothing." Finally, Haig found his family again and moved them to better accommodations. In 1942, at the age of forty-three, Haig died from complications of an ailment that could have been treated had there been money enough to pay for an operation. Nazeli, just thirty-two, was left alone with two children under ten.

One of those children, Boghos (Paul), who had been born in the Sanjak in 1934, recounted with some emotion how, as a child, he had been deprived of schooling, mainly because of poverty. Eventually, he entered a school with an accompanying orphanage that was funded by the Calouste Gulbenkian Foundation. Most, if not all, children in the school were orphans or from indigent or single-parent families. Paul was a good student, even though he worked after school for a shoemaker as a paid apprentice. But his mother was able to earn scarcely enough to pay for their meagre lodgings and for food for the three of them. Often there was hardly a scrap of bread for lunch. She needed him to work full-time. Much against his will he was compelled to quit school at the age of thirteen. Even the intervention of a teacher promising to waive the tuition did not change her decision. "Every day, I would go to the school yard and see my friends. Then I would sit and cry. This went on for weeks."

Continuing his trade, he eventually became an expert shoemaker. In the early 1950s, considering the political instability in Syria, he left for Beirut, not yet twenty years old. In 1966, Paul successfully applied for immigration to Canada as an independent immigrant. He knew that Canada was a young, strong, and democratic country, and he felt he could risk starting a new life in this new land. Before he left, Paul visited Ardashes Der Hovannesian, his principal from the Gulbenkian school, now retired and living in Beirut. When he heard that Paul was moving to Canada, Der Hovannesian, reflecting the fear of many Armenians, pleaded with him not to go. "I'm not afraid for you. I'm afraid for your children. You're going to lose your son and daughter [to assimilation]. Don't go. Even if you've bought your ticket, tear it up. Stay here." But Paul had made up his mind.

Paul, his wife Armenouhi, and their two children, Nazeli and Haig, joined his brother-in-law in Hamilton and found his first job, not surprisingly, at the International Harvester. From eight to four, he worked at the factory and then for a shoemaker until seven. In due time he left the factory and bought the shoe repair business from the elderly owner with a four-thousand-dollar loan from the bank. "We were so busy, I was up at five and worked until midnight. We had huge piles of shoes." By 1969 Paul had paid off all his debts.[59]

In many ways the stories of Migirdic and Paul differ dramatically. But they are also typical in geographic mobility, family fragmentation and separation, violence and refugeeism, childhood trauma, unrelenting poverty, and truncated family histories, where names of ancestors and information about work and life have all been lost. Both men were determined not only to rise above circumstances but to do well, and both have been active in Canadian and Armenian affairs. The most striking similarity, however, remains their steadfast conviction that Canada is the land of hope, peace, and fulfillment.

REFUGEES

The 1951 Geneva Convention was intended to clarify the legal status of the displaced in Europe after World War II, specifically those displaced before 1 January 1951. The Protocol of 1967 broadened the scope of the Geneva Convention by removing limitations of time. Eventually the Geneva Convention was applied to the displaced in any part of the world, not just in Europe. The Convention was important because it defined the category of refugee and established the principle of nonrefoulement, i.e., protecting an individual from being forced to return to a life-threatening situation. According to the Convention, refugees are those who, owing to a well-founded fear of persecution for reasons of their race, religion, nationality, political opinion, or membership in a particular social group are outside their country of nationality and are unable or, owing to such fear, are unwilling to return to that country. However, the Convention did not deal with asylum, determination of refugee status, admission requirements, or resettlement responsibilities: for all these problems it fell to each country to set up its own decision-making structures and processes. While international law prescribes human rights for all, nation states are the guardians of these rights and the communities in which they are realized. The basic dichotomy between the rights of the individual and the sovereignty of the state is not easily resolved, for states, including Canada, consider asylum to be a privilege, not a right.

Although Canada participated in drafting the 1951 Convention, the Canadian government was reluctant to limit its prerogatives and therefore did not sign the Convention or the 1967 Protocol. Canada's hesitation was influenced both by the question of sovereignty and by the tradition of linking immigration to the country's economic needs. As already indicated, the admission of refugees and "displaced persons" after World War II was associated with Canada's economic conditions and needs and with its ability to absorb the newcomers into the economy.

Following the war, the questions of the definition of a "bona fide refugee" and the validity of travel documents once again fell onto the agenda of Canadian government officials. Although Canada was not a signatory of the 1951 Geneva Convention, the government recognized the travel documents issued under that Convention, as it had done previously under the Convention in London in 1946.[60] As for the distinction between a voluntary immigrant and a refugee, for administrative purposes the term refugee was applied only to those displaced in Europe during World War II. Accordingly, Armenians suffering persecution in Turkey in the 1950s or in other Middle Eastern countries were not classified as refugees, and Jews in North Africa were defined as "quasi-refugees." External Affairs made no distinction between refugees and other immigrants, except for authorizing the acceptance of travel documents or certificates of identity from refugees in lieu of passports and insisting that they remain valid for return to the country of issue for at least six months after the date of arrival in Canada. Refugees granted landing privileges in Canada were to be treated no differently from other immigrants. The Department of Citizenship and Immigration emphasized an unwillingness "to support any extension of additional benefits to these people [refugees]."[61]

Finally, in 1969 Canada signed the Convention and Protocol, thereby committing the country "to a refugee policy based upon the needs of people in distress rather than those of the Canadian economy." Even after signing the Convention, however, Canada dealt with refugees on an ad hoc basis, until the Immigration Act of 1978. In this act, the Canadian government agreed to fulfill its international legal obligations with respect to refugees and to uphold its humanitarian tradition with respect to the displaced and the persecuted. The government also acknowledged the specific category of Convention refugee, assigned certain priorities to this status, established specific procedures for determining refugee status, and made provisions for assisting refugees in resettling in Canada. Thus, for the first time in Canadian history, refugees were granted a separate status in Canadian immigration law.[62]

Since the post–World War I period, the principle of humanitarianism has been established in Canada in practice, if not always in law. This principle played a significant role in the entry of refugees to Canada during the 1920s, particularly by means of the Minister's Permit. The Immigration Act of 1978 confirmed the ministerial prerogative and empowered the minister responsible for immigration to use his or her discretionary powers to classify certain individuals and groups as special humanitarian cases (as already indicated regarding Armenians in the early 1950s). These cases included people in need of resettlement who were not refugees according to the Convention definition but who had sponsoring agents in Canada and who were oppressed in their own countries or displaced by emergency situations such as war, revolution, earthquake, or flood. The ministerial prerogative has been a way of circumventing the constraints of the Geneva Convention.

Another provision of the 1978 Immigration Act significantly affected the entry of refugees. Any church, corporation, or group of five or more adult Canadian citizens or permanent residents was permitted to sponsor refugees. For decades sponsorship had been an important consideration in the admission of refugees, who were dealt with on an ad hoc basis: family, ethnic, or religious associations, employment agencies, industries, and nongovernment organizations facilitated the entry and initial adaptation of refugees to Canada, notably the displaced persons after World War II. The major difference after 1978 was in the composition of the sponsoring group. Under the aegis of Operation Lifeline, the government permitted small, unaffiliated or unrelated groups of five or more individuals to make a direct application for sponsorship. Legally binding contracts for a maximum of one year of financial and moral support were signed by these groups with the federal government.

In keeping with these priorities and regulations, the government issued visas under relaxed criteria to specified people in countries wracked by civil war. Canadians with close relatives in Lebanon, Iran, Sri Lanka, El Salvador, and Guatemala were allowed to sponsor relatives under family class if they could show that they were adversely affected by hostilities. Thus, if there were "urgent humanitarian family considerations," Armenians from Lebanon and, later, Iran were, accordingly, permitted to enter as immigrants under the family reunification program. At the same time, they were not obliged to meet all the points requirements. To enable administering to Lebanese and Iranians, offices were set up in Cyprus and Damascus. The immigration officers also had "the authority to issue Minister's Permits to allow immediate entry to Canada in cases of real need."

From 1980 to 1990 inclusively, approximately 5.7 percent of immigrants giving Armenian as their mother tongue entered Canada classified as Convention refugees.[63] In cooperation with the United Church of Canada, which acted as a liaison with the Canadian government, Holy Trinity Armenian Church in Toronto undertook to sponsor Armenian refugees and to help in resettling them in Canada under its Refugee Aid Committee, headed by Haig Misakyan. The church sponsored approximately 150 to 175 refugees, primarily from Turkey, Iran, and Lebanon.[64] Except for a travel loan from the government and a small grant to produce an Armenian-English immigrant guidebook, the church received no outside assistance in this work. With the termination of the government travel loan, the effort to assist refugees was inevitably jeopardized because of the financial strain on the church. In any case, the church discontinued this work in 1992 to focus on its commitment to help Armenians in the former Soviet Union after the collapse of communism, to help in the creation of the independent Republic of Armenia, and to deal with the Azerbaijani attack on Karabagh and Armenia and the combined Azeri and Turkish blockade on the newly created states.

THE MOVEMENT OF ARMENIANS TO CANADA

To a remarkable extent over the past hundred years, the movement of Armenians has been sparked by political, economic, and religious violence. The pogroms of 1894–97 and 1909, the Genocide of 1915–23 in Turkey, and upheaval in the Middle East since the 1950s have precipitated Armenian emigration.[65] Persecution has remained a push factor. For example, in 1982 a group of three to four hundred Kurdish-speaking Christian Armenians from Anatolia was stranded in the Netherlands. Having entered as guest workers, they were pressed by the Dutch government to return to Turkey because of unemployment in Holland. Their refusal on the ground that to return to Turkey would be suicide, led to the intervention of the AGBU to facilitate the migration of some of them to Canada.

Principal source countries changed as different Middle Eastern countries were in upheaval. According to applications submitted by the congress to the ministry from 1 October 1964 to 29 February 1968, the majority of immigrants came, in order of numbers, from Egypt, Turkey, Syria, and Lebanon.[66] Statistics indicate that emigration from Egypt peaked in the mid-sixties and that more than half the immigrants sponsored by the CAC during 1964–65 came from Egypt.[67] Forty-seven percent of Armenian immigrants in 1954 came from Greece; this percentage dropped to 16 percent in 1958. From 1946 to 1966, the number of Armenian immigrants who came to Canada from the United Arab Republic (Egypt and Syria) was 2,864, or 45 percent, and from Turkey, 673, or 11 percent. Three-quarters of Armenian immigrants to Canada from 1946 to 1966 originated in Egypt, Turkey, Syria, Greece, and Lebanon.[68] The numbers from Lebanon increased during the civil war in the 1970s and well into the 1980s. The Armenian community in Lebanon, which in the early 1960s numbered perhaps as many as 280,000, was reduced to between 50,000 and 70,000 by 1990, mainly because of emigration.

In its turn, the Canadian immigration program has shaped the patterns of Armenian immigration to Canada. Major changes in immigration policy after World War II, especially with respect to racial preferences and categorization, and the creation of a points system led to increased movement of Armenians to Canada. At the same time, Canadian immigration policy continued to be based on such fundamental bulwarks as family reunification, sponsorship, health (both mental and physical), political affiliation, terrorism, and criminality.[69] Canada's economic development and the country's labour requirements also remained a critical underpinning in the choice of immigrants. From the turn of the century until immigration virtually ceased during the Depression, agricultural and domestic labour were preferred occupations, while in the post-World War II period, industry, trades, and the professions played an increasingly more important place in the selection process. The aggregate numbers for the years 1945–1966 and 1980–1990 are set out in the following list.[70]

Year	Entries	Year	Entries	Year	Entries
1945	3	1956	181	1980	725
1946	11	1957	272	1981	613
1947	8	1958	189	1982	671
1948	10	1959	231	1983	344
1949	7	1960	143	1984	419
1950	35	1961	769	1985	480
1951	80	1962	769	1986	579
1952	71	1963	899	1987	858
1953	70	1964	841	1988	823
1954	68	1965	887	1989	955
1955	131	1966	1,174	1990	1,438

The immigration of Armenians from 1950 to 1988 was marked by circumstances unique to a dispersed people. It included the movement of people from one diaspora to another, the flow of people from several diasporas to a single new destination,[71] and the phenomenon of multiple migrations. For example, many of the elderly immigrants had been deported from their ancestral homeland in Turkey to a country of asylum during the Genocide, usually in the Middle East, and they were later obliged to move yet again. People fled from one Middle Eastern country to another during times of violence, conscription, or economic, political, or religious persecution. In the 1950s, for instance, political instability in Syria drove Armenians to Egypt or Lebanon where insecurity and war drove them out once again.

Both Pasdermajian and Bedoukian were very conscientious about choosing "quality" immigrants who would be an asset to Canada and contribute to Canadian development. Even the stateless immigrants from Greece, who were, on the whole, selected, according to

Bedoukian, "on the basis of their shortcomings, e.g., no money, no education, no English or French and no trade,"[72] were carefully screened. Much to their credit, neither Pasdermajian, who was pro-Dashnak and a member of the Cilician Church, nor Bedoukian who belonged to the AGBU and the Echmiadzin Church, allowed their political differences to interfere in their goal to choose "quality" immigrants.

Their work in general, however, generated debate in the Armenian world. Armenians were being drawn away from countries close to the homeland, thus dispersing even further abroad potential immigrants, should a regime change occur in Soviet Armenia. The selection criteria of Armenian Canadian leaders, furthermore, spawned a brain drain from the active and dynamic communities in the Middle East. Rather than bringing Armenians to Canada or the United States, it was argued, it would be far more constructive to spend the time, energy, and money in building up the communities in the Middle East. Indeed, opposition to emigration was so great in certain circles that violent action was taken against the Beirut office of the World Council of Churches in 1975.[73]

Thousands of newcomers, nevertheless, resettled in Canada. They came from different countries of origin, immigrating as single individuals or as parts of families. They came from different socioeconomic backgrounds with different educational levels, belonged to different religious denominations, had different political loyalties, and spoke different languages. The following chapters trace their experiences in regrouping in a new land, adjusting to Canada, and contributing to Canadian society.

18

Settlement of the Third Wave: 1950–1988

Armenians chose to immigrate to Canada to find political and economic stability, religious freedom, and educational and occupational opportunities and to rejoin family members. Because of the sponsorship structures, immigrants did not always enter Canada as part of a family or kin network. Several thousand newcomers had entered Canada sponsored by the Canadian Armenian Congress (CAC) and had no family links in Canada before immigration. This critical component of the immigration movement of the 1950s and 1960s meant that newcomers, unlike the Keghi pioneers, came from different countries of origin, with decidedly different backgrounds and without the bonds of kith and kin – an Armenian melting pot in Canada, so to speak.

DEMOGRAPHICS

Records of the CAC indicate that, at least until 1968–69, when the organization virtually ended its operations, the immigration consisted both of entire families and of single men and women. According to applications submitted to the ministry by the CAC from 1964 to 1968, the number of men slightly surpassed that of women. Both single men and single women spearheaded the immigration of their families by sponsoring family members, depending on the "tap-on, tap-off" regulations governing sponsorship of first- and second degree relatives. Between 1980 and 1990 inclusive, 7,905 immigrants listed Armenian as their mother tongue, and the majority entered as family class and assisted relative class.[1] Obviously, family reunification was as important to these later immigrants as to the old-timers who had waited for decades to rejoin relatives who had been separated from them by the Genocide. Eventually family solidarities began to play an increasingly important role in group formation and direction.

Most post–World War II newcomers were destined for the provinces of Quebec and Ontario. From 1953 onwards, excluding 1955, the majority of immigrants settled in Quebec. Estimates indicate that from 1950 to 1966 (excluding 1965) almost 4,000 Armenians were destined for Quebec and approximately 1,500 for Ontario.[2] Preference for the province of Quebec in recent years is linked to the immigration services that were under the auspices of Pasdermajian and Bedoukian. For many prospective immigrants, Montreal represented Canada – and the possibility of employment and relatively smooth adaptation to a new land. But their preference for Montreal was also related to the French language. Of 372 immigrants questioned in 1972, approximately 30 percent (115) gave "l'amour pour la francophonie" as their principal reason for settling in Quebec.[3] A 1961 study showed that 23 percent of Armenians in Montreal knew English and French well and that 40 percent had some knowledge of both languages. In a 1979 study, about 50 percent claimed a good knowledge of French and English. In addition 13 percent had good French but poor English, and another 4.5 percent revealed that their French was good but their English was nonexistent. In short, more than two-thirds of Armenian settlers in Montreal could communicate in French.[4] This predilection for French can be traced to their countries of provenance in the Mediterranean region, where Armenians attended French schools and/or used French in business. Unlike many other immigrants, Armenians, once settled in Quebec, tended not to resettle in other parts of the country. For them Montreal was their home town and Quebec their belle province.

The 1981 census confirmed that 95 percent of Armenians in Canada resided in Ontario and Quebec. According to a survey published in 1962, almost 75 percent of Armenians resided in Ontario and approximately 25 percent in Quebec.[5] In the 1986 census data, which were based on Armenian ethnic origin, Ontario continued to be the province of principal settlement.[6] By the time of the 1991 census, however, the immigration of the previous forty years had borne results, as Quebec surpassed Ontario as the main province of residence. British Columbia and Alberta ran a distant third and fourth.

Post–World War II immigrants were mainly urban dwellers from such cities as Cairo, Alexandria, Istanbul, Aleppo, Teheran, Athens, and Beirut, and they settled in big urban centres in Canada, primarily Montreal and Toronto and to a decidedly lesser degree in Calgary,

Edmonton, Ottawa, Vancouver, Hamilton, Cambridge, Windsor, and St Catharines. In 1960 the pioneer settlements of Brantford, St Catharines, Hamilton, Galt, and Guelph combined retained a numerical superiority over Montreal and Toronto. However, the largest *single* Armenian settlement was Metropolitan Montreal. By 1981, Montreal and Toronto dominated settlement: over 97 percent of Armenians in the province of Quebec lived in Metropolitan Montreal and almost 74 percent of those in Ontario resided in Metropolitan Toronto.[7]

One of the factors that contributed to this preference was the role played by the leadership of the Canadian Armenian Congress in meeting newcomers, arranging for temporary lodgings, and helping them find initial jobs. Both Yervant Pasdermajian, owner of Yervant's Oriental Rugs, and Kerop Bedoukian, owner of Ararat Rugs, provided jobs in their businesses. Both men were generous in their dealings with newcomers and neither was criticized for exploiting a naive newcomer. Interviewees made a point of praising both businessmen for giving them a good start in the New World. In addition, the leaders also signed loans at the bank to help newcomers get started. According to his own report to the CAC, Bedoukian personally extended loans amounting to eighteen thousand dollars, "all borrowed from the bank at 6 percent interest, which can not be charged to the immigrant by Immigration ruling." His accounts show that most, but not all, repaid him and he himself recognized that 20 percent would be "uncollectable."[8] Naturally, he took precautions requiring cosponsors to sign a notarized letter of guarantee for the repayment of loans advanced by him and for assurances that newcomers would not become public charges while in Canada.[9]

Many others, too, helped immigrants start off, as revealed in the following account:

When I arrived at the airport, I had three hundred dollars American in my pocket and the knowledge that an additional five hundred dollars was forthcoming from _____. I also had the names of three or four Armenians and their addresses. Complete strangers. When we got off the plane, I called one of the people ... and he said he would pick me up in ten minutes ... He took us to his home. I was surprised to find that I knew his wife. We'd attended the same school. When I recognized her, you'd think God had sent a light. It was a wonderful feeling to see someone I knew in a strange land. At that moment, the world was mine. Mr _____ began phoning Armenian families to find us a place to stay. Finally he found a home which we rented ... The next day, an Armenian goldsmith who had come to Canada ten or twelve years before, who had a shop downtown, heard about me. He didn't know me, but he called and offered me a job. That was a stroke of luck, bearing in mind that I didn't know any English – to find a job and lodgings with Armenians! I was lucky. It was a common thing for Armenians to help each other, perfect strangers.[10]

Newcomers entered Canada, not as sojourners like their predecessors, but as permanent settlers. Unlike the young, down-and-out refugees, this movement was composed of tradesmen, skilled workers, businessmen, and professionals. Many were well-educated and cosmopolitan, and they came with their own sizeable private funds. In 1963, 899 Armenians entered the country, of whom 404 were classified as follows: manufacturing and mechanical, 159; clerical, 116; engineers, teachers, health professionals, and other professionals such as architects, 129.[11] In both Toronto and Montreal, the population was largely youthful. A 1961 Montreal study indicated that about 68 percent of settlers were between the ages of fifteen and forty-nine. This trend continued: according to 1981 statistics, about 66 percent of settlers in Montreal fell below the age of forty-five. The 1981 census material for the Toronto Census Metropolitan Area also reveals a young immigrant group, with the majority of settlers being in the age categories from twenty to thirty-nine. According to 1986 census statistics, more than 55 percent of Armenians in Toronto fell below the age of forty.[12]

Statistics for Canada based on the 1981 census show that the largest single group of those giving Armenian as their ethnic origin were born in Canada: about 20 percent. Of the remaining 80 percent, about 19 percent were born in Turkey (a group composed of past and recent immigrants), 17 percent in Lebanon, and 15 percent in Egypt. A 1981 study reveals that more than 84 percent of Armenians in Montreal were foreign-born. This ratio is similar to a demographic and ethnocultural profile of 1986 census data showing that almost 85 percent of Toronto Armenians were born abroad. Clearly, the Armenian community in Canada was predominantly young and foreign-born, with a growing proportion born in Canada.[13]

RESIDENTIAL PATTERNS

In Toronto, with no recognizable Armenian neighbourhood and with settlement scattered throughout the city, the newcomers fell into the same residential pattern of dispersal throughout the city, in effect sustaining the community without a neighbourhood. For a time, they showed a preference for the Lawrence/Avenue Road, and Lawrence/Bathurst/Dufferin areas, and a small number moved in along Danforth

Avenue, since these locations were relatively close to Holy Trinity Church on Woodlawn Avenue near Yonge Street and to the Armenian community Centre on Dupont Street near Avenue Road. In spite of this focus, Toronto remained a community without a well-defined neighbourhood.

With the building of Armenian community centres and churches in the northeast part of the city (see below), a large number of Armenians settled in the boroughs of North York and Scarborough, particularly from the Don Valley Parkway, east along Highway 401, to an area east of Morningside Avenue. They also gradually moved to the towns of Mississauga, Thornhill, and Markham. But even within this concentration, largely in the northeast part of Metropolitan Toronto, the general pattern of settlement in Toronto remained marked by dispersal.

In 1991 the Armenian population of Montreal was estimated at between ten thousand (1991 census) and forty-five thousand (community figures). Regardless of these discrepancies, Montreal ranks as the largest Armenian community in Canada, a position it has enjoyed since the 1960s. A tabulation of Montreal Armenians based on 1981 census data found, not surprisingly, a predominantly immigrant population, with only about 16 percent born in Canada. Almost 24 percent were born in Egypt; almost 20 percent in Turkey; about 16 percent in Lebanon; and 10 percent in Syria.[14]

The small number of Armenians in Montreal before 1914 had been augmented by the arrival of refugees after the Great War. After World War II, Armenians in Montreal numbered approximately 100 people.[15] Gradually, Park Avenue (avenue du Parc) evolved as the main artery of Armenian settlement and enterprise. During the interwar years, Armenian shops dotted Park Avenue and the side streets, notwithstanding the dispersal of a small number of Armenians in Westmount, Verdun, LaSalle, Lachine, and Ste Adèle in the Laurentians. Post–World War II newcomers consolidated the already existing pattern of settlement. By 1960, the majority of Armenian immigrants lived in a "corridor-shaped area" within a one-mile radius of the corner of Park Avenue and Bernard Street. This area provided work for newcomers, primarily at Ararat Rugs, relatively cheap housing, and a multitude of services, including a YMCA, shops, and proximity to the newly purchased Surp Hagop Church on the corner of St Zotique and Jeanne-Mance. As an added bonus, the area was near the Greek settlement of Montreal, enabling Armenians from Greece to speak and carry on business with the local Greeks. Chain migration added to the location's desirability, as more kith and kin joined the early post–World War II immigrants.[16]

During the 1960s, settlement pushed northward along Park Extension (Park Avenue north of Jean-Talon and along boulevard de L'Acadie). Unlike the poorer "core" area, Park Extension attracted more affluent settlers.[17] The northwestward push continued into Ville St-Laurent and Nouveau Bordeaux.[18] By the early 1970s, more than 60 percent of Montreal Armenians lived in a 1.5-square-mile area comprising four subsections: Ville d'Outremont, Park Extension, St-Laurent, and Nouveau Bordeaux.[19] Settlers were also moving to the Ville de Laval (Chomedy), Mount Royal, and the South Shore, notably Longueuil and Brossard. The push northward into Laval, marked by the purchase of single-family dwellings, was clearly evident in 1988, when approximately 13 percent of Armenians in the Montreal region resided in Chomedy/Laval. The same estimates show that roughly two-thirds of Armenians in Metropolitan Montreal lived in Laval, Nouveau Bordeaux, Ville St-Laurent, and along Park Extension.[20]

This ethnic concentration was not prompted by prejudice on the part of the host society. In fact, knowing French enabled Armenians to spread out into both English- and French-speaking sections of Montreal, unlike previous cohorts, which had lived primarily in immigrant or English-dominated areas. Settlement patterns were dictated by jobs, transportation and communication networks, socioeconomic factors pertaining especially to housing, and internal preferences related to proximity to relatives, Armenian shops, and sociocultural facilities. Preferences for being near family and close to other Armenians have generated broad *internal* segregation within the Armenian corridor, segregation that is related to the immigrant's country of last permanent residence, as well as to socioeconomic factors.

THE COMPOUNDS

Proximity to ethnic structures such as churches, schools, or community centres has also influenced residential concentration. Usually, community buildings follow settlement. For example, Montreal Armenians organized a church on St Zotique near Park Avenue in 1958 and ran an "Armenian home," i.e., a community centre, on Park Avenue. These structures were located in the heart of the Armenian "colony," like St Gregory's church on Carlton Street in St Catharines and the Hamilton community centre on Princess Street.

However, another totally different phenomenon began to emerge with the third wave. In both Toronto and Montreal, Armenians established or relocated organizational and institutional structures in *new* areas and thereby created the nucleus of settlement in *new* districts. Settlement followed structure. Such an initiative was possible because the cities themselves were expanding and suburban areas were receiving increasingly better services. Continued immigration expanded the Armenian communities, which required more and larger facilities, and better facilities, in turn, attracted both newcomers and older residents.

The relocation of Surp Hagop Church in 1968 from St Zotique to Rue Olivar Asselin in Ville St-Laurent and the relocation of the Armenian community centre from Dupont Street in downtown Toronto to Highway 401 and Victoria Park Avenue in 1979 are prime examples. These new structures galvanized new locations of settlement in Ville St-Laurent and in northeast Toronto. In turn, these new settlements both expedited the relocation of existing organizations and institutions and stimulated the establishment of new ones. A snowballing effect occurred. By the 1990s most Armenian organizations and institutions were located west of boulevard de l'Acadie and between boulevard Metropolitain and Rivière de Prairie in Montreal and in Toronto, along Highway 401 east of the Don Valley Parkway towards Morningside.

In its compound, Surp Hagop of the Cilician See has within its immediate vicinity a community centre, the Horizon Press, and various levels of educational facilities ranging from preschool to high school, in addition to a host of political, cultural, athletic, social, and charitable organizations. Similarly in Toronto in 1981 the Armenian General Benevolent Union built the Alex Manoogian Community Centre at Highway 401/Markham Road/Progress Court and inaugurated the Daniel and Alice Zaroukian Day School in 1985. Two years later, the Church of the Holy Trinity relocated from Woodlawn Avenue in downtown Toronto to its new premises next to the centre and the school. As a response to the absence of the early type of tightly knit neighbourhood and as a counterpoint to residential dispersion, such a concentration of resources brings together Armenians of all ages, from different socioeconomic classes, various immigration cohorts, and various source countries.

While these complexes or compounds cut across a number of potentially divisive interests, we rarely find different political ideologies or religious affiliations sharing the same facilities, since the perimeters between the complexes are usually delineated along political or religious lines. In Toronto, for instance, the Echmiadzin Holy Trinity Church, the Armenian General Benevolent Union Alex Manoogian Community Centre, and the Zaroukian Armenian Day School are all in the same complex, which is supported by the Armenian Democratic Liberal Party, or Ramgavar organization. A few miles away, the Cilician St Mary's Church, the Armenian National Committee Community Center (ARF, Dashnak), and the Armenian Relief Society Day School form another nucleus of activity.

The complexes provide restaurants for Armenian and Canadian cuisine, as well as facilities reminiscent of old coffeehouses for men to play cards and backgammon. While such informality occurs, the real heart of these structures is a robust emphasis on organizational and institutional activities, ranging from regular church services, seniors clubs, men's clubs, women's societies, political associations, choirs, theatrical and dance groups, scouts and guides, sports teams, youth groups, full-day schools, and Saturday and Sunday schools. Some centres also offer information about jobs and housing, as well as counselling and social services. A visit to any of the community centre complexes strikes the visitor with the sound of children playing outside in the grounds, young people practising basketball in the gym, seniors meeting in one of the rooms, men organizing a fundraising banquet, women planning a bazaar, and the church choir practising in one room while a theatre group rehearses in another. The variety and level of activity is astounding.

In their own fashion then, these complexes have replaced the neighbourhoods as the locus of community activity. While they lack the breadth of the old neighbourhoods – the streets and verandas and the proximity of living space – they nevertheless provide a meeting ground and gathering place for community members to congregate and to maintain and enhance linguistic, cultural, and religious customs and traditions. These powerful networks offer participants opportunities to develop their potential in myriad ways, while still keeping them within the invisible boundaries of the community. And they link Armenians with each other, strengthen Armenian identity in Canada, and enhance Armenian ethnocultural development and progress. This environment gives Armenian communities a measure of autonomy within Canadian society that is somewhat reminiscent of the self-regulation and mutual help in former countries of residence. Accordingly, the rate of crime and indigence is noticeably low, almost nonexistent. As a mechanism for adjustment to Canadian society, furthermore, the complexes and their services act as a cushion for newcomers as they move into the mainstream. While these complexes offer intimacy and group cohesion, they also allow for a great measure of flexibility. Community members can enjoy privacy at the same time that they have every opportunity to integrate into the larger society.

On the other hand, the absence of a physical neighbourhood where men could walk to a corner coffeehouse to play cards or to a local shoe repair shop or barber shop to gossip prompted a group of men to meet at a local Toronto mall. For some time, they congregated at the Fairview Mall, which was within walking distance of their residences, and played cards and backgammon. The mall authorities, however, frowned on this informal gathering, and eventually the men were obliged to leave. They found a more hospitable environment at the local library, which offered them a meeting room. About forty men, calling themselves the Fairview Library Armenian Seniors Association meet three afternoons a week to chat, read, and play cards and backgammon in a smoke-free environment.[21]

While immigrants who arrived after World War II built on the work of their predecessors and while leadership remained in the hands of the pre–World War II immigrants for a number of years, the newcomers, with their numbers, youth, and dedication were comparatively such a powerful group that they moulded the settlements in Montreal and Toronto according to their needs. The newcomers brought with them their organizations and foods and the characteristics and behavioural patterns relating to their countries of origin.[22] The issue of language is a case in point. The Armenian language has two different forms, the Eastern, spoken in Armenia and Iran, and the Western, spoken in all other places. Initially, Western Armenian was the language of communication in Canada. With the movement of Armenians from Iran, and later from Armenia, the Eastern form has been introduced into Canada.

EMPLOYMENT

Armenian participation in the Canadian labour force kept pace with the economic developments in the country. Interestingly, many who entered Canada as tradesmen such as tailors, shoemakers, or seamstresses initially worked in the rug business – cleaning, dyeing, repairing, and selling rugs – and some eventually chose to remain in rug-related work. A businessman from Aleppo, Syria, is a case in point. After graduating from the Mkhitarist Armenian Catholic College in Aleppo, he had received his electro-technician's diploma in 1948 from the Institut Electro-Radio in Paris and worked at electroplating, specializing in nickel, copper, chrome, gold, and silver plating. He was married with a family, spoke five languages, and could pay his own passage and bring in twenty-five thousand Canadian dollars to start his own business. In a letter he notes that he visited Canada to study "the working and living conditions" and was convinced he would be self-supporting in a short time and would be "helpful" to Canada. Immediately after his arrival, he began working for a rug merchant and eventually opened his own very successful store.²³

A brief account of some immigrants from Greece also gives a sense of initial work experiences. In 1957, a year after arrival, they were all gainfully employed and most were attending evening English-language classes, and had joined the local YMCA. Bedoukian speculated that their keen desire to adjust readily to Canada could be related to the fact that "they are not coming from their own country, but from a place where they never felt permanent. Given the opportunity to make Canada their permanent home, they are eager to fit in as quickly as possible." The following profiles have been chosen at random.

_____ was employed at Yervant's Oriental Rug cleaning plant, where he was in charge of carpet installation, was attending night school, and spoke English quite well.

_____ worked at the Hamilton Steel Works, had a son born in Canada, and recently purchased his own home for $10,000.

_____ a hard worker, was employed in a laundry, had learned some English and French.

_____ worked at Ararat Rugs as a carpet cleaner, was helping his parents in Greece, just beginning to understand English.

_____ had four workers in his family, made "great strides financially," paid off their loan promptly, purchased modern appliances, was attending night school, active in YMCA, children spoke English fluently. (No reference to type of work.)

_____ was working at Ararat as an on-location carpet cleaner, very valuable worker, could not get driver's licence because of poor English.

_____ was doing well as a jeweller, a promising young man.

_____ was a watchmaker, had brought out his parents and sister to Canada, was attending night school at university, a very bright and intelligent boy.

_____ was working at Yervant's Oriental Rugs, in charge of a crew of carpet cleaners, sponsored and brought his family to Canada, purchased land to build a home, spoke English fluently, was attending school and was active in YMCA.²⁴

Out of the above eight references that reveal the type of work, 50 percent of the immigrants were employed in the rug business and 25 percent in the jewellery business. As earlier cohorts had used the factory and the carpet trade as a channel for work, so also many post–World War II newcomers used the rug or jewellery business as a vehicle with which to enter other employment or as a means of establishing their own business in these fields.

Armenians gradually moved into a niche market: manufacturing, importing, retailing, setting, and repairing jewellery. In Montreal in 1983, it was found that about 50 percent of the gem-stone setting ateliers were operated by Armenians.[25] Another increasingly popular line of work was related to the automotive industry – automobile, truck, and bus repairing and painting, car rentals, new and used car sales, and foreign car imports. In both the jewellery and automotive industry, Armenians brought with them considerable expertise and funds from their businesses in the countries of emigration.

Other lines of endeavour included printing and photography; real estate sales, building, and development; trades, including carpentry and shoe repairing; picture framing; and the manufacture of precision tools and of leather goods. Food-related enterprises such as bakeries, restaurants, and grocery stores and the manufacture of Armenian foods such as bulgur catered not only to Armenian clientele but also to many others who had recently arrived from the Middle East. Medicine, engineering, and teaching have remained popular professions among Armenians. In 1990–91, it was estimated that Montreal had about 70 Armenian doctors, more than 25 dentists, as many pharmacists, and 134 engineers. The 1992 Armenian telephone directory in Toronto listed 20 physicians and 17 dentists.[26] Armenians have also branched out into other professions, including, in particular, law and pharmacy.

THE WANING OF THE PIONEER SETTLEMENTS

While the Montreal and Toronto communities flourished with the post–World War II wave of immigration, what became of the old pioneer settlements in Brantford, St Catharines, Galt, and Hamilton? Before World War I, Brantford anticipated a prosperous future as a bustling industrial city. For a number of reasons, Brantford's fortunes declined, companies relocated or closed down altogether, immigrants shunned the town, and local young people fled to employment, educational, or marital opportunities elsewhere. Without a strong and determined core element or active leadership, with internal conflict, exogamy, and a typically low Canadian birthrate, the Brantford Armenian community continued on a downward spiral that had started in the post–World War I period. If membership in a political party is any indication of general decline, we can readily see this transformation in the rolls of the Dashnak Party. In 1910 Brantford boasted 114 members, by 1918 membership had dropped to 87, and by 1925 it had plunged to a mere 11. Community cohesion gradually disintegrated. Eventually, both the Progressive and the Dashnak clubs were sold. No political party or church held the community together. Today just a small number of Armenian names dot the telephone directory. Only the gravestones in the city cemetery stand as silent monuments to the existence of a once robust Armenian community.

St Catharines, on the other hand, remained a good place to live and work, but the community in St Catharines was shattered by the 1933 church crisis. Still, in St Catharines, job prospects not only kept many of the younger generation in the city but also attracted some newcomers of the third wave. Both Dashnaks and the church group, moreover, have had a dedicated core and diligent leadership that has managed to preserve a measure of community cohesion. The church has remained intact; in fact it has expanded. In their turn, the Dashnaks have sold their hall across from General Motors and built a larger and more beautiful community centre in a new subdivision. Many local residents have rejoiced about these obvious signs of group stability and progress; others see them as problematic, citing the unrelenting demands on a small community to support two facilities. A profile of the community, based on 1986 census data reveals that the single largest group of those giving Armenian as their mother tongue was in the fifty-five to sixty-four age group, about 25 percent of the total. Only 32 percent of the total were born abroad (no doubt mostly in the pre–World War II period). Thus, according to census data by the mid-1980s St Catharines had an aging Armenian-speaking population that had not been rejuvenated by a big influx of young newcomers. The composition of both the church and the Dashnak organization confirms these findings, as both old-timers and newcomers shared membership.

The communities of Galt, Hespeler, and Preston have amalgamated as the city of Cambridge. Here the influx of newcomers revitalized the old community. Cambridge received settlers descended from the survivors of Musa Dagh (Mt. Moses) (see Franz Werfel's *Forty Days of Musa Dagh*), mainly from the villages of Kessab and Anjar (Syria). Famous for their resistance to the Turkish attack on their region in 1915 and their final deliverance by French ships in the Mediterranean, the settlers commemorate their victory every September with the traditional feast of *harisa* (wheat and veal). This new type of cultural dimension reflects a general decline in the predominance of Keghi culture and Keghetsi ways, which had characterized the old communities for half a century. In Cambridge, too, the little community centre has given way to a much larger complex (1980) incorporating the church of St Nshan.

Hamilton was also able to retain some of its youth and attract a small number of immigrants of the third wave. Initially newcomers joined relatives in the Armenian neighbourhood. Thus, in the 1950s and 1960s the Armenian community in Hamilton, and indeed the Armenian neighbourhood, was marked by a mix of old-timers and newcomers. A demographic and ethnocultural profile of those giving Armenian as their mother tongue in Hamilton, based on 1986 census data, reveals an aging population, with the largest single group in the 40–54 age group (slightly more than 40%). Approximately 80% of those giving Armenian as their mother tongue were born outside Canada, indicating on the one hand an aging population over 65 and a growing number of newcomers, on the other.[27] Indeed, the leadership of St Mary's church and the Armenian National Committee (Dashnak) is shared by newcomers and old-timers alike. However, as Canadian-born Armenians leave the organizations and institutions, the new arrivals are gradually taking over leadership roles in the community. Old age, death, exogamy, and conflict between cohorts have weakened community solidarity, as indeed have assimilation and rejection of the community itself.

The old Armenian neighborhood in Hamilton lasted about eighty years, roughly from 1910 to 1990 – a mark of some distinction considering the small size of the Armenian community. For the most part, the elderly remained in little Armenia in the Sherman/Princess/Gibson/Birch area around the Armenian community centre in the working class north end of the city. But for the younger members of the community, other considerations and experiences dominated their choice of residence. Since neighbourhoods were arenas of human activity, they were as much a place of constraint, envy, hostility, and fractiousness as they were of harmony, friendship, mutual aid, and neighbourly love. The very strengths that gave the neighborhood and the community it housed its raison d'être also became its weakness. Neighbourhoods facilitated integration into mainstream society, to be sure, but even as they did so, young people began to reject what they considered the stranglehold of neighbourhood life.

Canadian mores and behavioural patterns, furthermore, highlighted the often stifling atmosphere of the neighbourhood, its taboos, "old-fashioned" customs, and narrow moral standards. Young people yearned for the privacy and liberty of the larger world just as the call of career opportunities and marriage prospects broadened their horizons. The "eyes" that had protected them in childhood were seen in young adulthood as intrusion and interference. The equilibrium that had existed between public and private spheres and between public and private behaviour became imbalanced when immigrants and their native-born children and grandchildren diverged over what was and was not acceptable. Young people fled from the group and its space, craving instead anonymity in mainstream society.

The unbridled growth of suburbia has destroyed many downtown cores and left emptiness and danger where once attractive buildings had watched the engaging activity of the city scene. Young Armenians in Hamilton abandoned the old working class "homeland" and moved to other cities or to more affluent sections of Hamilton. As the second, third, and fourth generations grew up, improved their socioeconomic standing, took jobs outside the factory, opened their own businesses, or entered the professions, they began to move away from the working-class area, from the noises and smells of industrial Hamilton, and away from the poverty that seemed to personify Armenian town. They sought bigger and better housing, better access to amenities, better schooling for their children elsewhere.

What is noteworthy is that Armenians did not attempt to reconstitute neighbourhood life in another, more affluent part of Hamilton but, rather, moved in a dispersed fashion. They bought homes in middle-class areas, such as on Hamilton Mountain or in small towns around Hamilton, like Dundas, Burlington, and Stoney Creek. The advantages and the intrinsic value of neighbourhood life were lost, as residents conformingly dispersed to houses lined row upon row upon row and as malls emerged as the locus of shopping. While once Armenian women had walked to the grocery store, shopped, chatted, socialized, and gossiped along the streets, people drove to shops, mostly non-Armenian ones at that, for items like *bulgur* and *gorgod, lahmajun* and *beorag*. The automobile became the only means of getting around and together with the telephone enabled residents to keep in contact with other Armenians, the Armenian community centre, and the newly founded St Mary's Apostolic Church. The old ambiance faded away and gradually vanished.[28]

The migration away from the core neighbourhood and the influx of non-Armenians into the area prompted Dashnak community members to sell the community centre on Princess Street in 1995 and to purchase a building far from the old settlement in Stoney Creek for a new community centre. While this centre has neither the flavour of the old neighbourhood nor the concentration of activity of the Toronto and Montreal complexes, it is working in conjunction with St Mary's Church (Echmiadzin) to fulfill community needs.

In reviewing one hundred years of Armenian settlement in Brantford, St Catharines, Galt/Cambridge, and Hamilton, it might be worthwhile to sum up why these Armenian communities declined. At the forefront was the Canadian immigration program, which profoundly affected the size, composition, and geographic location of Armenian settlement. Restrictions kept the communities small, and numerical size can make a dramatic difference to a community's vitality. Indeed, in a country of immigration, Armenian communities in Canada received no great impetus from new immigration from roughly 1914 to the late 1950s, a period of about forty years, discounting the small number of refugees permitted to enter after 1918. Initially these cities attracted immigrants partly because Canadian immigration authorities discouraged Armenians from settling on Western land and partly because jobs in southern Ontario were available and accessible. But when employment opportunities dwindled and when companies relocated elsewhere or closed down altogether – as in the case of Brantford, Armenians moved to other places in search of work. The fate of the Armenian community in Brantford, then, is very closely linked to the growth and prosperity of the city itself and to its decline. The same cannot be said about St Catharines, for here General Motors continued to thrive, but the community was shaken from within. St Catharines remains an example of how internal conflict can reshape the structure and dampen the vigour of community life. Hamilton and Cambridge, on the other hand, continued to offer employment and were not severely undermined by the rancor of the church crisis; yet they have not expanded and flourished. Unlike Brantford and St Catharines, where a single dominant force played havoc in the community, Hamilton and Cambridge show how a combination of external and internal factors can sap community cohesion: small numbers, tensions between old and new cohorts, intermarriage, attrition, departure from the city, and assimilation into the larger Canadian society.

As leading actors in Armenian community life in Canada these pioneer communities have been replaced by Montreal and Toronto. Here women and men from all over the Armenian diaspora – people who were different in myriad ways – came together in Canada and together forged new social, economic, political, religious, cultural, and educational foundations based on the common denominator of their Armenian heritage. Their sense of Armenianness united these people and promoted organizational and institutional development, which not only nurtured and enhanced Armenian culture in the diaspora but also strengthened their loyalty to Canada and deepened their sense of a Canadian identity.

19

Institutional and Organizational Life

In the Armenian diaspora, loyalty to the homeland has been a consistent and enduring force, regardless of political or religious affiliation. Yet no word exists in Armenian or, for that matter, in English to define this frame of mind. Neither *azgaser* (love of nation) nor nationalism grasp the subtleties of the diaspora/homeland dimension. To refer to a diasporan allegiance to a homeland or to the idea of a homeland, I have chosen to use the word "ethnopatriotism." As we have seen throughout this study, one of the principal characteristics of the Armenians in Canada has been their attachment to the homeland, which has been driven by feelings about the insecurity of the nation and its people and about the fragility of their culture and identity. Before World War I, Armenians in Canada were troubled by the oppression and persecution of their people in the Ottoman and, at times, the Russian Empires. After the Genocide they were tormented by the fear of national extinction. In more recent times, while they rejoiced at the creation of an independent Armenian state, they knew that it was not free of danger. As in the past, its precariousness has again mobilized Armenians to help the homeland.

All opposing factions considered themselves *the* true patriots, a belief that was shared by many other ethnic groups, especially those whose homeland fell behind the Iron Curtain. Indeed, Communist propaganda itself drew lines between "the 'bourgeois nationalism' of the non-communist world, which it condemned, and 'proletarian nationalism,' which consist[ed] solely in loyalty to the Soviet Union as a socialist fatherland."[1] What remains significant, though assuredly not unique about the Armenian case is that organizations and institutions, each in their own fashion, became engaged in a determined effort to preserve Armenian identity in the diaspora and to raise the community's consciousness about Armenian issues. In fact, their strength and popularity often depended on the degree of commitment to the Old World and its traditions.

Eventually, different interpretations evolved as to what it meant to be an Armenian. Brantford Progressives, St Catharines Hnchaks, Hamilton Dashnaks, Montreal parishioners, and Toronto AGBU members, each regarded themselves as *the* true Armenians, whether they defined their Armenian ethnopatriotism in terms of an all-engrossing national political consciousness or as a deeply felt ethnocultural heritage. The reverse side of this ethnopatriotic coin was as fervent a belief that "the other kind of Armenian" was not a true Armenian. Thus, the different political, religious, and cultural groups kept a close watch on developments in the Old World at the same time that they endeavoured to uphold Old World culture and language in North America. Their rivalry strengthened a sense of Armenian identity in the New World, but their divisiveness also served to undermine the very identity the immigrant generation sought to entrench.

Participation in Armenian-Canadian organizations and institutions remains a major bellwether of the strength and vitality of the community. It has also been an important indicator of heritage retention. For many, institutional and organizational participation has been the principal venue for expressing their Armenianness, keeping dynamic individuals inside the fold, providing an outlet for talent, training young leaders, and transmitting to the new generation not only a spirit of camaraderie but also the group's principal priorities. Whatever their motives and whatever their deeds, the variety, degree, and intensity of community participation have been monumental. This success also reflects the fertile environment in Canada, which, far from being hostile or indifferent, has permitted ethnocultural enhancement. In turn, organizations and institutions have forged a strong liaison with the host society, have helped ease the transition for the immigrant generation, and have enabled the Canadian-born to have access to a rich ethnocultural heritage.

Shortly after they set foot on Canadian soil, Armenians created various types of organizations to meet their different needs. They started regional, political, charitable, cultural, and youth associations whose origins can be traced to Canada, the village, the homeland, or another place in the diaspora. Over a period of one hundred years these organizations have interacted with each other and with their host society. Invariably, as with any viable and dynamic force, they have overlapped and have been superimposed on one another. As they responded to new conditions and demands, they were transformed; or when they became anachronisms in a changing world, they dissolved and disappeared altogether. Others continued, even flourished. By and large, the organizations and institutions carry on activities with more than a single focus and in more than one geographic area. The Armenian Relief Society and the Armenian General Benevolent Union, for instance, work in charitable, cultural, and educational arenas both in Canada and abroad. This fact emphasizes yet again the extent and importance of Armenian networks in holding together a vast diaspora.

The institutions and organizations have brought together Armenians with different Old World traditions and customs and reshaped and remoulded them into Armenian Canadians. From this orientation, Armenian Canadians refined Armenian ethnoculture in Canada.[2] Within this context, I touch on two other characteristics of Armenian institutional and organizational life in Canada. First, in the early years of the twentieth century, Armenians in Canada relied on their counterparts in the United States, but over the span of the twentieth century, a gradual independence from their American confreres developed. A Canadian focus and a growing desire to "be Canadian" is evident in the churches, organizations, and schools and in the press. The second characteristic is also typically Canadian and pertains to the Anglo-French fact. Although Armenian communities exist in different parts of Canada, Montreal has clearly become the "headquarters" of Armenian organizations and institutions in Canada. This fact adds a unique dimension to Armenian community life, because it keeps Armenians in touch with developments in Quebec and within the francophonie. It also gives a place to both official languages, which is evident in full-day schools where both official languages are taught, in newspapers such as *Horizon* and *Abaka*, which are trilingual, and in efforts by community leaders to enhance communication in both official languages.

During the twentieth century, the nature of community leadership gradually changed. In the early years, wealthy rug merchants like Levon Babayan, Yervant Pasdermajian, and Kerop Bedoukian or businessmen like John H. (Jack) Mooradian guided the young settlements. They shared leadership with ordinary factory workers and small businessmen who ran the day-to-day affairs of churches, political organizations, and regional associations. In the Canadian milieu these men were not seen as important or influential, but in the community their role was particularly significant, for they established the foundations of Armenian organizational and institutional traditions in Canada. With the third wave, more professional men, both those educated abroad and those educated in Canada, took the reins of power. They, in turn, shared leadership with prominent families, business interests, and strong religious headship centred in the diocese and prelacy in Montreal. Although descendants of earlier cohorts continue to participate in community organizations, their marginalization will no doubt intensify without meaningful inclusion by the dominant group and without the use of English at meetings and church services.

THE CHURCHES

The Armenian Apostolic Church

The rapprochement among the various political and church factions during World War II was sustained for a short time after the war. From 1945 to 1954, Rev. Khoren Mamigonian, with his headquarters in St Catharines, was the itinerant priest serving Canada and Niagara Falls, New York. Services were invariably held in Anglican churches, except, of course, in St Catharines. The diocesan primate in New York, Bishop Tiran Nersoyan, conducted a pastoral visit to various Canadian cities in 1947–48. Prompted by his visit, local leaders organized elections for religious councils that were somewhat reminiscent of the pre–1933 initiatives. In Hamilton and Brantford, where the old religious councils of the post-Tourian period had fallen into disuse, and in Montreal, elected representatives were drawn from different political factions.[3] In Montreal, for example, the parish council included Yervant Pasdermajian, Kerop Bedoukian, Archie Shiroyan, and Vahan Dirado(u)rian.

Echmiadzin The elected committees started working towards building a church. In 1953 Toronto Armenians built their own church on Woodlawn Avenue near Yonge Street. Finally, after more than twenty years, St Catharines had a sister church in Canada. Toronto Armenians named their church Holy Trinity, in recognition of the hospitality they had received at the Anglican church with the same name for almost twenty years. For Armenians, Holy Trinity, which was the first Armenian-owned community structure in the city, became not only a place of worship, a meeting home for friends and relatives, and a magnet for future immigrants but also a centre for cultural, athletic, social, and educational activities, especially for young people. Holy Trinity looked to Echmiadzin, but here all Armenians could participate in church functions. For a time the church had only a visiting priest, but in 1961 the community, swelled by new immigrants, could support a full-time priest. In the meantime, Very Rev. Vazken Tatoyan took up the pastorship in Montreal, where by then the community had grown to include about one thousand Armenians.

By the 1960s, as less rigid immigration regulations admitted an increasing number of Armenians, three parishes under the jurisdiction of Echmiadzin served Ontario and Quebec (St Catharines, Toronto, and Montreal). In 1967, the Diocesan Vicarage was founded in Canada; it was situated in Montreal under the jurisdiction of the Diocese of North America (Echmiadzin), with Bishop Vatché Hovsepian as the first vicar general (1967-71). The following year, His Holiness Catholicos Vazken I of Echmiadzin paid his first pontifical visit to Canada, an occasion of great celebration and joy.

The Cathedral of St Gregory the Illuminator in Ville d'Outremont in Montreal, formerly St Giles United Church, was purchased for $250,000, renovated by the Armenian-Canadian community, and consecrated in 1970, with Patriarch Shenork Kaloustian, patriarch of Constantinople; Archbishop Torkom Manoogian, primate of the Armenian Diocese of North America (New York); and Bishop Vatché Hovsepian. During the 1970s, as more immigrants entered Canada and as their religious needs required greater attention, church members in Canada negotiated with the Holy See in Soviet Armenia to establish their own separate Canadian diocese. In 1980 they received an encyclical from the catholicos consenting to an independent diocese in Canada, and three years later, Very Rev. Vazken Keshishian, the first primate in Canada, presided over the initial meeting of the diocesan assembly of the Canadian diocese held in Toronto. When His Holiness Vazken I, Catholicos of all Armenians, made another pontifical visit to Canada in 1987, he held services in St Gregory the Illuminator in Montreal, the mother cathedral of the Canadian diocese and consecrated the new building of the Church of the Holy Trinity, at Highway 401 and Markham Road in Toronto.

In the meantime, other communities initiated efforts first to establish a parish (usually with services in an Anglican church and often under the care of an Armenian visiting or itinerant priest) and then to buy or build their own church structure. By 1998 the diocese (Echmiadzin) had five churches in Canada: St Catharines, Toronto, Montreal, Vancouver (St Vartan, 1984), and Hamilton (St Mary, 1985). In addition, four communities were designated as parishes with parish councils, auxiliary organizations, and a regular schedule of church services, festivities, and activities: Ottawa (St Mesrob, parish in 1978), Laval (Holy Cross), Mississauga (St Vartan), and Windsor (Holy Resurrection). Even small communities, which nevertheless wished to maintain relations with the diocese, organized mission parishes under the direction of Archbishop Hovnan Derderian, primate of Canada (to 2002): namely, Halifax, Winnipeg, Edmonton, and Calgary. Both those designated as parishes and those designated as mission parishes received regular visits from clergy for Divine Liturgy.[4]

Cilicia When the Armenian factions in the United States clashed in 1933, the pro-Dashnaks, deprived of church services, formed the prelacy in New York City, and its future was subsequently closely linked to the Great House of Cilicia (see the section titled "Prelude," in the introduction to this book, and chapter 7). When the Cilician See was transferred from Sis in Turkey to Antelias, near Beirut, Lebanon, it retained its original historic name and maintained, under its jurisdiction, four dioceses: Aleppo, Lebanon, Damascus, and Cyprus. These dioceses became progressively more important after the Great War, when they emerged as major centres of refugee settlement. The strong Dashnak presence in Lebanon and Syria, the tensions of the Cold War, and the democratic structure of the Armenian Church, with lay and clerical voting privileges to elect the catholicos, all had an impact on it. Once again, politics rather than doctrine or theology drove a wedge into the Armenian community.

In early 1957, the National Representative Assembly of the prelacy convened at St Gregory the Illuminator's Cathedral in New York City to consider the situation of the "unaffiliated diocese," a diocese that had been "deprived of holy *muron* [chrism], longed for the blessings of Echmiadzin, and only through the assistance of a few priests, [had been] able to take care of the spiritual needs of its adherents."[5] In spite of Echmiadzin's opposition, the Representative Assembly appealed to Cilicia in 1957 "to accept our Diocese in the structure of the Hierarchy of the Cilician Catholicosate, as a separate diocese of Cilicia." The Cilician Catholicosate, under the newly elected pontiff, Zareh I (Payaslian), agreed to accept the United States diocese under its authority, despite Echmiadzin's condemnation of this move as a defiant encroachment on its territorial jurisdiction and an illegal dilution of its authority.

In 1957, His Holiness Catholicos Zareh I sent as his legate Bishop Khoren Paroyan, later catholicos of the Great House of Cilicia, to visit diasporan communities in Canada and the United States. The following year, Montreal Armenians converted the building on St Zotique and named it Surp Hagop [St. James]. The growing needs of the community heralded a major drive to build a new church in Montreal, which was constructed on rue Olivar Asselin and which fell under the jurisdiction of the prelacy in New York City, which itself looked to Cilicia. Rev. Armen Ishkhanian served Surp Hagop from 1974 until well into the 1990s. In the meantime, Rev. Sempad Der Meksian served as an itinerant priest in southern Ontario and Niagara Falls, New York. The second church in Canada under the jurisdiction of the prelacy in New York and of Cilicia, Surp Astvadsadsin (St Mary, Mother of God) started services in Toronto in 1983; the building was consecrated by His Holiness Catholicos Karekin II in 1990. Six years later Bishop Khajag Hagopian, formerly the priest in Toronto, was appointed the first vicar general of Canada under the wing of the prelacy in New York. In 2004, the Canadian vicarage separated from New York and formed the Canadian prelacy with direct affiliation to the Great House of Cilicia in Antelias, Lebanon. Currently Archbishop Hagopian has five parishes in his care: Montreal, Surp Hagop (St James); Toronto, Surp Astvadsadsin (St Mary); Laval, Surp Kevork (St George); Cambridge, Surp Nshan (Holy Sign); and Vancouver, Surp Krikor Lusavorich (St Gregory the Illuminator).[6]

While having two churches allows outlets for different ideological and political perspectives, the division does weaken well-meaning efforts at community building, because it promotes a proliferation and repetition of services and dissipates limited financial, moral, and other resources. However, the two churches are not irreconcilably polarized. Major events, such as the commemoration of the Genocide, bring the two groups together in an official capacity, not to mention the many circumstances in which individuals co-operate outside the formal sphere. When the community split in 1933, one faction remained outside the church. But today, those who choose to leave one group can usually join the other side, so that if a conflict arises an individual is not obliged to forsake his Armenian heritage or be ostracized from the Armenian church. Individuals can move from one side to the other and still "be Armenian."

Armenian Evangelical Churches

As already indicated, a small number of Protestant students and families (e.g., Courian, Utudjian, Charkoyan, Posigian) immigrated to Canada before World War II, but they were not numerous enough to found their own church and usually attended Canadian Protestant churches, most notably the United Church of Canada (after 1925). The third wave of immigration brought more Protestants, and in 1960 they established the First Armenian Evangelical Church in Montreal and the Armenian Evangelical Church in Toronto, under the leadership of Rev. Soghomon Nigoghosian. Both churches are affiliated with the Armenian Evangelical Union of North America (founded 1971).[7] The Armenian Evangelical United Church of Montreal (founded 1964) and the Armenian Evangelical United Church of Cambridge, Ontario (founded

1970), are associated with the United Church of Canada. These four churches organized the Armenian Missionary Association of Canada in 1984, in order to encourage religious, educational, literary, and philanthropic work. The Armenian Brotherhood Bible Churches in Toronto and Montreal date back to the early twentieth century in the spiritual revivals in Cilicia, and gathered momentum in Aleppo, Syria, in the 1920s, under Abraham Seferian, an Armenian Evangelical layman. In less than two decades the Armenian Brethren Church branched out in Aleppo, Beirut, and Cairo, and in South America and the United States.[8] The Armenian Brotherhood is a Bible-centred, evangelistic, and nonecumenical movement associated with the General Union of Armenian Brotherhood Churches (founded 1980–81, in Pasadena, California). While the Armenian Protestant congregations may be linked to larger entities in North America, they are autonomous churches.

This tradition of autonomy has led to serious controversy in the United States but has not rent the evangelical churches in Canada. In the United States, some members advocated relinquishing the unique Armenian characteristics of their churches in favour of community churches open to all nationalities, of dropping the word "Armenian" from the church name, of using only English in the services, and of abandoning the Armenian ethnic heritage altogether. Others strongly opposed these changes and argued that the preservation of the Armenian heritage and culture was a major responsibility of the Evangelical churches. While some churches in the United States experimented with the concept of community churches, their efforts have proven counterproductive.[9]

The Catholic Church

The small group of Armenian Catholics from Mardin who settled in the province of Quebec before 1914 were joined by relatives after the Genocide. The post–1950 immigration brought more Armenian Catholics to Canada, principally to Montreal. Initially they were served by an itinerant priest from the United States, Father Grégoire Guerguerian. Three hundred families in Montreal, primarily from Egypt, attended the Greek Melkite church of St Sauveur. In 1966 they received recognition as an Armenian congregation by His Eminence Cardinal Léger, and under the guidance of their first priest, Rev. Msgr. Edouard Kurdy (Edward Kortigian), the community held services in the chapel of St Antoine until they constructed their own church and centre, Notre Dame de Nareg, in 1983.[10] In Toronto, the Armenian Catholics, organized as a congregation in 1974, held services in St

Edward's Catholic Church until they built their own church complex, St Gregory the Illuminator, in 1993. Combined, they have a church membership of more than one thousand families. The two Catholic churches in Canada are of the Bzommar Order (Beirut) and fall under the jurisdiction of the Apostolic Exarchate for Armenian Catholics of North America (1982), located in the United States, which, in turn, comes under the authority of the Armenian Patriarch in Beirut and, ultimately, the pope in Rome.[11]

Armenian churches sponsor a host of ancillary organizations, including schools, ladies auxiliaries, youth and sports groups, senior citizens groups, and theatrical, dance, and choral groups; they also publish periodicals. They face the usual problems confronting other ethnic churches in Canada, such as competition from Canadian mainstream churches, the tensions between different cohorts of immigrants, recruitment of the young, the place of women in the church hierarchy, the lack of faith, the work of the church in social/secular areas, and the role of the church as an agent in preserving ethnic identity and maintaining the ethnic heritage and culture. In addition Armenian churches must cope with difficulties that are specifically Armenian, such as the unity of the churches, their relationship with Armenia, the revitalization of the Armenian Apostolic Church in Armenia after years of Communist repression, and the separation/integration of the Church and Armenian political organizations.[12] Language use is particularly problematic. As Armenians are a dispersed people, they bring with them many languages, including Arabic, Turkish, and French. These, added to English, the vernacular and classical forms of Armenian, and the Eastern and Western forms of the language render the medium of church services the subject of ongoing and serious debate. However, a measure of renewed interest in religion, in spirituality, and in traditions gives hope of overcoming impediments to church harmony.

POLITICAL ORGANIZATIONS

Although Armenian political factions began as political "parties" with specific ideologies, they have evolved in the diaspora more as political community organizations with a host of ancillary subgroupings involved in all aspects of community life, including schools, the arts, the press, and youth, sports, women's, and seniors' groups. In addition to their involvement in Canadian political life, the organizations have adopted a double-pronged approach to Armenian affairs: they have focussed both on the diaspora and on the homeland. On the one hand, they have perpetuated Armenian culture and traditions, an Armenian consciousness, and an Armenian identity in the diaspora and on the other, they have endeavoured to strengthen the old country and to publicize concerns about Armenia worldwide.

In a century of genocide, displacement, and political turmoil, the fate of the homeland has emerged as a major thrust of activities. Before 1915 diasporan Armenians helped their persecuted countrymen in the Ottoman and Russian Empires by raising funds for victims of pogroms and petitioning Western political and religious leaders on behalf of their compatriots. Following the Genocide, during the peace negotiations, and to the present day, Armenians continue their humanitarian assistance and political intercession on behalf of Armenia and of Armenians. The recognition of the Genocide has occupied their energies, particularly in view of the Turkish government's stubborn denial of the crime and its powerful lobby to distort the truth. The central objectives of Armenian political mobilization are to obtain, as a minimum, full recognition by Turkey of the crime, in order to restore dignity to the one and a half million Armenian victims and, further, to obtain compensation for survivor losses of family, property, and territory.

In the 1970s and 1980s, changes in Soviet Armenia encompassing cultural and economic progress, greater religious tolerance, and a more open attitude to the West improved ties between Armenia and Armenian Canadians. Exchanges and visits became more numerous, the transatlantic press more accessible, and the relationship between the Dashnak party and Soviet Armenia less acrimonious. With the renewed turmoil in the Caucasus beginning in February 1988, the political organizations have been obliged to reappraise their relationship with each other and with Armenia, as well as to reexamine the role of the diaspora vis-à-vis Armenia and her neighbours.

Currently, the Dashnaks form the largest political organization in Canada. In the mid-1990s, the organization sustained eight branches: Hamilton (founded ca 1903), St Catharines (1906), Toronto (1921), Cambridge (Galt, 1907, and Guelph, 1913), Montreal (1956), Vancouver (1969), London and Windsor (combined, 1975), and Laval (1992). (The Brantford branch had dissolved some years before). Already by 1962, the Montreal Mihran Papazian chapter was the largest with forty-five members. Over a span of almost one hundred years in Canada the Armenian Revolutionary Federation (ARF) has changed in many respects, particularly by moving from left to right, but it has never veered from its nationalist course. The party has enunciated a straightforward and single-minded platform: the creation of a free, independent, and united Armenia. The Armenian Democratic Liberal organization, or Ramgavar Party, was established in Canada in the 1960s with Dr Arshavir Gundjian and Yeznig Boyadjian forging the new party. Currently the ADL has branches in Montreal (Eugene Papazian and

Parounag Tovmassian chapters), Toronto (Yessai Yaghoubian chapter), and Ottawa (Kersam Aharonian chapter). A small but culturally active Hnchak group set down new roots in Montreal and Toronto with the formation of the Nor Serount Cultural Union in the mid-1970s under the leadership of Bedros Mouchian and with the creation of a renewed political component in the early 1980s. All three political organizations have their ancillary constituents, community centres, and press.

In the past, community activity centred around the little clubs or halls and, more recently, around large compounds. Because these conglomerates are so all-encompassing, they have tended to entrench the political polarization of Armenian settlers. On the other hand, they have created rivalries that have stimulated a striving for excellence and group solidarity around powerful symbols and loyalties. For these political factions, two levels or channels of power emerged. On the one hand, a leadership with its specific ideology and priorities kept an eye on affairs from a distant foreign place and maintained contact with the various chapters through correspondence, conferences, and regular visits and lectures by fieldworkers. In the 1980s Dashnaks still praised the inspirational speeches of Reuben Darbinian, Garegin Njdé (Garegin Ter Harutunian), Simon Vratsian, and Kopernik Tandurjian, while Hnchaks extolled the patriotic lectures of the hero Murat, who visited Canada in 1908, of Pandkht, and of Stepan Sabah-Gulian. On the other hand, local leaders and the rank and file, with their own values and motives, did not always agree with the thinking and actions of distant interests. The fluctuation between these two forces – the international and the local – as one played off against the other, became an integral feature of Armenian community life in Canada. Thus, while Armenian Canadian political groupings are part of world-wide organizations, they also have distinctive Canadian characteristics and interests. For example, early Hnchaks and Dashnaks held annual party conventions of the Canadian chapters. St Catharines hosted the first Dashnak regional meeting in 1912 and the seventh in 1921. The Dashnaks revamped their branches in 1937 as the Canadian Regional Committee and in 1975–76 as the Canadian Central Committee. They created the Armenian National Federation to participate in the Canadian Ethnocultural Council and set up the Armenian National Committee of Canada (ANCC) as an advocacy group with governmental and non-governmental jurisdictions.

SCHOOLS

It is somewhat symbolic that the first Armenian known to have entered Canada (ca 1887) was probably a student. For the next hundred years

Armenians in Canada continued to demonstrate a commitment to education, learning, and schooling. When the early settlers arrived, one of the first organizations they founded was not a mutual benefit or sick and burial society; rather, it was a village educational association. Acutely aware, furthermore, of their own stunted education, they took advantage of the freedom in Canada to establish their *gradarans*, or reading rooms, which, as we have seen in earlier chapters, were places for camaraderie, learning, and self-improvement. Settlers also showed an eagerness to learn English and attended English-language classes provided by the local school board or by religious missions.

Refugees of the second wave also set about trying to learn English and to familiarize themselves with Canadian ways. They studied Armenian-English guidebooks and dictionaries, attended movies, read newspapers, talked to their non-Armenian neighbours, and gradually learned more and more about the world around them. They took English-language classes and joined non-Armenian-speaking organizations like church or mission groups.

As the number of children increased in these early communities and as the notion of permanent settlement became entrenched, the concern for learning took on a different focus. Grateful that their children could attend Canadian schools, Armenians encouraged them to study and do well. They were anxious to see their children well-versed in English and familiar with Canadian customs. The children could then act as family interpreters with government officials, life insurance agents, or health clinic personnel. They could also help the family partake of the benefits of its new society. A knowledge of English was the stepping-stone to a better education, and it provided a sound economic base for the community. Parents were prepared to work hard and sacrifice their own comfort to ensure that their children had a good education. Out of 104 second-generation young people living in Hamilton in 1945, for example, at least 13, or more than 10 percent, completed university; this number excludes those who pursued postsecondary education in nursing or elementary school teaching careers, which at that time did not require university training.

Immigrants were also keen to preserve and pass on their fragile culture. In the Ottoman Empire, Armenians had been identified by their religion; they were a Christian minority in a Moslem world. When they came to Canada, they ceased to be a religious minority but became an ethnic and linguistic one. Language took on major prominence. Learning Armenian was not a simple matter of generational transfer. As a group the earliest wave of settlers had come to Canada with a limited knowledge of the language, the result of Ottoman suppression, especially due to the closure of Armenian schools. Many improved their reading and writing skills in Canada. The Genocide survivors also suffered language loss. Not only had the schooling of children been disrupted by the Genocide, but Armenian women and children who had been abducted had been forced to speak Kurdish and Turkish. Many had forgotten their mother tongue. After the war efforts were made to locate these children and place them in orphanages where they relearned Armenian. Under these circumstances the language suffered immeasurably, rendering schools all the more indispensable.

Immigrants were determined that their children would learn to speak, read, and write Armenian. The little informal classes that were held for the small number of children before 1914 were transformed after 1918 into structured little supplementary schools. The schools' mandate was to make the children more than bilingual; it was to make them biliterate and bicultural. Language and literature were seen as important factors linking and unifying the disparate Armenian communities. The language was thus more than a symbol of ethnic identity or a tool of communication between the generations. Because they believed that language was a critical agent of ethnonational survival, they put much time, money, and energy into their Armenian schools

School committees or local school boards, composed of both men and women, ministered to the school's needs. They engaged teachers, decided on honoraria and, later, salaries for the teachers, set fees for the children, inspected the school, sat in on examinations, and assisted teachers and parents with concerts and plays. Both girls and boys attended school, which was held regularly three evenings a week for two hours each evening. Nominal fees were expected, perhaps twenty-five cents a month per child, but they were abrogated in times of unemployment or indigence. The curriculum, usually based on an Armenian textbook, consisted of reading, writing, grammar and composition, literature, history, and music.

Armenian schoolteachers have always enjoyed the respect of the community. But in the early days in Canada, they were faced with the growing influence of Canadian society and the concomitant fear that Armenian ethnoculture was doomed. Their commitment, self-sacrifice, and diligence helped to create an Armenian consciousness among the young in southern Ontario and to sustain a strong bond among group members.

Armenian schools in Canada have traditionally reflected the political and/or religious affiliation of the parents. The small community of St Catharines, for example, had two Armenian supplementary schools in the early 1920s: one organized by the Social Democratic Hnchakian Party and the other by the Armenian Revolutionary Federation, or Dashnak Party. In Brantford in the 1930s and 1940s, the schools operated under the auspices of the Dashnaks and the Armenian Progressive League. As a point of clarification, however, it would have been inconceivable for any school, though supported by a specific interest group, to turn away a child whose parents had a different affiliation. In this respect, then, all were community schools, and in fact, children often attended the school operated by the "other" group.

Still, the Armenian supplementary schools, comparatively the most effective instruments of language transfer to the young, were undermined by inadequate funding, comparatively backward pedagogical methods, often ineffective discipline, and texts that were outdated or culturally inappropriate for meeting the important challenge of their mandate. Because they would have preferred to be playing outside, many children did not attend Armenian school, and if they did, they resented parental pressure "to make us go to learn our Aip, Pen, Keem [ABCs]." To the extent, moreover, that the language did not include words for ideas, processes, and events in a Canadian milieu and to the extent that it did not modernize, it became fossilized. As the language failed to meet the changing needs of the young people, they found it easier and more efficient to speak in English. Except in conversations with elders (when they spoke a broken Armenian mixed with English and Turkish words), in church services, and during certain meetings, by the mid-1950s young people were speaking English in their political, cultural, and social encounters in the Armenian environment, partly by necessity and partly by choice.

Their speech was marked by lexical transfers from English to Armenian in their conversations with each other, with younger siblings and even with their parents, notably in areas where their Armenian vocabulary was limited. As they grew older, the code switching was more clearly drawn. At home and in the Armenian community, with their parents and with their parents' friends, young people spoke broken Armenian. Outside, in the school yard, at play, or in sports, they spoke to each other in English. As a rule, children of the early immigrants acquired at best an understanding of spoken Armenian and an ability to speak the language but only a rudimentary ability, if that, to read and write Armenian. The 1981 census shows the decline in language use. About 64 percent of Armenians in St Catharines were born in Canada, and of them only 14 percent spoke Armenian as the main language in the home. According to the 1991 census (single responses), 10,745 individuals gave Armenian as their ethnic origin in Ontario, but only 7,735 indicated Armenian as their home language.

By contrast, children of survivors who had settled in the Middle East attended full-day Armenian schools and lived in self-sufficient Armenian quarters where Armenian was the language of communication in everyday life. As a cohort, then, the post-1950s immigrants – even though they too were from the diaspora – had a better grasp of the Armenian language and Armenian culture than the same age group of Armenians born in Canada. This fact, all the more, raises the old debate about the future of the North American diaspora, which has consistently supported communities in and near the homeland on the assumption that they, more than the North American diaspora, were likely to maintain their ethnocultural heritage.

As for the general level of education of the third wave, it is reasonable to assume that they compared favourably with the average educational attainment of mainstream Canadians in the urban areas where they settled. Many undertook postsecondary schooling in Europe, the United States, or Canada. Their broad educational background, coupled with the variety of countries of provenance, enabled them to acquire expertise in several languages and familiarity with a number of different cultures. The third wave was thus remarkable for its cultural and linguistic scope and flexibility.

Armenian schools have always reflected the attitudes, origins, backgrounds, sophistication, and prosperity of the parents. Thus, Armenian supplementary schools were overshadowed in the 1970s by the concept of full-time day schools. Immigrants from the Middle East, who were accustomed to operating their own schools, transferred this tradition to Canada. As they prospered, they were able, albeit with considerable sacrifice, to establish full-time day schools. In Montreal, the Armenian General Benevolent Union founded the AGBU Alex Manoogian/Armen-Quebec School in 1970 (six hundred students were enrolled in 1995, from nursery school to grade eight). Surp Hagop Church started a full-day school in 1973 (it was serving nine hundred students, from nursery school to grade eleven in 1995). In 1983 the Congregation of the Armenian Sisters of the Immaculate Conception opened an Armenian school in Montreal. When the Sisters left the school in 1988, it was renamed the Armenian Catholic School of Notre Dame de Nareg. In 1993–94, the school offered classes from kindergarten to grade six to a student population of 250.

Similarly, three full-time day schools were established in Toronto. The Society of Armenians from Istanbul was the spirit behind Surp Khach (Holy Cross) school; it opened its doors in 1978, and in 1995, under the able principalship of Diana Hanimyan, offered nursery school to grade six to 100 children. The Armenian Relief Society founded the Babayan nursery and Kololian elementary school in 1979; in 1993–94 it operated classes from preschool to grade eight, with a student enrolment of 375. The Armenian General Benevolent Union inaugurated the Daniel and Alice Zaroukian School in 1985, and by

1993-94 it offered classes from nursery to grade six to 125 students. The combined *full-time* student population in Montreal reached over 1,700 in 1995; for the same period Toronto full-day schools enrolled over 600 students.

While Armenian schools are open to all children, the ideas of the parents may differ and they may be reluctant to send their children to schools with different political viewpoints. Granting that the aims of the schools are to preserve Armenian language and heritage, Hasmig Kurdian adds: "the fact that one [school] is politically oriented (the ARS School) and the other (Holy Cross Day School) accommodated mainly Armenians coming from Turkey, has made it difficult for many parents who have been raised in the traditions of the AGBU to accept the idea of sending their children to either school ... A survey conducted at the time among AGBU members, most of whom were graduates of AGBU schools themselves, convinced the leaders of the necessity of having a school."[13]

Day-care centres and publicly subsidized heritage-language classes extend the range of available services. In 1983-84 twenty-nine heritage-language classes had an enrolment of 550. In 1991-92, statistics for Ontario revealed that thirty-seven Armenian heritage-language classes in both public and separate school boards provided services to almost 780 students. Saturday classes and schools are usually run by one organization but bring together children from different socioeconomic classes, geographic locations, and affiliations.

The largest and oldest of such schools in Toronto is the St Sahag and St Mesrob Saturday School founded in 1956 by the Church of the Holy Trinity in Toronto; its enrolment in the mid-1990s ran between 250 and 300 students per year. One of the newest Saturday heritage-language schools in the Toronto area is St Gregory the Illuminator School, started in 1981 and administered by the Armenian Catholic Church. In 1992-93 it served about 140 students from preschool to grade eight. Heritage-language classes and schools have also functioned in North York, Mississauga, Ottawa, Hamilton, St Catharines, and Cambridge, and in Brant County, Ontario, and in Montreal and Vancouver. Saturday schools or heritage-language programs have made important contributions to language learning and maintenance. Because of government funding, the organization running the program has paid no rent to the host school; teachers with more than twenty students have received a salary; supplies have been provided; and professional development classes have been available without charge. In Toronto the principal at St Sahag and St Mesrob School was classified as head-instructor, thus strengthening ties with the Toronto Board of Education, which provided professional assistance for curriculum development through the Heritage Languages Program.[14]

Almost every Armenian church or congregation maintains a Sunday school or a summer school, adding still more dimensions to the educational landscape. In some places different groups offer different services. In St Catharines, for instance, St Gregory the Illuminator Church has a Sunday school, while the Armenian Relief Society administers the Saturday morning school. In other instances, a group may operate more than one type of educational facility. In 1992–93, in Montreal, Surp Hagop Church maintained a day-care centre (for children from two and a half to four years of age), an elementary and secondary full-day school, a Saturday school, a summer camp, and a Sunday school. The total enrolment of these various schools in 1992–93 was approximately 1,200 students. While nursery and elementary schools form the backbone of Armenian-language education in Canada, Armenians have been moving towards building private secondary schools, starting with Surp Hagop in Montreal, followed by the Armenian Relief Society secondary school in Toronto, opened in 2003.

Not only has there been a proliferation of Armenian schools, but the number of Armenian students has escalated with the increase in immigration and the improvement of facilities and programs. For example, Holy Cross started with eighteen students in 1978–79; in 1981–82, the enrolment skyrocketed to 130. In 1983–84, the AGBU School in Montreal had a student enrolment of 550; by 1988, it had reached 600. Similarly, Surp Hagop enrolled 500 students in 1985 in its elementary and secondary school; seven years later 275 more pupils were in attendance, an increase of more than 50 percent. The preschool classes are particularly popular in the community; in 1974–75, there were 25 students in the Surp Hagop preschool program; in 1991–92, about 160 children attended. It has been estimated that at least 65 percent of elementary- and secondary-school-age youngsters of Armenian heritage in Montreal attend an Armenian language school. Such an enrolment clearly reflects not only the emphasis placed on the language and culture but also the conviction that these schools are extensions of family and community life.

Armenians are able to sustain such a vigorous level of educational programming partly because of the combination of autonomy and means and the powerful role of political affiliation. But their success depends equally on a high degree of dedication and voluntarism. In the early days, supplementary school teachers usually taught without remuneration. In Galt and Toronto, where no Armenian school existed in the 1930s and 1940s, young men travelled from house to house at their own expense to teach the basics of Armenian reading and writing to children living in various parts of the city.

Since their arrival in this country, Armenian women and their organizations have done indispensable work for Armenian language education, particularly in teaching and fund raising. In Hamilton, St Catharines, and Brantford, Armenian women like Astghig Melkonian not only organized the schools but also taught in them. In Montreal, the Armenian Women's Benevolent Association operated a supplementary school from 1930 to the mid-1940s under the able leadership of Isgouhi Hazarian, Rébéca Kalpakdjian, Yevnigé Karibian, Lousvart Kouyoumdjian, and Armèn(ouhi) Melconian.[15] The Armenian Relief Society of Montreal (ARS) administers the Garderie St Jacques and has provided a twenty-five-hundred-book library for Surp Hagop School, while in Toronto the ARS is the force behind the Babayan/Kololian School. The ARS has operated Saturday schools in various cities, including Cambridge, Hamilton, and St Catharines.

The intense activity around Armenian schools is costly and makes heavy demands on the community. In 1984–85, the ARS day school in Toronto served 270 students with a budget of $250,000; in the same year, the AGBU School in Montreal had a student enrolment of 572 utilizing a budget of $1 million; in 1992–93 Holy Cross in Toronto served 125 students with a budget of $350,000. In this respect, another tradition marks the Armenian schools in Canada. Just as men like Senator James McGill and Senator William McMaster have endowed Canadian universities in the past, so wealthy Armenians sponsor Armenian schools. Armenouhi Kololian and Kevork Kololian and the Babayan Foundation are benefactors of the ARS school in Toronto; Levon and Sophia Hagopian, of the ARS Surp Hagop nursery in Montreal; Astghig and Vartkes Sarafian, of Surp Hagop primary school in Montreal; and Daniel Zaroukian and Alice Zaroukian, of the AGBU school in Toronto. Yervant Pasdermajian, the beloved elder statesman in Montreal, and his brothers, Hrant and Hagop, have made regular donations to Surp Hagop, and the late Alex Manoogian, president of the AGBU, was an ardent benefactor of the AGBU schools. Aside from generous donations, the viability of the schools depends on a very high level of community and parent mobilization.

Support from wealthy Armenians, from provincial government subsidies whenever available, along with tuition and support from the community at large have enabled Armenians to build or purchase their own school structures. The first effort to construct an Armenian school house occurred in 1925, when a group of St Catharines Armenians organized the Raffi *varzharan* (school) and began to raise money for a building. The focus on this secular institution changed when the community decided to build a church instead, incorporating a hall in the basement that would provide school facilities. From the little Armenian supplementary schools that occupied a room in someone's house, Armenians then moved to using a portion of the Armenian hall.

With the trend to full-time schools, more space was required than was available in church basements or community centres. Armenians first rented quarters from a local school board and then bought or built their own school structure. In Toronto, for example, the Armenian Evangelical Church summer school met at Bedford Park elementary school. Holy Cross School started in the basement of All Soul's Anglican Church and moved to a school leased from the Scarborough Board of Education, and it has recently purchased its own building. The ARS and AGBU schools in Toronto are incorporated within their respective community-centre complexes.

Armenian schools are not without their problems. Because of the dispersed nature of settlement, especially in Toronto, where families live in Aurora, Thornhill, Richmond Hill, Unionville, and Ajax, in addition to Metropolitan Toronto, bussing has become a major consideration and a serious cost.[16] In addition, such issues as tuition for children of indigent parents, the education of non-Armenian-speaking children and of children of mixed marriages, the acquisition of up-to-date equipment and teaching materials, the certification of teachers, the evaluation of programs, the opposition between family values and Canadian media values, obstacles to keeping graduates within the bosom of the community, and the overpowering impact of English continue to confront schools and school boards.

Inevitably, the quality of education is linked to teachers, teacher education, and pedagogy. In the past, a teacher's knowledge of Armenian and his or her ability to maintain a measure of discipline and willingness to assume responsibility for the class were acceptable criteria for the position. Depending on individual teachers and school settings, teaching methods ranged from authoritarian Old World models to more liberal Canadian ones. More recently, particularly in the full-day schools, teacher qualifications and pedagogical methodology are recognized as integral to the school's performance, and more and more Armenian-language teachers are upgrading their qualifications in Canadian education faculties.

Textbooks and the curriculum recurrently emerge as major issues. In the supplementary schools, the textbooks *were* the curriculum, for they were used not only to enhance the language but to teach the history and literature as well. Texts often imported from the United States, from the Middle East, or from the former Soviet Republic of Armenia were frequently inappropriate or pedagogically unsuitable for Canadian students. The stories in the texts from Armenia, for example, were often about topics that were unfamiliar or uninteresting to Canadian children, like the worker's struggle, and they were frequently politically charged, condemning, for example, ancient Armenian monarchs as exploitative. The dependence on out-of-Canada texts is beginning to diminish as Armenian educators are producing textbooks and teaching aids that both reflect the life of youngsters in Canada and fulfill the educational requirements of Armenian-Canadian schools.[17] With respect to the curriculum, the day schools follow provincial guidelines, teach both French and English, and incorporate an additional one to one and a half hours a day for Armenian-language instruction. For Armenian linguistic and cultural components, no uniform guideline exists among schools.

The importation of texts and the creation of a viable curriculum are issues that affect a very broad-based school clientele. Since each school operates under the auspices of different diasporan affiliations, it has strong links with its counterparts around the world. Thus, the AGBU schools in Montreal and Toronto liaise with the AGBU central educational authorities in the United States. Since the schools have become more firmly established, efforts are being made to link up teachers, administrators, and students in the same city, regardless of affiliation. The day may come when Armenians in Canada will create their own board of education to standardize curriculum, authorize the preparation of textbooks, and delineate certain schools for specific grades, to avoid duplication. In this manner the school may become a unifying element – a countervailing force to political and religious polarization.

Today Armenian schools have a dual mandate: to educate children within an Armenian framework and to prepare them for their role in Canadian society. Each school is part of an intimate society, a large family, where parents, grandparents, and community members contribute their time, talents, energy, and money to "produce a flourishing harvest," as one school brochure noted. Many students would agree with the graduate who commented that she loves her school and will miss her second home.[18] In spite of the sacrifices, most community members favour Armenian day schools because they provide a well-disciplined environment that is praised by parents as "drug-free." A recent letter from a principal of a local high school confirmed that students from the Armenian day schools "average about 5 percent higher than their peers"; demonstrate "cross-curricular" proficiency; display a strong work ethic, politeness, and good values; and are involved in the total life of the school.

Traditionally, the principal focus of Armenian schools has been to teach Armenian language, history, and culture. These goals may still be appropriate for the part-time schools, but the full-day schools – especially the secondary schools – must enlarge their vision of education. Principals, teachers, school committees, and parents are actively debating about their expectations of the school, its philosophy, its broader goals, and its role in Canada. Parents are asking questions about the quality of education and their children's preparedness for study in Canadian universities and for life in Canadian society. Concern about such issues reflects shifts in the community itself. For decades Armenians concentrated on heritage maintenance. But now, as the community is maturing, the retention of ethnic heritage has become one component of a larger agenda. The ethnic minority is finding its place in Canadian society.

REGIONAL ORGANIZATIONS

While Armenians may identify themselves in the North American context as Armenians, within their own communities they often identify themselves by their old-country origins, especially the immigrant generation. Regional loyalty and regional identity have played and continue to play a defining role among Armenians in the diaspora. The bonds of kith and kin and the attachment to village and region generated far-flung networks of *yerkiratsis*, or countrymen. This network, in turn, led to a proliferation of village, town, and city compatriotic associations, which helped to transmit the bonds of Old World loyalties to subsequent generations. Typical foods, sayings, dialects, folkways, and songs and dances strengthened the link between the old land and the North American Armenians themselves. As a result, Canadian- and American-born children frequently identified themselves as Erzerumtsis, Vanetsis, or Kharputsis, depending on where their parents or grandparents were born, i.e., in Erzerum, Van, or Kharput. In California, people still ask (in English), "What *tsi* are you?" i.e., where do your parents or grandparents come from?

Almost from the day Armenians entered Canada, they established regional associations. The Village Educational Associations, the first among them, were grassroots attempts to improve the education of the children in the village. While the need for these associations emanated from the Ottoman Empire, the impetus came from the diaspora. Regardless of their place of settlement or of their political or religious affiliation, émigrés from each village joined their association. When the villages were destroyed in 1915, some associations continued to function in North America with a social, benevolent, and educational focus, particularly for survivors in countries of refuge. The Osnag Village Association, for example, continued to operate with six branches in Canada and the United States, but with the disappearance of the village and the harsh realization that it would not be reborn, villagers accepted the anachronism of their goals. In 1941 members revised the constitution and changed the name of the organization to the Osnag Benevolent Society. Like other such compatriotic associations, it collected dues, organized fund-raising events for specific projects, and held annual conventions, but its aim was to help displaced villagers abroad. As village friends and relatives became rehabilitated in countries of asylum, the association assumed a more social role. Annual picnics and reunions brought together the villagers and their children. By the 1960s, like most of the compatriotic associations the Osnag Benevolent Society began to peter out. In 1967 the society closed its books. Its final press statement recalled that in their original constitution villagers had agreed to send the treasury to St Minas Church, in the village, should the organization disband, but since no village existed, the members were faced with two alternatives: to send the money to New Keghi in Soviet Armenia or to send it to the Armenian Church. Because villagers had acted harmoniously for sixty-two years, regardless of political affiliation, they agreed that as the symbol of the nation the church should receive the remaining funds. Accordingly, members divided the treasury (approximately fourteen thousand u.s. dollars) between the two Sees of the Armenian Church: Echmiadzin in Soviet Armenia and Cilicia in Lebanon. The villagers, the last remnants of Osnag, requested that each see put up a memorial plaque to their village.[19] It is of great interest that the villagers' priority was not to help students or families in North America but rather to assist their people abroad. Even in the final division of funds the money was sent overseas rather than used for the new churches being built in Canada.

In 1917, with the destruction of the villages of Keghi, Keghetsis organized a pan-Keghi union to help the refugees. With the political strife in 1933, the pan-Keghi group split on political lines. Pro-Dashnaks aligned with the Compatriotic Society of Keghi (1934), while Progressives supported the Pan-Keghi Association, later called the Reconstruction Association of Keghi. Both operated from the United States, with headquarters in Detroit, Michigan and East St Louis, Illinois, respectively. Very active branches in Canada, notably in Brantford, St Catharines, Galt, and Hamilton continued the Keghi tradition in Canada. Ever mindful of their history, of their lost villages, and of their own role as the remnant of the villages, they published histories of the region, of villages, and of renowned individuals from the area.[20] Like the village associations, these larger organizations maintained an overseas focus, helping their scattered compatriots, particularly through charitable and educational work. The Reconstruction Association directed its aid primarily to Soviet Armenia, and the Compatriotic Society of Keghi helped Keghetsi refugees in the Middle East.

In 1969, on the occasion of the thirty-fifth anniversary of the Compatriotic Society of Keghi, the association announced that over the years, it had contributed U.S.$150,000 for the purposes of education, primarily in the Middle East. An editorial in the *Hairenik Daily* praised the society, noting that like sixty other such associations, it had helped save a generation of survivors. The contribution rendered by compatriotic societies for the rehabilitation and education of survivors was monumental. Within this framework, the editorial then discussed the omnipresent and contentious issue of sending such large sums of money abroad, instead of using them in North America. It concluded that in the Middle East the numbers and potential for ethnocultural retention would have been great were it not for massive poverty and destitution. For such reasons, financial support from the diaspora would be vitally necessary to rebuild and empower these communities that were close to the homeland.[21] In 1972, continuing to abide by their original educational mandate, the two pan-Keghi organizations joined forces as the United *Nor Keghi* (New Keghi) Committee and raised $50,000 to build a school in the village of New Keghi, Soviet Armenia, which had been established in 1962, also through their joint efforts. But this momentum was not sustained. By the 1970s, as the first-generation villagers were dying off and as their children were dispersed or pursuing their own careers or losing interest in a faraway place, the Keghi associations had begun to decline. In the 1980s both pan-Keghi associations ceased operations and divided their remaining funds between the two sees of the Armenian Church.

Attrition and indifference weakened these compatriotic societies as much as the political/nationalist organizations which viewed them as agents of ethnic fragmentation undermining their mandate of promoting pan-Armenian loyalty.[22] But they have not been successful in stamping out regional affiliations. Currently, new and different regional identifiers mark the community. Armenians from Iran, for instance, are Barskahai (Persian Armenians), and Armenians from Egypt are Egyptahai (Egyptian Armenians).

The focus and interests of current regional associations have been primarily educational and cultural. The Raffi Armenian Cultural Association, established in Montreal in 1988, serves Armenians from Iran by sponsoring Armenian cultural endeavours. The Union of Marash Armenians, with branches in Toronto and Montreal, provides scholarships for deserving students. By far the largest and most active group is the Society of Armenians from Istanbul. Although Armenians from Constantinople and vicinity were among the first to settle in Canada and although some of the first Keghetsi pioneers came to Canada via

Constantinople, they founded no regional society until the more recent wave of Armenians from Istanbul organized an association in Montreal in 1967 and in Toronto in 1988.²³ This organization seeks to promote the Armenian language and culture, to aid immigrants from Turkey, and to help Armenian students. In both Montreal and Toronto, the organization has operated its own community centre, with groups for women, the arts, youth, and sports; it publishes a literary periodical in Montreal, and in Toronto it supports Holy Cross full-day school.

CHARITABLE ORGANIZATIONS

Relations between Armenians in North America and their confreres abroad are perhaps most sharply revealed by the activities of benevolent societies. Two global Armenian organizations, each associated with different political groupings, stand out in providing relief during times of crisis and in nurturing and enhancing Armenian educational and cultural life.

Armenian General Benevolent Union

In 1906 in Cairo, Egypt, "on the free soil of a foreign country," a group of affluent Armenians led by Boghos Nubar Pasha founded the Armenian General Benevolent Union (AGBU). "With sufficient capital and resources for emergency relief" and a "long-range program of philanthropy, with a strong emphasis on education," the AGBU directed its efforts to help Armenians in both the Ottoman and Russian Empires. From 1906 to 1914, the AGBU encouraged literacy by establishing or subsidizing schools and assisting or building orphanages. It sent machines, implements, food, and seed to the Armenian peasantry and dispatched relief funds and supplies for Armenian victims of the Armeno-Tatar clashes (1905, Russia) and of the massacres in Adana (1909, Ottoman Empire). Following the Genocide, the AGBU changed its focus to care for the dispersed refugees and orphans in the countries of asylum, to assist in the reconstruction of Soviet Armenia, and to support the movement of diasporan Armenians to Soviet Armenia, especially after World War II.²⁴ As Armenian refugees in a vast diaspora rebuilt their lives and strengthened their communities, the AGBU redirected its efforts from relief measures to "reviving and preserving Armenian national identity." From 1950 to 1970, the AGBU set up an infrastructure of institutions and programs serving the scholastic and cultural needs of Armenians in the Middle Eastern and Mediterranean countries. The upheaval of Armenian communities resulting from the civil strife in these countries, the exodus of Armenians, and their resettlement in the West shifted part of the AGBU focus of activity once more. Since the early 1960s, AGBU-supported schools and community centres have been established from Australia to Argentina and Brazil, from France to Canada and the United States. The 1988 earthquake in Armenia, followed by the Azeri blockade and the Karabagh war of independence, once again prompted the AGBU to change its course. General relief, assistance to schools and to the Armenian Apostolic church, promotion of the American University of Armenia, and material, medical, and economic aid to Armenia and Karabagh consume much of the AGBU energies at the beginning of the twenty-first century.

In 1922–24 the AGBU moved its headquarters from Cairo to Paris, partly reflecting France's role as one of the largest countries of sanctuary after the Genocide. In the early 1940s, at the height of World War II, the headquarters was moved to New York and remains in that general area today. Membership has grown from 8,500 in 1913 to 22,000 in 1991, with 66 chapters worldwide.[25]

The first Canadian AGBU chapter was started in Toronto in 1924, but it was virtually dormant until the mid-1930s. From then to the late 1940s, the Central Board of Directors in the United States spearheaded four major campaigns. Toronto members raised an estimated $37,000 in Canadian Armenian communities for relief in the Middle East and the Caucasus, for the David of Sasun tank regiment during World War II, and for facilitating the movement of Armenians in the diaspora to Soviet Armenia.[26] However, the AGBU did not flourish in Canada until after World War II. The revitalized Toronto branch received a provincial charter in 1967, and in Montreal a new branch, started in 1957, was granted a provincial charter in 1969. Three chapters in Canada (Montreal, Toronto, and Vancouver) had a combined membership of approximately 800 in the mid-1990s.

Two large community centres are the hub of activities in Montreal (built 1978) and Toronto (1981). Throughout its history in Canada, the AGBU has been a conservative force; it has balanced a global and local focus, remained open to both men and women, and sponsored a host of auxiliary activities for women and men, youth, and seniors, activities ranging from social, athletic, and sports events to cultural endeavours. The AGBU supports two full-day schools and offers scholarships to worthy students. The work of Kerop Bedoukian, a founder and leader of the AGBU in Montreal who started social-service and immigrant-aid work among Armenian newcomers in the 1960s, partly under the auspices of the AGBU, has already been discussed, as have the efforts of the AGBU in assisting refugees in Toronto in the late 1970s.[27]

The Armenian Relief Society

The other major charitable organization in Canada is the Armenian Relief Society. From the 1890s on, small groups of concerned Armenian women and men founded local committees to serve the educational, health, relief, and social needs of their fellow Armenians. During the first decade of the twentieth century, Armenian immigrant women in North America formed such committees in association with the Armenian Revolutionary Federation. Their purpose was to raise funds for needy Armenians in the Ottoman and Russian Empires. In 1910–11, primarily through the efforts of the ARF fieldworker Edouard Aknuni (Khachatur Malumian), these Dashnak women's relief committees were amalgamated as the Armenian Revolutionary Federation Red Cross. By the time it held its first convention in 1915 in Boston, its headquarters, it had thirty-two chapters throughout the United States and Canada. The dispersal of the Armenians during and after World War I led to the creation of chapters in countries of asylum in Europe, the Middle East, and South America. From 1920 to 1946, the organization was known as the Armenian Relief Corps, and in 1946 it changed its name to the Armenian Relief Society (ARS). Although men can and do belong, the ARS has remained a women's organization, the most significant Armenian women's association in the world. In 2003 there were chapters in twenty-five countries with a membership of eighteen thousand. The ARS has five priorities: charity, education, social services, enlightenment of members, and relations with the host society and non-Armenian organizations. The top priority of the ARS has been to aid Armenians in distress. During and after the Genocide, ARS chapters raised funds for Armenia and for Armenian refugees in countries of exile to be used for hospitals, orphanages, and schools. Whenever a crisis loomed, the ARS immediately mobilized to provide assistance. During the upheavals in the Middle East, for instance, particularly in Lebanon, where a large Armenian community existed before the wars, the ARS organized relief projects. With the cataclysmic events in Armenia and Karabagh since 1988, the ARS has sent medical and heating supplies; it has subsidized housing, schools, food, and clothing; and it has undertaken to minister to the sick, to orphans and the homeless, and to the soldiers at the front.

The ARS has also nurtured educational and cultural development: it has organized Armenian schools; sponsored plays, choirs, and lectures; and assembled the community for Armenian historical or festive events. As the post-Genocide refugee settlements in the Middle East stabilized and became self-supporting and as Armenians left those communities and resettled in North America, the ARS centred its attention and resources more and more on North America, in an effort to preserve the ethnic heritage and identity, particularly through education. As an indication of its focus, the society donated the entire proceeds from its sixtieth-anniversary fund-drive (1970) to the ARS full-day school in Detroit, Michigan.[28]

Four chapters pioneered the movement in Canada: Brantford, which was a founding member of the Armenian Revolutionary Federation Armenian Red Cross (in 1910), and St Catharines, Hamilton, and Galt, which joined in 1915. With the entry of refugee women during the 1920s, the number of ARS chapters increased to include ones in Guelph, Toronto, and Windsor, and the membership expanded to approximately eighty-five by 1930.[29] As the women reached old age in the 1950s and 1960s, their daughters continued the work. In Brantford, however, which had lost a good part of its Armenian population, and in Windsor, Guelph, and Toronto, where the communities were small to begin with and where they were further depopulated as the younger generation moved away, the ARS began to decline. However, the young women coming from the Middle East after 1950 rejuvenated the organization, bringing their vigour and talents, especially to Montreal and Toronto.

In the mid–1990s there were ten ARS chapters in Canada: in St Catharines (founded 1915, Araz), Hamilton (1915, Arev), Toronto (1924, reconstituted in 1963, Roubina), Cambridge (formerly Galt and Guelph, 1915 and 1923 respectively, reconstituted in 1962, Meghri), Windsor (1926, reconstituted 1978, Roubina), Montreal (1957, Sossé), Vancouver (1977, Araz), Mississauga (1991, Arakasd), Ottawa (1993, Sevan), and Laval (1993, Shoushi). The combined membership was over twelve hundred. In 1990 the Canadian chapters formed the ARS Canadian Regional Board of Directors, with headquarters in Montreal. The Canadian region chapters hold an annual convention, and from time to time a Canadian chapter hosts the international ARS convention.

The Canadian ARS branches have consistently balanced the needs of the Armenian people outside Canada with the requirements of those in the local communities. ARS members give relief and help, both financial and moral, to individuals and families in Canada. They visit the ill and dying and help the indigent. In 1987, to formalize social work activities, the Toronto community established the ARS Social Service Office to provide assistance to Armenian newcomers, the unemployed, and the aged. Two years later the Toronto branch organized the ARS Home for the Aged in a wing of the Seven Oaks Senior Citizens Home. The Montreal branch organized a similar facility at the Manoir Cartierville.

Working voluntarily, ARS members contribute their energies and time to Armenian educational endeavours. In the past, they operated and taught in supplementary schools. Currently, the organization supports full-day schools, nursery schools, summer camps, and Saturday schools. In keeping with a tradition established in the early 1920s, when the ARS contributed funds to help the boys of the Georgetown farm/home/school and later provided scholarships for young Canadian Armenians to attend high school, the society now offers scholarships for deserving students and enables young people to attend the ARS Summer Studies Program, which is held every year in the United States. To enlighten its own members and to facilitate their integration into Canadian society, the ARS arranges lectures, field trips, and annual seminars. The organization has also contributed to non-Armenian causes. For example, during World War II members spearheaded campaigns to send parcels of food and clothing to the Allied forces at the front. In an attempt to bring about mutual understanding, the society participates in local Canadian projects and keeps in contact with non-Armenian women's groups.

Both the AGBU and the ARS are worldwide charitable, cultural, and educational associations that thrive because of the members' voluntarism and commitment. In a century of upheaval, the two organizations have met the daunting challenge of helping their fellow Armenians both in Canada and abroad. Other political groupings had their charitable/cultural/educational components. Like the Dashnaks, the Hnchaks had an active women's wing, but it met the same fate as the Hnchak Party itself. It was subsumed by the Hai Oknutian Gomide (HOG, the Relief Committee for Armenia) and by its women's branch, the Hai Petakan Karmir Khach (the Armenian National Red Cross). The HOG and the Red Cross were conceived with the sole purpose of helping the reconstruction of Soviet Armenia. With the demise of the HOG in the mid–1930s, the Red Cross in St Catharines, the most active branch in Canada, gradually evolved into the Ladies Auxiliary of St Gregory's Church.

A more recent charitable organization is the Armenian Missionary Association of Canada, founded in 1984 and affiliated with the Armenian Missionary Association of America (AMAA), established in Worcester, Massachusetts, in 1918. At first, the AMAA worked with the American Board of Commissioners for Foreign Missions but gradually took up the mission and philanthropic work on its own. It has developed missionary outreach in thirteen countries, serving underprivileged Armenians in projects ranging from child education sponsorships, college and seminary scholarships, and the provision of medical and general relief.[30]

With the events in the Caucasus towards the end of the twentieth century, new charitable organizations have sprung up focusing primarily on efforts to rebuild Armenia and Kharabagh. The most remarkable of these new endeavours is the All-Armenia Fund, a nonpartisan group engaged in fund-raising to reconstruct areas in Armenia and Kharabagh that have been devastated by the war with Azerbaijan.

CULTURAL ORGANIZATIONS

In the pre–1950 period, cultural and educational work in the community was generally undertaken by the women's groups, such as the Armenian Relief Society and the National Red Cross. Today, most institutions or organizations have their cultural adjuncts, many of which were imported to Canada by recent immigrants from the Middle East, namely the Hamaskayin Educational and Cultural Union (Dashnak), the Tekeyan Cultural Union (Ramgavar), Nor Serount Cultural Union (Hnchak), and the MEG (the cultural alumni association of the Mkhitarian, Esayan, and Getronagan Colleges in Constantinople, sponsored by the Society of Armenians from Istanbul). They support choirs, theatrical troupes, folk dance groups, literary and fine arts exhibits, and public lectures and debates on Armenian art, literature, and history. They launch books, operate libraries, sponsor television and radio programs, publish newsletters, and organize book sales. These cultural organizations also play a major role in providing venues for promoting and displaying the work of young Armenian Canadian artists, photographers, and writers,

YOUTH/SPORTS

Most churches and organizations sponsor religious, educational, athletic, and social activities for youth. The first youth group in Canada started in 1926, when several young people in Toronto founded the Canadian Armenian Young Peoples' Association (CAYPA). A nonpartisan, self-help group, it was composed of refugees ranging in age from sixteen to twenty-eight who were trying to come to terms with loneliness, uprootedness, and unfamiliar surroundings. In addition to engaging in social, literary, theatrical, and musical pursuits, members of the association acted as itinerant teachers helping the growing number of children in Toronto to read and write Armenian. The CAYPA did not survive the conflicts that split Armenian communities in the early thirties, but men continued to teach children on an individual and personal basis.[31]

Another early youth group was the rather loosely organized Georgetown Boys' club. When the children were dispersed to Ontario homes and after their terms of indenture were fulfilled, the young men kept in contact with each other on an informal basis. Gradually the young people joined together to create a more formal structure, the Georgetown Boys' Association, with a largely social emphasis.

The longest-standing and enduring youth group in Canada is the Armenian Youth Federation (AYF), which is affiliated with the Dashnak organization. The AYF started in the United States in 1933, and by 1940 several chapters had been established in southern Ontario, particularly during the Canadian tour in 1934 of Garegin Njdé, the founder. Galt and Hamilton started chapters in 1934, followed by St Catharines, Brantford, and Windsor. In an effort to keep alive an Armenian heritage and to encourage a sense of fraternity, the AYF supported educational, political, athletic, and social activities. Canadian members participated in the yearly Olympic Games, in the annual convention, and in social and educational functions held in different cities throughout Canada and the United States. In 1975 the AYF created its own Canadian region and four years later changed its name to the Armenian Revolutionary Federation-Canadian Youth Association and turned its focus to the Armenian cause. In 1995, there were eight chapters in Canada with approximately eight hundred members.

During the 1940s, the Armenian Progressive League in Brantford founded a youth group, the Armenian Youth Association (AYA), which was affiliated with the Progressive Youth movement in the United States. Like the AYF, it engaged in political, social, cultural, and athletic activities, but it suffered from the exodus of Armenians from Brantford, the aging of those who remained, and the bigotry of the Cold War. Less prominent were the Social Democratic Sparks (Hnchaks) and the Democratic Liberal Juniors (Ramgavars).

The Armenian Church Youth Organization of America (ACYOA), founded in Providence, Rhode Island, in 1946, is affiliated with the Armenian Apostolic Church (Echmiadzin). Young people at St Gregory the Illuminator Church in St Catharines established the first chapter in the 1950s, and Toronto and Montreal followed shortly afterwards. The youth groups provide members with religious, educational, and athletic programs. When the Canadian diocese was created in 1980, the name was changed to the Armenian Church Youth Organization of Canada (ACYOC).

Several athletic organizations serve the youth, such as the Hai Marmnakrtakan Endhanur Miutiun/Kamk, or HMEM (the Armenian General Sports Union – Dashnak). Founded in Constantinople in 1918, the General Sports Union promotes physical fitness and athletic competition for men, women, and children. Five chapters (in Montreal,

Toronto, Cambridge, Hamilton, and St Catharines) serve approximately sixteen hundred members, including athletes, scouts, and guides. In 1974 the Canadian chapters formed their own regional association and organized regular games, and in 1993, Toronto and Montreal hosted the HMEM world championships.[32]

Youth organizations regularly bring together young people from different cities and countries for athletic, religious, educational, or political purposes. Not only do these gatherings strengthen group cohesion, but they also help build friendships and broaden the scope of choice for young people of marriageable age.

CANADIAN ARMENIAN UNION AND THE ARMENIAN UNION OF MONTREAL

In 1925, Toronto Armenians, who were determined to maintain their Armenian culture, to have an Armenian school and church, and to protect the interests of Armenian Canadians, established the Canadian Armenian Union (CAU). In rented quarters, first on King Street and then on Bond Street, they set about organizing cultural and educational events and social gatherings. Gradually a network of small branches was established in southern Ontario. As a spokesman for Armenians in Canada, the CAU tried unsuccessfully to persuade government officials to change the Asiatic designation for immigration purposes, and, also unsuccessfully, it tried to purchase the Armenian boys' farm/home/school in Georgetown, Ontario, when the Armenian Relief Association of Canada decided to divest itself of the responsibility of caring for the Armenian children. The CAU stands as the first nonpartisan pan-Armenian organization in Canada and the first such entity to have its roots in Canada.

The principal aim of the Armenian Union of Montreal (AUM), still another non-political organization (founded in the late 1920s) was to bring the small number of Armenians together for various national events, particularly for the commemoration of the Genocide on 24 April. The Armenian Women's Benevolent Association of Montreal (founded 1930) focused on social and educational activities, like organizing picnics, community gatherings, and plays. Its most notable contribution was the creation of an Armenian supplementary school that functioned from 1930 to 1944.

Nonpolitical organizations were more common in places where the Armenian community was small, such as in Toronto and Montreal. Under such conditions, Armenians bonded together regardless of their political sympathies. As the communities grew, however, factions became more polarized. With the conflicts that split the Armenian diaspora in the early 1930s, each individual was obliged to take a stand. In Toronto the CAU and the CAYPA and in Montreal the AUM, all very popular organizations, dissolved after 1933. Only the Montreal Women's Benevolent Association survived as the women's auxiliary of the church of St Gregory the Illuminator.

WOMEN'S ORGANIZATIONS

To the three specifically women's organizations that existed before World War II, namely, the Armenian National Red Cross, the Armenian Women's Benevolent Association in Montreal, and the Armenian Relief Society – can be added the many women's auxiliaries associated with various churches, political groupings, schools, and regional associations. In the past, whether women pursued secular or religious community work, they generally followed in their husbands' footsteps. If their husbands belonged to the Compatriotic Society of Keghi, so did they; if their husbands belonged to the Social Democratic Hnchakian political party, they joined the women's group of that party. Women's organizations evolved as one of the few legitimate channels for their self-expression and service to the community.

In their pursuit of ethnocultural goals, women's organizations, both secular and religious, invariably have become vital channels in the education of women and important agents in the creation and preservation of Armenian identity in Canada. While it is true that many women were and are engaged in fund-raising work – cooking meals for and serving at banquets, selling raffle tickets, preparing handmade fancywork for sale, contributing food and articles for bazaars – it is also true that there has been another very critical dimension to their endeavours: women in churches, for instance, have participated as organists, in the ladies' auxiliary, the altar guild, the choir, and on the board of trustees. One of their most outstanding contributions has been fashioning the lacework in the church: exquisite episcopal vestments and fair linen for the altar. By means of their enterprises the women have created a forum for developing both their administrative and Armenian-language skills. Through their meetings and activities they have become familiar with parliamentary procedure and discipline; they have learned to write and respond to minutes, correspondence, and reports; and they have had the opportunity to speak publicly among friends on topics other than home and family. In these associations, members have made deliberate and determined efforts to purify the language of Turkish and Kurdish borrowings. Some who were artistically inclined have produced plays and directed poetry recitations. At the same time, educated or bright women were able to fulfill intellectual needs and leadership roles through their involvement while remaining within the bosom of community life.

Because these organizations were international in scope, with branches in many different countries, members were exposed to issues affecting other Armenian communities in the diaspora. In this regard, women were encouraged to read the Armenian press, to improve their ability to read and comprehend their language, to enhance their knowledge of Armenian history, politics, and literature, and to learn more about issues and events outside the local sphere. Women who were engaged in Armenian activities and women's associations were presumed to be safe from harm and from the corrupting influence of the mainstream society. They operated within controllable boundaries and within permitted behavioural patterns, and because they were at the same time serving the national cause, their participation was approved by Armenian men and viewed by themselves as praiseworthy.

Like the ARS, the only women's group to have survived from the first wave and expanded with the third, women's organizations have changed and developed with the times. The women of the recent wave, having come to Canada with a good Armenian-language education, have brought a different dimension to the organization. More and more frequently, professional women have become active participants and have assumed leadership roles. The focus on self-improvement through lectures and the like and on integration into Canadian society give modern women's groups a broader perspective. Their concern, for instance, with the future of the family in Canada and their exposure to Canadian culture reveal a willingness and a need to step beyond the confines of the Armenian community.

PROFESSIONAL AND BUSINESS ORGANIZATIONS

Until recently, Armenians did not create business associations. Although they had an informal worldwide network, rug merchants, for example, did not establish their own guilds or associations. The closest Armenians came to acting on an ethnic/labour scale was in the foundries where they united to strike. These pre–trade union protests were usually sparked by prejudice or injustice against the workers *as Armenians*, and the men reacted as an ethnic force. These activities differed from their support for the union movement and from their involvement in industrial strikes during the 1930s and 1940s, which had a much broader ethnic base.

Partly because of the type of individuals chosen by the Canadian Armenian Congress and partly because of the selection criteria of the Canadian immigration program, many professionals entered the country and added their numbers to the cadre of professionals graduating from Canadian institutions of higher education. The contributions of this cohort to the solidarity of community life cannot be underestimated, both with respect to the creation of professional organizations and to the accessibility of professional services provided by Armenians for Armenians.

Armenian business and professional associations and lodges, some totally Canadian, others linked to larger North American or global entities, have developed in recent years: the Armenian Engineers and Scientists of America, the Armenian American Bar Association, Research on Armenian Architecture, the Canadian Armenian Business Council, the Armenian Jewellers' Association, the Armenian Medical Association of Ontario and of Quebec, the Armenian Rugs Society, the Canada Armenia Friendship Society, the Knights and Daughters of Vartan, the Zoryan Institute, the Armenian Studies Association of Quebec, and student associations at various universities. These associations allow like-minded people to come together, to raise funds for special community projects, and to strengthen links with the newly created Armenian Republic. By cutting across political, religious, and regional lines, through their networking with each other, and through their links with mainstream professionals, these bodies and their members are redefining "Armenianness" in different and distinct ways.

The growing number of professionals – both newcomers and young people educated in Canada – provide a field of services delivered by Armenians that were unavailable to earlier settlers. Today Armenian immigrants can seek counselling from the social services provided by the Armenian Relief Society or the Armenian General Benevolent Union; they may have their teeth tended to by an Armenian dentist, use the services of an Armenian general practitioner, or seek advice from an Armenian heart specialist or urologist. They may find communications with an Armenian lawyer and accountant much easier than with a non-Armenian professional. As a matter of interest, the 1996 Armenian telephone directory for Montreal lists 28 pharmacists, 8 psychiatrists, 24 dentists, 4 dental specialists, 25 general practitioners, and 37 medical specialists. The same source lists 76 Montreal-area members of the Canadian Armenian Business Council, as well as advertisements for Armenian bakeries and food processors, carpet stores, goldsmiths and jewellers, auto dealers and repairers, real estate agents, and lawyers.[33]

THE PRESS

The media have provided one of the most important means by which Armenians have communicated with their compatriots around the globe. In the pioneering pre- and post-Genocide period, Armenian Canadians sent local news items to the Armenian-language newspapers published in the United States by the various political organizations: the Dashnak *Hairenik* (Fatherland, founded in New York in 1899), the Social Democrat *Yeritasard Hayastan* (Young Armenia, Boston 1903), the Progressive *Lraper* (Reporter, New York 1937), and the Ramgavar *Baikar* (Struggle, Watertown, MA, 1923. The Armenian press in the United States also published in English: the *Armenian Weekly* (Boston 1934, Dashnak), the *Armenian Mirror-Spectator* (Watertown 1932, Ramgavar), and the *Armenian Reporter* (New York 1967). Scholarly journals published in the United States and read in Canada included *Hairenik Amsagir* (Fatherland Monthly), the *Armenian Review*, and the literary periodical *Ararat Quarterly*. The various presses also published books, pamphlets, and Armenian-language textbooks. In addition, various churches with their centres in the United States, notably the Armenian Apostolic Church Diocese and the Prelacy, published periodicals and newsletters.

The Armenian press in Canada started humbly with *tertiks* (flyers), short, hand-written notes of local news and announcements that were distributed locally and to nearby Armenian settlements by mail. The first periodical undertaking was the newsletter of the Armenian boys at the Georgetown farm/home/school. *Ararat* (Georgetown, Ontario, 1926–28), a monthly/bimonthly, was stencilled by the boys in English and later in Armenian, under the direction of their teacher, Aris Alexanian.

Gradually, flyers became more regularized newsletters and bulletins; and Armenian Canadians moved from typed mimeographed copies to more sophisticated printed ones. St Gregory the Illuminator Church in St Catharines published *Lusavorich* (The Illuminator). In Hamilton, the Hamaskayin Cultural and Educational Union published the periodical *Nor Arshav* (New Currents), and in Toronto the same organization published *Artsakank* (Echo). The oldest of these periodicals and the only one still publishing is *Nor Serount* (New Generation), founded in 1955 and published by the Armenian Church Youth Organization of America/Canada until 1975 and since then by Holy Trinity Church in Toronto. Interestingly, *Nor Serount* originally published in English, but with the flow of new immigrants who had a good grasp of Armenian, it gradually shifted to a mixture of English and Armenian and more recently has concentrated on publishing primarily in Armenian. This evolution perhaps reflects the emphasis placed on language retention and more widespread use of Armenian. Newsletters published in Armenian, English, and French on a monthly, bimonthly, or quarterly basis contain local news, including announcements and reports on events; articles on Armenian history, literature, art, and poetry; and major current news about Armenia and other places of the diaspora.

The tradition of newsletters, bulletins, and literary accounts continues to the present, as each organization or institution publishes its own tabloid. A sense of the activity in Montreal can be gleaned from the following list of publications in 1989: *Hayaved* (quarterly), First Armenian Evangelical Church of Montreal, founded in 1969; *Geghard* (Lance), Society of Armenians from Istanbul, founded 1969; *The Armenian Cause/La cause Arménienne*, sponsored by the Armenian National Committee of Canada (Dashnak), founded 1984; *Lousartsag* (Searchlight), published by the Armenian Evangelical Church of Montreal, founded 1981; *Lradou* (Newsletter, quarterly), Armenian Studies Association of Quebec, founded 1983; *Lra-kagh* (Reporter, bimonthly), Surp Hagop, founded 1958; *Nor Ayk* (New Dawn, monthly), AGBU, published from 1978 to 1993; *Purasdan* (Garden, monthly), St Gregory the Illuminator, founded 1962; and *Armash*, founded 1984, a biannual religious and cultural, privately operated and funded publication.

St Gregory's and St Mary's Churches in St Catharines and Hamilton, respectively, jointly publish *Avedaper* (The Messenger). The Ottawa community has published *Ottawa Hai* (The Ottawa Armenian). In Toronto, bulletins and newsletters that serve to inform, lead, and consolidate membership include *Canadahai Mamul Lradou* (Canadian Armenian Press Newsletter), published by the Armenian Evangelical church; *Hai Getroni Lradou* (Armenian Community Centre Newsletter), Toronto; *Khosnak* (Advocate), published by the AGBU Toronto branch); *Loussapatz* (The Dawn), Social Democratic Hnchakian newletter; *Massis* (Massis, i.e., Mount Ararat), published by Holy Cross School; *Zank* (Bell), a publication of the ARS Kololian primary school, Toronto; and *Lraper* (Reporter), published by the Armenian Catholic Church in Toronto. For a brief period, the Armenian Secret Army for the Liberation of Armenia (ASALA) published *Azad Hai* (The Free Armenian) in Toronto.

Two Armenian political organizations publish weekly newspapers: *Abaka* (Future), an organ of the Ramgavar organization, published in Montreal and founded in 1975, and *Horizon*, mouthpiece of the Armenian National Committee (Dashnaks), a trilingual weekly founded in 1979 and published in Montreal. Both newspapers focus on international and Canadian news, Armenian affairs, local announcements and events, and various topics of general interest, including architecture, history, and the arts. As a means of bridging the generations and of enhancing Armenian-language use among the young, they carry special pages to delight children and young adults. Regular literary supplements not only provide a platform for writers but also keep readers aware of literary developments in Armenian, English, and French that are contributed by Armenians or are about Armenians. In addition to the press, Armenians produce radio and television programs in both Montreal and Toronto, and more recently they have taken advantage of the internet.

Armenian organizational and institutional life, which is marked by a staggering number of activities, continues to flourish in Canada. Such dynamism reflects the autonomy and particularities of interest groups; the dedication and resilience of the leadership; the commitment to meet the needs of different gender and age cohorts; the perseverance required for fund-raising campaigns; and meaningful voluntarism. Perhaps the vitality of Armenian organizational life reflects a period of youthful optimism in the life-cycle of this community. Whereas in the past, Armenian organizations and institutions depended on their affiliates in the United States, in the last thirty years, successful efforts have been made to create strictly Canadian structures. Many may be part of world-wide organizations, to be sure, but they are autonomous and have distinct Canadian characteristics and objectives. This striving for independence shows that, along with its youthful energy, a measure of security and maturity distinguishes the Armenian community in Canada.

On the other hand, organizational and institutional proliferation may duplicate and dissipate community resources and impede community-wide cooperation. In her study of Armenians in the United States, Bakalian suggests that institutional and organizational abundance may be detrimental to effective community cooperation and unified action. Mobilizing an ethnic group en masse and promoting institutions with specific goals are not easily reconcilable, since their objectives call forth agendas that often pull in opposite directions. Organizational and institutional proliferation may thus prevent the development of strong and effective lobbying mechanisms that could coordinate the overarching interests of the community.[34]

Abaka, an Armenian-, English-, and French-language weekly published in Montreal by the Armenian Democratic Liberal party (Ramgavar). This edition announces the crucial vote in Armenia in favour of independence. Courtesy of Migirdic Migirdicyan and by permission of *Abaka*

Horizon, an Armenian-, English-, and French-language weekly published in Montreal by the Armenian National Committee. *Horizon* newspaper announces the passage of the Resolution in the Canadian Senate recognizing the Armenian Genocide, 24 June 2002. This resolution is viewed as a major step towards the approval of Motion m-380 in the Canadian House of Commons on 21 April 2004. Members of Parliament voted resoundingly in favour of acknowledging the Genocide. Photo, *from left to right*, Aris Babikian, Paul Douzjian, Senator Raymond Setlakwé, Senator Shirley Maheu, Roupen Kouyoumjian, and Apo Niziblian. Photographer, Aris Babikian. By permission of *Horizon Weekly*

Annual demonstration in Ottawa on 24 April protesting Turkey's unwillingness to recognize the Genocide. Courtesy of the Armenian National Committee

Armenian schoolchildren in concert, Toronto, 1990s. Inscription above reads, "We are few. But we are Armenian." The reference is to survival and rebirth. Hundreds of Armenian churches, monasteries, and cemeteries have been plundered and destroyed in Turkey; thousands of Armenian homes, farms, and schools were confiscated, looted, and demolished; countless manuscripts and books were burned and tens of thousands of people were murdered. But today, in Canada, Armenians have built new churches, they have opened new shops, and they have established new schools. They have written new books, created new music, and painted and sculpted new works of art. Courtesy St Sahag and St Mesrob Armenian Saturday School, Toronto

Armenian sculpture, one of the few remaining Armenian antiquities in Turkey, Armenian Cathedral at Aghtamar, 915–921. This sculpture of the Virgin and Child plays a significant role in Atom Egoyan's film *Ararat*, for it symbolizes the theme of the relationship between mother and son. Egoyan weaves together various artistic manifestations of the theme ranging in time (tenth century to the present) and in place (Canada, the United States, and Turkey). This sculpture, Arshile Gorky's painting of his mother and himself (reminiscent of the picture shown in part 1, and the tensions between a Canadian art historian and her son provide the mortar of the film's structure. Photo courtesy Armenian Genocide Memorial Committee, Montreal, 2000

Sculpture of a stone cross and eagle remembering 1915, St Gregory the Illuminator Catholic Church, Toronto. By permission of St Gregory the Illuminator Church

Statue erected by Armenians in Montreal to commemorate the genocide and man's inhumanity to man. Cover of an Armenian Telephone Directory of Montreal. By permission of the Armenian National Committee

Canadian stamp commemorating the seventeen hundredth anniversary of Armenia's conversion to Christianity as a state religion. Design, Debbie Adams; photos, Christine Guest, Brian Merrett, the Montreal Museum of Fine Arts. The stamp shows a leaf from an Evangelary, St Mark, the Entry into Jerusalem, attributed to Isit (Psak), c 1420, Stone cross, photo by Hrair Hawk Khatcherian. Courtesy of the Armenian National Committee of Canada

On April 21, 2004, Armenians expressed their appreciation to Canada for passing the parliamentary resolution recognizing the Armenian Genocide. The event symbolized the transition from stateless refugees to empowered citizens. Photo courtesy *Horizon* newspaper, Montreal

20

Armenian Integration, Group Maintenance, and Societal Recognition

The movement of peoples, whether temporary or permanent, voluntary or involuntary, does not necessarily lead to the loss of their identity as defined in terms of their culture, religion, or language. Over a period of time, ethnic minorities may lose their ethnocultural identity, but they may also adjust to the new environment, evolve, and reinvent and restructure themselves as viable minorities. The fate of minorities depends as much on their internal dynamics and on their collective will to survive as it does on conditions and attitudes in the host society. Like most immigrants, Armenian newcomers were eager to participate in Canadian society; they also wanted to preserve their ethnic identity. These two aspects of the immigrant experience and their implications, though not necessarily or always contradictory, generated tensions within the communities themselves and in their relationship with Canadian society.

THE TWO SIDES OF ETHNOCULTURAL LOSS

Canadian Society

The extensive control of the host society – the "mainstream" – and the imposition of its attitudes and policies on the newcomers are without question fundamental forces in the adaptation process of ethnic groups. Either by passing deliberate measures, such as restrictive immigration regulations, or by creating intolerant environments, the host society can promote assimilation and accelerate the diminution of ethnic identity. Every ethnic or racial group, especially those not sustained by new waves of immigration, has experienced major changes in group dynamics, as well as some loss of descent-group identity and solidarity. In some instances, the group has slowly and steadily disappeared.

At any specific time in Canada, ethnic visibility or invisibility appears to be closely associated with the degree of tolerance shown by the host society. During the early years of this century, Rev. M.C. Kinsdale reflected the attitude of Anglo-Canadian Protestant liberals when he exhorted his listeners "to abandon the idea of our infinite superiority over the foreigner; we are not their superiors but their equals, and we have to step down from our haughty standpoint and *assimilate them*" (italics mine). Those who could not be assimilated, like Asians and Blacks, were often excluded from the country. Central and Southeast Europeans were reluctantly allowed to enter but they were expected to assimilate into a homogeneous social order based on the English language, British customs, British political traditions, and Protestant doctrines.

Calling for a halt to non-British immigration as early as 1900, the *Calgary Herald* wondered what this country was coming to with Doukhobors pouring in by the thousands, Galicians swarming over the central portions, and rats taking possession of Dawson City. The newspaper complained that Canada had become "a veritable dumping ground for the refuse of civilization" and the country had a mean task ahead "if we are to preserve a preponderating British tone." Indeed, as the sociologist Raymond Breton has written: "Historically, nation-building in its symbolic-cultural dimension had been oriented toward the construction of a British-type of society in Canada. This was to be reflected in the cultural character of the political, religious, educational and other public institutions, in the language of the society, in the customs, mores, and way of life, and in the symbols used to represent the society and its people ... Thus 'being Canadian' was in the process of being defined as speaking English within a British-type institutional system."[1]

Canadian public schools became the focal point of the assimilationist drive. Children were instilled with pride about being part of the British Empire. Their flag was the Union Jack and their monarch sat on the British throne. Each morning they repeated the pledge of allegiance to the flag, the monarch, and the Empire. Their nationalistic songs were Rule Britannia and the British Grenadiers, and they enthusiastically praised "Britannia's flag on Canada's fair domain." Their history texts boasted about Alfred the Great, the Tudors, and the daring British pirates. Their heroines were Queen Elizabeth I and Queen Victoria, and their empire builders were Robert Clive and Cecil Rhodes.

The experience of a group of Armenian orphan boys (see chapter 9) best illustrates attempts at rapid assimilation and insensitivity to the unique personal history of newcomers. Shortly after the children arrived at their orphanage in Georgetown, Ontario, the administrators of the Armenian Relief Association of Canada tried to change their names to more easily pronounceable English ones, but the boys' resistance to losing the only shard they had salvaged from the ruins of genocide finally compelled the administrators to allow them to keep their own names. But the association came under heavy fire from its members and supporters for not carrying out its promise to "Anglicize" the children. This initial skirmish was the first shot in many battles between those who wanted to keep the orphans together and to preserve their identity as Armenians and those who wanted to disperse them and produce Anglo-Saxon farmers.

As late as the 1940s, while Armenian men were fighting and dying in the war, their brothers and sisters faced prejudice in Canada. In the factories, foreign names were synonymous with dangerous jobs, heavy work, and obedience. When "foreign" children tried to climb the job ladder, they encountered resistance. If, for example, they applied for office work, they were usually turned down or advised to anglicize their names. It was not until the late 1940s or early 1950s that persons with an Armenian name were allowed to work in the office of those same factories. Similarly, in seeking admission to professional schools, Armenians often found that their grades were not the only qualifying criteria. Armenians in southern Ontario were restricted from joining certain clubs and organizations, and residential segregation plagued them as much as in cities where Armenians were more numerous, such as Fresno, California and Boston, Massachusetts.[2]

For many immigrants and their children, the word "foreigner" still conjures up distressing memories of intolerance and contempt. Anglo-Canadians scorned those who were not descended of British stock – even if they were born in Canada – with such clichés as "those foreigners, they all reek of garlic and eat weird food." Or, "those foreigners, why don't they speak English?" Or, "those foreigners, they take jobs away from us." As foreigners, Armenians, like other minorities, were often harassed. An interviewee recalled the sound of shattering glass when a brick came hurtling through her front door as an angry mob of boys outside shouted, "Foreigners go home."[3] Another remembered how a neighbour grasped him by the collar and gave him a good shake while scolding him because his father, and others like him, were taking jobs away from her husband. "My father was doing the filthiest job in the factory. Her husband wouldn't go near such a job or risk his life. I guess she understood when my father had an industrial accident and couldn't work anymore."[4]

Not only were Armenians immigrants in a sophisticated, urbanized, industrial society that took no account of them or their culture, they were, at least in the early years, small farmers and refugees who entered Canadian society on the lowest rung of the socioeconomic ladder. To what avail that a refugee child's grandfather had been a well-off merchant in Istanbul or a newspaper editor in Smyrna? That life was in another world and in another time. In Canada, until the 1940s and 1950s, Armenians were struggling to establish an economic foothold. The message to the young was clear: to be Armenian was to suffer the stigma of poverty: to be Canadian was to enjoy opportunities, social mobility, and potential success.

The narratives that have been woven into this study reveal to some extent the impact of the Genocide on the psychology and emotions of survivors and their descendants. Their ethnic identity was deeply rooted in tragedy. Even more powerful was their confrontation with evil. Survivors had been shaken by the incomprehensible fury of evil. "Evil" was no longer a word they read in the Bible or heard in church. For them evil was real. The Genocide experience wrapped survivors in a shroud of fatalism and defeatism. It left them vulnerable, with a deep-seated "genocide complex" that was, unfortunately, too often passed on to their children, who were insidiously weaned on a sense of victimization. The painful legacy of torture and massacre and the agony of unredressed crimes scarred the entire community. The message to the young was, once again, obvious: to be Armenian was to be the victim of unspeakable horrors; to be Canadian was to be a member of the British Empire.

Forces within the Armenian Community

The Genocide and the pall of extinction had other ramifications. Some young people resented the attitude of their parents and community elders – the remnant survivors – for imposing heavy responsibilities on them. It was the *duty* of the young generation to save the nation – to attend Armenian school, speak the language, learn the culture, join partisan groups, and marry an Armenian. Many Canadian-born Armenians were unable or unwilling to cope with the burden of the hopes of a nation almost destroyed, and some rejected it altogether.

Far from the big Armenian settlements in the United States and the Middle East, the southern Ontario communities, those small, dispersed pockets of Armenian life, constantly faced almost insurmountable obstacles to group cohesion. Outmigration further diluted the community, as people moved away from the old neighbourhoods, either to suburban areas or away from the city altogether. Such emigration was prompted partly by marriage, improved socioeconomic status, and comparatively better opportunities elsewhere.

Events outside Canada – in the United States and in Soviet Armenia – also had profound repercussions on Armenian settlements in Canada. International developments generated internal conflicts, led to ugly quarrels and recriminations, and set brother against brother. Bitterness and vindictiveness left their indelible marks on the communities. Young people found their parents' fanaticism and the community's factionalism distasteful and simply turned their backs on the Armenian community and their Armenian heritage.

Internal divisions led to a proliferation and duplication of services, schools, organizations, and churches, each appealing to different political and religious interests and priorities and together providing a rich and active ethnocultural environment. But as has already been pointed out, such proliferation and duplication also taxed the limited resources of a relatively small group and in the long run may have been self-defeating, a consequence that was perhaps reflected in the extent of language loss for the first and second generations born in Canada during the first half of the twentieth century.

Endogamy is considered a pertinent index of cultural persistence, while exogamy is viewed as a significant index of the degree of assimilation or loss of ethnic identity, though it is certainly not the only such index, as is shown in Anny Bakalian's study, *Armenian-Americans: From Being to Feeling Armenian.*[5] Exogamy is not only a significant *indicator of* the degree of assimilation but it is also an active *contributor to* assimilation and loss of ethnocultural identity. When an Armenian girl, for instance, marries a non-Armenian boy, she has probably already slipped away somewhat from the Armenian community and its culture. The assimilation process will likely continue and intensify after such marriages, unless deliberate measures are put in place to combat the loss of the mother tongue and the home culture. In the Armenian community, exogamy has tended to hasten acculturation and withdrawal, partly because of the sometimes cruel rejection of non-Armenian spouses by Armenians. An examination of Armenian marriage patterns in Canada during the twentieth century reveals that intermarriage rates have risen over the past hundred years, that the increase is evident even among the foreign-born and in relatively new and large Armenian settlements like those in Toronto and Montreal, and that intermarriage rates will likely continue to rise.[6]

Not surprisingly, almost all immigrants to Canada before 1914 married Armenians. Of twelve marriages of Armenians consecrated in Grace Anglican Church in Brantford, Ontario, from 1905 to 1914, only one was exogamous. All Armenian marriage partners were foreign-born, almost all in Keghi. From 1917 to 1931, the same records reveal a marked increase in the number of marriages, reflecting the movement of Armenians to Canada in the post-Genocide period and their decision to settle permanently in the Dominion. The records show a slight move towards exogamy. Of sixty-eight marriages involving Armenians, two were exogamous, i.e., less than 3 percent. In both cases Armenian men married outside the group. The records of the itinerant Armenian priest Rev. Movses Der Stepanian again show the high degree of endogamy. All forty marriages performed by him in Canada and the northern United States from 1924 to 1929 were endogamous. A low incidence of exogamy during the 1920s is not abnormal given the traumas of the Genocide and the well-founded fear of national extinction, coupled with discrimination against Armenians by the host population and the resistance to marrying "foreigners." During the 1930s and early 1940s, records at St Gregory's in St Catharines reveal the same preponderance of endogamy; in 1946 none of the marriages consecrated in St Gregory's were exogamous (the couples were mostly first- and second-generation Armenians).

Following World War II and into the Cold War period, however, a different trend emerges as second-generation Armenians reached maturity, as World War II brought Armenians into closer contact with people from other ethnic, racial, and religious groups, as Armenians encountered less prejudice in the Canadian environment, and as movement into Canadian society through schooling, sports, the arts, and employment drew Armenian young people into a larger orbit of spousal choices. At no time were the tensions of a dual heritage so stark as in the choice of a marriage partner. Children whose families spoke Armenian, belonged to Armenian organizations, ate Armenian food, and thought "Armenian" met and fell in love with young people from non-Armenian backgrounds. Given the strong emphasis on personal choice and romantic love, it was inevitable that the second generation would intermarry, but the first few such unions caused immeasurable anguish for both parents and children.

From 1948 to 1980 the rate of exogamy as shown in the records of St Gregory's jumped to approximately 59 percent. From 1983 to 1987, inclusive, all marriages were exogamous. But church records and city registers are known to be incomplete and inaccurate. As a means of offsetting some of the imprecision of church records, a different kind of survey was undertaken in Hamilton. Using the names of Armenians in Hamilton in 1945 under the age of 30, I traced their marital patterns (first marriage only). Most, but not all, were first-generation Armenians born in Canada. Because the number of "acceptable" mates was limited and because the pressure on young people to marry Armenians was unrelenting, many never married at all. Out of 104 young people on the survey list, 12, or over 10 percent, remained spinsters or bachelors. Of the 92 who married, 41 chose Armenian spouses, and 51 took non-Armenian mates. Thus about 55 percent of marriages were exogamous, a ratio considered rather low by Canadian standards, but anathema among Armenians of the period. In Toronto, the marriage registers of Holy Trinity Armenian Church showed that in 1970, 19 percent of the marriages were exogamous. In Montreal, church registers revealed a similar trend: from 1958 to 1974, 24 percent of the marriages were exogamous. How do we account for these statistics, which are in striking contrast to the 59 percent exogamy rates in St Catharines and the 55 percent rates in Hamilton during roughly the same period?

These statistics bear out the findings of Aharon Aharonian, whose study of Armenian marriage patterns in the United States, using Apostolic Church records, showed that the older the community and the further removed from the immigrant generation, the more the likelihood of intermarriage. Anny Bakalian confirmed these findings in her analysis of Armenians in New York; and Matthew Jendian noted the same trend in his work on Armenian marriage patterns in Fresno, California.[7]

Inevitably, immigration makes an impact on marriage patterns, partly because immigrants are less likely to outmarry and partly because they increase the "critical mass" and thus provide a larger pool of eligible partners. After World War II, thousands of displaced persons were admitted to Canada, but Armenians were not among them in any appreciable numbers. The Armenian communities in Canada, therefore, received no "new blood" from the 1920s until the situation started to change in the 1950s. These immigration flows contributed to the discrepancies between the exogamy rates in places like St Catharines, an "old" community, and Montreal, a "new" community, during roughly the same period.

Place of birth has a bearing on marriage patterns. The Hamilton marriage survey mentioned above revealed that the vast majority of the marriage partners had been born in Canada. By contrast, a survey in Toronto yielded different results. Using the registers of the two Armenian Apostolic churches in Toronto (Holy Trinity and St Mary), the survey found that of thirty-five marriages performed in 1987, twenty-one were endogamous and fourteen were exogamous. Thus, about 40 percent of those married in the two Armenian churches were in exogamous marriages, compared to 55 percent of those in the Hamilton survey referred to above. Unlike the Hamilton group, most of the Toronto participants had been born abroad.

Size, too, has had an impact on marriage patterns. As we have already seen, Armenian communities in cities like Brantford, Hamilton, and St Catharines did not attract as many new immigrants as those in Toronto and Montreal. Declining populations with minimal immigration affected the size of the community, which in turn influenced marriage patterns. Those maturing in the postwar period, moreover, were part of the Depression generation, whose fertility rates were markedly lower than the rates of young couples of the previous decade. These two facts – low immigration flows and low birth rates – reduced the critical mass for a generation of young people who were already moving out into Canadian society.

Invariably, the study of marriage patterns raises questions about gender. Have there been differences between the rates of intermarriage of boys and girls? If so, what factors contribute to the differential? How have parents treated the intermarriage of their sons compared to their treatment of the intermarriage of their daughters? Parents strenuously resisted the intermarriage of their children, regardless of gender, and they often threatened to disown their children if they acted against their wishes. But societal forces became too strong for them to impose such constraints, especially on their sons, who enjoyed more freedom than their daughters in moving out into the Canadian world. Before World War II, most mixed marriages were between Armenian men and non-Armenian women. After the war, however, the incidence of female exogamy rose, a clear reflection of the growing autonomy of young women. Armenian society, particularly for the immigrant generation, was largely patriarchal. One might argue, then, that parents expected their sons, as potential heads of households, to be able to create an "Armenian home," regardless of the ethnic background of their spouse. Hence, there was less opposition to their sons' "aberrant" behaviour. In the last analysis, however, it seems more a question of control. Parents exercised more power over their daughters than over their sons and could be more assertive with daughters. However, as girls began to venture out into Canadian society, attain higher education, and take jobs in the "Canadian world," they, too, began to make their own decisions about marriage partners, even against their parents' wishes. Endogamy persists among immigrants of the third wave and their children, though the incidence of intermarriage is creeping into this cohort, despite family and community pressure. For example, 1981 and 1991 census data for Quebec reveal an increase from 14 percent to 18 percent of Armenians reporting multiple ethnic origins.

The financial records of the Keghi compatriotic societies reveal the old-timers' vision of the future of the Armenian heritage and Armenian culture in North America. Their children received good public school education in Canada and the United States, so it was not necessary for them to provide for their own schools, as they had done in the

Ottoman Empire. But instead, they sent their funds to help Armenian survivors in Soviet Armenia and the Middle East. And when their organizations disbanded in the 1980s, they divided their remaining funds between the See of Echmiadzin and the See of Cilicia. Their actions should be seen as symbolic gestures, for they epitomized the skepticism of the old-timers about Armenian group survival in North America. In spite of their own commitment, their deeds reflected the conviction that the future strength of the Armenian nation lay not in the North American settlements but in the numerically superior communities in the Middle East and in Soviet Armenia. How could they possibly have foreseen the disruption of the Middle Eastern communities, the dire conditions in Armenia today, and the increasingly critical role of the North American diaspora?

To sum up, the strong pull of Canadian society, a pervasive genocide complex, enormous pressures on the young, internal community conflicts, the small size of dispersed communities, and exogamy all played a role in weakening the collective viability of the older Armenian communities. But while the mechanisms and demands of Canadian society and the internal dynamics of Armenian community life sapped the strength of the early settlements, they did not destroy them altogether.

A DUAL HERITAGE

When Armenians came to North America, they were already aware of their cultural distinctiveness. They knew they could function as a distinct community, retain their heritage, and perpetuate their culture and at the same time contribute to Canadian society and enrich the Canadian environment. In every Armenian family, school, organization, and church the same lesson was repeatedly taught to the young, as it had been for generations in the Ottoman Empire: loyalty to their Armenian heritage and allegiance to the governing state.

Armenians repudiated total separation and isolation from the larger society. They were determined to be part of the Canadian world, to work and thrive in Canadian society, and to uphold Canadian values of democracy, civility, and respect for the law. Just as they had shown their loyalty to Canada during World War I and World War II by volunteering in the armed forces, Armenians sought to prove their patriotism and love of Canada and to show that loyalty to a dual heritage is not only possible but a potent force in Canadian development and progress. Their attempts to practice loyalty both to their ethnocultural past and to the country that offered them new hope were, however, complicated and thwarted by attitudes that Armenians encountered in Canada. They did not foresee that some Anglo-Canadians would reject them and their ancient culture and would expect them to surrender their identity, since many Canadians saw dual loyalty as a form of disloyalty or resistance or betrayal. In their view, ethnic culture had no prestige or status in Canadian life. Many Anglo-Canadians deemed cultural and linguistic self-maintenance by "foreigners" as contradictory to Canadian nation building and considered any form of diversity an obstacle to British conformity and an impediment to the objectives of the larger society, rather than a rich and worthwhile addition to it. While Armenians may have expected a measure of discrimination in Moslem countries, they did not expect the strident prejudice they encountered in a Christian country, particularly with respect to immigration regulations. Not only were they "undesirable," but their religion was of little consequence in the eyes of some Canadians, and their values, behavioural patterns, foods, and customs were often the butt of ridicule.

Links with Canadian Churches

Like other groups, Armenians tried to create a workable balance between adaptation to Canadian society and preservation of their ethnic heritage. For some Armenian Canadians a link with the host society was established through relations with other Christian denominations. As early as the 1890s, Canadian Protestant missionaries proselytizing among Armenians in the Ottoman Empire intervened with the Canadian government on behalf of Armenians wishing to emigrate to Canada. During World War I, expulsion and massacre captured the attention and compassion of the Canadian people. Churchmen and business leaders joined forces and in cooperation with the *Toronto Globe*, raised almost three hundred thousand dollars in 1920 to send abroad to aid the Armenian survivors. Canadian religious groups were also instrumental in bringing Armenian refugee orphans to Canada during the 1920s under the auspices of the Armenian Relief Association of Canada. Meanwhile, Canadian churches sent protests to the Canadian government urging Ottawa to act in favour of an independent Armenian state (see chapter 7).

All along, the Anglican Church, which has strong theological bonds with the Armenian Apostolic Church, offered church facilities for Armenian services and opened its doors to Armenians for worship, the rites of passage, and membership. The list is extensive: in Montreal, St John the Evangelist; in Ottawa, St Mark; in Vancouver, St Chad; in Toronto, St Stephen, Holy Trinity, and later, St Augustine of Canterbury; in Hamilton, St Philip until it was sold, then St Thomas; in St Catharines, St Barnabas and St Thomas; in Brantford, Grace Anglican; and in Galt/Cambridge, Holy Trinity Anglican Church. In its turn, the

United Church of Canada, which is affiliated with certain Armenian Evangelical churches, assisted the Georgetown young men and in the 1980s facilitated the movement of Armenian refugees to Canada. Armenians have also worked closely with the Canadian Council of Churches, not only to bring stateless Armenians to Canada but also to establish close ties with the Christian community in Canada.

Links through the Workplace

Armenians have also moved into Canadian society through the workplace. Aside from the fact that Armenians contributed to Canadian industrial development, men working in the iron factories took the lead in the trade union movement in the 1930s, 1940s, and 1950s. Many others joined the unions and gave them their unequivocal support. Armenians opened small businesses catering to an Armenian and non-Armenian clientele, but for a long time the major role played by the Oriental rug trade – a "niche" market – testified to the difficulty of moving into the mainstream of retailing. More recently, the concentration of a number of Armenians in specialty businesses, like the jewellery and automotive trades, represents a continuation of professional expertise gained abroad, rather than a response to societally limited opportunities in Canada. The formation of Armenian Canadian business and professional organizations, moreover, has created innovative ways of bringing Armenians together and strengthening ethnic-group cohesion within a wider Canadian professional and economic sphere.

The opening up of Canadian society since World War II, the popularity of the concept of multiculturalism, and by 1970, the national policy of bilingualism and multiculturalism as propounded by Prime Minister Pierre Elliott Trudeau coincided with greater professional and economic mobility for Armenian Canadians. Although ethnically based barriers against Armenians disappeared only gradually until the mid-1970s, they have disappeared almost completely in recent years. Armenian Canadians excel in every field of medicine and the sciences, architecture, engineering, law, and education. Professor Stephen Hanessian, for example, of the University of Montreal, was awarded the 1996 Canada Gold Medal for Science and Engineering by the Natural Sciences and Engineering Research Council of Canada for his outstanding work in organic, bioorganic, and medicinal chemistry.[8] Similarly, Dr Berge Minassian of the University of Toronto and the Hospital for Sick Children led a team of scientists in a ground-breaking study of the second gene associated with the most severe form of teenage-onset epilepsy, known as Lafora disease. Not only does the Armenian intelligentsia serve as a role model for the young, but it forms a professional bridge between the Armenian community and Canadian society.

Links through the Sphere of Politics

Until 1988 very few Armenians held high political office in Canada. As in the earlier period, Armenian entry into politics was initially through ethnic/multicultural organizations, as in the case of Dr Kévork Baghdjian of Montreal, who was president of the Fédération des groupes éthniques du Québec from 1975 to 1988, followed by Dr Arshavir Gundjian. Armenians continue to support multicultural initiatives through the political process. In 1988, for example, Sarkis Assadourian, Aris Babikian, Zohrab Malek, and Apkar Mirakian represented the Armenian community before the House of Commons Standing Committee on Multiculturalism. In the 1990s more Armenians began vying for office in mainstream Canadian politics. Although those years are beyond the scope of this study, it would be appropriate to mention municipal representatives Tom Jackson of Hamilton, Noushig Eloyan of Montreal, Hasmig Vasilian-Belleli of Montreal, and Jack Chaderjian of Ville St Laurent. Sarkis Assadourian, an Ontario Liberal, became the first Canadian of Armenian descent to be elected to the House of Commons, and Raymond Setlakwé, the first Canadian of Armenian descent appointed to the Senate.

Links through the Arts

As early as the pioneering period, Armenians engaged in musical and theatrical endeavours, but the Genocide altered the course of Armenian artistic development. At a time when the dispersed and destitute people needed the sustenance of their culture to reinforce their identity, their creative leaders had been murdered. Cut off from their past, the survivors cherished the fragments of their cultural heritage that they brought with them: perhaps a treasured song book or a booklet of favourite family recipes, perhaps a prayer sung by a lost parent, perhaps a childhood poem. The post-Genocide period was marked by a reliance on the pre-Genocide literary and musical repertoire, and only gradually did an Armenian Canadian/American artistic culture begin to take shape. In recent years Armenians have been trying to revive and reconstitute traditional Armenian forms in folklore, feasts and festivals, literature, music, architecture, and the arts, including Armenian embroidery and needlework. As a corollary, they are seeking to purge the arts of Turkish influences, particularly in language and music.

When earlier generations of Armenian Canadians took up the pen, they wrote poetry, autobiographies or memoirs, or village or regional histories. A single theme dominated these works: loss. Loss of home and property, of village, family, and country, and of identity.[9] The same theme permeates Armenian Canadian literary expression in English and in French: Aram Aivazian's *Armenia: Usurped by Genocide and Treachery*, Ara Baliozian's *Fragmented Dreams: Armenians in Diaspora*, Shant Basmajian's poetry, Kerop Bedoukian's *Urchin: an Armenian's Escape*, Agop Haikyan's *Un été sans aube* (1991), Gerard Pederian's *Armenian Massacres*, and Lorne Shirinian's *Quest*.

Since the 1920s Armenians have taken their artistic culture to Canadian society at large, mostly through music and the theatre. Their choirs and theatrical troupes have won awards in public competitions. Such groups have acted as ambassadors, bringing Armenian culture to the Canadian public, and equally important, they have introduced "mainstream" music and theatre to the Armenian community. Armenian Canadians of the third wave have continued this tradition and have contributed their artistic talents to the Canadian cultural scene. Music has conspicuously dominated Armenian artistic endeavour in Canada, as is evident in the achievements of violinist Peter Oundjian, conductor of the Toronto Symphony Orchestra, and Nurhan Arman, conductor of the New Brunswick Symphony Orchestra and musical director of the Toronto Sinfonia Chamber Orchestra. Conductor Raffi Armenian developed the Kitchener-Waterloo Symphony Orchestra into one of Canada's finest, and violinist Gérard Kantarjian was formerly concertmaster with the Toronto Symphony Orchestra. Raffi (Cavoukian) is a popular children's songwriter and performing musician. A new generation of outstanding young Armenian Canadian musicians like Isabel Bayrakdarian, soprano, Eve Egoyan and Serouj Kradjan, pianists, and Catherine Manoukian, violinist, and Levon Ishkhanian, guitarist, have excelled in mainstream performance. Other Armenians have also distinguished themselves in the musical arena: Norair Artinian, pianist; Raffi Bedrosyan, pianist; Mihran Essegulian, composer; Aline Kutan, soprano; Edik Hovsepian, choir master; Zabel Manoukian, pianist; Ludvig Philibosian, choir director; Ludwig Semerjian, pianist; Hrachia Sevadjian, violinist; Bedros Shoujounian, composer and choir master; David Varjabed, choir director; and Zaven Zakarian, clarinetist. Hasmig Injejikian and Maryvonne Kendergi are well-known musicologists.

In the visual arts, Anahid Aprahamian, Cavouk (Artin Cavoukian), Suren Chekijian, Hagop Khoubesserian, Berge Missakian, Gérard Paraghamian, Arman Tatossian, Michael Torosian, and Arto Yuzbasiyan are highly respected painters or photographers, while Arto Tchakmakchian is a noted sculptor. Hrant Aliank and Richard

Ouzounian have excelled in theatre; Khazaros Surmeyan in ballet; and David Alpy, Araz Artinian and Merj Fazlian in film. Atom Egoyan, the Canadian filmmaker, and actress Arsinée Khanjian, who has played a leading role in many of Egoyan's films, have brought international acclaim to Canadian cinema. Egoyan's movie *Exotica* (1994) won eight Genie awards, and *The Sweet Hereafter* (1997) won the Grand Prize of the Jury at the Cannes Film Festival, as well as making a sweep of the Canadian Genie top honours. Egoyan's film, ARARAT, released in 2002 won five Genie awards for the best motion picture, best supporting actor, best acress, costume design, and original score in music. Of all Egoyan's films, ARARAT is perhaps the most prominent artistic interweaving of Armenian and Canadian themes. While the action takes place in Canada and raises such contemporary Canadian issues as intergenerational tensions, the complexities of family reconfigurations, and homosexual relationships, the film focusses on the Genocide and on Arshile Gorky's painting in expressing a people's suffering and loss. The Canadian and Armenian threads are intricately entwined in the theme of mother and son. In English, French, and Armenian, Egoyan weaves this theme through time – the present, the past, and the distant past – and through literature, painting, and sculpture. In another dimension, but still focussing on the Genocide, the film grapples with the contradictions inherent in interpreting the past, with the nature of truth, and with the consequences of subverting the truth.

MAINTAINING ETHNIC GROUP IDENTITY

At the same time that Armenians have tried to integrate into Canadian society, they have also endeavoured to maintain their unique identity. Armenians, of course, have not been alone in trying to come to terms with their civic loyalty to Canada and their private loyalty to their ethnic heritage. It is noteworthy that various ethnic groups in Hamilton founded one of the first multicultural organizations in Canada, the Canadian National Unity Council (1947). It is even more noteworthy that the driving force behind the creation of this organization was an Armenian: John H. Mooradian, its founder and first president.

To an extent, ethnocultural preservation has been possible because, while a degree of nativism and intolerance prevailed in Canada for a good part of the century, overt suppression did not. Canadians may have disapproved of Armenians speaking their language in public places, but no laws forbade it. No regulations prohibited Armenian supplementary schools, Armenian churches, or Armenian communal gatherings. The Canadian government and the Canadian people were, by and large, indifferent to Armenians and did not interfere in the internal life of the Armenian community. While indifference can and frequently does lead to rejection and hence polarization, it also allows the ethnic group to express its own agenda. If Armenians operated their Armenian-language schools in the evenings, no objections were raised, provided that they did not interfere with attendance and performance in the Canadian public schools during the day and provided that Armenians ran and funded the schools themselves. As long as Armenians were hard-working and law-abiding and as long as they did not infringe on others' rights, the community could create and maintain its own institutions and associations, speak its own language, and pursue its own ethnocultural goals. A sense of the Armenian perspective is conveyed by the following observation:

We have lived outside our homeland for centuries – in Bolis [Constantinople], Tiflis [Tbilisi], Cilicia. You'd think that the Armenian has developed a sense, an ability, to live outside his fatherland but fulfill all the qualifications of living within the homeland. It is interesting to note that our culture in the eighteenth, nineteenth, and twentieth centuries has developed in Bolis and Tiflis. Neither is in Armenia. When you speak of literature and culture, you think of the fatherland; you have to be bound to that soil. Yet much of Eastern Armenian literature and drama was fostered in Tiflis and Western Armenian culture in Bolis. Even the political parties originated outside the fatherland. It is an interesting ability – to live outside the fatherland just as if we were living in it. We have lived outside Armenia but we have created, thought, and felt as if we had lived there. We in the diaspora have so much in common with each other – our mentality, our feelings, our craziness – that I ask myself, is it true that a nation cannot exist without a state?[10]

In the Canadian diaspora, two principal agents of preservation and community cohesion have, for almost a century, provided not only the institutional framework of Armenian community life but also the crucial element of leadership. While other organizations, once popular and vibrant, like the patriotic or educational associations, have all but disappeared, these agents have been and continue to be effective in translating group aspirations and discontent into collective action. Since the early part of the century, the Armenian National Committee, or Dashnak organization, and the Armenian Church, together with their ancillary associations, forged Armenian identity in Canada. In small towns like Hamilton, St Catharines, and Cambridge, the church and the political organization continue to be the principal forces that reinforce community cohesion.

The Armenian neighbourhood, the little urban villages, contributed to group cohesion as the locus of social integration and community activities. As inhabitants died or drifted away and as tensions grew between different cohorts, the old working-class neighbourhoods in Brantford, Hamilton, and St Catharines floundered or disintegrated altogether. The Progressive and Dashnak halls in Brantford were sold and not replaced. In cities where Armenian community life continued, changes in transportation and communications further rendered the neighbourhood obsolete as a mechanism for maintaining group cohesion. The Dashnaks in St Catharines and, more recently, in Hamilton sold the old halls and acquired new structures in the suburbs. Neighbourhoods are no longer de rigueur for maintaining group solidarity. Particularly in large cities like Montreal and Toronto, they have been replaced by extensive complexes that provide multiple services and facilities, generate outlets for cultural, political, and religious expression, and allow opportunities for leadership roles within the community.

Concerned about generational language loss, leaders encourage attendance at Armenian-language schools and participation in Armenian organizations where Armenian is typically spoken. The question of language use engages the community in ongoing discussion. Some argue that Armenian must remain the language of communication in the home, at church, and in community activities. Others concede the importance of language but fear that to insist on Armenian will discourage the young and eventually drive them away. Still, a desire to learn Armenian and an interest in Armenian affairs are evident among the young as is revealed by the growing numbers who attend Armenian Canadian schools and who travel regularly to Armenia to work and study. One consequence of the strength of Armenian-language schooling is that Armenians in both Montreal and Toronto are among the very few groups in which intergenerational ethnic-language transfer (transmission of the heritage language from parents to children) remains comparatively high.[11]

The Armenian press has also played a significant role in promoting language use. A 1981 questionnaire carried out by the Toronto-based *Canadian Armenian Press Newsletter* yielded pertinent information regarding language use and readership. Seventy-eight percent of respondents replied that they read both Armenian and English, 73 percent indicated that they read Armenian publications other than the *Newsletter*, and 59 percent specified that they read three or four other Armenian publications.[12]

The third wave of immigrants brought the same emphasis on family values and family cohesiveness. One of the principal areas of family and community solidarity has centred around both the preparation and the enjoyment of Armenian meals.[13] Both women and men have a tradition of preparing food together at church gatherings or community centres and at picnics. Women are often expected to contribute a dish for a bazaar or a "tea table," and they take great pride in preparing delicious and attractive dishes. In many ways, food is the last vestige of ethnoculture to be lost. It is not unusual to encounter people with Armenian backgrounds who do not identify themselves as Armenians but who prepare and treasure Armenian cuisine. Food, of course, has another dimension, for it also represents the migratory routes Armenians have taken on their way to Canada. One has only to visit an Armenian grocery store or bakery to find foods from the Middle East or Greece, foods such as *lahmajun* (Middle Eastern pizza) and *mohammara* (a Middle Eastern dip made of walnuts or pomegranates and red pepper). Conversely, Armenians manufacture foods such as bulgur, which immigrants from various countries enjoy, so that their clientele moves beyond the Armenian community itself. In a cross-cultural country like Canada, furthermore, Armenians have adopted typically Canadian dishes, giving them their own Armenian flavour at the same time that Armenian dishes have become part of "Canadian" cuisine, notably *madsun* (yogurt), *lavash* (unleavened bread), and *sarma* (rice wrapped in grape leaves). The changing cuisine has led to the publication of Armenian Canadian cookbooks.

Armenians have long recognized the link between marriage and survival and firmly believe that endogamy strengthens the community. Marriage statistics can be viewed from different perspectives. The Hamilton survey mentioned above showed that exogamy was as high as 55 percent. However, if we study the statistics from another angle, we find that only ten Armenians from Hamilton married Armenians from Hamilton, i.e., five couples. The remaining thirty-one married Armenians outside Hamilton, thus rendering the Armenian component much larger than would appear at first glance and than would be expected from local population figures. The numbers also show the efficacy of family, organizational, and institutional networks.

Armenian marriage patterns have been affected by the environment in which Armenians live and by the relationship between Armenians and their neighbours. Yet marriage patterns are more complex than intolerance or mutual acceptance, more complex even than individual autonomy and individual choice in a land of liberty. Armenian marriage patterns and family formation are also inextricably bound up with history, particularly with the Genocide and its aftermath. As a community, Armenians have, in principle at least, opposed intermarriage in North America on the grounds that this "white massacre" would eventually lead to extinction. Their attitudes to couples and families of mixed marriages have ranged from acceptance to polite distance to active rejection. Far too often non-Armenian speaking spouses have not been treated as welcome additions to the Armenian community, and part of the problem lies in attitudes that extend beyond family members. In her study of the Armenian experience in the United States, Anny Bakalian points to the importance of attitude:

> The marriage of men and women of Armenian descent with non-Armenians (odars) is assumed to be the key to assimilation that will obliterate Armenian presence in the United States – the final straw on the camel's back ... the culprit of all the woes of Armenian-Americans ... the cause of all the changes in the life-style that the immigrant generation had taken for granted.
>
> Armenian-Americans do not realize, as the evidence from the New York survey has shown, that statistically intermarriage is of secondary significance to the passing of generations in the United States and religious affiliation ... A non-Armenian parent decreases the likelihood of participation in the ethnic world; however, *the organized community's reactions are as significant, if not more so. Their attitudes and behavior send the message that odars are not welcome in their midst* [italics mine].[14]

Nowhere is Armenian resistance to exogamy more poignantly symbolized than in the use of the word "odar" coupled with "but," as in: "My daughter married an odar, but he's a good man" or "My son married an odar, but she's a nice girl." One might excuse a well-meaning parent for using such a loaded conjunction; nevertheless, the phrase speaks volumes about prejudice against mixed marriages.

The willingness to bring people of non-Armenian descent into the group is vital to its survival in North America. Relying on immigration to enhance the numbers and bolster Armenian community life seems both unrealistic and precarious, because immigration is subject to conditions and regulations beyond the control of the North American Armenian community. Nor can Armenians depend on natural birth increase, since their fertility rate is relatively low, probably averaging about 2 children per woman of child-bearing age. (Under current demographic conditions, an average of 2.1 children per woman is required for population *replacement*.) Gradually, very gradually, Armenians are accepting non-Armenian spouses into their midst, and many have been totally integrated into the Armenian Canadian community. They attend Armenian churches, engage in Armenian activities, participate in Armenian organizations, and learn the Armenian language; and their children attend Armenian schools and join Armenian youth groups. This trend increases the chances of ethnocultural survival. Mixed-marriage families may be one of the greatest assets in the diaspora, but an unrecognized, unappreciated, and unused asset. As a numerically small ethnic group Armenians cannot afford to lose anyone – neither those of Armenian descent nor their partners nor their children – if, as a community, they are to have any hope of retaining their ethnocultural identity.

For Armenians in Canada, probably history remains the most powerful force of group dynamism. The creation of the Armenian Republic in 1918 and its partition by the Communists and the Turks in 1920 galvanized opinion in the diaspora, either in favour of the irredentists or in favour of Soviet Armenia. The resulting polemics, while divisive, nevertheless served to keep Armenian issues at the forefront of daily life. In their own fashion, moreover, each faction proved to be useful in strengthening the homeland. On the one hand, the pro–Soviet Armenia and pro–Echmiadzin Church faction's moral and financial support of the homeland helped to improve facilities and introduce modernity into this Caucasian republic. On the other hand, the anti-Soviet Armenia faction acted as a protagonist; its scrutiny of Soviet policies and exposure of measures it deemed harmful to Armenia's interests served to keep Soviet Armenian authorities on the alert.

The overarching historical force has been twofold: the Genocide and survival The destruction starting in 1915 left not a single Armenian unscathed and generated a resolve among survivors to defy further loss of identity. Armenians have had a history of survival. Being geographically situated at the crossroads between East and West, North and South, Armenia has for centuries been in the path of warring armies but has managed to withstand repeated invasions. After each case of aggression, Armenians restored their churches and homes, rebuilt their farms and businesses, and revived their music, art, and literature. For the remnant survivors of the Genocide, however, the task and responsibility of saving the nation took on enormous proportions, since for the first time in recent history Armenians had been driven out of their homeland. An account by an elderly survivor gives the texture of that traumatic legacy:

In a big field there were thousands of Armenians ... From one of the nearby villages, five or six young Turks came among us and tried to abduct one of the girls. A youth, fifteen or sixteen years old, tried to stop those men from taking his sister. He hit a couple of them and threw them on the ground. They attacked him with axes and cut him to pieces. I can still see that incident before my eyes today. And that boy's mother and the other women, gathered up the pieces of his body and took them to a church. Weeping, they sang this hymn as they buried him:

The hour of death draws near.
I no longer must bear

All my sorrows.
I am departing from my loved ones
And the sweet flowers.
But no matter
God is my Lord.[15]

Only within the context of the Genocide and of the fear of extinction can we understand the Armenian psyche. For Armenians, survival and endurance are dynamic concepts embodying not just continued existence but the quest to rise above destruction and to triumph over adversity. The Genocide continues to have a major impact on Armenian Canadian group consciousness and remains a major basis for community mobilization. Since the 1920s, Armenians have commemorated Martyrs' Day each year on 24 April. At first these memorials took place within the community itself; only gradually did Armenians take their sorrow into the Canadian sphere, initially with services at the local cenotaph. In 1955, on the fortieth anniversary of the Genocide, Armenians in Ontario organized a mass march in Toronto and invited non-Armenians, including the mayor, to speak about the tragedy. In 1965, Mayor Chown of St Catharines signed a declaration designating 24 April as Armenian Memorial Day. And in the province of Ontario, Greek, Hungarian, Italian, Jewish, Polish, and Ukrainian leaders joined the Canadian Armenian Crusade to commemorate the fiftieth memorial services of the Genocide.

In 1980 the Ontario and Quebec legislatures unanimously voted to recognize the Genocide as a violation of human rights and decency. The Ontario legislature called on the Canadian government to recognize and condemn the atrocities "committed by the Government of Turkey upon the Armenian people who were victims of persecution and genocide during World War I" and to designate 24 April as a day of remembrance for Armenian victims of the Genocide. In its turn, the Quebec National Assembly called on the Québécois to set aside 24 April each year as a day of commemoration of the Armenian Genocide. Sixteen years later, after years of advocacy, the Canadian Parliament recognized the Armenian "tragedy" of 1915 and the loss of life of more than 1.5 million Armenians. The government was careful not to use the word "genocide" for fear of economic reprisals from Turkey, a position that disappointed many Canadians. Parliament passed a resolution designating the week of 20 to 27 April of each year as a remembrance of Man's Inhumanity towards His Fellow Man.[16]

Efforts to have the Genocide recognized by Turkey and, for some Armenians, to obtain reparations from the Turkish government have been pitted against a stone wall of unremitting denial thrown up by successive Turkish regimes. Following the events in 1915, a number of Turkish leaders responsible for the atrocities were tried and convicted. Future denial of the crime was unimaginable, both in Turkey and abroad, since it had been witnessed and reported on by Western military, political, and religious observers. However, later Turkish governments repudiated the very events themselves and launched a revisionist campaign, basing their position on both economic and moral grounds: they were unwilling to pay reparations, and they were unwilling to paint their forefathers, in particular Mustapha Kemal Ataturk, as murderers. In response, Armenians around the world campaigned to mobilize public attention on the Genocide, to alert international opinion to the atrocities, and to petition for recognition of the Genocide by various governments and international tribunals, including the Permanent Peoples' Tribunal (Paris, 1984). As in the past sixty years, their efforts were peaceful, but progress was slow and setbacks were many, as Turkey, a member of NATO, stepped up its propaganda of denial.[17]

Frustrated but determined, militant Armenian groups originating in the Middle East, including the Armenian Secret Army for the Liberation of Armenia (ASALA) and the Justice Commandos of the Armenian Genocide (JCAG), later transformed into the Armenian Revolutionary Army (ARA), took armed action against Turkish diplomats and Turkish interests. They aimed to force the Turkish government to accept responsibility for the Genocide, to return Armenian lands, and to pay reparations. They were also determined to bring the Genocide issue forward and expose the Turkish government's denial to world attention.[18] Their militancy was fed by a business-as-usual international climate that found it expedient to allow Turkish denials to stand unchallenged, as if crimes against humanity were a commodity to be exchanged for Turkish government contracts for military and industrial projects. Aggression by young Armenians was their response to the terrorism of the Turkish state against their people during World War I and to the denial since then. Their actions, however, split the Armenian community, for many were strongly opposed to the use of violence, and others, knowing that governments had condemned Turkey's actions during and after World War I, believed it should have been unnecessary to prove yet again what was common knowledge.

In Canada, anti-Turkish action centred on the wounding of one Turkish diplomat and the assassination of another in Ottawa in 1982 and on an assault on the Turkish Embassy in Ottawa in 1985. A guard was shot, and the three Armenian attackers, Hovig Noubarian, Kevork Marashlian, and Raffi Titizian were convicted of first-degree murder and imprisoned for twenty-five years without parole. Canadians reacted with horror to the events, denouncing the practice of bringing old-country quarrels to Canadian shores, just as they had condemned fights between Irish Catholics and Irish Protestants, between Serbs and Croats, and between Italian Fascists and Communists. But one of the main purposes of the activists was fulfilled: they had publicized the Genocide.[19] What a sad state of the media: violence achieved more in three years than peaceful advocacy had in seventy!

In the meantime, peaceful efforts by Armenians to bring the Genocide to the attention of Canadians came up against economic pressure from Turkey. During the 1980s Armenians proposed a teaching unit to the Ottawa Board of Education entitled "Man's Inhumanity to Man." It included a brief study of the Genocide and also incorporated a Turkish perspective. Turkish political pressure and the threat of economic reprisal, however, prompted the Department of External Affairs to intervene with the Ottawa board. Writing to Marjorie Loughrey, the Ottawa board chairperson, Jacques Roy, assistant deputy minister in charge of the department's European desk, discouraged the teaching of the unit because it would have a "negative impact" on Canadian-Turkish relations. Armenian Canadians protested, and the minister of external affairs, Joe Clark, apologized for the fact that the letter had been sent, while Roy continued to reiterate departmental policy, which was that "Canada should accept Turkey's claim there was no genocide, in order not to jeopardize 'millions of dollars' in trade contracts." Bureaucrats interested in trade rather than in truth used an argument frequently adopted by the government of Turkey: it was not "appropriate to describe an event retroactively and to give it a legal connotation which it did not have at the time." This comment refers to the fact that the term "genocide" was coined in 1943 (by Raphael Lemkin, 1900–59) and that the Convention on the Prevention and Punishment of the Crime of Genocide took place in 1948, both events obviously occurring well after the Genocide. This is casuistry. No one would think of denying the genocide of many Aboriginal peoples in North and South America, even if the events occurred in previous centuries.

The teaching unit was revised by local school authorities to present *primarily the viewpoints of well-known genocide deniers* and to cast serious doubt on the veracity of the Genocide. Aside from this outcome, many Canadians were scandalized that the federal government had interfered in an area of provincial jurisdiction and, more especially, that a foreign power had successfully meddled in a Canadian school curriculum. We can well imagine the outcry if the roles had been reversed and Canada had encroached on curriculum matters in Turkish schools on behalf of Kurdish children![20]

By putting pressure on foreign governments not to recognize the Genocide for fear of losing huge contracts with Turkey or in deference to Turkey as a NATO ally and by granting large sums of money in the field of higher education, especially in the United States, the Turkish government distorts the facts and perverts the truth. In Turkey itself, the government has changed the Armenian names of villages and towns and continues to tear down the remaining fragments of Armenian antiquities. Armenian churches and monasteries are systematically destroyed or converted to mosques or public buildings, in order to shroud the fact that Armenians once lived on those lands and prayed in those churches. As if the destruction of historical monuments in Turkey itself is not damaging enough, the government of Turkey attempts to obstruct Armenian efforts to erect cultural monuments in foreign countries where Armenians have lived for generations, including such an initiative in Montreal. After years of persistence by Armenian Canadians and unrelenting obstruction by the Turkish Embassy, the Armenian community of Montreal was finally permitted to erect a monument in 1998, with the inscription: "On the occasion of the 83rd anniversary of the Armenian genocide of 1915 where 1,500,000 Armenians fell victim, we dedicate this work to all martyrs of genocides and we call upon all citizens to work for tolerance and social harmony. This recognition is given in the spirit of the International Declaration of Human Rights."[21]

Where recognition of the Genocide is outside the control of states and big business, Armenians believe that truth has prevailed. The Permanent Peoples' Tribunal, the United Nations Sub-Commission on Prevention of Discrimination and Protection of Minorities (1985), and the European Parliament (1987) have all recognized the Genocide.

In Canada, mobilization spearheaded by the Armenian-Canadian community finally culminated in a victory of thirty-nine to one in a Canadian Senate vote to recognize the Armenian Genocide. On 13 June 2002, Senator Shirley Maheu sponsored the following motion:

Whereas on April 24, 1915, the Ottoman Turkish authorities arrested and later executed over 2,300 prominent leaders of the Armenian community in Istanbul, without cause or reason, but for their race and religion, signaling the beginning of the first genocide of the twentieth century;
Whereas using the First World War as a cover for their operations, Ottoman Turkish authorities ordered and carried out the systematic slaughter of Armenians living in six provinces of Eastern Anatolia and Cilicia, in an effort to exterminate the Armenian presence in those regions;
Whereas the Ottoman Turkish authorities exiled the survivors of the massacres from their homes and native lands;
Whereas the historical record clearly demonstrates that the events occurring between 1915 and 1918 that resulted in the massacre and exile of the Armenian

population of Eastern Anatolia and Cilicia constitutes a genocide as defined by international customary law and by the United Nations Convention on the Prevention and Punishment of Genocide of December 11th 1948;

Whereas the government of the Republic of Turkey distorts the historical record and denies that the Armenian Genocide took place;

Whereas the parliaments of Argentina, Belgium, France, Greece, Italy, Lebanon, Russia, Sweden, Uruguay and the European Parliament and the World Council of Churches have condemned the massacres of the Armenian population of the Ottoman Empire and recognized them as constituting a genocide;

Whereas the Armenian Genocide has also been recognized by the National Assembly of Quebec, the Legislative Assembly of Ontario and the Canadian Council of Churches;

Whereas thousands of Armenian Genocide survivors and their descendants now reside in Canada as Canadian citizens and enrich Canada's multicultural heritage;

Whereas Canada is a country which prides itself on the rule of law and of the respect of human rights and liberties;

Whereas April 24th has become a symbolic date of remembrance for Armenian-Canadians and for people of Armenian origin all over the world;

Whereas the resolution of the Armenian Genocide issue could help peacefully resolve several long-lasting conflicts in the Caucasus

BE IT RESOLVED

That this house calls upon the Government of Canada:

a) to recognize the genocide of the Armenians and to condemn any attempt to deny or distort a historical truth as being anything less than a genocide, a crime against humanity, and

b) to designate April 24th of every year hereafter throughout Canada as a day of remembrance of the 1.5 million Armenians who fell victim to the first genocide of the 20th century.

This resolution, seconded by Senator Raymond Setlakwé, was followed by a similar motion in the House of Commons. On 21 April 2004, members of Parliament voted 153/68 to recognize the Armenian Genocide and to condemn it as a crime against humanity. The success of this all-party motion, put forward by Bloc Québécois MP Madeleine Dalphond-Guiral (Laval Centre) and co-sponsored by Liberal MP Sarkis Assadourian (Brampton Centre), Conservative MP Jason Kenney (Calgary Southeast), and New Democratic Party MP Alexa McDonough (Halifax), placed Canada in the league of a growing number of nations that have defied Turkish pressure. Before the vote, Foreign Affairs Minister Bill Graham warned members about the negative consequences of approval, alluding to several Canadian contracts with

Turkey, such as Bombardier's $335 million contract for work on the Ankara metro. After many Liberal MPs broke with the government in support of Private Member's Motion M-380, Graham insisted the government was not bound by Parliament's decision. Responding to Graham's comments, former cabinet minister Stéphane Dion (Liberal, Saint-Laurent-Cartierville) argued that the government's position was "undermining the importance of Parliament." Canada's "confused" position in 2004 underscored the Canadian government's inability or unwillingness to resist Turkey's powerful economic lobby and to stand up consistently in defense of human rights.[22] The vote nevertheless proclaimed Canadian parliamentarians' heightened awareness of the critical issues – just as eighty-five years previously Canadian parliamentarians had condemned the Turkish atrocities and voiced support for an independent Armenian state. The readiness of members of Parliament to champion human rights was all the more courageous because it flew in the face of threats from the Turkish government and ran counter to the Canadian government's own position. Apart from any other factor, for Armenians the decision to seek recognition of the Genocide in the Canadian parliament not only galvanized the community but revealed, in a deeper sense, the growing involvement of the Armenian community in Canadian public life. And the victory – more than a show of political strength in the Canadian arena – highlighted the integration of this group into Canadian society at the same time that it reinforced group solidarity.

Conclusion and Epilogue

This study has examined the experience of Armenians in Canada for a period of one hundred years, starting in the late 1880s and continuing to the 1980s, when changes in Soviet Armenia reshaped and redirected the Armenian diaspora. I have structured the book, first of all, on the basis of the three major waves of immigration to Canada. The pre-1914, or pre-Genocide, movement was composed of male agriculturalists from the *kaza* of Keghi who settled primarily in Brantford, St Catharines, Galt, and Hamilton. Small groups of Armenians also settled in Thetford Mines, Montreal, and Toronto. The second wave occurred in the post-Genocide period and consisted primarily of women and children who were refugees with different geographic and socioeconomic origins in the Ottoman Empire. By and large, they joined the pre-1914 settlers. Following World War II, Genocide survivors and their descendents immigrated to Canada, largely from countries of exile and sanctuary.

Within the overarching structure of the three waves, I have focused on the experiences of Armenians in five different cities in order to show the ebb and flow of their dominance and to examine both external and internal forces that nurtured or weakened Armenian community development. Brantford, the first and most important settlement in the pioneer period, established the foundations of Armenian community life in Canada. In the interwar years St Catharines assumed the predominant position, leading to the founding of the first Armenian church in Canada. But St Catharines was weakened by the acrimonious struggle for the very institution that gave the community its prominent role. In the 1940s and 1950s Hamilton overshadowed the other settlements, and for that reason I turned to Hamilton for my discussion of family and social life. The third wave preferred to settle in Montreal and Toronto, where, building on the infrastructure established by previous settlers, newcomers created strong and vibrant communities.

My discussion of Armenians in Canada has integrated immigration, settlement patterns, work arrangements, organizations and institutions, family and community, and the arts. Within this scope I have also pursued four major themes that I thought were particularly relevant and perhaps even unique to the Armenian experience in Canada. The first is ethnopatriotism, which I define as a profound and engrossing attachment to the old country, its causes, and its survival. This focus has often led to conflict within the community, but it has always kept the homeland in the forefront of community activity. The motherland, whether lost territories in Turkey, the first Armenian Republic, Soviet Armenia, or the present independent republics of Armenia and of Karabagh, has been an intense motivator in the Armenian psyche. Proud of their history and their survival as a people in spite of "the fire and wreckage of history," Armenians derive a measure of assurance that their language, religion, and culture, indeed their unique identity, has survived for three millennia. Their neighbours, the Lydians and Circassians, have vanished; so too have the Ostrogoths and Visigoths, those "barbarians" who destroyed the western Roman Empire. Yet a small nation like the Armenians has managed to survive, despite conquest and genocide. Small though it has been, this nation has nurtured, invigorated, and inspired its diaspora and has embraced it in its bosom.

Secondly, I have emphasized what I call ethnoversion, which I define as a strong determination to retain an ethnic identity in the diaspora. As a minority in the Ottoman Empire and later in Middle Eastern and Mediterranean countries, Armenians were conscious of their religious, racial, and linguistic distinctiveness. They entered Canada as members of a collectivity, fully aware of their group identity that, in many ways, superceded their different places of origin, different educational backgrounds, and different socioeconomic status. The powerful desire not to lose their language, religion, culture, and history has been evident from the moment Armenians set foot in Canada and has been exemplified in institutional and organizational vitality and the many networks linking together a far-flung diaspora.

The third theme, closely connected to the previous ones, is the Genocide and its impact. One cannot understand Armenians outside the scope of the Genocide and its enduring legacy. In this examination of Armenian life in Canada I have tried to describe the many threads unravelled and broken by the Genocide and the ruined tapestry that emerged. I have also tried to show how a determined people – few in number – have set about to reweave the tapestry, how by helping one another to build and create, Armenians have made the tapestry whole and beautiful again.

The fourth important theme has been the attitude of Armenians towards Canada. Embedded in this book has been a confirmation of the constant and deep loyalty and love of Canada, a country in which Armenians found peace and safety, a country that allowed them to develop their potential and that now reaps the benefit of their talents, diligence, and commitment in the arts, sciences, professions, and business. Because Armenians in Canada are part of a world-wide Armenian diaspora, the interplay between international and local perspectives gives the community breadth without minimizing its Canadian focus, a fact that is evident in the steady drive to foster autonomous Canadian organizations and institutions and an independent Canadian Armenian press.

Juxtaposing a member of the Toronto "elite" with the young shoe shine boy mentioned in chapter 15 might highlight group dynamics. The Toronto millionaire rubbed shoulders with judges, cabinet ministers, and prime ministers. A glance at his business portfolio, showing bonds and stocks trading in New York, London, Paris, and Zurich, suggests wide-ranging and diversified business connections and contacts around the world: Abitibi Pulp and Paper, International Nickel, and Hudson's Bay Company shares are listed side by side with Brazilian Traction, Tokyo Electric Light, Great Northern Telegraph, United Sumatra Rubber, Imperial Tobacco of Great Britain, Crédit Foncier de France, and North Caucasian Oil, to name but a few.[1] Together, the wealthy investor, cultured and distinguished, and the bootblack, scrubbed and in his Sunday best, worshipped in the same church, enjoyed the same community festivities, and wept at the tragedy of their people. The old man and the young boy from different socioeconomic classes were bound to each other by their Armenianness, to be sure, but also by their Canadianness. Class distinctions remained, of course, but the poor man's son grasped the opportunities in the young country, and through education or business he too gradually became cultured, distinguished, and respected.

The history of Armenians in Canada owes as much to the social, economic, and political conditions that the immigrants found in the New World as to the experiences, mentality, and attitudes that they brought with them from their places of origin. This interaction has produced a different way of life, new traditions, and a new culture. Transformations and reinventions inevitably occurred.[2] In a new and foreign land,

Armenians created their own new homeland. As a diaspora, the Armenian community in Canada is an entity with a history of its own. It was built on the foundations of the old-country world, moulded in the Canadian milieu, and maintained for over one hundred years.

EPILOGUE: THE FUTURE

What, now, is the future of the Armenian community in Canada, numbering at least seventy thousand and perhaps as many as ninety thousand in 2003? Is language use, a lively press, church attendance, organizational involvement, or some subjective dimension the indicator of persistence? Or are behavioural patterns the indicator? Bearing in mind the weight of history and of the environment, what constitutes continuity? Is it genealogy, ideas, institutions, organizations, buildings, or myths and symbols? What length of time constitutes persistence? Is it twenty-five, fifty, or more than one hundred years? How many people or what percentage of the population involved in ethnic activities would be a reasonable indicator of the transfer of the ethnocultural heritage from one generation to the next?

An overview of Armenian settlement in Canada over a span of one hundred years reveals that in spite of considerable loss of group cohesion and ethnic identity, the spirit of community life is still vigorous, especially in those places that received new waves of immigrants and in those communities that have a dynamic and dedicated core group. Composed of both élites and rank and file, of old-timers and newcomers, this core has defined and continues to define the group's collective identity and to mould and restructure the group in the Canadian environment.

Ethnocultural communities are facing major changes in a dramatically changing world. Let us consider demographics. While individuals with a single heritage are declining in contemporary North American society, those with multiethnic, multiracial, multicultural, and multireligious backgrounds are multiplying.[3] In such a diverse society, boundaries that used to define, separate, and fragment people are dissolving. As boundaries melt away, North American society may become more homogenous and group differences more trivial. Arguing that a politics of groups' rights poses a fundamental challenge to liberal democracy, many would praise uniformity as a giant leap towards national unity: a neutralization of ethnic-based or group-based political power, an end to ghettoization, and the disappearance of ethnic and racial group inequalities and injustices. By the same token, an equally vociferous number would condemn homogeneity as the step-child of authoritarianism. They would regret the passing of a diverse and pluralistic society, which, they would contend, not only allows for group maintenance and group participation in the larger society, but more significantly, acts as the very foundation of democracy. They would suggest that ethnic and linguistic diversity is not in and of itself a source of disunity or national fragmentation. Rather, they would regard ethnic groups as vehicles for channeling aspirations, just as pressure groups and professional associations do for many citizens.[4]

These contradictory trends towards diversity and pluralism, on the one hand, and uniformity and assimilation, on the other, towards ethnic group formation, survival, and loyalty, on the one hand, and the tradition of the rights and freedoms of the individual, on the other, are a distinguishing mark of twenty-first-century North American society.[5] The difficulties of reconciliation become immediately apparent, be they between the individual and the community of descent or the individual and the state or between the community of descent and the state. These issues are now complicated by technological advances and the entrenchment of globalization and supranationalism. Technology has already transformed Armenian minority communities of descent. For generations, Armenian diasporan communities kept in touch with each other and the mother country through religious, political, and cultural exchanges and communications. In more recent times, the internet has revolutionized these networks and has instantaneously brought Armenians closer together, thus enhancing a pre-existing global Armenian "nation." The juxtaposition of such groups within a multiethnic, multiracial, and multicultural state like Canada, the United States, or France raises new challenges and problems and reveals the potential for new and different configurations.

Stacy Churchill, a Canadian educator, addresses the need to rethink and restructure the roles of minorities and majorities in this new world order: "The number one threat to the creation of humane solutions to common human problems comes from the survival of a nation-state model that legitimates state-imposed internal socio-linguistic-cultural conformity and the creation of national minorities with the attendant danger of ethnic-racial-cultural warfare." Churchill continues by referring to the politics of recognition:

The romantic nation-state based upon a philosophical matrix that equates "the people" with "the nation" [and the state] is an historical anomaly in today's world. Technically, it is dysfunctional ... The politics of recognition [of identity] in post-industrial societies produces a vast variety of minorities, so many that one is hard-pressed to find a mainstream or dominant group sufficiently numerous to be referred to as the "majority" ... The new rules of the globalized economic and technological communications game are creating a common problem shared by majorities and minorities in most nation-states: how to conserve their 'cultural symbolic communities' in the face of overwhelming transnational cultural and social trends.[6]

As society becomes increasingly more impersonal and as formerly clearly defined boundaries become fluid, resilient, and ambiguous, individuals and communities will need to redefine and realign themselves. Inevitably individuals will continue to have a pervasive need for group affiliation and will seek out solidarities and points of orientation. Their loyalties may revolve around religion, biology, the arts, sports, the professions, or – on the technological fringe – cyberspace. Individuals will decide for themselves how they will be identified and who or what will win their allegiance and participation. The structures may be as varied, as creative, and as manifold as the individuals and families themselves. The crucial fact remains that the choice will be theirs. They can be Greek *and* Armenian *and* Canadian or Chinese *and* Italian *and* American. Choice and inclusivity are not impossible in a society of many "we's."[7]

In such a world, each ethnocultural group is under great pressure if it wishes to survive. Some have argued that for any ethnic/racial community of descent to pursue its continued identity in North America is self-serving and segregationist and therefore contrary to the general good of the national state, be it Canada, the United States, or other multicultural countries. But it could be reasonably argued that in such a society civic and private identities can and do exist – even flourish – along with collective and personal loyalties. A Canadian national identity can flourish without relinquishing an individual's or a group's ethnic traditions and values. In such a society multiple accommodations and multiple identities can be sustained, though that is not to say that stresses and pulls, attractions and antagonisms, will not exist.

Inevitably the boundaries, composition, structures, and tensions of ethnic/racial groups will change as they respond and adjust to a changing world. Malleability is nothing new to them, for they are not, and have never been, static entities but have been evolving over time in geographic space and in the political arena. The Armenian collectivity of Toronto, for example, was not the same in 1995 as it was in 1925, nor is it the same today as the one in Montreal or Los Angeles. Ethnic communities may need to redefine what makes them tick. Will it be biology, history, religion, culture, the environment, or a combination of many factors? Ethnic groups may also reorder their priorities, move from a focus on culture to a focus on religion, business, status, or politics, and in doing so, they may find it necessary to redefine their nucleus and reshape the core. They will need to transform and reinvent themselves as they interrelate with massive economic, social, political, and cultural forces. This tradition of self-determination for the individual and the community is possible in Western democracies, where no laws prohibit the operation of minority-language schools or the construction of community churches and community centres. The underpinning of self-determination for both the individual and the collectivity is fundamental to private and civic identities. Armenians may retain their identity as Armenians in the private sphere while performing fully as Canadians in the public sphere. One approach does not negate the other.

Identities can be malleable both for the individual and for the community of descent. Momentous shifts in the world will have profound and widespread ramifications. If ethno/racial/religious communities wish to survive in such a "new" world, they must make conscious, prudent, and practical decisions, since they do have the power to exercise some control over their future. A reevaluation of goals, priorities, and strategies is fundamental if Armenians envisage surviving as an ethnic collectivity in a fast-changing world.

Contemporary society is taking its brutal toll on small nations, either through military defeat, assimilation, or the powerful impact of the internet. If the Armenian language, the principal vehicle of Armenian culture, is not to be among the five thousand or more languages destined for extinction by the end of this century, if Armenian culture is not to be reduced to an academic pursuit fit only for museums and archives, and if Armenian identity is not to disappear in what Jared Diamond calls "the tragic loss of diversity," then Armenians need to entrench their language, sustain their churches and their organizations, and keep alive their history.[8] Needless to add, such an approach requires a society that does not suppress its minorities and demands great commitment and sacrifice on the part of the ethnic group, especially of its leadership.

To assume that ethnic groups have been indoctrinated through some overarching conspiracy of the receiving society is to credit them with little intelligence and self-direction. Indeed, Armenians have displayed a very intense self-motivating dynamism – their own will to exercise a measure of control over their own destiny and, to a degree, to determine their own future. Armenian survivors thwarted the Turkish government's plans for annihilation. Through courage and resolve they forged a modern identity and laid the foundations for national cohesion that did not necessarily depend on a nation-state but flourished in different countries all over the world as integral parts of a "global nation." Avetis Aharonian recognized this fact when he declared that no outside power could annihilate the

Armenians: "Only we Armenians can destroy ourselves by committing national suicide."

If the diaspora is an entity unto itself, an entity with its own traditions, character, and history, then Armenians may wish to perpetuate that entity – their identity – and to offer their creativity to the new world of their world. Like their mountains, Armenians are a peaceful people. When they were many and when they were strong, even then they did not destroy any nation. Over no people have they held the tyrant's whip. If they ruled, it was only with their literature. And if they prevailed, it was only with their genius. Yes, Armenians are few. But wherever they have settled, they have been builders. Wherever Armenians have called home, they have contributed to the sciences and philosophy, fashioned art and architecture, and created music and poetry.[9]

Notes

INTRODUCTION

1 For examples of the Armenian diaspora in different parts of the world in the modern era, see Bournoutian, *History of the Armenian People*, vol. 2. For the definitive history of Armenians in the United States before 1914, see Mirak, *Torn between Two Lands*.
2 See, for example, Churchill, *New Canadian Perspectives*, and Breton, "Multiculturalism and Canadian Nation-Building."
3 See, for example, Gleason, "Pluralism and Assimilation," and Taylor, "The Politics of Recognition."
4 Studies of various ethnic groups in Canada include the following: Adachi, *The Enemy that Never Was*; Anderson and Higgs, *A Future to Inherit*; Chimbos, *Canadian Odyssey*; Dreisziger et al., *Struggle and Hope*; Higgs, *Portuguese Migration*; Lupul, *Heritage in Transition*; Perin and Sturino, *Arrangiarsi*; Renkiewicz, *Polish Presence*; Sturino, *Forging the Chain*; Tulchinsky, *Immigration in Canada*; Zucchi, *Italians in Toronto*; *From Immigration to Integration: The Canadian Jewish Experience*; and Weinfeld, *Like Everyone Else*. See also various issues of *Polyphony, Bulletin of the Multicultural History Society of Ontario*.
5 For a modern history of Armenia, see *Encarta Reference Library*, 2002, and *Encarta Encyclopedia Deluxe*, 2002, or visit the Encarta web site at http://encarta.msn.com.
6 Apramian, *Georgetown Boys*, 1976. Arslanian, http://www.geocities.com/~arslanm/arslanian/Keghiimmigrants.html and http://arslanmb.org/arslanian/KeghiImmigrants.html; Baghdjian, *Les Arméniens au Québec*, 1980;

La Communauté Arménienne, 1992; Bakalian, *Armenian-Americans: From Being to Feeling Armenian*, 1994; Chichekian, "Armenian Immigrants in Canada and their Distribution in Montreal"; Chichekian, *The Armenian Community of Quebec*, 1989; Hovannisian, *Armenian Van/Vaspurakan*; *Armenian Baghesh/Bitlis*; *Armenian Tsopk/Kharpert*; *Armenian Karin/Erzerum*; Kooshian, "The Armenian Immigrant Community of California, 2002; LaPiere "The Armenian Colony in Fresno County," 1930; Mesrobian, *Like One Family*, 2000; Minassian, "A History of the Armenian Holy Apostolic Orthodox Church," 1974; Mirak, *Torn between Two Lands*, 1983.

7 For a history of the Armenian people see Bournoutian, *A History of the Armenian People*, vols. 1 and 2, or his most recent book, *A Concise History of the Armenian People*; Hovannisian, *The Armenian People*, vols. 1 and 2; Kévorkian and Paboudjian, *Les Arméniens*; Kurkjian, *History of Armenia*. Lang, *Armenia*; Walker, *Armenia*.

8 Cited in Kurkjian, *History of Armenia*, 206–7.

9 Walker, Armenia, 374.

10 For a discussion of "subjective documents" see Yans-McLaughlin, "Metaphors of Self in History."

11 The symbolism of the cross is borrowed from Bedrosian, *The Magical Pine Ring*, introduction.

12 Communiqué from the Canadian Diocese, 3 September 2001; communiqué from the Armenian National Institute, www.armenian-genocide.org/affirmation/ resolutions/168.htm.

13 The term "Armenianizing Christianity" has been borrowed from Hacikyan et al., *The Heritage of Armenian Literature*, vol. 1, 86–91.

14 Kevork Emin, "Small," trans. Diana der Hovannesian, *Ararat* 13 (summer 1972): 5. Cited with permission of *Ararat*. Mashtots created thirty-six letters; two more were added in the eleventh and twelfth centuries.

CHAPTER ONE

1 For a discussion of the name of the district see Kasuni, "Kghi – Keghi – Geghi," 222–30. Translations of original titles will henceforth appear in parentheses.

2 Mirak, *Torn between Two Lands*, chap. 2. Mirak's descriptions are based on Mesrob, *L'Arménie*. See also Ubicini, *Letters on Turkey*.

3 Vratsian, ("Towards Keghi"), in (*Yearbook*), 49–72. Simon Vratsian travelled through Keghi in 1911 and likely included sojourners in his calculations of thirty thousand Armenians. In his *Church of Armenia* (206), Malachia (Maghakia) Ormanian estimates the number of Armenians in Keghi at about twenty-five thousand. Kévorkian found that before the

first World War, Keghi had approximately twenty thousand Armenians. Kévorkian and Paboudjian, *Les Arméniens*, 59–60. The decline is no doubt the result of large-scale emigration from the region, especially of the male population, and the concurrent fall in the birth rate. Kévorkian's statistics are based on the February 1913–August 1914 census. Bishop Hmayag estimated that in 1915 Keghi had forty thousand inhabitants, of whom thirty to thirty-five thousand were Armenian. Bishop Hmayag, ("Destruction of Villages in Keghi Township"), reprinted in *Nor Gyank* (New Life), 18 May 1995.

While most of my sources refer specifically to Keghi, I have also used material about other areas because they reflect conditions in Keghi.

4 Kévorkian, *Les Arméniens*.
5 For the patriarchal system, see Mazian, "The Patriarchal Armenian Family System." For Turkish joint families, see Duben, "Turkish Families"; and Stirling, *A Turkish Village* and "A Turkish Village."
6 Hoogasian Villa and Matossian, *Armenian Village Life*, 29.
7 For the figures on land holdings in Keghi, see Public Record Office (PRO), London, BT 15/103, 112569, Canadian/Armenian Claim. For land tenure in Turkey, see Steeg, "Land Tenure," 238–64; Lewis, *Emergence of Modern Turkey*, 90–2, 119, 449–50; United States Department of Commerce and Labour, *Monthly Consular and Trade Reports*, Feb. 1910, 233, cited in Mirak, "The Armenians in the United States," 18–19; Great Britain, House of Commons, *Sessional Papers*, vol. 96 (1896), *Turkey*, no. 5, Vice-consul C.M. Hallward to Consul R.W. Graves, enclosure in no. 212, to Sir P. Currie, Van, 10 November 1894, 166. Henceforth all such publications will be referred to as *Sessional Papers*. National Archives of Canada, MG 29 D38, Robert Chambers to Principal Grant [Queen's University], Bardezag, 20 February 1896. Henceforth, reference to the National Archives of Canada will be to NA. See also Kasaba, *The Ottoman Empire*; Islamoglu-Inan, *The Ottoman Empire* and Reşat, "Agricultural Policy of Turkey," 108–13.
8 Eghigian, ("A Brief Geographic Sketch"), 7–8. J. Papazian, oral interview, Hamilton, Ontario; H. Tashjian, interview, Brantford, Ontario. Unless otherwise stated all interviews were carried out by the author from 1978 to 2002.
9 V. Laligian, oral interview, Fresno, California. Gulnaz Bakaian, interviewed by Laurens Ayvazian, Granite City, Illinois, 1980, and Antranig Shamigian, interviewed by Laurens Ayvazian, Silver Springs, Maryland, 1979. My thanks to the Armenian Research Center, University of Michigan at Dearborn, for providing me with transcripts of the taped interviews of Bakaian and Shamigian.
10 Vratsian, ("Towards Keghi"), 69.
11 For capitalism, European industrialization, the peripheralization of the

Ottoman empire, and the public debt administration, see Kasaba, *The Ottoman Empire*.
12 Ruben Khan-Azad, ("Memoirs of an Armenian Revolutionary"), 63. See also Mirak "The Armenians," 1965, chap. 1; Berkes, *Secularism in Turkey*, 342.
13 N. Lazarian, oral interview, Hamilton.
14 *Sessional Papers*, vol. 96 (1896), *Turkey*, no. 5, C.M. Hallward to R.W. Graves, enclosure in no. 212, to Sir P. Currie, Van, 10 November 1894, 166.
15 *Sessional Papers*, vol. 80 (1879), *Turkey*, no. 10, Sir Henry Layard to Lord Salisbury, 15 July 1879, 108–16. Unless otherwise indicated, most of the following accounts of the actions of the Keghi *beys* have been extrapolated from a memorandum sent to Mr Malet by an anonymous person or persons on 14 April 1879 (henceforth referred to as Memo) and from a petition to the British Consul, Henry Trotter, signed by representatives from the village of Oghnud (no date, probably 1879, henceforth referred to as Petition). Strictly speaking, Oghnud was not in Keghi, but the bonds between this village and several Keghi villages remained strong through marriages and godparenting. Besides, conditions in Oghnud did not differ from those in Keghi. See also Lewis, *Emergence of Modern Turkey*, 119, 483.
16 Eghigian, ("Geographic Sketch"), 7, and Aram Norsigian, ("Passages of Tarman"), in (*New Keghi*), vol. 1, 16, and vol. 2, 62–4. See also Kitur, (*Hnchak History*), vol. 2, 394–95.
17 Even if the courts upheld the law, enforcement proved difficult, as indicated in the following account in another context. An interviewee described how his family had won a case against a *bey* who had confiscated their flour mill: "When our people were returning through the mountains [after the court case had been heard], they were set upon by that man's ruffians and beaten up. One of them died and the other was left for dead ... He got better but we lost the mill to the *bey*. Years later we tried court action again, but we never repossessed the mill we had built." H. Kaprielian, oral interview, Hamilton.
18 *Sessional Papers*, vol. 80 (1879), *Turkey*, no. 10, Layard to Salisbury, 108–16, and *Sessional Papers*, vol. 82 (1880), Captain Everett to Major Trotter, 5 Dec. 1879, 13, and Layard to Granville, 11 May 1880, 169. To confirm these accounts of conditions in the interior see also missionary documents cited in Robert Mirak, "Armenian Emigration to the United States to 1915," in *Journal of Armenian Studies*, vol. 1, no. 1, (autumn 1975), 5–42, and Mirak, *Torn between Two Lands*, chap. 2. For more details about Keghi in general and the Keghi land scandal and its outcome, see Kaprielian, "Sojourners from Keghi."

19 *Sessional Papers*, vol. 96, (1890–91), *Turkey*, no. 1, Lloyd to Sir William White, Erzerum, 6 April 1890, 28.
20 Vratsian, ("Towards Keghi"), 69.
21 Lewis, *Emergence of Modern Turkey*, 33, 450. H. Tootikian, Toronto, recounted how "the police were coming ... Either they were taking all your animals from your stable ... or they were pulling that rug which you have on the floor ... so as if your property [tax] is paid. But nothing written down, that you have paid ... no registration. And after that ... you see there's another group came over with the same request."
22 Report from Keghi, 25 January 1870. Letter signed by eighteen Keghi leaders, 23 September 1878. Copy in author's personal collection, donated by R. Norigian.
23 *British Blue Book*, no. 6 (1881) Capt. Everett, 23 September 1880, 185 cited in M. G. Rolin-Jaequemyns, *Armenia*, 66.
24 *Sessional Papers*, vol. 96 (1896), *Turkey*, no. 5, Hallward to Graves, enclosure no. 2 in no. 212, to Currie, Van, 10 November 1894, 166.
25 For accounts of tithes and taxes and the collusion and coalescence of taxfarmers with civil, judicial, and military officials, refer, for example, to the following: *Sessional Papers*, vol. 92 (1877), *Turkey*, no. 16, 4–5, 19, 61; *Sessional Papers*, vol. 79 (1878–79), *Turkey*, no. 53, 196–7; *Sessional Papers*, vol. 95 (1895–96), *Turkey*, no. 2, 14 August 1895; *Sessional Papers*, vol. 96 (1896), *Turkey*, no. 5, Hallward to Graves, Van, 27 August 1894, 182; *Sessional Papers*, vol. 95 (1895–96), Turkey, no. 2, Hampson to Cumberbatch, Mush, 9 October 1895, 98–9; *British Blue Book*, no. 6 (1881), Capt. Everett, 23 Sept. 1880, 185, cited in Rolin-Jaequemyns, *Armenia*, 66.
26 *Sessional Papers*, vol. 95 (1896), *Turkey*, no. 3, "Letter from Bitlis," June 1893, 158–9; *British Blue Book*, no. 6 (1881), Capt. Everett, 23 September 1880, 185, cited in Rolin-Jaequemyns, Armenia, 66.
27 Vratsian, ("Towards Keghi"), 69–72 (also in Memo); Varantian, (*History of the Armenian Revolutionary Federation*), vol. 1, 26, citing an article in the periodical *Massis*, 1872. For an account of the Sasun massacre of Armenians who resisted the double-tax demands of the local Kurdish tribal chieftains and of the Turkish government, see Walker, *Armenia*, 136–51; Memo; also *Sessional Papers*, vol. 109, part 1 (1895), *Turkey*, no. 1, "Report on the Relations of the Armenians with the Kurds," by H.S. Shipley, M. Vilbert, and M. Prjevalsky, Mush, 20 July 1895, 162–3.
28 *Sessional Papers*, vol. 92 (1877), *Turkey*, no. 16, Taylor to Granville, 4 July 1871, 62; *Sessional Papers*, vol. 106 (1898), Vice-consul Crow, "Report," 10 July 1897, 243–4.
29 Memo from St Petersburg, cited in Schopoff, *Les Réformes*, 103. *Sessional Papers*, vol. 106 (1898), Armenian Patriarch to the Porte, 92–3,

and "Report on a Journey through Sasun," by vice-consul Crow, 10 July 1897, 243–4; United States Consul Norton to David Hill, Assistant Secretary of State, Kharput, 14 March 1901, National Archives of the United States, RG 59, T579, Roll 1, cited in Mirak, "Armenian Emigration," 19. See also Kitur, (*Hnchak History*), vol. 2, 394–6.

30 Memo; Eghigian, ("Geographic Sketch"), 7.
31 *Sessional Papers*, vol. 92 (1877), *Turkey*, no. 25; Eghigian, ("Geographic Sketch"), 6–7; Safrastian, *Kurds and Kurdistan*, 9–10; Lynch, *Armenia Travels and Studies*, vol. 2, 418–421.
32 Eghigian and Kaprielian, (*History of the Village of Chanakhchi*), 151, 183–9. Henceforth referred to as *Chanakhchi*. My thanks to Tsaghig Der Krikorian of St Catharines for lending me a copy of this book. H. Kaprielian, interview, Hamilton. See also Bryce, *Treatment of Armenians*, 613–14.
33 Lynch, *Travels*, vol. 2, 419–20; H. Kaprielian, oral interview, Hamilton.
34 Lynch, *Travels*, vol. 2, 423; *Sessional Papers*, vol. 95, (1895–96), *Turkey*, no. 2, Hampson to Graves, Mush, 31 Aug. 1895; *Sessional Papers*, vol. 96 (1896), *Turkey*, no. 5, Hallward to Graves, Van, 10 September 1894, 140–1; *Sessional Papers*, vol. 92 (1877), Taylor to Clarendon, Erzerum, 19 March 1869, 18.
35 *The Survey* (4 December 1915), trans. by Alice Stone Blackwell.
36 For an account of the relationship between the central government and "social banditry" during the seventeenth century see Barkey, *Bandits and Bureaucrats*; see also Hobsbawm, *Primitive Rebels*, and Hobsbawm, *Bandits*.
37 Walker, *Survival*, 150; Eghigian, ("Geographic Sketch"), vol. 1, 6–7; *Sessional Papers*, vol. 92 (1877), *Turkey*, no. 25, Taylor to Clarendon, 19 March 1869, 22–6. Also refer to Setrag Shahen, ("A Brief Sketch of Keghi"), 11; *Sessional Papers*, vol. 106 (1898), Crow, "Report," 10 July 1897, 243–6.
38 Walker, *Survival*, 143–4
39 Safrastian, *Kurds and Kurdistan*, 67–8. For the Hamidiyeh refer to Nalbandian, *Armenian Revolutionary Movement*, 161, and the following *Sessional Papers*: vol. 96, *Turkey*, no.1 (1892); vol. 95 (1896), *Turkey*, no. 3; vol. 96 (1896), *Turkey*, no. 5, Hallward to Graves, Van, 31 July 1894; Hallward to Graves, Van, 10 Sept. 1894.
40 Walker, *Survival*, 134. See also (*Memoirs of the Armenian Revolutionary Federation*), 33–4. Lewis, *Emergence*, 342, 123–4, 142.
41 Ormanian estimates that twenty-four thousand Armenians in Keghi belonged to the Armenian Apostolic Church and one thousand to the Protestant faith (Ormanian, *Church*, 206). He also gives the number of parishes and churches.
42 Copy of letter from Mardiros Agha Alemian and a group of Keghi leaders

to the Armenian Archbishop of Erzerum, 22 July 1868, in author's private collection; *Sessional Papers*, vol. 95 (1895–96), *Turkey*, no. 2 (1896), Cumberbatch to Currie, Erzerum, 12 Dec. 1895, 270; *Sessional Papers*, vol. 106 (1898), Crow, "Report," 10 July 1897, 243–6; Walker, *Survival*, 158.

43 *Sessional Papers*, vol. 92 (1877), *Turkey*, no. 16, Taylor to Clarendon, Erzerum, 19 March 1869, 19; *Sessional Papers*, vol. 95 (1896), *Turkey*, no. 1, "Resumé of Report Received from Keghi," 28 October 1894, 24. Arshag Apkarian, "Hakstun," (*New Keghi*), vol. 2, 46–9.

44 *Sessional Papers*, vol. 80, (1879) *Turkey*, no. 10, Trotter to Salisbury, Diarbakir, 12 Jan. 1879; Memo.

45 See, for example, Kévonian, *Les Noces Noires de Gulizar*.

46 Memo; *Sessional Papers*, vol. 92 (1877), *Turkey*, no. 16, Zohrab to Sir Henry Elliott, 19 July 1875, 142–4. For Armenian/Kurdish relations, see Hofmann and Koutcharian, "Armenian-Kurdish Relations," 1–45.

47 Norsigian, ("Passages of Tarman"), 16.

48 *Sessional Papers*, vol. 82 (1880), *Turkey*, no. 1, Capt. Everett to Major Trotter, Erzerum, 5 Dec. 1879, 13; Layard to Granville, 11 May 1880 (enclosure), 169; and "Petition of Turkish and Christian Inhabitants of Keghi to the Vali," Keghi, 22 Nov. 1879, signed by fifty-three Moslems and forty-one Armenians, 14. "Vali" is the Turkish word for the governor of a province."

49 For the 1894–96 massacres, see Walker, *Survival*, chap. 5 and Melson, "Armenian Massacres of 1894–1896." See also Dolabjian (The Hamidian Massacre) *Horizon* (Montreal) 25 April 1994, insert. See also Hopkins, *The Sword of Islam*; Greene, *Armenian Massacres*; Bliss, *Turkey and the Armenian Atrocities*. For a bibliography of the 1894–97 massacres, see Shirinian, "The Armenian Massacres of 1894–97," 113–164. For Cumberbatch's letter: *Sessional Papers*, vol. 95, (1896), *Turkey*, no. 2.

50 Hairabedian, ("The Defiant Village of Khups"), 76–8. See also Arevigian, ("General Survey"), 20; Shahen, ("Sketch of Keghi"), 11–13; Norsigian, ("Tarman"), (*New Keghi*) vol. 1, 16–17. Also *Hushamatian Kghi Khups Giughi* (Memorial Volume of the Village of Khups in Keghi).

51 *Sessional Papers*, vol. 101 (1897), *Turkey*, no. 7, Memo from Fontana to Currie, Kharput, 14 Oct. 1896, 9–10.

52 *Sessional Papers*, vol. 95 (1896), *Turkey*, no. 1, Graves to Currie, 1 April 1895, 20–6; "Résumé of a Report Received from Keghi."

53 *Sessional Papers*, vol. 101 (1897), *Turkey*, no. 7, Williams to Currie, Van, 6 Oct. 1896, 20; Shahen, ("Kghi"), vol. 1, 11–12.

54 According to United States Air Force Aeronautical Approach Chart Erzinçan (340A 1) and Elazig (340 A IV), cited in Hewsen, "A Geographical Note on the Encyclical of Catholicos Aristakes II (1475)," 569–76. The Encyclical, addressed to the town of Keghi Kasaba, lists forty-four Armenian villages.

CHAPTER TWO

1 Levon Musheghian, ("Kulo's Branch of the House of Musheghian"), 55 and Der Matosian, ("History of my Clan"), 44–5.
2 P. Evarian, oral interview, Hamilton; Hagop Pasha was an "important" man in the capital. Eghigian, ("Aslan the Administrator"). See also Shemmassian, "The Sasun Pandukhts," 175–90.
3 Lynch, *Armenia Travels and Studies*, vol. 2, 427; Freely, *Istanbul*, 284–7, notes that in 1886 Constantinople had a population of 851,294, of whom 21 percent were Armenian. George Bournoutian gives the number of Armenians in Constantinople in the late nineteenth century as 250,000, in *A History*, vol. 2, 9.
4 P. Evarian, oral interview, Hamilton.
5 Poem translated by Eugenie Shehirian.
6 In the latter part of the nineteenth century, men from the interior found work in the capital city because of large-scale civic improvements, including the widening and paving of streets, the construction of sidewalks, the installation of water, sewage, and pipe lines, the building of gas street lights and tramways, and the erection of the first metal span of the Galata Bridge (1878).
7 Mirak, "Armenian Emigration," 26–7; Vratsian, ("Towards Keghi"), 68. The census carried out by the Armenian Patriarch of Constantinople in 1913–14 revealed that 4,043 people had left Keghi. See Kévorkian and Paboudjian, *Les Arméniens*, 59–60. Kévorkian also states that according to the same census, 129,786 Armenians had left the Ottoman Empire. Ellis Island statistics for Keghi immigrants can be found at http://www.geocities.com/~arslanm/arslanian/Keghiimmigrants.html and http://arslanmb.org/arslanian/KeghiImmigrants.html. Immigrants had registered at Castle Garden before the opening of Ellis Island in 1892; a fire at this immigration depot in 1907 destroyed countless records.
8 G. Raician, oral interview, Cambridge; P. Evarian, oral interview, Hamilton.
9 H. Kaprielian, oral interview, Hamilton.
10 R. Nahigian, oral interview, Hamilton.
11 A. Torosian, oral interview, St Catharines; N. Injeyan, oral interview, Brantford.
12 H. Kaprielian, oral interview, Hamilton.
13 For the movement of labour to capital see Thistlethwaite, "Migration from Europe"; Thomas, *Migration and Economic Growth*; *Migration and Urban Development*; and *The Industrial Revolution*.
14 Mirak, *Torn between Two Lands*, chap. 4; H. Tootikian, oral interview, Toronto. See also Kaprielian, "Sojourners from Keghi," chap. 3.
15 L. Eloyan, oral interview, Fresno, California.

16 A. Kh., collector and compiler of ("Biographies"), in (*Yearbook* (Keghi)), 112, 118.
17 United States, Immigration Commission, *Abstracts and Reports*, "Emigration Conditions in Europe," 11–12, cited in Roberts, *The New Immigration*, 15. Refer also to Commons, *Races and Immigrants in America*, 126.
18 Z. Norigian, oral interview, Detroit, Michigan.
19 The "bono" test refers to the eye examination required by immigration regulations.
20 Arakel Eghigian, ("Towards Sojourning"), 28–31.
21 Eghigian, ("The Town of East St Louis"), 32.
22 *Brantford Daily Expositor*, 24 December 1909.
23 In discussing the peripheralization of the Ottoman Empire during the nineteenth century, Kasaba states that peripheralization generated transformations: "Many existing groups and relations die out, many new groups and relations develop, but most of all existing groups in relation to one another are transformed." Kasaba, *The Ottoman Empire*.
24 Chakmakjian, (*Armeno-American Letter Writer*), 51–3. A summary of Ellis Island passenger lists from 1900 to 1914 indicates that at least forty-four Keghi immigrants were headed for Corey (modern Fairfield) and Ensley, Alabama, presumably to work in the Birmingham iron industry. For the Ellis Island statistics, see *http://www.geocities.com/~arslanm/arslanian/Keghiimmigrants.html* and http://arslanmb.org/arslanian/KeghiImmigrants.html.
25 For a more elaborate discussion of part-culture, see Kaprielian, "Sojourners."
26 Vratsian, ("Towards Keghi"), 59.
27 Eghigian, ("Women's Role in Everyday Life"), 26–7.
28 Shahen, ("The Keghetsi Wife's Letter"), 97–8.
29 Chakmakjian, (*Armeno-American Letter Writer*), 155.
30 Excerpt from an Armenian folk song, attributed to Nahabed Kuchag, translated by Diana Der Hovanessian, cited in Mirak, *Torn between Two Lands*.
31 Eghigian and Kaprielian, (*Chanakhchi*), 23.
32 See, for instance, Suny, "Populism, Nationalism and Marxism," and "Marxism, Nationalism, and the Armenian Labor Movement."
33 For more information about the educational associations, see chapter 5.
34 Kensagrakan, ("Biography" (of Setrag Shahen)), by Nor Geghi editorial board, (*New Keghi*), vol. 1, 95–6. See also Kitur, (*Hnchak History*), vol. 2, 403–4.
35 Ibid., vol. 2, 367.
36 For references to American Protestant missionaries, see Housepian, *Smyrna*; Grabill, *Protestant Diplomacy;* and Balakian, *Burning Tigris*.

37 Tootikian, *The Armenian Evangelical Church*, 13; from files of the American Board of Commissioners for Foreign Missions, Houghton Library, Harvard University.
38 Shrikian, "Armenians under the Ottoman Empire," 151–3. Shrikian states that the Protestants tried to change the Armenian Church "in form, character, design and mission and replace it with a puritanical New England Congregationalism." See also Sarkisian, (*Balu*), 265, and Mirak, "Armenian Emigration."
39 Grabill, *Protestant Diplomacy*, 22.
40 M. Jamkochian, ("Young Armenia at Euphrates College"), 249; Mirak, *Torn*, 24, citing Arpee, *Armenian Awakening*; Tootikian, "Armenian Congregationalists." Tootikian is citing Hadidian, "American Contribution to Armenian Culture," 3–4. See also Shrikian, "Intellectual and Social Renaissance," 151–3 and Sarkisian, (*Balu*), 265; Mirak, "Armenian Emigration." Numbers of Protestant churches, members, schools, and students vary. See Chambers, *Yoljuluk*, 111–13; Grabill, *Protestant Diplomacy*, 27.
41 Menejenian was the maternal great-grandfather of Antranig Shamigian, born in Keghi-Kasaba, 1898, interviewed by Laurens Ayvazian, Silver Springs, Maryland, 1979. Transcripts of interviews, Armenian Research Center, University of Michigan–Dearborn, Dearborn, Michigan.
42 Arevigian, ("General Sketch"), 18–19; Vratsian, ("Towards Keghi"), 55; Norsigian, ("Tarman"); (*New Keghi*), vol. 1, 15; Rahanian, ("Bits of Memory"), vol. 1, 48.
43 Shrikian, "Renaissance," 229–355. Also refer to Davison, "Westernized Education," 289, and Woodley, "Turkish Days."
44 H. Kaprielian, oral interview, Hamilton.
45 Mrs Setrag Shahen (Aghavni), oral interview, Los Angeles, recalled that young men were expelled from Euphrates College for their political activism.
46 Mirak, *Torn*, 26–7. See also Kitur, (*Hnchak History*), vol. 1, 221; Shrikian, "Renaissance," 172, 231, 311–12. Also, *Aspirations et Agissement Révolutionnaires*, 11, no author, no publisher.
47 NA, RG 76, vol. 300, file 279907, pt. 1, Constantinople, 20 March 1905. Newnham, a missionary in Constantinople, was the sister of the bishop of Saskatchewan (possibly Anglican) and worked in the Favre Boys' Home in Constantinople.
48 LBP (Lisa Boghosian Papas), "By Way of the Queen," AGBU *Magazine* (spring/summer 2000): 31 (no date is given for the founding of "Armenia," but it was probably after the 1894–96 massacres); Mirak, *Torn*, 107; "Armenians of Manchester," in Teodik, (*Everyone's Almanac*), 226–9. For more on Kamberian see George, *Merchants in Exile*.
49 Zarevand, *United and Independent Turania*, 38.

50 Cited in Mirak, *Torn*, 57.
51 Hayes, *Nationalism*, 112.
52 Vratsian, ("Towards Keghi"), 58, 62–3.
53 Shahen, ("Boghos"); (*New Keghi*), vol. 2, 86–8; Kitur, (*Hnchak History*), 394–416.
54 Hobsbawm, *Bandits*, 20
55 Kitur, (*Hnchak History*), vol. 2, 399; A.P., compiler, "Biographies, Part a: The Contribution of Keghi towards Armenian Emancipation" (*Yearbook*), 107.
56 For the most extensive study in English of the early Armenian political parties, see Nalbandian, *The Armenian Revolutionary Movement*; see also Walker, *Armenia*.
57 For further details about their debates, see Kaprielian, "Sojourners," chap. 2, and Kitur (*Hnchak History*), vol. 2, 404–8.
58 Suny, "Formation of the Armenian Patriotic Intelligentsia," 18–34.
59 *Sessional Papers*, vol. 92 (1877), *Turkey*, no. 25, Holmes to Elliott, Bosna Serai, 17 April 1871, 51.

CHAPTER THREE

1 Bagdasarian, a student at McMaster University in 1896 (then located in Toronto), was later to write *The Sunny Side of the Armenian People*.
2 P. Courian (grandson of the original settler), oral interview, Toronto.
3 Kitur, (*Hnchak History*), vol. 2, 79, states that "some Armenians came to Brantford to work in the iron factories in 1889." This citation may refer to those brought by Cockshutt or to another group, perhaps also brought in by the same family. In any case, I was unable to find other references to this group.
4 NA, RG76, vol. 368, file 488557, Harry Gourjian to Rt Hon. Sir Edward Grey, Brantford, 22 Jan.1906; RG76, vol. 368, file 488557, Shipley, British consul in Erzerum to British Ambassador in Constantinople, N. O'Connor, 29 May 1907, in response to a request for information by W.F. Cockshutt, conservative member of Parliament, Brantford, Ontario, on behalf of Armenians in Brantford. Henceforth Record Group 76 will be referred to as RG76. Also Great Britain, *Sessional Papers*, vol. 101, 1897, 90, citing proclamation by Turkish government to dissuade Armenians from emigration. Armenians wishing to come to Canada during this period often requested the intervention of British consular authorities in the Ottoman empire.
5 Krikor Parseghian, "Memoirs," in author's collection.
6 Mirak, "Armenian Emigration," 21; *Torn between Two Lands*.
7 Government authorities disliked the agents not only because they sometimes used unsavory tactics but also because they circumvented official efforts to exclude certain immigrants. Franc Sturino has argued that

agents side-stepped regulations that peasants considered to be unjust obstacles to their freedom of movement and opportunity. Agents and peasants, he concluded, formed a symbiotic relationship and a united front against the values and standards of the country of destination. Sturino, "Inside the Chain," 254–5. See also Harney, "The Commerce of Migration," 42–53.

8 For a more extensive examination of problems faced by Armenian migrants to Canada, see Kaprielian, "Sojourners from Keghi," and also, *Halifax Herald*, 12 March 1908.

9 RG76, vol. 531, file 803588.

10 RG76, vol. 431, file 642439, Allan Line to Bruce Walker, 11 December 1907.

11 For movement to the United States, see Mirak, *Torn*, chap. 4. Armenian newspapers, such as the *Hairenik* (Fatherland, Boston) not only related stories of corruption but also gave the names of men who charged the people high fees for writing letters and who stole their cheques and forged their signatures: *Hairenik*, 5 March 1904, 19 March 1904, 11 June 1904, 30 July 1904, 2 October 1905, cited in Mirak, *Torn*; RG76, vol. 531, file 803588, 1 July 1910, and RG76, vol. 431, file 642439, Report of Detective Inspector William Pierpoint, Liverpool, 11 May 1907.

12 P. Evarian, oral interview, Hamilton.

13 RG76, vol. 354, file 390480, J. D. Pagé, "Medical Inspection of Immigrants on Shipboard," paper delivered to the Canadian Public Health Association, Montreal, December, 1911. "Detention" was a reference to medical treatment provided at detention hospitals in Canada. For a concise account of Canadian immigration policy under Sifton and his successor, Frank Oliver, see Timlin, "Canada's Immigration Policy."

14 Dr C.K. Clarke, Medical Director, Canadian National Committee for Mental Hygiene, foreword to Smith, *Canadian Immigration*.

15 RG76, vol. 344, file 366144, *Ottawa Citizen*, 13 March 1908. Also vol. 307, file 284136, 1911.

16 RG76, vol. 354, file 390480, Bryce to MacFarlane, 24 August 1905; ibid., MacFarlane to Bryce, 22 January 1906; ibid., Memo to William Duncan Scott, June 1906; ibid., Bryce, "Report of the Sanitation of Emigrant Ships," chap. 3, "Summary of Results of Inspection of Immigrants and Immigrant Ships from 1905–1910," December 1910; RG76, vol. 531, file 803588, Memo, Bryce to Scott, 9 August 1910; ibid., Walker to Scott, Winnipeg, 21 May 1912; ibid., Bryce to Scott, 28 June 1912.

17 NA, Sifton Papers, vol. 255, 139, Sifton to Smart, 15 January 1904; ibid, 142, Sifton to Scott, 25 January 1904, cited in Hall, "Clifford Sifton," 76–7. The occupations of farmers, farm labourers, and domestics were classified as preferred occupations by legislation.

18 RG76, vol. 125, file 27114, J.N. Chambers (Woodstock) in a letter to the editor, *Montreal Daily Witness*, 23 March 1896, citing Rev. William Nesbitt Chambers, missionary in Erzerum. For a contemporary account depicting Armenians in Canada as primitive Christians who were lazy, burdensome, diseased parasites, and incapable of doing manual labour, see the work of fellow Protestant, J. S. Woodsworth, *Strangers within Our Gates*, 138–9; original published in 1909. The introduction to this reprint by Marilyn Barber examines Wordsworth's thoughts about immigrants in the light of the social gospel and Canadian nationalism.

19 Another Canadian missionary, Rev. Frederick W. MacCallum, suggested after the 1909 massacres that relief funds for Armenians would be better spent by transporting them to Canada, the United States, or Brazil, instead of keeping them alive in Turkey "with every prospect of a massacre" in fifteen years (cited in Mirak, *Torn*, 55). RG76, vol. 300, file 279907, part 1, Scott to Robert Reford Co., 29 April 1913. (See also ibid., Monahan to Grey, Erzerum, 19 Nov. 1912; ibid., Scott to Cory, memo, 7 Jan. 1913; see also RG76, vol. 125, file 27114, 28 January 1896; ibid., Harry H. Smith, in a Letter to the editor of the *Nor'Wester*, 16 April 1896.

20 RG76, vol. 125, file 27114, 4 April 1896, 5 August 1896, 14 August 1896; ibid., Chambers to the CPR, 4 April 1904. See also *Presbyterian Review*, 12 December 1895, 534; 25 June 1896, 1223; 27 Feb. 1896, 806–7; 19 March 1896, 891; Nahabedian, "Canadians and Armenians," 28–34; RG 25, A2, vol. 141, file C, Stevens to Lansdowne, 2 December 1904. Programs had also been initiated unsuccessfully to bring Armenian tobacco, silk, and grape cultivators to Canada.

21 RG76, vol. 300, file, 279907, part 1, Scott to Arfeuilly, 2 January 1913.

22 Ibid., vol. 431, file 642439, memo from Scott to the Minister, 16 January 1913; vol. 449, file 681314, *Montreal Daily Star*, 17 July 1909, quoting Minister Frank Oliver in England; vol. 480, file 745162, part 2, and vol. 531, file 803588.

23 Ibid., vol. 407, file 594511, part 2, part 2A, part 4, part 5; see also vol. 300, file 279907, part 2, Monahan to Grey, 14 June 1913; vol. 480, file 745162, part 2, Oliver to Scott, 11 April 1908; vol. 531, file 803588, Scott to Annand, 27 August 1909; vol. 507, file 783375, part 1, Circular, 8 May 1908. For the role of industry in recruiting unskilled factory workers see Avery, "Continental European Immigrant Workers," 53–64, and Avery, *Dangerous Foreigners*. Avery draws out the double-pronged approach of the Canadian immigration program: "Until World War I Canadian immigration policy had two determinants: the willingness of the Dominion government to give businessmen a free hand in the recruitment of the immigrants they needed for national economic development; and the determination of the Immigration Branch to recruit agriculturalists,

particularly for the settlement of Western Canada" (18). For the treatment of others classified as Orientals, see Buchignani, *Continuous Journey*, and Wickberg, *From China*.

24 RG76, vol. 578, file 817510, part 1, W. D. Scott to CPR Traffic Manager in Montreal, 16 July 1913. The Dominion Iron and Steel Company merged with the Dominion Coal Company of Glace Bay, Cape Breton Island in 1908 to form the Dominion Steel and Coal Company.

25 RG76, vol. 531, file 803588, Hetherington, Assistant Dominion Immigration Agent, Halifax, to W.L. Barnstead, Dominion Immigration Agent, Halifax; also vol. 431, file 642439.

26 For a study of other sojourners from former Ottoman territory, see Petroff, *Sojourners*. For the Ellis Island statistics, see http://www.geocities.com/~arslanm/arslanian/Keghiimmigrants.html and http://arslanmb.org/arslanian/KeghiImmigrants.html.

27 Mirak, *Torn*, 57–8, citing the newspaper *Asbarez*, 20 June 1913, and 27 June 1913.

28 Baghdjian, *La Communauté Arménienne*, 50–4; interview with Senator Raymond Setlakwé, grandson of Aziz; Chichekian, *The Armenian Community of Quebec*, 35–6, citing Dr Georges Saine, also a member of the Mardin group. See chapter 16.

29 K. Lalazarian, oral interview, and A. Lusikian, telephone interview, both of Toronto. It appears that Courian settled first in Montreal, where he opened a rug business in the 1890s, then moved to Toronto. It is not clear when he closed the Montreal store; the *Montreal City Directories* (1913–15) list Courian and Sons Oriental Rugs at 31a McGill College Avenue, under the supervision of D.M. Haig.

30 RG6A, vol. 209, file 1876, J.O. Pelland to Sir Charles Tupper, Montreal, 19 March 1896.

31 *Toronto Star*, 8 November 1999. For developments in Hamilton that attracted immigrant workers to the new industries at the turn of the century, see Wood, "Emergence of the Modern City," 119–37.

32 *Brantford Daily Expositor*, 8 June 1907.

33 RG76, vol. 368, file 488557, Harry Gourjian to Rt Hon. Sir Edward Grey, Brantford, 22 January 1906; ibid. Gourjian to W.F. Cockshutt, 5 April 1907; ibid., Shipley, British Consul in Erzerum to British Ambassador in Constantinople, N. O'Connor, 29 May 1907.

34 This figure was given by Louis Stander, missionary of the Evangelical Union, quoted in the *Brantford Daily Expositor*, 24 December 1909.

35 Perhaps this connection with the CNR is what has led to the idea that Armenians first came to Canada to work on the railways. It may be true, but I have found no documentation to show that they came to Canada in the 1880s for this type of work. Garo Chichekian checked the records of

36 Mardig (Mardiros) Der Vartanian, Memoirs, in author's personal collection.
37 For more on settlement patterns in Brantford, see Kaprielian, "Sojourners," chap. 5.
38 Indeed, so numerous were the Mush Armenians in St Catharines that the Dashnak club was called Darontsort, after the ancient name of the Mush region. Similar predilections are evident in Galt, which was favoured by people from Van; in Toronto, favoured by Armenians from Constantinople; and in Montreal, home of Armenians from the village of Khochmat, Balu region.
39 A. Takvorian, Hamilton; J. Kasoian, Brantford; A. Nahigian, Hamilton; oral interviews.
40 Hygus Torosian, E. Levonian, and M. Tavitian, all of St Catharines, oral interviews. By the twenties Brantford also had a loose form of political segregation. Hnchaks lived in the northern part of the city near the railway tracks, while the Dashnaks preferred to live further south around Alfred and Darling Streets. H. Nishanian, oral interview, Toronto.
41 RG76, vol. 368, file 488557, Harry Gourgian to Rt Hon. Sir Edward Grey, 22 January 1906; Kaprielian, "Sojourners," 206–63.
42 *Brantford Daily Expositor*, 25 August 1906, 13 September 1906, 17 June 1911.

CHAPTER FOUR

1 For details of the Brantford reconstitution project, see Kaprielian, "Sojourners," chap. 5. The principal sources used to reconstitute the Armenian settlement in Brantford included Brantford property tax rolls, city directories, membership lists of village educational associations, a census of the Armenian Revolutionary Federation, the records of Grace Anglican Church, and information gleaned from oral interviews. Marriage records of Grace Anglican Church in Brantford reveal that of the twelve marriages performed in the church among Armenians between 1905 and 1914, only one was exogamous: Manuel Der Manuelian, twenty-three, married Rowenzelina Morton, twenty-two, in 1906.
2 For home ownership, see *Brantford Daily Expositor*, 13 August 1906 and 8 June 1907. Also Brantford city tax assessment rolls.
3 P. Evarian, oral interview, Hamilton.
4 For the Canadian Expeditionary Force, see chap. 7.
5 Oral interviews with H. Tashjian, Brantford; N. Injeyan, Brantford; A. (Chichakian) Torosian, St Catharines.

6 For a view of Armenian boardinghouses and male domesticity, see John Barsamian's short story, "Ashod's Boarding House," *Ararat* 21 (spring 1980).
7 H. Torosian, oral interview, St Catharines.
8 Different views of the immigrant's moral fibre are presented in Valverde, *Age of Light, Soap, and Water*. Often, the host society viewed immigrants as morally depraved. In their turn, Armenians frequently saw sexual dangers in the open society of North America.
9 *Brantford Daily Expositor*, 8 June 1907.
10 See *Brantford Daily Expositor*, 10 August 1906, regarding a collection among Armenians to pay for treatment for a countryman suffering consumption in Providence, Rhode Island.
11 NA, RG76, vol. 368, file 488557, Harry Gourjian to Rt Hon. Sir Edward Grey, Brantford, 22 Jan. 1906; Shipley, British consul in Erzerum to British Ambassador in Constantinople, N. O'Connor, 29 May 1907, in response to a request for information by W.F. Cockshutt, conservative member of Parliament, Brantford, Ontario, on behalf of Armenians in Brantford.
12 M. Chichakian, oral interview, St Catharines. The incident occurred in Brantford shortly after Ms. Chichakian arrived in Canada in 1907.
13 Andranik Donoian, "Memoirs," 1967, in author's collection.
14 Commons, *Races and Immigrants in America*, 121; A. Torosian, oral interview, St Catharines. Galt, Preston, and Hespeler amalgamated in 1973 to create the city of Cambridge.
15 Eghigian and Kaprielian, (*History of the Village of Chanakhchi*), 30.
16 See Heron, *Working in Steel*; Walkowitz, *Worker City*.
17 Cited in Harney and Troper, *Immigrants*, 53; see also Walkowitz, *Worker City*, 35.
18 R. Nahigian, oral interview, Hamilton; Z. Lorisian, oral interview, Hamilton.
19 H. Torosian, oral interview, St Catharines.
20 See Guttman, "Work, Culture, and Society," 531–87; see also Avery, "Continental European Immigrant Workers," and *Dangerous Foreigners*.
21 Harutiun Chakmakjian, (*Armeno-American Letter Writer*), 91–5. The *Letter Writer* was a guide to the art of writing letters in Armenian and English but also reflected Armenian life in North America before 1914. For an account of Armenian guidebooks for immigrants, see Kaprielian, "The Armeno-American Letter Writer" and "Sojourners," conclusion.
22 P. Evarian, oral interview, Hamilton.
23 Unsigned diary, handwritten in Armenian, from East Providence, USA, March, 1915. Original in author's private collection.
24 Ontario Archives, A.G. 4 C-3, file 1143, 1912 (6), H.G. Symons to the

Provincial Attorney, Brantford, 18 August 1912. See also *Brantford Daily Expositor*, 10 July 1912.
25 A. Torosian, oral interview, St Catharines. As a rule, Armenians were neither seasonal migrants in Canada nor seasonal transoceanic migrants.
26 Kitur, (*Hnchak History*), vol. 1, 220.
27 Letter to the editor, *Brantford Daily Expositor*, 12 June 1907.
28 Their behaviour could lead to conflicts with other workers. In St Catharines in 1904, Armenian recruits, perhaps undercutting wages of Anglo-Saxon workers, were run out of town until McKinnon's management interceded to bring them back. From Mardig (Mardiros) Der Vartanian, *Memoirs*.
29 See Kaprielian-Churchill, "James Manoukian," in *Dictionary of Canadian Biography*, vol. 14, 741–2.
30 For the move from factory to business, see Mirak, *Torn*.
31 H. Thomasian, oral interview, Brantford; Brantford tax assessment rolls and Brantford city directories.
32 R. Melkonian, oral interview, Hamilton, and A. Mooradian, Hagersville. The coffeehouse was part of a long tradition among Armenians. According to Fernand Braudel, Armenians brought coffee and coffeehouses to Paris in the mid-seventeenth century. One of the first, if not the first, coffeehouses in London was founded by an Armenian in 1659: it was called Turk's Head. Braudel, *Structures of Everyday Life*, 257.
33 H. Nahigian, oral interview, St Catharines.

CHAPTER FIVE

1 In Brantford, Armenians attended Grace Anglican Church, St Philip's in Hamilton, and St Barnabas and St Thomas in St Catharines.
2 Elisaeus, *History of Vartan*, trans. C.F. Neumann (London: The Oriental Translation Fund 1830), 20, cited in Bedrosian, *The Magical Pine Ring*, introduction, 7–8.
3 H. Tashjian, oral interview, Brantford. Records of the Armenian Revolutionary Federation indicate that rather than a church, settlers had raised funds for a community centre. When they decided not to proceed with this major project, they returned money to all contributors.
4 Baghdoian, (*History of the Village of Astghaberd*), handwritten memoir of the village of Astghaberd.
5 Kitur, (*Hnchak History*), vol. 1, 220. For an account of sojourner mentality see Harney, "Men without Women."
6 For an account of sojourner impact on Keghi, see Kaprielian-Churchill, "Migratory Caravans," 20–38.
7 Sarafian, *History of Education in Armenia*, 205.

8 Hushamatian Kghi Khups Giughi (*Memorial Volume of the Village of Khups in Keghi*), 124–5.
9 Sarafian, *Education*, 216–35. On the association and schooling, see Ter Minassian, "Sociétés de culture," 7–30.
10 See Srabian, (Keghi), 61. ("Khups Educational Life and the United Association,") in (*Khups in Keghi*) states that Keghi Kasaba followed the example of Khups (17). Mamigon, Ashukian, *Memoirs*, 1973 (in author's possession).
11 A. Raffi, oral interview, Cambridge, Ontario.
12 Setrag Shahen, ("A Concise Sketch of Keghi"), 11–13. See also Great Britain, House of Commons, *Sessional Papers*, vol. 79 (1878–79), Rev. C. H. Robinson to Col. Trotter, 10 April 1892, 27.
13 "Azgain Gordser Kghi" ("National Endeavours in Keghi"), (*Khups in Keghi*), 190–1.
14 Ohannes Torosian, hand-written memoir, translated by his son, Hygus Torosian, St Catharines, Ontario.
15 Miatsial Enkerutiun Hayots (*The United Armenian Association*), 42.
16 A. Raffi, oral interview, Cambridge, Ontario.
17 See for instance, *Hairenik*, 9 December 1905. See also Srabian, ("A Few Pages from Levon Srabian"), 217. See also Eghigian and Kaprielian, (*Chanakhchi*), 68.
18 Very Rev. Suren Papaghian, ("Khups and its Compatriotic Union"), 151. The names changed from Educational Association before 1914 to Compatriotic Union or Society after the Genocide.
19 Part of the records of the villages of Osnag, Astghaberd, and Tarman have been examined for this account.
20 See *Hairenik*, 1900–1910. Almost every issue of the *Hairenik* during these years published appeals for membership by various Armenian educational and compatriotic societies.
21 Papaghian, ("Khups and its Compatriotic Union"), 153
22 Bertrand Bareilles, in preface to Ormanian, *The Church of Armenia*, xviii. Bareilles adds that the same goal was adopted for elementary education in France some twenty years later.
23 As there is some similarity in the constitutions, it is likely that the associations used a basic model provided by the Armenian patriarchate in Constantinople or by the United Armenian Association.
24 ("Compatriotic Union of Khups"), no author, in (*Khups in Keghi*), 31.
25 In a letter from Osnag, 16 March 1910, a roster of the *total* membership shows that of sixty-two members, only five were women.
26 These numbers probably reflect the North American membership and do not include members who were in the village.
27 A. Raffi, oral interview, Cambridge.
28 Reported in *Hairenik*, 11 November 1905; in Astghaberd records.

29 Osnag Village Educational Society records.
30 Ibid.
31 Tarman information from *Hairenik*, 22 April (1905?).
32 (*Khups in Keghi*). Although it is not stated, it is assumed that these funds were sent from 1900 to 1914.
33 Osnag Village Educational Society records.
34 Osnag Village Educational Society minutes. The vote against the teacher, Mr Mesrob, (Mesrob Der Vartanian?) was unanimous.
35 Letter from Osnag executive to comrades in Canada, 16 March 1910.
36 Letter from Rev. Khorenian to Rostom Zorian, General Director of the National Schools in Erzerum, 18 March 1911; letter in private collection; Sarafian, *Education*, 210, and Baghdjian, *La Confiscation*, 252. See also (*New Keghi*), vol. 2, 34.
37 "Hayots Miatsial Enkerutiants Karno Shrdjanak, 1910–1911" (Report of the United Armenian Association in the Region of Erzerum, 1910–11), in (*New Keghi*), vol. 1, 42–4. See also Baghdoian, ("History of Astghaberd"), 26.
38 In 1911, Simon Vratsian noted that every Armenian village in Keghi had a school because of the money sent by its "sojourning sons." ("Towards Keghi"), 59.
39 For instance, see Sarafian, *Education*, 221–2.
40 ("Compatriotic Union of Khups"), no author, in (*Khups in Keghi*), 31. Population statistics for Khups vary. In ("History"), in (*Khups in Keghi*), two thousand Armenians were said to be in the village in 1900 (13). In the same book (178), we find 185 Armenian households in 1879. In Pashigian, ("Traditional and Contemporary Reflections"), (*New Keghi*), vol. 1, 33–4, we see three hundred households and fifteen hundred people, including sojourners (no date given, probably early 1900s). See also ("On the Occasion of the Sixty-fifth Anniversary of the Compatriotic Union of Khups Village"), in (*Khups in Keghi*), 171
41 It would be interesting to study the similarities between the village educational societies and Armenian guilds.
42 For example, Bizian Amira, director of the Imperial Mint under Mahmud II, established the first industrial school for girls in Kum Kapu. For an excellent account of Armenian philanthropy and capitalism, see Zekiyan, *The Armenian Way to Modernity*.
43 Krikor Der Krikorian, ("Memoirs of an Arektsi Bolsetsi Pilgrim"), (*New Keghi*), vol. 1, 123.
44 Village and regional histories are indispensable sources for the historian. Several Keghi accounts have been cited in this study.
45 The first ARF chapter in Canada was formally founded in Brantford on 16 July 1904, with fourteen members (ARF Archives, Montreal, Quebec). Informally, the branch had started earlier; a citation in *Hnchak History*

notes that the Dashnaks already had a branch in Brantford in 1903. See also Seropian, ("Formation of the Armenian ethnic group in Canada"), 116; "H.H. Dashnaktsutian Canadayi medj gordsuneutian 95-amiak" (Armenian Revolutionary Federation in Canada, on Its Ninety-fifth Anniversary), *Horizon Weekly*, 5 January 1998, insert; Manoyan, ("A Sketch"). For Hnchaks, see Kitur, (*Hnchak History*), vol. 2, 77–86. Bedros Mouchian, of Toronto, stated that the first Hnchak chapter was in St Catharines.

46 Armenian Revolutionary Federation, Brantford chapter, minutes, ARF Archives, Montreal, Quebec. See Giro Manoyan, ("A Sketch").
47 The ARF records, ARF Archives, Montreal.
48 Acton, "Nationality," 166–95.
49 For a discussion of the political organizations, in English, see the definitive work by Nalbandian, *The Armenian Revolutionary Movement* and Dasnabedian, *History of the Armenian Revolutionary Federation*. For the Hnchak perspective, see Kitur, (*Hnchak History*), vols. 1 and 2; Walker, *Survival*. For an account of the parties in the United States, see Mirak, *Torn*. See also Lima, "Evolving Goals," vii–xix; Dasnabedian, "The Hunchakian Party," 17–39; Suny, "Populism, Nationalism and Marxism"; Suny, "Marxism, Nationalism,"; Ter Minassian, "Le Mouvement Révolutionnaire Arménien," 536–607; and Ter Minassian, "Aux Origines du Marxisme Arménien," 67–117.
50 Barton, *Peasants and Strangers*, 64.
51 ARF Records of Guelph, ARF Archives.
52 Kitur, (*Hnchak History*), vol. 2, 83; P. Evarian, oral interviews, Hamilton, and H. Torosian, St Catharines.
53 Kitur, (*Hnchak History*), vol. 2, 80–1. Murat had spent at least ten years in jail, imprisoned by the Turks in Tripoli. He was hanged in 1915.
54 Oral sources indicate that Windsor also had Hnchak and Dashnak chapters in the period before and during World War I, but I have not been able to verify this point.
55 Kitur, (*Hnchak History*), vol. 1, 221 ff.
56 *Hairenik*, 20 November 1913, 5 December 1911; 5, 7 August 1913; and 18 July 1914; and *Asbarez*, 6 October 1911. Cited in Mirak, "Armenians," 289.
57 From 1920 to 1946, the organization was known as the Armenian Relief Corps. In 1946, it changed its name to the Armenian Relief Society (ARS), a name it still carries today.
58 Constitution of the Armenian Red Cross, 1936.
59 Meruzhan Ozanian and Siranush G. Mkhitarian, (*Memorial Volume of the Armenian Relief Society: 1910–1970*), 17–24.
60 Their children were often sent abroad to study, and upon returning to the Ottoman Empire, they disseminated their learning to others.

61 Rev. Cannon MacColl, quoted in the *Presbyterian Review*, Toronto, 12 December 1895. Harry Woodley, Montreal, son of Rev. E. C. Woodley, Protestant missionary in Marash, Ottoman Empire, recounted how the missionaries were forbidden to teach chemistry on the grounds that the symbol for water, H_2O, represented Hamid II = 0.
62 Portukalian established one of the earliest teachers' colleges in Turkey, in Van in 1879. Under constant police surveillance, he was finally exiled from the Ottoman Empire and settled in Marseilles, where he published *Armenia*. Quotation from "Twenty-fifth Anniversary Brochure of Armenia."
63 Minutes, accounts, membership lists, and library contents of the Khrimian *gradaran* in Brantford, Ontario, from 1910 to 1913 are in the ARF Archives, Montreal. Of the thirty-two members in the 1910 Khrimian *gradaran* roster, twenty-nine were members of the ARF.
64 K. Topalian, oral interview, Brantford. Kitur, (*Hnchak History*), gives Dalhousie Street as the location of the first Hnchak club in Brantford.
65 A. Libarian, oral interview, Hamilton.
66 Kitur, (*Hnchak History*), vol. 2, 77–9. Oral interviews, H. Tootikian, Toronto; Z. Norigian, Detroit; and P. Evarian, Hamilton.
67 Referring to Hnchak reading rooms in the United States, cited in Mirak, "Armenian Schools and Lyceums," typewritten manuscript.
68 For a discussion of the *Armeno-American Letter Writer* as a reflection of immigrant life, see Kaprielian, "The Armeno-American Letter Writer," 26–30.
69 Mirak, "Armenian Schools."
70 On coffeehouses as reading rooms, see Ellis, *The Penny Universities*; Kelly, *Adult Education*; Lillywhite, *London Coffee Houses*.
71 St Catharines, ARF minutes, September 1911.
72 Archbishop Khoren Nar Bey de Lusignan, translated by Alice Stone Blackwell.
73 A. Libarian, oral interview, Hamilton.
74 Kitur, (*Hnchak History*), vol. 2, 82. The Hnchaks were often called Muratians after the Hnchak hero.
75 *Brantford Daily Expositor*, 4 April 1903, 5 September 1912, 23 October 1912, 7 October 1915. Hamilton Board of Education, Internal Management Committee Minutes, 1912–15.
76 Khazar Nubarian, from the village of Astghaberd.
77 Park, *The Immigrant Press*, 35.
78 P. Evarian, oral interview, Hamilton.
79 Park, *Immigrant Press*.
80 Kevorkian, (*Everyone's Yearbook*), 361
81 *Yeritasard Hayastan*, 19 December 1903, cited in Mirak, "Armenians," 288.

82 Park, *Immigrant Press*.
83 See for instance, Hairenik, 2 October 1905, and 5 March, 11 June, and 30 July 1904.
84 *Hairenik*, 23 October 1908, 10 June 1913, 8 January 1914.
85 Aknuni, (*Towards the Old Country*); Mirak, *Torn*, 264.
86 See Shanin, *Peasants and Peasant Societies*, for the "hinge man" concept.
87 RG6 A1, vol. 120, file 947, Gourjian to Rt Hon. Sir E. Grey, 22 January 1906; *Brantford Expositor*, 8 June 1907; ARF Minutes. For an examination of leadership and governance, see Raymond Breton's important work, *The Governance of Ethnic Communities*.

CHAPTER SIX

1 Article 61 of the Treaty of Berlin states: "The Sublime Porte engages to realize without further delay the amelioration and the reforms demanded by local requirements in the provinces inhabited by the Armenians and to guarantee their security against the Kurds and the Circassians. Turkey will periodically render account of the measures taken in this matter, reporting to the Powers which will supervise them." (Sublime Porte is the French translation of Babe Ali. It refers to the seat of Ottoman government and of the Ottoman courts.) Signatories included Austro-Hungary, Britain, France, Germany, Italy, Russia, and Turkey. For a discussion of international intervention in Ottoman affairs, the Armenian Question, and its relationship to the Eastern Question see Dadrian, *History of the Armenian Genocide*.
2 For a discussion of the massacre of Bulgarians, Maronites, and Macedonians, the events in Sasun, and the 1894–96 and 1909 massacre of Armenians, see Walker, *Survival*, and Dadrian, *History*. The term "sub-culture of massacre" is borrowed from Dadrian.
3 The junta is also referred to as the Ittihadists, or the Young Turks. At the time of the revolution, the Dashnak Party supported the Young Turk efforts at reform.
4 See Heyd, *Foundations of Turkish Nationalism*. Ziya Gokalp, who is regarded as the intellectual father of modern Turkey, defined the nation as "a society consisting of people who speak the same language, have had the same education and are united in their religious, moral and aesthetic ideals – in short, those who have a common culture and religion." Heyd, *Foundations*, 63. For an examination of the pan-Turanian movement (pan-Turkism), see Zarevand, *United and Independent Turania*; Landau, *Pan-Turkism in Turkey*; Williams, "Russia's Orphan Races."
5 Gooch and Temperely, eds., *British Documents on the Origins of the War 1889–1914*, part 1, vol. 9, doc. no. 181 (6 Sept. 1910 report): 207, 1926, cited in Dadrian, "Genocide as a Problem of National and International

Law." Robert Melson points out that the Armenian genocide was "at one and the same time a product of this nationalist revolution and a stage in its development." Melson, "Provocation or Nationalism," 73.

6 For a structural approach to the Genocide, see Dadrian, *History*, and Astourian, "Genocidal Process." See also Lepsius, *Le Rapport secret sur les massacres d'Arménie*, 271–81. Lepsius notes that 60 percent of foreign imports and 40 percent of foreign exports, as well as 80 percent of the interior commerce was in the hands of Armenians. Ronald Suny notes that of forty-two printing plants in the Ottoman Empire, only eleven were owned by Moslems and twenty-six by non-Moslems, including Armenians, Greeks, and Jews. Of the Bursa raw silk establishments, six were owned by Moslems, two by the government, and thirty-three by non-Moslems. Ronald Suny, "Rethinking the Unthinkable: An Historian's Reading of the Armenian Genocide," unpublished manuscript, 25, cited in Miller and Miller, *Survivors*, 48. Armenians were also more progressive than their Turkish and Kurdish neighbours in the spheres of medicine and education.

7 For a concise account of the Genocide see Hovannisian, "The Historical Dimensions of the Armenian Question." For the Armenian Reform Commission, 1913–14, see Davison, "The Armenian Crisis."

8 On the issue of blaming the victim and of the victim as provocateur, see Melson, "Provocation or Nationalism." Dadrian, in *History*, part 4, examines the various methods employed by the Young Turks to blame the victim.

9 As Armenians realized the intentions of the Turkish government, the surviving men formed regiments in the Caucasus, joined the Armenian Legion in Mesopotamia, or fought with the Greek army against Turkey.

10 Dadrian, *History*, 236–9. See also Walker, "World War I," 253, 269.

11 Americans and British on the scene, as well as Germans, notably Dr Johannes Lepsius, founder and director of the Deutsche Orient-Mission, came to the same conclusion. Refer also to Dadrian, *German Responsibility*. Dadrian's work is particularly relevant because he has examined German, Austrian, and Turkish primary sources.

12 After studying German Foreign Office documents in the United States archives, Ulrich Trumpener, author of *Germany and the Ottoman Empire, 1914–1918*, found that the extermination of the Armenian population was not the consequence of wartime security but a deliberate act to destroy an ethnic minority judged politically bothersome. Cited in "Note pour l'édition française," by Tessa Hofmann, in Lepsius, *Archives du Génocide*, 15. See also Beylerian, *Les grandes puissances*; Hovannisian, *The Armenian Genocide*, and Hovannisian, *Armenia on the Road to Independence*; Dadrian, *History*, chaps. 12, 13, and 14, and notes,

226–9, and Dadrian, "The Secret Young Turk Ittihadist Conference," 173–201. For a bibliography of publications and archival sources on the Genocide, see Papazian and Ottenbreit, *The Armenian Genocide*; Hovannisian, *The Armenian Holocaust*. Also see the *Armenian Review*, special issue, *Genocide: Crime Against Humanity*, vol. 37, no. 1 (spring 1984) and vol. 42, no. 4/168 (winter 1989); Sarafian, *United States Official Documents*, vols. 1–5. Also *The Armenian Review*, vol. 25, nos. 1–2/177–8 (spring/summer 1992), especially Tessa Hofmann and Gerayer Koutcharian, "'Images That Horrify and Indict': Pictorial Documents on the Persecution and Extermination of the Armenians from 1877 to 1922"; Mouradian, "Bibliographie," 558–67. For the Turkish point of view see, for example, Ahmed Rustem Bey, *La guerre mondiale et la question turco-arménienne* (Bern 1918); *Aspirations et agissements révolutionnaires des comités arméniens avant et après la proclamation de la constitution ottomane* (n.a. Constantinople: n.p. 1916). Stanford J. Shaw and Ezel Kural Shaw, *History of the Ottoman Empire and Modern Turkey*, vol. 2, *Reform, Revolution, and Republic: The Rise of Modern Turkey, 1808–1975*. Also Heath Lowry, *Ambassador Morgenthau's Story*, Istanbul 1990. Shaws take a revisionist perspective.

13 Surmenian, (*The Turkish-Armenian Soldier and the Military*) 16, 23. Numbers are discussed in Vartkes S. Dolabjian, "Portrayal of the Armenian Genocide in the *Encyclopedia Britannica*," paper presented at the International Conference of the Association of Genocide Scholars, 2001, 11. Approximately 150,000 Armenians fought in the Russian army. In a letter to German ambassador, Baron von Wangenheim, Johannes Ehmann, German missionary in Kharput, expresses his anxiety about the treatment of Christian subjects, of Christian soldiers between the ages of twenty and forty-five who enlisted in the Turkish army and of the Christian population, which responded to the appeal of the Red Cross for assistance and supplies. In Lepsius, *Archives*, 86–7.

14 Morgenthau, *Ambassador Morgenthau's Story*, 302–3. See also Kévorkian, "Récueil de témoignages sur l'extermination des *amele tabouri*," 289–303 (includes documents). For the "labour battalions" and prisoners of war, a topic that still requires considerable research, see Baldwin, *Six Prisons*, 187–90, 203–4. See also correspondence of Dr C.E. Clarke, American medical doctor in the American hospital in Sivas to Hoffman Philip, American chargé d'affaires in Constantinople, in United States National Archives, General Records of the Department of State, Record Group 59,867.4016/288/encl 31 May 1916, cited in Hairapetian, "'Race Problems' and the Armenian Genocide," 57. See also Rawlinson, *Adventures in the Near East*.

15 Taft, *Rebirth*, 32. See also Ussher, *An American Physician in Turkey*, 264–5, and Stürmer, *Two Years in Constantinople*, 115.

16 Morgenthau, *Ambassador*, 305.
17 See Kazarian, "Opening of the Turkish Genocide."
18 Arlen, *Passage to Ararat*, 226. Commenting on the use of torture, a high-ranking Turkish official reported to Ambassador Morgenthau that the Ittihadists had "delved into the records of the Spanish Inquisition and other historic institutions of torture and adopted all the suggestions found there." Morgenthau, *Ambassador*, 307.
19 Dadrian deals with the Temporary Law of Deportation (27 May 1915) and its unconstitutionality in *History*, 221. For the "official proclamation" read by the town criers, see Hairapetian, "Race Problems," 46.
20 Reported in the *Toronto Daily Star*, 7 October 1915, citing J. (Viscount) Bryce. Bryce later published documents of the Genocide in *The Treatment of Armenians*. Author of *The American Commonwealth* (1888), Bryce also served as British ambassador to the United States and as a member of the Hague Permanent Court of Arbitration.
21 For the most thorough account of the confiscation of Armenian property and bank accounts consult Baghdjian, *La confiscation*. For the terms of the Abandoned Property Law, 16 May 1915, see ibid., 255–60, and Dadrian, *History*, 222–25.
22 For the patriarchate statistics, see Kévorkian and Paboudjian, *Les Arméniens*; Aharonian and Nubar, *Arménie*. This account has also been published in Baghdjian, *Confiscation*, 261–9. See also Dalrymple, *From the Holy Mountain*.
23 Davis, *Slaughterhouse Province*, 55; United States Government Archives, RG 59,867.4016/148, Consul Jesse Jackson to Ambassador Morgenthau, 14 August 1915, cited in Hairapetian, "Race Problems," 49; United States Government Archives, RG 59,867.4016/74, Morgenthau to Secretary of State, 20 July 1915, cited in Hairapetian, "Race Problems," 47. For a discussion of the pillage motive for genocides, see Simpson, *The Splendid Blond Beast*.
24 Bryce, *Treatment*, 291–2. See also Dadrian, "Genocide as a Problem," 263.
25 Cited in Walker, "World War I," 256, quoting Lepsius, *Deutschland und Armenien, 1914-1918*, 80.
26 Bryce, *Treatment*, 291–2. For the events in Kharput, see the work of Rev. Henry Riggs, American missionary and principal of Euphrates College, in Riggs, *Days of Tragedy*.
27 Morgenthau, *Ambassador*, 333, 308–9. See also United States Government Archives, RG 59,867.4016/74, Morgenthau to Secretary of State, 20 July 1915, cited in Hairapetian, "Race Problems," 47.
28 Morgenthau, *Ambassador*, quoting Talaat, 342.
29 United States Government Archives, RG 59,867.4016/226/, encl. Johannsen to Morgenthau, October 1915, in Hairapetian, "Race Problems" 52–3. Also in Bryce, *Treatment*, 89.

30 Morgenthau, *Ambassador*, 351–2.
31 For other survivor accounts, see Miller and Miller, *Survivors*; Balakian, *Le golgotha Arménien*; Ternon, *Mardin*.
32 N. Topalian, oral interview, Detroit, Michigan. Koulakan was a big field in the region of Southern Keghi, where the inhabitants of several villages were gathered together and attacked.
33 Hovannesian, ("The Joyful Anniversary of New Geghi"), 41.
34 Charles Palvetzian, oral interview, Cambridge.
35 G. Elemian, oral interview, Toronto.
36 Agnacia Manuelian, *Unending Journey*, 204–11, 263.
37 I. Israelian, oral interview, Montreal, Quebec.
38 Baldwin, *Six Prisons*, 152–3, citing Mme Captanian, "Les memoirs d'une deportée Arménienne."
39 Niepage, *The Horrors of Aleppo*, 13. Dr Niepage was a teacher in the German Technical School in Aleppo.
40 Miss Y, a foreign resident at Adana, recorded her experiences there from September 1914 to September 1915, in Bryce, *Treatment*, 506.
41 United States Government Archives, RG 59,867.4016/225, Consul Jesse Jackson to Morgenthau, 16 October 1915, in Hairapetian, "Race Problems," 49.
42 Report by a neutral eyewitness, in Lepsius, *Deutschland und Armenien*, cited in Boyajian, *Armenia*, 119–121; also cited in Walker, *Survival*, 227–9, as testimony of Auguste Bernau, German representative of the United States Vacuum Oil Company in Aleppo. Dadrian, *History*, 242, refers to Bernau as a German employee of the American consulate at Aleppo. See also the account of Jesse B. Jackson, American consul in Aleppo, in Hairapetian, comp., "Documents: the State Department File," 127–45. See also Kévorkian, "L'extermination." On the Naim-Andonian documents, see also Dadrian, "The Naim-Andonian Documents."
43 Armin Wegner, in Chaliand and Ternon, *The Armenians*, 101. Wegner, who was with the German Red Cross, took an extensive series of photographs of the devastation. This quotation is taken from his letter of appeal on behalf of the Armenians to President Woodrow Wilson. See also Andonian, *The Memoirs of Naim Bey*.
44 Bryce, in *Treatment*, 650, gives the figure of 600,000 dead during the first year; Turkish accounts estimate that 800,000 had died by 1918. These numbers do not include those who died later in Turkey, in the Caucasus, or in the Middle East. Nor do they include those who were taken into captivity and lost forever as part of the Armenian nation. In October 1915, it was estimated that only 200,000 Armenians were left in Turkey.
45 See Walker, *Survival*, 230; Libaridian, "The Unltimate Repressions," 206.
46 For the definitive history of the Armenian Republic see Hovannisian,

Armenia on the Road to Independence; *The Republic of Armenia*, vols. 1–4.

47 Hovannisian, *Republic*, vol. 2, 300–2, discusses various estimates of refugees from Turkish Armenia and native indigents in the Armenian Republic. See also Hovannisian, *Republic*, vol. 1, 126–33.

48 The twelfth of Wilson's Fourteen Points states that the "Turkish portions of the present Ottoman empire should be assured a secure sovereignty, but the other nationalities which are now under Turkish rule should be assured an undoubted security of life and an absolutely unmolested opportunity of autonomous development." Great Britain, FO371/2488.630 95, cited in Walker *Survival*, 231.

49 *Parliamentary Debates*, House of Lords, 38, cols. 279–88, cited in Hovannisian, *Republic*, vol. 2, 436. United States Department of State, *Paris Peace Conference*, vol. 3, 795, cited in Hovannisian, "Historical Dimensions," 33. See also Walker, *Survival*, chap. 7. For an account of the war crimes trials see Dadrian, "Documentation," 549–76, and "A Textual Analysis," 1–36; Kévorkian, "Le procès des criminels," 166–205. See also Yeghiayan, *Trial*.

50 Khatissian, "La République Indépendente d'Arménie," 81.

51 For an example of the half-hearted Allied effort to supply the republic with arms and ammunition see Hovannisian, *Republic*, vol. 3, chap. 9. For Armenian attempts to share in the surplus Allied war materiel, see Hovannisian, *Republic*, vol. 2, 95–102. See also ibid., chapter 15, and Walker, *Survival*. For an examination of Britain's pledges to a free Armenia and its subsequent betrayal of the young state, see Nassibian, *Britain and the Armenian Question*.

52 Hovannisian, *Republic*, vol. 2, 325, 416. Hovannisian also refers to the British habit of "dumping" Armenian refugees from Arab provinces into Cilicia to be free of the obligation of feeding, sheltering, and protecting them (418).

53 See Walker, *Survival*, 292–303. Also Brémond, *La Cilicie en 1919–1920*, 46.

54 Du Véou, *La Passion de la Cilicie*, annex 13, "Proclamation du Général Gouraud," 405.

55 For an account of the Cilician tragedy, see Gotigian et Tachjian, "La Légion d'Orient"; Du Véou, *La Passion*; Macartney, *Refugees*; Mutafian, "La France en Cilicie"; Astourian, "Testing World-System"; Walker, *Survival*, 293. As an explanation for French action, Walker notes that France controlled 61 percent of the Ottoman public debt, the tobacco monopoly, and concessions for rail construction, mining, and ports. See also Hovannisian, *Republic*, vol. 2, 124–8.

56 In the postwar period, Constantinople was under Allied occupation, and in May 1919, at the invitation of the Supreme Council, Greece occupied

Smyrna. The Smyrna conflagration is covered by Housepian, *The Smyrna Affair*. The citation is from ibid., 159. For expulsion during the 1920s see Tachjian, "Etat-nation," 206–44.

57 See Hovannisian, *Republic*, vol. 1, 416–47.
58 Letter from Georges Burnier, delegate of the International Labour Office and of the High Commissioner for Refugees in Beirut to the Assistant High Commissioner for Refugees in Geneva, 22 December 1929. League of Nations, High Commissioner for Refugees, Reference Box C-1378.
59 Hovannisian, "The Armenian Genocide and Patterns of Denial," 111–34.
60 Walker, *Survival*, 347ff., argues that the United Nations is bound to be "guardian" of articles 38–44 of the Treaty of Lausanne, which guaranteed the rights of minorities, including Armenians.
61 Zaroukian, *Men Without Childhood*.
62 Bedoukian, *The Urchin*. Arlene Voski Avakian pays tribute to her grandmother, whose lion-hearted courage saved her family. Avakian, *Lion Woman's Legacy*.
63 L. Lorisian, oral interview, Hamilton.
64 A. Ungerian, oral interview, Fresno, California.
65 On the survival of children, see Kaprielian-Churchill, "The Armenian Genocide," 221–58. For example, see cipher telegrams from the Young Turk leaders: no. 537 to the administration of Aleppo, 29 September 1915; no. 603, 5 November 1915; and Order no. 691, 13 November 1915, in Andonian, *Memoirs*.
66 N. Topalian, oral interview, Detroit.
67 League of Nations, "Extent and Cost of the Rescue Work of 1925," A.61.1927.4; "Protection of Women and Children in the Near East," Geneva, 13 September 1927. Karen Jeppe, the commissioner, was a Danish educator.
68 A. Chorbanian, oral interview, St Catharines.
69 Riggs, *Days of Tragedy*; Kaprielian, "Genocide and the Survival of Children"; Koloian, ("We and the People of Dersim"), 94–6.
70 Eblighatian, (*A Life*). Eblighatian was the executive director.
71 See League of Nations, "Extent and Cost of the Rescue Work of 1925," A.61.1927.4; "Protection of Women and Children in the Near East," Geneva, 13 September 1927.
72 V. Pilafjian, oral interview, Toronto. Interviewed by Nadine Deshlian. For Donabedian, see Tachjian, "Etat-nation," 226–7; for Herian, see Jizmejian, *History*, 527–33.
73 The defense of Musa Dagh has been immortalized by Franz Werfel in *The Forty Days of Musa Dagh*. The defense of other places, like Van, Khups, Marash, and Urfa, has also been recorded. For Urfa, see (*Heroes of Urfa*); for Marash, see Kerr, *The Lions of Marash*; and for Van, see Mkhitarian, (*The Heroic Battle of Van*). A sense of the spirit of resistance

is found in the memoirs of a survivor from Van: "The Turkish artillery would demolish the Armenian positions during the day and the peasant workers would build new walls during the night's darkness. The Turks would be infuriated to find the resistance just as strong the following day ... Ten or twelve high school students went from one fortified position to another and played cheerful martial music ... Soon amateur chemists found means to make smokeless gunpowder – a workshop was opened and empty cartridges were reused." Archives of Ontario, Multicultural History Society of Ontario collection, Memoirs of Oksen Teghtsoonian.

74 Shahan Natali (Hagop Der Hagopian), a member of the Dashnak Party at the time, led the secret Nemesis network. He wrote *Turkism from Angara to Baku and the Turkish Orientation* (Athens 1928) and *From the Treaty of Alexandropol to the Caucasian Rebellions of the 1930s* (Athens 1928). On punishment of the Young Turks, see Hovannisian, *Republic*, vol. 1, 419–20; also Derogy, *Resistance and Revenge*. For more on the topic see Dadrian, *History*, "Documentation," and "Analysis," and Simpson, *Beast*. See also *The Case of Soghomon Tehlirian: Proceedings* (Los Angeles: Armenian Revolutionary Federation 1985) and Shiragian, *The Legacy*.

75 The majority of Armenian men had been jailed, dispatched to slave labour camps, or killed, or they had taken up arms.

76 League of Nations, *Monthly Summary*, vol. 2, no. 10 (Oct. 1922).

77 Barton, *Near East Relief*, 210–22. See also Elliott, *Beginning Again at Ararat*.

78 The French, Swiss, Danes, Norwegians, Germans, and British also had relief agencies. On the Near East Relief, see Barton, *Near East Relief*. Created in November 1915 as the American Committee for Armenian and Syrian Relief, it changed its name to the American Committee for Relief in the Near East in 1918, and a year later it adopted a new name, The Near East Relief, and a new mandate. In all, the NER spent $100 million in relief, mostly in Syria and Lebanon. Because Armenia did not receive de jure recognition until August 1920, the Armenian government was unable to secure private loans or government credits and was even deprived of a share of 823,202 metric tons of surplus goods distributed by the United States Liquidation Commission. Hovannisian, *Republic*, vol. 2, 397. On British relief, see Nassibian, *Britain and the Armenian Question*.

79 Wehrlin, "Mission en Arménie"; Barton, *Near East Relief*.

80 Barton, *Near East Relief*, 84, 103, 180–1. For more on the role of charitable organizations, see Hovannisian, *Republic*, vol. 1, chap. 5; vol. 2, chaps. 10–12.

81 Burnier, "L'Installation de réfugiés arméniens en colonies agricoles."

82 League of Nations, High Commissioner for Refugees, "Armenian and

Russian Refugees," A.48.1927.8 (5 Sept. 1927); League of Nations, RA/413/70/4.
83 See Bedoukian, *Urchin*, 119–25.

CHAPTER SEVEN

1 See also Teodik, *Golgotha of the Armenian Clergy*.
2 Minassian, "Armenian Church."
3 Dasnabedian, "The Hunchakian Party," 516.
4 Hunt, *Theory and Practice*, 156–8, 192–6.
5 For an excellent account of the activities and propaganda of the HOG in the diaspora and of its relations with the church and the compatriotic societies, see Mouradian, *L'Arménie*, chap. 7. See also Kitur, *Hnchak History*, vol. 1, 500ff.
6 Mardirosian, (*American-Armenians*), 53. See also *Banvor*, 28 July 1923.
7 See Roy, *Communism and the Churches*, 469n5, citing the *Daily Worker*, 28 September 1935, 4. The agreement between the Communists and the Hnchaks included joint support of Soviet Armenia and united hostility against the Dashnaks. The fortieth anniversary (1943) of the Hnchak newspaper, *Yeritasard Hayastan*, gives reports about Lenin, Stalin, the Soviet Union, and Soviet Armenia. For Hnchak-Communist Party relationship, see Kitur, *Hnchak History*, vol. 1, 498–525.
8 Mirak, "Armenians," 531.
9 (Minutes, Third Convention of the American-Armenian HOG). See also Kitur, *Hnchak History*, vol. 2, 324–8. For more on the HOG refer to A. Vartabedian, (*Relief Committee for Armenia*) and *Shinarar*, 1931, mouthpiece of the HOG in the United States.
10 For a brief account of the Ramgavar Party, see Arsen-Nubar Mamourian, (Sixty Years of the Armenian Democratic Liberal Organization).
11 Walker, *Survival*, 354; Leader of the Ramgavar Party cited in Phillips, *Symbol*, 140.
12 For the definitive work on the partition and sovietization of Armenia see Hovannisian, *Republic*, vol. 4.
13 Mirak, "Armenians," 529
14 Rev. Principal Caven, in *Massey's Magazine*, Toronto (March 1896): 97–103.
15 NA, MG29 D38, vol. 5, file 3420–3576, W.N. Chambers to Rev. G.M. Grant, Erzerum, 4 March 1896, "What is to Become of the Armenians? A Proposal." See also "Martyred Ministers of Mardin Station."
16 Hopkins, *Sword of Islam*, 423; Bliss, *Turkey*, 510–11. See also Greene, *Armenian Massacres*.
17 MacLachlan founded the International College in Smyrna.
18 Chambers, *Yoljuluk*, 1.

19 Chambers, "The Massacre of Armenia," 232–3. See also two other articles in the *Queen's Quarterly*: Robert Chambers, "Our Interest in Turkey," and Lawson P. Chambers, "The Armenian Deportations."
20 For newspaper accounts in the United States, see Kloian, *The Armenian Genocide*. For newspaper accounts in Canada, see *The Armenian Genocide in the Canadian Press*. Vols. 1 and 2.
21 For an account of the relations between Armenians and Canadian missionaries and churches, see Nahabedian, "Relations"; *The Canadian Churchman*, 28 October 1915, (published by the Church of England in Canada, now the Anglican Church), cited in Nahabedian, "Relations," 31.
22 *L'Action Catholique*, 20 October 1915; *Montreal Daily Star*, 7 October 1915, quoting Lord Bryce; *Berlin Daily Telegraph*, 7 October 1915 (Berlin is present-day Kitchener, Ontario); *Globe*, 26 August 1925, also *Toronto Daily Star*, 7 October 1915; *La Patrie*, 25 September 1915; *Manitoba Free Press*, 14 October 1915. (For newspaper coverage in Canada see *The Armenian Genocide in the Canadian Press*, vols. 1 and 2).
23 *Canadian Churchman*, 24 May 1917, cited in Nahabedian, "Relations"; *Halifax Herald*, 4 January 1919; *Gazette*, 15 April 1919. See also Dadrian, *Genocide*, chap. 18.
24 For reference to the Armenian Relief Association of Canada, see Apramian, *The Georgetown Boys*, 1976.
25 *Toronto Globe*, inaugurating the fund-raising campaign with "The Call from Armenia," 9 January 1920. All subsequent quotations are from the *Globe*, January and February 1920, unless otherwise indicated.
26 Smith, *At the Hands of the Turks*, 55. Smith wrote the articles in the *Globe* and later compiled them in the aforementioned book.
27 The criticism that missionaries were frontrunners of American economic imperialism and worked hand-in-hand with American commercial interests in Turkey is best understood from their attitudes and activities during and after World War I, when many of them seemed more concerned with safeguarding their vast real estate holdings in Turkey than with protecting the Christian minorities. Housepian, for instance, in *Smyrna*, points to the role the missionaries played in 1917 in convincing President Wilson not to declare war on Turkey for fear of jeopardizing their work and their properties. See also Grabill, *Protestant Diplomacy*, and Balakian, *Burning Tigris*.
28 *Presbyterian Review*, Toronto, 12 December 1895. See also *Presbyterian Review*, 6 February 1896, 27 February 1896, 19 March 1896, 25 June 1896, 10 September 1896, 5 November 1896, 19 November 1896, and 11 March 1897. My thanks to Michael Owen for drawing these articles to my attention.

29 NA, MG29 D38, vol. 5, file 3420–3576, Robert Chambers to Dr George Grant, Bardizag, 5 April 1896.
30 See Hovannisian, *Republic*, vol. 4, for the mandate controversy, the role of missionaries, American aid, and the contributions of James Gerard.
31 *Canadian Churchman*, cited in Nahabedian, "Relations," 33.
32 Clark, *Documents on Canadian External Relations*, vol. 3, 1919–1925, Documents 92–4, pp. 70–1. Hovannisian, *Republic*, vol. 2, 338, 396; RG 2, vol. 1240, Order-in-Council 400. The churches specifically mentioned in the supporting documents for the order-in-council were the Toronto Methodist Ministerial Association, the Toronto General Ministerial Association (representing all Protestant churches in Toronto), the Presbytery of Toronto, and the congregation of Brant Avenue Methodist Church, Brantford, Ontario. *Toronto Globe*, 20 February 1920. See also Nassibian, *Britain and the Armenian Question*, chapter 4.
33 *Gazette*, 17 April 1920; *Armenian Genocide in the Canadian Press*, vol. 2, 87; Clark, *Documents on Canadian External Relations*, vol. 3, documents 98–9, 73–4; Veatch, *Canada and the League*, 52, citing League of Nations, First Assembly Debates, 16 December 1920, 589; Hovannisian, *Republic*, vol. 4, 335. Newton Wesley Rowell, Canada's representative to the League, had been leader of the Liberal Party of Ontario, later became chief justice of Ontario, and was one of the authors of the Rowell-Sirois Report, the Royal Commission on Dominion-Provincial Relations.
34 NA, RG25 G1, vol. 1325, file 999, Christian Science Society of Western Toronto to the Secretary of State, 23 August 1922 and First Church of Christian Scientist, Edmonton, Alberta, to HRH the King, 15 September 1922.
35 Baldwin, *Six Prisons*, 203–4.
36 Polyphony, *Armenians in Ontario*, 38.
37 Kitur, *Hnchak History*, vol. 2, 82–3.
38 Ibid., 83; Gotikian, "La Légion d'Orient," 154.
39 NA, RG13 A–2, vol. 198, file 1716–1735, 1915; see NA, RG25 G1, vol. 1325, file. 999, George Alexander to Sir Joseph Pope, Undersecretary of State, Ottawa, 2 October 1922. Until 1917, Armenians from the Russian Empire were also fighting with the czarist forces in Eastern Europe. See also Thompson, *Ethnic Minorities*. For Armenians in the Canadian Expeditionary Force, see NA, RG150.
40 H. Kaprielian, oral interview, Hamilton.

CHAPTER EIGHT

1 Government of Canada, Department of Immigration and Colonization, *Sessional Papers, Annual Reports*. My thanks to Robert Mirak for his

statistics on Armenian entry to the United States in the post-Genocide period.
2 Eastman, *Canada at Geneva*; Veatch, *Canada and the League*.
3 Archives of Ontario, MU 9587. Letter from Mrs D. Miller to Rev. Ira Pierce, Secretary of the Armenian Relief Association of Canada, 6 August 1927.
4 National Archives of Canada, Department of Immigration and Colonization, Record Group 76, volume 300, file 279907, parts 1 to 3 (henceforth referred to as RG76); ibid., Frederick Blair to Lucien Pacaud, Joint Secretary, Office of the High Commissioner, London, England, 25 January 1923; ibid., Blair to César Raymond, Librairie Raymond, Constantinople, 5 December 1922.
5 Ibid., Blair to Turner, 25 Aug. 1925. See also ibid., Memo, Blair to the Minister of Immigration and Colonization, James Alexander Robb, 12 November 1924.
6 For a discussion advocating a system of selection not necessarily based on race, see Carrothers, "The Immigration Problem in Canada."
7 See, for example, Smith, *Canadian Immigration*; Government of Canada, Department of Immigration and Colonization, *Sessional Papers, Reports of the Deputy Minister*, 1923–25.
8 RG76, Blair to Mr G. Topakyan, General Secretary of the United Armenian Immigration and Welfare Societies, New York City, 30 July 1923; Blair to C.K. Morse, Secretary of the Armenian Relief Fund Association of Canada, 29 January 1921; J.S. Fraser, Division Commissioner, Ottawa, to Messrs Murphy, Sherwood, Clark and Robertson, barristers, 23 Oct. 1924; handwritten comment, initialed W.J.E. [Deputy Minister William John Egan] in margin of Memo from Blair to Egan, 10 November 1927.
9 In the prewar period, instructions from the Department of Immigration gave immigration officials at ports the liberty to enforce P.C. 918, the passport regulation, against anyone considered "rejectionable for any other reason." See RG76, vol. 480, file 745162.
10 NA, RG25 G1, vol. 1484, file 44T, Acting Deputy Minister of Immigration W.R. Little to Dr O.D. Skelton, Under-Secretary of State for External Affairs, 18 August, 1927. Immigrants from the British Isles and the United States could be deported "without any passport difficulty." See RG76, vol. 636, file 978450, part 6, Deputy Minister of Immigration, W.J. Egan, to Canadian Senator Raoul Dandurand, Chairman of the Assembly of the League of Nations, 6 May 1926. For a more detailed discussion of Canada's handling of the Nansen Passport and its role in the intergovernmental conferences, refer to Kaprielian "Canada and the Nansen Passport," 281–306.

11 RG76, Acting Deputy Minister Blair to Dr O.B. Price, Member of Parliament, 6 Feb. 1926; Mesag Rasmigian, oral interview, St Catharines.
12 See Tachjian, "Etat-nation," 206–44.
13 RG76, Blair to T.B. Willans, Special Immigration Commissioner, Antwerp, 28 November 1923; W.R. Little, Commissioner of Colonization, Ottawa to J. Bruce Walker, Director of European Emigration, England, 29 December 1926. To complicate the issue even further, Armenians in Syria or Lebanon were in territories that had been part of the Ottoman Empire *before* the war.
14 Vernant, *The Refugee*, 417, 431; R.P. Poidebard, "La Mission française des Camps Arméniens de Beyrouth," in *Extrait de la Revue International de la Croix-Rouge*, no. 85 (January 1926). See Tachjian, "Etat-nation," 206–44.
15 For an examination of the issue of humanitarian intervention as applied to refugees during the interwar period, see Kévonian, "Réfugiés." For a discussion of the thought of André Mandelstam, human rights, and the rights of minorities, see Kévonian, "Exilés politiques," 245–73.
16 Report by the High Commissioner for Refugees, League of Nations, 1927.XIII.3.1927, 3, cited in Hathaway, "Evolution of Refugee Status," 349. See also Kaprielian, "Nansen Passport." For the Arrangements see NA, RG25 G1, vol. 1465, file 160, and vol. 1484, file 44T.
17 Inter-Governmental Conference, High Commissioner for Refugees, 10–12 May 1926; RG76, Blair to W.N. Walker, Acting Under Secretary of State for External Affairs, Ottawa, 9 Dec. 1924; Memo, Blair to Egan, 29 April 1926; Blair to Sir Joseph Pope, Under-Secretary of State for External Affairs, Ottawa, 24 July 1924; NA RG25 G1, vol. 1484, file 44T, Acting Deputy Minister W.R. Little to Dr O.D. Skelton, 18 August 1927; NA RG76, vol. 637, file 978450, part 8, Blair to Riddell, 6 April 1928.
18 NA, RG25 G1, vol. 1484, file, 44T, T.F. Johnson to Dr W.A. Riddell, Dominion of Canada Advisory Officer in Geneva, 29 July 1927; League of Nations, International Labour Office, A.41.1925. IV. 6; NA, RG76, vol. 215, file 89310, Blair to Egan, 18 March 1927.
19 The statistics for Armenian refugees in Greece vary from approximately forty thousand to one hundred thousand. See Macartney, *Refugees*, chap. 3. Simpson, *The Refugee Problem*, chap. 3. Following the Lausanne Treaty, in the exchange of populations between Greece and Turkey, approximately 1.4 million non-Moslem refugees poured into Greece from Turkey, increasing the population of Greece by nearly 25 per cent to over 5 million. See Barton, *Near East Relief*, 139, 164. RG76, McKinnon and Munro, barristers, Guelph, to W.J. Egan, Deputy Minister, 27 November 1925. The reply from Acting Deputy Minister Blair, 4 December 1925.
20 NA, RG25 G1, vol. 1484, file 44T, Johnson to Riddell, 29 July 1927; see

also vol. 1465, file 160, Johnson to Dandurand, 5 October, 1928; RG76, vol. 637, file 978450, part 9, Riddell to Dandurand, 13 March 1929.
21 RG 76, vol. 480, file 745162, Frank Oliver, Minister of the Interior to Superintendent Scott, 11 April 1908. A regulation requiring *all* immigrants to show $250 landing money was passed in 1921 and rescinded in 1923. The money test continued to apply to Asians except the wife and children under 18 of a person legally domiciled in Canada.
22 *Toronto Globe*, 15 Jan. 1921, 7 Feb. 1920; RG76, vol. 215, file 89616, Memo, Blair to Egan, 18 March 1927; Blair to F.J. McClure of the Robert Reford Steamship Agency, Montreal, 29 May 1923. By contrast, British immigrants were not required to show landing money after 1923. Their transatlantic travel was subsidized by the British and Canadian governments, so that their tickets cost $50, but only $9.73 for agricultural and domestic workers. Epp, *Mennonite Exodus*, 243. When Armenians in Kharkov sought to found an agricultural settlement in the Canadian West, they were told that without the $250 landing money for each man, woman, and child, they would be ineligible for admission. These refugees could not afford to come to Canada. Their fate is mentioned by Paul Tabori in *Anatomy of Exile*, 396, who quotes Alexander Weissberg, *Conspiracy of Silence* (London 1952): "In Kharkov there were about six hundred Armenians; one day in the autumn of 1937 more than three hundred of them were arrested. About a month later the rest shared the same fate."
23 Lucy Lorisian, oral interview, Hamilton; RG76, Blair to Miss Esther M. Jaquith, Near East Relief, New York, 12 August 1924.
24 RG76, William Elliott to Egan, 2 June 1924, on behalf of Kaloust B. Kamourdjeian.
25 United Church Archives, Blair to Rev. Ira Pierce, 11 Jan. 1930. See also RG76, vol. 215, file 89616, Blair to Egan, 4 April 1927; vol. 215, file 89616, Blair to Rev. Ira Pierce, 5 April 1927.
26 Archives of Ontario, MU 9587, records of Kegham Babigian; Mrs D. Miller to Rev. Ira Pierce 12 July 1926; G. Bogue Smart, *Report*, 11 March 1927; Pierce to Kegham Babigian, 11 Dec. 1929; Babigian to Pierce, 25 November 1929; Babigian to Pierce, 15 December 1929, 23 Jan. 1930; RG76, Blair to Rev. D.N. McLachlan, Secretary of the Board of Evangelism and Social Service, United Church of Canada, 28 May 1931.
27 According to the *Revised Statutes of the Government of Canada*, vol. 2, 1927, chap. 93, section 38(a), the governor-in-council had the right to "prohibit" landing of "any immigrant" who did not come by continuous journey and on a through ticket purchased in that country or prepaid in Canada. RG76, vol. 480, file 745162, part 2, Frank Oliver to the Robert

Reford Company, Ottawa, 25 May 1909; also vol. 507, file 783375, Circular, 8 May 1908; RG76, James Alexander Calder, Minister of Immigration and Colonization to F.S. Scott, MP, 7 March 1921.
28 House of Commons, *Debates*, 19 March 1930, 756.
29 Government of Canada, *Sessional Papers, Annual Reports*, Minister of Labour, 1923 and 1927. See also *Toronto Globe*, 15 Feb. 1920; Privy Council Order-in-Council 182 (P.C. 182), 1923; RG76, Blair to F.S. Scott, Galt, 9 July, 1924; Blair to E. Blackadder, MP, 6 June 1922.
30 Ibid., Blair to Turner, 25 Aug. 1925; Blair to F.S. Scott, Galt, 9 July 1924; Blair to Price, 6 Feb. 1926; Departmental Memo, 24 July 1925. See also Blair to George Alexander, 5 Dec. 1922; Blair to Raymond, 5 Dec. 1922.
31 Ibid., Blair to George Alexander, 18 December 1922.
32 Ibid., Mihran Antreassian, Constantinople to the Secretary of Agriculture, 9 Jan. 1923, and the reply from Blair, 6 March 1923. See also Blair to Price, 6 February 1926. Efforts to establish a settlement of Armenian farmers in Ontario and another in the West met with the same obstructions as similar endeavours before the war. See ibid., W.J. Egan, to Armen Amirkhanian, Brantford, 10 Jan. 1924; Blair to F.J. McClure of the Robert Reford Steamship Agency, Montreal, 29 May 1923.
33 League of Nations, High Commission for Refugees, Box C 1378, L.B. Golden to John T. Lawton, 25 May 1929; League of Nations, "Armenian and Russian Refugees," A.48.1927.VIII.6; RG76, Blair to F.S. Scott, 9 July 1924; Blair to Raymond, 5 Dec. 1922; Blair to Dr O.B. Price, M. P., 6 Feb. 1926; Blair to G. Topakyan, 30 July 1923.
34 Ibid. These exchanges took place from 18 Nov. 1922 to 6 March 1923 between the Department and George Alexander, an Armenian, though not a representative of the Armenian community. Efforts to establish an Armenian farming colony met with resistance in spite of the immigration minister's comments that "Colonization rather than immigration is the most pressing need of the hour and colonization always involves directional effort and after-care, sometimes it necessitates assistance in land purchase and always, if developed on a large scale it involves heavy expenditure." *Annual Reports*, 1924–25, vol. 3, 7.
35 RG76, The Honourable George Gordon, Minister to Levon Babayan, 6 Nov. 1925; Memo from Blair to Cullen, private secretary of James Alexander Robb, Minister of Immigration, 29 September 1924. Der Stepanian's family eventually were allowed admission and indeed worked the farm, near Fonthill, Ontario. They planted thirty acres of grapes, which were selling at $85 a ton. In 1929, when they harvested their first crop, the price plunged to $8–10 a ton, and even at that they could not sell all their produce and faced bankruptcy.
36 Ibid., J.S. Fraser, Division Commissioner, Ottawa, to Messrs Murphy, Sherwood, Clarke and Robertson, 23 October 1924.

37 Armenians, mostly Urantzis from the Van region, had settled in the Galt/Cambridge area. John Ishkhanian, oral interview, Cambridge.
38 RG76, Blair to J.M. Stahl, Canadian Immigration Inspector, Boston, regarding a request from Hagop Bogigian of Boston, 29 July 1920; Blair to Turner, 25 Aug. 1925; Memo from Blair to Egan, 28 Jan. 1928.
39 Ibid., Blair to W.N. Walker, Acting Under-Secretary of State for External Affairs, 8 Nov. 1929. *Annual Report of the Immigration Branch*, 1941, cited in Irving Abella and Harold Troper, *None is Too Many*, 230.
40 Oral interviews in Hamilton and St Catharines.
41 Wolverton based his decision on race, culture, and colour. In 5th case of Level 1, printed in full format, *United States v. Cartozian*, District Court, D. Oregon, 6 F.2nd 919, 27 July 1925. See also "The Cartozian Case," *Armenian Review*, vol. 24 (1953) 125–29; Minasian, "The Armenian Immigrant Tide," 108–9. See also RG76, Memo from Blair to Egan, 28 Jan. 1928.
42 The regulation (Privy Council Order 534) allowing the immigration of a broader range of family members, along with more flexible labour requirements, was passed in 1926 and pertained to non-British but also non-Asian migration. RG76, Memo, Blair to Egan, 10 Nov. 1927; Memo, Blair to Egan, 28 Jan. 1928; Armen Amirkhanian to Minister Robert Forke, 4 Jan. 1927. For the nomination scheme, see House of Commons, *Debates*, 19 March 1930, 756.
43 RG76, handwritten remark in margin, initialed by Egan, 21 Jan. 1928. See also ibid., Memo, Blair to Egan, handwritten remark by Egan, 18 Jan. 1928; Departmental Memo, Blair, 30 Jan. 1928. For an examination of bureaucratic secrecy in the Department of Immigration see Reg Whitaker, *Double Standard*. See also Abella and Troper, *None Is Too Many*.
44 RG76, Memo, Blair, 30 Jan. 1928. During this period, immigration regulations were becoming generally more restrictive. *Toronto Globe*, 19 August, 25 August 1930. For ministerial permits awarded on humanitarian grounds, see chapter 17.
45 RG76, Memo, A.L. Jolliffe, Commissioner, 3 Sept. 1930; RG76, O.D. Skelton, for the Secretary of State for External Affairs, to the Secretary of State for Dominion Affairs, London, 18 May 1931; Departmental Circular, 22 Sept. 1930; Circular to Canadian Immigration Inspectors, Eastern Division, 3 Nov. 1930, from Assistant Division Commissioner, Congdon.
46 Statistics from Government of Canada, *Sessional Papers*, Department of Immigration and Colonization, *Annual Reports*, 1900 to 1930.
47 RG76, Memo, Blair, 28 January 1928; ibid., vol. 215, file 89616 Memo, Blair to W.J. Egan, 18 March 1927; ibid., Division Commissioner to Messrs. Murphy, Sherwood, Clarke and Robertson, 23 October 1924;

ibid., J. Obed Smith to the Secretary, Office of the High Commissioner for Canada, 18 December 1922.
48 Little is known about the Armenian Immigration Association group except the names of some of the members, including George Alexander, Charles Sheregian, Krekor Avedissian, Mesak Manoogian, Abraham Haksian, and Marsop Asadoorian.
49 RG76, Blair, Memo, 30 Jan. 1928. The Armenian Immigration Association of Galt made no headway with the government. Not until they established the Canadian Armenian Congress in 1948 did Armenians have an organization that represented the community and effectively negotiated with the government. Armen Amirkhanian, Congregationalist, was a World War I veteran from Brantford, Ontario, studying law in Montreal.
50 RG76, Memo, Blair, 18 Jan. 1928.
51 Ibid., vol. 673, file 978450, part 8, reply of Manager of the French Consulate in Montreal to the Commissioner of the Department of Immigration, September 1927; Roberts, "Shovelling out the Mutinous," 78–9, 84–5. See also, Roberts, *Whence They Came*.
52 RG76, Memo, Blair, 21 Dec. 1927; Blair to McKinnon, barrister, 4 Dec. 1925; Memo, Blair to Egan, 10 Nov. 1927; Blair to Minister James Alexander Robb, 12 Nov. 1924. Also Abella and Troper, *None*.
53 For the Minister's permit, see, for example, Immigration Act, 1927, section 4. See also Irving Horowitz, *Taking Lives: Genocide and State Power* (Transaction Books, 1980), cited in Strom and Parsons, *Facing History and Ourselves*, chapter 11. According to League of Nations, RA/413/40/4, 1929, Armenian refugees found asylum in the following countries: Bulgaria, 22,000; Poland, 1,000; Cyprus, 2,500. Simpson (*Refugee*, 318–19) notes that according to the Nansen Office census, there were 63,000 Armenian refugees in France in 1936. Vernant (*The Refugee in the Post-War World*, 257), gives the figure of 80,000 refugees in France in 1925. According to the annual reports of the United States Commissioner General of Immigration, 22,878 Armenian immigrants entered that country from June 1920 to June 1930.
54 With reference to this donation to the League for Armenian relief abroad, see NA, MG26, vol. 86, W.L.M. King Papers, King to Rev. Dr. A.J. Vining, 5 Dec. 1922. It would take another sixty years for the Canadian government to include refugees as a category in its immigration program and to provide initial assistance in settlement and adaptation.
55 NA, MG26, vol. 86, W.L.M. King Papers, King to Dr. A.J. Vining, General Secretary of the Armenian Relief Association of Canada, 5 Dec. 1922.
56 RG76, Chambers to Sir Horace Rumbold, British High Commissioner, Constantinople, 20 September 1922.
57 Considering their high level of literacy, the immigration literacy test

proved an ineffective mechanism for exclusion of Armenians. Government of Canada, *Sessional Papers, Annual Reports of the Department of Immigration and Colonization*, 1920–31. For entry statistics see also the *Royal Commission on Bilingualism and Biculturalism*, book 4, *The Cultural Contribution of the Other Ethnic Groups*, 239–41.

58 RG76, Blair to Deputy Minister W.J. Egan, 12 December 1923.

CHAPTER NINE

1 Oral interview, Toronto.
2 For refugee women see Cole, *Refugee Women and Their Mental Health*; Epp, *Women without Men*; Kaprielian, "Armenian Refugee Women," and *Pulse of the World*; Martin, *Refugee Women*.
3 Government of Canada, *Sessional Papers, Annual Reports of the Department of Immigration and Colonization*. Those entering by ocean ports alone numbered about 1,250.
4 For difficulties in refugee resettlement, see Murphy, *Flight and Resettlement*.
5 Disrupted developmental time is treated by Erikson in *Identity: Youth and Crisis*. Kasparian, *Armenian Needlework*, 122. Kasparian relates that her father, formerly a man of considerable wealth, found it humiliating to accept financial help from his children.
6 Indeed, seventy-five years after the beginning of the Genocide, survivors continued to search for their kin. *Horizon Weekly*, published in Montreal, ran an advertisement on 12 November 1990 submitted by Hratch Nersessian, in Armenia, seeking his two brothers and his cousins lost during the turmoil of the Genocide.
7 The Turks destroyed hundreds of churches, monasteries, schools, libraries, valuable ancient manuscripts, hospitals, monuments, and a countless number of homes. See chapter 10, "The Quest for Reparations."
8 H. Ergatian, oral interview, Hamilton.
9 M. Stepanian, oral interview, Hamilton: "My sister married him to come to Canada. To be saved. She didn't want to marry him. He was eighteen years older than her. But the go-between convinced her that after she got to Canada, after a few years, she could bring out the rest of us." By the same token, a man might prefer an orphan girl with no surviving relatives, so that he would not have to take on the additional cost and responsibility of bringing out her relatives to join her. Richard Kalinoski's play *Beast on the Moon* deals with the subject of Armenian picture brides. For more on Armenian picture brides see Kaprielian, "Picture Brides."
10 Physical problems were frequently associated with the eyes. Indeed, many

institutions cared for the large number of survivors who had become blind or almost blind as a result of the shortage of clean water, among other factors.

11 Kherdian, *The Road from Home*, 213–14, 228. In Armenian circles engagements were often performed in absentia, but never marriages.
12 K. Lorisian, oral interview, Hamilton. B. Raisian, oral interview, Galt.
13 These letters are in the author's personal collection. This literal translation accurately reflects the style and tone of the originals.
14 See for example, Kaprielian, "The Armeno-American Letter Writer," 26–30. Letters played an important role both in bringing together men and women and in reuniting surviving family members. The widespread use of letter writing was possible because of the prewar improvements in education and the concurrent spread of literacy among Armenians.
15 Cited in Bedrosian, *The Magical Pine Ring*, 57–8.
16 G. Halagian, oral interview, Hamilton. For Apcar, see Isabel Kaprielian, "Diana Apcar: Writer, Diplomat, Humanitarian," in *Hye Sharzoom*, May 1999.
17 Iskouhi Israelian, oral interview, Montreal, in Kaprielian, "The Saved," 6–7.
18 K. Lorisian, oral interview, Hamilton.
19 A. Takvorian, oral interview, Hamilton; V. Ludvigian, oral interview, St Catharines; B. Raisian, oral interview, Galt.
20 K. Tanelian, oral interview.
21 *Yergounk: Revue Littéraire Arménienne*, 1929–1930, Bibliothèque Nubar, Paris, France. In Armenian and French.
22 *Yergounk: Revue Littéraire Arménienne*, vol. 1, no. 10 (January 1930).
23 The exchange of money helped men recover their expenses and should not be construed as the sale of women.
24 An interviewee recounted how her betrothed introduced her to his friends before their marriage: "They were all short and fat. By comparison my fiancé looked like a prince."
25 M. Stepanian, oral interview, Hamilton.
26 E. Garabedian recalled how at his mother's funeral he learned for the first time in his life that she had had children by a Turk and had abandoned them when she escaped. Fresno, California.
27 A. Ungerian, oral interview, Fresno, California. For a novel dealing with similar issues see Hacikyan, *Un été sans aube*.
28 G. H. Karageulian, "The Question of the Islamicized Armenian Women," *Hairenik*, 5 May 1916.
29 F. Onassian, oral interview, Toronto.
30 A. Uvoian, oral interview, St Catharines.
31 As Erik Erikson has stated, "The danger of any period of large-scale uprooting and transmigration is that exterior crises will, in too many individuals and generations, upset the hierarchy of developmental crises

and their built-in correctives and that man will lose those roots that must be planted firmly in meaningful life cycles. For man's true roots are nourished in the sequence of generations and he loses his taproots in disrupted developmental time, not in abandoned localities." *Insight and Responsibility.*

32 Kherdian, *Road from Home*, 140, 209.
33 N. Haroutounian, oral interview, Fresno, California.
34 A. Uvoian, oral interview, St Catharines; K. Topalian, oral interview, Brantford.
35 A. Takvorian, oral interview, Hamilton
36 Because of United States immigration restrictions and the tight quota for Armenian immigrants after 1924, many Armenians destined to the United States waited out their time in Cuba, Mexico, Brazil, Argentina, Venezuela, or Canada.
37 Song sung by Kévork Baghdjian to the author, 1993.
38 L. Lorisian, oral interview, Hamilton.
39 Baghdasarian, (*National Almanac*), 186–90. In author's personal collection.
40 A. Takvorian, oral interview, Hamilton.
41 A. Lorisian, oral interview, Hamilton.
42 A. Takvorian, oral interview, Hamilton; T. Fanfarian, oral interview, Hamilton.
43 G. Elemian, oral interview, Toronto; I. Israelian, oral interview, Montreal. For love and the picture bride, see Kaprielian, "Marriage and Love in America."
44 Oksen Teghtsoonian, Memoirs, Archives of Ontario, Multicultural History Society of Ontario Collection, chapter 14; S. Tateosian, oral interview, Brantford; Osanna Kinosian, cited in Bedrosian, *Pine Ring*, 54–5.
45 M. Stepanian, oral interview, Hamilton.
46 A. Takvorian, oral interview, Hamilton.
47 For refugee family fragmentation, reconfiguration, and variability, see Epp, *Women without Men*, especially chapter 6.
48 Hapet M. Pilibosian, (*Practical Hygiene*).
49 For details about the ARAC, see the previous chapter. I am preparing an in-depth study of the Armenian children, both boys and girls, brought in by the ARAC and the UCC.
50 NA, RG76, vol. 215, file 89616, Memo, George Bogue Smart, Supervisor of Juvenile Immigration, to Mr. Featherston, 27 February 1923. See also Smart's letter to Rev. Dr A.J. Vining, Secretary of the Armenian Relief Association of Canada, 14 April 1923. Unless otherwise stated all National Archives references are in this file and will be indicated by RG76. It is unclear whether the term "of age" means sixteen or eighteen.

51 RG76, F.C. Blair to Vining, 28 May 1923; Vining to Smart, 31 May 1923; Vining to the Honorable Charles Stewart, Minister of Immigration, 27 November 1922. Around 1922 the Armenian Relief Fund of Canada changed its name to the Armenian Relief Association of Canada. Henceforth it will be referred to as the ARAC.
52 H. Injeyan, oral interview, Hamilton.
53 Onnig Shangaian wrote about his personal experience at Georgetown in a short piece, "The Nightmare," published in the boys' periodical *Ararat* (June 1926).
54 RG76, Memo, Smart to Egan, 26 December 1923.
55 K. Margarian, oral interview, Toronto.
56 United Church Archives (henceforth UCA), Pierce to Milley, 17 April 1930.
57 Rev. Andrew Lane, quoted in Apramian, *Georgetown Boys*, 48.
58 UCA, Minutes of the Board of Evangelism and Social Service, Minutes of the Sub-Executive Committee, 18 November 1927, 39.
59 *Toronto Globe*, 13 January 1928.
60 UCA, Minutes of the Board of Evangelism and Social Service, Minutes of the Sub-Executive Committee, 13 April 1928, 59; ibid., Minutes of the Board of Evangelism and Social Service, Minutes of the Sub-Executive Committee, 15 June 1928, 75.

CHAPTER TEN

1 NA, RG14 D2, vol. 242, file 98d. Printed copy. Errol M. McDougall, Commissioner, "Reparations 1930–31, Special Report upon Armenian Claims," Ottawa, 9 May 1931, 3. See also RG117, vol. 20, file 229, C.H. Cahan, "Report to Council: Armenian Claims," Ottawa, 20 January 1932. Unless otherwise stated, all references in this account are from McDougall's or Cahan's reports.
2 As a point of interest, Canada did not ratify the Lausanne Treaty, claiming that the Dominion had not been invited to the deliberations and had not signed the proposed treaty. Canadian authorities said Canada would not take exception to the treaty being ratified by Britain, but Canada would assume no obligation under the terms of the treaty, in particular the terms relating to the Straits of Bosphorus and Dardanelles. See NA, RG7 G21, vol. 636, pt. 2, 1924–25.
3 Cahan, 14. For terms of the Convention see, RG7 C21, vol. 2(b) and RG7 G21, vol. 636, pt. 2. See also Treaty Series, no. 3 (1924), Convention between the United Kingdom, France, Italy and Japan Relative to the Assessment and Reparation of Damage Suffered in Turkey by the Nationals of the Contracting Powers, Paris, 23 November 1923, 5. It seems

Japan was not actively involved in the actual proceedings in Paris, and Rumania may have been included later.

4 RG7 C21, vol. 2(b) and RG7 G21, vol. 636, pt. 2. See Byng's coded telegram to the Secretary of State for Dominion Affairs, Ottawa, 4 August 1925; telegram from Secretary of State for Dominion Affairs to Mr Hoare, the British Chargé d'Affaires in Constantinople, 6 August 1925; and letter from Secretary of State for Dominion Affairs to Governor General, Lord Byng of Vimy, 25 August 1925. Ironically, seven years later the then secretary of state, Charles Hazlitt Cahan, stated in his report that the Armenian claims should have been but *were not* filed with this tribunal.

5 Public Record Office, London, BT 15/103, 112569, F. Durrant to Keyes, Paris, 31 July 1925; Keyes to Paris Commission, St Catharines, 27 April 1926. To be on the safe side, Keyes sent copies of his claims both to Constantinople and to Paris. Shortly afterwards Keyes died and the claimants hired Grace Brown from Detroit to pursue their case.

6 Lausanne Conference on Near Eastern Affairs, 1922–23; *Records of Proceedings and Draft Terms of Peace* (London: HMSO 1923), 439, 669, 833.

7 By the terms of Article 58 of the Treaty of Lausanne, both Turkey and the Allied Powers renounced "all pecuniary claims for the loss and damage suffered ... as the result of acts of war or measures of requisition, sequestration, dispossession or confiscation." See also RG13, vol. 2215, file 405/1932, "Petition for the Appointment of a Royal Commission for the Examination and Assessment of Claims for War Damage Suffered in Turkey," addressed to the Governor General in Council, Ottawa, and signed by D. Windrum Carlisle and Louis Coté, 30 June 1931, "Right to Compensation," 11.

8 See Treaty Series, no. 3 (1924), Convention between the United Kingdom, France, Italy and Japan Relative to the Assessment and Reparation of Damage Suffered in Turkey by the Nationals of the Contracting Powers, Paris, 23 November 1923, 3. There was also the confiscation of battleships being built in England and paid for by the Turkish government.

9 McDougall, 3. Also PRO, BT 15/103, 112569. There is some discrepancy in the number of claims sent to Paris and considered by the Paris Commission. In his report, Cahan refers to 208 original claims. Order-in-Council 571, 12 March 1932, indicates that 204 claims were originally sent to Paris, followed by seventy others that arrived too late for consideration, making a total of 274 claims. In his statement to the prime minister, 27 January 1932, Cahan indicates that 201 claims were deposited with the Paris Commission and 73 late claims. The Paris Commission indicated that 267 had been received. See MG 26K, vol. 434, part 3,

microfilm M-1309, 383336–42, Cahan to Prime Minister R.B. Bennett, 27 January 1932. See also RG13, vol. 2215, file 405/1932, "Petition," Annex 1, List of Claimants. This list, prepared by Carlisle and Coté, confirms that 201 claims were adjudicated by the Paris Commission and 73 were not. There seems to be no explanation why 73 claims were dispatched by Canadian authorities to Paris too late for consideration.

10 Cahan, 7. See also PRO, London, BT 15/103, 112569.
11 RG13, vol. 2215, file 405/1932, "Petition," 13. Carlisle and Coté stress that these claims had been sent to Paris "without reference to the claimants" (underlining theirs). In "Petition," Annex 3, 2, the claimants also state that "in fact many of them were actually unaware that their claims were in Paris and not in Ottawa, as they had not received notice of the transfer from the Canadian Government, or Reparation Commission."
12 McDougall, 3.
13 See RG19, E2 (c), vol. 545, file 135-8-70. Grace Brown practised with the law firm of Leithauser, Brown, Lenehan and O'Donnell in Detroit, Michigan. It is unclear exactly when the Armenians engaged Brown or why they hired legal counsel from the United States.
14 RG13, "Petition," Carlisle and Coté, annex 3, 1–2.
15 RG117, vol. 20, file 229, Grace H. Brown to claimants, Detroit, 3 February 1930; file 231, "In the Matter of the Estate of Hampartz Daloo Kashian," 18 May 1932.
16 RG117, vol. 20, file 229, Grace H. Brown to claimants, Detroit, 3 February 1930. For the subcommissions and the examination of claims see RG7, C 21, vol. 2(b) and RG7 G21, vol. 636, Report by British Delegate, H.E. Garle to The Lords Commissioners, His Majesty's Treasury, 7 August 1925, 5–9. Fourteen representatives of the commission had been engaged in investigations in Turkey but not a single one for the Armenian Canadian claimants.
17 PRO, London, BT 15/103, 112569, Sir Eliot Colvin, Canadian Armenian Cases, 5 April 1929.
18 Cahan, 7.
19 RG7, C21, vol. 2(b) and vol. 636, Report by British Delegate, H.E. Garle to The Lords Commissioners, His Majesty's Treasury, 7 August 1925, 5–7.
20 Cahan, 7.
21 Cahan, 8.
22 RG13, "Petition," annex 3, 2–3. For a general account of Armenian losses, see Aharonian and Nubar, *Arménie*. See also Baghdjian, *La confiscation*, 261–69, and Gidel et al., *Confiscation*.
23 Bryce, *The Treatment of Armenians*.
24 The records are unclear as to how many expert reports were submitted

25 See RG25, series A-2, vol. 163, file C13/5, E.J. Elliot to Miss L. Secchi of the High Commissioner's Office, 26 October 1932.
26 McDougall, 12, Brown, op. cit., 2.
27 Questionnaire in author's possession.
28 Brown, op. cit. These included Philippe Roy, minister for Canada at Paris, Mr Desy, the chargé d'affaires, and Mr Dupuis, first secretary of the legation.
29 Cahan, 8; Brown, op. cit., 2.
30 At this point, two representatives from Britain sat on the Commission: Sir Eliot Colvin, president of the commission, and Mr Jesse-Curely, British delegate. The others were Mr Tripepi (Italy) and Mr Giraudoux (France, secretary general).
31 McDougall, 3, 10: Brown op. cit., 2.
32 See MG 26K, vol. 434, part 3, microfilm – 1309, Cahan to Bennett, 27 January 1932. Funds cited are in old currency.
33 PRO, London, BT 15/103, 112569, Reliquat, Canadian/Armenian Claim. The scale used by the commission was based on "minimum values of minimum quantities" set forth by experts. Thus, the minimum value of the smallest farm, with buildings, trees, and movables, capable of supporting five people, i.e., a farm of twenty-five to fifty acres, would be valued at about £T467, while a large farm of about 3,300 acres with buildings, timber, and movables would be valued at £T15,347. Most of the farms in this group were less than one hundred acres.
34 Brown, op. cit., 2.
35 PRO, London, BT 15/103, 112569, Sir Eliot Colvin, "Note to be placed with the Canadian-Armenian claims," 18 April 1929.
36 RG13, "Petition," annex 1, 5. Carlisle was incensed that out of a surplus fund of almost £300,000 sterling, only the modest amount of £4,000 sterling had been paid for the massacre of women and children. He unsuccessfully sought an allocation for the property claims from a distributable balance handed over by the Paris Commission to Britain. The British government, however, awarded this meagre amount to those who had already received payment by offering a further dividend of 2½ percent on the amounts of their grants. McDougall, 4, 8; Brown, op. cit., 2. Carlisle to Calouste Gulbenkian, Paris, 14 November 1930, in the Bibliothèque Nubar, Armenian General Benevolent Union Archives, Paris.
37 Macartney, *Refugees*, 59. "It certainly appears," adds Macartney, "as though the Armenians lost it and the Allies got it."
38 RG13, vol. 2215, file 405/1932, "Petition" for the Appointment of a Royal Commission for the Examination and Assessment of Claims for

War Damage Suffered in Turkey, Addressed to the Governor General in Council. Ottawa, signed by Carlisle and Coté, 30 June 1931, 7.

39 Bryce, *Treatment*, 229, document no. 54, "Erzeroum: Report, dated 25th September, 1915, drawn up by the American Consul-General at Trebizond, after his return from a visit to Erzeroum; Communicated by the American Committee for Armenian and Syrian Relief." The consul-general's visit took place in August 1915.

40 Bryce, *Treatment*, 227, document no. 53, "Erzeroum: Record (undated) of an Interview between the Rev. H.J. Buxton and the Rev. Robert Stapleton, a Missionary of the American Board, Resident at Erzeroum from before the Outbreak of War until after the Capture of the City by the Russians."

41 Alamuddin, *Papa Kuenzler and the Armenians*. Kuenzler was a Swiss national working for the German missionary movement primarily in Urfa.

42 For confiscation of Armenian property and bank accounts consult Baghdjian, *La confiscation*. For the terms of the Abandoned Property Law, see ibid., 255–60 and Toriguian, *The Armenian Question*, 135. For a discussion of government debates regarding the confiscation of Armenian property see Dadrian, *Armenian Genocide*, 222–5. See also Simpson, *The Splendid Blond Beast*, regarding the major beneficiaries of Armenian wealth: the members of the Young Turk party and their friends. See also, Dalrymple, *From the Holy Mountain*.

43 Davis, *Slaughterhouse Province*, 55.

44 On insurance policies see Morgenthau, *Ambassador*. See also Karagueuzian, "The Armenian Genocide," and Toriguian, "Armenian Insurance Claims." A class-action suit brought by Armenians in California against the New York Life Insurance Company reaped some compensation for beneficiaries. See "He Stands Up in the Name of Armenians," *Los Angeles Times*, 27 April 2001. New York Life finally settled on a payment of $20 million to the Armenian heirs, including $3 million to be given to nine Armenian civic organizations. See "Insurer Settles Armenian Genocide Suit," *Los Angeles Times*, 29 January 2004.

45 Cahan, 2.

46 Cahan, 2–3; McDougall, 4. Order-in-Council, P.C. 4032 (3 Nov. 1921) and P.C. 2100 (6 September 1930). It is not clear whether the terms of reference included all of annex 1 or only clause 9 of annex 1.

47 McDougall, 4; Cahan, 3.

48 RG13, vol. 2215, file 405/1932, annex 1, List of Claimants.

49 For Carlisle's position regarding McDougall's use of the Bryce report, see RG13, vol. 2215, file 405/1932, "Petition," Annex 4, 9–12, 22–3, and in particular, McDougall's use of Bryce's general conclusions as applying to the specific area pertaining to the claims.

50 In their "Petition," Carlisle and Coté raise this important point. See "Petition," op. cit., annex 4, 13–14.
51 McDougall, 4–8.
52 RG25, series A-2, vol. 163, file C13-5, Carlisle to the Secretary, Board of Trade, Ottawa, 4 December 1931.
53 Ibid., F. Durrant to Miss L. Secchi, London, 3 December 1931.
54 RG117, vol. 20, file 229, C.H. Cahan, "Report to Council: Armenian Claims," Ottawa, 20 January 1932, 12.
55 Ibid., 12.
56 RG13, "Petition," annex 4, 5–7. For instance, Carlisle refers to the case of Michael Khamis, no. 1332, James Friel, Commissioner, 16 February 1927, and Mrs Beatrice Aramian.
57 McDougall, 11.
58 Ibid., 11–12
59 See Kaprielian-Churchill, "Migratory Caravans," 20–38 and "Kghi Village Educational Associations in North America before 1915," 317–39.
60 RG13, vol. 2215, file 405/1932, "Petition," annex 4, 18, McDougall's Interim Report, 3 March 1931, and McDougall's Final Report.
61 "Petition," annex 4, 20, citing Sumner's Report, 26 February 1924, 8, clause 8.
62 At least eleven names matched in both lists: Martin Avakian, Manoug Avedisian, George Boghosian, Harry Bogosian, Ohannes Chichakian, David Goshgarian, Harry Mooradian, Siragan Siroonian, Edward Terzian, Artin (Hagop) Terzian, and Peter Vartanian.
63 RG19, E2 (c) vol. 544, file 135-8 (3), Royal Commission on Reparations, case 1332, James Friel, Commissioner, 16 February 1927.
64 See Canada Naturalization Act, R.S. 1914, chapter 44, which states that naturalized citizens "have to all intents and purposes the status of a natural born British subject."
65 Not only Armenians but others too expressed dissatisfaction with McDougall's evaluations. On 21 June 1935, the Prisoner of War Association wrote to members of Parliament complaining that their claims had been "improperly adjudged" by McDougall. Under the previous commissions the awards to prisoners of war had been "adequate and fair," but under the McDougall Commission 60 percent of the claims had been dismissed, and the awards he granted were minimal by comparison with the earlier decisions. See RG19, vol. 544, file 135-8 (3), Prisoner of War Association, Toronto, to the Honourable Members of His Majesty's Government of the Dominion of Canada. Earlier commissions included those established under Sir John Douglas Hazen, chief justice of New Brunswick, by Order-in-Council, P.C. 4032 (3 November 1921); Hon. William Pugsley, appointed 13

March 1923, and James Friel, K.C., of Moncton, New Brunswick, appointed 19 June 1925. McDougall was appointed on 6 September 1930.
66 RG117, vol. 20, files 229–31.
67 RG13, vol. 2215, file 405/1932, "Petition," 14–15, and annex 1. One of Carlisle's basic arguments in the "Petition" was that McDougall's mandate had been to examine the claims to ascertain whether or not he had jurisdiction over them and not, as McDougall had done, to treat the claims as if they were on trial. For the legal arguments pro and con see "Petition" and Cahan's report.
68 "Petition," annex 4, 24.
69 The British High Commissioner in Ottawa years later described Cahan as "generally accepted as the mouth-piece of the Holt, Gundy and other big business interests in Montreal." Kealey, "State Repression of Labour," 303n64.
70 NA, MG2 3 B1, vols. 2–5, Charles Hazlitt Cahan Papers.
71 Cahan, 15–17.
72 Cahan, 17–18. In this clause, Cahan made no mention of those who had owned property outright in the Ottoman Empire.
73 MG26K, vol. 434, part 3, microfilm M-1309, p. 383336–42, Cahan to Prime Minister R.B. Bennett, 27 January 1932. It is unclear why the amount was reduced from $350,000 to $300,000.
74 RG13, vol. 2215, file 405/1932, Thomas Mulvey, Under-Secretary of State and Deputy Custodian to Georges Gonthier, Auditor-General, Ottawa, 9 February 1932.
75 Ibid., Gonthier to Mulvey, Ottawa, 12 Feb. 1932, citing *Hansard*, 1931, unrevised edition, 4670.
76 RG13, vol. 2215, file 405/1932, Mulvey to Gonthier, Ottawa, 15 Feb. 1932.
77 Ibid., Memo (probably internal) from C.P. Plaxton, Deputy Minister of Justice, to Mr Edwards, 25 February 1932, 4, citing from Cahan's Report and from Despatch from Secretary of State for the Colonies to the Governor General of Canada, 27 April 1920.
78 Ibid., Memo from C.P. Plaxton, Deputy Minister of Justice to Mr Edwards, 25 February 1932, 4–6.
79 Ibid., draft of letter from Plaxton to Auditor-General, Ottawa, 25 February 1932.
80 Ibid., Cahan to Hugh Guthrie, Minister of Justice, 7 March 1932.
81 Ibid., Guthrie to the Auditor-General, 8 March 1932.
82 Order-in-Council 571. See also RG13, series A-2, vol. 2215, file 405/1932, and RG19 E2 (c), vol. 545, file 135-8-70.
83 By March 1932, Canada had received approximately $26,672,244.06 in reparations from Germany.

84 RG117, vol. 20, files 230–1. It is not indicated why only 257 claimants and not 274 received compensation.
85 RG150, acc. 1992–93/166, vol. 3343, no. 3031466, seq. 37.
86 These figures represented the lower amounts actually granted by the Paris Commission.
87 RG117, vol. 20, files 229–31.
88 Coté was a member of the law firm of Thompson, Coté, Burgess and Code of Ottawa. For the lawyer's percentage, see RG117, vol. 20, file 231, "In the matter of the Estate of Hampartz Daloo Kashian."
89 RG19, E2(c), vol. 545, file 135–8–70, Georges Gonthier, Auditor General, Report, 11.
90 See RG117, vol. 20, files 230–1.
91 RG13, vol. 2215, file 405/1932, Memo by D. Windrum Carlisle, 6 January 1931.
92 Vahakn Dadrian writes that the decision to destroy the Armenian community was already in place in the Young Turk party well before the war. See "The Secret Young-Turk Ittihadist Conference," 173–202.
93 Dadrian, *History*, 216–17, 312–14; introduction, xxviin14.
94 Ibid. Lord Kinross took the position that the Young Turks organized an official state campaign by force of arms as if the Armenians were a "foreign enemy," not Turkish citizens.
95 Cahan, 11.

CHAPTER ELEVEN

1 RG13, vol. 2215, file 405/1932, annex 1, List of Claimants.
2 *Vernon's City Directory*, 1941. The south side of Carlton St consisted largely of factories and fields. The Ontario Street names are from the rail lines at Kensington Place to Carlton Street.
3 J. Kasoian, oral interview, Brantford; A. Raffi, oral interview, Cambridge; Y. Lucasian, oral interview, Toronto; Rev. Arden Ashjian (*Tableau and History*). Jabaghjour, in the Bingol region, was often included as part of Keghi.
4 H. Torosian and A. Torosian, oral interview, St Catharines. Ashjian, (*Tableau and History*), 228, gives the total number of Armenian families in St Catharines before the war as five.
5 This same process was evident in the Armenian farming community in Fresno, California, where farmers often spent years elsewhere, working and saving until they could afford to buy farmland in the San Joaquin Valley.
6 G. Essayan, oral interview, Brantford.
7 Henry Ford's enticement of a five-dollar day (1914) combining wage and profit sharing attracted hundreds of Armenian workers to Detroit,

making Highland Park a major centre of Armenian settlement. See Meyer, *The Five-Dollar Day*.
8 *Population: Local Subdivisions, Census of Canada*, 1941, vol. 11, 190, gives the population of St Catharines in 1921 as 19,881 and in 1931 as 24,753. The same census gives the percentage increase in population from 1921 to 1931 for Brantford and St Catharines as 2.27 percent and 24.51 percent, respectively. *Census*, 1941, vol. 11, 210. In 1941, St Catharines had a population of 30,275 and in 1951, the population reached 37,984. *Census of Canada*, 1951, vol. 1.
9 *Vernon's City Directory*, 1931
10 See Avery, "Continental European Immigrant Workers." See also Brody, *Steelworkers in America*, chap. 3, "The Breakdown of Craft Unionism."
11 *Vernon's City Directory*, 1931.
12 Information about General Motors in St Catharines is from various articles in the *St Catharines Standard* and from documents in the General Motors Archives, St Catharines. I would like to thank Byron Blundell, Director of Public Relations at the time I was researching this material, for giving me access to these records and for arranging a tour of the foundries before their final closure.

The records showed some inconsistency about dates. For example, both 1893 and 1901 are given for the formation of the McKinnon Dash and Metal Works Company. McKinnon Industries changed its name officially to General Motors, St Catharines, in 1969. (I will use both names interchangeably.) The foundry was moved from the Ontario Street plant to the new site in 1952. Armenians continued to work in the foundries, even though the job site was now situated away from the Armenian quarter. Some continued floor moulding as pattern moulders, while others were retrained in the modern automated process of the new foundry. For an examination of Hamilton, see Dear, Drake, and Reeds, *Steel City*, particularly the article by Wood, "Emergence of the Modern City."
13 Oral interviews with H. Torosian, St Catharines; P. Kaprielian, Hamilton; A. Melkonian, Windsor.
14 Heron, *Working in Steel*, 165. For the Depression, see Safarian, *The Canadian Economy*; Horn, *The Dirty Thirties*, and "The Great Depression." For an account of social welfare in Canada during the Depression, see Struthers. "How Much is Enough?"
15 *St Catharines Standard*.
16 G. Raician, oral interview, Cambridge. N. Lorisian of Hamilton recalls: "When Mr _____ started working ... he was just a young kid. The work was heavy. Really heavy. So my dad who was an old pro did his own work as a moulder in the ... foundries, working extra hard, then helped Mr _____ do half of his job as well. Until he caught on."
17 J. Kasoian, oral interview, Brantford.

18 Armenians living in the vicinity of GM also complained about the drop hammer, which shook their houses and cracked the plaster.
19 H. Torosian, oral interview, St Catharines.
20 N. Lorisian, oral interview, Hamilton.
21 A. Torosian, oral interview, St Catharines. With respect to factory workers generally during this period, Heron writes, "Consent was probably the predominant consciousness of factory workers in Canada between the wars." Heron, *Working in Steel*, 173.
22 T. Rice, oral interview, Hamilton. Rice, former assistant superintendent of works at the Harvester, noted that, while the malleable was largely in the hands of Armenians, the Poles ran the grey-iron foundries at the Harvester. Oral interviews indicate that in 1945 about two hundred Armenians lived in Galt and about 90 percent of the men worked at the Galt Malleable. During the 1940s about 25 percent of the factory work force at Clare Brothers consisted of Armenians.
23 H. Torosian, oral interview, St Catharines.
24 See Kaprielian, "Earning a Living: 1900–29," 60–6.
25 Rice, oral interview, Hamilton. Everywhere, Armenian grocers helped the community if they were able. In St Catharines, an interviewee remarked that Avak Mooradian had given her family $9000 credit for food until her husband was back at regular work at GM.
26 A. Takvorian, oral interview, Hamilton. According to Thomas Rice, when the Depression was over, the company required repayment, but after a short time, forgave the "loans." Thousands of other workers resisted relief. For the attitude of unemployed workers see Bliss and Grayson, *The Wretched of Canada*. Also Struthers. "How Much is Enough?"
27 For "boondoggling," i.e., making sham public works projects in return for relief, like cleaning dandelions from boulevards, see Gray, *The Winter Years*, and Horn, *Dirty Thirties*.
28 H. Torosian, interview.
29 See Manley, "Communists and Auto Workers," 105–33. See also Morton, *Working People*. Unless otherwise stated, all references to union formation in St Catharines are from Hygus Torosian, both in oral interviews and in the article by Torosian, "Local 199 UAW-CIO St Catharines, Ontario, General Motors," in *News: the Bulletin of the Canadian Auto Workers ITCA Canada*, Local 199, St Catharines, 24, no. 6 (Sept. 1989).
30 Communists, working through their union organization, the Workers' Unity League (a cousin of the Trade Union Unity League in the United States and affiliated with the Red International of Labour Unions in Moscow), had already started activities at McKinnon's before 1935, the year the CIO got under way and the year the WUL was disbanded by orders of the Seventh Congress of the Comintern, which called for a united popular front against fascism. For the Workers' Unity League, see

Manley, "Communism and the Canadian Working Class. Refer also to Friesen and Taksa, "Workers' Education in Australia and Canada. For the relationship between the Communist party and the Canadian labour movement, see Abella, *Nationalism, Communism and Canadian Labour*; see also Avery, "Dangerous Foreigners," and Abella, *The Canadian Labour Movement*.

31 It was not unusual for "foreigners" to change their names. For example, John Navis, Communist leader of the Ukrainian Labour Farmer Temple Association, was born Navizivsky. See Avery, "Ethnic Loyalties," 70, and Avery, "Dangerous Foreigners," 135.

32 The McKinnon Employee Council wanted to shift from irregular paydays to a standardized system, so that paydays would consistently fall on either Fridays or Mondays. Their goal was to facilitate family budgeting, particularly for mortgage payments. See David Brody, "The Origins of Modern Steel Unionism," 13–29.

33 This move preceded the Flint, Michigan, sit-down strike which started later in December and ended on 11 February 1937, when GM recognized the UAW. *St Catharines Standard*, 27 June 1967; V. Ludvigian, oral interview, St Catharines.

34 The ratification took place at the time of the successful strike at GM in Oshawa (1937). Regarding company "agreement," see "McKinnon Doings," 6 May 1937, GM Archives, St Catharines.

35 The company and the government argued that the St Catharines plant was only an auto parts plant and did not fall under the same classification as the principal plants in Oshawa and Windsor. Consequently, workers in St Catharines were not entitled to the same package. Manley states that wage levels and working conditions were "appreciably inferior in the parts sector, which existed in an almost colonial relationship to the primary producer." "Communists and Auto Workers," 124.

36 Picketers included the United Coal Miners of Cape Breton and the International Wood Workers of Western Canada. *St Catharines Standard*, 11 to 29 September 1941.

37 See also NA, RG27, vol. 413, Strike no. 213. Also NA, MG30 A94/ vol. 27, J.L. Cohen Papers (Cohen was the lawyer representing the employees); UAW Local 199, 1941–42; Ontario Archives, RG 7–30–0–120. See also Heron, *Working in Steel*; Kealey, "Canadian Working-Class History"; Palmer, "'Taking It"; Manley, "Communists and Auto Workers"; Jack Scott, *Canadian Workers*.

38 In fact, workers had to wait many months before they received a wage increase.

39 Lawrence later was elected mayor of Hamilton (Rice, oral interview). Manley refers to a similar point of view: "Let the English workers join first." "Communists and Auto Workers," 119.

40 Armenians thought the Harvester responded more to their needs than many other big plants. By comparison, they said, Harvester had "more heart." Certainly, during the Depression, Harvester had a much better track record of helping its employees than most other major companies in Hamilton, and as a matter of course it provided some safety features, medical care, garden plots, and pensions. For a discussion of corporate welfarism in the Harvester, see Ozanne, *A Century of Labor-Management Relations*. According to informants, GM also gave the workers garden plots and supplied them with seeds during the Depression.

41 The Canadian Car and Foundry had taken over the old Pratt and Letchworth Malleable works in 1913, but people still referred to the plant as the Malleable or, more usually, as the "Mybil."

42 G. and V. Raician, oral interviews, Cambridge. Bejian wrote his memoirs, which were mysteriously "lost" by the publisher.

43 NA, RG27, vol. 443, Strike no. 192; *Brantford Expositor*, 26 August 1977, Centennial Issue. The bitterness of families was evident in interviews forty years later.

44 G. Raician, oral interview, Cambridge. Raician noted that H.J.B. Bassett, General Manager and 60 percent owner of the company, eventually dismissed the foreman.

45 G. Raician, oral interview, Cambridge; RG27, vol. 425, Strike no. 47; Ontario Archives, RG7-30-0-218; *Toronto Globe and Mail*, February and March 1943. The victory was incomplete, as Galt Malleable continued to recognize employer-sponsored "associations."

46 Letter addressed to "Whom It May Concern" from T.W. Price, Warden, Holybrook House Training Course, Reading, 31 December 1942. Torosian credits the Workers Educational Association and Drummond Wren of Toronto for giving the men "education in regards to unions, and how to get a better understanding of economics and politics and its influence on the working people." On one of his regular lecture trips to St Catharines, Wren suggested to Torosian that he apply for a scholarship for further study in England (Torosian, "Local 199"). For a discussion of the Workers Educational Association, see Radforth and Sangster, "Labour and Learning."

47 Torosian, in a note to the author, 1992.

48 For deportation from Canada, see Avery, "Dangerous Foreigners"; Roberts, "Shovelling out the 'Mutinous,'" 77–110, and "*Whence they Came*"; Petryshyn, "R.B. Bennett," 43–54; Drystek, "Deportation from Canada."

49 George Raician, oral interview, Cambridge, Ontario; H. Torosian, oral interview, St Catharines.

50 The change of tactics occurred after 1928, following the Sixth Congress of the Comintern. See Kolasky, *The Shattered Illusion*. This quotation is

taken from Diggins, *The Rise and Fall of the American Left*, 168. See also Avery, "Dangerous Foreigners."

51 For the activities of the Communists in Canada, see Avakumovic, *The Communist Party in Canada*; Avery, "Dangerous Foreigners," and "Ethnic Loyalties," 68–93; Balawyder, *Canadian-Soviet Relations*, chap. 10; Buck, *Thirty Years*; Beeching and Clark, *Yours in the Struggle*; Kolasky, *The Shattered Illusion*; Manley, "Canadian Communists." For the Workers' Unity League, see Manley, "Communism," and Petryshyn, "R.B. Bennett." See also Abella, *Nationalism, Communism and Canadian Labour*.

52 Mirak mentions their support for the Lawrence, Massachusetts, strike in 1912 and their support for striking Armenians at the Detroit Malleable Foundry in the same year. Mirak, *Torn between Two Lands*, 91.

53 Indeed, by 1946 Communists and their allies had won many top leadership positions in nearly half of all CIO unions in the United States, and they had their greatest success in Detroit, Michigan, particularly in the UAW at the Ford River Rouge plant. Stepan-Norris, "Communist Leadership."

54 Without union membership lists it is difficult to determine accurately the relationship between Armenian political affiliation and trade union membership and to ascertain the numbers and dates of affiliation. The UAW files housed at Brock University, St Catharines, do not provide these early lists. However, an informal survey disclosed that most of those who initially refused to join were Dashnaks.

55 The strike started approximately three months after Hitler invaded the Soviet Union. Communists in Canada vociferously and wholeheartedly supported the war effort and encouraged their affiliates to work hard "for democracy." Presumably, some Communists in the UAW in St Catharines participated in the strike with reluctance, for a strike slowed war production.

The All-Canadian Congress of Labour and the CIO amalgamated to form the CCL. In 1943, the CCL combined forces with the socialist CCF party.

56 By 1950, "Communist-dominated" unions had all been virtually expelled from the CIO. The purge in Canada was just as effective. By 1951 the Canadian Congress of Labour had been "cleansed" of Communist leadership. Abella, *Nationalism, Communism*, 221.

57 For a discussion of the changing relationship between industrialists and labour, with a focus on the impact on workers, see Meyer, *The Five Dollar Day*; Brody, *Steelworkers in America*; Thompson, *The Making of the English Working Class*; Hobsbawm, *Labouring Men*; Gutman, *Work, Culture, and Society*.

58 P. Lorisian, oral interview, Hamilton.

59 Elliott, *Beginning Again at Ararat*, 140.
60 For example, the *Antranik* newspaper, published in the province of Sivas, reported in 1905 that a group of Armenian women working in a rug factory agitated for an increase in wages. When the owner, an Armenian, refused, the women went on strike. Other women collected money to help them but the workers refused to accept their assistance. They won the strike and also won fame as the first group of women to go on strike in the Armenian provinces. Conversation with historian Ardashes Kardashian, Paris, 1987.
61 See, for example, Boudjikanian-Keuroghlian, *Les Arméniens*, 123–7. In the Rhone-Alpes region in 1926, Armenian refugees were hired by leather, mechanical, metallurgical, textile, dry cleaning, and weaving enterprises. The author notes that at Décines, about 88 percent of the Armenian women had a job. The percentage is given in G. Bardakdjian, *La communauté arménienne de Décines*, 1925–1971 (Université Lyon II, 1972), 132. Boudjikanian emphasizes that about 53 percent of working women were employed as skilled workers, largely in textile factories, and about 19 percent were hired as unskilled workers, and 18 percent were domestic servants. By contrast, about 47 percent of the men were employed in unskilled labour, 22 percent were in skilled work, and 20 percent were artisans (126–7). See also Mirak, *Torn between Two Lands*.
62 A. Takvorian, oral interview, Hamilton.
63 For a discussion of the interdependence of men and women, see Tilly and Scott, *Women, Work and Family*.
64 For Armenian women boardinghouse operators, see Kaprielian. "Women and Work."
65 M. Bedrosian, oral interview, Hamilton.
66 A. Kaprielian, oral interview, Hamilton. Armenian women were not the only ones who earned money in these ways. See, for instance, the *St Catharines Standard*, 27 June 1967, E15, "The Needle and Boarders Helped Earn Money."
67 Cottage industry was not limited to women, of course. In Galt, Manoog Avedissian, for example, made *bulgur* in his home and sold it to local Armenians. See Kaprielian, "Earning a Living."
68 For an examination of women and work, see Bradbury, "Women's History"; Creese, "The Politics of Dependence"; Kessler-Harris, *Out to Work*; Parr, *The Gender of Breadwinners*. For studies juxtaposing class, gender, and ethnicity, see Burnet, *Looking into My Sister's Eyes*; Iacovetta, *Such Hardworking People*; Lindström-Best, *Defiant Sisters*; Swyripa, *Wedded to the Cause*.
69 J. Tatoulian, oral interview, Galt.
70 R. Chamlian, oral interview, St Catharines.
71 A. Takvorian, oral interview, Hamilton.

72 A. Torosian, oral interview, St Catharines.
73 For women during the war see Ruth Roach Pierson, "'They're Still Women after All': The Second World War and Canadian Womanhood." See also Jean Bruce, *Back the Attack!*
74 S. Tateosian, oral interview, Brantford.
75 S. Tateosian, oral interview, Brantford.
76 A. Torosian, oral interview, St Catharines.
77 Mirak, *Torn between Two Lands*, 92–3. This initial focus is mentioned also in H. Khashmanian, *Amerikahai Hanragetakan Taregirk* (American-Armenian Encyclopedic Yearbook), 1924, cited in *Navasart Monthly* 9, no. 105 (April 1991).
78 A. Kaprielian, oral interview, Hamilton.
79 This, of course, does not include the 125 Georgetown and Fegan's young men and boys, who worked as farm labourers.
80 H. Torosian, oral interview, St Catharines.
81 See *Vernon's St Catharines City Directory*, 1915, 1919, 1921. For Armenians in business in the United States, see Mirak, *Torn between Two Lands*, 92ff.
82 For buying and selling property and businesses from each other, see chapter 16 with respect to Toronto. See also Phillips, *Symbol, Myth, and Rhetoric*, 107
83 Examples are the Sahagian and Krikorian families on Beech St (formerly Merritt) and the Asadoorian family on Ontario St.
84 *Vernon's St Catharines City Directory*, 1951.
85 For Armenian women running their own businesses in Cyprus, see Pattie, "Armenian Diaspora Life." For a woman whose family business took off when she decided to package a dry mix for Armenian pilaf, see Kalajian, *Hannah's Story*.
86 This same trend into the business world by both women and men was evident in the other Armenian settlements as well. Mesag Kaloostian, in Hamilton, for instance, opened a shoe repair shop, and his wife dealt with the customers when he was working at the factory. In Windsor, while her husband worked at the Windsor Auto Specialties factory, Lusintag Torigian ran a little restaurant in her home.
87 Using an old-country metaphor, an interviewee expressed the growing power of women: "she held the key to the larder."
88 Kate Houroian, oral interview, St Catharines.
89 For the interaction of family and factory see Hareven "Family Time and Industrial Time," and *Family Time and Industrial Time*.
90 With Senekerim Chichakian's election as a shop steward and Seth Bejian's election as chairman of the shop committee they were considered to have risen about as high as this first generation of men could aspire to, either in the factory or the union. Both men were coremakers. Hygus Torosian, a considerably younger man who had been educated in Canada, was

elected to the District Council representing the UAW locals in Windsor, Oshawa, and St Catharines.
91 R. Chaligian, oral interview, St Catharines.
92 They could all remember at least one community entrepreneur who had suffered bankruptcy during the Depression and lost his business and property.
93 This fact is also true of other factory towns. A study of the relationships between Armenian political affiliation, North American voting patterns, factory work, and business enterprise would likely reveal complex and unexpected loyalties. In one case, for instance, a moulder, a die-hard unionist and member of an Armenian leftist party, became a part-time merchant and voted, not for the socialist Co-operative Commonwealth Federation, but for the Liberal Party of Canada. Meanwhile, a co-worker with similar interests never wavered from the CCF.

CHAPTER TWELVE

1 For the subculture of church and politics see Bakalian, *Armenian Americans*, chap. 2.
2 Armenians well remembered the Armenian Church crisis in Russia (1903–7) when Russian authorities confiscated church property, closed down Armenian schools, adopted a policy of Russification, and imprisoned Armenian activists.
3 From *Guide to Subversive Organizations and Publications*, cited in Phillips, *Symbol*, 138.
4 Atamian, *Armenian Community*, 439.
5 Vahan Navassardian, cited in Atamian, *Armenian Community*, 340.
6 Kooshian, "Church Reform," 90.
7 For a discussion of the "theology of exile," see Tölölyan, "Apostolic Church in the Diaspora." For the church in Armenia, see Mouradian, *L'Arménie*.
8 Kolarz, *Religion in the Soviet Union*, 151.
9 Minassian, "Armenian Church," 401, citing a circular in *Gotchnag*, 31 August, 113. See also Bardizian, (Crisis in the Armenian Church).
10 Minassian, "Armenian Church," 317.
11 Armenians, of course, were not alone in coping with such divided loyalties. Roman Catholics were often accused of placing allegiance to the Papacy above allegiance to the United States.
12 For Der Hovannesian's period in office, refer to Minassian, "Armenian Church," 336, 371. See also Ashjian, (*Tableau*); Kooshian, "Church Reform."
13 Mrs T. Isahagian, "Letter to the Editor," *Mshak*, vol. 1, no. 29 (20 April 1926): 98–9, cited in Kooshian, "Church Reform."

14 Information about the Raffi school is from the school minutes, Armenian Collection, Archives of Ontario.
15 Torosian, "The First Armenian Church," *Polyphony*, 88.
16 Yervant Mesiayan, (*Babayan*), 51. Unless otherwise stated, information on the CAU, St Catharines branch, is taken from the minutes of the organization, Armenian Collection, Archives of Ontario.
17 V. Ludwigian (oral interview, St Catharines) recounted how her husband, chairman of the St Catharines council, collected money for these very important visits. Before building their own church, St Catharines Armenians used the premises of St Barnabas and St Thomas Anglican Churches for the visiting priests. Toronto Armenians used the facilities of St Stephen's on College Street and later the chapel of Holy Trinity Anglican Church, tucked behind the Eaton warehouses in the city's central core. See Kasparian, (*Vdag*); Ashjian, (*Tableau*), 228–33; Minassian, "Armenian Church," 423.
18 Hygus Torosian, notes to the author; Kasparian, (*Vdag*); Krikor Der Krikorian, memoirs; Der Vartanian, memoirs; also *Polyphony*, "Armenians in Ontario," 90.
19 See Torosian, "The First Armenian Church," Golden Jubilee.
20 Handwritten statement in author's possession dated 8 March 1930, from the collection of A.B. Davies; newspaper clipping dated 8 March 1930, no name of newspaper.
21 Mesiayan, (*Babayan*), 62. Newspaper clipping dated 8 March 1930, no name of newspaper. For copy of clipping see *Polyphony*, "Armenians in Ontario," 92.
22 The costs of land and building are unclear. Torosian states the building cost $12,989; Ashjian, (*Tableau*), 229, uses the figure $20,000, perhaps including land and building; V. Vartanian of St Catharines recalled that the church and land cost about $20,000, since members bought additional land over the years.
23 Arshak Karageuzian was a prominent carpet merchant and president of the Armenian General Benevolent Union.
24 Maas should not be confused with the Mass or with Communion.
25 Minutes of St Gregory the Illuminator Church, St Catharines. *St Catharines Standard*, 1 December 1930. See also Minassian, "Armenian Church," 424.
26 Bardizian, (*Crisis*), 323–5. My thanks to Nazareth Bidanian, Fresno, California, for lending me a copy of this rare book.
27 Minassian, "Armenian Church," 458, citing *Banvor*, 29 July 1933. Minassian, "Armenian Church," 450, 459, 493. See also Ashjian, (*Tableau*).
28 From Canada, only Babayan and Father Zkon voted with the Hotel Martinique group; the other four remained in Holy Illuminator Church.

29 Arzumanian, (*National History*); Minassian, "Armenian Church"; Ashjian, *Armenian Church in America*; Bardizian, (*Crisis*); Philips, *Symbol*; Mkund, (*Armenian Clergy*).
30 The United States recognized the Soviet Union in 1933.
31 V. Vartanian, oral interview, St Catharines.
32 Kasparian, (*Vdag*), 56–61.

CHAPTER THIRTEEN

1 T.S. Eliot, *Murder in the Cathedral*, 19–21.
2 *St Catharines Standard*, 19 April 1932; *Toronto Star*, 26 December 1933; *Brantford Expositor*, 21 April 1933.
3 *Documents on the Schism in the Armenian Church of America* (New York 1993), 36.
4 Bardizian, (*Crisis*), 180; *Toronto Star*, 18 April 1932; Mesiayan, (*Babayan*), frontispiece, 17. Babayan's mother had lived for some time in Canada, then returned to Turkey and died in Constantinople in 1917.
5 By mid–1931, Der Stepanian's name seldom appears in the St Catharines church minutes, and as we have seen Der Zkon was hired in the fall of 1931. Oral sources were unable to shed light on the change of priests. The question of political leaning is important, considering that in the crucial diocesan convention in September 1933, Der Stepanian sided with the Holy Illuminator group and Der Zkon with the Hotel Martinique faction. Der Stepanian was intimately connected with the Chicago/Racine region and led the building of St Hagop church in Racine, which was consecrated in 1938.
6 Torosian, "First Armenian Church," Golden Jubilee volume. Also parish council minutes.
7 The minutes indicate that the parish council bought *Hairenik, Yeritasard Hayastan, Baikar,* and *Banvor.*
8 ARF Minutes, St Catharines, 27 July 1920.
9 Torosian, "First Armenian Church," Golden Jubilee volume, 94.
10 A. Uvoian, oral interview, St Catharines.
11 Aside from Levon Babayan, the names of the other lay delegates from Canada are unfamiliar to me. Possibly they were proxies (Minutes of the Diocesan Assembly). See also *Documents on the Schism*, 88–91.
12 According to the records, the council eventually paid this quota.
13 This fact is particularly relevant, since the controversy between centralization and decentralization of the church had been the topic of heated debate in the United States all during the 1920s and early 1930s.
14 *Bagharch* is a meal made of whole wheat flour, *madsun* (yogurt), garlic, and hot clarified butter.
15 ARF Records, St Catharines.
16 At the time, the women's wing was called the Armenian Revolutionary

Federation Red Cross, not to be confused with the Armenian National Red Cross, which was an arm of the HOG.
17 V. Vartanian, oral interview, St Catharines.
18 Kitur, *Hnchak History*, vol. 2, 81; Krikor Der Krikorian, "Memoirs"; conversations with Bedros Mouchian, Toronto.
19 Kitur, *Hnchak History*, vol. 2, 77–87. For an account of state suppression see Kealey, "State Repression of Labour," 281–314, and *Workers and Canadian History*, chap. 12, 419–40.
20 Kitur, *Hnchak History*, vol. 2, 83–4; vol. 1, 499–501.
21 H. Uvoian, M. Laligian, V. Ludvigian, oral interviews, St Catharines.
22 V. Ludvigian, oral interview, St Catharines. *Shinarar*, 1931, 44.
23 From church minutes, 152; my synopsis. Obviously the St Catharines council was unaware of the 25 October decision of the Supreme Council in Echmiadzin.
24 The account in this section is pieced together from the church minutes, newspaper articles, the transcript of the court case, minutes of the Armenian Revolutionary Federation, and oral testimony. The transcript of the court case can be found in Archives of Ontario, RG 22, T. box 63, file no. 16, Supreme Court of Ontario, 1934, in Lincoln, *Akazarian vs Torosian et al.*
25 *St Catharines Standard*, 5 February 1934.

CHAPTER FOURTEEN

1 V. Ludvigian, interview, St Catharines.
2 Torosian, "The First Armenian Church," 89; Yervant Mesiayan, (*Babayan*), 55. Babayan would surely be aware that the oil magnate Mantoushian (Mantoushev) had built the Armenian church in Paris (1902–3). *L'Église-Cathédral de Paris Saint Jean-Baptiste* (Paris: L'Association Culturelle de l'Église Apostolique Arménienne de Paris et de la Région Parisienne 1994).
3 Father Zkon died in Toronto in 1938.
4 For *Diaruntarach*, or Christ's Presentation at the Temple, members lit a bonfire in the church garden and young people jumped over it.
5 Unless otherwise indicated, statistics of the parish council are from Torosian, *St Gregory Armenian Apostolic Church*, Golden Jubilee volume.
6 The first woman on the council was Lucille Chichakian, elected as assistant secretary in 1957. During the first fifty years of the board's existence, a total of three women were elected to the board. In 1992, by contrast, all members of the board except one were women.
7 Torosian, *St Gregory Armenian Apostolic Church*, Golden Jubilee volume.
8 See Stephens, *A Memoir of the Spanish Civil War*.
9 For a discussion of the purges in Soviet Armenia, see Minassian, "Armenian Church," 596.

10 See, for example, Minassian, "Armenian Church," 653.
11 F. Ohanjanian, oral interview, Toronto.
12 K. Topalian, oral interview, Brantford.
13 H. Torosian, oral interview, St Catharines. For a contradictory position see Kitur, *Hnchak History*, vol. 1, 501–2.
14 R. Chaligian, P. Tashjian, oral interviews, St Catharines.
15 Kasparian, (*Vdag*), 60, 120–1. Dashnak communities in Hamilton, Galt, Guelph, and Brantford also elected religious councils.
16 In 1951, Galt residents proudly participated in a "burning of the mortgage" ceremony.
17 Group interview, St Catharines.
18 See Ashjian, (*Tableau*), 145.
19 Z. Lorisian, oral interview, Hamilton.
20 For an account of some of these rituals, see Kaprielian, "Armenian Folk-Belief."
21 In Boettiger, *Armenian Legends and Festivals*, 62–6, citing Boyajian, *Armenian Legends and Poems*.
22 This stanza is a translation from the original in the author's personal collection. They are in Turkish, written in Armenian letters, and translated by Zivart and Eugenie Shehirian.
23 The opera Anoush by Hovannes Toumanyan is based on the *vijak* ritual.
24 Cited in Phillips, *Symbol*, 140
25 Such was the fear that when the author tried to interview a former Progressive League member in 1989, his daughter angrily refused to allow it.
26 Estimates typically indicate that from 1948 to 1956 approximately one-fifth to one-third of the members of the Communist Party of Canada left the party. Cited in Kealey, *Workers and Canadian History*, 54.
27 Z. Lorisian, interview, Hamilton.
28 A similar reciprocation occurred in Brantford in the late 1980s and early 1990s. When the Progressive hall was sold, the money was invested. From these funds Armenians made donations to Grace Anglican Church.
29 Roy, *Communism and the Churches*, 410; Walker, *Survival*, 355; Atamian, *The Armenian Community*, 390.
30 For an account of changes in Soviet Armenia, see Minassian, *Armenian Church*, 604–23; Roy, *Communism and the Churches*, 411. The most notable victim of the purges was Catholicos Khoren I. The attribution of his death to the KGB was long ignored as a Dashnak calumny. See Mouradian, *L'Arménie*, chap. 8.
31 Eugene Papazian, *Inknakensagrutiun yev Husher* (Autobiography and Memoirs) (Cairo 1960), 55–9, cited in Walker, *Survival*, 355.
32 See Atamian, *The Armenian Community*, 395.
33 The reports of the North American contribution vary between $105,000 (Minassian, *Armenian Church*, 641) and $115,000 (Walker, *Survival*,

356). Schahgaldian notes that by early 1944, the Catholicosate had raised over $U.S.1 million for the Red Army from several campaigns throughout the diaspora. "Political Integration," 97.

34 Department of State, Office of Research and Intelligence, "Notes on Armenian National Aspirations and on the Soviet Claims to the Eastern Provinces of Turkey." 12 March 1946, no. 3523.2, cited in Suny, "Return to Ararat."

35 Despite the Anglo-Franco-Turkish treaty of 19 October 1939, Turkey signed a nonaggression and trade pact with Nazi Germany, proclaimed neutrality in 1941, and closed the straits to all shipping at the beginning of the war. As Walker states, "Turkey ... maintained a grudging neutrality throughout the war, until it was won, when she joined the winning side" (*Survival*, 358). See also Schahgaldian, "Integration," 99. Walker also discusses the spread of pan-Turkism, the "unashamedly racist" policy, which, in effect, coveted the rich Baku oil fields. Walker, *Survival*, 358–9.

36 Most notable were the representations made by the Catholicos to the Yalta conference (1945) and by the Armenian National Council of the United States and the ARF to the first conference of the United Nations in San Francisco in 1945. See Schahgaldian, "Integration," 97; Suny, "Return"; Atamian, *Armenian Community*, 405–9.

37 R. Chaligian, oral interview, St Catharines. For repatriation see Suny, "Return"; Atamian, *Armenian Community*, 405; also Schahgaldian, "Integration," 91, and Mouradian, "L'immigration," 79–110.

38 Ashjian, (*Tableau*), 233.

39 The world-wide contribution of Armenians to the Allied war effort has not been fully examined. Aside from the fact that more than fifty Soviet generals were Armenians, including Marshal Hovannes Baghramian, who led the march into Berlin, it is estimated that three hundred to five hundred thousand Armenians fought in the Soviet armed forces. Thirty-two thousand Armenian soldiers were decorated in the war and over a hundred received the award Hero of the Soviet Union. Walker, *Survival*, 355–6, citing British government documents. According to Walker, the Armenian Army, the Eighty-ninth, also known as the Tamanian Army, after it liberated the Taman Peninsula under Major-General Nver Safarian, was "the only one of the Soviet national armies to enter Berlin in 1945." (As a point of interest, General Heinz Guderian, who spearheaded Germany's invasion of France, was also of Armenian descent.) Armenians were also in the forefront of the resistance movement in France. In the United States, the topic has been treated by Tashjian, *The Armenian-American in World War II*. Minassian gives the number of Armenians in the United States armed forces as 18,500 (632). Unfortu-

Notes to pages 321-34

nately, the contribution of Canadian-Armenians has never been fully studied.
40 A. Tashjian, oral interview, St Catharines.
41 A. Uvoian, oral interview, St Catharines.

CHAPTER FIFTEEN

1 Yeran, (*Armenian-English Conversation*). Yeran also published dictionaries, song books, histories, and books about hygiene.
2 L. Lorisian, oral interview, Hamilton.
3 Professor Chaké Minassian, oral interview, Montreal.
4 John Wilson, oral interview, Fresno, California.
5 Z. Lorisian, oral interview, Hamilton
6 A. Uvoian, oral interview, St Catharines.
7 The role of the Armenian grandmother has been raised by Armenian American writers like Arlene Voski Avakian, Peter Balakian, Carole Edgarian, Laura Kalpakian, and William Saroyan. They have all paid tribute to their grandmothers, often using the symbolism of the lioness.
8 Z. Zakarian, oral interview, Hamilton.
9 V. Arestakesian, oral interview, Hamilton.
10 Murat was hanged in 1915. Murat of Sivas, a member of the Dashnak party, was killed in the defence of Baku in 1918. Paramaz (Mateos Sarkisian), a Hnchak leader, was hanged in Constantinople in 1915, along with nineteenother Hnchakians. This group was known as the Twenty Hanged Men. Sepouh, (Arshak Nersesian) was a military commander and parliamentarian. As for the different spellings of names, I have normally used the Eastern form in my transliterations, except where the people themselves used the Western form. In the Eastern form, for example, the correct transliterations would be Murat, Andranik, and Sepouh, and in the Wstern forms they would be Murad, Antranig, and Sebouh.
11 J. Tatoulian, oral interview, Cambridge.
12 N. Kaprielian and P. Kaprielian, oral interviews, Hamilton. Two of the larger and more attractive houses on Gibson Avenue were occupied by "Harvester bosses."
13 Z. Lorisian, oral interview, Hamilton.
14 Sharambeyan, "Needle Arts," 165–174. See also Kasparian, *Armenian Needlework*. Sadly, the needle arts were not passed on to succeeding generations.
15 P. Lorisian, oral interview, Hamilton.
16 V. Arestakesian, oral interview, Hamilton.
17 Ibid.
18 As a point of interest, Toronto Armenians never formed an Armenian

neighbourhood. They established the Canadian Armenian Union and the Canadian Armenian Young Peoples' Association in the 1920s, and these organizations rented space on Bond Street, opposite St Michael's Cathedral, for a clubhouse and meeting place. Neither the organizations nor the clubhouse survived the upheavals of the early 1930s.

19 For an account of this hilarious play, see Kaprielian, "The Mooradian and Melkonian Family Collection," 69–71.

20 I have already referred to several published and unpublished village and regional histories of Keghi. These include, among others, the history of the villages of Khups and of Chanakhchi and three regional histories published by the compatriotic associations. For a more detailed list of village and regional histories consult Gaghjayan@aol.com, which provides a partial list and refers to the bibliography published by Sarkis Karayan, "History of Armenian Communities in Turkey," in *The Armenian Review*, and Hamo Vassilian, *The Armenians: A Colossal Bibliographic Guide to Books Published in the English Language*. For a discussion of the literature of genocide and exile, see Peroomian, *Literary Responses to Catastrophe*, Nichanian, *Writers of Disaster*, and Beledian, "L'experience."

21 Shahmouradian and Panosian sang under the Columbia label and Oudi Hrant performed under the Balkan label.

22 Vosbikian, the Nor-ikes, and the Aramite band each played under their own label; Barsamian played under the Mihran label; Boghosian sang under the Metropolitan label.

23 This song was written by William Saroyan and Ross Bagdasarian and translated into Armenian by Guy Chookoorian.

24 Robert Melkonian, the community violinist, collected approximately 160 of these melodies; his collection has been deposited with the Multicultural History Society of Ontario.

25 Hairenik Press, Boston, published *Empost Yerker* (Songs of Defiance) in 1915. This small pocket songbook of Armenian revolutionary songs and others like it became the foundation of the musical repertoire for diaspora communities in the post-Genocide period. For an account of Keghi folk songs see Hasmig Injejikian, "Musical Repertory."

26 For an account of a Hamilton picnic, see *Hairenik*, 13 September 1947.

27 I. Hovanesian, oral interview, Hamilton.

28 J. Tatoulian, oral interview, Cambridge.

29 Z. Lorisian, oral interview, Hamilton.

30 As he lay poised to attack Poland, Hitler discounted any concerns about the extermination of enemy races by asking the trenchant question, "Who now remembers the Armenians?" See Bardakjian, *Hitler and the Armenian Genocide*.

31 For newspaper coverage in Canada, see *Armenian Genocide in the Canadian Press*, vols. 1 and 2.

32 Shahnazarian, (*Study of Genetics*).
33 This thirty-five-page pamphlet was published by the Canadian Armenian Union, with a preface by Canon Gould, General Secretary of the Missionary Society of the Church of England in Canada, and with an acknowledgment by F.H. Cosgrave, provost of Trinity College, Toronto.
34 Z. Zakarian, oral interview, Hamilton.
35 For an account of the impact of the Depression on children, see Elder, *Children of the Great Depression*. "Conditions in the Depression," he notes, "denied some young people the protected, nonresponsible experience of adolescence by extending adult-like tasks downward to childhood." (28). For child labour, see Bullen, "Hidden Workers"; Copp, *Anatomy of Poverty*; Piva, *The Working Class in Toronto*.
36 V. Dro, oral interview, Hamilton.
37 Several women spoke in the same terms and showed their determination to provide a good education not only for their sons but also for their daughters.
38 Mooradian, *The Book of Life*.
39 Survey done by Norman Kaprielian and Paul Kaprielian, Hamilton.
40 G. Yeremian, oral interview, Toronto.
41 *McAlpine's Halifax City Directory*, 1920. Mgrublian and Ar(a)kelian were partners. Since the photography business was not always lucrative enough to provide for his growing family, Ar(a)kelian opened a restaurant beside his studio. A strong relationship existed between Boston and Halifax Armenians.
42 For the concept of the life-cycle of communities, see the seminal work on this topic by Breton, "Institutional Completeness."

CHAPTER SIXTEEN

1 Baghdjian, *Les Arméniens au Québec*. Material based on information from Armèn(ouhi) Melconian, 26–7. For a discussion of refugee resettlement, see Schahgaldian, "Ethnicity and Political Development."
2 K. Lalazarian, oral interview, Toronto.
3 J. Rustigian, oral interview, Toronto.
4 This number is quoted from an article in the *Brantford Daily Expositor*, 8 June 1907. Montreal city directories yielded work and settlement patterns.
5 Lovell's *Montreal City Directories*.
6 Baghdjian, *La Communauté Arménienne Catholique*, 54–64, citing the unpublished memoirs of Yervant Jrjoian (George Miller). Yervant Jrjoian's handwritten memoir, "Montreal Armenians before 1912," in author's private collection. Also, telephone interview with and questionnaire response from Paul and Rose Vartanian, Montreal.

7 Baghdjian, *Les Arméniens au Québec*. Baghdjian bases his figures on a list drawn up by Yervant Jrjoian and by Arménouhi Melconian. The *Census of Canada*, 1921, vol. 11, 502, shows 84 Armenians in the province of Quebec, ten years of age and over, including 60 males and 24 females.
8 Chichekian, *The Armenian Community of Quebec*, 57. Also, conversations with Yervant Pasdermajian and Harold Bedoukian, Montreal.
9 *McAlpine's Halifax City Directory*.
10 *Lovell's Montreal City Directory*, 1907.
11 Information about Stepanian was pieced together from Jrjoian, Baghdjian, and Melconian.
12 *Lovell's Montreal City Directories*. Street addresses are from the 1949 edition.
13 Oral interview and questionnaire, Vartanian family, Montreal; T. Goshgarian, oral interview, Ste. Adèle.
14 Senator R. Setlakwé, oral interview, Sherbrooke. The Mardin group continues to keep contact and every year has a golf tournament appropriately called the Mardin Open. See Baghdijian, *La Communauté*.
15 Guelph, Galt, and Windsor also became more popular after World War I. In Windsor, Armenians settled around Felix, Lena, Giradot, and Millen Streets.
16 For short pieces on Armenian domestics, see Kaprielian, "Women and Work: The Case of Finnish Domestics and Armenian Boardinghouse Operators" and "Refugee Women as Domestics: a Documentary Account."
17 In 1921 it was calculated that 18 percent of all employed women in Canada were engaged in domestic service, which represented the second most important category of female workers. From Leslie, "Domestic Service in Canada," 71.
18 Domestic service was already an accepted part of Armenian tradition, both before the Genocide and in the countries of asylum. In 1928, as I have already noted, the United Church of Canada took over the work of the association to facilitate the movement of Armenian refugees to Canada and assist in their resettlement in this country.
19 United Church Archives (UCA), Georgetown Boys; Mrs R.G. Dingman, York Mills, to Rev. Pierce, 7 April 1927.
20 E. Voskorian, oral interview, Hamilton.
21 K. Lalazarian, oral interview, Toronto.
22 K. Lalazarian, oral interview, Toronto.
23 K. Lalazarian, oral interview, Toronto.
24 Oral interviewees have suggested that while Babayan became rich by importing and selling rugs, his real wealth lay in buying and selling real estate in downtown Toronto. Armavir has since been demolished.

25 Y. Kerbekian, oral interview, Toronto.
26 A study of the St Catharines city directories reveals a similar proclivity to buy and sell businesses and property from each other.
27 Ghazarian, *Armenian Carpet*; Babayan, *Oriental Rug*. For an account of the oriental rug trade in the United States, see Mirak, *Torn between Two Lands*, 105–11. For more on oriental carpets, see Summers, *Oriental Rugs*.
28 Ghazarian, *Armenian Carpet*.
29 Der Manuelian, "Art and Economics," and *Weavers, Merchants, and Kings*.
30 Gantzhorn, *Le tapis chrétien oriental*, 11, translated by Stacy Churchill.
31 Like their father, Levon Babayan's older brother Pierre had been a lawyer in Constantinople. See Mesiayan, *Levon Babayan*.
32 Oral sources and the *Toronto City Directory* indicate that the break came before 1915. Babayan's biographer sheds no light on why and when Babayan broke with his brother-in-law. Yervant Mesiayan, *Levon Babayan*. Courian and Sons later became N. Courian and Company on King St, west of Bay.
33 According to Paul Courian, grandson of the original founder, the Courians had a shop opposite the King Edward Hotel, then on King St closer to York St, and finally on Yonge St. Paul Courian, oral interview, Toronto. A 1921 advertisement lists the store at 88 King St West.
34 In the *Toronto City Directory* for 1910, Utudjian is listed as foreman of Courian Babayan and Company.
35 G. Der Stepanian, interview, Brantford. Rugs woven by Armenian orphans after the 1894–96 massacres, the 1909 pogroms, and the Genocide now form a special genre of rugs known as "orphan rugs." Needless to add, the Genocide had a devastating impact on the Armenian carpet trade, from weaving to retailing. See Bedoukian. "*A Unique Armenian Silk Rug.*"
36 See Bedoukian's autobiography, *The Urchin*, published in the United States under the title *Some of Us Survived*.
37 Bedoukian, unpublished manuscript, sequel to *The Urchin*.
38 Oksen Teghtsoonian, *Memoirs*. Teghtsoonian remained part of the Ridpath organization for thirty-four years, until 1966. I am indebted to Mr and Mrs Teghtsoonian for giving me access to his manuscript.
39 Norma Chichakian from St Catharines, for instance, worked in the office of Babayan's in Toronto during the 1920s.
40 L. Postalian, oral interview, Toronto.
41 Armenian merchants established themselves in London, importing British goods to the Ottoman Empire and exporting oriental rugs and tobacco to England. Among the merchants were the Gulbenkians, the

Karagheuzians, the Oundjians, and the Tavshanjians. The Oundjian family has continued to excel in this line; the family opened a rug-importing branch in Toronto.

42 Y. Pasdermajian, oral interview, Montreal. See also the article about Pasdermajian by L. Tasso-Hovsépian in *La Presse*, 9 June 1986.

43 The *La Presse* article notes that Pasdermajian had as clients "important people such as the prime minister, judges of the Supreme Court, and presidents of banks and large corporations." My translation.

44 Y. Levonian, oral interview, Toronto.

45 Eaton's College Street was one of the few non-Armenian firms that sold Oriental carpets in Toronto; as early as the first decades of the twentieth century Courian and Babayan were supplying the department store with fine Oriental rugs. What strikes one as particularly interesting is that Armenians, who had manufactured rugs abroad, never undertook in any major way to weave carpets in Canada. The only exception that I found was the manufacture of reversible rag rugs, called Catalogne runners, by Bedoukian in Montreal in the early 1940s. The reason suggested by interviewees was that the Genocide had devastated the industry, that it was too costly to reestablish looms in Canada, and that Canadian wages would have made the rugs exorbitantly expensive. By contrast the Karagheuzian family manufactured rugs in the United States, notably the Gulistan, Karastan, and Sheffield carpets.

46 Babayan, *Romance*, 14.

CHAPTER SEVENTEEN

1 NA, RG76, vol. 854, file 554-6, Int. no. 51, Memo, Laval Fortier, Deputy Minister, to the Minister, Ottawa, 18 February 1950, citing the Prime Minister's statement of 1 May 1947. It is interesting that the prime minister's remarks regarding absorptive capacity always referred to economic absorptive capacity and not to cultural absorptive capacity. For an account of Canadian immigration policy see Hawkins, *Canada and Immigration*; Green, *Immigration*; Elliott, *Two Nations*; and Knowles, *Strangers at Our Gates*.

2 From a photocopied statement, "The Organization of the CAC," in author's files.

3 RG76, vol. 854, file 554-6, Int. no. 51, Memo, Hugh L. Keenleyside, Deputy Minister of Mines and Resources to the Minister (who also held the immigration portfolio), 9 August 1949.

4 Ibid., Memo, Keenleyside to F. P. Varcoe, Deputy Minister, Department of Justice, Ottawa, 22 March 1949. The draft to the governor general of the new regulations included the stipulation that "the term 'Asiatic race' as

used in this regulation shall not apply to immigrants of Armenian, Lebanese or Syrian origin."
5 Ibid., Memo, Minister of Mines and Resources to the Governor General in Council, 28 April 1949.
6 Ibid., Memo, Arthur L. Jolliffe, 12 May 1949. As early as 2 September 1948, Jolliffe had recommended waiving the provisions of P.C. 2115 to allow for the movement of some of the Armenian displaced persons.
7 Ibid., Keenleyside to Varcoe, 11 July 1949, with copy of draft to Governor General from Minister of Mines and Resources, Colin Gibson; Deputy Minister to Gibson, 9 August 1949.
8 Ibid., Memo, Deputy Minister to Minister, 10 February 1950. Also NA, Kerop Bedoukian fonds, MG30 D371, vol. 2, file 2–14, J.G. Levy to John H. Mooradian, 20 August 1952. Henceforth, these fonds will be referred to as MG30 D371 with volume and file numbers. The material is currently under certain restrictions.

Hawkins deals with the issue of the minister's discretionary powers, noting that the flood of correspondence on individual cases and representations on behalf of individuals were as time-consuming for the department as they were for the minister and inevitably led to a huge backlog. Hawkins, *Canada and Immigration*, 102ff.
9 RG76, vol. 854, file 554–6, Int. no. 51, Memo, Deputy Minister Laval Fortier to Minister, 18 February 1950; ibid., file 554-3, pt. 1, D.A. Reid (for Director of Immigration) to Dr J. Arzumanian, ANCHA representative in Milan, Italy, 20 April 1951. During this period the Canadian government was being strongly criticized for its racist immigration policies, its conflictual relations with the Department of Labour, and its unwieldy procedures.
10 Ibid., Jolliffe to the Minister of Citizenship and Immigration, Walter Harris, 24 March 1950. This department was created in 1950 with Harris as the first minister.
11 Ibid., John Mooradian to Walter Harris, 16 March 1951. For displaced persons see Aun, *Political Refugees*; Danys, *Lithuanian Immigration*; Epp, *Women without Men*; Isajiw, *The Refugee*; Radecki, *A Member*; and Luciuk, *Searching for Place*.
12 For example, 35 Armenians had been admitted to Canada in 1950, in stark contrast to the 1,592 admitted to the United States in the same year. U.S. statistics provided by Robert Mirak.
13 NA, MG30 D371, vol. 3, file 3–14, Bedoukian to Armen Atamian, 27 November 1951. Also RG76, vol. 854, file 554-3, pt. 1, which includes Report on Armenian Immigration. This document refers to a government decision on *8 November 1949* to provide a measure of relief by including the classes of relationships to sponsors that pertained to European

immigration. The report, undated, refers to the minister's permit and also mentions the lack of facilities in the Middle East for screening potential immigrants.

14 NA, MG30 D371, vol. 2, file 2–14, J. Mooradian to Walter Harris, 11 August 1952; ibid. J.G. Levy to John H. Mooradian, 20 August 1952.
15 RG76, vol. 854, file 554–3, pt. 1, J.G. Levy, private secretary to Walter Harris, Minister of Citizenship and Immigration, Ottawa, 20 August 1952, to John Mooradian. Clarification based on regulations of 4 July 1952 regarding the admissibility under P.C. 2856 and P.C. 2115. Also Department of Citizenship and Immigration – Immigration Policy. Summary of persons admissible under P.C. 2856 and P.C. 2115. The list of eligible relatives varied from time to time in a tap-on, tap-off arrangement.
16 RG76, vol. 854, file 554–3, pt. 1, Chief, Admissions Division, to Miss E. O'Connor, 3 October 1952. Also MG30 D371, vol. 2, file 2–14, J.G. Levy to John H. Mooradian, 20 August 1952.
17 RG76, vol. 854, file 554–3, pt. 1, Laval Fortier, Deputy Minister, to L.H. LaVigne, 1 September 1953.
18 Ibid., file 554–6, Int. no. 51, Memo, Deputy Minister to Minister, 10 February 1950. The *Report of the Royal Commission on Bilingualism and Biculturalism*, book 4, 1969, 243–4, has only 39 Armenians entering from 1944 to the end of 1949, 256 from 1950 to the end of 1953, and 773 from 1955 to 31 December 1958. In December 1950, P.C. 2115 was amended to include husbands and children under 21, rather than under the age of 18.
19 RG76, vol. 854, file 554–3, pt. 1.
20 As pointed out in MG30 D371, vol. 3, file 3–14, Yervant Pasdermajian to W.H. Neville, Department of Citizenship and Immigration, 2 February 1957.
21 RG76, vol. 854, file 554–3, pt. 1, Fortier to Pasdermajian, 29 March 1956.
22 Ibid., Immigration Directive to all Immigration Officers, 22 February 1960.
23 Ibid., Memo from Wallace R. Baskerville, Director of Immigration to George E. Davidson, Deputy Minister, 19 January 1960; ibid., Director of Immigration to George Perley-Robertson, barrister, 20 January 1960.
24 Ibid., pt. 2, Chief of Operations, Draft of Operations Memorandum to all Immigration Officers, 1 March 1962.
25 Y. Pasdermajian, oral interview, Montreal.
26 RG76, vol. 854, file 554–3, pt. 2, Davidson, Deputy Minister to Kerop Bedoukian, 14 December 1961.
27 Ibid., pt. 1, Memo, Fortier to Ellen L. Fairclough, Minister of Citizenship and Immigration, 20 October 1959.
28 Ibid., pt. 2, Baskerville, Director of Immigration Branch to Davidson,

Deputy Minister, 25 October 1961; Baskerville to Deputy Minister, 1 October 1962; Claude M. Isbister, Deputy Minister to Guy Favreau, Minister, 10 January 1964.

29 MG30 D371, vol. 2, file 2–14. Current restrictions apply.
30 RG76, vol. 854, file 554–3, pt. 2, Pasdermajian to Pierre Berton, Montreal, 9 March 1964.
31 Ibid., Confidential Memo, Isbister to the Minister, 10 January 1964; Confidential Memo, Isbister to Minister, 24 April 1964; Russell B. Curry to Claude Richardson, solicitor acting for the Congress, Ottawa, 1 May 1964. See also Operations Memo no. 32, 27 July 1964. See also MG30 D371, vol. 3, file 3–35, Pasdermajian to Department of Citizenship and Immigration, 4 August 1964.
32 RG76, vol. 854, file 554–3, pt. 2, Richardson to Curry, citing Pasdermajian, 26 June 1964.
33 Ibid., Revised Operating Memorandum, 17 November 1964. Of course, there was no reason for the CAC to sponsor applications when the sponsor was able to provide satisfactory settlement arrangements and the proposed immigrant fell within a sponsorable category. Congress was a sponsor in those cases where the co-sponsor was not financially able to assume full responsibility.
34 Hawkins, *Immigration*, 124.
35 Jean Marchand, Minister of Manpower and Immigration, *White Paper on Immigration*.
36 Richmond, "The Green Paper."
37 RG76, vol. 854, file 554–3, pt. 2, J. Anderson, Director, Eastern Region to Director, Canadian Service, 4 Nov. 1965.
38 Ibid., B.A. Gorman to Director, Special Services, 16 December 1965.
39 Ibid., Curry to Pasdermajian, 27 November 1967.
40 Roberts, *Canada's Immigration Law*.
41 "The Canadian Armenian Congress," an interview with Y. Pasdermajian.
42 MG30 D371, vol. 1, file 1–30. Current restrictions apply.
43 Ibid., vol. 2, file 2–11. Current restrictions apply
44 Ibid., file 2–26. Current restrictions apply.
45 "The Canadian Armenian Congress: An interview with Yervant Pasdermajian," *Polyphony* (fall/winter 1982), vol. 4, no. 2, 117–21.
46 K. Bedoukian, oral interview, Montreal.
47 For a brief summary of Armenians in Greece, see MG30 D371, vol. 2, file 2–27, Y.H. Djedjizian, Director of the Howard Karaghousian Commemorative Corporation, "Notes about Armenians in Greece," Athens, April 1955.
48 MG30 D371; Kerop Bedoukian, "A Report on Immigration from Greece to Canada of Stateless Armenians, sponsored by K. Bedoukian and the Canadian Council of Churches" (current restrictions apply); Archives of

the Zoryan Institute, Toronto, Yervant Pasdermajian Papers of the CAC. My thanks to Mr Pasdermajian for giving me the records of the Canadian Armenian Congress to deposit with the Zoryan Institute in Toronto.

49 Statements from Y.H. Djedjizian, "Notes." Figures for Armenians in Greece vary, as do figures for naturalized Armenians in Greece, which range from 1,500 to 5,000. For statistics, see also Tabori, *Anatomy of Exile*, 355–6.

50 For these individuals, blood, rather than place of birth, was the criterion used to determine citizenship. Armenian children born in Greece did not have the automatic right to apply for Greek citizenship upon reaching majority and were obliged to go through a naturalization procedure that did not always guarantee full citizenship.

51 RG76, vol. 854, file 554-3, pt. 1, Officer in Charge, Athens to Chief, Administrative Division, 13 March 1958; Leslie A. Goodyear, Deputy Representative, UNHCR, Athens, to Paul Fortin, 17 March 1958.

52 Ibid., Eastern District Superintendent to Admissions Division, with note from E.B. (E.P. Beasley?), 18 February 1958. From Chief, Administration Division, to Chief, Operations Division, 1 April 1958; Director of Immigration to Deputy Minister, 9 May 1958; Asian Section to Chief, Admissions Division, 27 May 1958.

53 Ibid., pt. 2, Baskerville to Davidson, Deputy Minister, 25 October 1961.

54 Maclaren, a Scot who emigrated to Canada in 1904 was familiar with Armenians, since he had been on the board of the Georgetown Boys' home and had later been superintendent of the home. MG30 D371, vol. 3, file 3–14, letter from Montreal to Alexander Maclaren, 16 September 1957. Current restrictions apply.

55 Bedoukian's work continued on AGBU mandate dating back to the genocide.

56 For an eyewitness account of the events in Van, see Ussher, *An American Physician in Turkey*.

57 From notes by Migirdic Migirdicyan sent to the author.

58 For a brief overview of events in the Sanjak of Alexandretta, see Walker, *Armenia*, 348–9.

59 Boghos [Paul] Seferian, oral interview, Hamilton.

60 Final Act and Agreement of the Intergovernmental Conference on the Adoption of a Travel Document for Refugees, London, 15 October 1946.

61 RG76, vol. 902, file 569-22-1, part 2, draft of proposed reply from Paul Malone, Under Secretary of State for External Affairs, to E.P. Beasley, Admissions Division, Department of Citizenship and Immigration, 27 May 1957. Reply from Baskerville, Acting Director, 30 May 1957.

62 For more on the Immigration Act and Canada's humanitarian tradition see Isabel Kaprielian-Churchill and Stacy Churchill, *The Pulse of the World*, chap. 3.

63 Statistics provided by Employment and Immigration Canada, Refugee Affairs to the author, 1991.

64 A. Davidian, oral interview, Toronto. See also Kurdian, *Organizing and Preserving*, 27. Kurdian states that many of the refugees had fled Iran and had found temporary refuge in India, Pakistan, Greece, and Germany.
65 This same phenomenon has continued since 1988, with the flow of immigrants from the former Union of Soviet Socialist Republics, notably from the Republic of Armenia, which has been afflicted by war and blockade.
66 Baghdjian, *La communauté Arménienne*, 80.
67 Yervant Pasdermajian, personal book with information about those sponsored by the CAC.
68 Baghdjian, *Les Arméniens*, 50; Chichekian, "Armenian Immigrants," 65–81.
69 Even when the CAC had carte blanche, potential immigrants were, by and large, required to pass medical and security checks.
70 Statistics from the *Royal Commission on Bilingualism and Biculturalism*, book 4, 244–5, and from the Department of Citizenship and Immigration. Garo Chichekian, who provides more refined statistics than the Bilingualism and Biculturalism Commission, gives a slightly higher number entering from 1954 to 1965 ("Armenian Immigrants," 65–81). These statistics for 1980–90 are based not on ethnic origin, which was no longer recorded, but on immigrants who gave Armenian as their maternal language. My thanks to Jim Versteegh of Employment and Immigration Canada for these data.
71 For an excellent article discussing subethnicity, i.e., the same ethnic group from different countries, see Der-Martirosian, Sabagh, and Bozorgmehr, "Subethnicity," 243–58. See also Bozorgmehr, Der-Martirosian, and Sabagh, "Middle Easterners," 345–78.
72 MG30 D371, vol. 1, file 1–28. Current restrictions apply.
73 The Armenian Secret Army for the Liberation of Armenia (ASALA) attacked the office of the World Council of Churches in Beirut, Lebanon in 1975, because it objected to the council's work in promoting the emigration of Armenians from the Middle East to the United States and, presumably, Canada. Cited in Shirinian, *Quest for Closure*, 118, quoting from "Nadim Nasir Report: Al-Majallah Visits an Armenian Secret Army Base in Lebanon," in Foreign Broadcast Information Service, *Daily Report* (Middle East and Africa), 1 September 1982. Also see Gunter, "Pursuing the Just Cause," 33

CHAPTER EIGHTEEN

1 Employment and Immigration Canada, Refugee Affairs, 15 March 1991 (to the author). Of those who entered, 1,901 came in as family class and 2,069 as assisted relative; the remainder, a slight minority, entered as "other independent."

2 Chichekian, *The Armenian Community*, 48; also "Armenian Immigrants in Canada," 65–81. No data for 1965 in Chichekian's review.
3 Baghdjian, *La Communauté Arménienne*, 94–9. Approximately 28.4 percent, or 105, had settled in Quebec because of the prior settlement of family. Also Seta Der Assadourian's study (1961), cited in Baghdjian, *Les Arméniens au Québec*, 45.
4 Chichekian, *Armenian Community*, 91.
5 Kevorkian, (*Everyone's Yearbook*) (1962), 336ff.
6 See Chichekian "Armenians in Canada," in *Horizon Weekly*, 19 July 1993, 9, based on ethnic origin, both single and multiple responses.
7 Chichekian, *The Distribution and Linguistic Acculturation of Armenians*, 10, citing 1981 census data. According to the 1986 census material, 98 percent of Armenians in Quebec lived in Metropolitan Montreal.
8 Personal record book, restrictions apply. Bedoukian, *Report*.
9 NA, MG30 D371, vol. 3, file 3–20, Guarantee to Reimbursement.
10 B. Der Simonian, oral interview, Toronto, 1984. In Toronto, Setrag Tatarian, who had operated a rug-cleaning shop in Ottawa before moving to Toronto, offered his home to many Armenian immigrants in the late 1950s and 1960s. Cited in S. Chilingirian, "Setrak Tatarian: A Love for People," *Nor Serount* (January/February 1975): 44; cited in Kurdian, *Organizing and Preserving an Ethnic Group*, 14.
11 Chichekian, *Armenian Community*, 47ff.
12 Seta Der Assadourian, "The Armenian Community of Montreal: A Statistical Study, 1961," unpublished manuscript, cited in Baghdjian, *Les Arméniens*, 42; Chichekian, *Armenian Community*, 131; multicultural data base, Province of Ontario, 1981 census tabulation.
13 Chichekian, "Distribution," 11. Statistics for 1981 for Hamilton, St Catharines, and Brantford indicate, not surprisingly, the growing proportion of the Canadian-born. Seta Der Assadourian, "The Armenian Community of Montreal," indicates that only 8.3 percent were Canadian-born in that city in 1961. Cited in Baghdjian, *Les Arméniens*, 41
14 Chichekian, *Armenian Community*, 54. Note that those born in Turkey would also include survivors of the Genocide who had been born in Turkey but had come to Canada from another country of provenance or citizenship.
15 Y. Pasdermajian, oral interview, Montreal. Baghdjian, *Les Arméniens*, 26–8, indicates that between 1930 and 1944, about 224 Armenians lived in Montreal. He also cites a prelacy document stating that Armenians in Montreal numbered about 20 families in 1949.
16 Chichekian, "Armenian Immigrants."
17 Ibid., 72–6.
18 Chichekian, "Armenian Community," 57
19 Chichekian, "Armenian Immigrants," 72–6, and Chichekian, *Armenian*

Community, 52. See also Boudjikanian, "Immigration et Milieux Urbains, 21–39.
20 Chichekian, *Armenian Community*, 82–5; Chichekian, *Distribution*, 34.
21 Movses Bazarian, 94 years old in 2001, organized the group at the Fairview Library. A survivor of the Genocide, he immigrated to Soviet Armenia from Greece in 1947. After many difficult years under the Soviet regime, he made his way to Canada in 1970. He published his memoirs in 1998 about his years in Soviet Armenia: *Letters from the Soviet Paradise*. From notes provided by Migirdic Migirdicyan, Toronto.
22 For a study of successive flows of Armenians from different countries of origin, see Der-Martirosian, Sabagh, and Bozorgmehr, "Subethnicity," 243–58.
23 MG30 D371, vol. 3, file 3–35, Letter to Department of Citizenship and Immigration in Canada. Current restrictions apply. Anthony Zadourian, oral interview, Toronto.
24 MG30 D371, vol. 2, file 2–3. Current restrictions apply.
25 Chichekian, *Armenian Community*, 135–6.
26 Montreal and Toronto Armenian telephone directories.
27 Ontario Ethnocultural Data Base. "Ethnographic and Ethnocultural Profile, 1986, Mother Tongue, Armenian." Obviously the census material is skewed, since many second-, third-, fourth-, and fifth-generation Armenians would consider English rather than Armenian to be their mother tongue. See Karakashian, ("The General's Breath").
28 For an account of the impact of dispersion on Armenian supplementary schools in American cities, see Meruzhan Ozanian and Siranush G. Mkhitarian, (*Memorial Volume of the Armenian Relief Society: 1910–1970*), 101.

CHAPTER NINETEEN

1 Hunt, *The Theory and Practice*, 243. Unless otherwise indicated, the statistics given in this chapter are based on information from the mid-1990s.
2 For a discussion of the importance of institutions and organizations, see the classic study by Raymond Breton, "Institutional Completeness of Ethnic Communities," 193–205.
3 Ashjian, (*Tableau and History*).
4 Keuchgerian, "The Armenian Diocese of Canada," 54–65.
5 Ashjian, *Armenian Church in America*, 32ff.
6 *Prelacy Yearbook*.
7 Also referred to as the Armenian Evangelical Union of Eastern States and Canada, before the amalgamation of this Union with the Armenian Evangelical Union of California in 1971. See Tootikian, "Armenian Congregationalists." The Armenian Protestant church has had a much longer

established history in the United States than in Canada. The first church was the Armenian Congregational Church of the Martyrs in Worcester, Massachusetts, 1881.
8 Tootikian, *Armenian Evangelical*, 133–41.
9 Ibid., 302–7; Tootikian, *Congregationalists*, 5.
10 Baghdjian, *La physionomie sociale de la Communauté Arménienne Catholique de Montréal*, 170.
11 This brotherhood is different from the Mkhitarist Brothers in Venice and Vienna.
12 See Aram I, Catholicos of Cilicia, *The Challenge to Be a Church*, especially "The Witness of the Armenian Church in a Diaspora Situation," 25–44.
13 Kurdian, *Organizing*, 20.
14 Ibid., 28–9. Since 1995 cutbacks have affected these heritage language schools.
15 Baghdjian, *Les Arméniens*, 28–31. Baghdjian informs us that Karibian was a graduate of Euphrates College and Kalpakdjian of the Protestant college in Marsovan.
16 See Kurdian, *Organizing*, 21.
17 Mher Karakashian, "Meg u Meag Siune," *Horizon*, 23 June 1992.
18 From *Massis*, newsletter of Holy Cross School in Toronto.
19 *Laper*, 1967 (newspaper clipping, in author's collection, no date).
20 For example, Eghigian and Kaprielian, (*History of the Village of Chanakhchi in the Region of Keghi in the Prefecture of Erzerum*); (*Memorial Volume of the Village of Khups in Keghi*) (Fresno, CA: Asbarez 1968), published by the Village of Khups Compatriotic Union; (Keghi)Taregirk (*(Keghi) Yearbook*) (Detroit: Compatriotic Society of Keghi 1937). *Nor Geghi* (New Keghi), (East St Louis: Reconstruction Association of Keghi, vol. 1, 1964; vol. 2, 1965).
21 Editorial, (*Hairenik Daily*), 23 May 1969.
22 Schahgaldian, "The Political Integration," 71ff, 84ff.
23 For an account of the founding of the Toronto chapter, see Kouyoumdjian, (*The Story of a Life*).
24 For a history of the Armenian General Benevolent Union in Soviet Armenia, see Melkonian, (*The Armenian General Benevolent Union*).
25 *Union Générale Arménienne de Bienfaisance*, published by the AGBU, France, 1991. *AGBU News*, (spring–summer 2000), 42.
26 Teghtsoonian, "Armenians in Toronto."
27 For a discussion of the changing focus of the AGBU Central Board of Directors after 1988 and especially after 1991, when Armenia gained independence, see Hasmig Kurdian, *Organizing and Preserving*, 17–18.
28 *Hai Sird* (Armenian Heart), Seventieth Anniversary Issue, 1980.

29 (*Album of the Armenian Red Cross on the Occasion of its Twentieth Anniversary*) (Armenian Relief Society). Also *Hai Sird* 21, 83 (July 1960): 28–9. *Hai Sird* contains a brief history of the Hamilton chapter, noting that Verkin Korkoian, Eghisabet Goshgarian, Satenig Chichakian-Srabian, Khumar Tosoian, and Shogher Yeramian were the founding members.
30 Tootikian, "Armenian Congregationalists," 6.
31 See chapter 15 for reference to their choir and the eugenics book that the CAYPA commissioned: S. Shahnazarian, (*Study of Genetics*).
32 Artinian, "Armenian General Sports Union," 38, and *Horizon*, 5 July 1993.
33 *Bottin Téléphonique Arménien*, Montreal, 1996. The list probably does not include every Armenian doctor and dentist in the Montreal area.
34 Bakalian, *Armenian-Americans*, chap. 3, citing Talai.

CHAPTER TWENTY

1 Breton, "The Production and Allocation of Symbolic Resources," 127–8.
2 The 1948 Supreme Court case of *Shelley vs Kraemer* outlawed restrictive land covenants in the United States. Similar restrictive land covenants existed in Canada. See J.C. Weaver, "From Land Assembly to Social Maturity: The Suburban Life of Westdale (Hamilton), Ontario, 1911–1951," cited in Vartanian, "Chine Drive."
3 Z. Lorisian, oral interview, Hamilton.
4 J. Kasoian, oral interview, Brantford.
5 Bakalian found generational presence the prime variable in assimilation.
6 Marriage statistics are based on research from the following sources: Grace Anglican Church, Brantford; Dr Edward Melkonian; Armenian Diocese, Montreal; Armenian Prelacy, Montreal; Hamilton survey by Norman Kaprielian and Paul Kaprielian.
7 For intermarriage among Armenians, see Aharonian, *Intermarriage*; Bakalian, *Armenian-Americans*; Jendian, "The Farming Community."
8 Richardson, "Epilepsy Gene Puzzle," 34. Dr Hanessian has won many other awards for his work, including the Alfred Bader Award in Organic Chemistry (1988), the Palladium Medal of the Chemical Institute of Canada (1988), a Killam Fellowship (1989), and the A.C. Cope Scholar Award of the American Chemical Society (1996).
9 For an examination of post-Genocide literature, see Peroomian, *Literary Responses*, and Beledian, "L'expérience de la catastrophe."
10 A. Barkevian, oral interview, Toronto.
11 R. Pendakur, *Speaking in Tongues*.
12 Questionnaires were sent to readers of *Canadahai Mamul Lradou* (The Canadian Armenian Press Newsletter), published by the Armenian

Evangelical Church in Toronto, in 1981. These data represent the views of fifty-eight individuals. *Lradou* 19, no.1 (Jan.–March 1981): 33–4.

13 For the role of food in Armenian family life, see Balakian, *Black Dog of Fate*; Avakian, *Lion Woman's Legacy*; and Bakalian, *Armenian-Americans*.

14 Bakalian, *Armenian-Americans*, 393–4.

15 Avedis Manougian, oral interview, Toronto; Taleen Varjabedian, interviewer.

16 For an account of various speeches and promises made by Canadian politicians and political parties, see Shirinian, *Quest for Closure*, especially chap. 5.

17 For an account of the Permanent Peoples' Tribunal session on the Armenian Genocide, see *A Crime of Silence: The Armenian Genocide*. The Tribunal, which follows in the steps of the International Tribunal on Vietnam, instituted by Bertrand Russell, was founded by the Italian senator and jurist Lelio Basso and was set up in Bologna in 1979. Its goal is to contribute to the formation of a transnational humanitarian order and to render justice to people who, according to international law and, notably, the Statute of the International Court, are prevented from access to interstate jurisdictions.

Members of the jury for the session on the Armenian Genocide included primarily jurists, lawyers, theologians, and university professors; among them was Adolfo Perez Esquivel, winner of the Nobel Peace Prize. Algeria, Argentina, Australia, Belgium, France, India, Italy, Sweden, and the United States were represented on the panel. The request to the Tribunal to hold a session on the Armenian Genocide was made by the following nongovernment organizations: Groupement pour les Droits des Minorités (Paris, France), Cultural Survival (Cambridge, MA), Gesellschaft für Bedrohte Völker (Göttingen, West Germany.)

18 See, for example, Tölölyan, "Terrorism in a Textual Community."

19 These activists have simultaneously been referred to as freedom fighters and as terrorists, depending on the political viewpoints of the speakers.

20 For an account of the Ottawa School Board controversy, see Shirinian, *Closure*, 136ff, from notes provided by Garbis Armen, who was actively involved in the stormy affair.

21 See Akçam, *Dialogue*, regarding the perpetrator's perspective. See Shirinian, *Closure*, for the controversy in Montreal regarding the memorial sculpture and the shameful role played by the Canadian Tribute to Human Rights. See also Ugurlayan, "The Protection of Cultural Property," 71–84.

22 See Graham Fraser, "Armenian Genocide Did Happen: MPs," *Toronto Star*, 22 April 2004. France defied Turkish pressure and today, ironically, France and Turkey enjoy excellent trade relations.

CONCLUSION AND EPILOGUE

1 Private records in the author's possession.
2 For reinvention, see Conzen et al., "The Invention of Ethnicity."
3 *Toronto Star*, 11 March 2000. Andersen, in *None of the Above*, examines the world of mixed racial heritage and the problems of classification in a society obsessed with race and categorization. Since the 1970s, approximately 80 percent of immigrants to Canada have been from non-European sources and from "non-white" races. Lawrence Fuchs has predicted the "browning of America" due partly to immigration and partly to mixed marriages, and Kendra Wallace predicts this "browning" will take place primarily in large urban centres. Others have spoken of the "whiting" of America, i.e., the "whiting" of economically successful and assimilated groups like Jews and Asian Americans.
4 Breton et al., eds. *Cultural Boundaries*, 9–10. For an analysis of ethnic and racial identity issues, the tensions between the right of equality and the politics of difference, and the question of ethnic/racial survival, see Taylor, "Multiculturalism." Taylor writes, "There is a form of the politics of equal respect, as enshrined in a liberalism of rights, that is inhospitable to difference, because (a) it insists on uniform application of the rules defining these rights, without exception, and (b) it is suspicious of collective goals" (60).
5 See Hollinger, *Postethnic America*, and Kymlika, "American Multiculturalism."
6 Churchill, "The Decline of the Nation-State," 265–90.
7 See Hollinger, *Postethnic America*, chapter 5.
8 Diamond, "Deaths of Languages," 30–8.
9 With all due respect, liberties taken from the poem "We Are Few but We Are Armenian," by Baruyr Sevag.

Bibliography

SELECTED PRIMARY SOURCES

Memoirs, Autobiographies, and Unpublished Village Accounts

Ashukian, Mamigon
Baghdoian, Dikran
Chichakian, Senekerim
Der Krikorian, Krikor
Der Vartanian, Mardig
Donoian, Andranik
Dzalian, Onnig
Jrjoyan, Yervant (George Miller)
Kaprielian, Paul Vardkes
Krekorian, Edward
Krikorian, Arshag
Mooradian (Davies), Alexander B.
Muradian, Manoog
Ohanian, Ohannes (John)
Parseghian, Krikor
Tatarian, Setrag
Teghtzoonian, Oksen
Torosian, Ohannes
Vetzigian, Yeghnig

Manuscripts and Miscellaneous Sources

Aghotagirk (Prayer Book). New York, 1923
Armenian General Benevolent Union. Records, St Catharines.
Armenian Mother's Guide. Boston, 1923.
Armenian postcards, calendars, yearbooks, telephone directories, family Bibles, newspaper clippings.
Armenian Relief Society. Constitution and Bylaws. Various years.
Armenian Revolutionary Federation. Constitution and Bylaws. Various years.
Armenian school textbooks, including A. Andonian, *Gandzaran* (Treasury), Constantinople, no date: *Armenian Reader*, 1911, no covers; H.H. Chakmakjian, *Gerakan-Entertsaran* (Grammar-Reader), Boston, 1916; Simon Simonian, and Onnik Sarkisian, *Aragats*, Beirut, 1957; *First Reader*, Armenian Soviet Socialist Republic, no covers; R. Zardarian, *Meghraget* (River of Honey), Boston, 1927.
Armenian song books, including (*Pocket Song Book*), Boston, 1937; (*People's Song Book*), Boston, nd; Bedros Torosian, *New National Song Book*, Hoboken, 1917.
Armenian Women's Benevolent Association of Montreal. Constitution and minutes.
Atenagrutiun, Amerikahai HOGi Hamagumare (Minutes, Third Convention of the American-Armenian HOG). Providence, RI, 1929.
Azganver Hayuhyats Enkerutiun (*Armenian Patriotic Women's Association*). Pamphlet. Constantinople, 1880.
Canada. Census and Statistics Office. Various years.
Canadian Armenian Union. Minutes.
Cemetery records.
Chakmakjian, H(arutiun). *Amerikahai Namakani* (Armeno-American Letter Writer). Boston, 1914.
Documents on the Schism in the Armenian Church of America. New York 1993.
Marchand, Jean. Minister of Manpower and Immigration. *White Paper on Immigration*. Ottawa, 1966.
Miatsial Enkerutiun Hayots (The United Armenian Association). Constantinople, 1911.
Nubarian, Khazar. Book of clippings and hand-written accounts. Brantford, 1911.
Patriotic Society of Keghi. Constitution, minutes, accounts.
Prelacy Yearbook. New York 1993.
Raffi School. Minutes. St Catharines, 1924–25.
Report of the Royal Commission on Bilingualism and Biculturalism, Vols. 1–4. Ottawa, 1967–69.

Reports and Abstracts of the U.S. Immigration Commission. 41 vols. Document no. 747, 61st Congress, 3rd Session. Washington, 1911. (Dillingham Commission, sections pertaining to Armenians).
Village Educational Association Records of Astghaberd, Osnag, and Tarman.

Selected Newspapers and Periodicals

Abaka Weekly, Montreal
Ararat, publication of the Georgetown Boys
Armenian Mirror-Spectator
Armenian Red Cross Quarterly (periodical of the Armenian Red Cross, later the Armenian Relief Society)
Armenian Review
Baikar
Banvor
Brantford Expositor
Canadian Churchman (Church of England)
Hai Sird (Armenian Heart) (periodical of the Armenian Relief Society)
Hairenik Daily
Hairenik Monthly
Hairenik Weekly; later, *Armenian Weekly*
Halifax Herald
Hamilton Spectator
Horizon Weekly, Montreal
Montreal Gazette
Polyphony. Toronto: Multicultural History Society of Ontario, 1977–85
Presbyterian Review
St Catharines Standard
Shinarar
The Armenian Cause/La Cause Arménienne
Toronto Globe
Toronto Globe and Mail
Toronto Star
Various church and organizational bulletins and newsletters
Yergounk, Revue Littéraire Arménienne, 1929–30
Yeritasard Hayastan

Archives and Libraries

Archives of the Anglican Church of Canada, Toronto, and of records of various Anglican churches in Hamilton, St Catharines, and Brantford
Archives of Ontario. The Armenian Collection; The Georgetown Boys Collec-

tion, MU 9587; Court records for Brantford, St Catharines, Hamilton, 1900–15; RG22, T box 63, file no. 16, Supreme Court of Ontario, 1934, in Lincoln, *Akazarian vs Torosian et al.*

Archives of St Catharines, Brantford, Hamilton, Toronto, and Montreal: Tax Assessment Records. City Directories

Armenian Cultural Foundation, Arlington, MA

Armenian Research Center, University of Michigan–Dearborn, Dearborn, MI. Transcripts of oral interviews

Armenian Revolutionary Federation, Montreal, Records of Brantford, Guelph, and St Catharines Branches; Records of Khrimian Gradaran; Membership Survey

Bibliothèque Nubar, Armenian General Benevolent Union Archives, Paris

Boards of Education Records, Hamilton and Brantford: Public School Registers

California State University Fresno, Madden Library

Canadian Armenian Diocesan Archives

Canadian Armenian Prelacy Archives

Cemetery records, Hamilton

General Motors Archives, St Catharines

Great Britain. House of Commons. *Sessional Papers*, 1868–1916, vol. 79, 1878–79, *Turkey*, no. 53; vol. 80, 1879, *Turkey*, no. 10; vol. 82, 1890, *Turkey*, no. 1; vol. 92, 1877, *Turkey*, nos. 16, 17, 25, 26, 28; vol. 95, 1896, *Turkey*, no. 1; vol. 95, 1895–96, *Turkey*, no. 2; vol. 95, 1896, *Turkey*, no. 3; vol. 96, 1890–91, *Turkey*, no. 1; vol. 96, 1892, *Turkey*, no. 1; vol. 96, 1896, *Turkey*, no 5; vol. 101, 1897, *Turkey*, nos. 1, 2, 3, 7; vol. 103, 1905, *Turkey*, no. 3; vol. 105, 1909, *Turkey*, no. 1; vol. 106, 1898, part 1 (continuation of *Turkey*, no. 7, 1897); vol. 109, 1895, part 1, *Turkey*, no. 1

Harvard University, Houghton Library. Records of the American Board of Commissioners for Foreign Missions

International Harvester Archives, Hamilton

League of Nations, Geneva, Switzerland

Library of the Ontario Institute for Studies in Education, University of Toronto

Multicultural History Society of Ontario: The Armenian Collection

National Archives of Canada. MG26 K, vol. 434, part 3, microfilm M1309; MG26, vol. 86, William Lyon Mackenzie King Papers; MG27 III B1, vols. 2–5, Charles Hazlitt Cahan Papers; MG29 D38, vol. 5, file 3420-3576; MG30, vol. D371, 1–3, Kerop Bedoukian Papers

National Archives of Canada. RG2, vol. 1240, PC 400; RG6 A, vol. 209, file 1876; RG7 C21, vol. 2(b); RG7 G21, vol. 636, pt 2, 1924–25; RG13, series A-2, vol. 2215, file 405/1932; RG13, vol. 2215, file 405/1932; RG13 A-2, vol. 198, file 1716-1735, 1915; RG13 A-2, vol. 198, file 1718/1918; RG14 D2, vol. 242, file 98d; RG19 E2 (c), vol. 544, file 135-8 (3); RG19 E2 (c), vol. 545, file 135-8-70; RG25 file 160; RG25 series A-2 vol. 163, file C 13/5; RG25 A2

vol. 141, file C; RG25 A-2 vol. 296, file P-10-13; RG25 GI vol. 1325, file 999; RG25 GI vol. 1416; RG25 GI vol. 1465, file 160; RG25 GI vol. 1484, file 44T; RG25 GI vol. 1776, file 153; RG76, vol. 125, file 27114 ; vol. 215, file 89310; vol. 215, file. 89616; vol. 300, file 279907, parts 1–3; vol. 307, file 284136; vol. 344, file 366144, part 1; vol. 345, file 367711; vol. 354, file 390480; vol. 368, file 488557; vol. 406, file 594511, part 1; vol. 431, file 642439; vol. 449, file 681314; vol. 474, file 729921, parts 1 and 3; vol. 478, file 740325; vol. 479, file 742102; vol. 480, file 745162 C.J. parts 2 and 3; vol. 481, file 745162, part 3; vol. 522, file 801591; vol. 531, file 803588; vol. 550, file 805806; vol. 578, file 817510, part 1; vol. 635-641, file 978450; vol. 636, file 978450, parts 5 and 6; vol. 637, file 978450, parts 7–10; vol. 854, file 554-6 Int. no. 51; vol. 854, file 554-3, parts 1 and 2; vol. 902, file 569-22-1, part 2; RG117, vol. 20, files 229–231; RG150, Canadian Expeditionary Force
Presbyterian Church Archives, Toronto
Public Libraries in St Catharines, Brantford, and Hamilton. Vertical files
Public Record Office, London, England
Robarts Library, University of Toronto
Stanford University, Herbert Hoover Institution on War, Revolution, and Peace
United Church Archives, Toronto. Georgetown Boys (Cedarvale Home); Acts and Proceedings of the General Assembly of the Presbyterian Church, 1905; Report of a Preliminary and General Social Survey of Hamilton, April 1915; Report of a Limited Survey of Religious, Moral, Industrial and Housing Conditions, 1915; Minutes of the Board of Evangelism and Social Service
Zohrab Information Center
Zoryan Institute of Canada Archives, Toronto: Pasdermajian Records of the Canadian Armenian Congress

Interviews

Selected taped oral interviews, telephone interviews, and responses to written questionnaires. Dates are given where available.

WOMEN
Alexanian, Siroon, St Catharines, 1990
Aloian, Alice, St Catharines, 1978, 1979
Apegian, Rose, Hamilton, 1977
Aprahamian, Alice, Hamilton, 1977
Artinian, Anoush, Cambridge, 1980
Artinian, Dikranouhi, Toronto, 1978
Asailian, Aghavni, Toronto, 1985
Ashukian, Victoria, Yerevan, Armenia, 1981
Avedissian, Mary, St Catharines, 1980

Bailey, Victoria, Brantford, 1987
Bakaian, Gulnaz, Granite City, Illinois, 1980
Ball, Audrey, Brantford, 1987
Bedrosian, Haiganoush (Rose), St Catharines, 1980, 1987, 1990
Boyagian, Mariam, Detroit, 1980, 1989
Boyajian, Mariam, Toronto, 1987
Bozoian, Nartouhi, St Catharines, 1980

Campbell, Margaret, Toronto, 1980
Chichakian, Mona, St Catharines

Der Aristakesian, Haiganoush, Hamilton, 1979
Der Krikorian, Tsaghig, St Catharines, 1981, 1987
Derderian, Angel, St Catharines, 1979
DeRoches, Victoria, Hamilton, 1976

Evarian, Takouhi, Hamilton, 1976, 1979

Griffiths, Jenny Kalagian, St Catharines

Hachigian, Alice, Hamilton, 1977
Hanimyan, Diana, Toronto, 1984
Hairabedian, Mary, Windsor, 1988
Hatch, Roxanne, Hamilton, 1977
Hazarian, Iskouhi, Montreal, 1984
Hodson, Elsie, Toronto, 1979
Houroian, Peprone, Detroit, 1980
Humpartzoumian, Nevart, Brantford, 1979

Kalagian, Baidzar, St Catharines
Kalagian, Mariam, St Catharines, 1980
Kaloustian, Vera, Fresno, CA
Kapousouzian, Violet, Toronto, 1985
Kaprielian, Anna, Hamilton, 1979–80
Kaprielian, Loussaper, Hamilton, 1972–73
Kaprielian, Margo, Hamilton, 1995
Kasparian, Kohar, Toronto, 1986
Khashmanian, Alice, Toronto, 1987
Khoubessarian, Dikranouhi, Toronto
Krekorian, Edna, St Catharines, 1979
Krikorian, Varsenig, St Catharines, 1987, 1992

Langton, Nora Halagian, Brantford, 1987

Marderosian, Miriam, St Catharines, 1987
Melkonian, Astghig, Hamilton, 1976, 1979
Minassian, Professor Chaké, Montreal
Mooradian, Nazen, Hamilton, 1976
Mooradian, Satenig, Brantford, 1984
Mooradian, Zabel, Brantford, 1983
Muradian, Valantine, Brantford, 1977

Nahabedian, Frances, Toronto, 1980

Ounjian, Betty, Toronto, 1990
Ounjian, Helen, Toronto, 1990

Palvetzian, Mary, Toronto, 1992
Palvetzian, Victoria, Cambridge, 2001
Papazian, Juliet, Toronto, 1986
Pargamian, Baidzar, Cambridge, 1980
Petti, Dixie, St Catharines, 1992
Postalian, Lucy, Toronto, 1990

Racian, Vergin, Hamilton, 1980
Rasian, Margaret, Hamilton, 1978

Sahagian, Manig, Brantford, 1979, 1984
Sahagian, Mariam, St Catharines, 1980
Sarkissian, Alice, Brantford, 1987
Sarkissian, Jean, Cambridge, 2001
Sarkissian, Khatoun, Brantford, 1977, 1987
Sarkissian, Nevart, Detroit, 1980, 1985, 1989
Seferian, Armenouhi, Hamilton, 2002
Seferian, Hasmig, Brantford, 1979
Serabian, Satenig, Brantford, 1992
Setlakwé, Louise, Sherbrooke, 1999
Shahen, Aghavni, Los Angeles, 1985
Shehirian, Shnorig, Toronto, 1980
Simigian, Armenouhi, Hamilton, 1977–78
Solomonian, Alice, St Catharines, 1977, 1987
Souin, Marziné, Toronto, 1977
Srabian, Araxie, Toronto, 1978
Stepanian, Rose, Hamilton, 1977

Tanielian, Eglantine, Hamilton
Tatigian, Rose, Montreal, 1989

Teghtsoonian, Shoushan, Toronto, 1979
Topalian, Ardemis, Fresno, California, 1997
Torosian, Alice, St Catharines, 1980, 1989, 1990, 1995

Vasoyan, Nver, Toronto, 1986

Yakmalian, Joyce, Hamilton, 1976
Yakmalian, Zarouhi, Hamilton, 1976

MEN

Abkarian, Markar, Yerevan, Armenia, 1981
Adams, Dr Michael, Hamilton, 1979
Adourian, Setrag, Toronto, 1978
Aivazian, Aram, Hamilton, 1980
Alexanian, Armen, Hamilton, 1987
Aloian, Berj, St Catharines, 1983, 1992
Apegian, William, Hamilton, 1977
Aprahamian, Jack, Hamilton, 1977
Ar(a)kelian, Leo, Halifax, 1989
Artinian, Antranig, Toronto, 1983
Artinian, Harry, St Catharines, 1987
Ashukian, Kevork, St Catharines, 1990
Aslanian, Hamazasp, Detroit, 1980
Avedissian, John, St Catharines, 1980
Avedissian, Reginald, St Catharines, 1980

Bazoian, Harry, Brantford, 1977
Bedoukian, Harold, Montreal, 2002
Bedoukian, Kerop, Montreal, 1991
Boghosian, Nick, Fresno, California
Boyajian, Maghakia, Toronto, 1987
Bozoian, Aristakes, St Catharines, 1987

Chami, Alexander, Toronto
Courian, Paul, Toronto, 1978

Davidian, Abraham, Yerevan, Armenia, 1981
Deirmenjian, Garabed, Toronto, 1985
Der Meksian, Rev. Sempad, Toronto, 1979
Der Stepanian, George, Brantford, 1979
Diran, Leo, Fresno, CA, 2002

Ekmekjian, Harutiun, Toronto, 1991
Evarian, Pilag, Hamilton, 1979

Fermanian, Tom, Ste Adele, Quebec, 1999

Garabedian, Charles, St Catharines
Goshgarian, George, Hamilton, 1989

Hagopian, Edward, Fresno, CA, 2000
Hagopian, John, Cambridge, 2001
Haktsian, Dr Arthur, Vancouver, 1980
Hatch, Harry, Hamilton, 1977
Hopian, Geghemes, Toronto, 1978
Houroian, Mampre, Detroit, 1981
Hovsepian, John, Brantford, 1987

Jrjoian, Yervant, (George Miller) Hamilton, 1979

Kalagian, Richard, St Catharines, 1993
Kaprielian, Hagop (Jack), Hamilton, 1977–80
Kaprielian, Norman, Hamilton, 1976–80, 1990
Kaprielian, Paul Vardkes, Hamilton, 1976, 1989, 1990
Karibian, Nahabed, Hamilton, 1978
Kasoian, Mihran, Hamilton, 1976
Kerbekian Yeprem, Toronto, 1990, 1994
Kloian, Ardash, Detroit, 1980
Kostigian, John, Cambridge, 2001
Krekorian, Migirdich, St Catharines, 1979, 1989
Kuderian, Art, Windsor

Magarian, Kirk, Toronto, 1981
Malatjalian, Dr Dickran, Halifax, 1989
Mavian, Zorig, Detroit, Michigan, 1980
Melkonian, Robert, Hamilton, 1978, 1980
Migirdicyan, Migirdic, Toronto, 2002
Mooradian, Alexander (Davies), Hagersville, 1977–1980
Mooradian, Harry, Toronto
Mooradian, Levon, Atlanta, Georgia, 1984
Mouchian, Bedros, Toronto, 1992

Ohanian, Ohannes (John), Hamilton, 1979
Osganian, Vahram, Toronto, 1985

Palvetzian, Garabed (Charles) Cambridge, 1980
Palvetzian, George, Cambridge, 1980, 1987
Pargamian, Arsen, Cambridge, 1980
Paroyan, Mesag, St Catharines, 1989

Pasdermajian, Hagop, Montreal, 1999
Pasdermajian, Yervant, Montreal, 1980–85, 1991
Postalian, James, Toronto, 1990

Rice, Thomas, Hamilton, 1977

Safarian, Professor Edward, Toronto, 1978
Seferian, Boghos (Paul), Hamilton, 2002
Seraganian, Harutiun, Brantford, 1983
Setlakwé, Senator Raymond, Sherbrooke, 1999
Shamigian, Antranig, Silver Springs, Maryland, 1979
Solomonian, Paul, St Catharines, 1987
Srabian, Harutiun, Toronto, 1977–79

Tatigian, Paul, Montreal, 1989
Tchilingirian, Bedros, Toronto, 1984
Teghtsoonian, Oksen, Toronto, 1978–79
Terzian, Vasken, Toronto, 1992
Torosian, Hygus, St Catharines, 1978–80, 1986, 1990
Tourikian, Hratch, Toronto, 1981

Yedigarian, Hrachia, New Keghi, Armenia, 1981
Yeremian, Georges, Toronto, 2000

SELECTED SECONDARY SOURCES

Abella, Irving. *Nationalism, Communism and Canadian Labour: The CIO, the Communist Party, and the Canadian Congress of Labour, 1935–1956.* Toronto 1973.
– *The Canadian Labour Movement, 1902–1960.* Canadian Historical Association, Historical Booklet, no. 28. Ottawa, 1975.
– ed. *On Strike: Six Key Labour Struggles in Canada, 1919–1949.* Toronto 1974.
Abella, Irving, and Harold Troper. *None Is Too Many: Canada and the Jews of Europe, 1933–1948.* Toronto 1982.
Acton, Lord. "Nationality." In *Essays on Freedom and Power.* Glencoe, IL 1948.
Adachi, Ken. *A History of the Japanese Canadians: The Enemy That Never Was.* Toronto 1979.
Adalian, Rouben Paul, ed. *Guide to the Armenian Genocide in the U.S. Archives.* Alexandria, VA, 1994.
Adelman, Howard, and John H. Simpson. *Multiculturalism, Jews and Identities in Canada.* Jerusalem 1996.

Aharonian, Aharon G. *Intermarriage and the Armenian-American Community.* Shrewsbury, MA, 1983.

Aharonian, Avedis, and Boghos Nubar. *Arménie: Tableau approximatif des réparations et indemnités pour les dommages subis par la nation Arménienne en Arménie de Turquie et dans la République Arménienne du Caucase.* Paris Peace Conference 1919.

Ahmad, Feroz. *The Young Turks.* Oxford 1969.

"Ailleurs, hier, autrement: Connaissance et reconnaissance du génocide des Arméniens." Special issue. *Revue d'histoire de la Shoah. Le monde juif.* 177–78. (January–August 2003).

Aivazian, Aram P. *Armenia: Usurped by Genocide and Treachery.* Toronto 1992.

Akçam, Taner. *Dialogue across an International Divide: Essays towards a Turkish-Armenian Dialogue.* Toronto 2001.

Aknuni, Edouard (Khachatur Malumian). *Depi Yerkir* (Towards the Old Country). Boston 1911.

Alamuddin, Ida. *Papa Kuenzler and the Armenians.* London, 1970.

Album Hai K. Khachi: Ir Ksanamiak Artiv, 1910–30. (Album of the Armenian Red Cross on the Occasion of Its Twentieth Anniversary), 1910–30. Boston 1930.

Alexander, June Granatir. "Staying Together: Chain Migration and Patterns of Slovak Settlement in Pittsburgh prior to World War I." *Journal of American Ethnic History* 1, 1 (fall 1981).

– "City Directories as 'Ideal' Censuses." *Western Pennsylvania Historical Magazine* 65, 3 (July 1982).

Altounian, Janine. *La survivance: Traduire le trauma collective.* Paris 2000.

Anderson, Erica Surat. "None of the Above." *Toronto Star,* 11 March 2000.

Anderson, Grace M., and David Higgs. *A Future to Inherit: The Portuguese Communities of Canada.* Toronto 1976.

Andonian, Aram. *The Memoirs of Naim Bey.* Originally published in 1919. Newton Square, PA. Reprint 1964.

Apkarian, Arshag. "Hakstun." In *Nor Geghi* (New Keghi). Vol. 2.

Aprahamian, Sima. "A Multitude of Overlapping Identities: A Lebanese Armenian Community in the Beka'a Valley of Lebanon." *Armenian Review* 43, 1/169 (spring 1990).

Apramian, Jack. *The Georgetown Boys.* Winona, ON, 1976.

– "The Georgetown Boys." *Polyphony: Armenians in Ontario,* 4, 2 (fall/winter 1982).

Aram I, His Holiness, Catholicos of Cilicia. *The Challenge to Be a Church in a Changing World.* New York 1997.

Arevigian. "Endhanur Aknark me Kghiin vra" (General Sketch of Keghi). In *Taregirk* (Yearbook). Detroit 1937.

Arlen, Michael J. *Passage to Ararat*. New York 1975.

Armen, Garbis, Vrej-Armen Artinian, and Hamo Abdalian. *Historical Atlas of Armenia*. New York 1987.

Armenian Genocide in the Canadian Press. 2 vols. Vol. 1, 1915–1916. Montreal 1985; vol. 2, 1916–1923, Montreal, n.d.

Armenian Youth Federation. *Blue Books*. Boston 1949–55.

"Armenians of Manchester." In Teodik, *Amenun Taretsuitse* (Everyman's Almanac). Constantinople 1921.

Armenians in Ontario. Verabrum (Revival). Special issue, *Polyphony* 4, 2.

Arpee, Leon. *A Century of Armenian Protestantism: 1846–1946*. New York 1946.

Artinian, Hagop. "Armenian General Sports Union." *Polyphony* 7, 1 (spring/summer 1985).

Arzumanian, Rev. Zaven A., compiler. *Azgapatum* (National History), 1930–1955. Vol. 2. New York 1997.

Ashjian, Archbishop Mesrob. *The Armenian Church in America*. New York 1995.

Ashjian, Rev. Arden, compiler. *Vdag Vijakatsuits yev Patmutiun* (Vdag: Tableau and History). New York 1949.

Aspirations et Agissement Révolutionnaires des Comités Arméniens avant et après la Proclamation de la Constitution Ottoman. Istanbul 1917.

Astourian, Stephan H. "Genocidal Process: Reflections on the Armeno-Turkish Polarization." In *The Armenian Genocide: History, Politics, Ethics*. Richard G. Hovannisian, ed. New York 1992.

Atamian, Sarkis. *The Armenian Community*. New York 1955.

Attarian, Varoujan. *Le génocide des Arméniens devant l'ONU*. Np. 1997.

Aun, Karl. *The Political Refugees: A History of the Estonians in Canada*. Toronto 1985.

Avakian, Arlene Voski. *Lion Woman's Legacy: An Armenian-American Memoir*. New York 1992.

Avakumovic, Ivan. *The Communist Party in Canada: A History*. Toronto 1975.

Avery, Donald. "Continental European Immigrant Workers in Canada, 1896–1919: From 'Stalwart Peasants' to Radical Proletariat." *Canadian Review of Sociology and Anthropology* 12, 1 (1975).

– *Dangerous Foreigners, European Immigrant Workers and Labour Radicalism in Canada, 1896–1932*. Toronto 1979.

– "Ethnic Loyalties and the Proletarian Revolution: A Case Study of Communist Political Activity in Winnipeg, 1923–1936." In *Ethnicity, Power and Politics in Canada*. Jorgen Dahlie and Tissa Fernando, eds. Toronto 1981.

– "Ethnic and Class Tensions in Canada, 1918–20: Anglo-Canadians and the

Alien Worker." In *Ukrainians in Canada during the Great War*. Frances Swyripa and John H. Thompson, eds. Edmonton 1983.

Ayanian, Jean. *Le Kemp: Une enfance intra-muros*. Marseilles 2001.

Azadian, Libarid. *Hai Vorbere Meds Yegherni* (The Orphans of the Armenian Genocide). Los Angeles 1995.

"Azgain Gordser Kghi" ("National Endeavours in Keghi"). In (*Memorial Volume of the Village of Khups in Keghi*). Fresno, CA, 1968.

Babayan, Levon. *The Romance of the Oriental Rug*. Toronto 1925.

Bagdasarian, Mesrob. *The Sunny Side of the Armenian People*. Toronto 1930.

Baghdasarian, K. (*National Almanac*). Constantinople 1912.

Baghdjian, Kévork K. "La physionomie sociale de la communauté arménienne catholique de Montréal. Montreal 1972.

– Les Arméniens au Québec: Aperçu historique. Montreal 1980.

– Le problème arménien. Montreal 1985.

– *La confiscation par le gouvernement turc, des biens arméniens ... dits abandonnés*. Montreal 1987.

– *La Communauté Arménienne Catholique de Montréal*. Montreal 1992.

Bailey, F.G. "Changing Communities." In *Gifts and Poison: The Politics of Reputation*. F.G. Bailey, ed. Oxford 1971.

– "The Peasant View of the Bad Life." In *Peasants and Peasant Societies*. Teodor Shanin, ed. Harmondsworth, England, 1971.

– ed., *Gifts and Poison: The Politics of Reputation*. Oxford 1971.

Bailyn, Bernard. *Education in the Forming of American Society*. New York 1960.

Bakalian, Anny. *Armenian-Americans: From Being to Feeling Armenian*. New Brunswick, NJ, 1994.

Balakian, Grigoris. *Le golgotha arménien: Berlin-Deir es-Zor, Mémoires*. Vol. 1. Trans. from Armenian by Hratch Bedrossian. Original title *Hai Goghtotan*, published in Vienna 1922. Chamigny, France, 2002.

Balakian, Peter. *Black Dog of Fate: An American Son Uncovers His Armenian Past*. New York 1998.

– *The Burning Tigris: The Armenian Genocide and America's Response*. New York: Harper Collins, 2003.

Balawyder, Aloysius. *Canadian-Soviet Relations between the World Wars*. Toronto 1972.

Baldwin, Oliver. *Six Prisons and Two Revolutions*. London 1924.

Baliozian, Ara. *Fragmented Dreams: Armenians in Diaspora*. Kitchener, ON, 1987.

Bamberger, Joan. "Family and Kinship in an Armenian-American Community." *Journal of Armenian Studies* 3, 1/2 (1986–87).

Barber, Marilyn. "Nationalism, Nativism and the Social Gospel: The Protestant Church Response to Foreign Immigrants, 1897–1914." In *The Social Gospel in Canada*. R. Allen, ed. Ottawa 1975.

Bardakjian, Kevork B. *Hitler and the Armenian Genocide*. Cambridge 1985.

Bardizian, A(rmen). *Hai Yekeghetsvo Tagnape yev Anor Pataskhanatunere* (The Crisis in the Armenian Church and Those Responsible for It). Boston 1936.

Barkey, Karen. *Bandits and Bureaucrats: The Ottoman Route to State Centralization*. Ithaca, NY, and London 1994.

Barton, James L. *The Story of the Near East Relief, 1915–30*. New York 1930.

– comp. *"Turkish Atrocities": Statements of American Missionaries on the Destruction of Christian Communities in Ottoman Turkey, 1915–1917*. Ann Arbor, MI, 1998.

Barton, Josef J. *Peasants and Strangers: Italians, Rumanians, and Slovaks in an American City, 1890–1950*. Cambridge, MA, 1975.

– "Eastern and Southern Europeans." In *Ethnic Leadership in America*. John Higham, ed. Baltimore and London 1978.

Basmajian, John V. *I.O.U.: Adventures of a Medical Scientist*. Hamilton 1993.

Baxevanis, John J. *Economy and Population Movements in the Peloponnesus of Greece*. Athens 1972.

Bazarian, Movses. *Soviet Armenia: Letters from the Soviet Paradise*. Toronto 1998.

Bedoukian, Harold. "A Unique Armenian Silk Rug: An Historical Document." *Revue des Etudes Arméniennes* 20 (1986–87).

Bedoukian, Kerop. *The Urchin: An Armenian's Escape*. London 1978.

Bedrosian, Margaret. *The Magical Pine Ring*. Detroit 1991.

Beeching, William, and Phyllis Clark. *Yours in the Struggle: Reminiscences of Tim Buck*. Toronto 1977.

Beledian, Krikor. "L'expérience de la catastorphe dans la littérature arménienne." *Revue d'histoire arménienne contemporaine* 1 (1995).

Belkin, Simon. *Through Narrow Gates*. Montreal 1966.

Bensoussan, Georges, Claire Mouradian, and Yves Ternon, eds. *Ailleurs, hier, autrement: Connaissance et reconnaissance du génocide des Arméniens*. Special issue of *Revue d'histoire de la Shoah: Le monde juif*. 177–78. (January-August 2003).

Bercuson, David. *Fools and Wise Men: The Rise and Fall of the One Big Union*. Toronto 1978.

Berkes, Niyazi. *The Development of Secularism in Turkey*. Montreal 1964.

Beylerian, A. *Les grandes puissances: L'empire ottoman et les Arméniens dans les archives françaises, 1914–1918*. Paris 1983.

Bianco, Carla. *The Two Rosetos*. Bloomington, IN, 1974.

Bienvenue, Rita M., and Jay E. Goldstein. *Ethnicity and Ethnic Relations in Canada*. 2d ed. Toronto 1985.

Bliss, Edwin M. *Turkey and the Armenian Atrocities: A Reign of Terror*. N.p. 1896.

Bliss, Michael, and L.M. Grayson, eds. *The Wretched of Canada: Letters to R. B. Bennett, 1930–1935*. Toronto 1971.

Bodnar, John. *Immigration and Industrialization: Ethnicity in an American Mill Town, 1870–1940*. Pittsburgh 1977.

Bodnar, John. "Immigration and Modernization: The Case of Slavic Peasants in Industrial America." *Journal of Social History* 4, 3 (fall 1976).

– *The Transplanted: A History of Immigrants in Urban America*. Bloomington, IN, 1985.

Boettiger, Louis A. *Armenian Legends and Festivals*. Minneapolis 1920.

Bonacich, Edna. "A Theory of Middleman Minorities." *American Sociological Review* 38 (October 1973).

Bothwell, Robert, Ian Drummond, and John English. *Canada since 1945: Power, Politics, and Provincialism*. Toronto 1990 (revised).

– *Canada: 1900–1945*. Toronto 1990.

Boudjikanian, Aida. "Immigration et Milieux Urbains, Lyon, Montreal: Deux Lieux, Deux Moments de la Diaspora Arménienne." *Ani: Cahiers arméniens* 6 (September 1994): 21–39.

Boudjikanian-Keuroghlian, Aida. *Les Arméniens dans la région Rhone-Alpes*. Audin-Lyon 1978.

Bournoutian, George A. *A History of the Armenian People*. Vol. 2, *1500 A.D. to the Present*. Costa Mesa, CA 1994.

– *A Concise History of the Armenian People from Ancient Times to the Present*. Costa Mesa, CA, 2002

Boyajian, Dickran H. *Armenia: The Case for a Forgotten Genocide*. Westwood, NJ, 1972.

Boyajian, Zabelle, ed. *Armenian Legends and Poems*. New York 1959.

Bozorgmehr, Mehdi, Claudia Der-Martirosian, and Georges Sabagh. "Middle Easterners: A New Kind of Immigrant." In *Ethnic Los Angeles*. Roger Waldinger and Mehdi Bozorgmehr, eds. New York 1996.

Bradbury, Bettina. "Women's History and Working Class History." *Labour/LeTravail* 19 (1987).

Braudel, Fernand. *Civilization and Capitalism from the Fifteenth to the Eighteenth Century: The Structures of Everyday Life*. Trans. from French by Siân Reynolds. Berkeley and Los Angeles 1992.

Brémond, Edouard. *La Cilicie, 1919–1920*. Paris 1921.

Breton, Raymond. "Institutional Completeness of Ethnic Communities and the Personal Relations of Immigrants." *American Journal of Sociology* 70, 2 (September 1964).

– "The Production and Allocation of Symbolic Resources: An Analysis of the Linguistic and Ethnocultural Fields in Canada." *Canadian Review of Sociology and Anthropology* 21, 2 (May 1984).

- "Multiculturalism and Canadian Nation-Building." In Alan Cairns and Cynthia Williams, eds., *The Politics of Gender, Ethnicity and Language in Canada*. Toronto 1986.
- The Governance of Ethnic Communities: Political Structures and Processes in Canada. New York 1991.

Breton, Raymond, et al., eds. *Cultural Boundaries and the Cohesion of Canada*. Montreal 1980.

Briggs, John. *An Italian Passage: Immigrants to Three American Cities, 1890–1930*. New Haven, CT, 1978.

Brody, David. *Steelworkers in America: The Nonunion Era*. Cambridge, MA, 1960.

- "The Origins of Modern Steel Unionism: The SWOC Era." In *Forging a Union of Steel: Philip Murray, SWOC and United Steelworkers*. Paul F. Clark, Peter Gottlieb, and Donald Kennedy, eds. Ithaca, NY, 1987.

Brown, Robert Craig, and Ramsey Cook. *Canada, 1896–1921: A Nation Transformed*. Toronto 1974.

Bruce, Jean. *Back the Attack! Canadian Women during the Second World War: At Home and Abroad*. Toronto 1985.

Bryce, P.H. "Immigration in Relation to the Public Health." *Canadian Journal of Medicine and Surgery* 19, 4 (April 1906).

Bryce, Viscount James B., and Arnold Toynbee. *The Treatment of Armenians in the Ottoman Empire, 1915–1916: Documents presented to Viscount Grey of Fallodon by Viscount Bryce*. London, H.M. Stationery Office 1916.

Buchignani, Norman, and Doreen M. Indra, with Ram Srivastiva. *Continuous Journey: A Social History of South Asians in Canada*. Toronto 1985.

Buck, Tim. *Thirty Years, 1922–1952: The Story of the Communist Movement in Canada*. Toronto 1952.

Bullen, John. "Hidden Workers: Child Labour and the Family Economy in Late Nineteenth-Century Urban Ontario." *Labour/Le Travail* 18 (fall 1986).

Burgess, Joanne. "Exploring the Limited Identities of Canadian Labour: Recent Trends in English-Canada and in Québec." *International Journal of Canadian Studies/Revue Internationale d'Études Canadiennes* 1–2 (spring-fall 1990).

Burnet, Jean, ed. *Looking into My Sister's Eyes: An Exploration in Women's History*. Toronto 1986.

Burnier, Georges. "L'Installation des réfugiés arméniens en colonies agricoles dans les états sous mandat français. *La Revue International de la Croix Rouge* (May 1928).

Calder, J.A. Government of Canada, House of Commons, *Debates* 3, 26 April 1921.

Campbell, Marjorie Freeman. *A Mountain and a City*. Toronto 1966.

Campbell, Peter. "Making Socialists." *Labour/Le Travail* 30 (fall 1992).

Caplan, G.L. *The Dilemma of Canadian Socialism*. Toronto 1973.

Carrothers, W.A. "The Immigration Problem in Canada." *Queen's Quarterly* 36 (1929).
Centennial Anniversary of the Establishment of the Armenian Apostolic Church in Canada, 1898–1998. Montreal 1998.
Chakmakjian, Harutiun. "Hairenik and Its Workers: Memoirs of Seventeen Years." *Armenian Review* 32, nos. 1–25 (1979).
Chaliand, Gerard, and Yves Ternon. *The Armenians from Genocide to Resistance.* Tony Berrett, trans. London 1983.
Chambers, Ada Pierce (wife of Lawson P. Chambers). *In an Anatolian Valley.* Toronto 1955.
Chambers, Lawson P. "The Massacre of Armenia." *Queen's Quarterly* 24 (1916).
– "The Armenian Deportations." *Queen's Quarterly* 25, 1 (1917).
Chambers, Robert. "Our Interest in Turkey." *Queen's Quarterly* 22, 1 (July–September 1914).
Chambers, William Nesbitt. *Yoljuluk.* London 1928. Reprint Paramus, NJ, 1988.
Chichekian, Garo. "Armenian Immigrants in Canada and Their Distribution in Montreal." *Cahiers de Géographie de Québec* 21, 52 (April 1977).
– *The Distribution and Linguistic Acculturation of Armenians in Canada: A Research Report to the Multiculturalism Directorate.* Montreal 1985.
– *The Armenian Community of Quebec.* Montreal 1989.
Chimbos, Peter D. *The Canadian Odyssey: The Greek Experience in Canada.* Toronto 1980.
Choldin, Harvey M. "Kinship Networks in the Migration Process." *International Migration Review* 7, 2 (summer 1973).
Churchill, Stacy. "The Decline of the Nation-State and the Education of National Minorities." *International Review of Education* 42, 4 (1996).
– *New Canadian Perspectives, Official Languages in Canada: Changing the Language Landscape/Les langues officielles au Canada: Transformer le paysage linguistique.* Ottawa 1998.
– *Language Education, Canadian Civic Identity and the Identities of Canadians.* Strasbourg 2003.
Clark, Lovell C., ed. *Documents on Canadian External Relations.* Vol. 3, 1919–1925. Ottawa 1970.
Clark, Paul F., Peter Gottlieb, and Donald Kennedy, eds. *Forging a Union of Steel: Philip Murray, SWOC, and United Steelworkers.* Ithaca, NY, 1987.
Cole, Ellen, Oliva M. Espin, and Esther D. Rothblum, eds. *Refugee Women and Their Mental Health: Shattered Societies, Shattered Lives.* Binghamton, NY, 1992.
Coleman, H.T. "Training for a New Citizenship." *Queen's Quarterly* (July 1919).
Commons, John R. *Races and Immigrants in America.* New York 1916.

Conzen, Kathleen Neils. "Immigrants, Immigrant Neighborhoods, and Ethnic Identity: Historical Issues." *Journal of American History* 66, 3 (December 1979).

Conzen, Kathleen Neils, David A. Gerber, Ewa Morawska, George E. Pozzetta, and Rudolph J. Vecoli. "The Invention of Ethnicity: A Perspective from the U.S.A." *Journal of American Ethnic History* 12 (fall 1992).

Copp, John Terry. *The Anatomy of Poverty/ The Condition of the Working Class in Montreal, 1897–1929*. Toronto 1974.

Corbett, David C. *Canada's Immigration Policy: A Critique*. Toronto, 1957.

Creese, Gillian. "The Politics of Dependence: Women, Work and Unemployment in the Vancouver Labour Movement before World War II." In Gregory S. Kealey, ed., *Class, Gender, and Region: Essays in Canadian Historical Sociology*. St. John's 1988.

Creighton, Donald. *The Forked Road: Canada 1939–1957*. Toronto 1976.

A Crime of Silence. The Armenian Genocide: The Permanent Peoples' Tribunal. Cambridge, MA, 1985. Original text published in Paris, 1984, ed. Gérard Chaliand in collaboration with Claire Mouradian and Alice Aslanian-Samuelian. First published in English in London, 1985. English text edited by Gerard Libaridian.

Dadrian, Vahakn N. "The Naim-Andonian Documents on the World War I Destruction of Ottoman Armenians: The Anatomy of a Genocide." *International Journal of Middle East Studies* 18, 3 (August 1986).

– "Genocide as a Problem of National and International Law: The World War I Armenian Case and Its Contemporary Legal Ramifications." *Yale Journal of International Law* 14, 2 (summer 1989).

– "A Textual Analysis of the Key Indictment of the Turkish Military Tribunal Investigating the Armenian Genocide." *Armenian Review* 44, 1/173 (spring 1991).

– "The Documentation of the World War I Armenian Massacres in the Proceedings of the Turkish Military Tribunal." *International Journal of Middle East Studies* 23, 4 (November 1991).

– "The Secret Young-Turk Ittihadist Conference and the Decision for the World War I Genocide of the Armenians." *The Journal of Political and Military Sociology* 22, 1 (summer 1994).

– *The History of the Armenian Genocide: Ethnic Conflict from the Balkans to Anatolia to the Caucasus*. Providence, RI, 1995.

Dalrymple, William. *From the Holy Mountain: A Journey in the Shadow of Byzantium*. London 1997.

Dandurand, Raoul. *Les Mémoires du Sénateur Raoul Dandurand*. Marcel Hamelin, ed. Quebec 1967.

Danys, Milda. *DP Lithuanian Immigration to Canada after the Second World War*. Toronto 1986.

Dasnabedian, Hratch. "The Hunchakian Party." *Armenian Review* 41, 4/164 (winter 1988).
– *History of the Armenian Revolutionary Federation Dashnaktsutiun, 1890–1924*. Milan 1989.
Davidian, Nectar. "The Seropians: First Armenian Settlers in Fresno County." *Armenian Review* 31, 2/122 (February 1979).
Davis, Leslie A. *The Slaughterhouse Province*. Susan K. Blair, ed. New Rochelle, NY, 1989.
Davison, Roderic H. "The Armenian Crisis, 1912–1914." *American Historical Review* 53, 3 (April 1948).
– "Turkish Attitudes Concerning Christian-Muslim Equality in the Nineteenth Century." *American Historical Review* 49 (July 1954).
– "Westernized Education in Ottoman Turkey." *Middle East Journal* 15 (summer 1961).
Dear, M.J., J.J. Drake, and L.G. Reeds, eds. *Steel City: Hamilton and Region*. Toronto 1987.
Denison, Merrill. *Harvest Triumphant: The Story of Massey-Harris, a Footnote to Canadian History*. New York 1949.
Der Krikorian, Krikor. "Bolsakan Arektsi Me Ukhdavori Hushere" (Memoirs of an Arektsi Bolsetsi Pilgrim). *Nor Geghi* (New Keghi). Vol. 1. East St Louis, 1964.
Der Manuelian, Lucy. "Art and Economics: The Rug Weaving Industry in Soviet Armenia." Paper delivered at conference, Soviet Armenia: Problems and Prospects, University of Pennsylvania, 7 October 1988.
Der Manuelian, Lucy, and Murray L. Eiland. *Weavers, Merchants, and Kings: The Inscribed Rugs of Armenia*, Emily J. Sano, ed. Fort Worth, TX, 1984.
Der Matosian, Garabed. "Im Kertasdani Patmutiune" (History of my Clan). In *Patmutiun Karno Kusakalutian Kghi Gavari Chanakhchi Giughi* (History of the Village of Chanakhchi in the Region of Keghi in the Prefecture of Erzerum). Arakel Eghigian and Soghomon Kaprielian, eds. Belleville, IL, 1977.
Deranian, Hagop Martin. *Worcester is America: The Story of the Worcester Armenians, the Early Years*. Worcester, MA, 1998.
Derderian, Archbishop Hovnan. *Hayastanyats Yekeghetsin Keanki Janaparh* (The Church of Armenia: The Road of Life). Montreal 2000.
Der-Karabetian, Aghop. "Armenian Identity: Comparative and Context-Bound." *Armenian Review* 34, 1/155 (March 1981).
Der-Martirosian, Claudia, Georges Sabagh, and Mehdi Bozorgmehr. "Subethnicity: Armenians in Los Angeles." In *Immigration and Entrepreneurship: Culture, Capital, and Ethnic Networks*. Ivan Light and Parminder Bhachu, eds. New Brunswick, NJ, 1993.

Derogy, Jacques. *Resistance and Revenge: The Armenian Assassination of the Turkish Leaders Responsible for the 1915 Massacres and Deportations*. A.M. Berrett trans. New Brunswick, NJ, 1990.
Diamond, Jared. "Deaths of Languages." *Natural History* 4 (2001).
Diggins, John Patrick. *The Rise and Fall of the American Left*. New York 1992.
Diner, Hasia R. *Hungering for America: Italian, Irish, and Jewish Foodways in the Age of Migration*. Cambridge, MA, 2001.
Dirks, Gerald. *Canada's Refugee Policy: Indifference or Opportunism*. Montreal 1977.
Dolabjian, Vartkes. "Hamidian Naghjire" (The Hamidian Massacre) *Horizon Weekly* (Montreal), 25 April 1994. Insert.
Dreisziger, N. F., with M.L. Kovacs, Paul Body, and Bennett Kovrig. *Struggle and Hope: The Hungarian-Canadian Experience*. Toronto 1982.
Drystek, Henry F. "'The Simplest and Cheapest Mode of Dealing with Them'": Deportation from Canada before World War II." *Histoire social/Social History* 15, 30 (November 1982).
Dsovikian, Hovannes. *Ho Yertas Amerikahayutiun?* (Where to Armenian Americans?). Boston 1940.
Du Véou, Paul. *La Passion de la Cilicie, 1919–1922*. Paris 1954.
Duben, Alan. "Turkish Families and Households in Historical Perspective." *Journal of Family History* (spring 1985).
Eastman, Samuel Mack. *Canada at Geneva: An Historical Survey and its Lessons*. Toronto 1946.
Eblighatian, Mateos M. *Keank Me Azgis Keankin Medj, 1903–23*. (A Life in the Life of My Nation, 1903–23). Antelias 1987.
Eby, D.C. *At the Mercy of Turkish Brigands: A True Story*. New Carlisle, OH, 1922.
Echeverria, Jeronima. *Home Away from Home: A History of Basque Boarding Houses*. Reno, NV, 1999.
Eghigian, Arakel. "Ashkharhagrakan Hamarot Gdser" (A Brief Geographic Sketch). *Nor Geghi* (New Keghi). Vol. 1. East St Louis 1964.
– "Aslan Varchaget" (Aslan the Administrator). In (History of the Village of Chanakhchi in the Region of Keghi in the Prefecture of Erzerum). Arakel Eghigian and Soghomon Kaprielian, eds. Belleville, IL, 1977.
– "Depi Pandkhtutiun" (Towards Sojourning). In (History of the Village of Chanakhchi in the Region of Keghi in the Prefecture of Erzerum). Arakel Eghigian and Soghomon Kaprielian, eds. Belleville, IL, 1977.
– "Ist Sent Luis Kaghake" (The Town of East St Louis). In (History of the Village of Chanakhchi in the Region of Keghi in the Prefecture of Erzerum). Arakel Eghigian and Soghomon Kaprielian, eds. Belleville, IL, 1977.
– "Kanats Dere Hasarakakan Keankin Medj" (Women's Role in Everyday

Life). In (History of the Village of Chanakhchi in the Region of Keghi in the Prefecture of Erzerum). Arakel Eghigian and Soghomon Kaprielian, eds. Belleville, IL, 1977.

Eghigian, Arakel, and Soghomon Kaprielian, eds. *Patmutiun Karno Kusakalutian Kghi Gavari Chanakhchi Giughi* (History of the Village of Chanakhchi in the Region of Keghi in the Prefecture of Erzerum). Belleville, IL, 1977.

Elder, Glen H. Jr. *Children of the Great Depression: Social Change in Life Experience*. Chicago 1974.

Eliot, T.S. *Murder in the Cathedral*. London, 1987. Reprint. Original 1935.

Elliott, Jean L., ed. *Two Nations, Many Cultures: Ethnic Groups in Canada*. Scarborough, ON, 1983.

Elliott, Mabel. *Beginning Again at Ararat*. New York 1924.

Ellis, Aytoun. *The Penny Universities: A History of the Coffee Houses*. London 1956.

Epp, Frank H. *Mennonite Exodus: The Rescue and Resettlement of the Russian Mennonites since the Communist Revolution*. Alto, MB, 1966.

– *Mennonites in Canada, 1920–40: A People's Struggle for Survival*. Toronto 1982.

Epp, Marlene. *Women without Men: Mennonite Refugees of the Second World War*. Toronto 2000.

Epp, Marlene, et al., eds. *Sisters or Strangers? Immigrant, Ethnic, and Racialized Women in Canadian History*. Toronto 2004.

Erickson, Charlotte, ed. *Emigration from Europe, 1815–1914: Select Documents*. London 1976.

Erikson, Erik. *Insight and Responsibility*. New York 1964.

– *Identity: Youth and Crisis*. New York 1968.

Etmekjian, James. *The French Influence on the Western Armenian Renaissance, 1843–1915*. New York 1964.

– "The Tanzimat Reforms and Their Effect on the Armenians in Turkey." *Armenian Review* 25, 1/97 (1972).

– "The Utilitarian Nature of the Western Armenian Renaissance." *Armenian Review* 31, 3/123 (March 1979).

Etmekjian, Lillian. "Armenian Cultural and Political Contributions to Reform in Turkey." *Armenian Review* 29, 2/114 (summer 1976).

– "The Reform Movement in Turkey: Background." *Armenian Review* 29, 3/113 (autumn 1976).

Fairchild, H.P. *Immigration*. New York 1913.

Fishman, Joshua A. *Language Loyalty in the United States*. The Hague 1966.

Fleury, Michel. *Des registres paroissiaux à l'histoire de la population*. Paris 1956.

Freely, John. *Istanbul: The Imperial City*. London 1996.

Friesen, Gerald, and Lucy Taksa. "Workers' Education in Australia and Canada: A Comparative Approach to Labour's Cultural History. *Labour/Le Travail* 38 (fall 1996).

From Immigration to Integration: The Canadian Jewish Experience: A Millennium Edition. http://www/bnaibrith.ca/institute/millennium/millennium00.html.

Gabaccia, Donna. "Italian Immigrant Women in Comparative Perspective." *Altreitalie International Journal of Studies on the Peoples of Italian Origin in the World* 9 (1993).

– *We Are What We Eat: Ethnic Food and the Making of Americans*. Cambridge, MA, 1998.

Gabaccia, Donna, and Franca Iacovetta, eds. *Women, Gender, and Transnational Lives: Italian Workers of the World*. Toronto 2002.

Gans, Herbert. *The Urban Villagers: Group and Class in the Life of Italian Americans*. New York 1962.

Gantzhorn, Volkmar. *Le tapis chrétien oriental: Une représentation de l'évolution iconographique et iconologique des débuts jusqu'au XVIIIème siècle*. Francine Evéquoz, trans. to French. Cologne 1991.

Garnett, Lucy M.J. *The Women of Turkey and Their Folk-Lore*. London 1893.

– *Turkish Life in Town and Country*. New York 1904.

George, Joan. *Merchants in Exile: The Armenians in Manchester, England, 1835–1935*. Princeton and London 2002.

Ghazarian, Manya. *Armenian Carpet*. Erebouni 1988.

Gidel, Gilbert, Albert de La Pradelle, Louis Le Fur, and André Mandelstam. *Confiscations des biens des réfugiés arméniens par le gouvernement turc*. Paris 1929.

Gilad, Lisa. *Ginger and Salt: Yemeni Jewish Women in an Israeli Town*. Boulder, CO, 1989.

Gjerde, Jon. *Major Problems in American Immigration and Ethnic History*. Boston 1998.

Glazebrook, G.P. de T. *A History of Canadian External Affairs: In the Empire and the World, 1914–1939*. Vol. 2, revised edition. Toronto 1966.

Gleason, Philip. "Pluralism and Assimilation: A Conceptual History." In *Linguistic Minorities, Policies, and Pluralism*. John Edwards, ed. London 1984.

Goodwin-Gill, Guy S. *International Law and the Movements of Persons between States*. Oxford 1978.

Gordon, Milton. *Assimilation in American Life. The Role of Race, Religion, and National Origin*. New York 1964.

Gotigian, Guévork, and Vahé Tachjian. "La Légion d'Orient, Le mandat français sur la Cilicie et l'expulsion des Arméniens, 1916–1929." *Revue d'histoire arménienne contemporaine* 3, 1999. *La Cilicie (1909–1921): Des massacres d'Adana au mandat français*. Special number prepared by Raymond H. Kévorkian.

Grabill, Joseph L. *Protestant Diplomacy and the Near East: Missionary Influence on American Policy, 1810–1927.* Minneapolis, MN, 1971.
Graves, Sir R. *Storm Centers of the Near East: Personal Memories, 1879–1929.* London 1933.
Gray, James H. *The Winter Years.* Toronto 1966.
Greene, Frederick Davis. *Armenian Massacres, or The Sword of Mohammed.* N.p. 1896.
Greene, Victor. "'Becoming American': The Role of Ethnic Leaders, Swedes, Poles, Italians and Jews." In *The Ethnic Frontier: Essays in the History of Group Survival in Chicago and the Midwest.* Melvin Holli and Peter d'A. Jones, eds. Grand Rapids, MI, 1977
Guinn, James Milton. "The Seropians." *Armenian Review* 31, 2/122 (February 1979).
Gunter, Michael. *"Pursuing the Just Cause of Their People": A Study of Contemporary Armenian Terrorism.* New York 1986.
Gutman, Herbert, "Work, Culture, and Society in Industrializing America, 1815–1919." *American Historical Review* 78, 3 (June 1973).
– *Work, Culture, and Society in Industrializing America: Essays in American Working-Class and Social History.* New York 1976.
Hacikyan, Agop J., Gabriel Basmajian, Edward S. Franchuk, and Nourhan Ouzounian. *The Heritage of Armenian Literature.* Vol. 1. Detroit 2000. Vol. 2, 2002.
Hacikyan, Agop, and Jean-Yves Soucy. *Un été sans aube.* Montreal 1991.
Hadidian, Yervant H. "American Contributions to Armenian Culture." *Armenian/American Outlook* 9, 1 (no date).
Hagopian, S. "The Armenian Community of Providence, Rhode Island, up to 1957." *Armenian Review* 35, 4/140 (winter 1982).
"H.(ai) H.(eghapokhakan) Dashnaktsutian Canadayi medj Gordsuneutian 95-Amiak" (Armenian Revolutionary Federation Activities in Canada, on Its Ninety-fifth Anniversary). *Horizon Weekly,* 5 January 1998, insert.
Haikakan Baregordsakan Endhanur Miutian Gordsapatume (History of the Work of the Armenian General Benevolent Union). Cairo 1919.
Hairabedian, Vahan. "Embost Khups Giughe." ("The Defiant Village of Khups"). In *(Yearbook).* Detroit, MI, 1937.
Hairapetian, Armen. "'Race Problems' and the Armenian Genocide: The State Department File." *Armenian Review* 37, 1/145 (spring 1984).
Halagian Langton, Nora. *A Culinary Tour of the Middle East.* Brantford 1984.
Hall, D.J. "Clifford Sifton: Immigration and Settlement Policy, 1896–1905." In *The Settlement of the West.* Howard Palmer, ed. Calgary 1977.
Handlin, Oscar. *The Uprooted: The Epic Story of the Great Migrations That Made the American People.* New York 1951.
– *Race and Nationality in American Life.* New York 1957.

Hansen, Marcus Lee. *The Immigrant in American History*. Cambridge, MA, 1940.
Hareven, Tamara. "Family Time and Industrial Time: Family and Work in a Planned Corporation Town, 1900–1924." *Journal of Urban History* 1, 3 (May 1975).
- "Family and Work Patterns of Immigrant Labourers in a Planned Industrial Town, 1900–1930." In *Immigrants in Industrial America, 1850–1920*. Richard L. Ehrlich, ed. Charlottesville, VA, 1977.
- *Family Time and Industrial Time*. Cambridge, England, 1986. Reprint.
Harney, Robert F. "The Padrone and the Immigrant." *Canadian Review of American Studies* 5, 2 (fall 1974).
- "Ambiente and Social Class in North American Little Italies." *Canadian Review of Studies in Nationalism* 2, 2 (spring 1975).
- "Chiaroscuro: Italians in Toronto, 1885–1915." *Italian Americana* 1, 1 (spring 1975).
- "The Commerce of Migration." *Canadian Ethnic Studies* 9, 1 (1977).
- "Boarding and Belonging." *Urban History Review*, 2–78 (October 1978).
- "Men without Women: Italian Migrants in Canada, 1885–1930." In *The Italian Immigrant Woman in North America*. Betty Boyd Caroli, Robert F. Harney, and Lydio Tomasi, eds. Toronto 1978.
Harney, Robert F., and Harold Troper. *Immigrants: A Portrait of the Urban Experience, 1890–1930*. Toronto 1975.
Harney, Robert F., and Vincenza J. Scarpaci, eds. *Little Italies in North America*. Toronto 1981
Hartunian, A.H. *Neither to Laugh Nor to Weep: A Memoir of the Armenmian Genocide*. Vartan Hartunian, trans. Cambridge, MA, 1986. Originally written in 1968.
Harvester Bulletin, Hamilton 1920.
Harvester World, Hamilton 1909–1910.
Harzig, Christiane, and Dirk Hoerder, eds. *Labor Migration Project, Labor Newspaper Preservation Project: The Press of Labor Migrants in Europe and North America, 1880s to 1930s*. Bremen Publications of the Labor Newspaper Preservation Projekt, 1985.
Hathaway, James. "The Evolution of Refugee Status in International Law: 1920–1950." *International and Comparative Law Quarterly* 33 (April 1984).
Hawkins, Freda. *Canada and Immigration: Public Policy and Public Concern*. Montreal 1972.
Hayes, Carlton. *Nationalism: A Religion*. New York 1960.
"Hayots Miatsial Enkerutians Karno Shrjanak, 1910–1911" (Report of the United Armenian Association in the Region of Erzerum, 1910–11). In (*New Keghi*), Vol. 1. 1964.

Hekimian, Kim. "Armenian Immigration to Argentina: 1909–1938." *Armenian Review* 43, 1/169 (spring 1990).
Herberg, Wil. *Protestant-Catholic-Jew.* New York 1955.
Heron, Craig. "The Crisis of the Craftsman: Hamilton's Metal Workers in the Early Twentieth Century." *Labour/ Le Travail* 6 (August 1980).
– *Working in Steel: The Early Years in Canada, 1883–1935.* Toronto 1988.
Heron, Craig, and Bryan D. Palmer. "Through the Prism of the Strike: Industrial Conflict in Southern Ontario, 1901–14." *Canadian Historical Review* 58 (December 1977).
Hewsen, Robert. "A Geographical Note on the Encyclical of Catholicos Aristakes II (1475)." *Revue des études arméniennes.* New Series 20 (1986–87)
– *Armenia: A Historical Atlas.* Chicago 2001.
Heyd, Uriel. *Foundations of Turkish Nationalism: The Life and Teachings of Ziya Gokalp.* London 1950.
Higgs, David. *Portuguese Migration in Global Perspective.* Toronto 1990.
Higham, John. *Ethnic Leadership in America.* Baltimore 1978.
– ed. *Strangers in the Land: Patterns of American Nativism, 1860–1925.* New York 1963.
History and Development of International Harvester. Hamilton: Harvester Education and Training. n.d.
Hnchakian Taregirk (Hnchakian Yearbook). (American Armenian Region). New York 1932.
Hobsbawm, Eric. *Labouring Men.* New York 1964.
– *Bandits.* New York 1969.
– "From Social History to the History of Society." In *Historical Studies Today.* Felix Gilbert and Stephen R. Granbard, eds. New York 1972.
– *Primitive Rebels: Studies in Archaic Forms of Social Movement in the Nineteenth and Twentieth Centuries.* Manchester 1974.
Hofmann, Tessa, and Gerayer Koutcharian. "The History of Armenian-Kurdish Relations in the Ottoman Empire." *Armenian Review* 39, 4/156 (winter 1986).
Hollinger, David. *Postethnic America: Beyond Multiculturalism.* New York 2000.
Hoogasian Villa, Susie, collector. *One Hundred Armenian Tales.* Detroit 1982.
Hoogasian Villa, Susie, and Mary Kilbourne Matossian. *Armenian Village Life before 1914.* Detroit 1982.
Hopkins, J. Castell. *The Sword of Islam, or Suffering Armenia: Annals of Turkish Power and the Eastern Question.* Brantford and Toronto 1896.
Horn, Michiel. *The Great Depression of the 1930s in Canada.* Ottawa, 1984.
– ed. *The Dirty Thirties: Canadians in the Great Depression.* Toronto 1972.
Horn, Michiel, and Ronald Sabourin, eds. *Studies in Canadian Social History.* Toronto 1974.

Housepian, Marjorie. *The Smyrna Affair.* New York 1971.
Hovanessian, Martine. *Le lien communautaire: Trois générations d'Arméniens.* Paris 1992.
- "Récits de vie et mémoire(s) de l'exil: Les enjeux à l'oeuvre dans l'histoire orale." *Revue du monde arménien moderne et contemporain.* Vol. 6 (2001).
Hovannesian, Pailun. "Nor Geghii Berkrali Taredardse yev Oghbergakan Kghin" (The Joyful Anniversary of New Geghi and the Tragedy of Keghi). *Nor Geghi* (New Keghi). Vol. 2 (1965).
Hovannisian, Richard G. *Armenia on the Road to Independence, 1918.* Berkeley 1967.
- *The Republic of Armenia: The First Year, 1918–1919.* Vol. 1. Berkeley 1971.
- *The Armenian Holocaust: A Bibliography Relating to the Deportations, Massacres, and Dispersion of the Armenian People, 1915–1923.* Cambridge, MA, 1980.
- *The Republic of Armenia, From Versailles to London, 1919–20.* Vol. 2. Berkeley 1982.
- "The Armenian Genocide and Patterns of Denial." In *The Armenian Genocide in Perspective.* Richard G. Hovannisian, ed. New Brunswick, NJ, 1987.
- "The Historical Dimensions of the Armenian Question, 1878–1923." In *The Armenian Genocide in Perspective.* Richard G. Hovannisian, ed. New Brunswick, NJ, 1987.
- *The Republic of Armenia: From London to Sèvres, February–August 1920.* Vol. 3. Berkeley 1996.
- *The Republic of Armenia: Between Crescent and Sickle, Partition and Sovietization.* Vol. 4. Berkeley 1996.
- ed. *The Armenian Genocide in Perspective.* New Brunswick, NJ, 1987.
- *The Armenian Genocide: History, Politics, Ethics.* New York 1992.
- *The Armenian People from Ancient to Modern Times.* Vol. 2, *Foreign Domination to Statehood: The Fifteenth Century to the Twentieth Century.* New York 1997.
- UCLA *Armenian History and Culture Series: Historic Armenian Cities and Provinces. Armenian Van/Vaspurakan,* 2000; *Armenian Baghesh/Bitlis,* 2001; *Armenian Tsopk/Kharpert,* 2002; *Armenian Karin/Erzerum,* 2003. Cost Mesa, CA: Mazda Publishers.
Hunt, Lynn, ed. *The New Cultural History.* Berkeley 1989.
Hunt, R.N. Carew. *The Theory and Practice of Communism.* Harmondsworth, England, 1983.
Hushamatian Hai Oknutian Miutian: 1910–1970 (Memorial Volume of the Armenian Relief Society: 1910–1970). Boston 1970.
Hushamatian Kghi Khups Giughi. (Memorial Volume of the Village of Khups in Keghi). Fresno, CA, 1968.
Hushapatum Hai Heghapokhakan Dashnaktsutian: 1890–1950. (Memorial Volume of the Armenian Revolutionary Federation: 1890–1950). Boston 1950.

Hyland, Francis. *Armenian Terrorism: The Past, the Present, the Prospects.* Boulder, CO, 1991
Iacovetta, Franca. *Such Hardworking People: Italian Immigrants in Postwar Toronto.* Montreal 1993.
– *The Writing of English Canadian Immigrant History.* Ottawa 1997.
Iacovetta, Franca, Paula Draper, and Robert Ventresca. *A Nation of Immigrants: Women, Workers, and Communities in Canadian History, 1840s–1960s.* Toronto 1998.
Iacovetta, Franca, Roberto Perin, and Angelo Principe, eds. *Enemies Within: Italian and Other Internees in Canada and Abroad.* Toronto 2000.
Iacovetta, Franca, Michael Quinlan, and Ian Radforth. "Immigration and Labour: Australia and Canada Compared." *Labour/Le Travail* 38 (fall 1996).
Injejikian, Hasmig. "The Musical Repertory of Early Armenian Settlers." *Polyphony: Armenians in Ontario* 4, 2 (fall/winter 1982).
Innis, Harold Adams. *A History of the Canadian Pacific Railway, 1894–1952.* Toronto 1971.
Isajiw, Wsevolod, ed. *The Refugee Experience: Ukrainian Displaced Persons after World War II.* Edmonton 1992.
Islamoglu-Inan, Huri, ed. The Ottoman Empire and the World-Economy. Cambridge 1987.
Jafarian, Boghos. *Farewell Kharpert: The Autobiography of Boghos Jafarian.* N.p. 1989.
Jamkochian, M. "Yeritasard Hayastane Yeprat Koleji Medj." (Young Armenia at Euphrates College), in *Karasnamiak* (1903–1943) *Yeritasard Hayastani* (Fortieth Anniversary Commemorative Book (1903–1943) of Young Armenia). New York 1944.
Jenanyan, H.S. *Harutune, or Lights and Shadows in the Orient.* Toronto 1898.
Jendian Matthew. "The Farming Community and Marriage Patterns of Armenians in Fresno County." Paper presented at symposium, Armenians in the Raisin Industry: 1890–1990, California State University at Fresno, California, 1997.
Jenks, Jeremiah W., and Jett W. Lauck. *The Immigration Problem; A Study of American Immigration Conditions and Needs.* New York 1913.
Jizmejian, Manuk, G. *Patmutiun Amerikahai Kaghakakan Kusaktsutiants: 1890–1925* (History of American Armenian Political Organizations: 1890–1925). Fresno, CA, 1930.
Johnston, Charles M. *The Head of the Lake: A History of Wentworth County.* 2d rev. ed. Hamilton 1967.
Kabadayan, Hovannes. "'Asbarez' and Its First Ten Years of Life." *Armenian Review* 51, 2/122 (February 1979).
Kage, Joseph. *With Faith and Thanksgiving.* Montreal 1962.
Kahvedjian, Yeghia. *Housher Urfayi 1915 Herosamarti u Hetaka Iratardzuti-*

enneru Masin (Memoirs of the Herioc Battles of Urfa in 1915 and the Subsequent Combination of Events). Yerevan 1995.

Kalajian, Hannah. *Hannah's Story: Escape from Genocide in Turkey to Success in America*. Belmont, MA, 1991.

Kalbach, Madeline. "Ethnic Intermarriage in Canada." *Canadian Ethnic Studies* 34, 2 (2002).

Kalousdian, Krikor H. *Marash gam Kermanig yev Heros Zeitun* (Marash or Kermanig and Heroic Zeitun). New York 1934.

Kaprielian, Isabel. "The Mooradian and Melkonian Family Collection." *Polyphony* 1, 2 (summer 1978).

– "The Armeno-American Letter Writer." *Polyphony* 3, 1 (winter 1981).
– "Armenian Folk-Belief with Special Emphasis on Veejag." *Polyphony: Armenians in Ontario* 4, 2 (fall/winter 1982).
– "Earning a Living: 1900–29." *Polyphony: Armenians in Ontario* 4, 2 (fall/winter 1982).
– "From Baronian to Adamov: A Brief Sketch of Armenian Drama in Ontario." *Polyphony* 5, 2 (fall/winter 1983).
– "Armenians in Toronto: A One Hundred Year Survey." *Polyphony: Toronto's People* 6, 1 (spring/summer 1984).
– "Women and Work: The Case of Finnish Domestics and Armenian Boardinghouse Operators." *Resources for Feminist Research* 12, 4 (1984).
– "Sojourners from Keghi: Armenians in Ontario to 1915." PHD diss., University of Toronto, 1984.
– *The Georgetown Boys: Armenian Orphans in Canada*. 1987. Video.
– "Refugee Women as Domestics: A Documentary Account." *Canadian Woman Studies* 10, 1 (1989).
– "Marriage and Love in America." *Ararat Quarterly* 42, 167 (summer 2001).

Kaprielian, Isabel, ed. *Polyphony: Armenians in Ontario* 4, 2 (fall/winter 1982).

Kaprielian-Churchill, Isabel. "Creating and Sustaining an Ethnocultural Heritage in Ontario: The Case of Armenian Women Refugees." In *Looking into My Sister's Eyes: An Exploration in Women's History*. Jean Burnet, ed. Toronto 1986.

– "The Saved: Armenian Refugee Women." *Canadian Woman Studies* 7, 4 (winter 1986).
– "Migratory Caravans: Armenian Sojourners in Canada." *Journal of American Ethnic History* 6, 2 (spring 1987).
– "Armenian Refugees and Their Entry into Canada: 1919–30." *Canadian Historical Review* 71, 1 (March 1990).
– *Rose's Triumph: The Story of an Armenian Refugee Girl in Canada*. 1990. Video.
– "Armenian Refugee Women: The Picture Brides, 1920–1930." *Journal of American Ethnic History* 12, 3 (spring 1993).

- "Give Me Your Mothers and I'll Give You a Nation: Diasporan Armenian Women at the Helm." In *Armenian Women in a Changing World*, Barbara J. Merguerian and Doris D. Jafferian, eds. Belmont, MA, 1994.
- "Canada and the Nansen Passport." *International Migration Review* 28, 2 (1994).
- "Armenians." In *An Encyclopedia of Canada's Peoples*. Toronto 1999.
- "Intermarriage in the Diaspora: Integrating Armenians or Alienating 'Odars'?" In *Voices of Armenian Women*. Barbara Merguerian and Joy Renjilian-Burgy, eds. Belmont, MA, 2000.
- "The Armenian Genocide and the Survival of Children." In *Anatomy of Genocide: State-Sponsored Mass-Killings in the Twentieth Century*. Alexandre Kimenyi and Otis L. Scott, eds. Lewiston, NY, 2001.
- "Kghi Village Educational Associations in North America before 1915." In *Armenian Karin/Erzerum*. Richard G. Hovannisian, ed. Costa Mesa, CA, 2003.
- "'Odars' and 'Others': Intermarriage and the Retention of Armenian Ethnic Identity." In *Sisters or Strangers? Immigrant, Ethnic, and Racialized Women in Canadian History*. Marlene Epp, Franca Iacovetta, and Frances Swyripa, eds. Toronto 2004.

Kaprielian-Churchill, Isabel, and Stacy Churchill. *The Pulse of the World: Refugees in Our Schools*. Toronto 1994.

Karagueuzian, Hrayr S. "The Armenian Genocide and the Unpaid Life Insurance Policies: Legal and Historic Perspectives." In *The Anatomy of Genocide: State-Sponsored Mass-Killings in the Twentieth Century*. Alexandre Kimenyi and Otis L. Scott, eds. Lewiston, NY, 2001.

Karakshian, Mher. "Zoravarin Shunche: St Catharinsi Nor Hai Kedroni Aradjin Taredardzin Aritov" (The General's Breath: On the Occasion of the First Anniversary of the New Armenian Community Centre in St Catharines). *Horizon*, 19 May 1992.

Karasnamiak (1903–1943) Yeritasard Hayastani (Fortieth Anniversary Commemorative Book (1903–1943) of Young Armenia). New York 1944.

Karoian, Gaspar M. *Meds Yegherni, Nahatak Hai Bzhishknere*. (The Great Catastrophe: The Martyrdom of Armenian Doctors). Boston 1957.

Kasaba, Reşat. *The Ottoman Empire and the World Economy: The Nineteenth Century*. Albany, NY, 1988.

Kasparian, Alice Odian. *Armenian Needlework and Embroidery*. McLean, VA, 1983.

Kasparian, Rev. Yeghishé. *Vdag Amerikahai Taretsuits* (Vdag: Armenian-American Almanac). Boston 1935.

Kasuni, Manuel S. "Kghi – Keghi – Geghi." in *Hushamatian Kghi, Khups Giughi* (Memorial Volume of the Village of Khups in Keghi). Fresno, CA, 1968.

Kazarian, Haigazn K. "Opening of the Turkish Genocide of 1915–1918: Arrest and Murder of the Armenian Intellectuals." *Armenian Review* 24, 3/95 (autumn 1971).
Kealey, Gregory S. "The Structure of Canadian Working-Class History." In *Lectures in Canadian Labour and Working-Class History*. W.J.C. Cherwinski and G.S. Kealey, eds. St John's, NF, 1985.
– "State Repression of Labour and the Left, 1914–20: The Impact of the First World War." *Canadian Historical Review* 73, 3 (September 1992).
– *Workers and Canadian History*. Montreal 1995.
– ed. *Class, Gender, and Region: Essays in Canadian Historical Sociology*. St John's, NF, 1988.
Kealey, Gregory S., and Peter Warrian, eds. *Essays in Canadian Working Class History*. Toronto 1976.
Keljik, Bedros, A. *Amerikahai Patkerner* (Armenian-American Sketches). New York 1944.
Kelly, T. *A History of Adult Education in Great Britain: From the Middle Ages to the Twentieth Century*. Liverpool 1970.
Kensagrakan (Biography (of Setrag Shahen)). By *Nor Geghi* editorial board, *Nor Geghi* (New Keghi). Vol. 1. East St Louis 1964.
Kerr, Stanley E. *The Lions of Marash: Personal Experiences with American Near East Relief, 1919–1920*. Albany, NY, 1973.
Kessler-Harris, Alice. *Out to Work: A History of Wage-Earning Women in the United States*. New York 1982.
Keuchgerian Arminé. "The Armenian Diocese of Canada: The History of the Community." *Centennial Anniversary of the Establishment of the Armenian Apostolic Church in Canada, 1898–1998*. Montreal 1998.
Kévonian, Arménouhie. *Les Noces Noires de Gulizar*. Présentations historiques de Anahide Ter Minassian et Kéram Kévonian. Original *Gulizar* published in Paris, 1946, and translated from Armenian to French by Jacques Mouradian. Marseilles 1993.
Kévonian, Dzovinar. "Réfugiés et diplomatie humanitaire: Les acteurs européeans et la scène proche-orientale pendant l'entre-deux-guerres." PHD diss., University of Paris, 1998. 2 vols.
– "Exilés politiques et avènement du "droit humain": La pensée juridique d'André Mandelstam (1869–1949)." In *Ailleurs, hier, autrement: Connaissance et reconnaissance du génocide des Arméniens*. Special volume of *Revue d'histoire de la Shoah: le monde juif*. 177–8 (January–August 2003). Georges Bensoussan, Claire Mouradian, and Yves Ternon, eds.
Kevorkian, Garo, ed. *Amenun Taregirke* (Everyone's Yearbook). Beirut 1963.
Kévorkian, Raymond H. "Récueil de témoignages sur l'extermination des *amele tabouri* ou bataillons de soldats-ouvriers arméniens de l'armée

ottomane pendant la première guerre mondiale." *Revue d'histoire arménienne contemporaine* 1 (1995).

- "L'extermination des déportés arméniens ottomans dans les camps de concentration de Syrie-Mésopotamie (1915-1916): La Deuxième phase du genocide." *Revue d'histoire arménienne contemporaine* 2 (1998).
- "La Turquie face à ses responsabilités: Le procès des criminels jeunes-turcs (1918-1920)." In *Ailleurs, hier, autrement: Connaissance et reconnaissance du génocide des Arméniens*, special volume of *Revue d'histoire de la Shoah: Le monde juif.* 177-8 (January-August 2003). Georges Bensoussan, Claire Mouradian, and Yves Ternon, eds.
- ed. *La Cilicie (1909-1921): Des massacres d'Adana au mandat français.* Special volume of *Revue d'histoire arménienne contemporaine* 3 (1999).

Kévorkian, Raymond H., and Paul B. Paboudjian. *Les Arméniens dans l'empire ottoman à la veille du génocide.* Paris 1992.

- "Les massacres de Cilicie d'avril 1909." In *La Cilicie (1909-1921): Des massacres d'Adana au mandat français.* Special volume of *Revue d'histoire arménienne contemporaine* 3 (1999). Raymond H. Kévorkian, ed.

"Kghi-Khups Giughi Hairenaktsakan Miutian 65-amia gordsuneutian" (Sixty-five Years of Activity of the Khups Village Compatriotic Union) written by the union's executive committee. In (*Memorial Volume of the Village of Khups in Keghi*). Fresno, CA, 1968.

Khan-Azad, Ruben (Nshan Karapetian). "Hai Heghapokhakani Husherits." (Memoirs of an Armenian Revolutionary). *Hairenik Amsagir* (Hairenik Monthly) 5 (June 1927).

Khatissian, Prime Minister Alexandre. "La République Indépendente d'Arménie et le rôle des Alliés (1918-1920)." *Les Temps Modernes* (July-Sept. 1988).

Kherdian, David. *The Road from Home: The Story of an Armenian Girl.* New York 1979.

Khungian, Toros A. "Origins and Development of the Fresno Armenian Community in the 1918 Year." *Armenian Review* 51, 2/122 (February 1979).

King, Desmond. *Making Americans: Immigration, Race, and the Origins of the Diverse Democracy.* Cambridge, MA, 2000.

King, Prime Minister William Lyon Mackenzie. "Statement to the Canadian House of Commons." Government of Canada. House of Commons, *Debates.* 1 May 1947, 2644-6.

Kiouzalian, Karnik. "Armenia before the Revolution." Vahram Pahigian, trans. *Armenian Review* 51, 1/121 (spring 1978).

Kitur, Arsen, ed. and compiler. *Patmutiun S(otsial) D(emokratik) Hnchakian Kusaktsutian, 1887-1962* (History of the Social Democratic Hnchakian Party, 1887-1962). Vol. 1. Beirut 1962.

- *Patmutiun S(otsial) D(emokratik) Hnchakian Kusaktsutian, 1887–1963* (History of the Social Democratic Hnchakian Party, 1887–1963). Vol. 2. Beirut 1963.
Kloian, Richard Diran, compiler. *The Armenian Genocide: First Twentieth Century Holocaust.* 2d ed. Walnut Creek, CA, 1981.
Knowles, Valerie. *Strangers at Our Gates: Canadian Immigration and Immigration Policy*: 1940–1997. Toronto 1997.
Kolarz, Walter. *Religion in the Soviet Union.* London 1961.
Kolasky, John. *The Shattered Illusion: The History of Ukrainian Pro-Communist Organizations in Canada.* Toronto 1979.
Koloian, Bedros. "Menk yev Tersimtsinere" (We and the People of Dersim). *Nor Geghi* (New Keghi). Vol. 2. Told by Bedros Koloian and written by A.E. (probably Arakel Eghigian).
Kooshian, George B. Jr. "Church Reform in America: The Diocesan Assembly of 1923." *Journal of Armenian Studies* 3, 1 and 2 (1986–87).
- "The Armenian Immigrant Community of California: 1880–1935." PHD diss., University of California, Los Angeles, 2002.
Kouyoumdjian, Jacqueline. *Keanki me Patmutiune.* (The Story of a Life: In Memory of Hovannes Kouyoumdjian). Toronto 2001.
Kulhanjian, Gary A. *An Abstract of Historical and Sociological Aspects of Armenian Immigration to the United States, 1890–1930.* San Francisco, CA, 1975.
Kuper, Leo. *Genocide: Its Political Use in the Twentieth Century.* New Haven, CT, 1981.
Kurdian, Hasmig. *Organizing and Preserving an Ethnic Group Away from the Homeland.* Montreal 1998.
Kurkjian, Vahan. *A History of Armenia.* New York 1958.
Kymlika, Will. "American Multiculturalism in the International Arena." In M. Cohen, D. Howe, and M. Walzer, eds., *Dissent* (fall 1998).
Landau, Jacob M. *Pan-Turkism in Turkey: From Irredentism to Cooperation.* 2d ed. Bloomington, IN, 1995.
Lane, David. *The Roots of Russian Communism: A Social and Historical Study of Russian Social Democracy, 1897–1907.* Assen 1969.
Lang, David Marshall. *Armenia: Cradle of Civilization.* London 1970.
La Piere, Richard T. "The Armenian Colony in Fresno County, California: A Study in Social Psychology." PHD diss., Stanford University, 1930.
Lepsius, Johannes. *Archives du Génocide des Arméniens.* Marie-France Letenoux, trans., from German. Originally published 1919. Paris 1986.
- *Le Rapport secret sur les massacres d'Arménie, 1915–1916.* Paris 1918. Reprint 1987.
Leslie, Genevieve. "Domestic Service in Canada, 1880–1920." In *Women at Work, 1850–1930.* Janice Acton, Penny Goldsmith, and Bonnie Shepard, eds. Toronto 1974.

Lewis, Bernard. *The Emergence of Modern Turkey.* 2d ed. London, 1968.
Libaridian, Gerard J. "The Ultimate Repression: The Genocide of the Armenians, 1915–1917." *Genocide and the Modern Age: Etiology and Case Studies of Mass Death.* Isidor Walliman and Michael N. Dobkowski, eds. New York 1987.
Lillywhite, B. *London Coffee Houses: A Reference Book of Coffee Houses of the Seventeenth, Eighteenth, and Nineteenth Centuries.* London 1965.
Lima, Vincent. "The Evolving Goals and Strategies of the Armenian Revolutionary Federation, 1890–1925." *Armenian Review* 44, 2/174 (summer 1991).
Lindström-Best, Varpu. *Defiant Sisters: A Social History of Finnish Immigrant Women in Canada.* Toronto 1988.
Lister, Herbert. "Hamilton, Canada: Its History, Commerce, Industries and Resources." *Hamilton Spectator*, 1913.
Luciuk, Lubomyr Y. *Searching for Place: Ukrainian Displaced Persons, Ottawa, and the Immigration of Memory.* Toronto 2000.
Lupul, Manoly R., ed. *A Heritage in Transition: Essays in the History of Ukrainians in Canada.* Toronto 1982.
Lynch, Harry Finnis B. *Armenia: Travels and Studies.* Vols. 1 and 2. Beirut 1965, reprint. Original, London 1901.
Macartney, C.A. *Refugees: The Work of the League.* London, n.d.
MacDonald, John S. "Chain Migration, Ethnic Neighbourhood Formation and Social Networks." In *An Urban World*, Charles Tilly, ed. Boston 1974.
MacDonald, John S., and Leatrice D. MacDonald. "Urbanization, Ethnic Groups, and Social Segmentation." *Social Research* 29 (winter 1962).
MacDowell, Laurel Sefton. "The Formation of the Canadian Industrial Relations System during World War Two." *Labour/Le Travail* 3 (1978).
– "Remember Kirkland Lake": *The Gold Miners' Strike of 1941–1942.* Toronto 1983.
MacFarlane, Alan, in collaboration with Susan Harrison and Charles Jardine. *Reconstituting Historical Communities.* Cambridge 1977.
Magarian, Horen Henry. "The Founding and Establishment of the Armenian Community of Richmond, Virginia." *Armenian Review* 28, 5/111 (autumn 1975).
Magrath, Charles Alexander. *Canada's Growth and Some Problems Affecting It.* Ottawa 1910.
Makal, Mahmut. *A Village in Anatolia.* Sir Wyndham Deedes, trans. London 1954.
Makdisi, Ussama. "Reclaiming the Land of the Bible: Missionaries, Secularism, and Evangelical Modernity." *American Historical Review* (June 1997).
Malcom, M. Vartan. *The Armenians in America.* Boston 1919.
Mamurian, Arsen-Nubar. *Ramkavar Azatakan Kusaktsutiun: R. A. K.i Azgan-*

ver Dsarayutian 60 Tarinere (Sixty Years of Patriotic Commitment by the Armenian Democratic Liberal Organization). Montreal 1981.

Manley, John. "Communism and the Canadian Working Class during the Great Depression: The Workers' Unity League, 1930–1936." PHD diss., Dalhousie University, 1984.

– "Communists and Auto Workers: The Struggle for Industrial Unionism in the Canadian Automobile Industry, 1925–36." *Labour/Le Travail* 17 (spring 1986).

– "Canadian Communists, Revolutionary Unions and the 'Third Period': The Workers' Unity League, 1929–1935." *Journal of the Canadian Historical Association* 5 (1994).

Manoyan, Giro. "Hai Heghapokhakan Dashnaktsutian Canadayi Shrdjani Ankatar Patmutiune" (A Sketch of the Armenian Revolutionary Federation in the Canadian Region). *Horizon* (Horizon), (1 December 1980).

Manuelian, Agnacia. *Unending Journey*. London 1939.

Mardin, Serif. *The Genesis of Young Ottoman Thought: A Study of the Modernization of Turkish Political Ideas*. Princeton 1962.

Mardirosian, Levon. *Amerikahayutiune: Yereg yev Aisor.* (American-Armenians, Yesterday and Today). Beirut 1973.

Marks, Lynn. "The Knights of Labor and the Salvation Army: Religion and Working-Class Culture in Ontario, 1882–1890." *Labour/Le Travail* 28 (fall 1991)

Marrus, Michael. *The Unwanted: European Refugees in the Twentieth Century*. New York 1985.

Martin, Susan Forbes. *Refugee Women*. London 1992.

Martynowych, Orest. "The Ukrainian Socialist Movement in Canada, 1900–1918." *Journal of Ukrainian Graduate Studies* 1, 1 (fall 1976).

Mazian, Florence. "The Patriarchal Armenian Family System: 1914." *Armenian Review* (winter 1983).

McCormack, A. Ross. *Reformers, Rebels, and Revolutionaries*. Toronto 1977.

McCormick, C. *The Century of the Reaper*. New York 1931.

McDonald, John S. "Italy's Rural Social Structure and Emigration." *Occidente* 12, 5 (september, 1956).

Mears, Eliot Grinnell, ed. *Modern Turkey: A Politico-Economic Interpretation, 1908–1923*. New York 1924.

Melkonian, Edward L. *Haikakan Baregordsakan Endhanur Miutiune Khorhtain Hayastanum: 1923–1937* (The Armenian General Benevolent Union in Soviet Armenia: 1923–1937). Yerevan 1999.

Melson, Robert. "A Theoretical Inquiry into the Armenian Massacres of 1894–1896." *Comparative Studies in Society and History* 24 (1982).

– "Provocation or Nationalism: A Critical Inquiry into the Armenian Genocide of 1915." In *The Armenian Genocide in Perspective*, Richard G. Hovannisian, ed. New Brunswick, NJ, 1987.

- *Revolution and Genocide: On the Origins of the Armenian Genocide and the Holocaust.* Chicago 1992.
Mesiayan, Yervant. *Levon Babayan: Ir Keankn u Gordsere* (Levon Babayan: His Life and Work). New York 1941.
Mesrob, Kevork. *L'Arménie au point de vue géographique, historique, ethnographique, statistique, et culturel.* Constantinople 1919.
Mesrobian, Arpena S. *Like One Family: The Armenians of Syracuse: The History of Armenians in America.* Ann Arbor, MI, 2000.
Meyer, Stephen III. *The Five Dollar Day: Labour Management and Social Control in the Ford Motor Company, 1908–1921.* Albany, NY, 1981.
Miller, Donald E., and Lorna Touryan Miller. *Survivors: An Oral History of the Armenian Genocide.* Berkeley 1993.
Miller, Randall M., and Thomas D. Marzik, eds. *Immigrants and Religion in Urban America.* Philadelphia 1977.
Mills, Allen. *Fool for Christ: The Political Thought of J.S. Woodsworth.* Toronto 1991.
Minasian, Edward. "The Armenian Immigrant Tide: From the Great War to the Great Depression." In *Recent Studies in Modern Armenian History.* Cambridge, MA, 1972.
Minassian, Gaidz. *Guerre et terrorisme arméniens.* Paris 2002.
Minassian, Oshagan. "A History of the Armenian Holy Apostolic Orthodox Church in the United States (1888–1944)." Part 2. PHD diss., Boston University, 1974.
Mirak, Robert. "The Armenians in the United States, 1890–1915." PHD diss., Harvard University, 1965.
- "Armenian Emigration to the United States to 1915." *Journal of Armenian Studies* 1, 1 (autumn 1975).
- "On New Soil: The Armenian Orthodox and Armenian Protestant Churches in the New World to 1915." In *Immigrants and Religion in Urban America.* Randall M. Miller and Thomas D. Marzik, eds. Philadelphia 1977.
- "Armenians." *Harvard Encyclopedia of American Ethnic Groups.* Stephan Thernstrom, ed. Cambridge 1980.
- *Torn between Two Lands: Armenians in America, 1890 to World War I.* Cambridge, MA, 1983.
- "Armenians." In *The Immigrant Labor Press in North America, 1840s–1970s: an Annotated Bibliography.* Vol. 2. Dirk Hoerder and Christiane Harzig, eds. *Bibliographies and Indexes in American History*, Westport, CT, 1987.
Mkhitarian, On. *Vani Herosamarte* (The Heroic Battle of Van). Sofia 1930.
Mkund, Tigran (Dikran Spear). *Hai Kghern Amerikayi Medj* (Armenian Clergy in America). Weehawken, NJ, 1945.
Mooradian, Alexander (A.B. Davies). *The Book of Life.* Hamilton, ON. n.p., n.d., probably 1930s.

Morgan, Jaques de. *The History of the Armenian People.* E.F. Barry, trans. from French. Boston. (Pub. in French, Paris 1918).

Morgenthau, Henry. *Ambassador Morgenthau's Story.* Plandome, NY, 1975. Originally published in 1919.

Morton, Desmond. *Working People: An Illustrated History of the Canadian Labour Movement.* 4th ed. Montreal 1998.

Mouradian, Claire. "L'immigration des Arméniens de la diaspora dans la RSS d'Arménie, 1946–1962." *Cahiers du Monde russe et soviétique.* 20, 1 (1979).

– *L'Arménie: De Staline à Gorbachev: Histoire d'une république soviétique l'Arménie.* Paris 1990.

– "Bibliographie" (of the Genocide). In *Ailleurs, hier, autrement: Connaissance et reconnaissance du génocide des Arméniens.* Special volume of *Revue d'histoire de la Shoah: Le monde juif.* 177–8 (January–August 2003). Georges Bensoussan, Claire Mouradian, and Yves Ternon. eds.

Murphy, Henry Brian. *Flight and Resettlement.* Paris 1955.

Musheghian, Levon. "Musheghian Dohmi Kuloi-Mialaki Jiughe" (Kulo's Branch of the House of Musheghian). In (*History of the Village of Chanakhchi*). Arakel Eghigian and Soghomon Kaprielian, eds. Belleville, IL, 1977.

Mutafian, Claude. "La France en Cilicie: Histoire d'un échec." *Les Temps Modernes* (May 1988).

Nahabedian, Harold. "A Brief Look at Relations between Canadians and Armenians: 1896–1920." *Polyphony: Armenians in Ontario* 4, 2 (fall/winter 1982).

Nalbandian, Louise. *The Armenian Revolutionary Movement: The Development of Armenian Political Parties through the Nineteenth Century.* 3d ed. Berkeley 1975.

Nansen, Fridthof. *Armenia and the Near East.* New York 1928.

Nassibian, Akaby. *Britain and the Armenian Question, 1915–1923.* London 1984.

Nichanian, Marc. *Writers of Disaster: Armenian Literature of the Twentieth Century.* Vol. 1, *The National Revolution.* Princeton and London 2002.

Nickoley, Edward. "Agriculture." In *Modern Turkey.* Eliot Grinnell Mears, ed. New York 1924.

Niepage, Martin. *The Horrors of Aleppo.* London 1917. Reprinted New York 1975,

Nor Geghi (New Keghi). Vols. 1 and 2. East St Louis 1964 and 1965.

Norsigian, Aram. "Tarmani Antskere" (Passages of Tarman). In (*New Keghi*). Vol. 1, 1964; continued in vol. 2.

Nurikhan, Minas. *The Life and Times of the Servant of God Abbot Mechtar (1670–1750).* Rev. John McQuillan, trans. Venice 1915.

Ormanian, Malachia. *The Church of Armenia: Her History, Doctrine, Rule, Discipline, Liturgy, Literature, and Existing Condition.* G. Marcar Gregory, trans. London 1910.

Ozanian, Meruzhan, and Siranush G. Mkhitarian, compilers. *Hushamatian Hai Oknutian Miutian: 1910–1970* (Memorial Volume of the Armenian Relief Society: 1910–1970). Boston 1970.
Ozanne, Robert. *A Century of Labor-Management Relations at McCormick and International Harvester.* Madison, WI, 1967.
P.A., compiler. "Biographies: Part A: The Contribution of Keghi towards Armenian Emancipation." In *Taregirk* (Yearbook). Detroit 1937.
Pagé, J. D. "Trachoma and Immigration: Our Detention Hospitals." Dominion Medical Monthly 25 (1905).
Palmer, Bryan D., "'Taking It.' Ontario Workers' Struggles." In *Lectures in Canadian Labour and Working-Class History.* W.J.C. Cherwinski and G.S. Kealey, eds. St John's, NF, 1985.
– *A Culture in Conflict: Skilled Workers and Industrial Capitalism in Hamilton, Ontario, 1860–1914.* Montreal 1979.
Palmer, Howard. *Patterns of Prejudice: A History of Nativism in Alberta.* Toronto 1982.
– ed. *The Settlement of the West.* Calgary 1977.
Papaghian, Very Rev. Suren. "Khupse yev ir Hairenaktsakan Miutiune" (Khups and its Compatriotic Union). In (*Memorial Volume of the Village of Khups in Keghi*). Fresno, CA, 1968.
Papazian, Dennis R., and Gerald Ottenbreit. *The Armenian Genocide: A Bibliography.* http://www.umd.umich.edu/dept/Armenian/fact/gen_bib 1.html.
Park, Robert E. *Old World Traits Transplanted.* New York 1921.
– *The Immigrant Press and its Control.* New York 1922.
Parr, Joy. *Gender of Breadwinners: Women, Men and Change in Two Industrial Towns: 1880–1950.* Toronto 1990.
Pashigian, Hovannes. "Avantakan yev Zhamanakagits Khoher Khupsi Masin" (Traditional and Contemporary Reflections about Khups). *Nor Geghi* (New Keghi). Vol. 1. 1964.
Patrias, Carmela. *Patriots and Proletarians: Politicizing Hungarian Immigrants in Interwar Canada.* Montreal and Kingston 1994.
Pattie, Susan. "Armenian Diaspora Life in Cyprus and London." *Armenian Review* 44, 1/173 (spring 1991).
– "Armenians in Britain." Ararat Quarterly. 32, 4 (autumn 1991).
– *Faith in History: Armenians Rebuilding Community.* Washington, DC, 1997.
Payaslian, Simon. "After Recognition." *Armenian Forum* 2, 3 (1999).
Pears, Edwin. *Turkey and Its People.* London 1911.
– *Forty Years in Constantinople. The Recollections of Sir Edwin Pears, 1873–1915.* New York 1916.
Pendakur, R. *Speaking in Tongues: Heritage Language Maintenance and Transfer in Canada.* Ottawa 1990.
Penner, Norman. *The Canadian Left: A Critical Analysis.* Scarborough, ON, 1977.

Perin, Roberto, and Franc Sturino, eds. *Arrangiarsi: The Italian Immigration Experience in Canada*. Montreal 1989.
Permanent Peoples' Tribunal. *A Crime of Silence: The Armenian Genocide*. Cambridge, MA, 1985.
Peroomian, Rubina. "Armenian Literary Responses to Genocide: The Artistic Struggle to Comprehend and Survive." In *The Armenian Genocide: History, Politics, Ethics*. Richard G. Hovannisian, ed. New York 1992.
– *Literary Responses to Catastrophe: A Comparison of the Armenian and Jewish Experience*. Atlanta, GA, 1993.
Peterson, Charles W. *Wake Up, Canada: Reflections on Vital National Issues*. Toronto 1919.
Petroff, Lillian. *Sojourners and Settlers: The Macedonian Community in Toronto to 1940*. Toronto 1995.
Philips, Jenny. *Symbol, Myth, and Rhetoric: The Politics of Culture in an Armenian-American Population*. New York 1989.
Pilibosian, Hapet M. *Gordsnagan Aroghdjabanutiun (Practical Hygiene)*. Boston 1911.
Piva, Michael J. *The Condition of the Working Class in Toronto, 1900–1921*. Ottawa 1979.
Porter, John. *The Vertical Mosaic*. Toronto 1965.
Portukalian, Migirdich. (Pamphlet on the Occasion of his Fortieth Anniversary Working for the Nation and Twenty-fifth Anniversary of Armenia). Marseilles.
Power, Samantha. *A Problem from Hell: America and the Age of Genocide*. New York 2002.
Pozzetta, George, ed. *Pane e Lavorno: The Italian American Working Class*. Toronto 1980.
Prelacy Yearbook. New York 1993.
Prentice, Alison, et al. *Canadian Women: A History*. Toronto 1988.
Radecki, Henry, with Benedykt Heydenkorn. *A Member of a Distinguised Family: The Polish Group in Canada*. Toronto 1976.
Radforth, Ian, and Joan Sangster. "A Link between Labour and Learning: The Workers' Educational Association in Ontario." *Labour/Le Travail* 8 and 9 (1981–82).
Rahanian, Anahid. "Hishataki Pshurner" (Bits of Memory). In *Nor Geghi* (New Keghi), Vol. 1, 1964.
Ramsaur, E.E. *The Young Turks. Prelude to the Revolution of 1908*. Beirut 1965.
Rasporich, Anthony W. *For a Better Life: A History of the Croatians in Canada*. Toronto 1982.
Rawlinson, A. *Adventures in the Near East, 1918–1920*. London 1922.
Redfield, Robert, and Milton B. Singer. "City and Countryside: The Cultural

Independence." In *Peasants and Peasant Societies*. Teodor Shanin, ed. Harmondsworth, England, 1971.
Reid, W. Stanford, ed. *The Scottish Tradition in Canada*. Toronto 1977.
Renkiewicz, Frank, ed. *The Polish Presence in Canada and America*. Toronto 1982.
Reşat, Aktan. "Agricultural Policy of Turkey." In *The Economic History of the Middle East, 1800–1914*. C. Issawi, ed. Chicago 1966.
Richardson, Karen. "Second Piece in Epilepsy Gene Puzzle Found." *Medical Post* 39: 34.
Richmond, Anthony H. "The Green Paper: Reflections on the Canadian Immigration and Population Study." *Canadian Ethnic Studies* 1, 7 (1975).
Riggs, Henry. *Days of Tragedy in Armenia: Personal Experiences in Harpoot, 1915–17*. Ara Sarafian, ed. Ann Arbor, MI, 1997.
Rischin, N. *The Promised City: New York's Jews, 1870–1914*. Cambridge 1962.
Roberts, Barbara. "Shovelling Out the Mutinous": Political Deportation from Canada before 1936." *Labour/Le Travail* 18 (fall 1986).
– "Whence they Came": Deportation from Canada, 1900–1935. Ottawa 1988.
Roberts, John. *Canada's Immigration Law: An Overview*. Employment and Immigration Canada. Ottawa, no date.
Roberts, Peter. *The New Immigration: A Study of the Industrial and Social Life of Southeastern Europeans in America*. New York 1913.
Rodney, William. *Soldiers of the International: A History of the Communist Party of Canada, 1919–1929*. Toronto 1968.
Rolin-Jaequemyns, M.G. *Armenia, the Armenians and the Treaties*. Translated from *Revue de droit international et de législation comparée* (Brussels), revised by author John Heywood. London. 1891. Originally published in *International Law Review*, part 1, 1887; part 2, 1889.
Roy, Ralph Lord. *Communism and the Churches*. New York 1960.
Russell, Peter, ed. *Nationalism in Canada*. Toronto 1966.
Rustigian, Stella Sachakalian. "The Armenian Day School Movement in the United States." MA thesis. University of Connecticut, 1979.
– "The Armenian Community of Hartford Connecticut." *Armenian Review* 54, 1/155 (March 1981).
Safarian, A.E. *The Canadian Economy in the Great Depression*. Toronto 1970.
Safrastian, Arshak. *Kurds and Kurdistan*. London 1948.
Sakayan, Dora, ed. *An Armenian Doctor in Turkey: Garabed Hatcherian. My Smyrna Ordeal of 1922*. Montreal 1997.
Sanasarian, Elizabeth. "Gender Distinction in the Genocidal Process: A Preliminary Study of the Armenian Case." *Holocaust and Genocide Studies* 4, 4 (1989).

Sanjian, Avedis K. *The Armenian Communities in Syria under Ottoman Dominion*. Cambridge 1965.
Sarafian, Ara, comp. *United States Official Documents on the Armenian Genocide*. Watertown, MA, 1993–96.
Sarafian, Kevork. *History of Education in Armenia*. Van Nuys, CA, 1950.
Sarkess, Harry Jewell. "The Armenian Renaissance 1500–1863." *Armenian Review* 26, 5/105 (autumn 1975).
Sarkisian, Harutiun. *Balu, Ir Sovoruitnere Krtakan u Imatsakan Vijake Yev Barbare* (Balu, Its Customs, Education and Intellectual Conditions and Its Language). Cairo 1932.
Sarkissian. A.O. *History of the Armenian Question to 1885*. Urbana, IL, 1938.
Schahgaldian, Nikola Bagrad. "The Political Integration of an Immigrant Community into a Composite Society: The Armenians in Lebanon, 1920–1974." PHD diss., Columbia University, 1979.
– "Ethnicity and Political Development in the Lebanese-Armenian Community, 1925–1975." *Armenian Review* 36, 1 (spring 1983).
Schopoff A. *Les Reformes et la Protection des Chrétiens en Turquie, 1673–1904*. Paris 1904.
Scott, Bruce. "A Place in the Sun: The Industrial Council at Massey-Harris, 1919–1929." *Labour/le Travail* 1 (1976).
Scott, J.W., and Louise Tilly. "Women's Work and the Family in Nineteenth Century Europe." *Comparative Studies in Sociology and History* 17 (January 1975).
Scott, Jack. *Canadian Workers, American Unions: How the American Federation of Labour Took Over Canada's Unions*. Vancouver 1978.
Sennett, Richard. *Families against the City*. Cambridge 1970.
Seropian, Varoujan. "Canadayi Hai Azgain Garuitsnere" (Formation of the Armenian Ethnic Group in Canada). *Horizon, 15 Amiaki Batsarik* (Horizon, 15th Anniversary Abstract), 30 May 1994.
Shahen Setrag. "Kghetsi Knkan Namake" (The Keghetsi Wife's Letter). In *Nor Geghi* (New Keghi), vol. 1.
– "Meroria Kghiin Ampop Gdserov" (A Concise Sketch of Keghi in our Day). *Nor Geghi* (New Keghi), vol. 1, 1964.
Shahnazarian, S. *Zharangagitutiun* (Study of Genetics). Boston 1930.
Shanin, Teodor. "Peasantry as a Political Factor." In *Peasants and Peasant Societies*. Teodor Shanin, ed. Harmondsworth, England, 1971.
– "A Russian Peasant Household at the Turn of the Century." In *Peasants and Peasant Societies*. Teodor Shanin, ed. Harmondsworth, England, 1971.
– ed. *Peasants and Peasant Societies*. Harmondsworth, England, 1971.
Shapiro, Leonard. *The Communist Party of the Soviet Union*. London 1964.
Sharambeyan, Anush. "Needle Arts." *Armenian Folk Arts, Culture, and Identity*. Levon Abrahamian and Nancy Sweezy, eds. Bloomington and Indianapolis, IN, 2001.

Shemmassian, Vahram, L. "The Sasun Pandukht in Nineteenth-Century Aleppo." In *Armenian Baghesh/Bitlis and Taron/Mush*. Richard G. Hovannisian, ed. Costa Mesa, CA, 2001.
Shiragian, Arshavir. *The Legacy: Memoirs of an Armenian Patriot*. Sonia Shiragian, trans. Boston 1976.
Shirinian, Lorne. "Survivor Memoirs of the Armenian Genocide as Cultural History." In Richard Hovannisian, ed., *Remembrance and Denial: The Case of the Armenian Genocide*. Detroit, MI, 1998.
- *Quest for Closure: The Armenian Genocide and the Search for Justice in Canada*. Kingston 1999.
Shrikian, Gorun. "Armenians under the Ottoman Empire and the American Mission's Influence on their Intellectual and Social Renaissance." PHD diss., Concordia Seminary in Exile, 1977.
Simpson, Christopher. *The Splendid Blond Beast: Money, Law, and Genocide in the Twentieth Century*. New York 1993.
Simpson, John Hope. *Refugees: Preliminary Report of a Survey*. Royal Institute of International Affairs 1928.
- *The Refugee Problem: Report of a Survey*. London 1939.
Smith, Oswald J. *At the Hands of the Turks*. Toronto 1931.
Smith, Roger W., Eric Markusen, and Robert Jay Lifton. "Professional Ethics and the Denial of the Armenian Genocide." *Holocaust and Genocide Studies* 9, 1 (spring 1995).
Smith, Timothy L. "Immigrant Social Aspirations and American Education, 1880-1930." *American Quarterly* 21, 5 (fall 1969).
Smith, W.G. *A Study in Canadian Immigration*. Toronto 1920.
- *Building a Nation: A Study of Some Problems Concerning the Church's Relationship to Immigrants*. Toronto 1922.
Srabian, Levon. *Kghi* (Keghi). Antelias 1960.
- "Kani Me Edj Levon Srabianen" (A Few Pages from Levon Serabian). In *(Memorial Volume of the Village of Khups in Keghi)*. Fresno, CA, 1968.
St Gregory the Illuminator Armenian Apostolic Church. *Golden Jubilee Commemorative Volume 1930-1980*. St Catharines 1980.
Stamp, Robert. "Urbanization and Education in Ontario and Quebec, 1867-1914." *McGill Journal of Education* 3, 1 (fall 1968).
- *The Schools of Ontario, 1876-1976*. Toronto 1982.
Steeg, Louis. "Land Tenure." In *Modern Turkey*. Eliot Grinnell Mears, ed. New York 1924
Stepan-Norris, Judith, "Communist Leadership and the Organization of UAW Local 600: 1920-1941." Paper delivered at the Social Science History Association's annual meeting in Chicago, November 5-8, 1992.
Stephens, Douglas Patrick. (Pat) (Patrick Stepanian, né Patrik Der Stepanian). *A Memoir of the Spanish Civil War: An Armenian-Canadian in the Lincoln Battalion*. St John's NF, 2000.

Stirling, Paul. *A Turkish Village*. New York 1965.
- "Turkish Village." In *Peasants and Peasant Societies*. Teodor Shanin, ed. Harmondsworth, England, 1971.
Strom, Margot Stern, and William S. Parsons. *Facing History and Ourselves: Holocaust and Human Behavior*. Watertown, MA, 1982.
Strong-Boag, Veronica. "The Girl of the New Day: Canadian Working Women in the 1920s." *Labour/Le Travail* 4 (1979).
Struthers, James. "How Much is Enough? Creating a Social Minimum in Ontario, 1930–44." *Canadian Historical Review* 72, 1 (March 1991).
Sturino, Franc. "Inside the Chain: A Case Study in Southern Italian Migration to North America, 1880–1930." PHD diss., University of Toronto, 1981.
- *Forging the Chain: Italian Migration in North America, 1880–1930*. Toronto 1990.
Stürmer, H. *Two Years in Constantinople*. E. Allen, trans. New York 1917.
Summers, Janice. *Oriental Rugs: The Illustrated World Buyer's Guide*. New York 1994.
Suny, Ronald Grigor. "Populism, Nationalism and Marxism: The Origins of Revolutionary Parties among the Armenians of the Caucasus." *Armenian Review* 32, 2/126 (June 1979).
- "Marxism, Nationalism, and the Armenian Labor Movement in Transcaucasia, 1890–1908." *Armenian Review* 33, 1/129 (1 March 1980).
- "Return to Ararat: Armenia in the Cold War," *Armenian Review* 42, 3/167 (autumn 1989).
- *Looking toward Ararat*. Bloomington, IN, 1993.
Surmenian, Galust. *Tajkahai Zinvor yev Zinvorakanutiune* (The Turkish-Armenian Soldier and the Military). Beirut 1967.
Sutherland, Neil. *Children in English Canadian Society: Framing the Twentieth Century Consensus*. Toronto 1976.
Svajian, Stephan G. *A Trip through Historic Armenia*. New York 1977.
Synge, J. "Immigrant Communities: British and Continental Europeans in Early Twentieth Century Hamilton, Canada." *Oral History* 4 (1976).
Swyripa, Frances. *Wedded to the Cause: Ukrainian-Canadian Women and Ethnic Identity, 1891–1991*. Toronto 1993.
Swyripa, Frances, and John Herd Thompson, eds. *Ukrainians in Canada during the Great War*. Edmonton 1983.
Tabori, Paul. *The Anatomy of Exile: A Semantic and Historical Study*. London 1972.
Tachjian, Vahé. "Etat-nation et minorités en Turquie kémaliste: L'expulsion des Arméniens et des Syriaques." In *Ailleurs, hier, autrement: Connaissance et reconnaissance du génocide des Arméniens*. Special volume of *Revue d'histoire de la Shoah: Le monde juif*. 177–8 (January–August 2003). Georges Bensoussan, Claire Mouradian, and Yves Ternon, eds.
Taft, Elise Hagopian. *Rebirth: The Story of an Armenian Girl Who Survived the Genocide and Found Rebirth in America*. Plandome, NY, 1981.

Tarbassian, Hratch. *Erzerum (Garin): Its Armenian History and Tradition.* Nigol Schahgaldian, trans. N.p. 1975. Published by the Garin (Erzerum) Compatriotic Union of the United States.
Taregirk (Yearbook). Detroit 1937. Published by the Patriotic Society of Keghi.
Tashjian, James H. The Armenians of the United States and Canada. Boston, 1947.
— *The Armenian-American in World War II.* Boston 1953.
— "The Armenian and the American Bicentennial: A Bicentennial History of the Armenian Community of Massachusetts, with a Prefatory on the Origins of the Armenian Settlement of America." *Armenian Review* 28, 5/121 (autumn 1975).
Taylor, Charles. *Multiculturalism and the Politics of Recognition: An Essay.* Amy Gutman et al., eds. Princeton, NJ, 1992.
Teghekagir Hai Azgayin Miutian Amerikai, 1917–1921 (Report of the Armenian National Union of America, 1917–1921).
Teghtsoonian, Oksen. "Armenians in Toronto: The Early Years." *Polyphony: Armenians in Ontario* 4, 2 (fall-winter 1982).
Tehlirian, the Case of Soghomon: Proceedings. Los Angeles 1985.
Témisjian Khatoune, Anna-Maria Folco, and Nourhan Ouzounian, eds. *La langue Arménienne défis et enjeux.* Montreal 1995.
Teodik. *Amenun Taretsuitse* (Everyone's Almanac). Constantinople 1921.
Ter Minassian, Anahide. "Le Mouvement Revolutionnaire Arménien, 1890–1903." *Cahiers du Monde Russe et Soviétique* 14, 4 (October-December 1975).
— "Aux Origines du Marxisme Arménien: Les spécifistes." *Cahiers du Monde Russe et Soviétique* 19, 1–2 (January-June 1978).
— "Sociétés de culture, écoles et presse arméniennes à l'époque d'Abd-ul-Hamid II." *Revue du Monde Arménien: Moderne et Contemporain* 3 (1997).
Ternon, Yves. *La cause arménienne.* Paris 1983.
— "Historiens d'état et vérités historiques." In *Les Temps Modernes* (July-September 1988). Special issue, *Arménie-Diaspora: Mémoire et modernité.*
— "Mardin 1915: Anatomie pathologique d'une déstruction." In *Revue d'histoire arménienne contemporaine* 4 (2002). Special issue on Mardin.
Thernstrom, Stephan. *Poverty and Progress: Social Mobility in the Nineteenth-Century City.* Cambridge 1964.
— "Immigrants and Wasps: Ethnic Difference in Occupational Mobility in Boston, 1890–1940." In *Nineteenth-Century Cities: Essays in the New Urban History.* Stephan Thernstrom and Richard Sennett, eds. New Haven, CT, 1969.
— "Working-Class Social Mobility in Industrial America." *Social Theory and Social History: An Approach to General Education.* Melvin Richter, ed. Cambridge 1970.

Thistlethwaite, Frank. "Migration from Europe Overseas in the Nineteenth and Twentieth Centuries." In *Population Movement in Modern European History*. Herbert Moller, ed. New York 1964.
Thomas, Brinley. *Migration and Urban Development: A Reappraisal of British and American Long Cycles*. London 1972.
– *Migration and Economic Growth: A Study of Great Britain and the Atlantic Community*. 2d ed. Cambridge 1973.
– *The Industrial Revolution and the Atlantic Economy: Selected Essays*. London 1993.
Thomas, William I., and Florian Znaniecki. *The Polish Peasant in Europe and America*. Vol. 1. Boston 1918.
Thompson, E.P. *The Making of the English Working Class*. New York 1963.
Thompson, John Herd. *Ethnic Minorities during Two World Wars*. Ottawa 1991.
Thompson, John Herd, with Allen Seager. *Canada, 1922–1939: Decades of Discord*. Toronto 1985.
Tilly, Charles, and Harold C. Brown. "On Uprooting, Kinship and the Auspices of Migration." In *An Urban World*. Charles Tilly, ed. Boston 1974.
Tilly, Louise A., and Joan W. Scott. *Women, Work and Family*. New York 1978.
Timlin, Mabel. "Canada's Immigration Policy, 1896–1910." *Canadian Journal of Economics and Political Science* 26, 4 (November 1960).
Titizian, Mary. "We Can No Longer Accept Politically Correct Answers or Sanctimonious Messages of Goodwill." Speech delivered in St Catharines, 21 April 1996.
Tölölyan, Khachig. "Terrorism in a Textual Community." *Critical Exchange* 22 (spring 1987).
– "The Role of the Armenian Apostolic Church in the Diaspora." *Armenian Review* 41, nos. 1/161 (Spring 1988).
Tomasi, Silvano M., and M.H. Engel. *The Italian Experience in the United States*. New York, 1970.
Tootikian, Vahan H. "Armenian Congregationalists Flee from Genocide and Find a Home in the U.S." From *Hidden Histories in the United Church of Christ: Armenian Congregationalists in Teaching/Bilingual Ed Hist/Armenian Evangelicals*.
– *The Armenian Evangelical Church: Yesterday, Today, and Tomorrow*. Southfield, MI, 1996.
Toriguian, Shavarsh. *The Armenian Question and International Law*. 2d ed. La Verne, CA, 1988.
– "Armenian Insurance Claims Arising from the 1915 Massacres." *Klatsor*. Special Issue (1989).
Torosian, Hygus. "The First Armenian Church in Canada: St Gregory the Illuminator Armenian Apostolic Church 1930, St Catharines." In *St Gregory*

the Illuminator Armenian Apostolic Church, Golden Jubilee, 1930–1980. Commemorative Volume.
- "The First Armenian Church in Canada: St Gregory the Illuminator." *Polyphony: Armenians in Ontario* 4, 2 (fall/winter 1982).
Totovents, Vahen. *Scenes from an Armenian Childhood.* Mischa Kudian, trans. London 1962.
Troper, Harold Martin. *Only Farmers Need Apply: Official Canadian Government Encouragement of Immigration from the United States, 1896–1911.* Toronto 1972.
Troper, Harold, and Morton Weinfeld, eds., *Ethnicity, Politics, and Public Policy: Case Studies in Canadian Diversity.* Toronto 1999.
Trumpener, Ulrich. *Germany and the Ottoman Empire, 1914–1918.* Princeton, NJ, 1968.
Tucker, Eric, and Judy Fudge. "Forging Responsible Unions: Metal Workers and the Rise of the Labour Injunction in Canada." *Labour/Le Travail* 37 (spring 1996).
Tulchinsky, Gerald, ed. *Immigration in Canada: Historical Perspectives.* Toronto 1994.
Tylecote, Mabel. *The Mechanics' Institutes of Lancashire and Yorkshire Before 1851.* Manchester 1957.
Ubicini, Jean Henri Abdolonyme. *Letters on Turkey: An Account of the Religious, Political, Social, and Commercial Conditions of the Ottoman Empire.* Trans. from French by Lady Elizabeth Easthope. New York 1973.
Ugurlayan, Anahid M. "The Protection of Cultural Property under International Law." *Armenian Forum* 2, 2 (2000).
Ussher, Clarence D. *An American Physician in Turkey.* Boston 1917.
Vandal, Albert. *Les Arméniens et la reforme de la Turquie.* Paris 1897.
Varantian, Mikael. *Hai Heghapokhakan Dashnaktsutian Patmutiune* (History of the Armenian Revolutionary Federation), Vol. 1. Paris 1932.
Vartabedian, A. *Hayastani Oknutian Komiten, 1921–37* (Relief Committee for Armenia, 1921–37). Yerevan 1966.
Vartanian, Hrag. "Chine Drive: An Arts and Crafts Suburb and its Context." In an *Exhibition in the Thomas Fisher Rare Book Library.* Toronto 1997.
Vassilian, Hamo B. *The Armenian Genocide: A Comprehensive Bibliography and Library Resource Guide.* Glendale, CA, 1992.
Veatch, Richard. *Canada and the League of Nations.* Toronto 1975.
Vecoli, Rudolph J. "Contadini in Chicago: A Critique of the Uprooted." *Journal of American History* 51 (December 1964).
- "Prelates and Peasants: Italian Immigrants and the Catholic Church." *Journal of Social History* 2, 3 (spring 1969).
- "European Americans: From Immigrants to Ethnics." *International Migration Review* 6, 4 (winter 1972).
- "Italian American Workers, 1880–1920: Padrone Slaves or Primitive

Rebels." In *Perspectives in Italian Immigration and Ethnicity*. Silvano M. Tomasi, ed. New York 1977.

Vernant, Jacques. *Refugees in the Postwar World*. London 1953.

Voskematian Haikakan Baregortsakan Endhanur Miutian, 1906–1931. (Golden Jubilee Volume of the Armenian General Benevolent Union, 1906–1931). Vol. 1. Paris 1956.

Vratsian, Simon. "Depi Kghi" ("Towards Keghi"). *Taregirk* (Yearbook). Detroit, MI, 1937.

– *Armenia and the Armenian Question*. James G. Mandalian, trans., 1990. Original published in Boston, 1943.

– ed. *Vatsunamiak, 1890–1950* (Commemorative Volume of the Sixtieth Anniversary of the ARF). Boston 1950.

Vucinich, Wayne. *The Ottoman Empire: Its Record and Legacy*. Princeton 1965.

Walker, Christopher J. *Armenia: Survival of a Nation*. London 1980.

– "World War I and the Armenian Genocide." In *The Armenian People: From Ancient to Modern Times*. Richard G. Hovannisian, ed. Vol. 2. New York 1997.

Walkowitz, Daniel J. *Worker City, Company Town*. Urbana, IL, 1978.

Wallace, Kendra R. *Relation/Outsider: The Art and Politics of Identity among Mixed Heritage Students*. Westport, CO, 2001.

Wangenheim, Elizabeth. "The Ukrainians: A Case Study of the 'Third Force.'" *Nationalism in Canada*. Peter Russell, ed. Toronto 1966.

Washburn, George. *Fifty Years in Constantinople and Recollections of Robert College*. 2d ed. Boston 1911.

Wehrlin, Voldemar. "Mission en Arménie." *La Revue International de la Croix Rouge* (August 1925).

Weinfeld, Morton. *Like Everyone Else ... but Different: The Paradoxical Success of Canadian Jews*. Toronto 2001.

Werfel, Franz. *The Forty Days of Musa Dagh*. Geoffrey Dunlop, trans., from German. New York 1967. Originally published in Berlin, 1933.

Whitaker, Reg. *Double Standard: The Secret History of Canadian Immigration*. Toronto 1987.

Wickberg, Edgar, ed. *From China to Canada: A History of the Chinese Communities in Canada*. Toronto 1982.

Williams, Maynard Owen. "Russia's Orphan Races." *National Geographic* 34 (Oct. 1918).

Wolf, Eric R. "On Peasant Rebellions." In *Peasants and Peasant Societies*. Teodor Shanin, ed. Harmondsworth, England, 1971.

Wood, Harold A. "Emergence of the Modern City: Hamilton, 1891–1950." In *Steel City: Hamilton and Region*. M.J. Dear, J.J. Drake, and L.G. Reeds, eds. Toronto 1987.

Woodley, Harry. "Je me souviens. Turkish Days, 1911–20." Typewritten account deposited in the Multicultural History Society of Ontario.
Woodsworth, J. S. *Strangers within Our Gates: The Problem of the Immigrant.* Toronto 1909. Reprint 1982.
Wrigley, E.A. *Nineteenth Century Society: Essays in the Use of Quantitative Methods for the Study of Social Data.* Cambridge, England, 1972.
– *Identifying People in the Past.* London 1973.
Yans-McLaughlin, Virginia. *Family and Community: Italian Immigrants in Buffalo, 1880–1930.* Ithaca, NY, 1977.
– "Metaphors of Self in History: Subjectivity, Oral Narrative, and Immigration Studies." In *Immigration Reconsidered: History, Sociology, and Politics.* New York 1990.
– ed. *Immigration Reconsidered: History, Sociology, and Politics.* New York 1990.
Yeghiayan, Vartkes. *The Trial of the Young Turks.* La Verne, CA, 1990.
Yeran, E.A. *Patkerazard Zrutsatrutiun Hayerene Anglieren* (Armenian-English Conversation). 4th ed. Boston 1910.
Yeretzian, Aram. "A History of Armenian Immigration to America with Special Reference to Conditions in Los Angeles." Unpublished MA dissertation, University of Southern California, 1923. Reprint by R. and E. Research Associates, San Francisco 1974.
Zarevand. *United and Independent Turania: Aims and Designs of the Turks.* Vahakn Dadrian, trans. Leiden 1971.
Zaroukian, Andranik. *Men without Childhood.* Elise Bayizian and Marzbed Margossian, trans. New York 1985.
Zekiyan, Boghos Levan. *The Armenian Way to Modernity: Armenian Identity between Tradition and Innovation, Specificity and Universality.* Venice 1997.
Zucchi, John E. *Italians in Toronto: Development of a National Identity: 1875–1935.* Montreal and Kingston 1988.
Zunz, Oliver. "American History and the Changing Meaning of Assimilation." *Journal of American Ethnic History* (spring 1985).

Index

Abaka, 418, 451
Abandoned Properties Law, 119, 215
abduction: of women and children, 19, 130, 183, 191, 198
Abdul Hamid II (Sultan), 4, 21, 83, 120, 507n61; abdication, 28, 34, 100, 115; dissolution of the United Armenian Association, 83; Hamidian massacres, 95, 114; persecution of minorities, 17–20
Aboghnag (Akbinek), 121
Adana, 28, 31, 41, 57, 106, 148, 439, 512n40
Aharonian, Avetis, 119, 485
Aintab, 127, 366
Akazarian, Mihran, 297, 311
Aknuni, Edouard (Khachatur Malumian), 33, 97, 99, 441
Alexanian, Aris, 275, 368, 369, 450
Alianik, Hrant, xxiv, 465
All-Armenia Fund, xxxi, 444
Almas, Nick, 343–5
American Board of Commissioners for Foreign Missions, 36, 142, 215, 443
Amirkhanian, Armen, 173, 524n49
Anglican Church. *See* churches and the Armenian community
Andranig. *See* Ozanian, Andranig
Apcar, Diana Agabeg, 187
Arakelian, Sarkis, 59

Aram I (Catholicos), xxxvii, 562n12
Ararat, 450, 541n60
Ararat Quarterly, 450
Arek (Eskikavak), 24, 27, 42, 66, 77, 83, 94, 151, 213, 306, 342
Arman, Nurhan, xxiv, 465
Armenian Apostolic Church, 80–1, 419; Canadian Central Board of Trustees, 277, 288–9, 296, 302; Cilicia, xxix, xl, 126, 138, 141, 407, 421–3, 437, 461; and Communist rule, 269–72; conflict in Canada, 269–71; conflict in the United States, 269–73, 271, 279–82; and the Dashnaks, 270; Echmiadzin, 271–3, 281, 287–8, 294, 296, 305, 419–21; and the Genocide, 137–8; governance, 272, 277, 284–90, 302–3; history, xxix–xliii; in Keghi, 18–19; parish councils, 284–7, 288, 294–5, 297, 303; political influence, 304–5; in St Catharines, 277–9; women and the church, 303–4
Armenian Canadian literature, 335–6, 464–5
Armenian Church Youth Organization of Canada, 445, 450
Armenian General Benevolent Union (AGBU), 134, 140, 269, 293, 306–7, 309, 391, 398, 417–18, 433–5, 439–40

Armenian General Sports Union (HMEM), 445, 446
Armenian independence: 1918–20, 147, 252, 270, 340; 1991, xxvii, xxxvii, xxviii. *See also* Armenian Republic
Armenian Missionary Association of America, 443
Armenian National Committee of Canada (ANCC). *See* Dashnaks
Armenian National Red Cross, 275, 287, 294, 306, 443–4, 447, 546n16
Armenian, Raffi, xxiv, 465
Armenian Relief Association of Canada (ARAC), 133–4, 144–5, 164, 172, 175–6, 354–6, 528n51; and the Georgetown farm/home/school, 182, 200–4, 312, 362, 446, 455, 462
Armenian Relief Society (ARS), 275, 292, 311, 321, 408, 418, 432, 433, 441–4, 506n57, 546n16; and school, 408, 430
Armenian Renaissance (*Zartonk*), xlii, 33–4, 82
Armenian Republic, xxvii, xxxviii–xxxix, 124, 125–6, 449, 471, 479; and the Dashnaks, 140, 146, 280, 294, 318, 320; Sovietization, xl. *See also* Armenian independence
Armenian Revolutionary Federation (ARF). *See* Dashnaks
Armenian Secret Army for the Liberation of Armenia (ASALA), 451, 473, 559n73
Armenian theatre, 335
Armenian Union of Montreal (AUM), 446–7
Armenian War Relief Committee, 319
Armenian Youth Association (AYA), 315, 445
Armenian Youth Federation (AYF), 311, 315, 445
Armeno-American Letter Writer, 32, 72, 74, 102, 186, 502n21, 507n68, 526n14
Armenian Women's Benevolent Association, 433
Arshagouni, Rev. Vagharshag, 276
arts: Armenian contributions, 336–8, 340–1, 342, 347, 464–6; and cultural preservation, 134, 331, 334. *See also* musical culture
Artsakh. *See* Karabagh
Asiatic classification. *See* immigration regulations

Assadourian, Sarkis, xxix, 464, 476
assimilation, 73, 115, 128–9, 394, 413, 415, 453–5, 461–6, 482, 484; and the church, 294; and education, 273, 454–5; and exogamy, 457, 470
Astghaberd (Adakli), 27, 31, 62, 65–6, 81, 83, 85, 87–8, 90, 248
Ataturk, Mustapha Kemal, 126, 128–9, 161, 473

Babayan, Levon, 288, 355, 360, 364–5, 368–9; and church governance, 301–2; church and politics, 276–8, 284–5, 288–9; as a conservative, 306–8; crisis in the church, 294–5, 297–9; and the rug business, 364–5, 367–9, 370–2, 418, 552n24, 554n45
Babigian, Kegham (George Mooradian), 164–5
Babikian, Aris, 464
Bagdasarian, Mesrob, 48, 275, 276, 341
bagharch (Keghi festive food), 290, 320, 545n14
Baghdjian, Kévork, xxvi, 464
Baikar, 140, 275, 307, 450, 545n7
Bakalian, Anny, xxvi, 457, 459, 470
Banvor (Worker), 139–40, 231, 251, 293; and church conflict, 280–1, 307–8
barbershops, 76–8, 134, 261–2, 330
Baronian, Bagharsak, 151
Barton, James L., 134
Basmajian, John V., 347
Bayrakdarian, Isabel, xxiv, 466
Bazarian, Movses, 561n21
Bedrosian, Mateos, 245
Bedoukian, Kerop, 129, 365–6, 369, 374, 378, 410, 418, 419, 465; and immigration, 386–91, 399–400, 402–3, 440
Bejian, Seth, 247–8, 542n90
Bennett, R.B., 170, 227, 252
Bingol Mountains, 23
Bird's Nest Orphanage, 136, 199, 357
birth control, 199–200
Blair, Frederick, 157, 162, 165–6, 168, 171, 173–4, 178
boardinghouses: as entrepreneurial activity, 78, 79, 256; as the social framework for settlement, 66–7, 78–9, 103, 327–8, 502n6
Boghos, Nubar. *See* Nubar Pasha

Boyadjian, Yeznig, 425
Boyajian, Zabelle, 313–14
Brantford, 66–79, 91, 95–8, 99, 104, 108; demographics, 66; industry, 48, 60, 241–2, 248, 259; and the Progressives, 307–8, 315, 417; settlement patterns, xxviii, xxx, 27, 29, 58, 60–4, 237–9, 351, 403, 411–12, 414–15, 468, 501n1
Brown, Grace: and the Paris Commission, 207, 210, 214, 230, 529n5, 530n13
Bryce, Viscount: Bryce Report, 211, 217; and the Paris Commission, 211, 215
Buck Stove, 62, 73
Buck, Tim, 251, 304
Buzbuzian, Moushegian, 267
Byng, Lord Julian of Vimy, 145, 206

Cahan, Charles Hazlitt: Cahan's Report, 206, 225–9, 231–3; and the McDougall Commission, 217; and the Paris Commission, 216
Calouste Gulbenkian Foundation, 394
Canadian Armenian Congress (CAC): and the Asiatic classification, 374–5, 377; and sponsorship of immigration, 379–83, 403; work on immigration, xxx, 369, 377, 386–8, 401, 403, 448
Canadian Armenian Union (CAU), 172, 274–7, 288, 291, 293, 302, 446–7
Canadian Armenian Young People's Association, 444, 447
Canadian Council of Churches, 387, 389–91, 463, 476
Canadian Expeditionary Force (CEF), 65, 224, 230, 232; Armenian members, 150–2, 213
Canadian Reparation Commission, 205–6, 218, 219, 221, 233. *See also* McDougall Commission
Carlisle, David Windrum, 220: and Cahan's report, 226–7; and the Paris Commission, 207–8, 209–10, 211, 212, 216–17, 220, 224, 230, 531n36
career patterns. *See* occupational mobility
carte blanche for Armenian entry, 383, 385, 559n69
Cartozian case, 169–70
Cavouk, 465
Chaderjian, Jack, 464

Chambers, Rev. Lawson P., 143, 148, 176, 177
Chambers, Rev. Robert: and Canadian immigration, 53–4; humanitarian efforts, 142–3, 147
Chambers, Rev. William N.: and Canadian immigration, 53; humanitarian efforts, 141–3, 146, 148
Chan, 121
Chanakhchi (Chanakchi), 23, 29, 35, 47, 85, 101, 550n20
charitable organizations, 439–44. *See also* Armenian General Benevolent Union, Armenian Relief Society, Near East Relief
Chichakian, Senekerim, 66, 276, 290, 300–1, 303, 542n90
Chichekian, Garo, xxvi, 559n70
Chickegian, Samuel, 151
children, 193, 198, 230, 314–16, 324–7, 331–4, 340, 343–5. *See also* Georgetown home/farm/school
Charkhougian, Rev. Zkon, 276, 277, 278, 285, 294, 302
church crisis, 1933, 269, 291–9; and Hamilton, 323; impact on the young, 314–16; polarisation in St Catharines, 300–1, 412, 415. *See also* Armenian Apostolic Church
churches and the Armenian community: Anglican Church, 80, 143–4, 188, 277, 310, 312, 317–18, 462; Armenian Evangelical Churches, 37, 422–4, 451, 463; Catholic Church, 80, 309, 313, 353; United Church, 203–4, 323, 355–8, 362, 397, 422–3, 463. *See also* Armenian Apostolic Church, United Church of Canada
Churchill, Stacy, 482–3
Cilicia, xxxix, xl, 99, 127, 146, 148, 217, 232, 421, 475–6. *See also* Armenian Apostolic Church
Cockshutt: Cockshutt Plow, 61; family members, 48, 63, 81, 241, 259
coffeehouse (*srjaran*), 76–8, 103, 327–30, 333–4, 408–9, 503n32
Colvin, Eliot: and the Paris Commission, 208, 212–13, 214
Committee of Union and Progress (CUP). *See* Young Turks
Communists, 252, 471, 474, 540n55; and the Dashnaks, 252–3; and the

Hnchaks, 139–40, 270–1, 281, 293, 342, 516n7
Congress of Industrial Organizations (CIO), 244–5, 248–9, 252–3, 537n30, 540nn53, 55, 56
Constantinople, 4, 17, 24–5, 35, 48, 59–61, 72, 79, 82, 86, 494n3
Coté, Louis, 224, 227, 230
Courian, Paul, 355, 364–5, 367, 535n88; biography, 48, 59, 364–5, 501n29; business, 365, 367, 544n45
cuisine, Armenian, 408, 468–9
cultural organizations, 343, 444, 464, 466, 467
Curry, R.B., 385

Dadrian, Vahakn, 233
Daily Clarion, 245
Dalphond-Guiral, Madeleine, 476–7
Daniel and Alice Zaroukian Day School, 407, 430
Dashnaks (Dashnaktsutiun, Armenian Revolutionary Federation, ARF, Armenian National Committee of Canada (ANCC)), 63, 109, 269, 388, 425–6, 429, 501n40, 516n7; and the Armenian Church, 270, 280–2; and children, 316; and the crisis in St Catharines, 291–2, 294–9, 301, 309–10; formation of Canadian branches, 94–5; founding, 42; functions, 96–100, 292; and the Genocide, 140–1; in Hamilton, 322; *Hairenak* newspaper, 106–7, 141, 280–1; ideology, 95–6, 107, 252–3, 270, 319; as modernizing agent, 43, 252; reading rooms, 101; and Soviet Armenia, 270, 280, 294–7, 308, 319–21; and unionization, 252–4, 540n54
David of Sasun Tank Column, 319, 446
Davies, Alexander. *See* Alexander Mooradian
Darbinian, Reuben, 426
Derderian, Hovnan (Primate), xxxvii, 420
Der el-Zor, 123
Der Hovannesian, Tirayr (Primate), 273, 278, 279
Der Krikorian, Krikor, 94, 262, 284, 290, 303, 306
Der Meksian, Rev. Sempad, 421–2
Dersim Mountains, 13, 14, 130–1

Der Stepanian, George, 311, 365, 370
Der Stepanian, Movses, 167, 276, 285, 295, 310, 458, 545n5
Diamond, Jared, 484
Dirado(u)rian, Vahan, 419
domestics, 356–9
Donabedian, Garabed, 131–2
Dzotsikian, Rev. Atig, 276, 278

education, 83–6, 427–36, 439, 444, 446, 460–1, 474; in Armenian schools in Canada, 432–6; of Armenians in Canadian schools and universities, 274–5, 345–7, 407, 427, 430–1, 432, 435–6, 449; and the ARS, 441–3; and ethnopatriotism, 428–31; and family life, 346–7; in Keghi, 36–7; language education, 429, 433, 434; and missionaries, 37–8. *See also* village educational associations
Egan, William John, 158, 171
Eghigian, Arakel, 30, 47, 48, 70
Egoyan, Atom, xxiv, 466
Egoyan, Eve, 465
Eloyan, Noushig, 464
endogamy. *See* marriage patterns
enemy aliens, 232
entrepreneurial activity, xxix, 76, 262–3, 265–6, 308, 359, 409–11; and women, 255, 263–4, 542n86. *See also* barbershops, boardinghouses, jewellery, rug business
Enver Pasha, 121, 132
ethnopatriotism, xxi, 416–18, 424–5, 427–8, 435, 438, 453, 461, 466–9; and ethnoversion, 479; and the Genocide, 456, 471–2
Euphrates College, 27, 28, 35, 36, 37, 38, 39, 40
evangelical churches, 37, 422–4, 451, 463
exogamy. *See* marriage patterns

factory labour, xix, 69–71, 109, 168, 172, 239–43, 354; accidents, 72–3; factory and neighbourhood, 260–6; industrial disputes, 73–4; and unionization, 74, 244–8, 251, 537n30, 540nn53–6, 542n90; wages, 72; and women, 258–60
family: formation, 177, 469–70; fragmentation, 177, 180, 191, 193, 326,

329, 394–5, 527n47; lost childhood, 193–4, 199; reconstitution, xxviii, 135–6, 183, 194, 255, 325; reunification, 163–5, 168, 170, 378–9, 385, 397, 399, 401–2
Fegan's Homes, 169, 182, 359, 362, 365, 542n79
Fermanian family, 353
fieldworkers, 7–8, 33, 43, 97–9, 426, 441
Forke, Robert, 170
Fresno, California, 40, 105, 275, 455, 459, 535n5

Galt/Cambridge, 70, 95–6, 292, 306; settlement patterns, 60, 237–8, 327, 403, 411, 412, 414–15, 501n38, 537n22
Galt Malleable, 61, 62, 241, 243, 248–9, 265, 537n22
Garle, H.E., 209
Garo, Mgrdich, 348
General Motors, 238, 241, 244–6, 250, 252–3, 321, 415, 536n12. *See also* Mckinnon Dash and Metal Works
Geneva Convention for Refugees, 395–7
Genocide, 1915–23, xxviii, 41, 113–24, 237, 510n13, 512n44, 525nn6–7; the Allied response, 125–7; and the Armenian Apostolic Church, 137–8; and Armenian Canadians, 149–52; and Armenian faith, 311–12; and Canadian humanitarians, 141–9; and the Canadian Tribute to Human Rights, 564n21; and children's names, 326; as crimes against humanity, 233, 511n18; and the Dashnaks, 140–1; death toll, 129; and ethnopatriotism, 471–2; and the *Globe*, 145, 148, 163, 462; and the Hnchaks, 138–9; and the Ontario and Quebec legislatures, 472; origins, 114–17; and Permanent People's Tribunal, 564n17; recognition by the Canadian House of Commons, 476–7; recognition by the Canadian Senate, xxiv, 475–7; relief and rehabilitation, 133–6; services for martyrs, 339; survival, 129–32; trauma, xxi, xxv, 175–82, 191–2, 339–40, 456, 458, 461, 472, 479–80, 526–7n31; and the Treaty of Sèvres, 128; Turkish refusal to recognize, 472–5, 564n22; Young

Turk plan, 117. *See also* massacres, picture brides, reparations
Georgetown farm/home/school, 446, 450; attempts at assimilation, 455; Georgetown boys, 164, 169, 175–6, 182, 200–4, 275, 320, 359, 360–2, 443; role of ARAC, 200–3; and the United Church, 203–4
Globe: and the Genocide, 145, 148, 163, 462
gradarans. *See* reading rooms
Graham, Bill, 476
Greece, 128, 133, 161–2, 380, 386–7, 389–90, 399, 410–11, 520n19
Green Paper on Immigration, 385
group identity, 290, 454, 466–72, 479. *See also* ethnopatriotism
Guelph, 70, 96, 241, 293, 425, 442; settlement patterns, 237–8, 403, 522n15
Guerguerian, Father Grégoire, 423
Gundjian, Arshavir, 425, 464

Hadjin, 127, 132, 143
Hagopian, Khajag (Prelate), 422
Hairik, Khrimian, 33
Hairenik, 101, 105–8, 141, 252, 275, 280–1, 438, 450
Haktsian, Arthur, 347
Hamaskayin Educational and Cultural Union, 444, 450
Hamilton, 258, 342; Armenian neighbourhoods, 101, 239, 327–31, 333–4; and the Dashnaks, 301, 310, 322; entertainment, 335–8; family life, 322–7; and the Hnchaks, 292–3; reading rooms, 334; settlement patterns, xxviii, xxx, 58–60, 62–4, 237–8, 322, 351, 411, 413–15; shoeshine shops, 343–5; street life, 331–3; and unionization, 247, 250, 252
Hanemian, Sarkis, 386
Hanessian, Stephen, 463, 563n8
Hanimyan, Diana, 430
Harvester. *See* International Harvester
Herian, Ruben, 131–2
Hnchaks (Hnchak Social Democratic Party), 63–4, 140, 150, 251, 274, 352, 417, 426, 443, 445, 501n40; and church politics, 281, 285, 291; and the crisis in St Catharines, 292–4; formation of Canadian branches, 94–5, 505n45; functions, 96–100; and the

Genocide, 138–9; ideology, 95–6, 270; as modernizing agents, 43; reading rooms, 98, 101; and Soviet Armenia, 138–9, 516n7. See also *Yeritasard Hayastan*
HOG (Relief Committee for Armenia), 139, 251, 274, 275, 281, 293; and church politics, 281, 293–4, 516n5; as a Communist front organization, 251, 294; founding, 139–40 and Soviet Armenia, 251, 294, 443
Holy Cross Day School, 430, 431, 432, 433, 434, 439
Holy Trinity Anglican Church (Toronto), 419, 462
Holy Trinity Armenian Church, 397, 405, 419, 420, 431, 450
Horizon, 418, 451
Hotel Martinique group, 281–2, 284, 295–6
Hovannisian, Richard G., xxv
Hovsepian, Vatché (Bishop), 420
humanitarians, Canadian: and the Genocide, 141–9

identity, Armenian. See ethnopatriotism, group identity
immigration to Canada: Asiatic classification, 54–5, 57; demographics, 401–2; financial requirements, 521n22; Keghi migration before 1914, 58; statistics, 177–8; travel agents, 49–51; Turkish barriers, 48. See also immigration regulations, refugees, sponsorship and immigration
immigration regulations, Canadian, pre-1914, xxviii, 51–3, 499n23; and the Asiatic classification, 54–5, 57
immigration regulations, Canadian, post-World War I, xxviii, 155–6, 373; and the Asiatic classification, 159, 163, 169–72, 173; family reunification, 162–4, 165–6; and labour requirements, 166–8; money qualifications, 163; Nansen passport, 160–2; passports, 159–60; and refugees, 156–8, 171–8
immigration regulations, Canadian, post-World War II, xxx; and the Asiatic classification, 373–9; and the Canadian Armenian Congress, 374–5, 377, 380–2, 386; changes, 1960s, 383–4,

385; changes 1976, 385; displaced persons, 459; *Green Paper*, 385; Immigration Act, 1978, 397; and patterns of immigration, 398–9; and patterns of settlement, 414–15; refugees, 395–7; and sponsorship, 379–83, 385, 397–401, 403, 557n33; *White Paper*, 383–4
Inter-Allied Commission for the Assessment of Damage Suffered in Turkey. See Paris Commission
International Harvester, 70–1, 241, 247, 328, 332, 345–6, 377, 537n22, 539n40; labour protests, 74–5, 247–8, 250
International Labour Organization, 128
Ishkhanian, Levon, xxiv, 465
Ittihad ve Terakki. See Young Turks

Jackson, Tom, 464
Jacobsen, Maria, 357
Janigian, Melkon, 59
Jemal Pasha, 132
Jerusalem, xxxvii, xli, 279
jewellery business, xxvi, 410–11, 463

Kaloustian, Shenork (Patriarch), 420
Kantarjian, Gerard, 465
Kaprielian, Hagop (Jack), 151
Kaprielian, Kapriel, 311
Kaprielian, Norman, 339
Kaprielian, Paul, 335
Karabagh/Artsakh, xxxi, 140, 398, 479; independence 1991, xxvii, xxxvii–xxxviii, 440–1
Kara Kilisia, 125, 340
Karekin I (Catholicos), xxxvii, xxxviii
Karibian, Dickran, 353
Karsh, Yosuf, xxiv, 348, 354, 374
Kasparian, Gregory, 361–3
Keghi, 488–9n3, 550n20; and Armenian-Kurdish relations, 14–17; economic conditions, 4–9; education, 83–5, 90–4; emigration, 21–2; government corruption, 9–10; intellectual and political ferment, 34–44; landholding, 6–7; massacres, 20–1; migration to Canada, 58, 60–2, 71, 87, 190, 238; pan-Keghi organizations, 437–9; sojourning as a tradition, xxxiii, 21–2, 23–33; tax burden, 10–13, 20–1, 106

Keghi Kasaba (Kiği), 5, 7, 23, 28, 62; schools, 83, 85, 89
Kenney, Jason, 476
Kerbekian, Yeprem, 360–2
Keshishian, Rev. Vazken, 420
Keynes, John Maynard, 233
Khan-Azad, Ruben (Nshan Karapetian), 8–9, 98
Khanjian, Arsiné, xxiv, 466
Kharput, xxviii, xxxix, 4, 7, 27, 28, 35, 38, 40, 43, 85, 128, 134, 203, 216, 248, 316, 327, 357
Khatissian, Alexandre, 125
Khor Virap, xxxvii, xxxviii
Khups (Yazgounou), 21, 82, 83, 85, 86, 91, 132; population statistics, 505n40
Kiernan-Mooradian, Anaid, 347
King, William Lyon Mackenzie, 156, 175–6, 373
kinship: in the Old World, 6, 29, 67; in the New World, 265, 325
Kololian, Armenouhi, 433
Kololian elementary school, 430, 451
Kololian, Kévork, 433
Komitas, 317, 336, 338
Korkigian, Mateos, 245, 275
Kortigian, Msgr Edward. *See* Kurdy, Edouard
Kostigian, Johnny, 337, 338
Koulakan, xxxiii, 121–2
Kozekian, Garegin, 43
Kradjian, Serouj, xxiv
Krekorian, Nishan, 309
Krikorian, Arshag, 245, 276
Krikorian, Migirdich, 303
Kuenzler, Jacob, 215
Kurdian, Hasmig, 431
Kurds, 2, 4, 5, 7, 18–19, 21, 131; and the Genocide, xxxiii, 114, 121–3, 129–30, 132, 145, 217; massacres of Armenians, 20, 208, 491n27; relations with Armenians, 14–17
Kurdy, Msgr Edouard (Edward Kortigian), 423

Lane, Rev. Andrew, 203
language loss, 428, 457, 468. *See also* ethnopatriotism
Lausanne, Treaty of, 128–9, 149, 158, 160, 205–7, 212, 218, 389, 528n2, 529n7
Laval, 406, 420, 425, 442

Lawrence, Sam, 247
leadership: in nascent communities, 108–10, 418, 467–8; and the "hinge man," 108–9
League of Nations, 130, 131, 134, 149, 156, 160, 162, 175
Lemkin, Raphael, 474
Levon and Sophia Hagopian Foundation, 433
Litvinoff, Maxim, 281
Lord Mayor's Fund (London), 133
Lraper, 139, 248, 251, 304, 307–8, 450, 451

McDonough, Alexa, 476
McDougall Commission, 206, 217–25, 227, 229, 231–3, 532n49, 533n65, 534n67
McKinnon Dash and Metal Works, 61, 71, 238–9, 240–1, 253–4, 264–5, 536n12, 537n30; industrial action, 74, 242–3, 245–6. *See also* General Motors
Magarian, Kirk, 311
Maheu, Shirley, 475
Malak (Malak Karsh), xxiv, 348
Malek, Zohrab, 464
Malzac, M.: and reparations, 209
Mamigonian, Rev. Khoren, 419
Manigian, Rev. Mateos, 276, 288, 310
Manoogian, Alex, 407, 430, 433
Manoogian, Torkom (Primate), 420
Manoukian, Catherine, xxiv, 465
Marash, 126–7, 136, 143, 351, 438
Mardin, 58, 59, 183, 348, 354, 423, 552n14
Marsovan, 40, 351
marriage patterns, 182–3, 460–1; endogamy, 65, 457–60, 469; exogamy, 348, 411, 413, 457–61, 469–71. *See also* picture brides
massacres, 1890s, 13, 20–1, 37, 53, 57; 1909, 31–2, 37, 57, 98, 148, 439, 499n19; and crimes against humanity, 141–4; and Sultan Abdul Hamid II, 95, 114. *See also* genocide
Massey-Harris, 62, 77, 241, 259, 354
MEG, 444
Melkonian, Astghig, 433
Melkonian, Garabed, 38, 41, 42
Melkonian, Hagop, 284
Melkonian, Hovannes, 27

Melkonian, Robert (Nubar), 334, 550n24
Mgrubalian, Manuel, 347, 551n41
Migirdicyan, Migirdich, 391–3, 394–5
Minassian, Berge, 463
Minister's Permits: post–World War I, 171; post–World War II, 397, 523n44
Mirak, Robert, xxv, 27, 39, 102, 260
Mirakian, Apkar, 464
missionaries. *See* Protestant missionaries
Mkhitarists, xlii, 33, 392, 409
Montreal, 387, 391, 415, 451, 475; Armenian Union of Montreal, 446–7; business enterprises, 352–4; rug business, 364–9, 372–3; settlement patterns, 59–60, 301, 351–4, 402, 403, 405–7, 423, 457–60
Mooradian, Alexander (A.B. Davies), 109, 277, 335, 346–7
Mooradian, Ara, 343, 347
Mooradian, Arevaluis, 325
Mooradian, Hagop, 262, 275, 276, 418
Mooradian, John H., 342, 343, 374, 377–8, 418, 466
Mooradian, Parantzem, 335
Mooradian, Setrag, 150, 274, 275
Mooradian, Yeghishé, 27, 77, 109, 311
Morgenthau, Henry, 117–18, 120–1, 216
Mountainous Karabagh. *See* Karabagh
Mouradian, Mgrdich, 63
multiculturalism, xxiv–xxv, 342, 417, 463–4, 466, 476, 481–5
Muradian, Manoog, 150, 335
Murat (Hambardzum Bayajian), 97, 426, 506n53
Murat of Sivas, 507n74, 549n10
Musa Dagh, 412
musical culture, xxiv, xxix, 103, 194, 336–8, 340, 342, 347, 464–5, 466, 471

Nakash(ian), Georges, 58, 361
names, 326–7
National Unity Council, 342, 466
Near East Industries (NEI), 134–5
Near East Relief (NER), xl, 134, 146, 148, 162, 189, 515n78
Nershabu, Rev. Seropé, 276
Nershoyan, Tiran (Primate), 419
networks, 418
New Keghi, 437, 438
Nigoghosian, Rev. Soghomon, 422

Njdé, Garegin, 426, 445
Nor Serount, 450
Nor Serount Cultural Union, 426, 444
Notre Dame de Nareg, 423, 430
Nubar Pasha, 119, 150, 269, 270, 341, 439
Nubarian, John, 338
Nubarian, Kapriel, 65–6

occupational mobility, xxxiii, 76–8, 110, 260–2, 266–8, 345, 353, 359, 463, 410–11
Ohanian, Mary, 338, 347
Oror (Gokcheli), 12, 32, 36, 42, 121
orphans, xxvi, 36, 392, 454–5, 533n35; entry to Canada, 145–6, 158, 163–4, 176, 357, 359; and the Genocide, 120, 124, 131–2, 134–5, 193; orphanages, 119, 128, 133, 181, 183–4, 189, 198–9, 366. *See also* Georgetown home/farm/school
Osnag (Harsak), 83–4, 85, 87–90, 94, 436–7
Ottawa School Board crisis, 474–5
Oundjian, Peter, xxiv, 465
Ounjian, Mike, 366
Ouzounian, Richard, xxiv, 465–6
Owen Sound, 169
Ozanian, Andranig (General), 132

Panosian, Zabel, 336, 550n21
Papazian, Eugene, 425
Papazian, Mihran, 425
Paris Commission, 218; assessment of claims, 205–16, 224, 227, 529n9; and the McDougall Commission, 218, 222
parish council. *See* Armenian Apostolic Church
Pasdermajian, Hagop, 369, 433
Pasdermajian, Hrant, 369, 433
Pasdermajian, Yervant, xxx, 368–9, 370, 380–1, 386, 399–400, 402–3, 418–19, 433
patriotism. *See* ethnopatriotism
Peet, W.W., 215
photography, xxiv, 28, 59, 347–8, 354
picture brides, 263, 352, 525n9; difficulties, 188–91, 193–5, 196–7, 199; effects of Genocide, 182, 183, 184–5, 198; and Genocide trauma, 191–3, 196, 200; and immigration, 186

Pierce, Rev. Ira, 312, 356, 357-8; and Georgetown farm/home/school, 164-5, 203
Plaxton, C.P., 228-9
pluralism and liberal democracy, 481-2; Stacy Churchill on, 482-3
Posigian, Michael, 312-13, 422
Postalian, Lucy, 368
Postian, Paul, 368
Pratt and Letchworth (P and L), 31, 58, 62, 72; origins, 61; working conditions, 242
pregnancy, 199, 200
prejudice against Armenians, 180, 259, 329, 448, 458, 462
press, Armenian, 105-8, 141, 251-2, 334-5, 449-52, 468, 480; circulation, 105-6; content, 106-8, 109, 418, 448, 468
professional and business organizations, 448-9, 463
Progressives (Armenian Progressive Party, Progressive League), 139, 248, 251, 301, 304, 417, 429, 445, 468; Brantford Progressives, 307-8; children of the Progressives, 315-16. See also Lraper
Protestant churches. See churches and the Armenian community
Protestant missionaries, xlii, 19, 38-9, 517n27; and Anatolia College, 40; and emigration, 40-1, 53, 176, 462; and Euphrates College, 26, 36; humanitarian efforts, 141-3, 181, 312; and social reform, 39; as symbols of democracy, 39-40; and the *Zartonk*, 33-4

Raffi (Raffi Cavoukian), 465
Raffi Armenian Community School, 273-4, 275, 286
Raffi Armenian Cultural Association, 438
Raician, Garo: and unionization, 248-9
Ramgavars (Ramkavars, Armenian Democratic Liberal Party, ADL), 275, 408, 425-6, 445, 450, 451; founding, 140; ideology, 270, 281, 319
rape, 19, 183, 191; and trauma, 180. See also abduction
Ras-ul-Ain, 123, 217
reading rooms (*gradarans*), 35; formation, 101; functions, 95, 98, 100-5,

109; in Hamilton, 334; membership, 102
regional organizations, 436-9. See also village educational associations
refugees, Armenian, xxviii, 127, 128, 171-2, 174-8, 180-2 478; adaptation, 182, 290, 346, 371-2, 373; and the Asiatic classification, 163, 171-2, 173; definition of, 379-80, 384, 395-8; entry to Canada, 145, 155, 156-8, 395-8; family reunification, 163-5; and the Geneva Convention, 395-6; and the Genocide, 131, 133; money qualifications, 163; Nansen passport, 160-2; and the passport ruling, 159-60; rehabilitation, 134-5, 179-80, 391, 427; survival guilt, 180-1, 342
Relief Committee for Armenia. See HOG
reparations, 205-6; and crimes against humanity, 232-3; the solatium, 229-34; and Turkey, 472-3; and war crimes, 232-3. See also Cahan, Charles Hazlitt, Canadian Reparation Commission, McDougall Commission, Paris Commission
Republic of Armenia: 1991 and after, xxvii, xxxix, 113, 160, 217, 269, 398, 434, 559n65. See also Armenian independence
residential patterns, 62-4. See also settlement patterns
restaurants (Montreal), 353
Riggs, Rev. Henry, 131, 511n26
Roberts, Barbara, 173
rug business, xxvi, 362-71, 409-10, 463, 533n35, 554n45; rug merchants, 59, 364-5, 366-70, 403, 418, 500n29, 552n24

Sabah-Gulian, Stepan, 97, 98, 139, 426
St Catharines, 536n12; and the Canadian Armenian Union, 275-7; church building, 277-9; entrepreneurial activities, 263-6; factory labour, 239-54; General Motors strike, 253; and McKinnon Dash, 264-6, 503n28; occupational mobility, 261-2; politics, 291-7, 300-1; settlement patterns, 237-9, 240, 411-12, 414-15; and unionization, 250-1; women and work, 254-60. See also Armenian Apostolic

Church, church crisis, St Gregory the Illuminator Armenian Apostolic Church (St Catharines)
St Gregory the Illuminator Armenian Apostolic Cathedral (Montreal), 391, 420
St Gregory the Illuminator Armenian Apostolic Cathedral (New York City), 281, 282, 421
St Gregory the Illuminator Armenian Apostolic Church (St Catharines), 273, 277–9, 284–7, 289, 290–1, 301–3, 320–1, 450, 458
St Gregory the Illuminator Armenian Catholic Church (Toronto), 424, 431
St Laurent, 352–3, 406, 407, 464
St Light, 3, 47
St Mary Armenian Apostolic Church (Hamilton), 413, 414, 420, 424, 451
St Mary Armenian Apostolic Church (Toronto), 408, 422, 459
St Mary, Feast of (Blessing of the Grapes), 291, 303, 339
St Philip's Anglican Church (Hamilton), 283, 317–18, 328, 344, 462, 503n1
St Sahig and St Mesrob School, 431
St Zotique, 353, 405, 406–7, 421
Safarian, Edward, 347
Sarafian, Astghig, 433
Sarafian, Vartkes, 433
Sardarabad, 125, 134, 340
sciences: Armenian contributions, xxvi, 347, 463, 480, 485
Seferian, Boghos (Paul), 394–5
Seferian, Hagop, 63, 76
Selyan, Yervant, 338, 342, 370
Setlakwé, Aziz, 58–9
Setlakwé, Raymond, 464, 476
settlement patterns, 402–4, 411–15. *See also* Brantford, Galt/Cambridge, Hamilton, Montreal, St Catharines, Toronto, Windsor
Sevag, Baruyr, 485, 565n9
Sèvres, Treaty of, 126, 128, 131
Shahen, Setrag, 32, 35–6, 97, 293, 335
Shahmourdian, Armenag, 336, 550n21
Shirajian, Rev. Aharon, 131–2
Shirinian, Mampre, 361, 362
Shiroyan, Archie, 353, 419
shoeshine business, 260, 263, 329, 343–4, 363, 480
Sivadjian, Paul, 368, 370

Smart, Geroge Bogue, 202
Smyrna (Izmir), 3, 49, 118, 146, 176, 208, 217, 232, 368
Society of Armenians from Istanbul, 430, 438, 444, 451
sojourning: xxviii; consequences for the home villages, 81–3, 86, 88; earnings in Canada, 72; from Keghi, xxxiii, 4, 24; and modernization, 34–6, 43, 91, 104; motivations for, 22, 114; sojourner society in Canada, 58, 59, 64, 65, 67–9, 77, 78, 79, 80–1, 238; as a tradition, 23–33, 314; and village educational associations, 82, 85, 86
solatium. *See* reparations
Soviet Armenia, xxvii, xxix, xxxviii, 250–2, 280, 305, 315–16, 318–20, 341, 389, 425, 439–40, 443, 461, 478–9; and the Armenian Church, 141, 272, 287–8, 294–8, 307, 308, 420, 471; and the Hnchaks 138–9, 270, 516n7; and the HOG, 140, 294
sponsorship and immigration, 57, 159–60, 175–7, 182, 359, 385, 391–5, 397, 399, 403; and the Armenian Relief Association of Canada, 355–6, 362; and Bedoukian, Kerop, 378, 386–91, 403; and the Canadian Armenian Congress, 379–83, 398, 401, 557n33; and the United Church, 357. *See also* immigration regulations
Stepanian, Nahabed, 353
Sumner Commission, 205, 220–1, 223, 233
Surp Hagop (St James) Church, xli, 405, 407, 421–2, 430, 432; and schools, 432

Talaat Pasha, 120, 129, 132, 133, 216
Tandurjian, Kopernik, 295, 426
Tarman (Baghlarpunaru), 7, 10, 19, 38, 61, 76, 83, 85, 122
Tatoyan, Rev. Vazken
Teghtsoonian, Oksen, 309, 366, 368, 370, 533n38
Tekeyan Cultural Union, 444
Terzian, Artin: and reparations, 213–14
Toronto, 275–6, 419–20, 431–3, 434; the elite, 308–9, 351, 354–5; the entrepreneurial class, 359–63; factory labourers, 354; female domestics, 356–9; marriage patterns, 457,

459–60; the rug business, xxix, 363–71; settlement patterns, 59, 237, 351–2, 354, 403–9, 411, 415, 479–80
Toronto Globe: and the Genocide, 145, 148, 163, 462
Torosian, Hygus; and unionization, 244, 247–50, 536n46, 542n90
Torosian, Ohannes, 262, 263, 284, 297
torture of Armenians: by Kurds, 21, 132; by Turks, 117, 119, 141, 317, 336, 456, 511n18
Tourian, Ghevont (Archbishop), 279–80, 281–4, 294, 295–6, 297–300, 310–11, 321
trauma. *See* Genocide
Trudeau, Pierre Elliot, 563
Tsermag, 28, 42, 122

unions. *See* Dashnaks, factory labour, United Autoworkers, St Catharines
United Armenian Association (UAA), 83–5
United Autoworkers, 244–9, 251–3, 265
United Church of Canada: assistance to refugees, 355–7, 362–3, 397; Board of Evangelism and Social Service, 204; takeover of Georgetown home/farm/school, 203. *See also* churches and the Armenian community
United Nations Convention on Genocide, 233
United Nations High Commissioner for Refugees, 390
Utudjian, Socrates, 355, 365

Varoujan, Daniel, 24–5
Vartanian, Ohanas, 151
Vasilian-Belleli, Hasmig, 464
Vazken I (Catholicos), 420
Versailles, Treaty of, 205, 206, 217–21, 225–6, 228, 231
vijak, 313–14, 547n23

village educational associations, 67, 86, 427, 436–8; formation, 81–5, 88–90; impact, 90–4; of Keghi, 35, 85, 86; and school closures, 83–4; structure and function in North America, 86–90; support of sojourners, 82, 85, 86, 88–9, 91; United Armenian Association (UAA), 83, 84
Vining, A.J.: and Georgetown boys, 202–3
Vratzian, Simon, 7, 43, 426, 488n3

Wakelin, Rev. Roy, 317, 318
Walker, Christopher, xxxi, 16, 319, 393
White Paper (1966), on immigration, 383–4
Wilson, Woodrow, 125, 126
Windsor: settlement patterns, 237, 365, 403, 552n15
women and neighbourhoods, 330–1
women and work, 182, 249–50, 254–60, 263, 331
women's organizations, 447–8
Women's Unity League, 251, 252, 537n30
Worker's Unity League, 251, 252, 537n30
World Council of Churches, 389–90, 400, 476, 559n73

Yakmalian, Zarouhi, 325
Yerevan, xxxviii, xl, 316, 341, 392
Young Turks: and the Genocide, 114–24, 231–2; revolution, 28, 41, 49, 84, 100, 115–16
youth organizations, 444–6
Yeritasard Hayastan, 97, 98, 105–7, 139, 248, 251, 275, 293, 306–7, 335, 450

Zareh I (Catholicos), 421
Zaroukian, Alice, 407, 430, 433
Zaroukian, Daniel, 433
Zartonk, xlii, 33–4, 82